THE ENGLAND OF ELIZABETH

A. L. Rowse has spent most of his working life at Oxford, where he was elected to an Emeritus Fellowship of All Souls College. His teaching and research has focused largely on the Tudor period, in particular the Elizabethan age, and he is the author of a number of books on the subject. He has also published volumes of poetry, biography, autobiography and essays. Dr. Rowse has now retired to Cornwall.

Books by A. L. Rowse

Ralegh and the Throckmortons
The Expansion of Elizabethan England
The Elizabethan Renaissance: The Life of the Society
The Elizabethan Renaissance: The Cultural Achievement
The Elizabethans and America
Sir Richard Grenville of the *Revenge*
Tudor Cornwall
The Early Churchills
The Later Churchills

Poems of a Decade
Poems chiefly Cornish
Poems of Deliverance
Poems partly American
A Cornish Childhood
West Country Stories
St. Austell: Church, Town, Parish

The Use of History
The Spirit of English History
The English Spirit
Discoveries and Reviews
Portraits and Views
The End of an Epoch
All Souls and Appeasement

A History of France
by Lucien Romier. *Translated and completed*

William Shakespeare: A Biography
Shakespeare the Man
Shakespeare's Sonnets
Edited with an Introduction and Notes
Christopher Marlowe: A Biography
Milton the Puritan

THE ELIZABETHAN AGE

THE ENGLAND OF ELIZABETH

The Structure of Society

by

A. L. ROWSE

FELLOW OF ALL SOULS COLLEGE, OXFORD

Quoniam zelus domus tuae comedit me

PSALM. lxviii

M

First published in 1950 by Macmillan and Company Limited
Reprinted 1951 (twice), 1959, 1961, 1962, 1964 (twice)

First published in 1981 by
PAPERMAC,
a division of Macmillan Publishers Limited
London and Basingstoke

Associated companies in Auckland, Dallas,
Delhi, Dublin, Hong Kong, Johannesburg,
Lagos, Manzini, Melbourne, Nairobi,
New York, Singapore, Tokyo, Washington
and Zaria

ISBN 0 333 31918 4

Printed in Great Britain by
Redwood Burn Limited, Trowbridge
and bound by Pegasus Bookbinding, Melksham

TO THE GLORIOUS MEMORY OF
ELIZABETH
QUEEN OF ENGLAND

PREFACE

For many years now I have been working in the field of Tudor, particularly Elizabethan, studies. But I should never have dared to attempt a synoptic view of the whole Elizabethan Age if it had not been for a word from Sir Richard Livingstone, then Vice-Chancellor at Oxford, who said to me one day going down Magpie Lane: " Why not give us a portrait of the Elizabethan Age? " Why not, indeed? It was, of course, in our age of specialisation — when it becomes increasingly difficult to see anything steadily and see it whole — to assault the impossible. I have often felt, under the strain of composing this book — now over some years — that I had undertaken an impossible task. All I can say is that, so far, the book has gone exactly as I intended it should go; so that, whatever its defects and shortcomings, the responsibility is mine. And I am as yet only half-way through.

This first volume is concerned essentially with the structure of Elizabethan society; not with social life as an end in itself, nor with the achievements of the age in action and the life of the mind: all that will come in the second volume. Here I am concerned to expose and portray the small society — tough, vigorous, pulsating with energy — that accomplished those extraordinary achievements and made the age the most remarkable in our history. Everything is related to this central purpose: when I am dealing, for instance, with government or economic matters, with Parliament or the Church, I am not treating them as disparate subjects, ends in themselves; but from the end of the society, as expressions of it, part and parcel — or rather bone and sinew — of its life. In every aspect and with every subject, I am engaged in extracting the juices of the social. Only so is it possible to write the book and give it a coherent form.

The book, then, has a logical plan. It begins with a Prologue designed to reveal, for those who have eyes to see, how much of the Elizabethan Age is alive all round us and within us, beneath the skin, the scars, the scoriations of the present. With that always in mind, one goes back to found the society, firmly and securely, on the land and its cultivation. Then one passes to the new developments characteristic of the age, in industry, commerce, finance: the accumulation of capital then — as against its erosion in a low-grade consumption now — the increasing prosperity that has left us such evidences in works of art and architecture from palaces to cottages, in the virtual rebuilding of English villages from Cornwall to Northumberland the new wealth that encouraged so much enterprise, expansion, achievement. One must then indicate something of the part played by London and the towns in what was an overwhelmingly agrarian community — more like modern France in that respect than our top-heavy, ill-balanced industrial England. That done, one can describe the social classes, from the bottom upwards. Now that we have the society in being, there follows logically its government, which we trace, naturally, from the top downwards; and that also gives us a converse curve, a contrasted rhythm within those two chapters. After government, the administration of the society naturally comes, following a similar rhythm, from the centre outwards to the localities. Law, treated again not as an end in itself but as an expression of the society, comes as the ligament binding it together as a whole. We next have to tackle the Church, not as a system of belief, but as a social institution — indeed as the whole of society regarded from one aspect, inextricably entwined with secular life at every level, indisseverable from it. Yet it was in this very time, as the result of the Reformation, that the unity and homogeneity of medieval society was broken; a measure of progress, it produced opposition on the right and on the left: which is dealt with in the chapter on the Catholics and the Puritans. After religion, there follows the education of the society: again not the content and matter of education, but its place in the community, its social affiliations.

Having in the first volume shown what the society of Elizabethan England was, I hope in the second to deal with what it did: to portray its expansion, its achievements both in the field of action and that of culture. I shall be dealing with the impact of its energies beyond its borders, in Wales and Ireland, the voyages of discovery, the opening up of commerce across the oceans, the projects and attempts at colonisation, the foundations of a trading empire in America, the Indies and the outer world; the war on land and sea; the growth of interest in cosmography and science; the creative achievement in art and literature; the beliefs and doctrines of Elizabethans, the mind of the age, the penumbra of the subconscious and irrational, their superstitions and credulities: all related to the social life of which they were coloured and revealing expressions. There will be an Epilogue, placing the whole in the framework of contemporary Europe — that of Renaissance and Counter-Reformation — and in the tradition of the English-speaking peoples. When the design is complete, its logical and symmetrical structure will stand revealed.

Within the work there are various dominant themes corresponding to the rhythms observable in the society. There is the impact of the Reformation, at first destructive, deleterious, darkening; there are the black years of the middle of the century, from the fifteen-thirties to Elizabeth's accession — years of dislocation, economic maladjustment, of social malaise and financial crisis. Then, the experience absorbed, the lands of the Church swallowed, the society generates constantly increasing energies, from which its astonishing achievement flowed. The Elizabethans had luck with them — they were on the up grade; but they made the most of it. Another leading theme is the rise of the gentry: of which the consequences may be observed in many fields, in Parliament and local administration, on the land and in the society of every county, in the pressure on the monarchy and the Church, the support for the Puritans, the growing ascendancy of the Common Law, in the universities and schools, everywhere. It is fascinating to observe the same rhythms at work, rising and falling, palpitating and alive, in so many different sectors: in agriculture, in industry and commerce, in politics and administration, in education and religion. These themes serve to knit the work together and give it unity, instead of being a series of separate studies of different subjects. I have taken a tip from the art of musical composition: often a theme is merely announced, in order to be developed later, sometimes with variations.

It has been a help to have had a previous experience of attempting a portrait of a (small) society with my *Tudor Cornwall*. That book was built up, like a mosaic, out of innumerable details largely from original material. Impossible to follow the same method here: it would take forty *Tudor Cornwalls* to cover the whole country. (But how fascinating it should be to have a *Tudor Yorkshire*, or *Norfolk*, or *Kent*, or *Wales*!) The method of this book must be synthetic, its detail illustrative. The problem therefore has been to keep a balance. I have tried to make the picture representative: not to be seduced by my West Country leanings; to do justice to North as well as South, to the Midlands as well as to the West. Still, I could wish that the East had come out a little more strongly, though I have not neglected it.

There has been a similar problem of proportion as to subject, and of texture in treatment, all the way through. One has to keep the balance in mind at every point: often I have had to restrain myself on subjects that interest me more, to do justice to those that interest me less. I hope it will not be too easily discernible which was which. Naturally one accumulates far greater material on some subjects than on others. But I have not chosen to neglect those that are well known for others that have the mere virtue of obscurity: that would be to get the proportions wrong.

I have drawn largely upon local and regional material for my picture. There are immense riches in local archives and in the published records and journals of antiquarian societies all over England — tribute to our domestic tranquillity, the absence of revolutions; the amount of work done by generations of local scholars and antiquarians in this country is astonishing and beyond all praise. I love their work and them for their devotion. I believe that the marriage of local with national history — and further, beyond the bounds of nations — has more to offer us than many more sought and over-cultivated fields.

My aim has been to reduce references to a minimum. Those acquainted with the subject will know how to interpret them; those who are not will not need them. I dislike books that make a parade of apparatus and then proceed to show that their authors do not know how to write a book. I regret that I have not simplified my references even a little more.

It has been a great pleasure to accumulate so many obligations in the course of my researches; the composition of such a book has been a revelation in friendship, I have been helped so generously by so many friends. But they must not be taken as necessarily agreeing with any expressions of opinion within: my crotchets, or perhaps my convictions, are my own.

There are two scholars, masters in this field, whose work in general has been a great stimulus and from whom I have constantly profited: Professor J. E. Neale and Dr. J. A. Williamson. All my generation has been influenced by the work of Professor R. H. Tawney; and I owe much to it, though I have emerged with rather a different emphasis. Dr. G. M. Trevelyan, master of my craft, has shown a constant interest in the progress of the book and encouraged me in a way that I deeply appreciate. Dr. W. G. Hoskins of Leicester, of whose work I am a great admirer, has been most generous in placing at my disposal the product of his own researches, both published and unpublished. Professor

A. G. Dickens of Hull has kindly helped me over Yorkshire; Sir Edmund Craster and Mr. L. H. Butler with suggestions on Northumberland and Worcestershire respectively. I can never sufficiently acknowledge what I owe to my friend, Professor Jack Simmons, who has ferreted out all sorts of material from the resources of his scholarship and his wonderful topographical knowledge; or what I owe to the conversation of my friend, Lord David Cecil, who has such an intimate bond with the Elizabethan Age and so many original and reflective ideas on it, which has been a great stimulus.

I am most grateful to the Dowager Duchess of Devonshire for her hospitality at Hardwick and for her kindness in arranging for me to see the Hardwick papers; to the Duke and Duchess of Buccleuch for their kindness at Boughton and showing me the Montagu MSS. there; to my friend, Mr. Wyndham Ketton-Cremer, from whose friendly house at Felbrigg I have worked agreeably at Norfolk; to Mr. Norman Scarfe, who introduced me to Suffolk, and to Miss Lilian Redstone for help with her father's transcripts in the Borough Library at Ipswich; to Mr. K. B. McFarlane from whose medieval — and other — conversation I constantly profit. I am indebted to my former research students, Mr. W. J. Rowe of Liverpool University, Mr. F. E. Leese of the Bodleian Library and Mr. L. L. S. Lowe, for placing material at my disposal; to the officials of the Bodleian Library, the London Library and the Public Record Office for their help and consideration, and, not least, to Mr. A. E. Whitaker and Mr. G. A. Webb, assistant librarians of the Codrington Library, for their unwearied attentiveness and courteous assistance over years. Professor Jack Simmons and Mrs. John Holdsworth (L. V. Hodgkin) have added to their many kindnesses by reading my proofs for me. It has been a great honour to have the proofs of my book passed by the same hand as corrected that classic of historical writing, *Italy and her Invaders*. I am much indebted to my publishers for their patience and help, and for the particular interest and encouragement of the Rt. Hon. Harold Macmillan and Mr. Daniel Macmillan in the progress of the book.

A. L. ROWSE

OXFORD,
Empire Day, 1950

CONTENTS

PROLOGUE

CHAPTER I

A LIVING AGE

THE Elizabethan Age is not something dead and apart from us; it is alive and all round us and within us. Wherever one goes in England there are the visible memorials of what those men and women were when they were alive, the houses they built and loved and lived in, the things they made and wore, the objects they cherished, the patterns they imposed upon the very landscape; wherever English people are gathered together, or — and here is the miracle — wherever they speak the language, something of the tradition goes on in them. They may be completely unaware of it: that is all the more amusing to the scholar or the discerning. But it is more rewarding, has greater depth of intellectual interest and inspiration, when it is conscious.

The English people in our time have been through a crisis of their fate to which the nearest parallel is that they passed through in the Elizabethan Age. Only ours was a nearer thing, and even more depended on it. The coolest and least impassioned historian must admit that the contribution of the English people in our generation to the world was even greater than that of our ancestors; for it was a more dangerous and exhausting struggle against worse odds and so much more was at stake, not only for ourselves but for the world. That is not my theme. What is to our purpose is to note how, in the moment of greatest danger, when all might so easily have been lost and the country gone down for ever to destruction, people turned for inspiration to that earlier hour, and were renewed and went on. It has indeed never been forgotten. It must have some secret for our people that cannot be put in words, though it is the hopeless business of the historian to try. (All this book can only be an attempt to coax, evoke, describe, rather than to explain.) Perhaps it was in that electric, charged moment that our people suddenly reached maturity and became aware of themselves as a people, first saw themselves in the mirror of their destiny, half glimpsed the extraordinary fate that lay ahead across the seas and in the world.

There is no doubt about the fact, when Londoners in the

tense hours of 1940, awaiting the issue of the Battle of Britain, thronged to hear Queen Elizabeth's Golden Speech to the Commons in 1601 recited by our most admired living actress; when the chief box-office draw throughout the war, the one dramatist that never failed to hold the stage was a Warwickshire man who made a successful career in London over three centuries ago; when on the famous morning of 6 June 1944 a company commander, as his landing craft approached the coast of Normandy, read Henry V's speech before Agincourt to his men; when people at home held their breath and felt that not to be there was, in his phrase, not to be there on Crispin's day. It is fascinating to observe, too, that in the moment of acute danger in the French Revolutionary war, in 1798 when the French had landed in Ireland and were expected to invade this country, Pitt's government published as a State Paper the preparations made to meet the Spanish Armada two centuries before. "It was some consolation to find", wrote Pitt's friend, Dundas, "that, in a period of as much energy as was that of Queen Elizabeth's preparation against the Spanish Armada, ideas and measures similar to those which I was meditating had been, many of them, anticipated by that able Princess." [1]

When one thinks of the Elizabethan Age a hundred images, a thousand memories crowd in upon the mind, of all those people (for it is life that we are writing about), the places where they lived, where they now lie sleeping, the objects they left behind them, so many evidences of their passions, conflicts, loves, discontents, of the humble routine of work and duty — all the manifold pathos and mystery of life. Perhaps it is Exeter that comes into mind, and one sees again that Renaissance front of the Guildhall upon the ruined High Street, built in 1593, and within it, upstairs in the Mayor's panelled parlour, the portrait of old John Hooker, Chamberlain of the city and its historian, who meant so much in its busy, homely life three centuries ago. Or one thinks of the pretty monument in the Cathedral to the young musician, Matthew Godwin: there he is a gowned and hooded youth of seventeen, with wavy gilt locks, kneeling with hands in prayer not at an altar, but at an organ (how much of the religious shift of the time is in that), in the background viols, lutes and trumpets, the sky decorated with angels awaiting him: *hinc ad caelos migravit XII Jan. 1586* (*i.e.* 1587). Above, the inscription placed by his long-forgotten friend: *aeternae memoriae posuit, G. M. Fr.* At the other end of the country one thinks of the rose-red

[1] H.M.C. *Fortescue MSS.* IV. 278.

sandstone building of the school at St. Bees, between the mountains and the sea, built by Archbishop Grindal in his native place in that same year 1587, with its motto, *Ingredere ut proficias*; and of the tiny one-arch bridge over Pow Beck with his arms in a panel. Or, not many miles away — we shall see later how active the age was in founding schools — the little school at Hawkshead, founded by Archbishop Sandys, looking down to Esthwaite water where Wordsworth skated as a boy. Or, a more affecting relic from those very years, reposing in the Catholic house of the Throckmortons at Coughton in Warwickshire, with all its memories of religious division within the family, of persecution and suffering — the young son of the house executed in London the year before, 1584, the room upstairs in which the women waited for news of Gunpowder Plot and the fate of their men folk — there in a corner is the nightgown of Mary Queen of Scots, with the crimson thread at the throat.

The truth is that, with the discerning eye of the historical imagination, under the layers of subsequent time one can pick out and piece together a picture of the age — or rather it begins to coalesce and form a coherent whole, a framework for the other evidences that remain. Impoverished as we have become in our time by two world wars, the old wealth and superabundance gone, the immense surpluses made in the nineteenth century by the Industrial Revolution and invested abroad now eroded away, the country yet retains its extraordinary wealth in houses and monuments from that earlier time. There is still something that is not lost to us. There must be many hundreds of Elizabethan houses of one kind and another, from palaces to cottages, up and down the land. That already tells us something important about the age: it was rich and prospering, wealth was increasing rapidly, above all in the hands of the gentry and the middle classes, who were the dynamic element in that society and made it what it remained right up to our time and the social revolution that has now engulfed it. These monuments are their shells, like the tracings of a coral reef left when the molluscs are departed. But if you listen closely they retain the whisperings, the faint rumours of their former life, echoing and shadowy now of what was busy, bustling and vital then.

These houses vary naturally with the environment, the available building materials of their respective counties. If it is Somerset one thinks of, there is the snuff-coloured Ham Hill stone of which such a house as Montacute, with its dreaming terraces and deserted galleries, is made. A few miles further south it is the whitish-grey chalk stone, with a touch of hard silver in it, of the Dorset down country: such a house as the little manor of Upcerne one catches sight of across the valley going up the road from Dorchester to Cerne Abbas — the road that Michael and Susan Henchard trudged in the opening chapter of *The Mayor of Casterbridge*. Or there is the darker grey of the local stone of which the many-windowed house at the town-end of Wheatley is built — as also a great deal of Oxford. In the Severn country, among the orchards of Worcestershire and Herefordshire there are the white-and-black timber-framed houses bobbing up among the seas of fruit-blossom in spring. Further north, the white and black becomes more pronounced and decisive, positively aggressive (like everything northern) with such houses as Moreton Old Hall or Gawsworth Old Hall in Cheshire, or Speke Hall in Lancashire, the timbers very elaborate and decorated, with upright and wavy diagonal lines and quatrefoils in horizontal bands. (Something of the age in that.) High up on the bleak moorlands of Yorkshire and the Pennines there is the hard weathered stone of such a yeoman's house as the Withins, above Haworth,[1] bleak and bare like the hard subsistence its builders won from the moor, with one feature upon which they spent themselves: the many-mullioned window of the big upstairs bedroom where the chief events of their lives passed, birth and death, the begetting of children, the lyings-in, sickness, the laying out of the dead.

Or there is the cream plaster and peach-coloured brick of so many parts of Southern England, notably East Anglia with its decorative pargetting of exteriors; the old rose brick of the Cambridge colleges. Cambridge is far more Elizabethan than Oxford: a true historical indication of the age, for the later sixteenth century saw Cambridge to the fore. Or there are the magnificent houses of Central England, of Nottinghamshire, Northamptonshire or Derbyshire limestone: such a palace as Wollaton, with the soaring fantasy of its central hall, like a keep, with the four grouped towers at the corners about it, astonishing and mysterious as one sees it looming in the autumnal mist across those ploughed parklands, like some evocation of a house out of the *Faerie Queene*. Or there is the perfection achieved at Kirby Hall — Smithson did not achieve it at Wollaton — that exquisite ruined house amid green level fields, with its lime and grey colouring and all its music of gathered gables and finials. Unique in design are the great coupled bow-windows at the end of the long garden wing, like galleons that have come to rest there in

[1] The situation of Wuthering Heights; the house now falling into ruin.

the Northamptonshire pastures, and of which Mr. Sacheverell Sitwell has written: "They are like the poops of two stone ships, never meant to sail, but only to catch the sunlight . . . they remind us of great vessels with their cabins made on the curve, and bound in, as it were, to the shaping of the hull".[1]

To come to an end, where there is no end — there is Hardwick, most wonderful of all Elizabethan houses, all glass and symmetry and towers, with its fantastic roof-line appearing above the trees from all quarters of the park: the great house that Bess of Hardwick built, and all but finished, only a stone's throw away from the house that she had already enlarged into an immense one, out of the sufficient and shapely dwelling of her yeomen forefathers. What pride, fantasy and ambition, like the pursuit of some insatiable dream, to build a second palace within a hundred yards of the first — and she a parvenue. But is it not expressly revealing of something in the character of that age? To its snobbery, from which no age is free — and Bess's was snobbery in the grandest manner — we must add its restless and unsleeping sense of beauty, which few periods can rival. Mr. Sitwell thinks that the great chamber on the top floor, with its coloured frieze of forest scenes, of spring and summer, flowers and corn, of the court of Diana and the story of Orpheus, is "the most beautiful room, not in England alone, but in the whole of Europe".[2] What a house, indeed, it is, with its memories and portraits, its Renaissance cabinets, one of them with the characteristic emblem, to which we have lost the key,

> The redolent smelle of eglantine
> We stagges exalt to the Divine,

with the long gallery in which hang so many familiar figures of the time, its tapestries and needlework — "no other house possesses such needlework".[3] I remember it unforgettably as I saw it one summer night, a dark towering shape high up on the escarpment, from deep down in the park, while a lemon moon came up from the east, and shadows of former huntsmen and deer moved in and out among the trees and the inscription upon the tablet of an ancient keeper in the church beyond echoed in my mind:

> Long time he chas'd the red and fallow deer
> But Death's strong dart at length hath fix'd him here.

It would be easy to reconstruct the Society of the age — its leading people, the fashionable, the powerful, who gave it so

[1] Sacheverell Sitwell, *British Architects and Craftsmen*, p. 24.
[2] *Ibid.* p. 27. [3] *Ibid.* p. 28.

much of its character — simply from their tombs and monuments. There is a subject the full value of which, aesthetic and historical, is only just beginning to be appreciated.[1] In each county we can draw together once again the very people who met together at quarter sessions and assizes, at musters and merry-makings, when invasion was threatened or forces had to be made ready for Ireland or the Low Countries or Normandy, who quarrelled or were friends, gave their children in marriage or went to law, and are now separate dust in their tombs in the churches. Or if they are grandees, we may bring them together again from all over the country. In the Beauchamp chapel at Warwick, having pushed their way so successfully, lie the Dudleys beside the Beauchamps — the connection tenuous and remote. A hand's breadth away from Richard Beauchamp, in whose wake Malory went to the French wars, lies the good-tempered, amiable Ambrose Dudley, to whom Elizabeth gave the earldom of Warwick. Across the way lies the magnificent Leicester, whom his last wife, Lettice Knollys — the woman that Elizabeth could least of all abide — has brought safely to bed at last, while Elizabeth lies alone in Westminster: the inscription one to still the wagging tongues: *Optimo et charissimo marito moestissima uxor Leticia Francisci Knolles ordinis Sancti Georgii equitis aurati et Regiae Thesaurarii filia amoris et conjugalis fidei ergo posuit.* There she is, looking as determined and uncongenial a character as she was in life. And up by the altar, Leicester's little boy Robert, " the noble Impe ", upon whom all the hopes of the family rested: [2] " A child of great parentage, but of far greater hope and towardness, taken from this transitory into everlasting life, in his tender age at Wanstead in Essex on Sunday the 19 of July in the year of our Lord God 1584, being the twenty-sixth year of the happy reign of the most virtuous and godly Princess Queen Elizabeth and in this place laid among his noble ancestors in assured hope of the general resurrection ". Wanstead, where Elizabeth used to visit Leicester in state, on one such occasion Philip Sidney writing the masque for her entertainment; a lame little boy, bright but sickly, page to the Queen (his tiny suit of armour is still there in Warwick Castle), dying that summer Sunday.

[1] We owe it largely to the work of Mrs. Katharine A. Esdaile; cf. her *English Church Monuments, 1510–1840*.

[2] The boy was heir both to Leicester and to his uncle Warwick, who was childless. Leicester had promised Bess of Hardwick, Countess of Shrewsbury, to marry him to her granddaughter, Arabella Stuart (H.M.C. *Salisbury MSS.* III. 52) — with who knows what ideas of eventual succession to the throne? The Dudleys in two generations could not keep their eyes off that glittering prize. The third failed them.

In another part of the same church at Warwick in his marble four-poster lies Fulke Greville: "Servant to Queen Elizabeth, Counsellor to King James, Friend to Sir Philip Sidney". The tomb takes up the whole of what was the chapter-house of the college of canons in pre-Reformation days: a speaking evidence of the change that had passed over church and society. A few miles away at Alcester there are his mother and father: she a Willoughby de Broke, in the strait tubular dress of the earlier years of the reign, he with long and elegant curled moustache and forked beard, in full armour, with many rings on his fingers; above him hangs his old helm and visor. At Sheffield is the splendid tomb of the Earl of Shrewsbury, keeper of Mary Stuart, who takes the opportunity in his epitaph to defend himself against the aspersions of his wife, the scheming, irresistible, intolerable Bess of Hardwick, who lies by herself alone in the church of All Saints at Derby. At Ashby-de-la-Zouch is the Earl of Huntingdon, immensely noble and, though inclined to Puritanism, with royal blood in his veins, in this world of *nouveaux*. Chief of all these, the brains and guiding hands of the régime, the Cecils: old Burghley with his staff of office by the altar in St. Martin's at Stamford; Robert his son upon his Italianate table, supported by the Virtues, at Hatfield.

There are lesser people in hundreds: ambassadors like Thomas Hoby at Bisham in Berkshire, Sir Henry Unton at Faringdon, comic old Elizabethan bundles of bishops, like Bishop Westfaling at Hereford, or a successful actor like Edward Alleyn at Dulwich, or his acquaintance, who wrote the plays, in the chancel at Stratford. Some miles further down the Avon, in the wind-swept cornfields between Avon and Severn, looking across to the Malvern Hills with those other memories of William Langland and the Vision of the Field Full of Folk, is the church of Strensham: there among his ancestors lies Sir Thomas Russell, Shakespeare's friend and executor of his will, in a tomb evidently from the same Johnson workshop as provided the bust of the poet. In a more remote and old-fashioned part of the country, high up on the thyme- and bracken-scented fringes of Dartmoor, there is the Speaker of the Parliament of 1563, Thomas Williams of Stowford, who made his career at the law, but is depicted on his brass (no doubt as he would have it) as an esquire in armour. At Portsmouth a fellow-soldier and follower of Essex, young Charles Blount, who began his service at fifteen under Leicester in the Low Countries, then fought in Brittany under Norris, was at Cadiz and on the Islands Voyage with Essex, and with him in

Ireland at the last as Captain of Cahir Castle. " But in his return home upon the sea he departed this life in his prime and flourishing years about the age of thirty-two. As his life was pleasing to his friends so his death yielded comfort to those that were present. With assured hope of his joyful resurrection he yielded up his soul to God that first gave it and his body to the earth whereof it was made." The two Norris brothers, the most admired soldiers of the time, Black John and his brother Tom in whose arms John died, are to be seen in Westminster Abbey: their figures the masterpieces of that most expressive sculptor, Isaac James, whose work has only recently been identified and revealed to us.[1] Not far away are the two mutually exclusive Queens, Elizabeth Tudor and Mary Stuart, whose duel filled the age with its alarms:

> Think how many royal bones
> Sleep within this heap of stones:
> Here they lie had realms and lands,
> Who now want strength to stir their hands . . .
> Here's a world of pomp and state,
> Buried in dust, once dead by fate.

The tombs of the time, and the wealth of them, suggest the secular bias of the age. Though the Elizabethans built hardly a church, after all enough churches already existed to serve their needs. In those the altars went down; the monuments went up, often in place of the altars. In innumerable parishes there was a family striving towards or, more delectably, enjoying the position of gentry, impressing themselves upon their neighbours with the pomp or decency of their monuments: a chief contact between the simple rural mind and the world of Renaissance art.

The impulse of the Renaissance is to be seen in a hundred ways, which it is not our purpose now to study, but to mark its presence along with the native impulses in craftsmanship and inspiration, in all their vigour and naïveté, whether in architecture, woodwork, plasterwork, needlework or jewellery. In needlework, Englishwomen of earlier centuries had made a contribution of recognised excellence to the decorative arts: *opus anglicanum* was known and valued abroad as something of its own kind. The tradition was not broken at the Reformation, but it certainly received a jolt: one can see it in the needlework at Hardwick where the Virgin and saints have been taken out of the Gothic niches of the copes and turned into panels with Renaissance figures of Justice and Prudence, Labour and Charity. Sir Walter

[1] *v.* K. A. Esdaile, *Country Life*, 1950, p. 464.

Raleigh, the professor, was right when he said " The World, not the Church, called the tune to which the Age of Elizabeth danced and sang ",[1] though we may have to qualify, or rather amplify, later.

Take the jewellery in which the time was so prolific, " one of the most prolific in our history ".[2] Elizabeth's reign saw an enormous increase in the wearing of jewellery, solid and heavy in design, elaborate and rich in effect. Everything indicates the striking increase in wealth, especially in the upper and middle classes. The Queen's own jewellers were French. But such a collection as the Cheapside hoard, the stock of an average middle-class jeweller of about 1600, shows that though the gems were of Italianate workmanship, the native inspiration was to be seen in the chains of enamelled roses and daisies, the English love of flowers. While the materials used speak of the astonishing expansion of the world going on before Elizabethan eyes: " Emerald from Colombia, topaz and Amazon-stone probably from Brazil, chrysoberyl cats'-eyes, spinel and iolite from Ceylon, Indian rubies and diamonds, lapis lazuli and turquoise from Persia, peridot from St. Johns Island in the Red Sea, as well as amethysts, garnets, opals and other stones from nearer home ".

The architecture of the time reveals a score of variations upon the same compromise, between native tradition and vigour, and classical form and integration. By the usual English way of trial and error, and without too much subordination to doctrine, their architects worked out a recognisable style of their own, a judicious and happy mixture of Italian state and English comfort, the vigour and individuality of the native temperament brought into line and symmetry, if not into complete classical *ordonnance* and integration — that had to wait till Inigo Jones built the Queen's House at Greenwich. In many a West Country or East Anglian church one can watch the transition in the woodwork of the bench-ends from medieval to Renaissance take place with the greatest ease and naturalness in the world: from Gothic peasant keeping his sheep on the hills or early Tudor cog under sail to Italianate roundel with a profile in relief or pure Renaissance decorative motifs.

Elizabethan portraiture, painting and, in particular, wall-painting are only now beginning to receive just appreciation and proper aesthetic discussion. How new a field of study this is may

[1] *Shakespeare's England*, pp. 1-2.

[2] R. E. Mortimer Wheeler, *The Cheapside Hoard of Elizabethan and Jacobean Jewellery*, pp. 3-10.

be seen when as recently as 1916 a high authority could say, " the arts of painting, sculpture and engraving in England during the latter half of the sixteenth century do not afford a very fruitful field for their historian ", and go on to regard the native school of painting as derived from imitation of the Low Countries.[1] This emphasis is being corrected now. Of course there was a prodigious foreign influence — never greater — in all fields of art during the sixteenth century. But there was also a long tradition of craftsmanship in the country, and the case seems to have been the same in this field as elsewhere, a mingling of indigenous tradition with the new foreign influences. The Elizabethans were much given to painting the wall surfaces of their houses, as the medievals were their churches. In this century over three hundred examples of such painted interiors have been discovered, when the nineteenth century knew of only a dozen.[2] We can now gather together in the mind such examples as the splendid panels of Cupid and Psyche after Raphael's designs from Hill Hall at Epping, the house built by Sir Thomas Smith, or the rich dining-room of Gilling Castle in Yorkshire with its painted frieze of forest-work with all the arms of the gentry in the different wapentakes of the county in 1585,[3] down to the simple rusticity of stencilled patterns and texts in churches, as at Bowness-on-Windermere. We can imagine once more those coloured interiors, rich and figured; in the case of great houses, with their tapestries and valences and hangings, their counterpanes and carpets and cushions, of crimson and blue and green and gold, blazing with brilliant colour. We should find it restless; but then the age was restless, the minds of those who were aware more expansive and on the move than at any time before or since.

Their self-awareness and pride may be seen in their portraits, of which many hundreds remain, of all kinds and qualities. There was evidently an enormous extension of portrait-painting to meet the twin demands of increasing wealth and increasing self-consciousness. But it was in the art of the miniature, particularly with the work of Hilliard and Oliver, that the greatest sensibility and refinement were reached and the Elizabethans achieved perfection in the plastic arts. When there was so much over-elaboration, and furniture and dress were alike stiff with richness and

[1] *Shakespeare's England*, II, 1-2.

[2] F. W. Reader, " A Classification of Tudor Domestic Wall Paintings ", *Archaeological Journal* (1941), p. 182.

[3] These had been taken out and sold, but are now happily restored.

extravagantly swollen in line — one sees the same inflation in the bulbous legs of tables as in the farthingales of the women — it is well to note that the Elizabethans could achieve elegance and simplicity of proportion as in so much of their silver. In particular their favourite design of the steeple cup is a model of precision and grace. Innumerable examples remain to attest the craftsmanship and art of the goldsmiths, though here we may cite only such an outstanding piece as the Pickering Cup at Westminster, with its beautiful free-flowing design of leaves and rosettes like patterns on cloth of gold both without and within the bowl, the whole design of a splendid confidence and firmness.[1] John Acton of the parish of St. Mary Woolnoth had reason to be proud of his handiwork: one can imagine the pride of that long-dead craftsman when the cup stood finished for his client in the year 1588. Or there is that masterpiece of Renaissance sophistication and beauty, the Vyvyan Salt that came from Trelowarren, the house of an ordinary small country gentleman: a piece apparently unique in England for its panels of glass decorated with gold and silver leaf and colour, of which the designs come, so characteristically, from a book of emblems. It was made in London in 1592–1593.[2] At the other end of the scale we may catch something of their spirit from the humbler craft of ironwork, when we look at their latches and door-knockers, such things as fire-irons, casement-fasteners and hinges: in these last alone, especially with the familiar pattern of the dolphin-hinge, there is honesty, fantasy, mastery, even a certain extravagance of personality.[3] Thousands of these things remain: they were wrought to last.

These objects are not mere shells: they still incorporate the skill, the intention of eye and hand, the love that went into them. The same lights lurk in the jewels for us as for them. In the needlework as in the scenes upon their coloured friezes we see that pastoral dream of life they cherished, as in much of their poetry and music; their own life so active, throbbing with vitality, vibrant, extravert. The dream of the medieval world lingered on in the world of pastoral romance, of chivalrous deeds and knightly adventure: it is the world of the *Faerie Queene* as it is that of the great chamber at Hardwick or the hall that Sir Richard Grenville made for himself, with its emblematic frieze, out of the church at Buckland Abbey. What do we learn from

[1] Cf. *Country Life*, 18 April 1947.

[2] *Twenty Five Years of the National Art Collections Fund*, p. 233.

[3] Cf. Tunstall Small and Christopher Woodbridge, *English Wrought Ironwork*, and *Mouldings of the Tudor Period.*

these external objects about the men who made them? Not everything; but a good deal already. We learn that theirs was a society that attached the greatest importance to work, in the fundamental sense of what a man puts into a thing, to honest labour, to skill of craftsmanship that things might endure and a man take delight in the creations of his hands. We see in the evidences of their handiwork honesty and strength, their uninhibited expressiveness and *bravura*, their homeliness and freshness, an evident naïveté.

I have already said that Oxford is not Elizabethan in character; many places in England are more so. For many years I lived in a room of which the oak panelling, though in date Caroline, was Elizabethan in character, for in these matters the style was apt to be continuous right up to the Civil War and Oxford craftsmanship was conservative. Next door to me the Old Library of All Souls College has a plaster ceiling of 1600, with pendants and coloured armorial shields, along with the Tudor emblems of rose, pomegranate, portcullis and Cap of Maintenance, and Elizabeth's personal device of crowned and sceptred falcon which was stamped on her books. A few steps across the quadrangle on entering the Chapel is the bust-portrait of Warden Hovenden, a Canterbury protégé of Archbishop Parker, who guided the College throughout most of her reign. In the Turl one enters the hall of Jesus to see the portrait of the Queen, painted in 1590: the red wig, two cherries at her ear, a tunic of black-work with a floral design, delicately worked cambric sleeves, herself alert, watchful, master of the situation as ever. There is the fine room with elaborate overmantel and ceiling over the gate at Corpus; the Renaissance doorway of St. Alban Hall in Merton Street; the tomb of Sir Thomas Pope, the Marian founder of Trinity, in the Chapel; in the Cornmarket the painted room, with its mottoes, that remain from the inn kept by Davenant's parents; at the Ashmolean a jewelled watch once worn by Elizabeth — watches were just beginning to come in for the great: Leicester once gave her a long chain and "hanging thereat a round clock fully garnished with diamonds".[1]

More intangibly than these objects with their appeal to the eye are the memories and associations, so many gestures of the time, that linger wherever we turn. Suppose it is London: by Chancery Lane we think of Ben Jonson as a lad helping his stepfather at bricklaying, or being noticed by Camden, then under master at Westminster and taken into it, to be schooled for what a literary

[1] R. E. Mortimer Wheeler, *op. cit.* p. 24.

career! Now it is Spenser, shaken to the core by his terrible experiences in Ireland, sick and needy, dying at the age of forty-six in an inn in King Street. Or it is years earlier and the young poet just down from Cambridge shares a bed in Westminster with Gabriel Harvey, capping each other's English hexameters. Now it is Bankside and Shakespeare — all round the cathedral at Southwark breathes of him still. Or it is Plymouth and the shadow of Drake's *Golden Hind* hovers in the summer haze between his Island and the Hoe, her belly stuffed with silver from the coast of Peru. In his study, the top of the tower at Naworth, the window open to the sound of the stream a hundred feet below, Lord William Howard stands at a table, a book of Catholic piety open before him upon the deep red of the velvet cloth. In the gardens at Gorhambury Francis Bacon walks, with the young Hobbes attending to jot down the definitions that occur to his enquiring, perambulating mind. Or Elizabeth sits once more in her pew at Rycote, the canopy painted with the stars of the firmament, listening (or not) to a sermon with Leicester — where now the rain seeps through the roof.

The Age is indeed all about us, as Elgar said of music: it is in the air all round, we have only to reach out and catch it.

Not only are these evidences of the Age around us but, more important, they are within us — part of our living experience, entering into our conscious tradition and into the secret channels of heart and blood. The memories of a people are all the more important for being unconscious: not a thing to disregard even in so simple a form as the country belief that Queen Elizabeth once slept in a bed here or there, all over the land, in fact in many places where she had never been in her life. It is a simple indication of the fact that her personality has left a far stronger impression on her people than any other sovereign. She is by far the best-remembered figure of any that sat on the English throne: thousands of simple people who can hardly remember any other monarch have heard of her. There is a deep reason, in the nature of our society perhaps, for that, which we shall come to later. It is not that things have been made altogether easy for her memory. The nineteenth century, for example, which had to translate everything into moral terms before it could understand them, was distinctly unfavourable, from Queen Victoria downwards — "So unkind to my ancestress the Queen of Scots". Macaulay was hardly favourable; and we all know the monstrously unfair verdict that Froude pronounced at the end of his great book, because she did not come up to his idea of a simple

Protestant heroine prepared to follow in the wake of her sea-dogs She was much too subtle for that, and had a far more difficult and intellectually exacting role to play: she was above all things a politician, determined to rule. And how she ruled, what a triumphant success she made of it! One of the grandest of her opponents, Sixtus V, had the magnanimity to appreciate her greatness: "She is a great woman; and were she only Catholic she would be without her match. . . . Just look how well she governs; she is only a woman, only mistress of half an island, and yet she makes herself feared by Spain, by France, by the Emperor, by all." [1] That was thirty years after she had succeeded to a much-weakened, much-questioned, inheritance.

Though she was very English — and made great play with that — she was a woman of the Renaissance. Subtle, highly educated, with many gifts and talents, tremendously exhibitionist, an actress from beginning to end, full of vitality and with an inexhaustible gusto for life, she was essentially secular. None of the trapesing about in Corpus Christi processions of that melancholy *dévote*, her sister, praying that Philip would come back, hoping against hope that God would give her an heir. Elizabeth relied on herself alone, and on her own cool brain. The Spanish ambassador at her Court early in her reign diagnosed the truth about a personality around which there has been too much discussion by people who do not know, that her fundamental intention was to remain master and not to give herself a master. That involved a sacrifice of her essential woman's life. But she had seen the disasters that overwhelmed her sister and her cousin by following their desires instead of their judgment; a tragedy — to which she never once referred — lay with her in her cradle and followed her childhood. She was schooled in danger and discretion. The historian in this century may well have the generosity to recognise a quality of heroism in the woman who held on her course alone for forty-five years, in a world of distractions and dangers, full of treacherous currents and many threats to her life. True, she was wonderfully served: she saw to that. But the astonishing devotion she elicited, the pride and admiration, the fantastic flattery, the exotic compliments — "Vous, madame, qui êtes le phénix du monde", as the French Lady Killigrew wrote (it was almost *de rigueur* to refer to the Queen as the phoenix of the world) — all this, which subsequent ages have found so difficult to understand, is it so very ununderstandable, given a little historical imagination and the circumstances of

[1] *Cal. S.P. Venetian, 1581–91*, pp. 344-5.

the time? Is it not an indication of what her people felt for her?

We in our time have no excuse for judging people or events by the comfortable standards of late Victorian security: we have known far too much danger. Though even so, the impartial historian must admit that she emerges from an ethical scrutiny more respectably, a humane, tolerant woman, who disliked cruelty, in a world of Catherine de Médicis and Mary Stuarts, of Philip II and Alva, of the Massacre of St. Bartholomew and the terrible Spanish persecution in the Netherlands. What is to our purpose here is that the Queen of England was, by a providential stroke of good fortune, singularly fitted both for her place at that juncture in her country's fate and to sum up in herself the age. "No elder statesman or famous captain in all broad Europe would have served so well to lead Englishmen back to harmony and prosperity and on to fresh fields of fame."[1] In touch with life at so many points, responsive to all the Renaissance impulses, of a nature and temperament equal to meet the challenge of her time, she left an undying impress of her personality upon it, and it is no wonder that for us she gave it her name.

But it is not the Queen alone who elicits our attention, though she is the centre of the galaxy.

"And best is loved of all alive I ween", as Spenser wrote in one of the many tributes he paid to her in the course of the *Faerie Queene*; there are others that go on in us, in our tradition. There is Philip Sidney — that "spirit without spot", as Shelley described him — in whom men of the time, and not in this country alone, saw the pattern of chivalry; wounded and thirsty at Zutphen, fighting for the Protestant cause and the freedom of the Low Countries, dying at Arnhem, that place of an unforgettable memory for our own generation. There is Drake, whose spirit surely haunts Plymouth Hoe, for he has no grave, being buried at sea off Portobello in the Spanish Main on that last tragic voyage to the Indies, those familiar haunts to the young adventurous lad from Crowndale. So much nonsense has been written against Drake that it is well to quote the last tribute to him by the man in the best position to speak, who checkmated his plans for severing the Isthmus and brought his last voyage to failure, Don Alonso de Sotomayor, who, when he heard the news of Drake's death, said of him: "One of the most famous men of his profession that have existed in the world, very courteous and honourable with those who have surrendered, of great humanity

[1] G. M. Trevelyan, *History of England*, p. 323.

and gentleness, virtues which must be praised even in an enemy ".[1] Or we think of, and have in our time been inspired by, the unquenchable fighting spirit of a Grenville, or that which speaks in a letter of Howard of Effingham — which might describe even more exactly the Battle of Britain in 1940 — " Their force is wonderful great and strong; and yet we pluck their feathers by little and little ".[2]

But, the horrid doubt assails us, is there such a thing as ' the Elizabethan Age '? Can we speak of it to any purpose?

The tendency of some recent literary research has been all to emphasise its continuity with the Middle Ages. It is a difficult point; if we are to be sceptical, our scepticism must be much further-going. It would be more true to the nature of history not to have to talk of ' ages ' at all. The truth has been expressed by Sickert: " There is no such thing as modern art. There is no such thing as ancient art. The antithesis is as senseless as would be division of history into centuries. History is one unbroken stream." It would no doubt give a truer picture of continuity to write history without the divisions into centuries, without once referring to ' the Elizabethan Age ', or the Victorian, or the Middle Ages. But would it be possible to write history at all without these indispensable supports for framework?

Nor are they mere conveniences: the conception of an age can be shown to have recognisable content. When we are told that the way of looking at life common amongst most people in Elizabeth's reign was fairly continuous with that in previous centuries, we can agree; [3] for the way of looking at life among simple people, who form the bulk of society, does not afford very much variety from one time and place to another. For — although in this book we hope to present a portrait so far as possible of a whole society — it is not ordinary simple people, who are apt to be much the same everywhere, that give it its character. It is always the leading elements, the governing class, the dynamic forces, the original, creative spirits, who act and think and portray, that give character to an age. It is the *difference* we must lay emphasis on, what distinguishes one period from another. And this is not only in conformity with common usage, but common sense.

Further, it enables us to answer the question of a more pro-

[1] A. K. Jameson, " Some New Spanish Documents dealing with Drake ", *E.H.R.* (January 1934), p. 28. We may contrast the travesty of Drake presented by Lope de Vega in his *La Dragontea*.

[2] J. K. Laughton ed., *The Defeat of the Spanish Armada*, (Navy Records Soc.) I. 341.

[3] Cf. E. M. W. Tillyard, *The Elizabethan World-Picture*, pp. 1-4.

found scepticism: how can we know anything of, how can we see into the minds of, these people so far away from us? But are they so very different? People of different casts of mind, of separate levels in time and development, co-exist contemporaneously. There are plenty of medieval people about us in the world today, with the same credulities and superstitions and certainties, as there are others more primitive, and not a few sub-human. Earlier, simpler worlds, like the medieval, are not lost to us. There is even something consoling and satisfying in that thought. It means that knowledge is possible to us, that we do not need to deliver ourselves over to complete scepticism about the past. We *can* know something of the world and mind of Elizabeth and Bacon, Marlowe and Shakespeare from the evidences they have left us. We know enough to know that the emphasis of the leading spirits of the age *was* secular, and it was they who made it the 'Elizabethan Age', not the humdrum and commonplace, the ignorant and stupid, or even the conventionally intelligent who think what it is usual to think in all times and places.

With some assurance, then, we may turn to the distinctive achievements of the Age, those that go on in us and are its most characteristic legacies to posterity.

In the first place, the English Church, which is a true reflection of that society and its adaptation to the upheaval of the Reformation. It is difficult for anyone without a knowledge of anthropology to appreciate fully the astonishing audacity, the profound disturbance to the unconscious levels upon which a society lives its life, of such an action as the substitution of an English liturgy for the age-long Latin rite of Western Christendom in which Englishmen had been swaddled time out of mind. No doubt there were factors that aided such a daring breach with the timeless past, notably the gradual introduction of English services, such as the singing of the Litany, in Henry's reign; and, perhaps most important, the increasing national self-consciousness, a most powerful psychological current of the time. All the same, nothing can detract from the revolutionary audacity of such an interference with the customary, the subconscious, the ritual element in life. This revolution was introduced by order of Edward VI's government, with the English Prayer Book, on Whit Sunday, 1549; it at once produced a rising in the West. There followed the brief interval of Mary's restoration of the old order and reunion with Rome. The revolutionary acts of the breach with Rome, the dissolution of the monasteries and the adoption of an English Rite for the Church, had been the work of Henry and Edward. When Elizabeth went back on Mary's work, restored the Prayer Book and once more cut adrift from Rome, it was in a sense a restoration and a return to the past of her father and brother, rather than a revolution. Certainly the forward-looking forces of her supporters regarded Mary's reign as a disagreeable interlude, never intended to last by God or themselves, an episode of reaction in the continuous movement of the Reformation.

It was this that made Elizabeth's religious settlement comparatively agreeable until Rome woke up to the danger of its permanence and declared war on it. But to the country at large the revolution was over, and the Elizabethan Church a return to Henry's legislation and Edward's Prayer Book. The country was the more easily reconciled to it and in time marshalled behind it. Indeed the Elizabethan Church represented a compromise, Catholic in order, Protestant in doctrine (though even here opportunities were left open for subsequent glosses), a compromise very true to the English genius. And not in this regard only: it represented a compromise between the monarchy and the dynamic social forces in the laity that in the next century were to overwhelm it, between the monarch and her advisers. Those people who think that the Queen was a mere cipher for Cecil are immediately disproved by the character of the English Church: it is largely as she wished it. If she had had her way wholly, it would no doubt have been more Catholic and conservative, certainly with a celibate clergy. But if her lay advisers in Council and Parliament had had their way it would have been far more Protestant and would probably have emerged Puritan in doctrine, Presbyterian in form. All her life the Queen resisted this tendency, the natural dynamic of the Reformation; she held it up, frustrated it, defeated it for her own lifetime. And thereby gave the English Church chance to take root, to grow into the minds and hearts of later generations who were born into it, who were brought up in its teachings, formed and lived their lives in its mould, died with its consolations, its majestic and tender phrases and uses printed indelibly upon the mind, even into death and unbelief.

So that all this too, a most significant product of that time, is an intimate part of the life we know. Our minds too respond, though falteringly and with decreasing conviction, to the ritual and the phrases which have worn a channel, like raindrops, upon the mind that is lulled by them. " Almighty and most merciful Father, we have erred and strayed from thy ways like lost sheep. We have followed too much the devices and desires of our own hearts. We have offended against thy holy laws. We have left undone those things which we ought to have done. And we have done those things which we ought not to have done. And there is no health in us." " O Lord our heavenly Father, high and mighty, King of kings, Lord of lords, the only Ruler of princes. . . ." " Because there is none other that fighteth for us, but only thou, O God." " Lighten our darkness, we beseech thee, O Lord; and by thy great mercy defend us from all perils and dangers of this night; for the love of thy only Son, our Saviour, Jesus Christ." All these and such phrases the English people have been accustomed to hearing Sunday by Sunday in their parish churches through the centuries going back to the time when it was " our most gracious sovereign Lady, Queen Elizabeth " who was prayed for throughout her kingdom.

Equally continuing and vital in our inheritance is the Elizabethan drama: something unique, that is at the same time comparable to the drama of Athens, which similarly expressed a great period of tension, of struggle and triumph in a small people's history. Though we are used in our day to seeing plays of Ben Jonson, Marlowe and Webster — and, especially in the universities, to occasional performances of other dramatists of the time, Beaumont and Fletcher, Dekker, Tourneur — the heart of the matter is the prodigious vitality of Shakespeare for us. It may be seen in two aspects: the continuous and continually shaping influence of the work of Shakespeare on the literature of his people and those who speak his language, though not those alone. And there is the effect he has had, and continues to have, on the minds of Englishmen. It is difficult to keep a sense of proportion about it, the phenomenon is so astonishing. No other literature has been so dominated by one writer as English literature has by him, not even Italian literature by Dante, or Russian literature by Pushkin — perhaps the nearest parallels.

It is the phenomenon that is extraordinary, the illimitable vitality of his creations, the boundless influence of his work; for as a writer he was nothing if not natural. It was observed at the time that he was a child of nature, that he wrote as if by instinct rather than by following the rules; he was not an academic, bred in the universities, like Marlowe and Spenser, Greene and Chapman and Ben Jonson; least of all was he what would be called in our time an 'intellectual' — another name for the sterile and uncreative, the failed writer. Nor are his influence and inspiration confined to one country or the art of literature:

one thinks of such works as *A Lear of the Steppes* or the plays of Victor Hugo, of Beethoven's *Coriolanus* overture, Verdi's *Otello* and *Falstaff*, Tchaikovsky's *Romeo and Juliet* and *Hamlet*, of Mendelssohn and Berlioz; or of our own Elgar's *Falstaff*, and Vaughan Williams's *Sir John in Love* and *Serenade to Music*. The source of inspiration is apparently inexhaustible; even Soviet Russia, a new field of conquest, has contributed, with Shostakhovitch's opera *Lady Macbeth of Mzensk*. Or there are the provinces of the ballet and the film, just beginning to open up for him.

But our concern is with his living part in our own tradition. In poetry one can trace his influence upon poet after poet, in some of them hear his accents — Milton, Dryden, Shelley, Keats, Tennyson. (One thinks of Tennyson lying dead in the moonlight, with *Cymbeline* open beside him.) The historical novel springs — if after a long interval, so potent was the seed — from his imaginative treatment of history, his mingling of chronicle with characters of his own invention, come to fruition with the work of the most Shakespearean of writers, Walter Scott. Such characters as Hamlet, Falstaff, Lady Macbeth, Justice Shallow, Sir Toby Belch, Henry V, inhabit the minds of millions of those who speak their language: they are part of our mental world, none more potent or living, and help to bind us together, who are not severed by the seas. His essential concern with the problems of political and social order has only just begun to be recognised in literary criticism in the last few years.[1] No other dramatist has devoted a whole cycle of plays to the history of the country, not only as a kind of dramatic epic, but as a morality, reflecting profoundly upon the problems of order and authority, the responsibility of kingship, the necessity of right governance in a community, of degree and difference of function, the punishment of guilty actions, retribution, the rough justice of time.

Or take the sphere of character, its values and tones, and our own tastes and predilections. There are, on the whole, two main types of women in Shakespeare: the spirited, quick-witted, independent Rosalinds, Beatrices, Portias, and the touching and tender Cordelias and Desdemonas who are the innocent victims of fate. They have remained the dominant types of female character in the English novel. (In France it is the passionate, tempestuous woman, ultimately deriving from Racine.) These

Cf. such works as E. M. W. Tillyard, *Shakespeare's History Plays*; J. Dover Wilson, *The Fortunes of Falstaff* and his editions of *Henry IV* and *Henry V* (The New Cambridge Shakespeare); John Palmer, *Political Characters of Shakespeare*; Lily B. Campbell, *Shakespeare's History Plays*.

Shakespearean types are really very English. It is sometimes asked, did he impose them by the power of his genius upon subsequent literature? Surely not: he must rather have expressed what was native to the English instinct, released preferences deeper and more subtle than of the mind, those of unconscious and natural choice.

In that lies the tremendous vitality and power of his work. There *is* something mysterious about Shakespeare to the English, as not a few of them have obscurely felt. It is nothing so crude as merely a concern with the facts of his life — about which we know as much as can be expected for the age; still less is it concerned with the harmless vagaries of the lunatic as to whether the townsman of Stratford could be the Shakespeare of the Plays, or whether he was not rather Francis Bacon or Queen Elizabeth, the Earl of Oxford or Rutland or the Man in the Moon. The real mystery is the explanation of the inexhaustible vitality and veracity of all that he wrote, plays, characters, poetry or prose, for us English; so that centuries afterwards, in the stress of fighting for existence, in theatres disturbed by falling bombs and rockets, or in quiet English fields while the planes go over to Normandy, it is still his words that come to our lips. The mystery the English feel may be that this man of centuries ago should express them so completely today, should have expressed them, perhaps, for ever.

I think the explanation is to be found in the Age. The Elizabethan Age was so much the most intense and electric experience of a young people suddenly coming to maturity, with new worlds opening out before them, not only across the seas but in the mind. It is incredible what intensity of experience was crowded into those two decades at the end of Elizabeth's reign: one can only say here that the English people, in that short span, gave evidence of all that they had it in them to achieve in the centuries to come. All the myriad influences of Renaissance Europe, from Italy, France, the Low Countries, Spain and Germany, had come pouring in upon them, like so many waters finding their level: this island the last virgin soil to be fertilised. The islanders were a vigorous stock, with a history and a cultural tradition of their own, the most efficient State in Europe. They put up a long and obstinate resistance; they did not take at once to the charms of Renaissance culture and the inspiration of revived antiquity as the French did after Charles VIII's return from Italy. The new influences in thought and art worked slowly, leavening the English lump. How slowly may be seen from the fact that the Elizabethan Age itself falls into two halves. In the earlier, one sees a definite naïveté in both literature and art; the new influences are not yet assimilated; movement is like that of a young animal not yet sure of its muscles or strength, learning to walk. There is a rawness and rusticity, a gawkiness and stiffness even among Court poets like Sackville or Gascoigne, or in such productions as *Ralph Roister Doister* or *Gorboduc*, or *Gammer Gurton's Needle*. It is like the stiffness and awkwardness in the earlier wall-paintings and tapestries. But there is nothing naïf about Shakespeare or Ben Jonson or Donne, any more than there is about Bacon or Hooker, William Gilbert or John Dowland. *There* is a great difference between the earlier and the later half of the reign.

By the latter, all these influences from abroad and at home, of Renaissance discoveries in the mind and the extension of actual experience in the world, of aesthetic and intellectual excitement as well as scientific and geographical exploration, of religious and philosophical questionings, had all come together and fused themselves with the strong slow English temperament, as in a crucible, with the testing time of the struggle for life against Spain. It is noticeable how the drama gets into its stride, and the madrigals begin, in those very years of war, the fifteen-eighties. Such intensity of experience found fullest expression in Shakespeare. The most absorptive and sensitive of instruments, he sensed all or most of what there was in the time, releasing hidden depths hitherto unexplored. He did not indeed express all that was latent: religion, for example, had little or no appeal for him; in that like the sceptical Montaigne. The truth and fidelity of his recording lay in his very naturalness. He trusted his instinct. If he had wanted to impose some intellectual construction of his own upon that upheaved world of crowded experience his people were living through (what an inspiration to a writer it must have been!), like Marlowe or Spenser or Jonson or Donne, he would thereby have limited himself. By not doing so, he has escaped limitation; his influence is therefore illimitable, is coterminous with the life of the people he expressed and goes on continuously with it. Therein lies the miracle. The release and *essor* there is in his work he owed to the intensity of that moment in our history — as we owe to it the unfading memory of Elizabeth and him and Drake and all who made it theirs.

In the end, Shakespeare had no intellectual view of life, to the unity of which he subjugated the richness and variety of experience: in that, too, a mirror of his own people. His was not a metaphysical view of life; it was a moral and aesthetic one.

Breaches of the moral order are brought home to the guilty; there is justice and retribution, even though the innocent suffer and there is much needless pain. There is a balance, a rough equilibrium in things. He is all for acceptance and conformity; after all, our souls are our own.

> Every subject's duty is the King's; but every subject's soul is his own.[1]

As for the stuff of life and experience we cannot lay hold of it; we cannot lay down rules for it; no religion completely contains or expresses or formulates it; at the heart of man is a dream.

> We are such stuff
> As dreams are made on, and our little life
> Is rounded with a sleep.[2]

Such are his words of farewell. The only possible expression of that attitude is poetry. And since in that, as in so much else, Shakespeare expresses the inner instinct of his people, it is natural that the poetic should be the characteristic medium of the English in the arts.

The language itself ultimately reflects that high excitement, the opening out of new horizons. It is today very largely what the Elizabethans made it. Helter-skelter the new words came. They poured in, especially from Latin, to such an extent as to make the language a half-sister of the Romance languages, a bridge between the Germanic and Latin families, the speech of greatest catholicity and widest extension in the modern world. Even the chaste philologist allows that " no other half century has done so much for the permanent enrichment of the language as that which is covered by Shakespeare's lifetime ".[3] The language itself was in a highly suggestible, fluid, expanding condition: a mirror of the contemporary condition of the country. Never has a language been so absorptive: new words it gobbled up in no time. The enormous borrowings that went on from Latin, French, Greek, have been described as " a more or less unique phenomenon in the history of language "; and the result as " a language of unsurpassed richness and beauty, which, however, defies all rules ".[4] In this too, we may add, like the compounds of their own that the Elizabethans made out of Renaissance influences and their own creative vigour in architecture and the arts, in the drama, music and in thought. In Shakespeare, we are told, there are

[1] *Henry V*, IV. i. 189. [2] *The Tempest*, IV. i. 156.
[3] Henry Bradley in *Shakespeare's England*, II. 565.
[4] L. Pearsall Smith, *The English Language*, pp. 54, 73.

more new words found than in almost all the rest of English poets, and that his influence is to be seen " in the multitude of phrases derived from his writings which have entered into the texture of the diction of literature and daily conversation ".[1] But I suspect that a good deal of this comes from the speech of the day, if only we knew — like such a phrase as ' All that glisters is not gold ' : the upwelling into literature from the natural sources of speech.

There was far greater variety and local divergence of speech then than now, very much less ' standard English ', though such a thing was in process of establishing itself at the universities and among the educated. Even in the inmost circle at Court local inflexions were to be heard : you could tell where a man came from. Ralegh, we know, " spake broad Devonshire to his dying day ". The whole effect of spoken English was broader, coarser and more masculine. There was a wider range in vowel sounds : ' o ' sounds were spoken as in ' broad ' not as in modern Oxford ' holy ' ; the vowel in ' rule ' and ' fruit ' was spoken as in Devon or East Cornwall today, ' riwl ' or ' friwt '. All ' er ' sounds were spoken broadly as in ' serjeant ', not as in modern ' servant '. One can hear the effect in reading aloud the ending of a letter from that poor woman the Marchioness of Exeter, to her unsatisfactory son, Edward Courtenay, Earl of Devon, " by your lowfyng mothar, Gartrude Exettar ".[2] Henry Bradley says that Elizabethan speech would sound to us like " a mixture of vulgarisms and peculiarities of various provincial dialects ".[3] I cannot help feeling that it would have more force and colour and character than the more refined and somewhat devitalised modern English. The vitality of a language is evinced by the number and picturesqueness of its swear-words and abusive epithets : in these modern English is enormously poorer than the Elizabethan.

We may indeed trace the history of the time in the rich endowment we have inherited from them, in response to new experiences and to express new thoughts and increased knowledge. We note the words that came in with the Reformation and the religious disputes, always prolific in words of objurgation ; the exotic words that entered, through Portuguese and Spanish seamen and travellers, from the Far East and West.[4] Or such words as *mulatto*, first found in the account of Drake's last voyage, and *breeze*, which first appears from the Spanish in the account of one of Hawkins's voyages. From the wars in the Low Countries we derive such terms as *furlough*, *cashier*, *drill*, *forlorn hope* ; from

[1] Henry Bradley, *The Making of English*, p. 230. [2] S.P. 11/16/51.

[3] *Shakespeare's England*, II. 545. [4] Cf. L. Pearsall Smith, *op. cit.* p. 196 foll.

the war with Spain *embargo* and *contraband*; from the Dutch many sea terms. And all the time there is the immense importation going on from Latin and Greek to express the abstract ideas, the new notions seething in Elizabethan brains. There are large accessions to our literary and aesthetic vocabularies, to political terminology and that of science. The increasing national self-consciousness expresses itself; but most significant of all is the growth of words expressing self-awareness and personality, fancy and instinct, acuteness of observation, the psychological consequences of the sense of individuality that is at the core of the Renaissance experience.

It is pleasant to conclude with two examples of Elizabethan phrases that stand out from the unobserved multitude that pass upon our lips every day. An old friend of mine visiting a townswoman of Oxford during the 1914–18 war asked for the husband who was away in France; at that moment he came in. "Marry come up, here's John!" said she. Another friend during the recent war heard a Cotswold shepherd say, "I shall be seventy-five come Gunpowder eve".

Elizabethan music is an experience that we can share better today, thanks largely to the wireless and the gramophone, than at any time since the seventeenth century. As recently as 1938 Sir Donald Tovey wrote: "The time has long since passed in which any reasonable musician could doubt that the music of the sixteenth century indeed deserved its title of the Music of the Golden Age, and ought as such to be made the foundation of our musical experience and culture. It has not yet attained that position. . . ." [1] We can now say, only a decade after, that it has. There has been a notable revival of sixteenth-century music in our time, and not merely a revival but a genuine extension of our musical experience to include it. It was by far the greatest period there has ever been in English music. Actually it owed a great deal to the Reformation, which, as in other spheres, beginning with disarray and loss, in the end gave an immense new stimulus. Its first consequence was to end the monastic choirs and singing and throw a number of musicians out on the world, along with the printers and other craftsmen previously employed. That had the effect of stimulating secular music, comparable to the movement in architecture from building churches to houses. And musically, too, it was time for a change from the elaborate and timeless complexities of the settings of the Mass: Tridentine

[1] Sir D. Tovey, "The Main Stream of Music", *Proceedings of the British Academy* (1938), p. 116.

Rome had to order a reform in Church music. In England there was all the stimulus of having to find ways of setting English words for the services, far quicker, lighter and more varied than the staid and sonorous rhythms of Latin. The polyphony of the Church had become over-complex and esoteric, like the Church itself. The Reformation effected a simplification; there was the invigorating impulse of simplicity and a new world of English uses and words to explore with their quick and tripping rhythms. With all this there came in the Italian influences of madrigal and keyboard music. All gets going together, as in the drama and literature, upon a flood-tide of creative activity in a society which, as we shall see, was very propitious for and encouraging to the arts. The result was a splendid epoch in music, such as we have never known before or since, comparable only to the drama with which it was contemporary.

Now at last we can hear and appreciate that music: more and more is being brought out from the libraries where it has been buried for so long, studied and performed, given a renewed life. It is there, in the music of the Age, that one can hear its inner voice at its most affecting, breathe in its very breath, feel its pulses beating still. There is an extreme poignancy and beauty in it, in a motet of Tallis, a Mass of Byrd, a madrigal or an air of Dowland, to an extent that is hardly accountable. Is it that in their music we hear, more clearly than in anything else, their sense of the brief transitoriness of life; that in an age so extravert, so full of strain and effort and achievement, we hear in those falling cadences, those strangely disturbing harmonies, the quieter voices of regret, the human heart seeking its own stillness and rest from labour? It is very understandable in Byrd, greatest and most catholic of English musicians, for he was an adherent of the old Faith, and we hear in his settings for the Mass the fervour of his belief and affirmation against the evidence of the secular world in triumph, and in the motets he wrote for Corpus Christi day, *Ave Verum Corpus*, his personal devotion to the Blessed Sacrament. But there is the same nostalgia and pathos in the austere spirit of Tallis, in the touching and tender strains of Dowland and the madrigalists, in the sighing cadences of such a popular melody as "Greensleeves". It must be something in the time: the reaction of the spirit against a world in action.

> What if a day, or a month, or a year
>   Crown thy desire with a thousand sweet contentings;
> Cannot the chance of a night or an hour
>   Cross thy delight with as many sad tormentings?

Fortune, honour, beauty, youth,
Are but blossoms dying;
Wanton pleasures, doting love,
Are but shadows flying.
All our joys are but toys,
Idle thoughts deceiving.
None have power of an hour
In their lives' bereaving.[1]

It is a great gain to us that, more and more, Elizabethan music is entering into the stream of modern English experience, and with all the force of rediscovery. Already it may be said to have become " the foundation of our musical experience and culture ". A prime impulse in the Renaissance of English music, it has yielded rich returns in the inspiration given to a great composer, Vaughan Williams, to mention no others. His genius has been formed by it and permeated by it, as much as Keats's was by Shakespeare.

There are many other evidences of the Age that are active in us, activities of theirs that are continuous with us, which might be cited. Industrial England, that created the whole basis of modern industrial civilisation, the most dynamic power in modern history, goes back to Elizabeth's reign. It was then, particularly in the last decades, that coal-mining — the whole basis of this development — took a rapid and striking rise.[2] A minor consequence was the use of railways to carry the coal, the original wooden tracks for wagons from which modern railways have developed.[3] These years saw, too, the invention, by a Nottinghamshire clergyman, a Cambridge graduate, of the stocking-knitting frame, " which was the basis of all subsequent inventions in the field of knitting and lace-making machinery ".[4] These things pointed forward to the industrial future of the country.

It is only at this moment that we are beginning to understand, largely as the result of the work of American scholars, the importance and value of the scientific work done in this country in the latter part of the sixteenth century. Hitherto it has been thought of as a mere curiosity, an ante-room to the golden age of Hervey and Newton. We now know that Elizabethan science is of great interest in its own right, that activity was intense, and that, for example, one in ten of all the books published were on some

[1] Perhaps by Thomas Campion; cf. Norman Ault, *Elizabethan Lyrics*, p. 160.
[2] J. U. Nef, *The Rise of the British Coal Industry*, I. 21-5.
[3] C. E. Lee, *The Evolution of Railways* (2nd ed.), pp. 21-5.
[4] A. Wolf, *A History of Science, Technology and Philosophy in the 16th and 17th Centuries*, p. 465.

branch of science.[1] There was the mathematical and geographical work of John Dee and Thomas Hariot, the latter the foremost algebraist of the age, who left a mass of papers behind him and a posthumous book, making many advances, particularly in the theory of equations, and taking some steps in the direction of analytic geometry.[2] These men were at the centre of Elizabethan society, friends and acquaintances of its leading spirits, known to and backed by Queen and courtiers. There was the indefatigable work of Hakluyt, which bore such long-term fruits. Or the astronomical studies of Thomas Digges, with their practical consequences for navigation investigated by such men as Hood and Blundeville; the practical work on lenses by William Bourne; the astronomical instruments and gadgets of John Blagrave.[3] There are the naturalists, such men as William Turner, founder of English botany, Dr. Caius and Thomas Penny the botanist, not to mention the popular herbalists.[4] At the end of the age, in the reign of James I, John Napier of Merchiston invented logarithms; an invention of revolutionary import for arithmetic and commercial mathematics, one that apparently " affects the world with constantly increasing power ".[5] While East Anglia produced a great scientist in William Gilbert of Colchester. We certainly have not yet exhausted the significance of his book *De Magnete*, published in 1600: the foundation of the study of electromagnetism, its subject the properties of the magnet, of magnetic bodies and of ' that great magnet, the earth '. In it Gilbert propounds a whole theory of physics in terms of magnetism, the *Physiologia nova*, he calls it.[6] What is fascinating is that his position with regard to the magnetic properties of all large rotating bodies seems to be at this moment becoming the starting-point for a new line of development in physics. Gilbert was a great man whose work was known to, and approved by, Galileo. It was unfortunately depreciated by Bacon, who proclaimed the scientific method of experiment and induction, of which Gilbert's work is the greatest example in the Age, but which Bacon did little to explore.

The final achievement of the Elizabethan Age, its most en-

[1] F. R. Johnson, *Astronomical Thought in Renaissance England*, p. 9.

[2] D. E. Smith, *History of Mathematics*, I. 388.

[3] Cf. R. T. Gunther, " The Uranical Astrolabe and other Inventions of John Blagrave of Reading ", *Archaeologia* (1929), p. 55 foll.

[4] Cf. R. T. Gunther, *Early British Botanists*; C. E. Raven, *English Naturalists from Neckham to Ray*.

[5] D. E. Smith, *op. cit.* I. 389-90.

[6] Cf. Silvanus P. Thompson, *Notes on the ' De Magnete ' of Dr. William Gilbert.*

during monument — the decisive factor in the history of the modern world — is the English expansion overseas, the fact that North America is inhabited by English-speaking stock. What could be of more immediate impact upon every Englishman or woman alive today than this achievement of our forefathers, for to it we owe our very survival twice over in the course of one generation? The history, even of three centuries ago, is no remote thing; it comes home to us today, in the fruits of their efforts then. It is a popular legend, and dangerously misleading, to suppose that the English expansion overseas came about in a " fit of absence of mind ".[1] It is usually presented as a series of brilliant, adventurous episodes. There was plenty of adventure in it, infinite endurance, high courage and enterprise; but it was in fact a reasoned unity, a national venture. All the leading spirits of the age were concerned and interested and took part in it. The Queen herself was closely connected with the great Voyages, put money into a number of them, kept in touch with their plans and results, apparently knew more of what Drake intended on his Voyage round the World than was vouchsafed to her Lord Treasurer, gave him her support. Most of the leading men at Court were concerned, financially and intellectually: Burghley, Walsingham, Leicester; Sir Philip Sidney wanted to go to America, but was prevented, as was Essex later. We all know the cardinal importance of Ralegh, in planning the Virginia colony, and an empire in Guiana. He brought in Grenville, but before him was his half-brother, Humphrey Gilbert. The leading scientific minds of the time were engaged, Dee, the Hakluyts, Hariot, who wrote the *Brief and True Report of the new-found land of Virginia*, the first scientific report from the New World. And of course there were the capitalists, the merchants, the gentry and the sailors. In one way or another all the nation was involved, certainly men of all classes and conditions.

It is not surprising that the emergence of the New World is by far the greatest thing in the history of the Old. It mattered infinitely to the whole future course of history who took the opportunities the newly discovered world offered, and what they made of them. The English entered late, but in the end most effectively of all — and that was the work of the Elizabethans. Earlier in the century the distractions of the Reformation held us up. Once a new equilibrium was struck and society adapted itself, a working harmony established, new forces were released by the

[1] Cf. J. A. Williamson, Introduction to G. B. Parkes, *Richard Hakluyt and the English Voyages*, p. xv.

change — the surplus capital from the more productive employment of the country's resources, the increasing wealth and energy of the class which profited from the Dissolution and from trade: all raced forward together with a new momentum into progressive expansion beyond seas. The fact that North America was peopled by English-speaking stock is the greatest living monument to the Elizabethan Age: for that was the prize of the twenty years' warfare with Spain, fought not over religion (that was the flag each side fought under) but for power: the Spaniards to keep the monopoly of their Empire, the English for the gateway to the future. And not in North America alone. The Elizabethan voyagers entered the Pacific, they projected the quest for *Terra Australis*, the great continent they supposed to exist in the South Seas; they knew the West African coast and the coasts of South America, they rounded the Cape, they made the acquaintance of the Levant, the Middle East, of India and the East Indies. They foreshadowed the ways their people were to take in the centuries to come.

None of these evidences of their activities can be without interest for us; for they were the work of our forefathers. And we are still to some extent what they made us, all those who speak our tongue — even when we do not know.

CHAPTER II

THE ELIZABETHAN DISCOVERY OF ENGLAND

THE chroniclers and antiquaries of the Tudor period, various as they were in style and talent, shared the same sentiment, the same ambition. There breathed in each one of them the spirit of nationality. They recognised that the most brilliant discovery of a brilliant age was the discovery of their own country." So — perhaps a little too robustly — Mr. Charles Whibley. All the same, there is truth in what he says.[1] The increasing self-consciousness of the nation may be regarded as the fruit of the twin impulses of Renaissance and Reformation. For if the one meant a ripening intellectual climate leading to the self-awareness of the individual man, the other gave an edge, an aggressiveness, to the country's sense of itself, since its leaders were taking it along an independent course contrary to traditional Europe. Those who were in favour of the new course set — and these were the dynamic elements in the nation — were acutely conscious both of its dangers and its hopes, and Englishmen were defiant about it.

It is not so surprising, then, that the prime discoverers of the English past and present, the chroniclers and topographers, the antiquarians, surveyors and map-makers, were a strongly Protestant lot. It is indeed striking. One might have expected them, students and lovers of the past, to have been Catholics. But they were not. I have suggested the reason: they were looking back into the past for support on the new uncharted course; the course itself appealed to the spirit of national independence and elicited hidden resources of national pride.

The deeper one goes into these movements of the human spirit, the less one likes abstractions about them, even such necessary abstractions as Renaissance and Reformation, and the less one feels able to impute those movements and developments to any one strand in so complex a pattern. These things are

[1] *Cambridge History of English Literature*, III. 313.

really the fruit of men's experience; they grow out of men's lives and circumstances, out of what they are and do in a changing world. But there is an increasing awareness of the land itself, a matter of geography and history, that ultimately affects the realm of the imagination. And here we have a starting-point, for it all goes back to Leland.

It is impossible to exaggerate the importance of Leland as topographer and antiquary, as the discoverer of his own country — though so far from anyone trying, most merely literary estimates of him fail to grasp the astonishing character of his endeavour and what he achieved.[1] The flood of Tudor work in chronicles and surveys, topography and antiquities, the immense volume of publications that arose to meet the insatiable curiosity of Englishmen about their country and its past, scholars like Laurence Nowell and William Lambarde, geographers like Humphry Lluyd and Dee and Norden, chroniclers like Holinshed and Harrison, John Hooker and Stow and Speed, map-makers and antiquaries such as Saxton and Ralph Agas, or Carew and Ersdeswicke, above all, the magistral Camden, with whose *Britannia* Tudor scholarship attained its majority — it all went back to Leland. Not the less so, but the more, because he did not live to finish his work or even to put his immense collections of notes together: they remained a rich quarry for succeeding generations to rifle, like the abbeys he saw go down before his eyes.

Leland was a very characteristic scholar of the Renaissance and — though not a man of genius like More — the greatest in his kind that England had yet, or perhaps has ever, produced. Think what he achieved, and what he had it in mind to accomplish. As he wrote in his "New Year's Gift" to Henry VIII in 1546, inspired by reading the chroniclers of the English past, "I was totally inflamed with a love to see thoroughly all those parts of this your opulent and ample realm that I had read of in the aforesaid writers: in so much that, all my other occupations intermitted, I have travelled in your dominions both by the sea coasts and the middle parts, sparing neither labour nor costs, by the space of these six years past, that there is almost neither cape nor bay, haven, creek or pier, river or confluence of rivers, breaches, washes, lakes, meres, fenny waters, mountains, valleys, moors, heaths, forests, woods, cities, boroughs, castles, principal manor places, monasteries and colleges, but I have seen them;

[1] Cf. Charles Whibley, *Camb. Hist. of Eng. Lit.* III. 328-30, and the article on Leland by Sir Sidney Lee in *D.N.B.*

and noted in so doing a whole world of things very memorable ".[1] The extraordinary thing is that he practically accomplished it: we have the evidence in his celebrated *Itinerary* — what remains of his topographical notes, which had to wait until this century for a satisfactory edition.

The fact is that Leland saw the country at a poignant historic moment, when all the monasteries were going down, their libraries and precious possessions being dispersed, the churches unroofed and destroyed, monuments and tombs defaced and laid open to the weather. It was, like our time, the end of an age: we ought to be able to view his predicament with sympathy. He must have been torn in two. Like most sensible men, his sympathies were with the new order; on the other hand, he loved the past and its visible memorials. He was a poet, and evidently had the temperament of one. A kind friend of his tells us: " I much do fear it that he was vainglorious, and that he had a poetical wit, which I lament, for I judge it one of the chiefest things that caused him to fall beside his right discernings ".[2] It was a gigantic task that Leland proposed himself: to publish the acts of the King's progenitors, to set forth " your world and empire of England " upon a quadrate table of silver, the four books of Famous Men out of British writers, the six books on the islands adjacent to Britain, the fifty books, one for each shire, concerning the antiquity of Britain. There seems to have been a megalomaniac streak in Leland, as in his monarch, as perhaps in the Renaissance itself. No wonder he went off his head, leaving his books unpublished, unfinished — he was one of those authors — but leaving volumes of débris for others, more fortunate, to rout in.

In truth, it is a wonderful picture of the country that the *Itinerary* conveys, in spite of what has been lost. It is absurd, and anachronistic, to charge Leland with a lack of the sense of the picturesque, the absence of descriptive detail. Such a criticism shows no sense of the time: Leland would have thought it inappropriate: he put that into his Latin poems, especially the " Cygnea Cantio ", which is a specifically descriptive poem. But there is everything else one could expect: the towns, the churches with their monuments, castles, the houses going up and for whom, the industries, clothing, coal-pits and quarries, agriculture whether champion or enclosed, the lie of the country — a whole picture of England, fresh, concrete, piquant, sparkling like

[1] *The Itinerary of John Leland* (ed. by Toulmin Smith), I. xli.

[2] John Bale's Preface to " The New Year's Gift ", in *The Lives of Leland, Hearne and Wood*, 1772.

quartz. We see him ranging about the country, insatiably curious, taking in everything with his eye, getting access to the monastic libraries, copying extracts from their chronicles before it is too late.[1] Now he is at Deene in Northamptonshire taking down what Mr. Brudenell can tell him from old records, or asking questions from the vicar at Weedon; now he tells us the strange tale of the end of the house of Paynells, with two Johns, " both knights and great lechers " and how the son " begot abominably a daughter of his own daughter ". Now he is in Cornwall, stopping at Fowey with Thomas Treffry, who tells him the story of the town; or in Yorkshire at Wressle Castle, where he " liked exceedingly " the Earl of Northumberland's study called Paradise, in one of the towers, with an ingenious arrangement of book-rests upon the desks, calculated to seduce the heart of a scholar. Or he notes the sculptures upon the abbey church at Bath, or the gardens and orchards with " mounts *opere topiario* writhen about with degrees like turnings of cockleshells to come to the top without pain ".

For all his close adherence to fact, one knows that he must have been obsessed by a passion, the passion for seeing the country, the love of the road, of sky and wind and weather. He belonged to the select class that includes Celia Fiennes, Defoe, John Wesley, Cobbett, George Borrow: the first of them all. Patriotism was the motive that spurred him on and kept him single-handed on his course until the spirit broke under the strain. He wrote a Defence of Geoffrey of Monmouth against Polydore Vergil, who denied the legendary foundation of the realm of Britain by Brutus. No love was lost between Leland and Polydore: he was an Italian. Another Latin tractate Leland devoted to asserting the historicity of King Arthur.[2] He could not bear to think that foreigners, especially Italians, should think us barbarous and unlettered, and he promised the King " I trust so to open this window that the light shall be seen so long, that is to say, by the space of a whole thousand years, stopped up, and the old glory of your renowned Britain to reflourish through all the world ".[3] Then the light in himself flickered and went out.

But not before he had handed it on to his successors: all that came after him were his followers, the chief among them his direct debtors. " No student of the antiquarian activities of the

[1] These form the bulk of Leland's *Collectanea* (6 vols.), ed. by Thomas Hearne, 1774.

[2] Both these are printed in *Collectanea*, vol. V.

[3] *The Itinerary*, I. xlii.

second half of the sixteenth century", Mr. Flower tells us, "can fail to perceive Leland's ideals at work."[1] In truth, by the turn of the century they were in various ways and by different hands carried out. "The vain attempts of Bale and Sir Robert Cotton and his associates to persuade Queen Mary and Queen Elizabeth to erect a Royal Library for the preservation of England's antiquities, the creation by Archbishop Parker and Cotton of the great libraries which served as a substitute for this defeated design, the histories of Holinshed and others, the publication by Parker and his associates of English chronicles, the *Britannia* of William Camden, and the magnificent development of Elizabethan cartography — all these vigorous enterprises hark back to Leland, and his name is always on the lips of the participants in this great movement for the rediscovery of the English past and the depiction of the physical face of England."

An interesting intermediary between the generation of Henry VIII and that of Elizabeth is Laurence Nowell, brother of the better known Alexander, Dean of St. Paul's. Laurence Nowell is rightly regarded as the chief reviver of the Anglo-Saxon language and learning; he left an Old English Dictionary in manuscript, now in the Bodleian. But his aims were wider, his mind set upon the mapping of England, the bringing into light and use of the earlier sources for English topography. In the sixties Nowell was a member of Cecil's household as tutor to the latter's young ward, the Earl of Oxford. Cecil himself had a passion for the acquisition of information about every aspect of the realm in his paternal care and there must have been much discussion about the need for new and better maps of the country. In 1563 Nowell made a formal proposal to Cecil for his aid in undertaking maps of the whole country and of all the separate shires.[2] Nothing came of this; but Cecil gave support in the next decade to Christopher Saxton who achieved what Nowell proposed. Nevertheless, evidences of Nowell's work remain: a group of exquisitely finished maps, one of which Cecil seems to have carried about with him. His map of Scotland is regarded as much in advance of that of the great Mercator.

During these years in London when Nowell was in close touch with the circles of Cecil and Parker, both much interested in the collection of manuscripts and the illumination of the past, he

[1] R. Flower, "Laurence Nowell and the Discovery of England in Tudor Times", reprinted from *Proc. British Academy*, XXI. 5.

[2] *Original Letters of Eminent Literary Men* (ed. Sir H. Ellis, Camden Society), pp. 21-3.

made large transcripts from Bede, Geraldus Cambrensis, Matthew Paris and Higden. Like Cecil himself, he was interested in finding out all he could learn about Ireland: he prepared a Description of Ireland, now lost. He worked away at the laws of the Anglo-Saxons, along with his dictionary of the language. But he published nothing: he preferred the pleasures of church preferment to the grind of producing his books.

Fortunately, he left a pupil and disciple, to whom he passed on his books and collections: William Lambarde, author of the *Perambulation of Kent*, " famous as the first of the great series of county histories which are one of the glories of English antiquarian scholarship ".[1] That book provided a model for the group of county surveys which are such a delightful feature of the last decade of the reign. (They increased rapidly in number in the next.) But that is not Lambarde's only claim to fame. He first finished off his master's work on the Anglo-Saxon laws and published it in 1568 under the title *Archaionomia*. The first draft of the *Perambulation* was completed in 1570, read in manuscript by both Parker and Burghley, and published in 1576. Lambarde also intended a survey of the whole country, for which he made a Topographical Dictionary, " out of which I meant in time (if God granted life and leisure) to draw (as from a certain store house) fit matter for each particular shire and county ".[2] But no amount of leisure could complete the whole country on the scale of his *Kent*. So he concentrated on that by way of encouraging " some one able man of each shire to undertake his own ".[3] He went on to publish his *Eirenarcha* in 1581, a complete treatise in four books on the office of Justice of the Peace, which had the success it deserved in a time when the powers and responsibilities of the local gentry were constantly increasing. He wrote another book *Archeion*, on the high Courts of Justice, besides a number of useful tracts on kindred subjects, before becoming immersed in the delights of playing a part in the life of his county as J.P. and of the country as Master in Chancery and keeper of the records in the Tower.[4]

In this capacity Lambarde had an audience of the Queen in the Privy Chamber at Greenwich, not many months after Essex's conspiracy. Since this is her first appearance — a very character-

[1] Flower, *ibid.* p. 13. [2] q. in Flower, *ibid.*

[3] W. Lambarde, *A Perambulation of Kent* (ed. of 1596), p. 527. All quotations are from this edition.

[4] For Lambarde's life *v.* article in *D.N.B.*; John Nichols, " Memoirs of William Lambarde ", *Bibliotheca Topographica Britannica*, I. 493 foll.

istic one — in this book, and Lambarde wrote an account of it, here it is.[1] He had brought her his *Pandecta* (in Latin) of all her rolls, bundles, membranes of documents reposing in the Tower. The Queen received his gift saying: "'You intended to present this book unto me by the Countess of Warwick. But I will none of that; for if any subject of mine do me a service, I will thankfully accept it at his own hands.' Then opening the book said, 'You shall see that I can read,' and so with an audible voice read over the epistle and the title so readily and distinctly pointed that it might perfectly appear that she well understood and conceived the same." She then politely asked the meaning of such terms as *oblata*, *litterae clausae* and *litterae patentes*, giving the old scholar the opportunity to expound what she perhaps understood, and assuring him "that she would be a scholar in her age and thought it no scorn to learn during life, being of the mind of the philosopher who in his last years began with the Greek alphabet". Then, casting her eye down the list of reigns of the kings, "her Majesty fell upon the reign of King Richard II saying, 'I am Richard II. Know ye not that?'" (Essex's friends made much of the deposition of Richard II; one of them put down money to have Shakespeare's play performed the afternoon before the outbreak.) Lambarde answered: "Such a wicked imagination was determined and attempted by a most unkind gentleman, the most adorned creature that ever your Majesty made." The Queen: "He that will forget God will also forget his benefactors. This tragedy was played forty times in open streets and houses."

Next she asked, What was *praestita*? Lambarde explained — moneys lent by her progenitors to their subjects upon bond for repayment. The Queen: "So did my good grandfather King Henry VII, sparing to dissipate his treasure or lands." But the old woman could not get Richard II out of her mind, she turned back to ask "whether I had seen any true picture or lively representation of his countenance and person". Lambarde: "None but such as be in common hands." The Queen: "The Lord Lumley, a lover of antiquities, discovered it fastened on the backside of a door of a base room: which he presented unto me, praying, with my good leave, that I might put it in order with the ancestors and successors. I will command Thomas Knyvet, keeper of my house and gallery at Westminster, to show it unto thee."

She then came to the rolls and asked "if redisseisins were unlawful and forcible throwing of men out of their lawful

[1] *Ibid.* App. VII, I. 525.

possessions ". Lambarde replied: " Yes, and hence the rolls of fines levied upon such wrong-doers." The Queen: " In those days force and arms did prevail; but now the wit of the fox is everywhere on foot so as hardly a faithful and virtuous man may be found." When she came to the total of all the records, she gave Lambarde great praise, " not only for the pains therein taken, but also for that she had not received since her first coming to the Crown any one thing that brought therewith so great delectation unto her. . . . And so being called away to prayer, she put the book into her bosom, having forbidden me from the first to the last to fall upon my knee before her, concluding: 'Farewell, good and honest Lambarde!' "

A touching interview in its way, between an old and famous woman and an ancient faithful scholar. One sees how badly her confidence had been shaken by Essex's treason, the mood of distrust and despair of men that settled on her from now until the end. But there was the same royal graciousness that had always marked her. A couple of weeks and the old man was dead; two years on and she too was no more.

Lambarde was not by origin a Kent man; his family came from Ledbury, to which his father left a legacy for paving the town-end. The father had prospered in trade in London as a draper, one of the new middle class, became alderman and sheriff of the city, married a woman of some property, and bought the manor of Westcombe near Greenwich. This made the son a Kent man, and he displayed a proper Kentish pride not only in his life but in his book. He recognises that the gentry of Kent are not of such ancient stocks as elsewhere, for merchants, lawyers and courtiers were continually being transplanted thither from London. Thomas Wootton, to whom the book was dedicated and who was of an old Kent family, recommended it to his " Countrymen, the Gentlemen of the County of Kent . . . and thus, as of yourselves, do you see what they are now, and thus of this book may you know why they were, and by whom they were, and what they were long agone ". He asserts, what was a commonplace with Elizabethans, the value of the study of history, especially for gentlemen, upon whom the good estate of England principally rests.

Lambarde is as proud of his county as any one of the most ancient stock in it. No part of the realm has so many orchards, or so many parks — though one-half of the latter have been disparked within living memory. The peculiar custom of gavelkind prevailing there meant that " in manner every man is a freeholder, and hath some part of his own to live upon ". We are given a considerable list of Kentish writers, and of free schools to the number of eleven. The Kentish people " by an ancient prerogative of manhood, challenge the first front in each battle ". It is when he comes to Gillingham and the Queen's ships riding there that he is most moved: " No town, nor city is there (I dare say) in this whole shire comparable in right value with this one fleet: nor shipping anywhere else in the whole world to be found, either more artificially moulded under the water, or more gorgeously decked above ". That we can well believe: they were the ships that were to beat the King of Spain.

He has a strong Protestant patriotism. He is proud of the way the affairs of the country have been managed both at home and abroad under Elizabeth's good government. Henry VIII is his hero, the

Majestic lord that broke the bonds of Rome.

Open contempt runs through his account of the old monastic superstitions, the delusions of the Nun of Kent, by whom " the silly people were miserably mocked ". He enjoyed the exposure of the Holy Rood of Boxley, rigged up by a clever carpenter to roll its eyes and impress the idiot people. One sees that Protestantism marked a certain advance in rationality. As with Leland there is the same patriotic sentiment with regard to the past. The Britons embraced Christianity long before Gregory sent his mission from Rome. But it is an error to say, as Julius Caesar did, that the Britons were indigenous, for " that would but lead us to distrust the infallible Scriptures of God concerning the creation and propagation of mankind ". Lambarde has a short excursus on the authority of Geoffrey of Monmouth's British history, in which he defends him against Polydore and replies shrewdly that if Polydore is to " deprive this nation of all manner of knowledge of their first beginning ", this opens the way for us to call in question the origin and antiquities of Spain, France, Germany and even of Italy, Polydore's own country.

From the *Perambulation* we can see something of Lambarde's circle of antiquarian friends, all alike fired with zeal to learn about their country. He refers to " Master Stow mine old friend ", who lent him some of Leland's notes. He cites the opinion of Master Twyne that a land-bridge once existed between Dover and Calais. This was the interesting, if occasionally inebriated, antiquary who was Master of the King's school at Canterbury and wrote a work *De Rebus Albionicis, Britannicis atque Anglis*. He produced a son and grandson who were also given to these studies Philip Symonson, superintendent of Rochester bridge and mayor of Rochester, was another friend: he published a description of the shire and surveyed the Bridge estates.[1] Most agreeable of all are the friendly references to Camden, " the most lightsome antiquary of this age ". When Lambarde learned that Camden was engaged upon his *Britannia*, he gave up his own project of a general survey. Though, one may be sure, not without a pang, from his letter to the younger (and greater) scholar: " In reading of these your painful topographies, I have been contrarily affected; one way taking singular delight and pleasure in the perusing of them; another way by sorrowing that I may not now, as I wanted, dwell in the meditation of the same things that you are occupied withal. And yet I must confess that the delectation which I reaped by your labours recompensed the grief that I conceived of mine own bereaving from the like: notwithstanding that in times past I have preferred the reading of antiquities before any sort of study that ever I frequented."[2] Lambarde wrote " in the midst of our preparation for the country musters and other services that withdraw my mind. . . . And so praying God to bless your studies, and eftsoons wishing that you would spend a week at Halling with me." He offered Camden the use of his notes, and, sure enough, when his *Britannia* appeared, it contained a tribute to Lambarde as " eminent for learning and piety ". The 'piety' referred in particular to Lambarde's charitable foundation of almshouses, the College of the Poor of Queen Elizabeth, at Greenwich, upon which he spent a small fortune. It is an agreeable feature of the antiquarian society of the Elizabethan Age, and a rather unwonted one, that scholars were on such friendly terms with each other. It would seem that they felt there was so much work to be done, and in honour of the country, that they were only too anxious to co-operate.

It was in the fifteen-eighties — those wonderful years that saw so many things burst into a flame of activity, the war with Spain, the beginning of the madrigals, the maturing of the young poets, Greene, Spenser, Marlowe — that the antiquaries came together to form a society, which met in London to explore and discuss the past of their own country.[3] For the next twenty years the

[1] *Archaeologia Cantiana*, XXXI. 271. [2] Nichols, *op. cit.* App. II, I. 512.

[3] The account of the Society in *Archaeologia*, vol. I, says that " its foundation may be fixed to the 14th year " of the reign, *i.e.* 1572; and that has been usually followed since. It seems to be based only on reading back from a reference of Spelman's in 1614 to " about 42 years since ". But I do not know of any evidence of continuous activity until the fifteen-eighties.

varying company, according to who happened to be in London, met in the house of Sir Robert Cotton in Westminster. Those who lived in or near London saw most of each other: Camden and his rich young pupil and friend, Cotton; Sir William Dethick, Sir John Doddridge, Serjeant Fleetwood, all of them holding official positions; Francis Thynne, George Hakewill, John Stow. These were occasionally joined by such men as William Lambarde, Richard Carew from Cornwall, Sampson Erdeswicke from Staffordshire, Arthur Agard from Derbyshire, Sir John Davies when over from Ireland; Sir Henry Spelman came up from Norfolk to live near Cotton and enjoy the pleasures of these pursuits. The friends never became a formal Society, though they very much wished to. About 1589 they resolved to apply to the Queen for a grant of incorporation, and some public building in which to meet. There was a tradition that some such grant was promised; but the government had other things to think of, and was now far too hard pressed financially to found anything. Nor, when peace came, with a king who plumed himself upon his scholarship, was anything done: James was too much taken with the unrewarding conceits of theology; he was too generous to his favourites.

Though the project of a formal Society came to nothing, the influence of the circle was immeasurable. They encouraged each other's work; they set going the tradition of English antiquarian learning which has been continuous ever since. We can trace the immediate influence of the circle in the contributions of its members to county history, which is one of the peculiar glories of English scholarship. The books that emerged from it have marked common characteristics in method and treatment. They were in touch with similar work going forward on the Continent, as were the geographers and cosmographers; in this case with such a book as Guicciardini's *Description of the Low Countries*, and the works of Bodin and De Thou.

Lambarde's *Kent* was the first of the county surveys, but I hope it will not be taken for partiality if I hold that Carew's *Survey of Cornwall* is the most readable and delightful. Though not published until 1602, it was taken in hand in the eighties: the first edition of Camden's *Britannia* in 1586 promised it. It had for some time circulated in manuscript. Carew was an excellent linguist and literary scholar, well read in modern literature, who had translated Tasso and Juan de la Huarte from the Italian.[1] His

[1] Cf. article in *D.N.B.*; my *Tudor Cornwall*, pp. 421-6; Carew's *Survey of Cornwall* (ed. 1811), for "Life of Richard Carew", by Hugh C—.

book is a charming minor masterpiece of Elizabethan prose, written with a pleasant facetiousness, a quaintness of humour and a certain flavour of archaism that give one the character of the man. Carew was not so learned in antiquities as Lambarde and Camden, but his book is more alive and appealing: it lives still in its own right. He was a good scholar and followed an admirable method: the first Book is a general survey of the character and commodities of the shire, the second a particular survey of it place by place.

In Cornwall he had a good subject, a county with an individuality of its own, like no other, and with certain marked peculiarities. He made the most of it. He gives us a first-class account of tin-mining, the prime industry of Cornwall and one of the foremost of the realm: "with such plenty thereof hath God stuffed the bowels of this little angle, that (as Astiages dreamed of his daughter) it overfloweth England, watereth Christendom, and is derived to a great part of the world besides".[1] Carew goes into vivid detail about methods of working; much of his information he derived from his friend, Sir Francis Godolphin, the leading tin magnate in West Cornwall which was forging ahead at this time. The pilchard industry was another that was practically peculiar to Cornwall, with its large export of *fumados* (smoked and pressed pilchards) to Spain and Italy: of this too Carew gives us a valuable description. Similarly with Cornish weights and measures: almost every county offered varieties of its own, but Cornwall also varied within itself. There are excellent accounts of prevailing tenures and Cornish agriculture, of their distinctive games, hurling and wrestling, and of the miracle plays that were still performed. Then too there was the language. It is a pity that among the languages which, according to the inscription on Carew's monument in Antony church, he knew, Cornish could not claim a place. It is clear that, though he gives us common phrases of conversation and a number of words, he did not know it: it had died out in East Cornwall by his time. But he more than made up for this defect by his good scholarship, his human interest, the freshness and charm of his English. His book is full of such passages as this: "Of all manner of vermin, Cornish houses are most pestered with rats, a brood very hurtful for devouring of meat, clothes and writings by day; and alike cumbersome through their crying and rattling, while they dance their gallop galliards in the roof at night".[2]

Carew's book is very characteristic of its time: in its curiosity

[1] *Survey*, p. 25. [2] *Ibid.* p. 73.

and good sense, with streaks of the usual credulity that made him accept the natural history of the barnacle and several tall stories, the legends about the origins of Cornwall with Corineus, and about Goneril, " one of King Lear's daughters and heirs ", in its county pride and interest in ancient custom and folk-lore. Carew spent the whole of his life in Cornwall and so was cut off from enjoying much of the society he delighted in: " Sir," he wrote to Cotton in 1605, " I pray you give me leave to impart unto you my grief that my so remote dwelling depriveth me of your sweet and respected antiquarian Society, into which your kindness towards me and grace with them made me an entrance, and unto which (notwithstanding so long discontinuance) my longing desire layeth a continual claim ".[1] Of Camden: " I must confess, I am tainted with a spark of envy or rather applaud to his good fortune, which, beyond mine, hath assisted his industry with the sight and use of so many antiquities and antiquarians ". One could not expect much intelligent conversation in Cornwall: dear Carew made the most of his limited opportunities. But he was appreciated in a wider sphere: Spelman dedicated his *Epistle on Tithes* to him; John Dunbar and Fitzgeffrey addressed to him Latin epigrams; he is enshrined in a famous poem of Ben Jonson's: the latter is speaking of a work of his own,

> Wherein was oil, beside the succour spent,
> Which noble Carew, Cotton, Selden lent.[2]

It has hitherto escaped notice that Carew had an imitator in George Owen with his *Description of Pembrokeshire*.[3] There are many similarities between this book and Carew's *Survey*, both in general plan and in detail. Owen followed Carew's plan of devoting a first Book to a general survey of the county, which he completed — and an admirable book it is. For the second Book, he made out a detailed questionnaire to be sent to the gentlemen of every parish to answer. Not unnaturally he got no further. Carew did the job for himself. The *Survey* came out in 1602; Owen wrote his *Description* next year. It is a thorough and excellent piece of work. George Owen of Henllys was much the same kind of man as Carew: a country gentleman of old stock, a busy J.P. and Vice-Admiral of his county, a patriotic Pembrokeshireman. He had certain advantages over Carew: a more learned antiquarian, much more given to searching rolls and records, a good geologist, who has an honoured name as such. He

[1] *Letters of Eminent Literary Men* (ed. Ellis), pp. 98-9.
[2] " An Execration upon Vulcan ", in *Works* (ed. Herford and Simpson), VIII. 207.
[3] Ed. by Henry Owen, 1892.

was more of a pure historian, interested in legal documents and in monuments, of which he had an extensive knowledge. He too was a friend of Camden: "A dear friend of mine and famous for his learning".[1] It was Camden who had encouraged them both. There was a common method and cast of mind running through their investigations. Pembroke too had its peculiarities which are well brought out. For one thing, it was almost equally divided between the Welsh and the English of 'Little England'. In the latter, a man would say, "Look; there goeth a Welshman".[2] Owen's point of view, in spite of his name, was not that of the Welsh: he belonged to the gentry, his patriotism was that of a Pembrokeshireman against the Welsh. He took pride in the fact that it was men of Pembroke who had subdued both Wales and Ireland for the kings of England. That made him regret only the more the ending of the palatine jurisdiction of Pembroke by the Tudors and the county's assimilation to Wales by Henry VIII's Welsh Statutes. Like Carew, Owen has a section devoted to the notable men of the county, from Geraldus, "our dear and loving countryman to whom above all other our country is most beholding"[3], to Bishop Davies, translator of the New Testament and the Prayer Book into Welsh, who planted the diocese with his relations and naturally had many troubles.

Owen's survey is just as thorough as Carew's — if anything more so: admirable accounts of Pembrokeshire agriculture, industries, weights and measures, tenures, pastimes, sports. The characteristic game of 'knappan' was the same as hurling in Cornwall, and we have a vivid description of how it was played, often ending up with a free fight for all concerned: Owen still bore the old scars on him of former games. He had Carew's eye and ear for customary life; on the different tithe-customs, "I might write a whole book".[4] They had in truth an extraordinary similarity of outlook: to picture the mind of an Elizabethan country gentleman of more than average intelligence and piety, of learning and of antiquarian pursuits, we need only compare their books. The marl-beds which were being increasingly used for fertiliser, the fossils of fish left in the geological strata in the sides of hills, were evidences of Noah's Flood — if evidences were needed. But they were not: the Bible, extraordinary as it seems to us, explained everything to them. The abundance of woodcock (alas, for those days!) was such that it may be "they are engendered and raised by the mere easterly wind of some substance

[1] Owen, *Description of Pembrokeshire*, p. 68. [2] *Ibid.* p. 47.
[3] *Ibid.* p. 231. [4] *Ibid.* p. 194.

here in the country; the like whereof you may read of divers other fowls and other worms in Pliny ".[1] And all is said with the unconscious freshness, the natural eloquence with which men spoke and wrote at the time. Here are two kinds of furze: " This last kind blossometh with the heath in the latter end of harvest against winter, whereas the former accompanieth the broom and bloweth in May against the summer ".[2] Here is clover: " The herb called *Trifolium*, or three-leaved grass, and of the country people honey-suckles both white and red; so that in the summer time the land will be all covered with these flowers and look with a claret colour mingled with white and red, and will yield a most pleasant and fragrant odour and smell, proceeding from these sweet flowers ".[3] And of the alteration in the church, as witnessed by the spoil of St. David's: " So are the minds of men altered with the time until time turn men into dust ".[4]

Another of the circle to write a survey of his county was Sampson Erdeswicke, author of the *Survey of Staffordshire.* His book has nothing of the comprehensiveness of Carew's or Owen's, and is in fact on quite different lines; but it has its interest. A Catholic of an old stock, with the dislike of a man of the old order for the new, Erdeswicke was interested in families and the places where they lived. From this point of view he gives us a valuable record of the changes effected by the Reformation. He never fails to tell us when some new man managed to come by a desirable bit of church property, or to install himself in place of an old family. Something like a third of the properties in the county had changed hands in those ways during the century: in itself evidence of the social upset of the Reformation. At Colwich, a Lancashire gentleman, now the owner of the dissolved cell, " (as I have heard) hath made a parlour of the chancel, a hall of the church and a kitchen of the steeple, which may be true for I have known a gentleman in Cheshire who hath done the like '.[5] It sounds a very sensible arrangement: much what Sir Richard Grenville did at Buckland Abbey. A good clutch of estates around Beaudesert that had belonged to the Bishops of Coventry and Lichfield were now in the hands of the Catholic Lord Paget. The fact that you were a Catholic did not prevent you from getting and making the most of Church lands. Nor did it prevent Erdeswicke from new glazing and repairing his parish church, or from being buried there along with his forefathers under a vast monument.

[1] *Ibid.* p. 130. [2] *Ibid.* p. 94. [3] *Ibid.* p. 72. [4] *Ibid.* p. 85.
[5] Erdeswicke, *A Survey of Staffordshire* (ed. 1717), p. 179.

Erdeswicke was writing his book in the nineties; he died in 1603. In the next decade there appeared, under the name of John Coker of Mappowder, a *Survey of Dorsetshire.* But now we are in the reign of James, and the full harvest of the antiquarian enthusiasm of the Elizabethans is being reaped in book after book: Tristram Risdon's *Survey of Devon,* Westcote's *View of Devon,* Habington's *Survey of Worcestershire,* Burton's *Leicestershire,* culminating in the work of Dugdale later, from which these studies have never looked back.

Parallel to all this, and linked with it, is the interest in the geographical illumination of the country. That in turn was part of the immense and specific geographical excitement of the time. It has been said that geography is in a sense the characteristic science of the modern age as astronomy was of antiquity. Certainly it held a cardinal position in that revolutionary extension of knowledge which was the Renaissance. And for the best of reasons: the world was expanding before men's eyes. We are not concerned with all that here, but merely with something of its effect upon the discovery of England. The prime centre of geographical study, of cartography and map-making, had passed in the course of the Renaissance, along with much else, from Italy and the Mediterranean to the shores of Northern Europe: another of the profound movements of the time which underlie the modern age. In these years the Low Countries and the Rhineland, above all Antwerp, were the centre of the most advanced geographical thought: the leading figures, Sebastian Münster, Gemma Phrysius, Abraham Ortelius, the great Mercator.[1] The chief intermediaries between them and this country were the two Welshmen, Humphry Lluyd and John Dee.

The influence of Dee was far-reaching, but he was mainly concerned with oceanic discovery and overseas voyages. Humphry Lluyd was an interesting link between Antwerp and London on one hand, supplying Ortelius with information for maps of this country, and, on the other, between Leland again, whom he had known as a young man, and the Elizabethans. A handsome, red-headed North Welshman of Denbigh, Lluyd married the sister of Lord Lumley, first of Elizabethan connoisseurs. It was his fellow townsman Richard Clough, the right-hand man of the great financier Gresham at Antwerp, that first introduced Lluyd to Ortelius. They became fast friends, united

[1] Cf. E. G. R. Taylor, *Tudor Geography, 1485–1583,* pp. 75-88.

by their passionate interest in the new geography. From his deathbed, still a youngish man of forty, Lluyd sent his friend the maps of England and Wales to which he had devoted his last days, along with his chief writing, the *Commentarioli*, afterwards published at Cologne and translated as *A Breviary of Britain*. " Dearly beloved Ortelius," Lluyd wrote, " neither the daily shaking of the continual fever, with a double tertian, neither the looking for present death, neither the vehement headache without intermission could put the remembrance of my Ortelius out of my troubled brain. Wherefore I send you my Wales not beautifully set forth in all points, yet truly depainted, so be that certain notes be observed, which I gathered even when I was ready to die. . . . Take therefore this last remembrance of thy Humphry and for ever adieu, my dear friend Ortelius. From Denbigh, in Gwyneth, or North Wales, the XXXth of August 1568. Yours both living and dying, Humphry Lluyd." [1]

This ardent Welshman comes across to us a very affecting and a living person, though we know little about him. He was a physician and a cultivated gentleman, who cared for music and the arts as well as for science. He wrote in Latin, but what gives his book its chief value is the Welsh knowledge he is able to draw upon, his Celtic angle upon the past. He gives a brief description of the country shire by shire, with the English and Latin names and also the Welsh (for example, Derbyshire is Dwr gwent = white water). Sometimes he adds interesting information from Welsh sources, such as that after Strathclyde was overthrown by the conjunction of English, Danes and Scots, the inhabitants joined their Welsh countrymen and settled between Dee and Conway. He makes the sound — and welcome — point that derivations of the early names of the island are not to be sought for in Greek or Latin but in the ancient British tongue. It is curious that this was not appreciated by the scholars of the time: dominated as they were by the classics they were apt to derive any obscure name from Latin, if they could, or if not, from Greek.

Lluyd understood the relation of Brittany to Britain, and reproves Bede the Englishman and Polydore the Italian for getting it the wrong way round. " Our countrymen say that the Cornishmen and those [Bretons] were one nation, which both the kings' names, being like in both countries as Conan, Meriadoc, Hoel, Alan, Theodore, Rywallon . . . and also the proper words and names for all things almost one . . . do prove manifestly." [2] He

[1] Humphry Lluyd, *A Breviary of Britain* (trans. by Thomas Twyne, 1573).

[2] *Ibid.* p. 10.

has all the traditional lore of Wales behind him: there is the detestable arch-heretic Pelagius; he carries on the feud of the Welsh bishops with Augustine of Canterbury; he remembers St. David and St. Samson, and adopts Gerald's patriotic line about the see of St. David's; and, of course, in the valley of Rosea St. Patrick was born. He is moved with indignation at Polydore's strictures against the Britons. He concludes with an array of tributes to their prowess, a paean of Celtic patriotism: how they bravely resisted Caesar, winning recognition from Tacitus and Dion Cassius, the courage of Boadicea, how they produced Constantine. And what of Arviragus [1] who preserved his liberty in spite of the Romans? or Caractacus or the Emperor Maximus and, last, of King Arthur? Or there was the bravery of Llewelyn the Great. "And not these only, but also the Cornishmen, being the remnants of the old Britons, as they are the stoutest of all the British nations, so are they accounted to this day the most valiant in warlike affairs." [2]

In fact there was a patriotic consciousness of the Celts growing, to match that of the English. The Welsh were very proud of having the Tudors on the English throne — as well they might be, for never have we had a dynasty to equal them. Lluyd wrote for Ortelius a description of Anglesey where they came from; and translated a version of the *Brut y Tywysogion*, the Welsh histories "which of late so far as I suppose were by me first translated into English". Sir John Price, one of Henry VIII's visitors of the monasteries, also had a patriotic interest in British history and wrote a defence of it against Polydore. His *Description of Cambria* was revised and enlarged by Lluyd. After his death a manuscript of it came into the possession of Sir Henry Sidney, Lord President of the Council of Wales, at whose request it was edited by David Powell and published in 1584. Powell was one of the Welsh contingent at All Souls, numerous at this time: the first person to print Geraldus. Elizabeth's reign saw a considerable increase of Welsh scholars at Oxford; in 1571 Hugh Price founded Jesus College for them, of which the Queen accepted the title of foundress. She did not provide the funds.

Lluyd, as we have seen, intended his material for Ortelius, though he left, of his own, one of the earliest maps of Wales. This was very much a map-making decade. In 1564 Mercator published an important map of England and Wales, in 1572 his great map of Europe; in 1570 Ortelius had brought out his historic

[1] We remember that this is the name of one of the king's sons in *Cymbeline*.

[2] Lluyd, *op. cit.* p. 92 b.

atlas of the world. Englishmen were anxious to see their own country properly mapped. They were rewarded at the end of that decade with a masterpiece, Christopher Saxton's atlas of England and Wales, " the first national atlas produced by any country, and Saxton deserves a place beside Shakespeare as an interpreter of the national consciousness, unity and pride . . . of Elizabethan England ".[1] Little is known of Saxton, except that he was a Yorkshireman and worked under the patronage of Thomas Seckford, second son of that many-gabled rose-red Tudor house lying below the road into Woodbridge from the west. Master of Requests and of the Court of Wards, and therefore rich; unmarried and, as it happened, public-spirited, Seckford encouraged this enterprise and was in a position at Court to enlist the interest of the Queen and official backing for Saxton. The Privy Council gave special orders to the J.P.s to assist him " in all places where he shall come for the view of such places to describe certain counties in charts, being thereunto appointed by her Majesty's bill under her signet ".[2] Saxton's first two maps were engraved in 1574, the rest appeared in rapid succession until the atlas was completed in 1579. It seems that it was originally intended to illustrate Holinshed's *Chronicles*; for Reginald Wolfe, the Queen's printer, for whom Holinshed worked, designed — in the expansive manner of those times — a universal history and cosmography with maps. It proved impossible of achievement, and Wolfe died in 1573. But two fragments of his design achieved immortality: Holinshed's *Chronicles* and Saxton's *Atlas*.

The *Atlas* is indeed a work of great beauty with its hand-coloured engravings. There is the frontispiece of the Queen upon her throne in coronation robes of scarlet and ermine: a good portrait, aquiline nose, tight-lipped, red-wigged. Around her is a Renaissance construction with columns, cameos and rich incrustation; above, the royal arms supported by lion and gryphon, with delightful cherubs demonstrating wreaths upon the scene beneath, verses — said to be by Alexander Nowell — in praise of the peace of Elizabeth's rule while others war:

> Tristia dum gentes circum omnes bella fatigant;
> Caecique errores toto grassantur in orbe,
> Pace beas longa, vera et pietate Britannos. . . .

The map of England and Wales, engraved by an Englishman — Augustine Rhyther — is " both artistically and cartographically

[1] E. Lynam, *British Maps and Map-Makers*, p. 20.
[2] *A.P.C. 1575–7*, pp. 94, 159.

a masterpiece ".[1] The title ' Anglia ' is placed in a magnificent baroque cartouche tricked out with loops and lobsters and the fruits of the sea — under Elizabeth's rule " placidissima pace annos iam viginti florentissima ". (The years of peace were now coming to an end.) Ships and sea-monsters disport themselves; in the Irish Channel Neptune with his trident makes love to a mermaid. Each map has the royal arms and Seckford's decoratively displayed.

Then follow the maps of the counties, usually with their dates. Dorset has a most beautiful cartouche with birds, jewels and vases of flowers, and a fine big galleon off Swyre. Devon (1575) has two ships in action off Plymouth — one thinks of the future not far away now. Suffolk (1575) displays a fine three-masted ship off the Orwell — as it might be Cavendish's but a few years ahead, with Trimley, Walton, Felixstowe, the places just around where he was living then, all marked. The truth is that the *Atlas* is not only a masterpiece of decoration; it combines remarkable clarity and detailed information with beauty. No wonder it remained the most authoritative atlas of England for the next century. Owen tells us that Saxton's maps " are usual with all noblemen and gentlemen, and daily perused by them for their better instruction of the estate of this Realm ".[2] Most of the maps were engraved by Flemings who had been brought over to London, or who had taken refuge there from the religious madness raging in the Low Countries: a great gain to the English environment, which deserved it for its sanity and relative immunity from doctrinal fanaticism. The first English atlas, then, is a monument of the joint enterprise of England and the Low Countries which was in so many ways changing the world and ushering in the modern age.

John Norden was a more homely figure, his efforts largely unaided: which makes them all the more remarkable. All his life long he laboured with the idea of making a complete survey of the country, shire by shire, the *Speculum Britanniae*. Poor but honest, he could not expect the support of the great. Independent-minded and very middle-class, he maintained himself by pouring out numerous works of Protestant exhortation.[3] It was not for want of trying: he did his best, like everybody else, to find a patron. For years he tried to elicit the active support of Burghley. The great man was interested, but it was now towards the end of

[1] Lynam, *op. cit.* p. 20.
[2] Owen, *op. cit.* p. 2.
[3] The *D.N.B.* article is wrong in making two John Nordens out of these: they were one and the same; cf. *The Chorography of Norfolk* (ed. C. M. Hood, 1938), p. 28.

his life and he had other things, including the war, on his hands. He did what little he could. In 1593 the Privy Council issued an order authorising Norden to travel through the country " to make more perfect descriptions, charts and maps ", and requesting the local J.P.s to help him.[1] In that year he published his description of Middlesex, the first part of the intended design. Next year there was a further order from Burghley asking for voluntary contributions from the gentry towards it. But Norden was not one of them, and his scheme languished for want of backing. In 1596 he issued his prospectus, dedicating it reproachfully to Burghley: " Although (Right Honourable) I have been forced to struggle with want, the unpleasant companion of industrious desires and have long sustained foil, enforced neglect of my purposed business and sorrow of my working spirit . . . and the rather for that mine endeavours in this general business sprang from your honourable good liking ".[2] By two years later he had spent 1000 marks of his own and five years' work, was in debt, his family distressed and begged the bounty of the Queen. She gave him something: the surveyorship of Crown woods in certain counties. James gave him something more. But his real recompense must have been in the delightful learned vagabondage, the passion for sightseeing with which he was bitten and that had crazed Leland's wits. (One understands the madness.)

The remains of Norden's project are considerable, the value of his work even more. Mr. Lynam tells us that his maps " were more original than any which preceded or followed them for a long time, and embodied that spirit of independent scientific research which arose among . . . men of the middle classes in the 1590's ".[3] His maps contained many new features, some of which had come from the Continent. They were the first to show roads; they had marginal numbers along the sides to enable one to find any place one wanted; they supplied a simple scale, and he was the first to introduce the symbol for a battle. In addition, his maps please the eye by being very pretty: for example, the charming map of Westminster in his *Middlesex*, with the deer leaping in St. James's Park and the river banks opposite Whitehall lined with trees. From this time on, maps become numerous, " including plans of towns, estate plans and many maps of coastal districts and harbours carried out for the government. Ralph Aggas executed some fine estate maps, while the plans of Robert

[1] *Ibid.* pp. 28-31.
[2] Norden, *Speculum Britanniae: Description of Middlesex and Hertfordshire* (ed. 1723).
[3] Lynam, *op. cit.* p. 20.

Adams, a Royal surveyor, are perhaps the most delicate and lovely ever drawn in this country."[1]

Norden's interest in county surveying went back to the early eighties when we find him travelling back from Cornwall with the Portuguese Pretender, Don Antonio, and his party.[2] And Norden's *Description of Cornwall* is the most complete of his surveys to be printed. It follows Carew's so closely that one cannot but think he had a sight of Carew's manuscript. And yet he adds things of his own that he had seen or heard about, the mines and fisheries, the language or Cornish morals. He has a passage about the voluptuous life of the Cornish — the sweetness of the sin and the ease of its remission making it so general — that reminds one of the bourgeois Puritan strain that was to come to the top for a time in the next century.[3] His *Chorography of Norfolk*, only recently printed, is almost equally full and valuable. Half a dozen other counties, Essex, Middlesex, Hertfordshire, Northamptonshire, have been printed since his time; others remain in manuscript. Two other books attest Norden's part in the discovery of his own country: *An Intended Guide for English Travellers*, of which the aim was "to conceive some rule of ease (being myself a traveller) to find as near as I could the certain distances of towns"; he gives tables, county by county, with names of places down two sides, with lines intersecting making little squares giving the distances.[4] Then there is his classic *Surveyor's Dialogue*, an admirable treatise on the art of surveying in all its aspects. In his modest way, Norden was a part of the scientific movement of the time, and refers with respect to the work of Master Norman, Mr. Dr. Hood, Mr. Borough, Mr. Blagrave and others on the compass, and other instruments. He explains the use of the theodolite for planimetry and in some detail, for "quickest conceits do soonest forget".[5] I fear I have forgotten it already.[6]

Along with all this activity in discovering the England of the present went an equal enthusiasm for the discovery of the past. Only this was less new and original to the age: it was a continuation of the medieval tradition of chronicle and annal.

The name of Holinshed in this connection has had great *réclame* because of its association with Shakespeare. But his fame was largely fortuitous. Holinshed was a hack writer, like many others in that age — even the hacks were apt to be good then. He was

[1] Lynam, *op. cit.* p. 21.
[2] Dedication to King James, *Description of Cornwall* (ed. 1728).
[3] *Ibid.* p. 27. [4] Edition of 1625. [5] Edition of 1607, p. 128.
[6] But *v.* E. G. R. Taylor, *Tudor Geography, 1485–1583*, p. 140 foll.

employed by the printer Wolfe upon his projected " universal cosmography of the whole world and therewith also certain particular histories of every known nation ", which came down in the end to the Chronicles of England, Scotland and Ireland.[1] Behind Wolfe stood Burghley, who was " ever so especial good lord to Master Wolfe ". Almost everywhere we look in the Elizabethan Age we see the hand of Burghley. No place here to describe his systematic exploration of the economic resources of the country: he had a hand in every scheme for their development.[2] But he was also by nature a man of learning, whose great recreation was books, of which he was a collector. And he was deeply concerned that the country's past—as well as what it was good people should know about the present — be brought into the light.

Wolfe had spent most of his time on the maps, which, after his death, Seckford provided for, as we have seen. Many materials had been gathered by Wolfe for his enterprise, including Leland's note-books, though some were already damaged and others missing.[3] We see that the Holinshed group too profit from Leland, though they rest mainly on the material of the medieval chronicles. Holinshed lived long enough to see the immediate success of his first edition, two fat volumes well illustrated by portraits and battle-pieces; the main part of the book, the Chronicles of England, dedicated to Burghley. The Protestant patriotism of the book, the note of national pride and justification, assured its success: it was in line with the dominant temper of the time. Even so, it was irresistibly readable. No wonder Shakespeare was so fascinated by it, and Spenser too — " Master Holinshed hath much furthered and advantaged me " — along with so many other folk.[4] The stories there are in it! — reading that of Wolsey, for example, which made such an impression on the dramatist, one can still hardly leave off. Holinshed died about 1580, as steward at Bramcote in Warwickshire, not so far from Stratford, leaving all his papers to his master there.

On Holinshed's death, John Hooker of Exeter was called in to supervise a new edition and bring it up to date. It was this edition, of 1586–7, that Shakespeare used and this is the standard text. It is a composite work, full of varied interest and a rich quarry to dig in. Prefaced to the whole thing are two books by William Harrison, chaplain to Lord Cobham and Rector of Radwinter in Essex: a Description of Britain, for which he relied

[1] Dedication to Burghley, *The Third Volume of Chronicles* . . . (ed. 1586–7).
[2] Chap. IV, below. [3] Harrison's Dedication to Lord Cobham, vol. I.
[4] q. in *Camb. Hist. of Eng. Lit.* III. 320.

on, and often misread, Leland, with a Description of contemporary England, racy, homely, sharp as home-brewed cider, a work justly celebrated and which we shall often have occasion to cite. Harrison strikes the patriotic note at once with his description of the misery of the English under the Norman Conquest. What a career that theme was to have with the Parliamentarians of the next century, the Whigs of the eighteenth, the Radicals and early socialists of the nineteenth, Cartwright and Paine and Cobbett! The description of Ireland was based on a work by the Jesuit Edmund Campion, edited by his pupil Richard Stanihurst, who goes out of his way to praise his master, " so rare a clerk, who was so upright in conscience, so deep in judgment, so ripe in eloquence ".[1] It is odd to find this tribute, only a few years after Campion's execution, coming in a work that was part of the forward march of English Protestantism. It is like the fact that one of Parsons's devotional works was one of the most popular with Protestants in an approved guise, though they would have executed the author if they could have caught him. Truly the age is less simple, more richly mixed and contradictory, than it appears in the books: it has the variegated and coloured subtleties of life.

Hooker translated Geraldus's account of the conquest of Ireland, which he had written at the request of Henry II. One observes how little difference comparatively there is between Geraldus and the Elizabethan chronicler: it brings home to us the continuity of the time with the Middle Ages. Holinshed had brought up the story to the reign of Henry VIII, which was then covered by Stanihurst, who dedicated his work to Sir Henry Sidney: " How cumbersome (Right Honourable) and dangerous a task it is, to engross and divulge the doings of others, especially when the parties registered or their issue living. . . ." And so they found: various passages were held to reflect upon ministers, the book was called in and expurgated. Uncastrated copies of this famous book are very rare in the world. Hooker took up the story from 1546 to 1587, dedicating it to the young Ralegh just arrived in favour. He also took part in the work, with Abraham Fleming, Francis Thynne and John Stow, of bringing the rest of the book up to date. Hooker made a number of original contributions to the text. He was a distinguished antiquary in his own right, deep in the antiquities of his native city of Exeter, of which he left a description, along with a Discourse of Devon and Cornwall which has never been printed, and much else. Perhaps his best work of all was providing for the

[1] Stanihurst's Dedication to Sir Henry Sidney, vol. II.

education of his nephew, Richard Hooker.

Practically all these men who were engaged in meeting the insatiable demand of the Tudor middle-class public for patriotic history were themselves men of that class, imbued with its outlook.[1] This is particularly noticeable with the London group of chroniclers, Edward Hall, Richard Grafton, John Stow, John Speed: all of them citizens, immensely proud of the city and its fame, the last two — both of them tailors — so filled with its love that they were prepared to face poverty in order to dedicate their lives to its glory. (Elizabethan authors received very little for the books they wrote.) Hall produced his chronicle, *The Union of the Two Noble and Illustrious Families of York and Lancaster*, in the reign of Henry VIII. It was a popular work and very operative; his hero was Henry VIII, his account of that reign a valuable first-hand one; his theme may be gathered from his title: the ending of the civil broils of the fifteenth century by the union of the two dynasties in the Tudors. Can anyone deny that his was a sensible theme? — the unique contribution of the Tudors to the well-being of the country. The tendency of recent scholarship is to emphasise the importance of Hall's Chronicle as an independent source of Shakespeare's English history-plays.

"We are beholding to Mr. Speed and Stow", wrote Aubrey, "for *stitching* up for us our English history. It seems they were both tailors — quod N.B."[2] Stow, a "merry old man", if poor, never seems wholly to have deserted his craft — he probably had to resort to it occasionally to support himself; but his time he gave chiefly to his researches, having to go on foot about the city and in the country to look up records. He did a mass of work, some of it editing medieval chronicles for Archbishop Parker, printing Chaucer, helping with Holinshed, producing a summary of English Chronicles, over which he quarrelled with Grafton. It was in 1580 — again that dividing line — that he published his own original contribution to history, which became later known as the *Annals*. In 1598 he brought out the book by which he still lives, the delightful *Survey of London*, the basis of all later histories of London. He impoverished himself to write it; the citizens do not seem to have responded to the government's appeal to make him kind gratuities; he does not seem to have minded. Nothing in his eyes could diminish the glory of the city he loved and had celebrated. His portrait-bust in the church of St. Andrew Undershaft has happily survived the terror of our

[1] Cf. Louis B. Wright, *Middle Class Culture in Elizabethan England* chap. ix.

[2] Aubrey, *Brief Lives* (ed. Clark), II. 232.

time; and still the Lord Mayor places a new quill in his old hand every year.

Speed was set free from the drudgery of daily labour at his trade by the patronage of Sir Fulke Greville. He used his leisure to make maps of the counties, and in 1611 he brought them together, with some of Saxton's and Norden's, in the *Theatre of the Empire of Great Britain.* These maps have the interesting feature of a perspective view of the chief town of the county in the corner, from which one sees the completely articulated character of Elizabethan towns, still medieval, the design not obscured by modern developments. Encouraged by Camden and the antiquaries whose society he enjoyed, Speed undertook and — what was more — produced his enormous *History of Great Britain . . . from Julius Caesar . . . to King James.* This was dedicated to the King: the " Enlarger and Uniter of the British Empire; the Restorer of the British Name ". An ancient Briton has the place of honour on the title-page. One observes the gathering cult of Britain with the accession of James, the union of the island. The very first paragraph on Britain as Admiral of the Seas sets the tone: " Being by the Almighty so set in the main Ocean, as that she is thereby the High Admiral of the Seas, and in the terrestrial globe so as that she is worthily reputed both 'The Garden of pleasure' and 'The Storehouse of profit', opening her havens every way, fit to receive all foreign traffic and to utter her own into all other parts. . . ." Speed writes like the middle-class man he was; the long career of maritime expansion into commercial empire opens before us.

The culmination of all this scholarship and research comes with the great Camden. For a number of reasons. He had the classical background to put it into shape, and the immense range of learning to give it perspective. He was not only the acknowledged head of English scholars — the Headmaster of his Age — but he had an extensive European correspondence. And he wrote in Latin so as to put the new country, the latest conquest of the Renaissance, on the map of Europe, to give it its place in the mind of Europe. Both his great works, the *Britannia* and his *Annals of the Reign of Queen Elizabeth,* have a magistral authority, a quasi-official character. The age saw in them a presentation of itself and of the country, of its past and present, as its guiding spirits saw it and wished it to be seen. Burghley's library was always open to Camden, and he encouraged his work. Camden dedicated his *Britannia* to him. In the last year of Burghley's life, anxious that there should be a reliable account of the reign that was also a responsible one, he urged Camden to undertake the *Annals*, and handed over a mass of official papers to aid him in the work.

As a mere boy at Oxford — where he was a candidate for a fellowship at All Souls, but was frustrated by the popish party in the College — he gave all his spare time to the study of antiquities. As under-master, and later master, at Westminster, he spent his holidays in travelling about England. From time to time a phrase penetrates through the rhetorical prose — he wrote a florid, grandiloquent Latin style — that reveals he was responsive to the delights of perambulating the country — the air, the sun, clouds, the inexpressible pleasure of the road. (One remembers the fields in Bedfordshire by Hockley in the Hole " smelling sweet in summer of the best beans which with their redolent savour do dull the quick scent of hounds and spaniels not without fuming and chafing of hunters ".[1]) The book, in its final form, represented a lifetime's work. And not Camden's only. No scholar has ever had a greater gift for friendship: there was no *odium archaeologicum* with him. The result was that his friends and disciples all over the country were proud to make their offerings to the great work: which he in return graciously acknowledged — no-one more generously — as the slow equipage moved on its magnificent way: the pageant put up by the English contingent as their contribution to the procession of Renaissance scholarship.

Camden had no false modesty, such as our age affects, about his qualifications: he knew better than anyone else what they were. At the end of his address to the reader he appended a Renaissance Latin motto: " Books receive their doom according to the reader's capacity ". The Elizabethans passed this test with honour: they gave the enormous book five editions in the author's lifetime. It is indeed a wonderful book, so wide in its scope and so interesting throughout, that one cannot do it justice in brief. There were those, he said, who attacked the study of antiquity as a " back-looking curiosity "; to those he replied that there was the glory of their native country to uphold, besides which the study of history offered a sweet food to the mind. His deepest interests were archaeological and topographical; his aim to draw the whole shape and past of the country, so far as evidence remained, out of the mists of antiquity into the light of the Renaissance world. The range of evidence he drew upon was very wide. He knew not only all the classical authorities and all the medieval chronicles, but he had been collecting Roman

[1] Camden, *Britannia* (trans. by Philemon Holland, ed. 1637), p. 402.

inscriptions and coins *in situ* or through his friends all his life. What is most characteristic of the book is the way he uses archaeological evidence to build up a picture of the forgotten past, to bring it into relation with written evidence; his deepest aim to depict Britain once more as an integral province of Roman civilisation. Everywhere his critical sense is apparent; he does not build on fables, yet he understands the value of myths. He has a comprehensiveness and tolerant good sense that reminds one of that other good Anglican, Richard Hooker. Of course there is an occasional intermixture of contemporary credulity with scientific sense — or it would not be the Renaissance. Camden was sabotaged by the supernatural authority of Holy Scripture: the Britons must be descended from Gomer, one of the sons of Japhet, the son of Noah. The Ark of the Covenant was a mare's nest for most Renaissance scholars. After Camden extricates the Britons from that, all goes well: an excellent account of Roman Britain drawn from all the authorities then available; of the confused story of the Anglo-Saxon invasions Camden's outline remains in essence not much changed; he includes a spirited and excellent account of the Norman Conquest he had written much earlier. Then we come to the whole survey of the British Isles, county by county: a gigantic task carried through with complete confidence and candour. Mr. Collingwood sums up Camden's work as being in the best Renaissance tradition, a demonstration of how unremembered history could be reconstructed from data as natural scientists used data as the basis of scientific theories.[1] From this point of view we may regard Camden as the parallel to the great scientist, William Gilbert.

Naturally, the work being so successful, Camden aroused an enemy. In 1599 Ralph Brooke published *A Discovery of Certain Errors* . . . of Camden's, "whose reputation for learning is so great and beard of antiquity lately grown so long that the goodly Britannia, Mother of us all, is become his daughter, trained up and taught to speak Latin in his school", etc. How well one recognises the tone: in short, Brooke was jealous. (He was York herald, and Camden had been appointed Clarenceux king of arms over him.) Camden had garnered whole sheaves out of Burghley's library and had made great use of Leland's notes. Of course: he would have been no scholar, and a great fool, if he had not. Camden replied in his fifth edition; superfluously, for who remembers Brooke now? The taste of the public was right: Camden has never been forgotten. Indeed, and exceptionally,

[1] R. G. Collingwood, *The Idea of History*, p. 58.

Camden was highly honoured in his own age: the age was proud of him. He was not the man to accept mere distinctions; he refused a knighthood. He had a happy temperament, a ruddy, healthy complexion; he made himself well-off by his own exertions; unmarried, he had a host of friends and disciples at home and abroad, among the best men of the time — not only the scholars, but the poets and musicians. He could not prevent them giving him a magnificent funeral in Westminster Abbey, or stop them from writing him poems like his boy Ben's:

> Camden, most reverend head, to whom I owe
>   All that I am in arts, all that I know,
> (How nothing's that?) to whom my country owes
>   The great renown and name wherewith she goes.

One of the poets who prefaced verses to Philemon Holland's translation of *Britannia* commented that now Great Britain had no parallel. A specific British patriotism is one of the leading themes of the work. Camden praises the Welsh, the remnants of the Britons, for having preserved their ancient tongue. No Victorian Teutonism about him: his aim is to display the historic continuity of the islands and their peoples. " Even while we are perusing this work ", he says, preparing a new edition, England has become Britain again with James' accession.[1] In a way that would be thought unbecoming today, he boasts of Britain and vaunts the good qualities of its inhabitants. But that was the sixteenth century, and very necessary for a backward country that was just coming into the centre of the picture and the march of civilisation.

Impossible as it is to give any full idea here of the effect of this passionate interest in the past upon the literature of the time, one cannot but notice it at work in the choicest spirits. It is a leading theme in its literature. It provides the body to the work of the laureate, Michael Drayton. In Mary's reign first appeared the *Mirror for Magistrates*, a volume telling the tragic tales in verse of great people in our history from the time of Richard II onwards.[2] It was several times re-issued in Elizabeth's reign with additions, one of them the celebrated *Induction* by Thomas Sackville, finest of early Elizabethan poems.[3] On one hand the book looked back to Lydgate and his *Falls of Princes*, on the other to the outburst of historical poetry and plays that came with the war against Spain. It provided a useful source for the dramatists and inspired

[1] *Op. cit.* p. 141.
[2] Ed. by Lily B. Campbell, 1938.
[3] This was contributed to the edition of 1563.

other poets. Drayton, who was the recognised successor of Spenser as the head of his profession, mirrored the changing moods of the time in the clear smooth waters of his poetry as much as Shakespeare in the greater and more disturbed depths of his.

In the nineties Drayton devoted himself almost entirely to historical poetry. Beginning with the boring *Battle of Agincourt* and the *Barons' Wars* — almost as tedious to read about as they must have been to fight, though (I am assured) not without fine passages — Drayton at length hit upon his most successful work, *England's Heroical Epistles.* These were a series of letters, with their answers, passing between celebrated royal lovers, not always — or even usually — married; for example, Henry II and Fair Rosamund, Mortimer and Queen Isabella, Edward IV and Jane Shore. (One can imagine some amusing additions from our own time.) This work was frequently reprinted in Drayton's lifetime, and more often than any other of his works since.

But his greatest work did not achieve success. This was the famous *Polyolbion.* Only an Elizabethan, one feels, would have attempted anything so monumental, so vast: it is like one of those houses of theirs, Audley End or Burghley or Holdenby, of which there seems no reason why it should ever come to an end. It was nothing less than an attempt to put the whole of Camden's *Britannia* into verse. And that impossible task Drayton practically achieved. The poem consists of thirty songs or cantos surveying the whole country. He did not succeed in including Scotland; not that he gave out: the stationers did. And yet it is a great poem. It has always had its admirers, few but judicious: Lamb, Landor, Hardy. In our time, when topographical verse is coming back into favour, it should find more.

For, like Wordsworth and Hardy, Drayton was a topographical poet: he was inspired by places and their associations. Still his main motive was to raise a monument to the love of his country:

> Of Albion's glorious isle the wonders whilst I write,
> The sundry varying soils, the pleasures infinite
> (Where heat kills not the cold, nor cold expels the heat,
> The calms too mildly small, nor winds too roughly great,
> Nor night doth hinder day, nor day the night doth wrong,
> The Summer not too short, the Winter not too long). . . .[1]

So he ambles along for 30,000 lines. We may demur to his complacency about the weather, but we are conquered by him in the end, in spite of the *longueurs* — we can always skip, plenty

[1] "Polyolbion", Tercentenary Edition of Drayton's *Works* (ed. J. W. Hebel), IV. 1.

remains. For that slow ambling pace, jogging along like one of his own nags, is exactly right for his purposed view of the whole lie of the land: no use being in a hurry. He begins with Cornwall: one recognises his sources, Carew, Norden, Camden, to whom he adheres closely. He does not seem to have been there; nor do I derive the impression that he had travelled about the country much: his work was one of learning, based on literary sources rather than of observation. From Cornwall the work progresses through the West Country and Wales, then back through the western Midlands to Kent. The second part takes the reader up the east of England to the North. His method is to follow the course of the rivers: the usual one with the map-makers and surveyors like Lambarde, until Norden appeared and said let there be roads.[1]

Such good things by the way reward the attentive reader; especially when Drayton gets on to his own native ground, the sweet Warwickshire countryside where he was born, and to which he, like another countryman of his, used to retire for the summer. He has a charming passage about the Forest of Arden, on the edge of which he was brought up — one remembers what his countryman made of it in *Midsummer Night's Dream* and *As You Like It*. The truth is that Elizabethans had a sense of romance about the countryside: no knowing what you might find there, Queen Mab and the fairies, Robin Goodfellow, a translated weaver, an Autolycus or a rusticated philosopher, the fairy-land of the *Faerie Queene*. Drayton kept his Muse pretty close to the ground — though he too discovered a delicate, minute fairy-land in his *Nymphidia*. Even he becomes lyrical about the birds of the Forest of Arden and the hunting, the flowers of the Cotswolds, Robin Hood in Sherwood Forest, dropping down in a boat on the Thames from Windsor to London. He had the lore of the country at his finger-tips, and an instinctive understanding of country people:

> As an unlettered man, at the desired sight
> Of some rare beauty moved with infinite delight,

[1] Mr. B. H. Newdigate (*Michael Drayton and his Circle*, p. 165) thinks Drayton got this from Harrison's Description, but it was, as we have seen, common form. Mr. Newdigate is wrong in thinking that "Harrison's account, though supplemented from Leland and from other sources, is largely written from notes made by himself in his travels in and about the island". Harrison himself says that "until now of late, except it were from the parish where I dwell unto your Honour in Kent, or out of London where I was born unto Oxford and Cambridge . . . I never travelled forty miles forthright and at one journey in all my life" (*Elizabethan England* (ed. L. Withington, with Introduction by F. J. Furnival), p. xlviii). Harrison's topography is entirely based on Leland's notes.

Not out of his own spirit, but by that power divine,
Which through a sparkling eye perspicuously doth shine,
Feels his hard temper yield, that he in passion breaks,
And things beyond his height, transported strangely speaks.[1]

The poem has much else too: admirable story-telling, as in the case of Guy of Warwick, philosophical argument, prospects, economic information about flocks and herds and soils. Like Camden, Drayton had Welsh sympathies; he knew something of the poetry of the Welsh bards, doubtless from his early days when

John Hughes' lyre
Which oft at Polesworth by the fire
Hath made us gravely merry.[2]

The poet was unfortunate in that by the time his vast poem was finished the great age was over and James was on the throne, "that it cometh out at this time when verses are deduced to chambers, and nothing esteemed in this lunatic age, but what is kept in cabinets and must only pass by transcription".[3] But there it is still, a solid monument to the heroic years, "as the book is laid down, its chief attraction, after all, is seen to be the pathetic bravery of the whole scheme — the voice of the dogged old Elizabethan raised amid an alien world, to sing the old song in the old way, to proclaim and preserve the glories of his beloved country in the face of a frivolous, forgetful age".[4]

A comparable poem, based on the legends and tales of history, won much favour in the nineties: *Albion's England* by William Warner. He was an admired poet then; it is difficult for us to admire him now. Francis Meres tells us how Warner, "in his absolute *Albion's England* hath most admirably perused the history of his own country from Noah to his time . . . I have heard him termed of the best wits of both our universities our English Homer".[5] They must have been easily pleased; in the end, whatever one's good-will, the lagging fourteener is too much for one. Beginning with the Flood, the first two books end with Brutus's exile and arrival in Albion. Next we have the story of King Lear and his three daughters. The fourth book has "The Story of Curan and Argentile", a pleasing pastoral episode which

[1] Drayton, *Works*, IV. 285.
[2] Dedication of the Odes and Lyrics to Sir Henry Goodere, *Works*, II. 344.
[3] Preface to the General Reader, IV. v.
[4] Harold H. Child in *Camb. Hist. Eng. Lit.* IV. 192.
[5] Francis Meres. *Palladis Tamia*, q. in Gregory Smith, *Elizabethan Critical Essays*, II. 317.

was the most popular thing in the book and was taken up by other poets, among them Shakespeare in *The Comedy of Errors*.[1] So Warner jogs through English history up to contemporary times, Queen Elizabeth's persecutors and troubles, the overthrow of the Armada, the voyages of discovery.

But there were greater poets to pay their tribute to the historic and legendary past.

Spenser, least historically minded of poets, whose imagination inhabited naturally a visionary dream-world, made his obeisance to contemporary taste with " The Ruins of Time ". The poem begins with a vision of the past as seen by the spirit of the ruined city of Verulamium: the Roman rule in Britain, Boadicea's resistance, Rome's ruin, the Saxon Conquest. All comes straight out of Holinshed and Camden. The poem has a stanza in praise of the latter:

> Camden the nourice of antiquity,
> And lantern unto late succeeding age,
> To see the light of simple verity,
> Buried in ruins, through the great outrage
> Of her own people, led with warlike rage.
> Camden, though Time all monuments obscure,
> Yet thy just labours ever shall endure.[2]

A curious canto of the *Faerie Queene* is entirely given up to this legendary " matter of Britain ".[3] It is rendered as being what Sir Guyon and his squire —

> Whereat they burning both with fervent fire,
> Their country's ancestry to understand —[4]

read in the books of antiquity which were kept in the library of the House of Temperance. We hear how the land

> In antique times was savage wilderness,
> Unpeopled, unmanured, unproved, unpraised,
> Ne was it island then, ne was it poised
> Amid the ocean waves, ne was it sought
> Of merchants far, for profits therein praised,
> But all was desolate, and of some thought
> By sea to have been from the Celtic mainland brought.[5]

That we have seen was the opinion of John Twyne. Then we go on to the usual story to be found in Carew, Norden, Camden, everybody, of Corineus wrestling on Plymouth Hoe, conquering

[1] Cf. H. Huf, *William Warner, Albion's England: Quellenuntersuchungen.*
[2] *Complaints* (ed. W. L. Renwick), p. 10.
[3] Book II. x. [4] *Ibid.* IX. 60. [5] *Ibid.* X. 5.

and calling Cornwall after him. We do not escape Brutus, nor Locrine, nor King Lud who founded London; to these Spenser adds a fantastic rigmarole of names of his own invention. We are given the story of Lear, from which Shakespeare, with that infallible instinct, got the name of Cordelia in that form. Spenser does not omit to celebrate in verse the proper pride of the historians in the repulse of Caesar by the Britons: Elizabethans were not self-conscious about that sort of thing. Then we have Cymbeline and Arviragus, Boadicea, Constantine and Uther Pendragon, with whom the book ends abruptly, leaving Prince Arthur to cry out:

> Dear country, O how dearly dear
> Ought thy remembrance, and perpetual bond
> Be to thy foster child, that from thy hand
> Did common breath and nouriture receive?
> How brutish is it not to understand,
> How much to her we owe, that all us gave,
> That gave unto us all, whatever good we have.[1]

Shakespeare, whose job it was as a man of the theatre to give the public what it wanted, responded in the fullest measure to the demand for history. At the very beginning of Elizabeth's reign Sackville and Norton had produced *Gorboduc*, the first English tragedy, out of the legendary history of Britain. Marlowe had made a masterpiece out of the story of Edward II. But what are we to say of the astonishing cycle — the sheer tenacity of purpose apart from anything else — of Shakespeare's English history plays, covering with unforgettable intensity of imagination the whole story from Richard II to Henry VI, with its two outriders in *King John* and *Henry VIII*? Later in life, Shakespeare turned back to the legendary matter of Britain. All the world knows what he made of the stories of *Macbeth* and *King Lear*. And towards the end he took up the subject of *Cymbeline*. There the familiar names come out at us from the chroniclers: Cymbeline, Arviragus, Imogen. It is touching to find here the same simple pride that all men of the age took in their country's history and good fortune:

> A kind of conquest
> Caesar made here; but not made here his brag
> Of " Came, and saw, and overcame ": with shame —
> The first that ever touched him — he was carried
> From off our coast, twice beaten; and his shipping —
> Poor ignorant baubles! — on our terrible seas,

[1] *Faerie Queene* X. 69.

Like egg-shells moved upon their surges, cracked
As easily 'gainst our rocks: for joy whereof
The famed Cassibelan, who was once at point —
O giglot Fortune! — to master Caesar's sword,
Make Lud's town with rejoicing fires bright
And Britons strut with courage.[1]

They might indeed be the Armada bonfires. While all that had happened since bore out the lines

Our countrymen
Are men more ordered than when Julius Caesar
Smiled at their lack of skill, but found their courage
Worthy his frowning at: their discipline,
Now mingled with their courages, will make known
To their approvers they are people such
That mend upon the world.[2]

[1] *Cymbeline*, III. i. [2] *Ibid.* II. iv.

CHAPTER III

THE LAND

If we would think back to what the face of the country looked like then, what are the chief differences we should notice?

We must first think away the horrid agglomerations — the nodules, ganglia, tentacles — of an industrial and dominantly urban civilisation: the sprawl of our towns whether large or small. Elizabethan towns were beautifully integrated into the agrarian society of which they formed the markets and the local links. We must think away the Black Countries, the factories, mines, outcroppings, rubbish-tips; the scars of industry in the valleys; the railways and most of the roads; the telegraph wires and electric cables; around the coasts, the great docks and ports and shipbuilding centres; and — latest of additions — the air-fields. Having thought all these away, we arrive at a country infinitely less crowded and more spacious, less affected by man: a country in which, though there are far fewer people, it is much easier to be lost. It is a country that offers more scope to the imagination, not less — as those who are under the cult of mere size and numbers might suppose. It was in fact the country that inspired the imagination of Spenser and Drayton, Shakespeare and the young Milton.

What positively should we find if only we could go back to that land as it once was?

I suppose that the chief alteration in the appearance of the countryside is that which followed upon the enclosure of much of central England in subsequent centuries. In Elizabeth's time a great deal of this, and more outside the area, was open, champion country; that is to say, it was cultivated by the villagers upon a common system of agriculture in great open fields, in which they held strips and patches. The fields ran endlessly to the eye over the gentle undulations of the landscape, like the famous fields of Laxton in Nottinghamshire, which are the best known survivors of that earlier system.[1] The much greater extent of woodland and forest then is perhaps the next thing we should be struck by.

[1] *v.* C. S. Orwin, *The Open Fields*, Part II.

The Elizabethans were very anxious about the diminution of the woodlands by the increasing demands of the time for building, shipbuilding, industry — in particular for iron and glass-making. The State Papers are filled with apprehensions and complaints, and many writers voice the growing concern. The woods of Sussex, the Forest of Dean and of the west Midlands were particularly affected by the requirements of the new industry. Camden notices that the woods of North Wiltshire were just now beginning to thin, while the Forest of Blackmore in Dorset — which had been a chase of the medieval kings — was much thinner.[1] (It is the country of *The Woodlanders*.) Drayton laments the shrinking of the Forest of Arden in Warwickshire:

> For, when the world found out the fitness of my soil,
> The gripple wretch began immediately to spoil
> My tall and goodly woods and did my grounds enclose:
> By which in little time my bounds I came to lose.[2]

But there was still enough of it for Jacques and the courtiers of the Duke in exile to wander in, and for the moonlit lovers of *Midsummer Night's Dream* to be lost in it. Robin Hood in Sherwood Forest was a more popular figure than ever to the Elizabethan imagination.

Much more of the country was then 'waste' and 'wild' — as it appears in their maps: rough pasture or swampy bottoms, marsh or fen. There was much more moor and downland. Cultivation was constantly encroaching upon it. One can see the process at work if one looks down from the height of the Marlborough Downs, or above a Derbyshire dale or from a Devon tor, to see the settlement in the valley below creeping up the hillside with its pattern of fields.[3] (A point to remember here is that extensions of the cultivated area, from common fields, were apt to be in several, *i.e.* separate and enclosed fields, worked not in common but by their individual owners.) In place of the parks and gardened landscape which we owe to the eighteenth century, the older settled countryside of the Elizabethans would make an impression at once less tidy, more variegated and more curious. Around the villages and even the country houses of the gentry there would be a patchwork quilt of small gardens and closes.[4]

[1] Camden, *op. cit.* pp. 241, 212. [2] Drayton, "Polyolbion", *Works*, IV. 276.

[3] One can see the thing beautifully exposed all along the escarpment above the Vale of the White Horse, from Wantage to Swindon. But indeed one can observe it in hundreds of places.

[4] For a particular example cf. Port Eliot at St. Germans in Cornwall, my *Tudor Cornwall*, pp. 202-3.

No Kent or Capability Brown had yet decreed their levelling out under the smooth miles of turf, or the removal of whole villages outside the park pale.[1] On the other hand, there were many more, if scraggier, deer-parks; a great number of houses had two parks, one for the red, one for the fallow deer. Great castles still stood up and dominated the landscape, until the Civil War came and wrote *finis* to such places as Kenilworth and Ashby-de-la-Zouch, Basing and Corfe, Ludlow and Raglan. The gashes were but recent upon the great monastic churches, like that at Luton where Camden noticed the choir roofless and overgrown with weeds.[2] Red deer roamed the isle of Purbeck, and wandered from Exmoor across North Devon into Cornwall.[3] The country was wilder, more untamed and exciting. The last wolf had not yet been killed in Wales, the great bustard still flocked on the heaths of the eastern counties. Wild life, especially birds of every kind, teemed: no doubt of that from all the Elizabethan regional writers. The towns were a modest part of the landscape, not imposed upon it by the nineteenth-century development of a world market. The Elizabethans stood just upon the threshold of all that story, though a few of their forward spirits — the Hakluyts, Dee, Ralegh — had dreams of what might be.

In the physical configuration of the country the size of the Fens and marshes would most surprise us, for there an enormous work in the subjugation of nature has been accomplished in the centuries since. It was in 1600 that the Act was passed which set in motion the ultimate draining of the Fens.[4] This came as a culmination of a good deal of activity in similar improvements throughout the reign. There was, for example, the draining of Plumstead and Erith marshes down the Thames by Woolwich;[5] the latter seem to have been successfully 'inned' by the middle of the reign. Plumstead marsh gave much more trouble: from 1563 onwards there was a series of Acts to advance the project, which was delayed by floods and tides, the difficulty of getting experienced workmen over from the Low Countries during the restraint of trade, and, most of all, by "the huge greatness and charge of the work itself".[6] We must remember always how small were the instruments the Elizabethans had at hand to help

[1] As at Milton Abbas in Dorset.

[2] Camden, p. 402.

[3] Camden, p. 211; Carew, *Survey of Cornwall* (ed. 1769), p. 23.

[4] 43 Eliz. c. 11. And cf. Darby, *An Historical Geography of England*, chap. xii, "The Draining of the Fens, 1600–1800".

[5] The work of reclamation seems to have been started in Henry VIII's reign. (Ernle, *English Farming: Past and Present*, p. 115.)

[6] 5 Eliz. c. 36; 8 Eliz. c. 25; 14 Eliz. c. 14; 23 Eliz. c. 13; 27 Eliz. c. 27.

them in their struggle with nature, how little control they could exercise: it put a term to many a hopeful enterprise, ruined many gallant expeditions. Improving works of a lesser kind went forward, like the new cut in the River Lea, deepening and straightening the river from Ware to London, making the River Welland navigable, cutting a new channel to bring the haven to Chichester.[1] Important coast works were undertaken at Dover and the sea-banks maintained on the coast of Norfolk.

We can derive a general picture of the look of the land from Camden. He was impressed by the strangeness of the Fen country, seventy miles long and thirty broad — the size of a county — drowned in water; where the soil was so soft that the horses went unshod and where the people walked on stilts.[2] He was well content to dwell on its curiosities. Croyland had been "much haunted in times past with I wot not what sprites and fearful apparitions". The town was built like Venice, the streets severed by water-courses and raised on piles. The inhabitants kept their cattle a great way off and, when they went to milk them, went in skerries, little punts carrying two apiece. Enormous quantities of wild duck were taken there in summer. North Cambridgeshire resembled an inland sea in winter, he says, covered with water further than man kens: sixty-eight miles from the Suffolk border to Waynflete in Lincolnshire.[3] The land was prolific of a gross hay called 'lid'; the people burned what they did not want of it, to come up in great abundance next spring. Their chief occupations were fishing and fowling. The land grew turves for fire, reeds for thatch, willows to hold the banks. The draining of the Fens had often been discussed and even come before Parliament; but perhaps it was wisest not to intermeddle with what God had ordained. After all, the Pontine marshes had lapsed to their former state. It was fortunate that the government was not impressed with this classical example. The country people in Northamptonshire complained that the great drains were neglected and had been turned to private uses.[4] There may have been some deterioration since the Dissolution. In other spheres, too, one watches the State taking on former works of the Church.

Camden was enthusiastic about Northamptonshire, all champion country and "exceeding populous": perhaps his enthusiasm ran away with him when he tells us that in some places twenty or thirty church towers or spires could be seen, the

[1] 13 Eliz. c. 18; 13 Eliz. c. 13.
[2] Camden, pp. 529-30.
[3] *Ibid.* pp. 491-2.
[4] *Ibid.* p. 512.

country all over besprinkled with villages and little towns.[1] He was eloquent about the rich vales: of Evesham, which was the granary of all the country round about; of the Red Horse with its good red soil, the Feldon country of Warwickshire of which you have a goodly and pleasant prospect from Edgehill; of Aylesbury, with its soft and white fleeces in request as far as Turkey.[2] These great flocks of sheep were a principal commodity of the Buckinghamshire gentry, especially those of Quarrendon belonging to Sir Henry Lee, a familiar figure at Court, of whom Aubrey tells us a charming story.[3] Richest soil of all and very populous was the vale of Taunton: which "country here most delectable on every side with green meadows, flourishing with pleasant gardens and orchards and replenished with fair manor houses, wonderfully contenteth the eyes of the beholders".[4] The Isle of Wight was enclosed, with rich and prosperous cornfields. Worcestershire produced plenty of corn, perry and excellent cheeses. East Suffolk, which was enclosed country and pastured cattle along the coastal flats, produced large quantities of cheese for the London market and especially for victualling ships on long voyages. The best cheeses in England were made in Cheshire.[5]

The hilly and mountainous North and Wales did not appeal to the Elizabethan sense of the picturesque: Craven, Camden says, was "rough all over and unpleasant to see to, with craggy stones, hanging rocks and rugged ways".[6] But he was appreciative of Yorkshire agriculture. In Elmet they burned limestone to manure the land with. Best of all was the rich yellow marl of the Aire valley by Pontefract which, when spread over the fields, enabled them to bear corn for years together. There was soft marl too about Knaresborough and abundant liquorice-growing. He speaks with pleasure of the gardens and orchards of York and "behind them fields even hard to the walls, for exercise and disports". At Northallerton, Bartholomew Fair provided "the greatest fair of kine and oxen, and of most resort, that ever I saw in all my life". Lancashire and Cheshire had both greatly increased their crops of corn of late by marling. The Bishopric of Durham was fertile on the coastal side, with meadows, pastures

1 Camden, p. 505.

2 *Ibid.* pp. 577, 561, 395.

3 "He was never married, but kept women to read to him when he was abed. One of his readers was Parson Jones's wife of Wotton. I have heard her daughter (who had no more wit) glory what a brave reader her mother was and how Sir Harry's worship much delighted to hear her." And more to the same effect. (Aubrey, *Brief Lives* (ed. A. Clark), II. 31.)

4 Camden, p. 223.

5 For the above sentences cf. *ibid.* pp. 273, 573, 459, 601.

6 For the following pars. cf. *ibid.* pp. 694-5, 702, 723, 734, 745, 800, 806.

and cornfields, " beset everywhere with towns and yielding plenty of sea-coal, which in many places we use for fuel ". The Borders had their own way of life: small patches of intensive tillage in the dales, on the high fells and mountains pasturing, a nomadic existence; thieving, cattle-raiding, fighting and scuffling with the Scots occupied most people out in the wastes. " In the Wastes as they term them, as also in Gilliesland, you may see as it were the ancient Nomads, a martial kind of men who, from the month of April into August, lie out scattering and summering (as they term it) with their cattle, in little cottages here and there, which they call sheils and sheilings." Upon the Roman Wall, at Busy Gap, " a place infamous for thieving and robbing ", Camden had wished to inspect a fort, " but I could not with safety take the full survey of it, for the rank robbers thereabout ".

Camden was, as usual, attracted by Wales, but not by the scenery.[1] He praises the Golden Valley in Herefordshire, with the cornfields lying under the wooded hills, and the gay and gallant meadows below the cornfields. But the vast wilderness of Radnor was " hideous after a sort to behold, by reason of the turning and crooked by-ways and craggy mountains ". In Denbighshire they burned turves to fructify the soil and produced abundant rye. Flintshire was equally fruitful, " especially every first year that they [the fields] be broken up and sown "; they bear " in some places barley, in others wheat, but generally throughout rye, with twentyfold increase and better, and afterwards four or five crops together of oats ".

Let us look a little more closely into the picture: into some of the counties illustrated by contemporary evidence, especially the more advanced districts, those most characteristic of the progress of the age. Economic historians have accustomed us to the abstract phrase ' commercialisation of agriculture ' to describe what was happening in these areas at the time: the mercurial influence of trade and money and urban markets, above all the proximity of London and the ports, in disturbing the old settled customary system of rents largely in kind and labour services, of an agriculture dominantly for subsistence rather than geared to the market: the transition to new methods at once more specialised, more economical — for the land can thereby be devoted to the crop it grows best — and more efficient. Naturally these influences and trends can be seen at work best in the counties round London. The necessity — and the profit — in feeding London, which was growing at a rapid rate, exerted a pull over

[1] For the following par. cf. *ibid.* pp. 617, 624, 675, 679.

a large radius. Some historians think that the evolution of a metropolitan market may be regarded as a distinct phase on the way to a national economy.[1]

These abstractions can be brought down to earth concretely in Norden's homely accounts of the Home Counties. Of "the means most usual how the people of Middlesex do live, not meddling with the higher sort, I observe this of the meaner": those living by the Thames "live either by the barge, by the wherry or ferry, or by the sculler or by fishing, all of which live well and plentifully, and in decent and honest sort relieve their families".[2] Inland from the Thames the people lived by a prosperous husbandry, for "these commonly are so furnished with kine that the wife twice or thrice a week conveyeth to London milk, butter, cheese, apples, pears, frumenty, hens, chickens, eggs, bacon and a thousand other country drugs, which good housewives can frame and find to get a penny. And this yieldeth them a large comfort and relief." Here there were prosperous farmers who seldom or not at all set their hand to the plough, but fattened cattle for Smithfield and other markets. They were very well-to-do and commonly became rich, able to "wade in the weeds of gentlemen". The Meal-men and Malt-men were a feature of this shire: "the Meal-men for the most part buying their wheat at the best hand and so convert it into wheat and carry it to the market and bring it home in money. . . . The Malt-men for the most part carry for other men by the quarter, and yet profit greatly, but especially before the barges did pass the River Lea."[3]

Underneath the wilderness of bricks — and ruins — of modern London one can see with the historian's eye what Middlesex was once like, the fields and villages now covered with rubble, with the submerged churches that once were the centres of a rural parish life. Norden saw these places smiling with golden corn. Harrow "seemeth to make ostentation of its situation in the Pure-vale, from whence towards the time of harvest, a man may behold the fields round about so sweetly to address themselves to the sickle and scythe, with such comfortable abundance of all kind of grain, that the husbandman which waiteth for the fruits of his labours cannot but clap his hands for joy to see this vale so to laugh and sing".[4] The best corn of all grew at Heston, now an

[1] Cf. N. S. B. Gras, *The Evolution of the English Corn Market.*

[2] Norden, *The Chorography of Norfolk* (ed. C. M. Hood), p. 57.

[3] Norden, *Speculi Britanniae Pars: Description of Essex* (ed. Ellis, Camden Society), p. xii.

[4] Norden, *Speculum Britanniae: Description of Middlesex and Hertfordshire* (ed. 1723), p. ii.

airfield, then " a most fertile place of wheat, yet not so much to be commended for the quantity as for the quality, for the wheat is most pure, accounted the purest in many shires. And therefore Queen Elizabeth hath the most part of her provision from that place for manchet for her Highness' own diet, as is reported." [1]

Hertfordshire and Essex were similarly prosperous, irrigated by the fruitful streams of money and commodities coming from the markets and by commerce. Ware was flourishing more and more owing to the turning of the highway to London away from Hertford.[2] Hitchin had a very bountiful corn market and great store of malt was made in the town. Around the town was a deposit of marl, good for enriching the cornfields. " About the town of Walden groweth great store of saffron, whose nature in yielding her fruit is very strange and bindeth the labourer to great travail and diligence." [3] Yet it yielded a commensurate advantage. The use of saffron in those days was wide and various, though mainly medicinal. It was grown largely in Essex and Cambridgeshire.

Reyce's *Breviary of Suffolk* gives us a similar picture of prosperity and for the same reasons : " so quickly and commodiously it can vent and make return of such commodities which it affordeth " due to its " navigable rivers, diversity of commodious havens for exportation and importation, nearness unto the quickest and readiest markets of best trade ".[4] Reyce shows Suffolk divided between enclosed country on the east, open champion on the west ; the east living mainly by pasture and feeding of cattle, the middle by tillage, the west by tillage and flocks of sheep. Hops were of recent introduction on any considerable scale in Suffolk and had been grown to great advantage, the more so since they employed unprofitable, marshy grounds. Timber was being diminished, and deer-parks were not what they had formerly been, " the necessities of this latter age hath given such a downfall of the pleasures of this kind that necessary profit is had in a more general estimation ". (One thinks of the herd, survivors from an earlier world, in the medieval park around the moated manor of Helmingham.) Pigs were vastly more profitable : droves of them went up to furnish the London markets and served to victual the navy and ships voyaging from eastern ports. So also with the excellent Suffolk cheeses, which the county produced in large quantity. Reyce refers to " the late-born trade of cheese-mongers, which yearly from

[1] *Ibid.* p. 25. [2] Norden, *Description of Hertfordshire* (ed. 1903), pp. 18, 19.
[3] Norden, *Description of Essex* (ed. Ellis), p. 8.
[4] Reyce, *The Breviary of Suffolk* (ed. Hervey), p. 13 and foll.

London at all seasons flock hither to buy it at any hand". He tells us that in one ordinary year from one haven alone 900 loads of butter and cheese were carried to London; and that was but a quarter of the total for the county. His greatest enthusiasm was for the horses of Suffolk: he had seen them in time of service in the wars overseas and been proud of their firm carriage, "their quickness and readiness in all necessities, but of all for their continuance in time of battle, never giving in, but when other the choicest of all other countries, especially if the march have been anything long or the skirmish anything hot, have soon fainted and tired". Since these must be the ancestors of the Suffolk Punch we can all share his enthusiasm.

Norfolk was almost entirely open champion, with corn in great plenty in most parts of the shire. "Some part of the ground in it is wonderful fat and comparable for goodness with the Woodland in Suffolk, so much renowned for the fertility thereof."[1] At Tilney Smith "are fed above 30,000 sheep and the place is so fruitful as the inhabitants affirm that if overnight a wand or rod be laid upon it, by the morning it shall be covered with grass of that night's growth and not to be discerned".[2] But this was a commonplace of Elizabethan rustic lore. About Winterton on the coast the grounds were "the most fruitful fat and mouldy of any part in England" and requiring the least labour "as one horse though but a jade". Northamptonshire was no less prosperous. Norden remarked on the great herds of cattle belonging to every small parish and village, such main flocks of sheep — foundation of the fortunes of the Spencers — and "what made me most to marvel were the great herds of swine, a beast altogether unprofitable till he come to the slaughter. Then his rusty ribs in a frosty morning will please Pierce the ploughman and will so supple his weather-beaten lips that his whip and his whistle will hammer out such harmony as will make a dog dance that delights it."[3] The baser sort prospered well enough in this shire and were less beholden generally to the monied men of any shire he knew.

Much of London's food supplies came from these counties and from the southern Midlands, the corn coming down the Thames, making the towns upon the river prosper as it went — Abingdon, for instance, lived mainly by its malt.[4] Fattening stock was a gainful occupation in all these counties north of the Thames. To the south of the river Kent was already the 'garden of England':

[1] Norden, *Norfolk* (ed. Hood), p. 67. [2] *Ibid.* pp. 165, 170.
[3] Norden, *Description of Northamptonshire* (ed. 1720), pp. 31-2.
[4] Camden, *Britannia*, p. 279; and for Henley, *ibid.* p. 389.

Lambarde tells us that no part of the Realm had so many orchards.[1] The Weald used to drink cider only, for want of barley; it was now plentifully supplied with oats, and hops were rapidly increasing. Half the deer-parks had been disparked in living memory for tillage. The result was that Kent had now a surplus of corn to send to London, and was in fact the leading coastwise supplier.[2] Black conies were bred for their skins, and Kent had a good sale for young rabbits to the London poulterers.

Going further afield we note that Norden had a high opinion of Western husbandry. The secret of it was to take great pains to break up the turf and make channels: " their hearts, hands, eyes and all their powers concur in one, to force the earth to yield her utmost fruit ".[3] Oliver Cromwell, a generation later, held the same opinion: " I have been in all the counties of England and I think the husbandry of Devonshire is best ".[4] Indeed the county gave its name to this treatment of the soil, beating the turves with mattocks, burning them and spreading the ash over the land: it became known as Denshiring and was taken up in many parts of the country. Risdon tells us that the north and west of the country were lean and barren, except around the towns, where improvement had enforced fertility, and near the coast where sea-sand was used to better the soil.[5] Many parks had been converted to tillage. Sheep were plentiful, if they did not make as much show as elsewhere, because " the enclosures bereave the eye of its knowledge "; yet they supported a rapidly growing clothing industry. Similarly with cattle: great droves did not go as elsewhere to London, " for the great navigation in these western ports requireth store of victuals, which is fully supplied by our own breed ". Timber was diminishing, " what with good husbandry and cleansing of the ground, and what with ill husbandry in felling and selling ".

Much the same holds good of Cornish agriculture, of which Carew gives us an admirable account.[6] A marked improvement in husbandry had taken place, particularly in East Cornwall, during the latter half of the century. Denshiring the ground had become regular and the tillers of the soil took great pains over it. Sea-sand was much used. Rye was grown on the poorer

[1] Lambarde, *The Perambulation of Kent*, pp. 10-11.

[2] F. J. Fisher, " The Development of the London Food Market ", *Econ. Hist. Rev*. V. No. 2, 47.

[3] Norden, *The Surveyor's Dialogue* (ed. 1607), p. 227.

[4] q. in G. N. Clark, *The Wealth of England*, p. 97.

[5] Risdon, *Survey of the County of Devon* (ed. 1811), p. 5 foll.

[6] Carew, *Survey of Cornwall* (ed. 1811), pp. 62-81.

grounds; barley was of fairly recent cultivation and had much amended the Cornish drink, "which (to the ill refreshing of strangers) in former times they made only of oats". Four of the Duchy parks had been disparked for tillage. Timber had taken "an universal downfall". The Devon and Somerset graziers fed yearly great droves of cattle in the north quarter. Cornish animals were small and hardy. There had been a vast improvement in the well-being and standard of living of the husbandmen. No doubt this held good of East Cornwall, which Carew knew best, rather than of West Cornwall. The proximity of Plymouth and other ports was an important factor. Humberstone's survey of Leigh-durrant manor near the estuary of the Tamar points out that the "lands are very fineable, by reason there is such utterance and sale of all manner of victuals to the town of Plymouth".[1] The bloodless categories of the economic historian are seen to have substance after all.

Pembrokeshire, Owen tells us, was bare and champion country, and consequently had the worst 'manred' (*i.e.* manhood) — from a J.P. and Deputy Lieutenant's point of view — of all Wales.[2] This was because the principal means of livelihood was in herding cattle: "I have by good account numbered 3000 young people to be brought up continually in herding of cattle within this shire, who are put to this idle education when they are first come to be ten or twelve years of age and turned to the open fields to follow their cattle". There follows a vivid and unflattering account of their appearance in consequence, "more like tawny Moors than people of this land". The Welsh were poor husbandmen and so applied themselves to tilling oats, where the English inhabitants grew wheat and barley. Around St. David's was good cornland, but it was oaty and not so fine as it should be owing to negligence and sowing bad and oaty seed. But even the Welsh were now improving. The abolition of gavelkind had encouraged the purchase and exchange of lands, their hedging and enclosing in separate holdings, and thereby promoted better tillage. There was some corn for export now, as in Cornwall. This would seem to be from the English half of the shire; in the Welsh there was a great increase in cattle-breeding. Owen's enthusiasm, like a sensible landlord, was all for improved manuring, and he has a detailed account of the various new methods in use, Denshiring, applying sea-sand, burning limestone; above all, seeking out and treating with various kinds of marl. As a geologist,

[1] *Topographer and Genealogist*, I. 227.

[2] Owen, *Description of Pembrokeshire*, pp. 42-62.

Owen was all for marling, and he quotes the country saying that " a man doth sand for himself, lime for his son, and marl for his grandchild ". Great profit arose from their sheep, for though they were small and their wool coarse, they were no charge and could feed out in winter. South Pembroke sold its wool to Bristol, the north to Cardigan, thence to North Wales where it was made into white cloth and sold to Shrewsbury. One observes the commercialisation of agriculture already getting under weigh in these westernmost extremities of the land.

The essential difference marking off the North from the South in our period was its poverty and backwardness. At a time when the South was making rapid economic advances the disparity was all the more marked and awkward. Actually there was agrarian decline upon the Borders in the first half of the century, which called forth the Tillage Act for the Northern Counties in 1555 in the hope of arresting it.[1] The West Riding, still more the East Riding, had good arable land ; and a broad strip of cultivable land went up the east coast of Durham into Northumberland. But most of this large area was moorland, mountain and high fells, with cultivation confined to the dales : a country of great spaces and difficult communications, a world of its own looking towards Scotland and its hereditary enemies across the Border. Its society was still feudal, with an admixture of moss-trooping and cattle-raiding ; the peasantry and tenantry looked to their nobles and gentry, not to the distant government in the South, for leadership. The government could not conjure " the old good-will of the people deep-grafted in their hearts, to their nobles and gentlemen ", and could not have heard with any pleasure that in Northumberland " they knew no other Prince but a Percy ".[2] Henry taught them. Elizabeth completed the lesson.

Economic changes were affecting Border society adversely and the peculiar conditions and discontents prevailing there reflected the economic circumstances of life. All Border tenures were upon condition of military service upon the Borders when necessary. This applied to freeholders as strictly as to customary tenants and was no cause of discontent. Causes of decay were held to be, rather, the long peace, the exactions of the lords, the leasing of Crown lands and possessions to non-local men and their absenteeism. The country was essentially pastoral and not therefore affected by the enclosure movement of the South. But the government wished to extend enclosure for tillage, and Crown

[1] R. R. Reid, " The Rebellion of the Earls, 1569 ", *Trans. R.H.S.* (1906), p. 179.
[2] *Ibid.* p. 176.

lands were now being let on condition of " enclosure by quickset hedge ". More important was the substitution of profitable sheep and cattle for unprofitable horses, and the increase of fines upon tenants.

We have a shaft of light into what things were like there from the official Survey of the lands forfeited by the Northern Rebels of 1569.[1] ' Simple Thomas ', Earl of Northumberland, had been simple enough to allow himself to be led into rebellion against Elizabeth by his wife; the Earl of Westmorland was such a waster that he thought he had nothing to lose. But he had — his ancient estates. The Surveyors, Hall and Humberstone, report that on Northumberland's estates in Cumberland the tenants had earlier been well content, " till now of late years the greediness of the lords hath been such and their practices so horrible by making conveyance and devises of their lands to cause the poor tenants to make fine sometimes once in two, three or four years as to them seem good, as the poor tenants are so ransomed as they are neither able to live and maintain their family . . . so as that custom which heretofore they most desired is now become so odious unto them as they are not able to endure it ". At Kirby Moorside in Yorkshire, the poor copyholders " have no lands or other commodities to their cottages so as their rents must of necessity decay, unless the commons which Henry late Earl [of Westmorland] took from the tenants about 8 or 9 years past and enclosed them, which was the only relief of the inhabitants of the town, wherein they kept every man one, two or three kine for the relief of themselves, their wives and children ". The fact that the Westmorlands were Catholics did not prevent them, any more than it did the Treshams or the Rodneys, from being enclosers of commons with poor men's rights. The government was consistently on the side of the poor man, but there was little that it could do.

Something of the special conditions prevailing up there may be seen from what is said of the Forest of Westward, between Cockermouth and Carlisle, " so thick of wood as poor men used in all dangerous times to drive their cattle into the said forest, and when they were in the wood the enemy could not chase them without great company and great time to do it, by means whereof the country always had knowledge and gathered company to the rescue ". Of late years the wood had been spoiled and the deer partly decayed. The barony of Alnwick, though the soil was somewhat better and the people more given to tillage and labour, was " yet very poor, because they are able to keep no greater

[1] Excheq. K.R. Misc. Books, xxxvii, xxxviii.

number of cattle of any kind than may lie in house at night, because it is so near Scotland of one part and the thievish country of Tynedale of the other part, whose whole life and delight is only in stealing, robbing and spoiling their poor neighbours and more harm is done to the poor countrymen by the riders of Tynedale than by the open enemies the Scots ". The town of Bywell whose trade was in ironwork, making bits and bridles for all that country, was so subject to incursions from Tynedale that the inhabitants were forced " to bring their cattle and sheep into the street at night and watch both ends ". Something of the economic reason for this state of affairs may be seen from the custom in Tynedale of dividing tenements among all the sons upon the father's death, thus forcing youths to become thieves for lack of sustenance.[1] Though Cumberland was poor yet it was very populous in the dales and " breedeth tall men and hard of nature ".

The striking contrast between the value of North Country lands and those in the South may be seen by comparing the Survey of Northumberland's estates, or Westmorland's, with those of the Earl of Bedford. Though Northumberland lived like a prince in his castle at Alnwick, with his feudal retinue of Constable of the Castle, Porter, Castle-greave, Receiver, Feodary, Steward, Clerk of the Courts and Foreign Bailiff, when the Rising caught him he could raise hardly any ready money and was forced to pawn his George and let off his Yorkshire demesnes on lease. The total rents of the barony of Alnwick were £79 : 10 : 9¾ per annum, of which the fees to the above officials took £62 : 8 : 10, leaving the Earl £17 : 1 : 11¾ net. A very different state of affairs is revealed with regard to the Bedford estates in the South.[2] Several of their individual manors were worth more than the gross value of Alnwick, or almost as much; for example, the old Russell property in Dorset, the manor of Kingston Russell at £140 p.a., Berwick, £60; in Devon — Clyst Satcheville, £105 : 9 : 1, Werrington, £128 : 1 : 9½, Plymstock, £94 : 0 : 8½, while Cowick was worth £75 : 15 : 8½; in Bucks — Amersham, £76 : 4 : 2, Chesham, £74 : 10 : 10; in Hertfordshire, the manor of Moore was worth £239 : 2 : 11; in Hunts, Connington, £101 : 6 : 6; in Middlesex, Covent Garden, £79 : 4 : 10; when one comes to the enormous grant the Russells got of the possessions of Tavistock Abbey from Henry VIII, they were worth a gross annual value of £631 : 12 : 0½. It is true that upon these estates very considerable sums were charged for reserved rents to the Crown and for

[1] D. L. W. Tough, *The Last Years of a Frontier*, p. 58.
[2] S.P. 12/195/48, 49; S.P. 13, Case G.

the payment of vicars and officers, in all a sum of £556 : 11 : 11 p.a. But that left the Earl a clear £1496 : 18 : 9½ p.a. to himself. In fact, for all the princely position of the Percys in Northumberland and Cumberland, the new southern Earl could have bought them up several times over. That, in a world in which money values were coming increasingly to the fore and ancient liberties and dues were becoming reduced to them, was a significant pointer to the future.

It is impossible to sum up Tudor agriculture in a chapter — a subject that would take a whole book. Fortunately there are good books on it.[1] We have to keep before the imagination the idea that it has its own complexity and manifold variety, just as today: there is still every kind of difference of tenure and of farming systems found. So then. But we have always to remember that the complexity and variety emerge from, and are apt to disguise, a fundamental and a consoling simplicity: the men and their beasts, their implements and their operations according to the nature of the soil, the seasons and the weather. The things themselves are simple enough: it is the relations they set up in society, the social and legal arrangements, that are so various and complex.

Here we are concerned rather with the general factors affecting agriculture: what was specific to the time. The fundamental fact is the decay of subsistence husbandry.[2] This had been going on in select areas, under the influence of commerce and urban demand, especially around London, in the later Middle Ages. On the other hand, there are still today remote farms and small areas where the farming is more for subsistence than for the market: one knows such small producers living with their bellies close to the soil. But the sixteenth century, and in especial the second half of it, saw a rapid and concentrated transition from the more static conditions of medieval agriculture, that express themselves so deeply in the medieval experience of life and religion, to the freer, more mobile conditions of agriculture carried on on the basis of money and markets, the exchange of goods rather than of services. This is what we mean at bottom when we say that society is ceasing to have a feudal basis. The social effects, to take only one example, could hardly be more

[1] *E.g.* Ernle, *English Farming: Past and Present*; Tawney, *The Agrarian Problem in the Sixteenth Century*; Gonner, *Common Land and Enclosure*; Orwin, *The Open Fields*.

[2] Tawney, p. 404.

important: the process of change from bond to free labour is essentially completed in the Elizabethan Age.[1]

There is first the influence of money itself, and here the background to keep in mind is the Price Revolution of the sixteenth century: a world-wide phenomenon, though its effects are mainly to be seen in the Atlantic area of Western Europe. The flood of silver coming in from the New World sent prices up, encouraged production and trade, and helped to unfix the old foundations of a stable agrarian economy.[2] Increasing trade and population meant a demand for more production from the land — at a time when productivity was flagging, the old tillage areas under constant cropping and inadequate manuring, becoming less fertile and exhausted.[3] Agriculture was very inefficient in the earlier sixteenth century: it seems that ground had been lost since the thirteenth and fourteenth centuries. For one thing, marling appears to have gone much out of use until the renewed campaign for it by Tudor agriculturists. The increasing demands of trade and population could only be met by improved agriculture: greater mobility and flexibility, more efficiency and a better division of labour. That was coming about in a hundred different ways all over the progressive parts of the country: a tendency towards the enclosure of separate holdings and their concentration — which, no-one can deny, made for more efficient cultivation; a very great extension of cultivation at the expense of waste and woodland; a certain amount of conversion from arable to pasture — and this was what caused the outcries and the agrarian discontent of the time, very understandably when it led to depopulation and the tillers of the soil being thrown out of their holdings upon the markets and the roads. This consequence has been a great deal exaggerated as to its effect: it was really important only in a limited area, the southern Midlands, particularly Oxford, Bucks, Northants, Leicester. But naturally such a problem constituted one of national importance, and Tudor government addressed itself constantly to it. Not perhaps very efficiently: the effectiveness of government was limited in those days. At any rate it tried and never ceased trying. Heckscher tells us that English governments right up to the nineteenth century fostered agriculture more than any governments abroad.[4]

Then, too, there is the local influence of towns and growing industry stimulated by these wider factors international as well as

[1] *Ibid.* p. 43.

[2] Cf. Keynes, *Treatise on Money*, II. 152 foll.

[3] Cf. Ernle, p. 64.

[4] Heckscher, *Mercantilism*, I. 225.

national. We have seen something of the influence of the London market for food radiating out into the nearby counties; in other ways, its influence was far more extensive; and growing until it reached a national scale. Other towns exerted a similar pull upon their localities: Exeter and Norwich were each the metropolis of its area, and both linked with London. We have seen something of the effect that the growing cloth industry had upon agriculture in the case of Devon. This, with the improvement of communications or at least their greater use, enabled such areas to devote themselves to the crops they grew best instead of to subsistence.[1] Some specialisation meant much greater efficiency. The growing strength of markets multiplied this factor.

The Dissolution of the monasteries and chantries, with the consequent throwing of one-sixth of the whole cultivable area of the country upon the market, had an important effect in this direction. It was in the first instance disturbing and possibly disadvantageous, in so far as it threw existing arrangements out of gear. But with the second generation, and the settling in of numerous hard-headed, hard-fisted families to screw the utmost return out of the land in innumerable places where idle monks had droned away their lives, there must have been a considerable increase in productivity, as certainly there was a far greater emphasis upon it. The Elizabethans did not approve of the contemplative life. The immense activity of the age had its economic roots, though that is not the whole of its explanation.

With these general forces in mind, all of which could be illustrated illimitably, perhaps we could look at the country again and scrutinise it more closely, narrowing the scope.

It is usual to delimit a V-shaped area running from Wiltshire in the south-west to Norfolk in the east and the East Riding in the north as the area where the open fields with their common system of agriculture were dominant, the standard pattern. This pattern of things was by no means confined to this area: it extended far beyond it and the whole thing was more complex. Some counties, for example, were divided between the two systems: East Somerset had open fields, West Somerset was enclosed;[2] East Suffolk was enclosed while West Suffolk was open. We have seen that Pembrokeshire, far outside the area, was champion. Cornwall, which used to be supposed to have had none, is now known to have had some open fields.[3] We now appreciate that it was the

[1] Gonner, p. 36. [2] *V.C.H. Somerset*, II. 304.
[3] Cf. my *Tudor Cornwall*, pp. 32-5; *Topographer and Genealogist*, I. 346.

necessary exigencies of cultivating the land in very poor and primitive conditions that produced the open fields and the common system of farming. It was not political and constitutional ideas, still less the emphasis upon freedom or equality — as the liberal-minded nineteenth century thought — it was the very poverty of small agricultural communities and the necessity of mutual defence in their struggle for existence against the severity of nature and the violence of men that forced them to work together with their common plough and plough team. Co-aration in fact produced co-operation, not the other way round. We understand how little men's actions derive from any thinking but conversely how dependent their thinking is on their actions.

The open field system was then the standard pattern of medieval tillage, without as well as within the area of Central England. Sussex, for example, was mainly downland or woodland, but where there was cultivation in the valleys there were open fields. The distinction between one area and another is not the presence of open fields — for they were liable to be present anywhere — but between one kind of agriculture and another. Central England was the area overwhelmingly of tillage and therefore of open fields. The North, Wales and the South-west were dominantly pastoral, though they grew corn for their own subsistence (in the far North not enough, in the South they had occasional surpluses to export). What happened was immediately dependent on the weather: one county may be enjoying a surplus when the next has a serious dearth: the government has to step in to direct corn from one to the other, often enforce it by strict measures. One cannot over-estimate the directness and simplicity of the condition of things then: bad weather and a bad harvest meant a starving people. After the halcyon period of a beneficent world market in the past century, we are now beginning to understand a bit better what life was like in the sixteenth century.

It stands to reason that it would be in this area of Central England where the common field system was dominant that the impact of the new forces would be most felt. And such was the case. Elsewhere they could take them better, absorb the impact and profit by it. The large areas that had but lately come into cultivation were fairly free from the complicated arrangements of the common system. Where these existed they were a force for conservatism; the whole process was too complicated to overthrow: you needed the consent of a whole community, a thing almost impossible to obtain in this mortal life. The common system of open field cultivation, though not immovable, meant a tremendous *vis inertiae* against the new forces. The whole thing made for a static society and held up change: it formed "a complex of intermixed and mutual rights which, consecrated by immemorial usage, made conscious change well-nigh impossible, save under the pressure of strong forces".[1] These forces hit this area most strongly in the form of the drive towards enclosure.

The movement towards enclosure is, perhaps, the most characteristic as it is certainly the most noticeable — and noticed — trend in later Tudor agriculture. Enclosure meant several different things, most of them beneficial in their effects. There has been so much sentimentalism among historians on this subject, based on the literature of professional complaint, that it is essential to insist from the first that enclosure arose from agricultural causes and was a part of normal agricultural development.[2] Some enclosure was essential to the working of the open field system. No-one could object to the enclosure of new land for cultivation from the waste, provided that enough was left for pasture for the animals of the community. That was sheer gain for everybody. Take, for example, the enclosure of Grindleton Moor, or a part of it, within the manor of Slaidburn that belonged to the Duchy of Lancaster — it still does — that magnificent wild country on the borders of Yorkshire and Lancashire.[3] The inhabitants of Grindleton had petitioned for it. Warrant for it to be carried out was sent down to the steward of the manor and to Ralph Assheton, "our particular receiver" — there is still a Ralph Assheton there. "Whereas the said town of Grindleton is of late greatly increased in buildings and dwelling-houses and thereby much more populated than heretofore it hath been, by reason whereof the ancient grounds used and employed to pasture meadow and tillage are in no sort able or sufficient to maintain our said freeholders and copyholders . . ." it would be "a far greater relief to our freeholders and copyholders and especially to the poorer sort if some reasonable part and portions of the best and most fruitful part of the said common might by our favour be enclosed and fenced in and in some reasonable manner apportioned and divided". Order was accordingly sent down for a Commission of the officers and men of the best credit to view and tread out the portions, allowing the poor cottagers 20 acres each, paying no rent for the first 21 years,

[1] Gonner, p. 35. [2] *Ibid.* pp. 107-8.
[3] Tawney and Power, *Tudor Economic Documents*, I. 81 foll.

and 4d. an acre thereafter. This kind of enclosure was obviously popular and encouraging to enterprise.[1]

Fitzherbert, the leading writer on agriculture in the early sixteenth century, implies that the most part of the lords have already enclosed their demesnes and meadows so that their tenants have no common with them, *i.e.* rights to pasture their cattle on the lord's demesnes.[2] This must have meant some gain to the landlords at the expense of their tenants. Every motive of efficient management must have impelled them towards enclosing their demesnes and making them a going concern separate from, but not cut off from, the community of yeomen and peasants around them. The desire of the lord to build up and round off his own estate around him, what became his park and home farm, was often carried out by exchange and agreement.[3] Often the agreement led to disputes so that its interpretation came before the courts to settle.[4] That the tenants had a spirit of their own and were no oppressed and down-trodden peasantry as abroad, is evident from their readiness to bring such matters before the courts and the expectation that they would get justice. Often a process of exchange or purchase among themselves would enable them to build up a concentrated holding out of their scattered strips in the great field and to enclose it. There were such enclosed holdings in the midst of the common field though it was obviously more convenient and usual for them to be on the edge of it, especially of new land taken in or of meadow, which was easier to enclose into separate holdings than the open arable.

The enclosure of which we hear so much complaint is that of tillage for conversion into pasture.[5] If that involved the depopula-

[1] For a similar case of enclosure, of Chailey Common near Lewes in Sussex, by mutual agreement between the lord and the tenants, cf. *The Book of John Rowe*, ed. W. H. Godfrey (Sussex Record Soc. vol. XXXIV), p. 8.

[2] Cf. Fitzherbert's *Surveying* (ed. 1767).

[3] There is an interesting description of the process of enclosure of most of a manor by agreement between the tenants and the lord in the case of Iwerne Courtenay in Dorset in 1548, reported by Humberstone, *Topographer and Genealogist*, I. 47. In the case of West Coker in Somerset, Humberstone feared that the farmer of the lord's demesnes, Sir John S., " who being confederate with the freeholders of the manor maketh such enclosures for his own lucre and suffereth the freeholders to do the same, nevertheless surcharge the common with their cattle, that in process of time it will be the destruction of the customary tenants and utter decay of the lord's fines if remedy be not provided therein " (*ibid.* p. 150).

[4] Cf. the case of the inhabitants of Westangmering, Sussex *v.* John Palmer, and that of the inhabitants of Draycote and Stoke Gifford, Somerset *v.* Sir John Rodney (Tawney and Power, *Tudor Econ. Docts.* I. 19-39).

[5] Mr. Gonner thinks that the popular grievance was not necessarily due to conversion from arable to pasture so much as to the enclosure of commons and the deprivation of common rights (*op. cit.* p. 136).

tion of a village, it was obviously intolerable and everybody said so — even if it did mean a more economic use of the land in question; for example, if the land were more suited for pasture and yielded a better return as such. That was where the factor of international price came into an increasingly commercialised agriculture. Towards the middle of the century the prosperity of the cloth industry and the increasing demand for wool made it profitable for owners to convert tillage into pasture. The government was dead against it and passed a series of Tillage Acts to force the upkeep of as much tillage as before, and placing heavy penalties on lords who allowed land to go out of cultivation. The government had a double motive: the maintenance of man-power and the assuaging of agrarian discontent. But it could not contain economic movements within the framework of a statute. What was much more effective was that later in the century the markets moved in favour of tillage again, and not until the last years of the reign, with the ravages of war and bad harvests, was there anything like the agrarian discontent that marked the middle of the century, the upheaved sombre years of the Reformation.

We can see pictorially what was happening, catch the changes of the time on the wing, by inspecting the maps that Elizabethan surveyors made of their manors. No better maps than theirs have ever been made: they are so reliable and clear that today, nearly four centuries later, one can go to a place they surveyed and still tell one's whereabouts within a few feet. In addition they made them things of beauty, with their swags and decorations of fruits and flowers. Many of these survive; but it so happens that a particularly satisfying and well-known set exists of the estates of All Souls College, made at the command of Warden Hovenden.[1] From these one can watch every variety of happening to the fields and townships. Take the map of Padbury in Bucks, made by Thomas Clerk in 1591.[2] I remember some years ago tracing with the aid of that map the very furrows in those fields which marked the strips of long-dead Elizabethan tenants of the College. And one noticed from the gravestones in the churchyard how some of the old names continued. One sees the picture of the whole manor as it was then, the township in the centre, each tenement with its little house and toft marked. Several large holdings belong to Thomas Harris — a name that

[1] All Souls Muniment Room, Hovenden Maps.

[2] Thomas Clerk signs himself "gent of Stamford St. Martin's" — Burghley's parish.

remains — and one to the parsonage. Then in every direction all round are the furlongs, the strips of arable in the open fields, lying at all angles according to the lie of the land for drainage etc., the twisting ways giving access to them. Down by the stream are the meadows with an occasional 'tithe-dole' marked — the parson's holding. It is low-lying here: in one place a 'gog-mire' is marked and there are 'venny pool' furlongs: one remembers the primitive drainage of the times, the state of the ways in winter on heavy clayey soil on which so many writers remark. The names of holders are not specified on the strips in this general map of the whole manor, only of tenements in the township; but they often are on the detailed maps that follow illustrating the state of affairs in each section of the manor. Padbury is an absolutely typical undisturbed township, its inhabitants engaged mainly in tillage on their strips in the open fields with their necessary appendages in meadow and pasture.

At the other end of the scale a very different state of affairs is revealed at Whatborough in Leicestershire, from the map of 1586. There has been a profound disturbance here. The neighbouring monastery, Launde priory, had been snapped up by Thomas Cromwell. His comfortable son, Gregory, made a pleasant thing of it, lived, died and was buried there in his fine Renaissance tomb. There is the house depicted, three sides round a quadrangle with a gate-house in the fourth. Between the house and the fields of Whatborough are several large closes with the tell-tale inscriptions: "These grounds have likewise been arable", "These grounds do likewise lie ridge and furrow", "These grounds do appear to have been arable also". In the centre of the Whatborough fields we read: "The place where the town of Whatborough stood". Today, the guide-book tells us, the abbey "lies in a pretty park with beautiful gardens". There, in short, is the story of many a piece of English country landscape. The sentimental historian, Catholic or socialist in sympathy, would rush to the agreeable and obvious conclusion that the Cromwells had converted the old arable fields near the house to pasture. In fact it was the priory that had enclosed Whatborough many years before, in 1495.[1] The priory had leased it from the College. No doubt it was more suitably employed as pasture, for the country is hilly and contains the highest points in East Leicestershire, Whatborough hill and Robin-a-Tiptoe.

[1] I owe this information to my friend Dr. W. G. Hoskins, who has studied this area in detail along with the muniments at All Souls.

Between these two we find considerable variety of condition on the original pattern. The detailed map of Chattelfield at Maids Moreton in Bucks (1587) enables us to see the intermixture of strips.[1] John Harris, the College farmer (*i.e.* farmer in the original sense: he farms the College land), Mistress More, Abbot of Osney, Leonard Piggott, John Lambert and others alternate somewhat after that order, with an occasional strip for the parson. Of woodland Mrs. More has most; the College has a gorsy close and a park, "wherein the tenant has the furze and bushes in severalty but the feed thereof goeth in common along with Almead furlong". One sees the innumerable variations on the simple theme. Of the manor of Greenhams at Maids Moreton John Harris farmed some 230 acres, including the site of the manor just east of the church — the manor-house had disappeared: the College had no use for it. Some Lammas ground, *i.e.* meadow, was enclosed. Arable lying scattered abroad in the fields amounted to 157 acres; lea ground abroad in the fields 37 acres; lot meadow averaged each year 13 acres. There was common of pasture in Almead and Fursan. Such was the College farm there. Such are the shifting patterns one catches sight of.

At Weedon Weston in Northamptonshire, the next manor to Sulgrave, were two small townships. The parsonage tenement lies next the church at Weedon Pinckney. The Church close and the Rye lands, with the stream running through, belong to the College. To the south-west is Sulgrave Field. All round, the north-west corner of the furlongs is 'the Wild': two parts belong to the College, each of 40 acres, the other to Mr. Lovett, the next largest holder. Beyond his large holding east of Weedon Pinckney part of the 'new digging' is College land. The detailed map of the western furlongs shows College land bordering again on Sulgrave Field. (It was but ten years since Lawrence Washington, who got a grant of the priory of St. Andrew's, Northampton, from Henry VIII, had been laid to rest beneath his brass in the church at Sulgrave, leaving his manor-house unfinished. His son Robert Washington was living there now, the College's neighbour until 1610, when he and his son sold Sulgrave.)

A brief glance at the remaining estates will serve to illustrate our themes. The manors of Edgware and Kingsbury in Middlesex were wholly enclosed and in separate fields. In the former, evidently a good deal of enclosure had been made from Brockley Wood — new arable. The woodland was in the College's own

[1] The following maps in the series are by Thomas Langdon.

tenure; among the tenants were copyholders who paid fines upon transfer or demise at the lord's will. This put them at the mercy of the increasing value of land: they were the people liable to be squeezed out by it. At Harlesden in Middlesex we see the process of enclosing going on; there is a mingle-mangle of small fields and of small strips still in the open. The Kentish manors, Horsham and Scotney, were enclosed, as we should expect. Crendon in Buckinghamshire, in process of being enclosed, was half and half. But the farm at Wheatley in Oxfordshire was unenclosed; so was the manor of Alberbury in Shropshire.

It was in the south Midland counties that enclosures in our period created most outcry and even some disturbance. The disturbance did not amount to much, the gentry had things too well in hand. But in times of dearth and scarcity a few bold spirits arose who thought it would be a good thing to lop off the gentlemen's heads. It would be a mistake to dignify such outbursts with the name of a rising. In the lean year 1596 there were such murmurings in Oxfordshire; it was under the stress of scarcity that they came to the surface.[1] The ringleader was Bartholomew Steer, a carpenter, of Hampton Poyle who said that he would not always live like a slave and planned a meeting on Enslow hill, whence they would spoil the gentlemen's houses of arms and horses, cut off their heads, march on Lord Norris's house at Rycote and take his ordnance, and so to London to link up with the apprentices. It was a crack-brained scheme of young single men, who were not of the poorest. The ringleaders were sent off to London, their legs tied under the horses' bellies, there to be tortured for information as to any further complicity there might be. Bartholomew, like the bold fellow he must have been, refused to confess anything.

What the government found was that there had been considerable enclosure with some depopulation thereabouts. "Mr. Power has enclosed much; Mr. Frere has destroyed the whole town of Water Eaton; Sir William Spencer has enclosed common fields, and many about Banbury and other places have done the same."[2] True it is that there is nothing now at Water Eaton except that lovely fragmentary house of the Lovelaces that looks out between its pavilions across the water-meadows of the Cherwell to Wood Eaton and Islip. Sir William Spencer sleeps in the church at Yarnton beside his manor-house, just across the main road into Oxford. Hampton Poyle has forgotten that Bartholo-

[1] *Cal. S.P. Dom. 1595–7*, p. 316 foll. [2] *Ibid.* p. 343.

mew Steer the carpenter ever existed, while continuing in its name the medieval memory of Simon of Apulia.

Some years later, in 1607, there was a real rising in these counties beginning in Northamptonshire, the county chiefly affected by enclosures, spreading to Warwick and Leicester, those next most affected. There was an outbreak at Newton, which belonged to the Treshams, " where 1000 of these fellows who term themselves Levellers were busily digging, but were furnished with many half pikes, piked staves, long bills, and bows and arrows and stones ".[1] How this points forward to the later Levellers of the Commonwealth. The peasants were dispersed by the gentry, mounted and armed, who killed some forty or fifty of them. In spite of the government's commission, enclosures soon went steadily forward in the centre of this very area. It was not possible to arrest the economic advantages they offered, while the power of the gentry was enough to obstruct all the good intentions and the efforts of the government, which was, as usual, thinking of the well-being of the people. As the power and competence of the central government weakened under the Stuarts so the gentry got their way. Their bitter opposition to attempts of the Crown to control them, which culminated in the Civil War, began under Elizabeth. The geological fault in society which underlay the Revolution of the seventeenth century had its beginnings in the Elizabethan Age.

The intentions of the government may be read in the Statute Book and in the commissions of inquiry into enclosure. In 1563 the government directed the attention of Parliament to the question and a new statute was enacted for the maintenance of tillage and husbandry on the ground that the previous Acts being " imperfect and in some places too mild and gentle have not brought to the decayed state of tillage and of houses of husbandry that long looked for remedy which was then hoped for ".[2] All lands tilled successively for four years since 1529 were to be kept in tillage on a penalty of 10s. per acre. All tillage lands converted to pasture between 1516 and 1529 were to be restored. A couple more Acts were passed in the Parliament of 1597–8, which was much concerned with the land and with the problems of poor relief.[3] One Act was against the decaying of towns and houses of husbandry, providing that one-half the number of such houses decayed for more than seven

[1] E. F. Gay, " The Midland Revolt and the Inquisitions of Depopulation of 1607 ", *Trans. R.H.S.* (1904), p. 216.

[2] 5 Eliz. c. 2.

[3] 39 Eliz. c. 1 and c. 2.

years should be rebuilt. Impossible aim! The other Act, stating "whereas the strength and flourishing estate of this kingdom hath been always and is greatly upheld and advanced by the maintenance of the plough and tillage . . . being a principal mean that people are set on work", admitted that in the last four years "have grown many more depopulations by tillage into pasture than at any time for the like number of years". The government's point of view may be readily seen in the notes jotted down by Robert Cecil for a speech in the House: "The balancing of the misery of the people and the decay of the realm's strength with some trifling abridgement to gentlemen hath no proportion".[1]

It has been observed that legislation against enclosure coincided with periods of dearth, and in these last years of the reign the government was worried by the increase of unemployment and vagabondage, the strain of too long a war. It is difficult to get this whole question of the effects of agrarian changes in proper proportion, and we have already devoted too much space to them. For in fact the actual acreage of land and the number of people affected were astonishingly small: of the five Midland counties chiefly touched, the percentage of acreage returned to the commissions of inquiry of 1517 and 1607 was respectively 1·72 per cent and 2·46 per cent.[2] It is important not to exaggerate in these matters; it is even possible that the enclosure which took place, though some of its consequences were bad for simple folk, helped the open field system to continue as the standard pattern in all this central area by giving it added flexibility. For it continued to dominate Midlands agriculture till the great enclosure movement of the eighteenth and early nineteenth centuries. Even Mr. Tawney admits: "We must compare our sporadic enclosures with the two thousand six hundred Enclosure Acts which were passed between 1702 and 1810".[3] What is of far greater importance is the slow, continuing, diurnal routine of the land, the processes of agriculture, which we have to assume like the climate and the weather; and the life bound up with it.

> Round and round the fire
> Leaping through the flames, or joined in circles,
> Rustically solemn or in rustic laughter
> Lifting heavy feet in clumsy shoes

[1] Tawney and Power, *Tudor Econ. Docts.* I. 89. [2] Gay, p. 234.
[3] Tawney, *Agrarian Problem*, p. 401.

Earth feet, loam feet, lifted in country mirth
Mirth of those long since under earth
Nourishing the corn.

The routine on the land was essentially unchanged from medieval ways. What we have to keep in mind is our principle of infinite variation upon a ground-base of fundamental simplicity. There is no point in our going in detail into the rotation of crops: it has been often described, and in any case it varied from county to county, district to district, township to township, from one farm to another — as today. Tusser, for example, tells us that in Middlesex a crop of barley was followed by a crop of wheat, but that was not the usual practice:

First rye and then barley the champion says,
  or wheat before barley be champion ways,
But drink [1] before bread corn with Middlesex men,
  then lay on more compost and fallow again.[2]

Or again:

To harrow the ridges ere ever ye strike
  is one piece of husbandry Suffolk doth like.[3]

Underneath the diversities of practice there was little change. No new crops were introduced, on any scale, except the cultivation of hops. Turnips were beginning to be grown in gardens; but their field-cultivation, which has been described as being "as truly the parent of social revolution as the introduction of textile machinery", had not yet been thought of.[4]

And so the great limiting factor of medieval agriculture remained: the problem of winter keep for cattle. Until the introduction of turnips and root crops the true value of sheep could not be realised on arable. Hence the two branches of agriculture that are now combined were then dissevered. The secret of mixed husbandry had not been found, with its extraordinary increase in efficiency and productivity. Elizabethan agriculture therefore lived very near the margin; it alternated between the plenty of harvest and the leanness of Lent. "As in farming routine excessive cropping alternated with fallows, so, in the consumption of food, feasting trod on the heels of famine." [5]

[1] *I.e.* barley.
[2] T. Tusser, *Five Hundred Points of Good Husbandry* (ed. Payne and Herrtage), p. 50.
[3] *Ibid.* p. 39.
[4] Ernle, *English Farming*, p. vii.
[5] R. E. Prothero, "Agriculture and Gardening" in *Shakespeare's England*, I. 356.

For Easter at Martilmas hang up a beef,[1]

Tusser tells us; and

At Hallowtide slaughter time entereth in
and then doth the husbandman's feasting begin;
From thence until Shrovetide kill now and then some,
their offal for household the better will come.[2]

He conjures up for us a pleasant picture of Christmas cheer:

Beef, mutton and pork, shred pies of the best,
pig, veal, goose and capon, and turkey well drest;
Cheese, apples and nuts, jolly carols to hear,
as then in the country is counted good cheer.[3]

Christmas was kept up until Twelfth Night; and it was as well, for after that the lean time entered in when men were clemmed and beasts were famished. How difficult it was to provide for the latter through the winter may be seen from the great care that was taken of the loppings from the trees and the very moss from the boughs. Fitzherbert lays down: " If thou have any trees to shred, lop or crop for the fire wood, crop them in winter, that thy beasts may eat the browse, and the moss of the boughs, and also the ivies ".[4] This explains what might otherwise be surprising, the insistence of the parson in some parishes upon his right to tithe such loppings, which may be seen in various tithe disputes.

The primitive simplicity at rock-bottom on the soil is brought home to us by the fact that everything has to be used: they can afford to throw away no natural product. It is a state of affairs that we in our day can appreciate better than in previous decades with the advantages we once enjoyed in world markets. (We may be forced to appreciate still more closely the exigencies of the Elizabethan economy.) Everything had its use; everything was used. Of the trees growing about your holding, Fitzherbert tells us, " if there be ashes in it, to sell the small ashes to coopers for garches, and the great ashes to wheel-wrights, and the mean ashes to plough wrights, and the crab trees to millers to make cogs and rungs ".[5] In the winter evenings by the fire the house-

[1] Tusser, p. 57. [2] *Ibid.* p. 55. [3] *Ibid.* p. 70.

[4] Fitzherbert, *op. cit.* p. 78. It may not be generally realised that cattle will eat these things. But I am assured by my old friend, Mr. John Peters, formerly farmer of Little Pinnock in the parish of Tywardreath, Cornwall, that this is the case.

[5] *Ibid.* p. 79.

hold carved its own wooden platters, bowls and spoons; the husbandman prepared his implements for spring.

Yokes, forks and such other let bailiff spy out
  and gather the same as he walketh about.
And after all leisure let this be his hire
  to beat them and trim them at home by the fire.[1]

The extreme simplicity of equipment of the average farmer can be read in the many wills and inventories that remain. For harrow an old thorn-bush often served. From the withies they made their own baskets, from hides their leathern jacks and jugs, from the horns of cattle their mugs. They grew their own flax and hemp from which they made their sheets, smocks and towels; from coarse hemp, shoe threads, candle-wicks, halters and girths. Nettles were largely used in the manufacture of linen for sheets and clothes. Tusser tells us to gather in sloes at the end of October

And keep them in bed straw or still on the bough
  to stay both the flux of thyself and thy cow.[2]

Verjuice, or the juice of crab-apples, was used for sick cows: it must contain vitamins. For medicines people resorted to the herbs that grew in the fields or cultivated round the house: one still notes some of them growing round old habitations. One finds numerous recipes like that which Fitzherbert gives us to make broom-salve for sheep in place of tar: "Take a sheet full of broom crops, leaves, blossoms and all . . . seethe them in a pan of 20 gallons with running water, then take 2 lb of sheep suet molten and a pottle of old piss and as much brine made with salt. . . ."[3] Urine was used for many purposes: one understands the habit of preserving it that lingers in remote country places. Cinders made paths, as they still do, across the muck of the farmyard. Sir Hugh Platt, who made himself a leading authority on manures, recommended the use of blood, bones, the hair of the head, garbage, street-water, along with marl, sand and lime, the subsoil of ponds, in different proportions for different soils.

As in so many other respects, the later sixteenth century got the advantages that came out of the difficulties and disturbances of the earlier years. There was an undoubted improvement in the productivity of the land and in the standard of living of the bulk of the people. All the evidence of every kind goes to show

[1] Tusser, p. 62. [2] *Ibid.* p. 45. [3] Fitzherbert, p. 39.

this. The activity, the prosperity of the age is an expression of it. It is profitable to own land; there are capital surpluses to be employed in industrial enterprises, trade, voyages, colonisation. Harrison says: "Certainly it [the soil] is even now in these our days grown to be much more fruitful than it hath been in times past. The cause is for that our countrymen are grown to be more painful, skilful and careful through recompense of gain than heretofore they have been: insomuch that my *synchroni* or time-fellows can reap at this present great commodity in a little room; whereas of late years a great compass hath yielded but small profit, and this only through the idle and negligent occupation of such as daily manured and had the same in occupying."[1] Increased profits that came from improved methods of arable farming restored the preponderance of tillage over pasture: one notices at the end of the century that pasture loses the competitive advantage it had in the middle years. Increased size of farms and concentration of holdings, greater differentiation, were features of sixteenth-century changes. Fitzherbert urged every man "to change fields with his neighbour so that he may lay his lands together", to keep more livestock, improve the soil by composting and to rest cornland when impoverished.[2] He thought that natural fertility was exhausted by the common system of open fields, that it took too much out of the land and put little back. He was strongly in favour of enclosing on grounds of agricultural improvement. No man that had a fallow field several to himself would fold his sheep on the common field.[3] It was far better, even if more expensive, to fence your field to keep the cattle in than to employ the common herdsman.[4] It was evidently no improvement to the stock to allow them to run together and breed anyhow. Livestock would cost least and thrive best on enclosed land held in several; "and then shall his farm be twice so good to the tenant as it was before".

Tusser was of the same opinion:

> Good land that is several, crops may have three,
> in champion country it may not so be. . . .[5]

and he devoted a whole poem, "A Comparison between Champion country and several", to detailing the advantages of the

[1] Harrison, *Elizabethan England* (ed. Withington), p. 133.
[2] Cf. Ernle, p. 50.
[3] Fitzherbert, p. 20.
[4] *Ibid.* p. 70.
[5] Tusser, p. 50.

latter.[1] These are not viewed from the point of view of the lord, but from that of the small tenant such as Tusser himself was:

> The country enclosed I praise,
> the other delighteth not me,
> For nothing the wealth it doth raise
> to such as inferior be. . . .
>
> The flocks of the lords of the soil
> do yearly the winter corn wrong;
> The same in a manner they spoil
> with feeding so low and so long.
> And therefore that champion field
> doth seldom good winter corn yield.

He concludes:

> The one is commended for grain,
> yet bread made of beans they do eat:
> The other for one loaf have twain,
> of maslin, of rye or of wheat.
> The champion liveth full bare,
> when woodland full merry doth fare.

Tusser, who was a practising farmer himself, was in keeping with the whole of agricultural opinion. Norden thought moderately that the return on enclosed land was one and a half that on champion. The author of a tract on the "Complaints of divers of our countrymen" (1581) says: "Experience showeth that tenants in common be not so good husbands as when every man hath his part in severalty".[2] And, indeed, it is but common sense: a man normally will look after what is his own far better than what he has along with others. The countryman who had invested part of his profits from the London theatre in a share of the tithes upon the common fields at Stratford knew well the condition arable could get into

> with rank fumiter and furrow weeds,
> With burdocks, hemlock, nettles, cuckoo-flowers,
> Darnel, and all the idle weeds that grow
> In our sustaining corn.[3]

As the result of these changes the yield from the land was rising. The yield of corn now averaged 20 bushels per acre, barley sometimes reached 32, oats and beans 40.[4] The improvement in stock in the course of the century was notable: for 1500

[1] Tusser, pp. 140-46.
[2] Cf. Prothero, *Shakespeare's England*, I. 361.
[3] *Lear*, IV. iv. 3-6.
[4] Ernle, *op. cit.* pp. 97-8.

an average figure for sheep has been given of 28 lb., for cattle 320 lb.; for 1610 an average — true, of stock for the Prince of Wales — for sheep 46 lb., for cattle 600 lb. When we make all allowances it is still notable. The increased productivity meant an improved standard of living; and though no doubt that went in greater proportion more to the higher classes, all the evidence shows that the bulk of the peasantry, still more the yeomanry, were having more to eat.

The bread they ate throughout the land was " made of such grain as the soil yieldeth. Nevertheless the gentility commonly provide themselves sufficiently of wheat for their own tables, whilst their household and poor neighbours in some shires are forced to content themselves with rye or barley, yea, and in time of dearth, many of bread made either of beans, peas or oats, or of all together and some acorns among, of which scourge the poorest do soonest taste, since they are least able to provide themselves of better." [1] It may not be generally realised that the bread of the bulk of the people was not made of wheat, and that there was variation from district to district and region to region here too. England is not naturally a corn-growing country like France; it belongs geographically to the rye-growing areas of Northern Europe: only a highly developed capitalist agriculture later enabled our people to eat white bread.[2] In Shakespeare's time, when he saw the lover and his lass

> That o'er the green corn-field did pass

it was

> Between the acres of the rye,
> With a hey, and a ho, and a hey nonino,
> These pretty country folks would lie.

In most of these central areas of England rye was the dominant crop; there were exceptions and variations within each district and county.[3] Oxfordshire, for example, grew mainly wheat; so did North-east Suffolk and South-east Essex. Norfolk grew far more rye than wheat. Nottinghamshire was divided between the North-east where rye was the chief crop, and the South where wheat was. In Wiltshire wheat and barley drew level, but in the wetter West there was more barley. In Lancashire and the North, oats was the chief cereal, along with some rye. In Yorkshire rye was the main crop, three times the amount of

[1] Harrison, *op. cit.* p. 133.
[2] Sir William Ashley, *The Bread of Our Forefathers*, p. 137.
[3] *Ibid.* p. 38 foll.

wheat grown. It is characteristic that wheat was delivered at Sheffield for the Earl of Shrewsbury's own use. The garrison at Berwick lived on rye. Still in 1641, according to Henry Best's Farming Book, the poor folk in Yorkshire ate bread of four-fifths rye to one-fifth peas.[1] Wheat provided the chief bread corn of London, though it took considerable quantities of rye. There was the chief concentration of the professional and business classes, in addition to the Court and the households of the great. We see that the differentiation in consumption was, quite naturally, a class one.

Towards the end of the sixteenth century one observes a new impulse gathering strength in the realm of agriculture: the steady growth of farming improvement as a conscious aim.[2] With this there went a marked growth of agricultural literature, books of instruction on various aspects of the subject, so much propaganda for farming improvement. In the early part of the century only one book of importance was produced, Fitzherbert's *Book of Husbandry*, which continued to be popular and was several times reprinted under Elizabeth. The book has a delightful character of its own, shrewd, sensible, earthy; one senses the centuries of medieval experience behind it: Fitzherbert's is still the medieval world, the Catholic routine as yet unbroken, the old calendar and observances intact. He was a Derbyshireman who had bred horses all his life; towards the end of it, for he tells us he had been a householder forty years, he wrote his book and at the time of writing he had over sixty brood mares.[3] One derives a clear impression of his personality from his writing: a conservative old-fashioned type, pious, moralistic in the manner of the schools, making great play with the tags he learned at grammar-school, *Sanat, sanctificat et ditat surgere mane*. He was well-grounded in the sayings of the Fathers, but even more usefully in every kind of country lore and old sayings: " He that hath both sheep, swine and hive, sleep he, wake he, he may thrive ".[4] His principal motto, appropriate to the restricted condition of life in his time (as in ours), was *Eat within tether*. He deplored the prodigality of modern apparel and the great increase in household

[1] Sir William Ashley, *The Bread of Our Forefathers*, p. 33.

[2] Gonner, *op. cit.* p. 137.

[3] It used to be thought, cf. *D.N.B.*, that Sir Anthony Fitzherbert, the judge, was the author of this book and of that on Surveying. But I regard the arguments in favour of his elder brother John as conclusive; cf. R. H. C. Fitzherbert, "The Authorship of the *Book of Husbandry* and the *Book of Surveying* ", *E.H.R.* (1897), p. 225 foll.

[4] Fitzherbert, ed. cit. p. 68.

expenditure in his time. We leave him with his instructions to a young gentleman how to thrive, advising him to read a chapter out of his book to his servants according to the season of the year.

Undoubtedly the most popular — and deservedly — of Elizabethan writers on agriculture was Thomas Tusser. The more one reads the jog-trot verses of this old singing man the more one loves him. No wonder Kipling had such a fondness for him.[1] The Elizabethans read him to bits: thirteen editions of his book by 1600 and yet a copy is scarce to find. He was brought up a singing-boy in the chapel of the Duchy castle at Wallingford, where he was much thrashed. This did not extinguish his love of music: he left his books of music and his virginals to his son, and precious little else.[2] One sees the influence of his singing days in the Sternhold and Hopkins canter of his measures. It must be confessed that, like some other writers on agriculture, he did not make much out of farming:

> His counsel had I used
> and Ceres' art refused
> I need not thus have mused,
> nor droop as I do now. . . .
>
> By practice and ill-speeding
> these lessons had their breeding
> and not by hearsay or reading
> as some abroad have blown. . . .[3]

No doubt he had read Fitzherbert: there are one or two things he may have got from him. But the value of his book comes from the fact that at every point it springs out of his own experience as a farmer, the practice and the lore of the land. All his adult life he farmed. Ten years in the household of Lord Paget at Court, probably as a musician, then he left the service of the great, married and knew the sting of poverty. He settled in the parish of Brantham in Suffolk, where he first grew barley as a crop:

> In Brantham where rye but no barley did grow
> good barley I had, as a many did know.[4]

It was here that he wrote his *Hundred Points of Good Husbandry* and published it in 1557. Later he expanded it to *Five Hundred Points of Good Husbandry*, which he published in 1573, and it was in that

[1] It may not be generally realised that Kipling took the title for a famous story, " An Habitation Enforced ", from a poem of Tusser's.

[2] T. Tusser, *Five Hundred Points of Good Husbandry*, ed. cit. p. xxx.

[3] *Ibid.* pp. 8, 9.

[4] *Ibid.* p. 48.

form that it held the field. He was more successful as an author than a farmer; but, alas for him, Elizabethan authors made little out of their labours.

> My music since hath been the plough
> Entangled with, some care among:
> The gain not great, the pain enough
> Hath made me sing another song.[1]

Everything about Tusser is amiable and appealing: his charity and piety, his lack of success, his very apprehensiveness — for it reveals to one his touching sense of the insecurity of life; his friendliness, his chumming up with the Dean of Norwich, his affection for his college at Cambridge, Trinity Hall, his 'resting plot'. Then, too, he liked the friendly good cheer of life —

> Old customs that good be let no man despise.

He was all in favour of the old feast-days, keeping up Christmas and harvest-home; he wrote a poem "Against Fantastical Scrupleness" — of Puritans and such who despised these things:

> For oftentimes seen no more very a knave
> than he that doth counterfeit most to be grave.[2]

He loved Hallowmas and the time of feasting and (no doubt) singing:

> When Frost will not suffer to dike and to hedge
> then get thee a heat with thy beetle and wedge;
> Once Hallowmas come and a fire in the hall,
> such slivers do well for to lie by the wall.[3]

It is not likely that that observant reading man, William Shakespeare, should not have known the most popular countryman's book of the day:

> When icicles hang by the wall
> And Dick the shepherd blows his nail,
> And Tom bears logs into the hall,
> And milk comes frozen home in pail.

The remedies for the great difficulties of Tudor farming — lack of winter keep and the want of means for restoring the fertility of the soil — are beginning to be suggested in Elizabethan writers. An interesting example is Barnaby Googe, the poet and translator of Mantuan. A Lincolnshire man, kinsman and follower of Burghley, he translated the *Four Books of Husbandry* of Heresbach.[4]

[1] T. Tusser, *Five Hundred Points of Good Husbandry*, p. 220. [2] *Ibid.* p. 69.
[3] *Ibid.* p. 61. [4] First published in 1577; five editions appeared up to 1600.

Googe tells us that in translating he altered and increased the work with his own readings and observations and with the experience of his friends. Heresbach was Dutch and the value of the book is that it opened up foreign experience for the benefit of English agriculture. The farming of the Low Countries was much in advance of ours. This book was the first to mention a new reaping machine; it emphasised the importance of manure. The Low Countries had found that turnips were good food for livestock, and sown at midsummer made good winter feed. This book then was the first in English to suggest " that field cultivation of turnips which revolutionised English farming ".[1] At the same time Googe imbued it with characteristic nationalist spirit — the inferiority complex of the early Elizabethan Age coming out, as it does in so many works. He did not wish to detract from " Master Fitzherbert and Master Tusser, whose works may in my fancy without any presumption compare with any their Varro, Columella or Palladins of Rome ".[2] Of the grains and plants dealt with that were yet strangers to us he did not doubt that " they may in short time so be denizened and made acquainted with our soil ". It was not many ages since the peach, cypress, almond, the apricock and musk-rose had been brought in. The cultivation of the vine was rather a point of honour with these people touched with the Renaissance spirit. Good experience of its culture had been made of late years by Lord Cobham and Lord Williams of Thame (at Rycote) " who both had growing about their houses as good vines as are in many places of France ". If they answered not in all points, that was to be put down to the malice and disdain of the Frenchmen who kept them!

A similar spirit of enthusiasm for improvement and determination to catch up on the foreigner may be seen in Reginald Scott's *A Perfect Platform of a Hop Garden*.[3] This, like Googe's book, was dedicated to Serjeant William Lovelace, Reader of Gray's Inn. Scott sought to persuade him to lay out a hop-garden at his place at Bethersden in Kent where Lovelace was making many improvements. To the general reader, Scott commended his work " as a recompense to the labourer, as a commodity to the housekeeper, as a comfort to the poor and as a benefit to the country or commonwealth . . . there cannot lightly be employed ground to more profitable use, nor labour to more certain gains ". The book is a practical guide, with pleasant woodcuts of figures

[1] Ernle, *op. cit.* p. 99. [2] Preface to the edition of 1577.
[3] First published in 1574; I quote from this edition. Two more editions followed in 1576 and 1578.

illustrating the various operations, to planting and maintaining a hop-garden. Scott's is an original work, and he was an original man — as he showed with his remarkable book, *The Discovery of Witchcraft*. But he was acquainted with the practice of the Low Countries: he draws his description of an oast-house from that at Poperinghe. This does not prevent him from saying, rather disagreeably: "I see the Flemings envy our practice herein, who altogether tend their own profit, seeking to impound us in the ignorance of our own commodities, to cram us with the fruits and wares of their country and to do anything that might put impediment to this purpose, dazzling us with the discommendation of our soil, obscuring and falsifying the order of this mystery, sending us into Flanders as far as Poppering for that which we may find at home in our own backsides".

It is fascinating to watch how this humble literature of the soil itself springs from the Renaissance impulse and links up with similar expressions of it abroad. Thomas Hill produced several books; among others *The Profitable Art of Gardening*[1] and *A Profitable Instruction of the Perfect Ordering of Bees*. These were both compiled out of classical and Renaissance authors: one sees the influence of the civilised ancient world in the new art of horticulture, when one reads Hill's chapters on the siting of gardens, the advantage of their being near a city, the quarters and beds; the way to deal with pismires, moles, gnats, the flies "with the long hinder legs"; and the new vegetables and herbs that were being introduced. Hugh Platt, of Lincoln's Inn, was interested in all kinds of inventions and experiments, "the most curious man of his time".[2] The second book of his *Jewel-House of Art and Nature*[3] deals with the properties of salt in the soil and the uses of manure: "Divers new sorts of soil not yet brought into any public use". He refers to Bernard Palissy's *De la nature des eaux*, and it is clear that he was well acquainted with the salt-marshes of the Saintonge. He too shared the nationalistic spirit and deplored the "Dutch and drunken devices" for the draining of Erith marsh in which were "buried many thousands of English pounds, when some English wits offered to perform it and yet could not be heard". One would think that he was one of them. He urged upon those living in the London suburbs to "step into the Dutchmen's rooms" and use their wood-ash upon the land like the Flemings, "who will not lose so much as the

1 This went into at least six editions before 1600; I quote from that of 1574.
2 According to Sir Richard Weston in the next generation.
3 First published in 1594, dedicated to Essex. I quote from the Preface.

parings of their nails, much less the use of so rich a commodity ".

Leonard Mascall, of a Sussex family from just under the escarpment of the Downs by Lewes, who wrote a popular book, *The first Book of Cattle*, dealing with their diseases, was also in touch with French agricultural practice and writing.[1] In 1572 he produced *A Book of the Art and manner how to plant and graft all sorts of trees, how to set stones and sow pippins . . . By one of the abbey of St. Vincent in France, with an addition of certain Dutch practices set forth and Englished by Leonard Mascall.*[2] He seems to have made use in his writings of Charles Étienne's *L'Agriculture et maison rustique.*[3] All this is as characteristic as — indeed part of — the cross-fertilisation in literature that led to such an incomparable harvest. Little books began to be put out like *The Fruiterer's Secrets* — directions for gathering, packing, carrying and keeping fruits; how to lay up wardens and pippins: " pippins, John-apples, pear-mains and other such long lasting fruit need not to be turned until the week before Christmas ".[4] There was a great growth of interest in grafting and all the other delightful pleasures of gardening. When Justice Shallow invited Falstaff into an arbour in his Gloucestershire orchard it was " to eat a last year's pippin of my own grafting, with a dish of carraways and so forth ". Horticulture was a new interest of the age; its leading spirits, in particular Burghley, Walsingham, Bacon, were interested and concerned to advance it. But it was going ahead rapidly anyway: it had caught on. We see that Bacon's famous essay had all this for its background. " When ages grow to civility and elegancy men come to build stately sooner than to garden finely: as if gardening were the greater perfection." [5]

We can get an intimate close-up of the routine of agricultural life from a rare Elizabethan diary, that of a Cornish gentleman, William Carnsew of Bokelly within view of Rowtor on the moor, for 1576–7: just the time when these books of Scott and Mascall, Hill and Tusser were coming out.[6] We note from it that the new cultivation of hops had already reached Cornwall. I have portrayed elsewhere Carnsew's varied interests of mind and way of life as they are vividly revealed in his entries.[7] Here we will keep to his agricultural routine. In January he sowed his pulse. In February he had two ploughs at work, sent wheat to be sold at Bodmin, and dunged his beans in the mead park. In March

[1] There were six editions between 1587 and 1610.
[2] Six editions between 1572 and 1596.
[3] Woodward, *The Countryman's Jewel*, x.
[4] Edition of 1604.
[5] Bacon's *Essays* (ed. W. Aldis Wright), p. 186.
[6] S.P. 46/16.
[7] Cf. my *Tudor Cornwall*, pp. 426-33.

some of his bullocks miscarried and he finished tilling oats. His horse had the botts, a serious disease which was rarely cured, according to Fitzherbert.[1] Carnsew's medicine did no good; the horse died next day and was skinned. At the end of the month sheep were dying still. Carnsew watched his hedgers at work one day, on another he removed trees, and set hops and raisin trees, *i.e.* currants. In April he was making his gardens and poling his hops; he carried ashes, *i.e.* wood-ash, to the meadow. His lambs were still dying, and he had his sheep told. At the end of the month he sent his cattle to the moor; that is, they were 'summering' out on Bodmin Moor, beneath Rowtor. In May his servants rooted and trimmed the meadow, and he had home his furze: two days were spent on that. His sheep were shorn and sorted, and he rode to his outlying property at Danand chapel on the coast to see his corn: it "failed much".

June saw him beginning to make his sand-ridge. He washed his wool, set it to dry in the green lane and sold it for £6: 17s. "Wheat sold for 10/4 in Bodmin." He sold wood to various people and gave his great elm at Lansegy to his kinsman and neighbour, Thomas Roscarrock, whom he constantly visited and played bowls with. They were building at Roscarrock just at this time: the mullioned windows remain at the back of the house looking out on the passing wings of gulls, Pentire Head and the silver estuary of the River Camel. At Danand chapel they were beginning to burn, as they still do on the moors in the west to clear the ground for fresh growth. At Bokelly Carnsew had in his garden hay and his folks threshed. On the 18th he "began to carry dung, 30 loads a day, to my sand ridge". Next week he made a conserve of roses, and, setting his still in the garden, began to distil rose water. This month he received three heriots.[2] He walked about his grounds from time to time — one remembers the old saying which all the books enforce that the best manure is the foot of the master — but found his beans were not fully ripe.

In July his folks cut the meadow above, and next day sheared his lambs. On the 6th, "made my hay up into cocks in the mead park; rode to Danand chapel and went down under the cliff to see the quarry; was well wet for my labour". He bargained for a large number of pigs and hens. This done he went into Devon to see the Bishop, came back through Plymouth and paid several genial visits, at Port Eliot among others. Coming home he

[1] *Op. cit.* p. 63.

[2] Payment to the lord of his tenant's best beast on the tenant's death. The plague was at its height about this time in Cornwall.

paid more visits, at Lanherne where he played bowls and supped with the Arundells and Lord Stourton, but lay at Trerice. The last day of the month he " walked to Lansegy, saw my meadows cut, my oats almost ripe, my wheat thin, thin ". He consoled himself that evening by reading Luther's Commentary on *Galatians*.

August 1st saw his oats ripe and he was hay-making at Lansegy. A few days later : " Great harm done to the corn by winds. . . . Began to malt my oats which was razed more than was sowed in the ground." He rode to Danand chapel " where Richard Hambly was reaping, reckoned with Thomas Michell and we parted ; must build a house at my hall-door ". On St. Lawrence's day he rode to the fair at Bodmin — up to our fathers' time it was the leading horse-fair in Cornwall. There " George Lower hurt William Courtenay " — a characteristic event. Inch cut his corn at Danand chapel. At home " two great swine died . . . of eating poisoned rats I think ". " My harvest folks wrought little or nothing for wet weather at home or at Danand chapel, yet some of them took their wages." Next day was dry : " Cut all my wheat at home in fair weather with a 3^s [three score ?] hooks ". Meanwhile a great to-do had blown up because of Jewel of Davidstow's sheep having been taken feeding on the moor : 145 of them had been taken with 23 divers marks. This led to a dispute about the rights of pasture on the moor. Jewel sued out a precept on account of his sheep being taken — which led to much business and Carnsew's brother having to pursue the suit in London. In the last week of the month he cut and carried his wheat at Danand chapel, " which is but sorry corn ", and at home. One wain was sent to help in Mr. Budockshide's corn. Carnsew made his oats up, cut all his beans and peas, then rode to Bodmin, where the plague was coming to an end now, to buy necessaries.

The corn being inned Carnsew was free to go off for a ten-day round of visiting in Devonshire, to Adrian Gilbert, Lord Edward Seymour, George Cary of Cockington, the Bishop — who spent all his substance in farming at Newton Ferrers and ultimately bankrupted himself — and back to Port Eliot to a family party. The news there was of " 400 marks offered and fine for 32 acres of land in Lanrake " — a sign of the rise in land-values. Carnsew came home to find his men at the sand-ridge. He rode out across the moor — one can imagine the September colourings, all blue and purple, brown and gold — to Brown Willy, where he found a sick bullock and missed a stoned (*i.e.* gelded) colt. He gathered his hops and went off to visit Lord

Mountjoy in Devon, where he read Sir Humphrey Gilbert's discourse on the North-West Passage to Cathay. Mountjoy lent him a book on magic and told him Court news of Dr. Julio and how he fled into France.

At the beginning of October Carnsew returned from these delights to plough at Danand chapel. He sent quinces to Lanherne, and rode down to Carnsew in the west to hold his court-leet there; a tenant was presented " for waste, felling five trees and rooting them up ". He noted — what seems incredible — that " Thomas Roscarrock made above £1000 fines of £10 rents in Delye manor ". At the end of the month he finished tilling wheat and made up the planching (ceiling) in his stable. In November he rode about and visited a good deal. At Danand chapel he saw " 15 kine, 5 calves, 8 steers, a mare and 6 colts, but not all of an age ". On a stormy day he set the berries in the higher hedge and the garden. The masons were at work on a new stile at the high gate. There were many wrecks on the coast from the storms at the end of November. On December 1st some of his house was blown away. December 6th: " Up in the morning, sent to the fair, reckoned with my servants, paid them wages and so to bed again, when I left but 2s. 6d. in my purse ". Next day he had a shepherd to look over his sheep. He spent much of this month at home reading. On the last day of the year he planted pear-trees. In January his men began to plough again in Fentonridge and to delve in Fenton-mead. Carnsew was out and about overlooking them. The routine of the year had begun once more.

This little diary of an Elizabethan gentleman, unknown to the great world or to posterity, sums up with the lively detail and clarity of a miniature all the themes of this chapter, portrays — as hardly anything else — the routine of country life dictated by the seasons and the crops. I have indicated little of Carnsew's mind, his reading and his dreams, his gaming and gossiping, his family concerns.

As for the impact of these things, the land and its life, " the country facts, the country acts " — as Tusser called them — upon the imagination and the life of the mind, it is written across the face of the literature of the time. When an Elizabethan poet, in his last hours, thinks of the ill-success of his life, he says:

> My crop of corn is but a field of tares.

The greatest of English poets remained always, for all that he prospered in London, essentially a countryman.

CHAPTER IV

THE NEW WEALTH: ECONOMIC ADVANCE

DURING the sixteenth century the medieval world was unfixed from its foundations and lost the security of its ancient limitations. It underwent a revolution more far-reaching, a series of experiences more disturbing, than those of which we are so conscious in our time. In this particular sense, among others: it initiated that expansion of Europe which made the modern world as we know it. The discovery of a new and unsuspected continent in America was only one part, though the most spectacular, in the process of expansion. In that process the lead was taken — mainly by reason of geographical position, partly accidentally — by Portugal and Spain. For them, especially for Castile, it was a golden age of miraculous achievement: "within three generations Spaniards discovered, subdued and colonised the most extensive territorial empire the world has ever seen".[1]

> Este mar que de Atlante se apellida,
> en immensas llanuras extendido,
> que a la tierra amenaza embravecido,
> y ella tiembla a sus olas impelida . . .[2]

Part of this profound process, with its pulls hidden and overt, that was changing the world as the medievals knew it, was the shift of gravity from the Mediterranean to the Atlantic, westward to Spain, and ultimately north-west to the English Channel. All this is more important than the Reformation, profound as the effect of that was: indeed it may profitably be viewed as part of the larger process, the pull of the northern peoples away from the apron-strings of their ancient mother, Rome. It is the shift of gravity north-west that interests us. Its full development takes us long beyond our present period and occupies the

[1] C. H. Haring, *The Spanish Empire in America*, p. 4.
[2] Francisco de Rioja, in *Poetas de los siglos XVI y XVII*, p. 337.

centuries that follow, until with the eighteenth and nineteenth the island power emerges as the leading power in the modern world. That nineteenth-century perspective has made it difficult for us to appreciate the full greatness of the Spanish achievement. (Our Elizabethan ancestors made no such mistake, for they were up against it.) For, indeed, the Spanish achievement in the outer world has its lasting character, and there remains an interesting dichotomy between it and the English: the two great systems of colonisation and empire overseas.

We have to see the Elizabethan effort against this background. It was a couple of generations later that the impulse which had excited Castile reached the English and touched them to fire and fever:

> Avid of life, with dream and fever of mind possessed.

The Elizabethans awoke to the new world to find the Spaniards and Portuguese already entrenched in it. All the more striking that they caught up with them, in a rush of energy and enterprise. It is rewarding to investigate how the shift of power came to rest with England, when Spain had had such a lead; how the lasting advantages of the new economic trends, in trade and treasure, came to this country, leaving Spain, their initiator, impoverished and discouraged. The contrast between the economies of the two countries, the policies followed in one and the other and their subsequent fortunes, is exceedingly instructive. By the end of the Elizabethan Age people were already reflecting on it.

The most striking of these new economic forces, by its very newness, was the rise in prices throughout Western Europe consequent upon the immense import of treasure from the American mines into Spain from the middle of the century. The amounts went on increasing with each decade until 1600, when they reached their apogee — Spanish power was already showing symptoms of over-strain.[1] The stream of silver pouring into Europe had consequences unsettling, stimulating, uncontrollable: upsetting old ties and established relationships of value, stimulating new enterprise, reinforcing pressures creative of a new order. The rise in prices differed from one country to another; there was a different time-sequence. In Andalusia prices increased fivefold during the century; in France two and a half times; in England the threefold rise did not culminate until 1650. That

[1] Earl J. Hamilton, *American Treasure and the Price Revolution in Spain, 1501–1650*, pp. 34-6: Haring, *op. cit.* p. 268.

gives us an under-swell of a slower, more gradual duration, a long wave of profit inflation and capital accumulation which bore up the expansive achievements of the age in every sphere. "Never in the annals of the modern world has there existed so prolonged and so rich an opportunity for the business man, the speculator and the profiteer."[1] So thought Lord Keynes: one may wonder whether the nineteenth century was not as good a time for them. Some people have thought that the earlier period saw the birth of modern capitalism. Lord Keynes lent the authority of his name to this fancy; but capitalism goes much further back into the Middle Ages. Still the rise in prices greatly strengthened the forces transforming the old economic order.

It is a mistake to over-estimate the purely monetary factor — or any one other for that matter. Historic movements of this kind are so complex that one despairs of capturing the subtleties of life and rendering them on paper. We can only do our best to suggest them. Equally important, even on the economic plane, was the aggressive nationalism of the time — of which no people had a larger share than the English — which drove men to break into preserves of trade hitherto monopolised by others, to open up new routes and markets in the outer world. There was the drive — consistently encouraged by government and carried out by a new class of entrepreneurs, nowhere more effectively than in this country — to open up and exploit its own natural resources. There were the striking improvements in industrial and financial technique; the increased mobility of labour, particularly in the iron, coal and glass industries, special fields for the new capitalist; the growth of investment in new enterprises, the opening up of markets in America, Asia, Africa. In all these things England, at length, caught up and went ahead. This may be concretely brought home in the contrast between this country and Spain, which may be taken as an illustration of the argument. We went in for the real things of substance: building up the nation's resources, not consuming them profitlessly; accumulating capital; a healthy balance of trade. The facts of economic life are more important than their monetary symbols.

One effect of the rise in prices was that wages lagged behind. We must not exaggerate the effect of this either, for those who lived mainly by wages, though a growing element with the growth of capitalism, were a minority of the nation. In so far as they were producers, as the bulk of them were, they shared to some extent

[1] Lord Keynes, *Treatise on Money*, II. 159.

in the increasing prosperity. But not proportionately: the greater proportion of the surpluses made went into the pockets of the richer classes. The Elizabethan Age was a period of increasing class disparity, of subtler class differentiation, of more marked contrasts and greater ostentation. Some people with a contemporary prejudice may regard this as a defect. We may reflect that upon this rested the many achievements of the age — the voyages, the colonial experiments, the building, the arts, the conspicuous consumption of the time which has left us such permanent memorials as against the evanescent ephemera of our own; the interesting extravagance upon luxuries that have lasted, jewels, stuffs, fabrics, music; the demand for books, literature, the drama: those unforgettable responses to the demand for a richer, more varied life of the mind. It is open to us to prefer the consumption of what the society produces on one dead level, a shared and equalised mediocrity, offering no excitements, no inducements, no interest even — dreary tenements in place of Elizabethan palaces, the ability of all to go to the cinema instead of an elect society that made the music and drama of that age. Though this may have its easy satisfactions for the mass of a population of fifty millions it offers no hope of the glittering achievements of their population of five.

The increased rate of accumulation of capital came not so much from this source as from the growth of wealth out of returns from land and commerce. Improved methods of farming, we saw, produced larger yields. The Dissolution gave an incalculable incentive to more efficient cultivation all over the country: men will do for and with their own property what they will not do for others. Then, too, there was a notable influx of investment from abroad. There was the capital that useful religious refugees from Flanders and France brought with them, not only fixed capital and money, but their industrial skill. Italians, like Spinola and Palavicino, invested in English enterprises; the Augsburg mining firm of Haug put money into starting the copper mines and mineral works of Cumberland — not all of which they saw back. There was the part played by the bullion brought into the country in the course of the duel with Spain by the capture of rich prizes and exploits of which the most resounding example was Drake's raid upon the treasure-route off the coast of Peru. Much of that money went to support Elizabeth's policy in the Netherlands. A small portion of it was enough to float the Levant Company.[1] Members of the Levant Company

[1] Cf. J. R. Scott, *Joint-Stock Companies*, I. 70.

in turn fostered the East India Company, from which grew an Empire. It is an interesting concatenation. Even so, it was not so much the absolute value of the bullion brought in that mattered as the indirect effect upon profit and enterprise, the increment of the country's wealth in buildings, equipment, improvements.[1] Individuals gained and lost; but they had every incentive to be up and doing; they were not left without the incentive to achieve anything. Drake made a fortune; the family he established lasted right up to our own less fortunate time. Ralegh spent £40,000 on his voyages of discovery and gained nothing from them. Humphrey Gilbert ruined himself, spent his own patrimony and his wife's in pursuit of his mirage. The Earl of Cumberland, a man of vast estates, pledged himself heavily over his privateering enterprises: sometimes he caught a prize, more often he saw no return on his outlay. No doubt he enjoyed himself. The adoption of the joint-stock technique enabled the unavoidable losses in establishing new enterprises to be borne.

This method of collecting and regulating capital — more important in itself than the new mechanical inventions — enabled the necessary outlay to be made for industrial development at home and opening up trades abroad. Economic life under the early Tudors proceeded on a simple medieval basis; shortage of capital was its chronic limiting factor. Elizabeth's reign saw an expansion of credit and an extension of credit facilities along with the growth of capital. The popular outcry against usurers was constant — and sometimes justified. *The Merchant of Venice* was written, as usual with that author, on a theme that much appealed to its audience. The disputes about the rate of interest played the part in that age which disputes about wages play in ours: interest or 'usury' was a more acute matter for a community with a need for more capital for its growing concerns and in which wages were a secondary consideration. Lenders came in for much mud-slinging, though they performed an invaluable function, in the absence of banks, in enabling trade to extend its basis. Proposals were made for establishing a bank; but Elizabethan England got no further forward than to throw up a number of interesting financiers, speculators and entrepreneurs: such men as Sir Thomas Gresham, Sir Horatio Palavicino, Thomas Sutton, Customer Smythe and his son Sir Thomas. Among these the Countess of Shrewsbury, Bess of Hardwick, makes an unexpected figure with her four great coffers of money and evidences in her

[1] Keynes, *op. cit.* II. 157.

bedchamber at Hardwick.[1] The rustic mind of the parson of Radwinter, inured to hard and simple pleasures, noted about the middle of the reign "the great store and plenty of treasure which is walking in these parts of the world, far more in these our days than ever our forefathers have seen in times past".[2] We may observe the more forceful fixation of Drake's mind on treasure: he told his faltering men at Nombre de Dios in 1572 that he had "brought them to the mouth of the Treasure house of the World".

The industrial development of the country was equally remarkable — and has only recently come to be appreciated. Professor Nef, who has made it his subject, thinks that it amounted to a sort of 'Industrial Revolution'.[3] He thinks that England achieved the position of leadership in industrial technology and heavy industry she held till the late nineteenth century largely during the century between the Dissolution and the Civil War; that Elizabeth's reign saw a shift in the centre of progress in both science and technology from the Continent here, where more fresh industries were started and more new kinds of machinery and furnaces were developed than in any other country. The Renaissance impulse signalised itself in a host of new inventions: the printing press, the blast furnace, furnaces for separating silver from copper ore, for using coal in glass-making, steel and brick-making, for drying malt in brewing; boring rods for exploring underground strata, horse and water driven engines for draining mines — an immense field of development here as new mines were opened up and old workings deepened; the stocking knitting frame, the Dutch loom for knitting small wares, besides more specialised scientific devices and inventions.

Here there was a time-lag: naturally the impulse took longer to reach the island. But when it eventually arrived it found a peculiarly propitious soil. The discoveries, the experiences of a century were for the English crowded into those last decades of Elizabeth's reign. What must it have been like to have been alive then, sentient and intelligent? — alas, the mirage the historian pursues! One is tempted to say that England was the New Country were it not liable to be misinterpreted, for indeed she was even then an old one with a long and hardy history

[1] Hardwick MSS. at Chatsworth.

[2] Harrison, q. in E. Lipson, *Econ. History of England* (3rd ed.), II. xvi.

J. U. Nef, "War and Economic Progress, 1540–1640", *Econ. Hist. Rev.*, 1942.

behind her. But she was a new field for investment, of the most rapid development and of the greatest promise for the future in Europe. She had some great advantages favouring her, which all the writers of the time cried up and made the nation conscious of. The island had an abundance of natural products, corn, wood, coal, timber, iron. Here was the basis of industry. In the woollen industry it had a long-standing tradition of manufacturing skill and commercial experience. The traditional skill of the many hundreds of smiths and nailers, scythe-makers and cutlers of the Black Country and Sheffield formed the basis for the later expansion of industry in those areas. The makings were already there. What was necessary was that the wind of the spirit of creative enterprise should blow upon them.

The circumstances of English society were propitious: a social flexibility that was always greater here than anywhere else, save possibly the Netherlands — our nearest likeness. Then, too, there was the natural energy, inventiveness, enterprise of the people, that was elicited, encouraged and rewarded by the arrangements of society and the policies of government, not discouraged, thwarted and stifled by over-regulation. One of the clues to the early industrial success of this country is that there was far less regulation here than abroad; the rivers and internal communications were free of the crippling tolls that cramped navigation on the Rhine and the Loire. Still freer was the sea — and much of English traffic was coastwise. The country presented in short a large free-trade area, where abroad innumerable tolls interfered with domestic trade. This already suggests — a factor that we must allow for — the good sense of the English, who kept their internal jars and broils at a minimum. The American Professor says, perhaps too kindly, of us: "In a variety of ways the industrial losses of the warring countries were peaceful England's gains".[1] Too kindly, for it was our insularity, then as now, that gave us our comparative immunity from invasion. We took advantage of it; we made the most of it — as long as Elizabeth lived, and until Stuart incompetence brought down the Civil War upon us. By then the new forces were so strong that it did not do much harm. But when one thinks of what the Netherlands — the most highly industrialised area in Europe — lost by the religious wars, the ruin of Antwerp, the commercial and financial capital of Northern Europe, the destruction of her trade and the gain to London — one realises something of what we owed to insularity and good sense. Whole areas of

[1] *Ibid.* p. 25.

the Continent were overrun, and so much of its energy taken up, by wars, while there were no battles on English soil till the Civil War. One remembers how proud of it the Queen was, and how she wept to the French Ambassador at the record being even slightly soiled by the flurry of the Northern Earls in 1569. (No doubt her tears were political or even financial, for she counted the cost; on the other hand, they may equally well have been genuine.) We must lastly take into account the fortunate geographical situation of the country in relation to the outer world and for the strategy of commerce: a country, naturally rich and skilled, athwart the main ocean-routes at the entry to Northern Europe.

German scholars, particularly the gross Sombart, have attached the greatest importance in the development of the new industrial capitalism to the factor of war. So like a German! In fact we do not find this to be so in the Elizabethan experience. Peace was more propitious for the development of large-scale industry. The striking increase in coal output taking place was due to the shortage of timber and charcoal, and the profitability of mining, not to war. In the early years of the reign London got its refined sugar from Antwerp. After it was sacked, the sugar refining was moved to London. Several large refineries were built, haberdashers, grocers, merchant tailors, ironmongers combined with Dutch refiners to invest in the new industry here. Richard Carmarden, "perhaps the best informed and most reliable of Queen Elizabeth's customs officials", wrote with some satisfaction: "Now the English can supply Germany and the Low Countries better cheap than they can supply us".[1] The right spirit: a clear economic gain. Such were the rewards of political security and good sense. The textile industry of the Spanish Netherlands was permanently hit by war. By the end of the century the output of copper and metals in Central Europe, the production of iron in Burgundy, had declined. Only in England (and perhaps Sweden) was the production of iron, copper, brass increasing rapidly. The foundries of Sussex and Kent were able to supply guns to the Continent. The manufacture of woollens and cottons in Lancashire spread on such a scale that the changes brought about were scarcely less important than those of the Industrial Revolution of the late eighteenth century. The coal trade from Newcastle to London saw an astonishing growth: coal shipments from the North multiplied tenfold between 1545 and 1625. In the same period the tonnage of the

[1] U. Nef, "War and Economic Progress, 1540–1640", *Econ. Hist. Rev.*, 1942.

Navy doubled, while the number of the country's merchantmen, perhaps the tonnage also, increased fivefold. Peace, at any rate internal peace, stimulated the growth of the population, which was more marked in England than anywhere. And nowhere more than in London, which grew from some 60,000 at the time of the Reformation to over 300,000 before the Civil War. By then it had succeeded to something of Antwerp's position as the commercial capital of Northern Europe.

From about the middle of the century, after the English had worked out their characteristic compromise in settlement of the Reformation conflict, the new industries began to be introduced from abroad or set on foot.[1] The discovery of calamine, the ore of zinc, with the first effective mining of copper made brass-making possible and battery works were set up in London and elsewhere. By the end of the reign the soap-building industry of the capital, which was carried on in factories, supplied most of the kingdom. The new salt-making industry was mainly concentrated on the Tyne and the Wear, the older brine-pans of Cheshire and Staffordshire were extended. The first paper-mill was set up at Dartford by a German immigrant: its operation was characteristically described in a long poem by Thomas Churchyard. Steel works were set on foot, with German workmen, in Sussex; the glass manufacture was started there by Huguenot immigrants, later it was carried to the Black Country. The wire works of Tintern were employing a hundred 'hands' by 1581. There was a constant search to solve the problem of smelting ores with coal: its solution takes us long beyond our period, but the preliminary steps were taken in it. Before 1612 coal had been successfully substituted for charcoal in making glass: an English invention which was introduced on the Continent. Largest and most important of all industries, the woollen manufacture was expanding rapidly: the increase of the population gave it greater markets, above all in London, and a stronger basis still for its exports.

Professor Nef tells us that not till the later eighteenth century was the rate of expansion as fast again as it had been during Shakespeare's lifetime. "The rise of industrialism in Great Britain can be more properly regarded as a long process stretching back to the middle of the sixteenth century . . . than as a sudden phenomenon associated with the 18th and early 19th centuries."[2] The expansion was more continuous than in any

[1] Cf. J. U. Nef, "The Progress of Technology and the Growth of Large-Scale Industry in Great Britain, 1540–1640", *Econ. Hist. Rev.*, 1934. [2] *Ibid.* p. 22.

other country: that gave it its naturalness and strength. We must, however, remember its small scale, its localisation: the land was vastly more important than any other interest, indeed than all the others together. We can hardly expect to get the right perspective from Camden, who was old-fashioned and antiquarian-minded, fired even more by Roman Britain than Elizabethan England. If we judged by him, industry occupied a small space on the map. But even though the larger space it was beginning to occupy was small enough in relation to the roomy countryside of those days, it was the cloud no larger than a man's hand that portended a tremendous future. Here were the dynamic forces that were to transform the whole.

During the middle decades the English export trade and, in consequence, government finance enjoyed not only the closest liaison with, but a state of dependence on, the Antwerp market. In the sixteenth century Antwerp developed into a trading centre such as the world had never seen.[1] Never was there a market that so concentrated the trade of all the important commercial nations. Its trade was almost wholly in the hands of foreigners; colonies of foreign merchants were permanently settled there. The basis of its unparalleled prosperity was that it possessed the international cloth market and the monopoly of the East Indian spice trade, since the King of Portugal sold the cargoes of his argosies to the syndicates there.[2] On this basis it developed an international money market, first of the modern world. The English cloth trade, which formed the bulk of our exports, was concentrated upon Antwerp. It was in the hands of the Merchant Adventurers, the great government-backed body of exporters, who had succeeded to the dominating position of the Merchant Staplers during the last two centuries: a natural development with the change-over from exporting raw wool and unfinished cloth to woollen manufactures. Tudor government did everything in its power to encourage this change-over, and rightly: from a more primitive to a more advanced economy, from other people making money out of us to our making money out of them. It was a policy of retaining wealth within the country and developing it, of strengthening our bargaining position to get a larger share of the international wealth that was going. A policy that aimed

[1] R. Ehrenberg, *Capital and Finance in the Age of the Renaissance*, p. 234 foll.

[2] Cf. G. Unwin: "It was not only the London but the Manchester of the sixteenth century" (*Studies in Economic History*, p. 162).

not only at wealth but even more at employment — and much criticised by Victorian free traders under the name of Mercantilism — it was right for the circumstances of the time, while the circumstances of ours are forcing us to appreciate its point.

The disarray into which we were plunged at the Reformation, the weak benevolence of Protector Somerset's government, the dismal and unsuccessful wars we were entangled in during these middle decades, but most of all the currency depreciation of Henry VIII and Edward VI, brought the financial affairs of the country into confusion and weakened our position in international trade. Where in 1520, 20 English shillings were worth 32 Flemish shillings, in 1551 they were worth only 16: a striking index of the weakening of our economic position *vis-à-vis* the outer world. This made it very difficult to maintain the finances of government, which threatened to become bankrupt. The English government during the later years of Henry, both reigns of Edward and Mary and for the first decade of Elizabeth's, was dependent on the Antwerp money market for loans to tide over the gaps between its revenue and its expenditure — which in effect meant at any crisis or emergency. And this very state of affairs meant that the loans were raised at exorbitant rates of interest — a constant drain on the wealth of the country. The work of putting this to rights, of recovering our position in the international market, re-establishing our credit, was an indispensable prerequisite of successful government: it was the first work Elizabeth's government had to set its hand to after liquidating the war and the Catholic restoration, both alike unsuccessful, which were Mary's legacies. In this work the leading part was taken — supported by the Queen and Cecil at every point — by the greatest English financier of the century, the government's constant adviser and Royal agent in Antwerp, Sir Thomas Gresham.[1] He was a remarkable man: a sort of combination of a Pierpont Morgan and Keynes in his day.

He had not had to do everything for himself: his achievements rested upon the substantial position acquired by his family in trade, as mercers, and in finance. They were a Norfolk family, coming originally from Gresham, got a start in service with the Pastons and moved to Holt, where they lived in the manor-house, which Gresham's uncle charitably turned into a school. The family was engaged in the Low Countries trade and Gresham's father, Sir Richard, was frequently employed as financial agent by

[1] The following account is based on J. W. Burgon, *Life and Times of Sir Thomas Gresham.*

Henry VIII. He acquired five successive grants of Church lands, mainly in East Anglia, for which no doubt he paid cash. He was the first to project a Bourse or Exchange, after the Antwerp fashion, in which the merchants could meet instead of gathering twice a day, rain or fine, in Lombard Street: a project which his son carried out thirty years later. Young Thomas was bound as an apprentice the better to gain experience. He grew into a tall good-looking man with an intellectual expression; later on in Antwerp he numbered Ortelius and Verstegan among his friends, he was the patron of Thomas Churchyard, poet and journalist, and was three times painted by Anthony More.

He was a man of great energy and of an intense concentration on business, particularly the exchanges: he had the advantage of being one of the few Englishmen who fully understood the subject, besides having the practical experience to manipulate them. He conducted a vast correspondence, besides his increasing journeying — forty times in two years between the Court and Flanders on government business at the worst period of Edward's reign. In his letters one can read his character and sometimes overhear the very accents of the man: one fancies one hears his voice in his old-fashioned East Anglian 'a' for 'he': "I cannot see which way King Philip can annoy her Highness this year [1560]; considering a hath neither money, ships, nor men; nor munition, nor armour".[1] And there is his favourite phrase constantly on the tip of his pen — "which I will not molest you withal" — a convenient way of covering up a multitude of considerations. For, of course, he was immensely diplomatic and *rusé*. In character he was a moderate, reliable man, temperate in his habits. He did not like drink: he complains that the Captain and searchers of Gravelines will banquet him, "and all their cheer is in drink, which I can very ill away withal; but it must needs be done, for the better compassing of my business hereafter".[2] So he sends his treasure on beforehand. He allowed himself a little more latitude in more enjoyable respects: he left a natural daughter who, very well-dowered, married Sir Nathaniel Bacon and now sleeps with him in the church of Culford in Suffolk. Otherwise, he was a man very much after Cecil's own heart: living so much abroad he could permit himself a little more freedom.

Gresham became financial agent to the Crown in Antwerp in 1551, at a desperate moment for Edward VI's government. The Crown owed large sums there and its credit was so low that

[1] Burgon, I. 295. [2] *Ibid.* p. 143.

they were renewed on exceedingly unfavourable terms: sometimes at 14 per cent and more. The effect of this on the rate of exchange was deplorable. But Gresham was full of resource and engaged himself to bring the King out of debt in two years. Which he performed. His first exploit was to persuade the government to hold up the cloth fleet of the Merchant Adventurers until they agreed to lend the government a large sum of money from Antwerp, to be repaid in London at a fixed rate of exchange. Meanwhile Gresham played the exchange for all he was worth, raising smaller sums of money every day in his own name so as not to lower further the credit of the English government. He was a past master at this game and knew all its tricks. One clue to his success was his intelligence service, " having the brokers of exchange, as I have, at my commandment, for there is never a bourse but I have a note what money is taken up by exchange, as well by the stranger as Englishman ".[1] Another clue was his insistence that the King's debts should be honoured: sometimes — " I was fain to give forth my own word that this money should be paid at the just day, or else the King's Majesty should never have had it ".[2] The word of this Englishman was enough in Antwerp. By the end of Edward's reign the pound had recovered from 16 Flemish shillings to 22. Though Unwin insists that this was due to a normal recovery of mint-par, and not to Gresham's operations, even he admits that Gresham had made the exchange favourable to England instead of unfavourable.[3]

With the accession of Mary, who thought religion more important than money, Gresham was displaced. She appointed another agent whose religion, let us hope, was impeccable, for his financial operations were not. Her need for loans was clumsily and openly handled; the rate of interest went up from 10 per cent to 13 and 14 per cent; the exchange began to move against us. It needed Gresham to play poker with a Jew like Lazarus Tucker. Gresham had to be reappointed — he was indeed indispensable, and Mary had to reward him with Church lands. It is revealing of her incompetence as a ruler that she had to pay so much more for men's services, where Elizabeth attached them with fair words and promises, occasional gifts and a constant appeal to their sense of service to the State. At Gresham's first interview with Elizabeth she promised him " she would not only keep one ear shut to hear me, but also if I did her none other service than I had done to King Edward her late brother, and Queen Mary her late sister, she would give me as much land as ever both they

[1] *Ibid.* p. 99. [2] *Ibid.* p. 90. [3] Unwin, *op. cit.* p. 156.

did: which two promises, I will assure your honour, made me a young man again and caused me to enter upon this great charge again with heart and courage ".[1] Needless to say, she did not give him more land: she no doubt considered him sufficiently rewarded — which he was. But she listened very intently to his advice, which he proffered immediately upon her accession: " An it please your Majesty to restore this your realm into such estate as heretofore it hath been: First, your Highness hath none other ways but, when time and opportunity serveth, to bring your base money into fine, of XI ounces fine. And so gold after the rate. Secondly, not to restore the Steelyard to their usurped privilege. Thirdly, to grant as few licences as you can. Fourthly, to come in as small debt as you can beyond seas. Fifthly, to keep your credit; and specially with your own merchants; for it is they must stand by you, at all events in your necessity." [2] In the course of the reign we can watch the following out of this programme: one more respect in which Elizabeth's reign was continuous with Edward's, and Mary's but an unfortunate interlude.

The first task of Elizabeth's government was to arm the country for its defence: Mary's dependence on Philip had landed her unprepared in his war. Gresham was busily employed procuring arms and munitions, thousands of corselets and cargoes of gunpowder, in the Low Countries and Germany and shipping them over. His intelligence service was of the greatest importance: " There is not one word spoken by the customers, and what they intend to do but I have perfect intelligence ".[3] He was already a power of his own in Antwerp, able to buy arms on his own credit when funds were slow in arriving. But his greatest boast was that " it will not be a little spoken of through all the world that her Majesty, in her wars, doth make payment of her debts, when neither King Philip, the French King nor the King of Portugal in peace time payeth nothing, who oweth no small sums of money ".[4] The demands of State finance were beginning to ruin the Antwerp money market; its best chance lay in developing a system of primarily mercantile credit. And in time London did just this.

The second task of the government was the restoration of the currency, or at any rate its stabilisation. This had been purposed from Edward's days, and if he had lived he would have carried it out: Cecil and Gresham, with the backing of Lord Treasurer Winchester, provided the continuity.[5] Plans were well laid for

[1] Burgon, I. 217. [2] *Ibid.* p. 234. [3] *Ibid.* p. 364.
[4] *Ibid.* pp. 344-5. [5] Cf. A. E. Feavearyear, *The Pound Sterling*, p. 70 foll.

a bold, if conservative, measure of recoinage: various people tendered their advice, including the Queen who — versatile intellectual — put in a memorandum of her own. Gresham's advice was taken. "The enterprise is of great importance and the sooner it is put in use, the more honour and profit it will be to the Queen's Majesty and the Realm: for doubtless this will raise the exchange to 26s. 8d. at the least."[1] A far cry from the days when he had to bolster up the pound at 16s.! Gresham's mind was set upon the exchange; in his advice to the Queen he said: "As the exchange is the thing that eats out all princes to the whole destruction of their common weal, if it be not substantially looked into, so likewise the exchange is the chiefest and richest thing only above all others, to restore your Majesty and your Realm to fine gold and silver, and is the means that makes all foreign commodities and your own commodities with all kinds of victuals good cheap, and likewise keeps your fine gold and silver within your Realm".[2] The governing minds in Elizabeth's England had the root of the matter in them. The elaborate operation of the recoinage was swiftly and successfully carried through — the government even made a small profit on it. There was a stable monetary foundation for the gathering prosperity of the country.

It was well that things were in hand, for simultaneously there came the premonitory symptoms of the religious storm that was to lay waste the industrial and financial heart of Northern Europe. "At this instant I can write you of nothing certain; but every man speaks according to his religion."[3] Men were in for one of those gusts of convulsive idiocy when they kill one another for what they cannot know about, destructive of all peace and concord, of culture and common sense. The troubles of the Low Countries were beginning that ended their commercial ascendancy. It was decades before common sense regained its hold; when the clouds lifted, it was found that their old ascendancy had passed to England and Holland. Gresham was well prepared for this; in these latter years he was transferring his interests to this country, leaving his agent Richard Clough to look after his affairs in Antwerp. On one of his last visits there he wrote that the "country . . . is ready one to cut another's throat for matters of religion".[4] Next year, 1567, there were 20,000 Protestants in arms in Antwerp. The city was being deserted by the well-to-do, who were flying the country. The nomination of

[1] Burgon, p. 356. I have corrected Burgon's text here.
[2] *Ibid.* p. 485. [3] *Ibid.* II. 8. [4] *Ibid.* p. 161.

Alva increased the flight, not without reason: he ordered some 6000 executions. A good time was being had by both sides. Clough wrote home wishing that the arts and artisans might be transported to England. In time they were, in considerable numbers, and London's prosperity was directly increased by the ruin of Antwerp. By this time we were involved in a strenuous duel with Alva in the Netherlands: it was at bottom a political struggle on behalf of their independence and our own security, conducted by commercial and economic measures: the first round in the struggle with Spain. In this the most resounding *coup* was the English arrest of Philip's treasure — on loan from Genoese bankers — on its way up Channel to pay Alva's forces. The Queen had another use for it. Meanwhile Alva's troops mutinied, the forces of independence gained a breathing-space in which to establish themselves. An embargo was placed on all English goods there. To which the English replied with an embargo on goods of all Spanish subjects here. Gresham proposed that the Spanish treasure be used to pay off all the Crown's debts. There was the closest understanding between Cecil and Gresham in all this exciting passage. In the end Cecil won; the Spanish and Flemish goods arrested here were of greater value than the English goods arrested abroad: he had out-manœuvred Alva and provided Philip with a resistance movement to occupy him for the rest of his days.

By now English resources were sufficient of themselves to finance the government's needs, and Gresham advised: " I would wish that the Queen's Majesty in this time should not use any strangers, but her own subjects; whereby he [Alva] and all other princes may see what a Prince of power she is ".[1] A loan was accordingly raised from the principal merchants in the City. And later, in 1570: " Her Majesty cannot lack in money matters, if it were for £40 or £50,000 within her City of London ". In these same years Gresham had carried out his father's project to build a Bourse, and to accommodate the influx of foreign merchants from abroad. In 1565 the ground was purchased by 750 of the leading citizens, and by 1567 the building was complete at Gresham's charges: visible symbol that London had attained its majority as a financial centre. Its origin stood revealed in its design: planned by a Flemish architect, carried out by Flemish workmen and master carpenter, the materials brought from Flanders, it was modelled upon the Antwerp Bourse, with its internal piazza and open loggias. On the top of a tall column

[1] Burgon, II. p. 341.

was sculpted Gresham's famous crest of the grasshopper. In 1570 the Queen dined at his magnificent house in Bishopsgate Street — a consolation for having cut down his official rate of remuneration earlier — and paid a visit to the Bourse, which she caused to be proclaimed by herald and trumpet the Royal Exchange.[1]

Gresham passed his last years in England, dying in 1579 still only sixty. He lived in great magnificence, chiefly at Mayfield, which had formerly belonged to the Archbishops of Canterbury. The furniture of this house alone was worth £7550. He had accumulated a large number of manors, among them Osterley, where his enclosure of land for a park was very unpopular. At his death his widow was left the enormous income of £2388 : 10 : 6½ a year — double that of an ordinary peer. Gresham also left numerous charitable legacies, besides the almshouses at the back of his house in the City.[2] The splendid house he left for a college with full endowment for professors[3] — of whom Christopher Wren was later the most famous — and lectureships that continue even today. So that his name goes on, not only in the too celebrated Gresham's Law — a later invention anyway.

Though Gresham was the expert, actual policy was in the hands of Cecil. Unwin warns us against " the tendency to overestimate the active part which wise forethought and the deliberate pursuit of clear ideas has played in the economic history of nations ".[4] We may agree, but William Cecil remains always an exception. There are few examples in our history of a more clearly conceived and thought-out policy applied to our circumstances, and none that had the chance to be applied by the same hand over so long a period. Its leading features were to build up the country's capital resources, plant new industries and encourage old ones, to make the country economically independent and as far as possible self-sufficient. In sixteenth-century circumstances a measure of guidance and control at the centre was indispensable, and Burghley's exercise of it has often been described as a beneficent paternalism. He did indeed exercise an incessant watchful scrutiny over all aspects of the State's well-being. Those familiar with his papers know that no detail of administration, or of useful information, was too minute or tiresome for his infinite care. No wonder the Queen trusted him as she did: no ruler in Europe had such a servant, and contemporary opinion abroad recognised it.

[1] Stow's *Survey of London* (ed. C. L. Kingsford), I. 193.
[2] *Ibid.* pp. 76, 177. [3] *v.* below, pp. 527-9. [4] Unwin, *op. cit.* p. 158.

What is more remarkable than his exercise of a paternal authority is the extraordinary moderation with which he used it, keeping in touch with opinion, consulting the interests of merchants and producers, himself always bearing in mind the larger well-being of the people. Emphasis has been placed on the degree to which Elizabethan economic affairs, under his aegis, were regulated. But that was common form to the time; what strikes one more is the greater freedom from regulation that industry enjoyed in England compared with anywhere else. Burghley's activity was one of guiding, encouraging, scrutinising; he left business concerns and industries very much to run their own affairs, himself only weighing in in case of necessity. He kept his own authority as a residual court of appeal, all the more effective for not being over-used; his advice and guidance were always available.

We have seen that the first necessity of government in 1558 was arms for defence. By 1562, owing to Cecil and Gresham's efforts, the country was rearmed. But Cecil was looking further ahead: he did not want England to be dependent on foreign supplies; he aimed at self-sufficiency in armaments. The inventions and technical advances of the Renaissance had left us behind in these, as in other matters. England had no brass industry; copper was not mined on any effective scale; little gunpowder was made. From the sixties these things were taken in hand. Licences were given to dig for saltpetre; in 1561 an agreement was entered into with a German who undertook to make it. In 1565 a patent for manufacturing sulphur was granted to Wade and Herle for thirty years: a useful example of the way in which many monopolies started as a means of introducing new trades.[1] About the same time George Evelyn got a monopoly for the manufacture of gunpowder and set up several mills in Surrey. His grandson John Evelyn wrote: "Not far from my brother's house [Wotton] upon the streams and ponds since filled up and drained, stood formerly many powder mills erected by my ancestors, who were the first who brought that invention into England; before which we had all our powder out of Flanders".[2] George Evelyn made a good thing of it and extended his estates considerably in the vicinity where the Evelyns have been ever since. It is curious to think that the foundation of the equable Evelyn's family rested on gunpowder. By the end of the reign English cannon had won such a good name on the Continent

[1] W. Cunningham, *The Growth of English Industry and Commerce*, II. 60.
[2] H. Evelyn, *History of the Evelyn Family*, p. 19.

that there was keen competition to get them, licensed or unlicensed, and Ralegh was able to complain: "Heretofore one ship of her Majesty's was able to beat ten Spaniards, but now, by reason of our own ordnance, we are hardly matched one to one".[1]

For the new development of mining that was planned German enterprise was called in, not only mining experts and workmen but the capital and experience of a well-known Augsburg firm. As early as 1561 there were negotiations with Steinberg to form a company, twenty English and ten Germans, to explore and open up mines in the Lake District.[2] But Steinberg refused to agree to allow engines and equipment constructed by Germans to be left in England at the dissolution of the company: he said that no artificers would come on such terms. It is interesting to observe this conflict: the determination of the English to learn new methods and the reluctance of the Germans to impart their secrets. In 1565 William Humphry, Assay Master at the Mint, had to report to Cecil that Hans Loner, the best German brass manufacturer, had refused to bring the art of battery into England in spite of Humphry's allurements: "Already fearing casualty of death in this man I have secretly prepared such Englishmen as shall more suddenly learn than he expecteth . . . young goldsmiths that are of the best hammer men. . . . And lastly I have provided for geometricians skilful in metals, for speedy conceiving how to make the mills and engines for forging and drawing: all which artificers, being skilful in these several parts of goldsmithery are most apt people . . . so that if God did spare life but one year I did nothing doubt of the full recovering of manual working latten within this realm into all forms."[3] With such determination it was impossible to stop the English from learning the art of brass-making. Three years later it was successfully achieved; though English brass for a century more was inferior to foreign, so long does it take to build up a traditional skill.

What was necessary for brass-making within the country was to discover calamine, or ore of zinc, to mix with the copper. Search was set on foot, and its swift success was very satisfying. Daniel Höchstetter had told Humphry that there was calamine in England, "but he would not tell me where he had found it, for he is very secret and so is Hans Loner".[4] So Christopher Schütz was sent westward to look for it: the business was kept secret from everyone except Cecil and Leicester. In June 1566

[1] q. H. Hamilton, *The English Brass and Copper Industries*, p. 6.
[2] S.P. 12/18/18.
[3] Tawney and Power, *Tudor Econ. Docts.* I. 242-3.
[4] S.P. 12/37/73.

Humphry wrote Cecil: "Since February last a stranger and an Englishman have ranged by direction to the most likely places for the finding of the calamine, and now, thanks be given to the Creator of all things, it is found and yet unknown to the finders, for they have brought it by resemble of such description as have been given them. Christopher have brought of the several mines of calamine out of Germany, and by the assay we can find none comparable to this of England, which is found in Somerset."[1] From now on for two and a half centuries this source provided the largest amount of the best calamine raised in England.[2] The find was close to Bristol, where was a coal mine within four miles and whence transport to the Forest of Dean with its iron was easy.[3] So the wire works was set up at Tintern, in the abbey grounds; it was very lucrative and employed a hundred workmen — an early example of large-scale enterprise.

The search for copper in Cumberland was equally successful. The Augsburg firm of Haug and Langenauer was sufficiently impressed by the prospects to invest heavily — £20,000 in the first four years — and to place a leading member, Daniel Höchstetter, in charge of operations. The first contingent of forty or fifty miners from the Tyrol arrived at Newcastle in 1565.[4] Next year a rich copper mine was opened up at Newlands, and that autumn Höchstetter was able to report to the Queen, who was following these developments with interest, that they had at last made "fine and perfect copper". The time had come to place the organisation on a regular footing. In 1568 two companies were incorporated. The first, the Mines Royal, had the sole right of mining for precious metals and copper in the main copper-bearing areas of the North and West. The second, the Mineral and Battery Works, had the sole right to mine calamine and make brass. Relations between the two were complex and complementary, for a number of members were common to both. Each of them had a considerable Court element among its membership: Cecil, Leicester, Pembroke, Norfolk took shares.[5] It does not seem that they made any money out of it, certainly not out of the Mines Royal which demanded a great outlay of capital. One gets the impression that the Germans did things on a lavish scale, and it may be that they enjoyed a higher standard of living at home: they certainly paid out very high wages to their master workmen. At the beginning the English members of the company

[1] Tawney and Power, I. 245-6.
[2] *V.C.H. Somerset*, II. 389.
[3] Tawney and Power, I. 246.
[4] H. Hamilton *op. cit.* p. 10 foll.
[5] W. R. Scott, *Joint-Stock Companies to 1720*, I. 68.

were willing enough to pay up on their shares: Höchstetter expressed his joy that " Master Secretary hath showed himself so friendly and forward in this our works of our mineral, and that his money hath been so ready with the first and also so willing for the next payment ".[1] But as time went on money difficulties became acute for the company. It produced plenty of copper, but there was not a sufficient market for it. In 1575 the Mineral and Battery Works came to its aid by allowing it to make battery goods on its own, and we find a useful copper-smith's industry set going, making pots and pans and kettles, while Höchstetter exports copper for the Muscovy Company and to Bordeaux. By 1579 the Germans were ready to get out and Customer Smythe took over the mines, managed to pay a large rent and the Queen's royalty and to make them pay. The Germans cannot have extricated themselves without losses; but the industry was now established.

It so happens that the account books of this German community up there in the Lake District have survived in far-away Augsburg: from which we may trace something of their life like the workings, lined with the best oak, that they left behind them.[2] We learn of the German who was killed in a row — perhaps for some such reason as Hazlitt was set upon, for we note the christening of an illegitimate child of one of the Germans in Crosthwaite Register. But soon they settle down into the life of the country: next year there were no less than fourteen marriages with the dalesfolk. They sent home to Germany for books, mining compasses, fishing tackle; they sell the dalespeople drapery. A large sum is spent on mending Hans Loner's great clock; fifteen ells of canvas are bought for the dining-room to keep bats out. Then Vicar's Island in the Lake is purchased, and they set to work rooting up stumps and bushes, and planting apple and pear trees. Soon they have a windmill, a brewery and a pig-house built. There is archery on St. George's day and mumming at Christmas; several times there are comedies or plays, or players with fiddle and pipe, or bear-baiting which the children are taken to see. In winter they run their loads across the frozen lake or pay money to break the ice. They go to church at Crosthwaite, though it would be good to have a preacher to preach to the workmen in their own language. They send home money — those that have wives and families — to far-away Tyrol.

About the same time search for these ores, copper, lead, silver,

[1] Hamilton, *op. cit.* p. 16.
[2] W. G. Collingwood, *Elizabethan Keswick.*

was made in Cornwall; but not much progress was made until Customer Smythe took over the Cumberland mines and sent the master-miner Ulrich Frosse down to Cornwall to explore old workings and open up new ones. His correspondence gives us a vivid picture of the difficulties they had to encounter in these early days of mining: the water for ever breaking in, the dangers of the Cornish cliffs, the naughty habits of the workmen, above all the shortage of capital.[1] I have elsewhere given some idea of the technical and personal aspects of this; [2] let us here concentrate on what is of interest from the point of view of nascent capitalism. In 1584 Customer Smythe, from his house in Fenchurch Street, doles out money from his partners in small driblets to William Carnsew to keep Frosse and his men at work. Hovering about between the company in London and its various operations in Cumberland, Wales and Cornwall is a Mr. Weston, who acts as part supervisor, part promoter — all is rather undefined in these early operations. We learn, however, what Smythe's expectations are: " That we shall now after awhile receive our own stock back again with a yearly commodity during our lease, whereof I think can be no doubt (God blessing our mines and labour) if things be well ordered and followed ".[3] Here, too, the German miners proved much more expensive than the innocent Cornish, who, Carnsew wrote, " out of all peradventure be as skillful in mining, as hard and diligent labourers in that kind of travail as are to be found in Europe ".[4] Good veins of copper and lead were opened up and the minerals shipped across to Neath to be smelted: already here coal was used along with charcoal in the process. But there was a good deal of irregularity in the supply of ores; it may be that the costs were too great, certainly production was not profitable and Smythe and his partners closed down their Cornish operations.

The tin industry offers something of an exception to the general argument of this chapter; there are, however, points of similarity as well as of contrast. In the first place it was one of the oldest of English industries; throughout the Middle Ages this country had something like a monopoly in Europe in producing tin. This ceased to be so in the sixteenth century, with the rise of German and Bohemian production, though we remained by far the largest exporting country. Contrary to the general trend of industry, tin production declined in the latter half of the century and ended up with a severe depression. Two main factors

[1] S.P. 12/163/99, *passim*.
[2] *Tudor Cornwall*, pp. 55-9.
[3] S.P. 12/172.
[4] S.P. 12/163/74.

adversely affected it. The rise in prices put up the costs of production while the price of tin fell. Cornish gentlemen like Edgecumbe and Carnsew seem to have lost money by going into it: it was very speculative and chancy. At the same time alluvial deposits were giving out, and historic tin-streaming upon those western moorlands and in the valley bottoms was of necessity giving way to mining. Here came in the indispensable Germans. The Godolphins, the leading tin-producing family in the west, used the advice of a German master-miner with success; Peter Edgecumbe got not much advantage from consulting an odd German, whom he called, uncompromisingly, Burcot. There was a constant shift westward in production, from Devon to Cornwall, and from East Cornwall to West Cornwall. In our period Cornwall produced on average eight times as much as Devon, and paid ten or fifteen times as much in coinage duties.[1]

The organisation of the industry was extremely disadvantageous to the poor tinners: perhaps it could hardly have been otherwise, since they were so many individuals with no means of protection or of asserting themselves, and with the usual Celtic incapacity to hold together. The trade came into the hands of the merchants, money-lenders and rich tinners within the county, who formed a ring with the London interests, haberdashers and pewterers, who controlled the trade. Of the tin retained in the country — perhaps one-fifth of that exported [2] — the bulk went into the making of pewter, and the Pewterers' Company in London enjoyed a period of great prosperity. Meanwhile the poor tinners were often forced to sell their tin for £15 or £16 per thousand weight,[3] which the dealers sold again for £28 or £30. Worse still, the tinners were frequently forced to subsist on loans and credit, from one coinage to another, so that they could never extricate themselves from the toils of debt and obligation. Hence again the importance that usury, the rate of interest, had in all the discussions and disputes to which conditions in this industry gave rise: much more important than wages to many tinners. These conditions gave rise to a whole literature of complaint and suggested remedies which fill the State Papers towards the end of the century: it needs not a page, but a book to itself.

In the depression of the nineties the government was anxious to do what it could — even though, harassed by war and financial strain, it could not do much. The Queen agreed to advance £8000 a year free of interest to the industry, and ultimately the

[1] G. R. Lewis, *The Stannaries*, Apps. J and K.

[2] Cf. H.M.C. *Salisbury MSS.* XIII. 514-15.

[3] *I.e.* 1200 lb.

government decided to try the experiment of pre-emption, of buying the whole annual output at a reasonable fixed figure, round about £28 per thousand weight. The pre-emption, like other monopolies, was leased to and operated by patentees, and as such criticised by the growing class of business men who were not disinterested parties in the discussion.[1] The Queen expressed what she thought about them in her famous last speech to the Commons: " And for them I think they speak out of zeal for their countries, and not out of spleen or malevolent affection as being parties grieved ".[2] Ralegh claimed in the Debate that his exercise of the pre-emption had doubled the tinners' wages, from 2s. to 4s. a week, and he was not denied.[3] What the poor tinners themselves thought about it may be gathered from their petitioning the government that the pre-emption might continue. The most successful of these tin merchants — whose usury, after all, performed a function as necessary to the industry, in the absence of a bank or other credit facilities, as it was profitable to themselves — may be seen portrayed on his coloured monument, out of Janssen's workshop, in St. Mary's at Truro: Richard Robartes' son moved up to the grange of the Bodmin monks at Lanhydrock, built there his fine Jacobean house and purchased a peerage from Buckingham. His son became a very eminent, religious-minded and sour-faced Presbyterian and Parliamentarian leader. It is a nice concatenation, but a forward-looking one: so English history is advanced.

In the lead-mining of the Mendips there was a marked increase in extent and output, especially about Chewton, from the middle of the century: it reached its maximum in the next century.[4] Agreeable profits accrued to the Bishops of Bath and Wells: " Bishop Still had the harvest, Bishop Montagu the gleanings, and Bishop Lake the stubble ".[5] There was a considerable export from Bristol; some of it went illicitly to Spain, whence — in spite of the Council's constant pressure — " doubtless many an ounce of Mendip lead found its billet in Englishman or Netherlander ".[6] William Humphry claimed that he had invented a method of smelting lead-ore in a furnace worked by a foot-blast and a sieve of a particular fashion.[7] He obtained an injunction

[1] " The rich tinners opposed it, ' since they make money out of the necessity of the poor men, who cannot wait for a better market, but are forced to borrow at 20 per cent and to sell their tin cheaply ' " (Lewis, *op. cit.* p. 220).

[2] q. in J. R. Tanner, *Tudor Constitutional Docts.* p. 577.

[3] Sir Simonds D'Ewes, *A Compleat Journal* . . . (ed. 1693), p. 646.

[4] J. W. Gough, *The Mines of Mendip*, p. 112.

[5] *Ibid.* p. 115. [6] *V.C.H. Somerset*, II. 374. [7] Gough, *op. cit.* p. 144

against the Derbyshire lead-owners for infringing his patent in 1582. Problems of drainage brought the North Country mining adventurer, Bevis Bulmer, into the Mendips, where he introduced new methods of draining the mines. He is first heard of in connection with mining in Scotland in 1566;[1] an interesting example of the new type of entrepreneur, part projector, part capitalist, he was interested in hydraulic inventions, one of which he installed on the Thames. Among his other interests were the silver mine at Combe Martin in North Devon, where a good vein of silver was opened up under the aegis of Adrian Gilbert, Ralegh's half-brother and a crony of Carnsew's, in 1587. Bulmer rushed to take a share in the mine and for the next two years he and his partner netted £10,000 each from it. In 1590 the profit was £1000. When the silver ran out he had the last piece smelted made into a goblet for the City of London. Having become a gentleman, he was knighted: James was less particular than Elizabeth.

The most spectacular spurt was made in coal-mining. Before the sixteenth century coal was little used as household fuel; but with the diminution of the woodlands and the growth of towns, especially that of London, there came a great extension of demand. London's coal came from Newcastle — by the end of the reign the Newcastle Hostmen had gained the monopoly of the supply — hence it is as sea-coal that it becomes known there and makes its appearance in literature. "The cost of Mrs. Quickly's 'sea-coal fire' went up steadily, while Shakespeare was in London, from four shillings the chaldron to nine."[2] The impression that coal pits made on the impressionable minds of poets may be seen from Webster, in the curse that the Duchess of Malfi's brother proclaims on her and her lover:

> I would have their bodies
> Burnt in a coal-pit, with the ventage stopped
> That their cursed smoke might not ascend to heaven.

It seems that England was the first country to exploit coal intensively, and by 1597 it had already grown to be "one principal commodity of this realm".[3] Professor Nef tells us that "Elizabeth's reign marks the beginning of an epoch in the history of British coal-mining".[4]

[1] H. M. Robertson, "Sir Bevis Bulmer", *Journal of Econ. and Business History* (1931), p. 101.
[2] Unwin in *Shakespeare's England*, I. 336.
[3] q. in J. U. Nef, *The Rise of the British Coal Industry*, I. 3.
[4] *Ibid.* p. 14.

What is noticeable is the rapidity of the development: extraction was much easier than in the case of tin or copper, and there were no problems of treatment after. Transport was the limiting factor and carriage by water always the cheapest: hence the great advantage the Tyne coalfield had in the London market. The figures are remarkable all the same. From 1565 to 1625 "shipments of coal from Newcastle probably increased at a more rapid rate than at any other period in their history. . . . The annual shipments doubled every fifteen years, but it was almost a century and a half after 1625 before they doubled again."[1] Winlaton colliery alone produced more than 20,000 tons for shipment in the year 1581–2. At this rate one is almost inclined to place the beginning of the Industrial Revolution, with Professor Nef, in the Elizabethan Age! He tells us that in the century following Elizabeth's accession the production of coal increased almost as much as in that after 1775 — the golden age of the nineteenth century.

Naturally, profit was the incentive and profitability the secret of success. A water-front colliery at Benwell — one must visualise these early 'collieries' as quite small affairs, just one pit and its workings — which was farmed from the Crown at £10 a year rent, returned £1200 a year to its operators.[2] Such were the advantages of favourable transport: the opening up of many inland pits had to wait for the steam railway. Two further factors stimulated Tyneside coal-mining, and both came into operation about the same time. The first was salt-making, the second was the Reformation. The shortage of timber turned people's minds to using coal for boiling down sea-water in the large brine-pans at work on the coast here and across the Border in Scotland. Robert Bowes, Treasurer of Berwick, invested a large sum in these operations, followed by the Delavals, landowners hereabouts, who first came into industry this way.

As for the Church, Professor Nef thinks that if it had retained control in the Bishopric of Durham the growth of the industry would have been hindered: it had restricted at every turn the freedom of lessees, thereby retarding the investment of the large capital sums necessary to growth, and it had resisted the town merchants' attempts to control and expand the trade. Now the Reformation had put an end to the conflict between the ecclesiastical authorities entrenched on their hill at Durham and the townsmen of Newcastle: the latter had won their independence. Elizabeth added to their prospects by taking into her hands

[1] J. U. Nef, *The Rise of the British Coal Industry*, I. 25. [2] *Ibid.* pp. 27, 147.

from the see of Durham lands worth £1000 a year.[1] Both the Crown and the laity were more ready to encourage the development of coal resources by granting leases on favourable terms. The Crown notably so: commissioners were so much impressed by the hazards of coal-mining and anxious to encourage enterprise that rents were fixed enticingly low. Bishop Barnes granted leases of certain of his manors " in return for a fixed yearly income which bore no relation to the true value of the property ".[2] It happened that a bright young sprig of the Sutton family, a servant of the Dudleys, when surveyor of ordnance in the North, noticed these possibilities and obtained the leases. One of the manors, Whickham, was destined to produce over 100,000 tons a year in the next century. Thomas Sutton became one of the richest men in England and — contrary to what many might suppose likely for a protégé of the Dudleys and a *nouveau riche* — became the founder of Charterhouse.

The Newcastle coal trade had the further advantage of being a nursery of trained seamen, which would recommend it much in the eyes of the government. Before 1600 " nearly as many vessels were engaged in the carriage of coals from Newcastle to foreign countries as were engaged in the carriage of all commodities from foreign countries to London ".[3] In the year ending 1594, 852 ships carried 35,934 tons of coal from Newcastle to foreign ports; but presumably many ships made more than one journey. Progress was marked elsewhere, though it was less rapid. In Lancashire there was the same activity in surveying for coal as in Yorkshire, and the same eagerness to invest in coal pits. Shipments from Liverpool to Ireland were growing. Further north in Cumberland a small export trade was developing; the Lowthers built up their position in the industry upon lands at Whitehaven of the dissolved priory of St. Bees. Bristol, where coal was becoming the ordinary fuel of the poorer inhabitants, had its own field close by at Kingswood. Staffordshire saw a rapid increase in the second half of the century; so too South Wales and in Yorkshire and Derbyshire where " between 1550 and 1615 we find references to nearly 100 different collieries, most of which appear to have been recently started ".[4]

The Midlands came second to the Northumberland and Durham coalfield: here production was less concentrated and the increase less rapid. The Trent rendered communication easy, and that was advantageous to such a coal-producing manor as Wollaton next Nottingham where Sir Francis Willoughby was

[1] *Ibid.* p. 149. [2] *Ibid.* p. 151. [3] *Ibid.* p. 239. [4] *Ibid.* p. 57.

working his coal pits, within the park and outside, here and at Strelley. (From those fantastic towers, which the returns from the pits enabled him to build, one still sees them.) It so happens that a good many of his accounts remain,[1] some of them bound up with leaves of medieval manuscripts: from useless theology to coal, a transition eloquent of the time. As usual, it is impossible to make out the exact rate of profit, but it must have been pretty considerable. Sir Francis turned his attention to iron-making, and here on a turnover of £600 for the half-year he made a clear profit of £125.[2] A restless individual with an unhappy domestic life — perhaps the right type for an early speculative enterpriser — he went in for glass-making too, and for growing woad to establish a dye industry. Apparently he purposed to go in for arras-making, like the Sheldon tapestry-weaving at this time. But he overspent himself in building and, infatuated with his second wife, made over a good deal of his property to her, leaving impoverished estates.

No growth in the output of coal was comparable to that in England: by the eve of the Civil War this country produced perhaps three or four times as much as the whole Continent.[3] Professor Nef tells us that only the failure to solve the problem of smelting ores with coal prevented us achieving leadership equally in metallurgy. We shall see later the tale of the efforts made, and the patents taken out, for making iron by the use of coal. But though this process was not achieved until long beyond our period, coal was successfully substituted in calcining ores prior to smelting, in extracting silver, in converting iron into steel, in battery and wire work, and in nearly all finishing processes. It had also taken the place of charcoal in brick-making, brewing and dyeing.[4] Earlier it was in use among blacksmiths, in the Black Country and elsewhere.[5] By 1612 glass-making was transformed by the discovery of a method of closing the clay crucibles and so substituting coal for wood fire. Here was an English invention that was subsequently introduced into the Continent: some small return for what we had absorbed from abroad, but a harbinger of what a future! The cheapness of coal, its readiness to hand, underlay every other industry: the foundation of subsequent industrial development.

[1] H.M.C. *Middleton MSS.*

[2] *Ibid.* p. 496. For contemporary comparison multiply by 25.

[3] Nef, " The Progress of Technology and the Growth of Large-Scale Industry in Great Britain ", *Econ. Hist. Rev.* (1934), pp. 14-15.

[4] T. S. Ashton, *Iron and Steel in the Industrial Revolution*, p. 10.

[5] W. H. B. Court, *The Rise of the Midland Industries*, p. 102.

During our period the Weald of Sussex, Surrey and Kent, was the centre of the iron industry.[1] It is curious to think of it as an industrial district, but it has left its relics in those remote hammer ponds up in the hills among the woods, in those agreeable houses the iron-masters built for themselves — such a house as Batemans at Burwash, which Kipling lived in, or the manor-house at Crippenden that Richard Tichborne built in 1607, or the fine house at Cowden built about 1597; or in such humbler mementoes as the fire-backs and andirons one sees in Sussex farmhouses, the iron graveslabs, like the elaborate one to Anne Forster in Crowhurst church, dated 1591. This was the time when the industry reached its peak; owing to the exhaustion of the woodlands the next century saw a long slow decline, and a transference to the Black Country. Now the Weald enjoyed supremacy and the technical advantage of having introduced the blast furnace from the Continent. Of the two methods of making iron, the bloomery process, in which the lump of malleable iron is directly hammered out into the required shape, is very ancient and primitive. The blast furnace, which runs the molten metal into a shape, producing cast-iron which needs working in a forge to convert it into wrought-iron, requires capital equipment and a capitalist. The process was introduced into the Weald in Tudor times and there practically superseded the bloomeries.[2] The first casting of iron cannon in England at Buxted in 1543 brought the Wealden industry into the forefront.[3] At its height there seem to have been about a hundred forges and iron mills at work in the Weald.[4]

What is interesting socially is the close connection between the landowners and the industry. London merchants were willing to invest and speculate in iron furnaces, but in addition " the lesser gentry, yeomen and skilled tradesmen who had charge of actual management became an important and wealthy middle class ", who built " many substantial houses, equalling or surpassing the manor houses of the same period ".[5] Not less than 7000 men are thought to have been employed in the industry. From the moment Sir William Sidney got possession of Robertsbridge priory he set to work mining for iron and building a forge, with the vicar of Salthurst in charge. It is fortunate that many accounts and forge-books remain, some of them covered with leaves from the priory psalters.[6] Miners were brought in from

[1] *v.* E. Straker, *Wealden Iron.* [2] *Ibid.* p. 26. [3] *Ibid.* p. 48.

[4] Norden's estimate of 140, accepted by Nef, seems to be an over-estimate (Straker, p. 60). [5] *Ibid.* p. vii. [6] H.M.C. *De L'Isle and Dudley MSS.*

abroad. The forge was set up in the abbey gate-house; the abbot's lodgings served to house the workers; when steel-making was tried out the steel forges were set up in the brewhouse. The output was respectable: beginning with 6 tons of iron in the first year, it went up to an average of 130 tons, and reached its highest in 1562 with 202 tons.[1] We are more interested in the profits, which were very considerable: something over 40 per cent on the total turnover.[2] From prayer to profit, we might sum up the history of Robertsbridge; or perhaps, from profit in the next world to profit in this. The forge there was still in use up to the mid-eighteenth century. Now there is little left: not much in the way of remains: abbey and forge, monks and iron-workers are alike gone. In 1565 Sir Henry Sidney ventured upon steel-making, and for this purpose brought in a number of German workers under the command of two experts.[3] He laid out a large capital sum on the works, nearly £2000, and then met with set-backs. It is the specific function of the capitalist to support losses as well as to enjoy profits; in this case the enterprising capitalist was a nobleman, brother-in-law of Leicester, Lord President of Wales, Lord Deputy of Ireland, one of the innermost governing circle.

In 1588 Bevis Bulmer took out a patent for a new instrument to cut iron by machinery; two years later the first slitting-mill was set up at Dartford, introduced from Liège.[4] Before the end of the century the blast furnace for iron-making had made its appearance in Shropshire and Worcestershire.[5] Thomas, third Lord Paget, set up works in Cannock Chase: his Catholicism was no bar to his taking a hand in the new industrialism. South Staffordshire and North-east Worcestershire formed the largest nail-producing region in the country.[6] The Forest of Dean had about fifty nailers and half a dozen iron-founders in it. Nailing was a widely distributed industry, which used coal possibly earlier than the sixteenth century. The country round Walsall was full of iron-stone pits, and the trade of the town was in all kinds of iron work for horses — bits, stirrups, spurs, buckles and so on:[7] one forgets what a large demand for such there must have been in earlier ages dependent on the horse for transport. Belbroughton produced, as it still does, scythes and sickles: the pools and dams of former works may still be seen there. The industrial development of the Midlands sprang naturally out of a society dominantly

[1] Straker, p. 311.
[2] H.M.C. *De L'Isle and Dudley MSS.* p. 311.
[3] *Ibid.* p. 316.
[4] Court, *op. cit.* p. 105.
[5] *Ibid.* p. 82.
[6] *Ibid.* p. 101 foll.
[7] *Ibid.* p. 29 foll.

agrarian, with coal, iron, nailing interests interwoven; and the industrial craftsmanship that made English prosperity arose naturally from the inherited skills in metal-working of these early artisans. Capital was what gave it its expansion, the enterprise of capitalists the main motive force. Again what is so interesting about English society is the mixture of sources from which the impulse came: the landowners were as much to the fore as the capitalist *pur sang* — if ever his blood was pure — the gentry as much as the middle classes. In this area the lead was taken by Lord Dudley, who sensibly used his industrially-minded illegitimate son, Dud Dudley, a young man down from Balliol, to supervise his works.[1] Altogether movements too subtle to trace set the Elizabethan Age in motion towards the industrial age.

Similarly in Hallamshire around Sheffield the lead was taken by the Earl of Shrewsbury, to whom the great manor belonged. The ordinances governing the cutlers of the district were sanctioned by him as lord of the manor and enforced in his manor court. Up to Elizabeth's reign " the best continental cutlery was greatly superior to the English both in material and workmanship ".[2] Among the foreign workers who came into the country some settled at Sheffield: their terms remained long in the industry, *couteau* till the nineteenth century. During the reign the reputation of English cutlery rose rapidly and by James I's time the best and finest knives were made in England. In 1575 Shrewsbury sends Burghley a case of Hallamshire whittles and speaks of their fame throughout the realm.[3] Before 1600 they are being exported to Ireland. " A right Sheffield knife is best ", became a household word; Nashe says, " Then tell me if our English sconces be right Sheffield or no ". By 1606 workmanship is becoming more decorative: Lady Shrewsbury, Bess of Hardwick's daughter, sends Robert Cecil, now Lord Salisbury, a case of knives from " my poor town of Sheffield ", representing figures of Christ with the twelve Apostles, their names between the hafts and blades.[4] With the death of her husband, the last earl of his line, way was made for the incorporation of the Cutlers of Hallamshire to govern their own affairs, an independent body strongly organised against outside competition.

In the Weald, glass-making had taken a new lease of life.[5]

[1] Dud Dudley, *Metallum Martis* (ed. 1855), p. 4.

[2] G. I. H. Lloyd, *The Cutlery Trades*, p. 93.

[3] *Ibid.* p. 96.

[4] *Salisbury MSS.* XVIII. 445.

[5] S. E. Winbolt, *Wealden Glass.*

By the middle of the century there was a sad decline, after four centuries in which it had been the chief glass-making centre of the kingdom. Edward's government had made attempts to establish Italian glass-makers in London; the civil war in the Netherlands was more effective. Antwerp was the most important centre of glass-making after Venice, and from there Jean Carré came to London, bringing with him Huguenot workers and later bringing in Venetians to apply Venetian technique in the works at Crutched Friars. In 1575 Verzelini got a monopoly for making drinking and other glasses.[1] We hear of quarrels between the Carré workers and other aliens who refused vehemently to teach the English their art. The Carrés made window glass; and, indeed, a great deal must have been necessary to glaze the vast many-windowed houses going up everywhere — no wonder the Willoughbys of Wollaton, the Sidneys of Penshurst started glass-making on their own. In the Weald the Carré furnaces may be traced following the woods, and as these became exhausted by the demands of the iron industry, the glass-makers trekked westwards into Hampshire, where Huguenot names may be traced in the parish registers. Thence they moved to the Forest of Dean, window glass still their main product. There at Newnham Sir Edward Mansell erected the first glasshouse to be worked by coal. This brought a new technique and a fine English speciality of flint-glass. There you are: the first step to industrial power brings its own rewards.

France was the chief supplier of salt for North-western Europe: 'bay-salt' evaporated from the salt-marshes of the western coast.[2] We had a certain source of supply in the brine deposits of Cheshire and Staffordshire, but we were mainly dependent on France. Here, too, Cecil was anxious to develop our own resources. Several projects for introducing a process of manufacture were discussed, and in 1563 Cecil obtained a licence for Jasper Seeler of Augsburg, whom he invited over, to make white salt for the whole kingdom. This patent does not seem to have come to much, nor that which Cecil obtained for Francis Bertie, a Frenchman, two years later. But already English supplies of salt were increasing, by the use of coal to evaporate salt from sea-water on Tyneside and along the Northumberland coast into

[1] S. E. Winbolt, *Wealden Glass*, p. 16.

[2] The above account is based on E. Hughes, *Studies in Administration and Finance, 1558–1825*.

Scotland; and on the coast of Cumberland. The wars of religion in France very much disturbed the salt trade and sent up prices; the Huguenots seized on production in the Biscay provinces to raise loans: production went down. It was this that gave a "lasting impetus to salt production in England": once more one observes the rewards of common sense. From the middle of the century Scots and Shields salt began to compete with bay-salt; from 1600 our own cured bloaters were shipped direct from Yarmouth to Italy, as pilchards already were from the West Country. Within the area of the brine industry Northwich, which was freer from regulations, was outstripping its older rivals; production was coming more into the hands of the business-minded gentry in place of the haphazard democracy of burgess-owners: "The industry . . . had already undergone a revolution by the end of Elizabeth's reign".[1] By the end of the next century, with the discovery of rock-salt, English salt took the place of French in the European and American markets. Truly, at the end of the Elizabethan vista, one sees the commercial Empire and the Industrial Revolution.

The same development may be seen in the history of the fisheries. Their story reflects the changing economies of Europe, and ultimately the encouragement of the government as part of its navigation policy "gave the Atlantic maritime régime a crucial position in the struggle between the mercantile systems of Europe".[2] The outcome of this lay well ahead, but the essential positions which gave supremacy in the end were won in this period. The discovery of North America by Cabot brought no immediate advantages to the English. French and Portuguese fishermen were first to explore the inexhaustible riches of the Newfoundland fishing grounds — those fertile mist-shrouded waters more than a thousand miles away across the Atlantic, offering their challenge to the courage and daring of western-looking seamen in their small boats along a hundred bays and creeks. The conquest of those waters is an epic story. The English were behind, still concentrating on the Iceland fishery from east coast ports. The French had a great advantage in their bay-salt; soon they were exporting Newfoundland cod to England. "It is a certain maxim", wrote William Wood in 1722, "that all states are powerful at sea as they flourish in the fishing trade."[3]

It was a matter of great importance, and one very near to Cecil's heart, to encourage the fisheries: they helped to pay for

[1] *Ibid.* p. 28. [2] H. A. Innis, *The Cod Fisheries*, p. ix. [3] q. *ibid.* p. x.

our imports, an export of fish brought in specie, they trained sailors and increased shipping, they were the indispensable foundation of the fleet: they *were* maritime power. Here again Elizabethan government, under Cecil's inspiration, was the direct continuation of Edwardian. It was essential to provide as large an internal market as possible for the fisheries: as a good thing in itself and as a basis for export. An Act of 1548 had appointed Fridays and Saturdays as enforced fish-days, upon which no meat was to be eaten. The fact that the country had ceased to be Catholic meant not less, but more fish-days — for the best and most sensible of reasons. The moment Cecil returned to power we find among his memoranda for Parliament: "Let the old course of fishing be maintained by the straitest observation of fish-days, for policy's sake; so the sea-coasts should be strong with men and habitations and the fleet flourish more than ever".[1] In 1563 he followed this up by a very ably-argued paper in favour of adding Wednesday to the number of fish-days,[2] and this proposal was enacted in Parliament. Now, what with three fish-days a week, plus Ember days and Lent, more than half the year consisted of fish-days: a great saving of stock, nor was it any deprivation to poor people who ate little meat anyway. It was the well-to-do classes upon whom this sacrifice fell for the well-being of the nation, and they enforced it, on the whole fairly strictly, upon themselves.

Henceforward the Newfoundland fishery grew slowly but steadily, until after the defeat of the Armada, the English gained the first place in it. There was a complex scuffling of interests in that misty region; the English came out on top, with the Portuguese under their protection; the Spaniards were driven out, and the French forced into the outlying areas. The English fishermen turned their weakness in the supply of salt to a positive advantage by concentrating on drying the fish. Their dry fish had excellent keeping qualities, was much more suitable for sailors on long voyages and for export to the Mediterranean. And so an export trade was built up from the West Country, which now came to the fore: in 1594 the Newfoundland fleet was estimated to number 100 vessels, Plymouth providing 50 sail. Fish were sold to France, and through France to Spain: the tables were turned. At the same time there was growing up in the West a successful in-shore pilchard fishery.[3] Seine-fishing was becoming

[1] *Salisbury MSS.* I. 165. [2] Tawney and Power, *Tudor Econ. Docts.* II. 104 foll.

[3] Cf. my "Dispute concerning the Plymouth Pilchard Fishery, 1584–91" *Economic History* (1932), p. 461 foll.

prevalent; this meant larger boats, several of them co-operating, the domination of the market by the merchants and curers, the development of a considerable export to Spain and Italy. Something like 6000 hogsheads a year went abroad: the impost on them provided half the money for the fortification of Plymouth.

The temperamental herring chose this century to leave the eastern coasts of the North Sea for the western.[1] At the same time the Dutch discovered an improved method of curing him. This made the foundations of the merchant marine of Holland. The catch was of enormous value, enabled the Dutch to pay for all their necessary imports and — it is not too much to say — to resist the power of Spain successfully. Hundreds of Dutch boats fished off the east coast. These thoughts inspired Robert Hitchcock, encouraged by John Dee, to put forward his *Politic Plat* outlining an organised fishing fleet on a national scale to rival the Dutch: 400 large ships of 70 tons or more after the manner of Flemish busses, each of them employing a master, twelve mariners and twelve lusty beggars.[2] One sees the double motive of the enterprise: the Elizabethans were dogged by the fear of unemployment. The scheme was worked out in detail: 5000 lasts of herring to serve London (one remembers that red-headed, fork-bearded Robert Greene died after a supper of pickled herrings), 5000 lasts for the rest of the country; employment for 10,000 men. Hitchcock had all the M.P.s from the ports to dinner at Westminster before Parliament met in 1576 and read them his *Plat*: it was well approved. But it was too big and too costly: better the securer conquests of private enterprise. These were celebrated by Greene's scape-grace friend Nashe in his *Lenten Stuff: The Praise of the Red Herring*: so much publicity for Yarmouth in return for kind entertainment and money lent him when he took refuge there one autumn from London.[3] This has all Nashe's sense of the picturesque and brings back the vanished scene before us: the women and children in the sun spinning twine to make nets, at one moment £5000 worth of nets drying upon the Green, 40 mackerel boats departing in the spring, and "this last fishing 600 barks and boats sheltering there, most riding abreast before the quay"; and "that which especialest nourished the most prime pleasure in me was after a storm when they were driven in swarms and lay close pestered together as

[1] A. M. Samuel, *The Herring: its Effect on the History of Britain*, p. 101.
[2] Cf. Arber's *English Garner*, II. 133 foll.
[3] Nashe, *Prose Works* (ed. McKerrow), III. 146 foll.

thick as they could pack; the next day following if it were fair, they would cloud the whole sky with canvas, by spreading their drabbled sails in the full clue abroad adrying and make a braver show with them than so many banners and streamers displayed against the sun on a mountain-top ".

There was no doubt about the effect of the government's measures to encourage the industry — certainly not in the minds of those who knew, of the government itself and of Parliament. The towns on the east coast certified in March 1576 that since the passing of the Statute in 1563 fishing boats and barks of 10 tons to 30 tons had increased by 140 sail: " and if the said law had not been made . . . so many in number or rather more would have been decayed within this realm ".[1] The number of merchant ships of over 100 tons increased with the growth of trade from 35 ships to 135 in 1577, 177 in 1582, 183 in 1588, and in 1624 to 350.[2] It is open to argue that there would have been an increase anyway; there certainly would of merchant ships, but the fisheries could not have made such notable progress without the constant support they got — which the nation was agreed in giving. Even Cecil had his failures. He was anxious to establish the weaving of sailcloth, and a colony of foreign artisans wanted to settle in his own town of Stamford.[3] He was willing to let them have the use of a house of his, but he seems to have got no encouragement from the townsmen. It was left to a later generation of French refugees to introduce the art into Suffolk, where hemp was plentiful and sackcloth had long been made.[4]

Little enough space remains to deal with the most important industry of all, England's prime industry from the twelfth century to the nineteenth: the clothing trade. The mass of material relating to it in our period is enormous: it needs a book as thorough-going in its research as Professor Nef's on the coal industry. That book it has not yet had. Here again it is not my purpose, even if it were possible, to survey the industry as a whole, but to give some indication of the new developments that characterised it. Of these, the most general and widespread was the trend away from the old corporate towns to the newer towns and villages of the countryside. Into such a complex movement, which is to be

[1] Tawney and Power, *op. cit.* II. 122.
[2] Nef, *The Rise of the British Coal Industry*, I. 173.
[3] *Cal. S.P. Dom. 1547–80*, p. 293.
[4] *V.C.H. Suffolk*, II. 271.

seen in every clothing region, no doubt a number of factors entered: greater facilities of water power, cheapness of labour and victual. But above all it was freedom from excessive regulation that encouraged enterprise in the new areas where the cloth industry leaped ahead. And thereby hangs a moral for our own time. The decay of the cloth industry in the corporate towns was due to the rigidity of its structure, the excessive regulations — these were so numerous and so minute that it is a hard study to know what was permitted and what was not, industry would have been throttled if they had not been more honoured in the breach than in the observance — and to the burden of taxation and rates upon the product of the industry.

Wherever you look it is the same tale: towns like York and Beverley, Coventry and Bridgnorth were losing ground, their industry decaying.[1] In Yorkshire, Halifax, Leeds and Wakefield were coming up, the first particularly so: it was, according to Camden, already " a famous town ", its great trade in kerseys, shalloons and russets. In Lancashire, the corporate towns Wigan, Preston, Lancaster gave way to new centres like Bolton, Bury, Rochdale, Manchester. In Suffolk, new centres such as Lavenham and Hadleigh rose along with industrial capitalists like the famous Spring family, or in Wiltshire at Malmesbury with the Stumpes. The expansion of the export market for Wiltshire broadcloths brought about an extension of the industry down the Wylye valley to Salisbury.[2] In Somerset and Gloucester it spread out into the country, in Devon along the rivers Exe and Culm with centres like Tiverton and Cullompton.

Another general factor is constituted by the immense and complex changes in the character of the manufacture. It is impossible to sum these up, but I do not know that they have been sufficiently related, so far as the internal market is concerned, to the expanding demand from a population that was increasing and more prosperous. The large expansion of the industry in the West Riding and Lancashire, which is such a feature of the time, was based on the home market, which it served with cheap coarse cloth, fustians and cottons, for the people. On this basis it rapidly built up a remarkable export towards the end of the century: some 30,000 new kerseys a year.[3] Into East Anglia the valuable — and valued — refugees from religious persecution in the Netherlands brought the 'new draperies': bays and says,

[1] E. Lipson, *History of the Woollen and Worsted Industries*, p. 224.
[2] G. D. Ramsay, *The Wiltshire Woollen Industry*, p. 22.
[3] Wadsworth and Mann, *The Cotton Trade and Industrial Lancashire*, p. 12.

arras, grogram and mockado: " Many slight and vain commodities wherein the common people delight ", said the old-fashioned Suffolk clothiers in 1577.[1] But the new draperies had come to stay; they were lighter and more variegated woollens compared with the old, heavy kerseys and broadcloths. These held their own and came to be concentrated chiefly in the West Country, whence they increased their export abroad: Wiltshire broadcloths, Devon and Somerset kerseys. One observes that there is already a considerable measure of concentration and specialisation in the leading national industry.

There was a more economic division of labour on a national scale, with wool grown in one county, spun in another, woven in a third, finished in a fourth. As trade expanded so the London capitalists invaded the local preserves, or local men with push and ability, like Peter Blundell of Tiverton, made their way in London. Sir Nicholas Mosley, representative of the Manchester family business in London, became Lord Mayor in 1599: his doggerel epitaph outlines the story of the successful entrepreneur.[2] Back in Manchester Anthony Mosley, clothier, in 1607 left cloth at home and outside to the value of £1856 : 2 : 8.[3] There are the origins of the Mosley fortune. The Chethams were successful enough to be able to buy Clayton Hall from the impoverished Byrons, who had been there since the thirteenth century. They were predecessors of the country banker. Everywhere the growth of the industry brought up the clothier, the capitalist with his specific organising function. As it expanded, the wool-grower and clothier found themselves in different counties; there was also the need of capital to tide over the periods of waiting. The broker collected the wool and supplied it on credit, " an indispensable link between the small producers of wool and of cloth ".[4] There was a great variety among clothiers from large employers to those who were only just above the level of the labouring class through their thrift and alertness. But there was an important rough distinction between the organisation of the industry in the North and in the South. In the latter the clothier functioned chiefly as a capitalist entrepreneur: he directed the work, handed it out and took the risks; he did not manufacture himself. In the North the majority of the clothiers were small men engaged in manufacture themselves; therefore they needed the middleman to buy wool and sell cloth for them. The organisation was

[1] *V.C.H. Suffolk*, II. 267.
[2] Wadsworth and Mann, *op. cit.* pp. 7-8.
[3] B. Hewart, " The Cloth Trade in the North of England in the 16th and 17th Centuries ", *Econ. Journal* (1900), p. 25.
[4] *V.C.H. Suffolk*, II. 257.

more primitive and democratic, and perhaps had its part in forming, or was equally an expression of, North Country independence of mind.

The new draperies were brought into East Anglia by the Flemish immigrants. It was an enlightened and far-seeing government that encouraged immigration on so large a scale, against all the difficulties, the popular dislike of foreigners in Elizabethan England, the natural antagonism of local weavers. It was a good thing that Elizabethan government, not having to answer to the people, could afford to take no account of this last. By 1572 there were some 4000 aliens in Norwich weaving away like anything; they were very industrious and anxious to make good.[1] It seems to have been from one of these families that Thomas Deloney sprang, most popular of Elizabethan novelists, whose stories are the chief expression of the craft in literature, and with whom the business man first enters as the hero of romance.[2] Dekker, who developed to such advantage the theme of the apprentice who makes good, must have been another of immigrant stock. In 1561, 406 aliens were allowed to settle at Sandwich;[3] there were other communities at Maidstone, where they introduced the thread-manufacture, and at Canterbury, where an old-fashioned and musty chapel in the cathedral, given over to the Huguenots for their services, still perpetuates their tradition.

Colchester, a decayed town in the early part of the century, was given a new lease of life by the arrival of the immigrants: over 200 of them in 1571; by 1573, after being given incorporation and allowed to run their own affairs, there were 534.[4] The bailiffs of the town were, wisely, very willing to receive them; they anticipated that "great profit might arise to the common estate of the town" — in which they were not wrong. Forty households were allowed to settle at Halstead. While they were there eight or nine score of bays were sent to London every week and £250 came into the town.[5] But the idiot people resented their presence and drove them out. After which the trade sank to seven or eight single bays a week, leaving the poor folk of the town without employment. They then wanted the Dutch to come back; the Council did its best, but they would not return: the end of Halstead's brief prosperity. Even at Colchester there

[1] Lipson, *op. cit.* p. 23.
[2] Deloney's *Works* (ed. F. D. Mann), p. vii; Abel Chevalley, *Thomas Deloney*.
[3] W. Cunningham, *Alien Immigrants to England*, p. 150.
[4] *V.C.H. Essex*, II. 385 foll. [5] *Ibid.* p. 331.

were stirs against the immigrants by the working class, jealous of the Dutch who were already prosperous. The better class realised the great gain they were to the town and to the country; the meaner sort, as usual, not. The new arts of weaving were not the only things we owed to the immigrants: they brought new potteries, glass-engraving, printing into London; silk-weaving to Canterbury; linen-weaving and printing to Norwich; needles and parchment-making to Colchester; the manufacture of sail-cloth to Ipswich.[1]

The manufacture of the best quality broadcloths became concentrated in the West, especially in Wiltshire. From Newbury to Kent, kerseys and coarser fabrics were made. In the West there was a good deal of variety and specialisation from town to town. Devonshire made kerseys from Devon, Cornish and Dorset wool; Totnes concentrated on narrow-pin-whites, Cullompton made kersey stockings, Barnstaple bays.[2] A weekly market for wool, yarn and woollens had been established at Exeter in 1538; it grew with great rapidity and helped to make that prospering city rich. Fortunes were made in Exeter by the merchants of that time; their memorials are to be seen still on the walls of those rose-red churches. In the early years of Elizabeth Exeter gained the third place among the ports of the kingdom for its exports of cloth and imports of wine.[3] Westcote's account of the organisation of the trade is well known: how the farmer sent his wool to the market; it was bought by the comber or spinner, who next week brought in the spun yarn, which the weaver bought and next week brought back as cloth. It was then sold to the clothier, who after fulling and sometimes dyeing it, transported it to London or exported it. The process remained the same up to the eighteenth century without much change; just as a family like the Fabians, who appeared in Ashburton in the middle of the century, carried on serge-making there till 1815. By then, the conservatism of the West Country industry, the antagonism of the workers to the introduction of machinery, lost it its lead for good to Yorkshire.

The foundations of the ascendancy of the North in textiles were laid in this period. The quality of their fabrics was altogether coarser and cheaper, and there were constant complaints against the false practices of the Northerners: "In the north

1 Cunningham, *op. cit.* p. 177.

2 P. F. S. Amery, "Sketch of Ashburton and the Woollen Trade" (*Trans. Devon. Assoc.*, 1876), p. 323 foll.

3 Cf. figs. in S.P. 12/30/8. "Account of Customs and Subsidies on woollen cloths and new impost on wine in all ports 1559–1563."

parts no true cloths are made ".[1] They seem to have been up to every sort of dodge, stretching and tentering their cloths, fulling them with flocks or chalk, selling them wet for the buyer to discover them altogether lighter when dry. But this may be regarded as the reverse side of a healthy North Country readiness to experiment: " They despise their old fashions if they can hear of a new, more commodious, rather affecting novelties than allied to old ceremonies ".[2] At any rate these were the cloths for the people. Leeds and Wakefield, which made under 500 cloths a year in the reign of Edward VI, made 5000 at the end of Elizabeth's.[3] York recovered some measure of activity through the exports of the Merchant Adventurers. The county drew upon most of the Midland counties for its wool.

Even more interesting was the rise of Lancashire 'cottons'. The development of fustians was a feature of the period in Western Europe. They were not much taken up in East Anglia; but with the shrinkage of the old woollens in Westmorland and Lancashire, fustians were imitated in the new centres there. A new departure called 'cottons' — a mixture of wool and linen — was made in the neighbourhood of Manchester.[4] The two great northern counties had the inestimable advantage of being free from the restrictive legislation that controlled southern industry, so that it was free to experiment.[5] By 1610 Lancashire was making fustians of cotton proper, " a kind of bombast or down, a fruit of the earth growing upon little shrubs or bushes, brought into this kingdom by the Turkey merchants . . . commonly called cotton wool ".[6] We all know to what an astonishing future that led. Nothing is more remarkable in the age than its readiness to experiment in anything, in what it ate or read or wrote, in what it wore or made, its passion to learn new arts. An English factor in Turkey in 1582 receives the instruction — " to amend the dyeing of England, learn to know all the materials and substances that the Turks use in dyeing " and he is to send home samples of any cloth not made here.[7] We shall see later that what this country owed to its material acquisitions and gains from abroad is exactly and entirely paralleled in the realm of the mind, in literature, science and the arts.

Other, smaller, industries testified in their quiet way to the

[1] q. Wadsworth and Mann, p. 12.
[2] H. Heaton, *The Yorkshire Woollen and Worsted Industry*, p. 77. [3] *Ibid.* p. 79.
[4] *V.C.H. Lancaster*, II. 296. [5] Wadsworth and Mann, *op. cit.* p. 69.
[6] *V.C.H. Lancaster*, II. 380. [7] Lipson, *op. cit.* p. 85.

rising standard of living, the demands of luxury, the better exploitation of the country's resources. There was the straw-plaiting of Berkshire, the pillow-lace-making of Buckinghamshire traditionally brought in by Katherine of Aragon — which probably means that it was brought in at that time. Glove-making went forward in Somerset, where it still is. The pin industry developed rapidly from the mid-century; it had not much importance before.[1] Mrs. van der Plasse introduced the art of starching — which so annoyed the irritable Puritan Stubbes, and out of which she made a nice little fortune.[2] At Stonesfield in Oxfordshire the discovery of the process of splitting the 'green' rock, with the sap in it, by frost was made before the end of the century.[3] Hence arose that small delightful Cotswold industry, which came to an end, alas, in our time, leaving those memorials of itself, the roofs of Cotswold villages and of Oxford colleges. At Canford in Dorset, Camden tells us that Lord Mountjoy, studious in mineral matters, had begun to make copperas (vitriol) and to boil alum; so too Sir Thomas Chaloner, a learned searcher into Nature's works, at Guisbrough in Yorkshire.[4]

The Sheldons of Beoley, a Catholic family, were responsible for acclimatising the art of tapestry-weaving here.[5] William Sheldon sent his servant, Richard Hicks, abroad to learn it. His motives were characteristic: "For that this trade will be greatly beneficial to this commonwealth to trade youth in and a means to store great sums of money within this Realm that will issue and go out of this Realm for the same commodities to the maintenance of the foreign parts and to the hindrance of this commonwealth". Catholic or Protestant, they had the economic advantage of the country always before their eyes, and were they not right? On such foundations its subsequent greatness was built. There was equally the motive of employment. When Fisher, the town clerk of Warwick, came to see Leicester at Greenwich about his town's poverty, Leicester replied: "I marvel you do not devise some ways among you to have some special trade to keep your poor on work such as Sheldon of Beoley devised, which methinketh should be not only very profitable but also a means to keep your poor from idleness".[6] From Sheldon's works at Beoley and at

[1] Hamilton, *op. cit.* p. 46.
[2] Cunningham, *op. cit.* p. 148.
[3] W. J. Arkell, *Oxford Stone*, p. 131.
[4] Camden, *Britannia*, pp. 217, 721.
[5] E. A. B. Barnard and A. J. B. Wace, "The Sheldon Tapestry Weavers and their Work", *Archaeologia* (1928), p. 255 foll.
[6] T. Kemp, *The Black Book of Warwick*, p. 48.

Barcheston came the well-known tapestry maps of English counties, and their *chefs-d'œuvre*, the Hatfield Seasons.[1] William Sheldon had made his fortune out of the suppression of the monasteries;[2] upon his tomb in Beoley church his son inscribed with just pride: "eo animo in patriam ut tapetum texendi artem in Angliam suo sumptu advexerit, certasque pecuniarum summas ad fovendos in eo genere artifices testamento legaverit". To what more agreeable purpose could the spoils of the monasteries be devoted?

Cloth continued to constitute the bulk of the export trade, but a great change took place in its organisation and direction. The large part that the foreign merchants of the Hanse had in the export was extinguished and the native Merchant Adventurers gained a virtual monopoly.[3] It was one more indication of the country's economic advance and greater strength. The Merchant Adventurers represented the bulk of the leading merchants engaged in the export trade: some 3500 of them from the commercial and maritime towns mainly along the east and south coasts. This was their heyday, when they "won English trade from the foreigner and laid for Englishmen the basis for their later commercial supremacy".[4] There was a prolonged duel between the Hanse and the Merchant Adventurers; we have seen Gresham advising the Queen to rely on her own merchants — as against Mary's continental leanings — and to abate the privileges of the foreigners. These had actually enjoyed the privilege of paying slightly lower export duties than the native English, an anomaly Elizabethan England could hardly be expected to continue. But the Hanse obstinately refused to abandon its former privileges in England or its claim to privileges over English traders in Germany. A declining organisation, hugging the illusions of the medieval into a different age, it hoped to go on having the best of both worlds: in the event it got the worst of both and went the way of all

[1] These will be discussed in Vol. III.

[2] Sheldon took part in the suppression of Pershore, acquired many of the properties and made large purchases of the contents of Bordesley abbey, and was receiver of monastic estates for the Crown in Warwickshire. He bought Weston manor, where he built a splendid house, and emparked 300 acres. The looms were set up in the buildings of Bordesley abbey. He died a good Catholic in 1570, his son "in the verities of the Catholic church" in 1613; both were buried in Beoley church. Their great house at Weston is no more (John Humphreys, "Elizabethan Sheldon Tapestries", *Archaeologia*, 1923–4, p. 181 foll.; Barnard and Wace, *loc. cit.*).

[3] For figs. cf. A. Friis, *Alderman Cockayne's Project and the Cloth Trade*, p. 62.

[4] W. E. Lingelbach, *The Merchant Adventurers of England*, pp. xvi, xx.

institutions that fail to adapt themselves, to ossification and decay.[1]

The Merchant Adventurers came to be attacked by the end of the reign, as it has been in our time by the economic historian,[2] as a monopoly. In a sense the contemporary criticism was a tribute to its very success. It had so enormously expanded the export of cloth abroad that a great many more merchants and traders at home were anxious to jump on the band-wagon. The trade was full of interlopers ready to insert themselves into every crevice afforded by the disturbed conditions of the duel with Spain and the long war. But it is precisely the disturbed conditions of the time that made such a strong organisation with its virtual monopoly necessary. To criticise it in terms of the halcyon conditions of late Victorian free trade is quite unhistorical. So much of economic life, indeed of social life, in the sixteenth century was organised, regulated, controlled. It had to be, or there would have been economic anarchy and circumstances would have run away with them. That is not to say that an increasing measure of freedom and flexibility was not the way of progress. Burghley was aware of that: he moved with the times, more than most. So that John Wheeler, the Secretary of the Merchant Adventurers, in his well-known *Defence* of them, had no difficulty in answering the critics.[3] His bias against " a private, irregular and straggling trade " was in sixteenth-century circumstances well justified. There was, for one thing, the necessity of defence in seas upon which piracy and privateering were rife and lands in which war was endemic. For another, he showed that when organisation had been suspended and the stragglers had their way, the price of cloth fell and " the trade was utterly spoiled ". He established the point that the Merchant Adventurers were well able to buy up all the cloth available for export and sell it abroad so that no-one need complain of lack of vent. (No doubt what they might more legitimately complain of was the difficulty in becoming a member of the Fellowship.) He estimated the total exports as being 60,000 white cloths worth not less than £600,000 sterling, and 40,000 coloured cloths worth one with another £400,000 per annum. A little later Camden valued it at a million and a half. The importance of finding new markets for English cloth in the

[1] Cf. Lingelbach, p. xxviii: " It was a struggle between the representatives of the medieval organisation and federative system of the Hanseatic League on the one hand, and exponents of the growing nationalism and the centralised monarchy of England on the other ".

[2] Cf. G. Unwin, " The Merchant Adventurers' Company in the Reign of Elizabeth ", in *Studies in Economic History*.

[3] Wheeler, *A Treatise of Commerce*; Tawney and Power, *op. cit.* III. 280 foll.

outer world is well to the fore in Hakluyt's propaganda for colonising enterprise overseas and appears again and again in the preliminary publicity for voyages of discovery.

The leading themes of this chapter are given concrete, coloured illustration in the story of the companies for overseas voyages and trading which are such a memorable feature of the age: the growth of capital and its operations, the development of joint-stock enterprise, the fruitful incentives of profit, the advantages and disadvantages of regulation as against a free trade. We have to keep in mind the three periods into which the reign falls. The first twelve years, 1558–69, are a period of recovery and consolidation, experiment and new enterprise. They are followed by three years of crisis and tension, 1569–72, in which the various strains and conflicts internal and external come to a head: Elizabeth's government surmounts them successfully, and is enabled to take a more independent road in the world: the pattern of our external relations changes, a new course is set. There follows the high tide of Elizabethan prosperity, 1574–85, in which the Crown's debts are reduced, the burden of taxation is very light, enterprise of every kind leaps ahead. Then comes the great war with Spain, 1585–1604: the heroic age, followed like all such by disillusionment, doubt and difficulties, the familiar symptoms of overstrain, debt and impoverishment, too great an expenditure for the country's resources. But ours was then an expanding economy and, once the war was over, the country went ahead again.

At the beginning of the age, we have seen, scarcity of capital was the limiting factor in the expansion of the economy if not in enterprise. (For they made up in enterprise what they lacked in resources.) Hence a great deal depended on the results of the early companies.[1] It has been shown that the profits they made on balance, as against their losses, were already increasing the capital of the country. By 1569 some £100,000 were invested in them, or rather under 50 per cent of the net ordinary revenue. The indirect advance of joint-stock enterprise was even more important, for it increased the flow of capital and its mobility out of all proportion to the amount. The Russia Company, the first of the great joint-stock companies, went back to the Edwardian impulse. Founded in 1553 with a capital of £6000, it came to have some 200 to 240 members: the mercantile middle class

[1] The above account is based on Scott, *Joint-Stock Companies*, I. 42 foll.

were very much in the majority, where the Mines Royal and the Mineral Works were more mixed, with a strong Court element. It was the merchants who made the profits. Through Archangel as their port the English were the first in the field of Russian trade; they had the expectation of the entire monopoly of imports and exports into and from Russia. The capture of Narva in 1558 altered this, gave a new and shorter route via the Baltic, which later gave the Dutch their opportunity. The English Company wanted the Czar to exclude them; disappointed of his hopes of an English alliance, he refused. But the trade prospered and was very profitable up to 1585. In the earlier years the Company had almost a monopoly in Oriental commodities and in imports of naval stores. The Persian expedition of 1568–73 showed how profitable the former were: although two-thirds of the goods were lost on the journey the profit made equalled the whole capital.

The Russia Company was the pivot of English maritime enterprise northward — to which the Spaniards desired it to be limited — in these early years. Already by 1556 exploration had been carried as far as the Obi in the attempt to find an English North-Eastern route to the Far East. Defeated along this line, the London merchants gave their backing to Frobisher's voyages to find a North-Western route through North American waters. By 1582 £20,000 had been spent, with nothing to show for it. Drake had by now shown a better way: to attack the Spanish monopoly of southern routes and waters and to enter boldly their privileged seas. There was never a more successful or celebrated exponent of the belief in *la carrière ouverte aux talents*. The capital invested in his voyage round the world was some £5000. The results of this modest outlay were startling, and resounded, like the voyage itself, round the world. The treasure brought back was some £600,000; the dividends to shareholders some 4700 per cent. Burghley was in favour of returning all the overplus to Spain; but the Queen, who had invested in the voyage — as we now know, the Spaniards merely suspected it — overruled him. Most of the proceeds went on a more vigorous policy in the Netherlands, subsidising Alençon against the Spaniards. The freedom of the Netherlands was a crucial matter for us, not for Spain: the struggle with Spain was therefore inevitable since Philip insisted on their subjugation. War by joint-stock enterprise was proving very successful and even profitable; its diplomatic advantages were corresponding, as the Queen could reply to Mendoza's protests against Drake: "The gentleman careth not if I disavow him". Hawkins thought that the wealth of England had trebled since the Queen's accession, and even the cautious Burghley admitted in 1579 that the country was "abounding in riches".

Next year Philip's acquisition of Portugal and the Portuguese Empire made it urgent to get spices independently of Lisbon. Two important London merchants — one of them Edward Osborne, ancestor of Danby — took the initiative in sending William Harborne, with the government's backing, to make contact with Turkey and open the trade routes of the Levant to English commerce.[1] Harborne was notably successful: his vein of patriotic assertion yielded returns at the Porte: Nashe pays appropriate tribute to him: "Mercurial-breasted Mr. Harborne . . . who hath noised the name of our island and of Yarmouth so tritonly that not an infant of the cur-tailed skin-clipping pagans but talk of London as frequently as of their prophet's tomb at Mecca". Harborne won generous capitulations for English trade against the opposition of both French and Venetians, who wanted to keep us out; he became both diplomatic and commercial representative at the Porte and even secured a reduction of customs duties in our favour: "The Englishman had firmly laid the foundations of his country's influence in the Near East, and never again was it in any real danger of extinction by rival influence".[2] On this basis the trade was organised under the aegis of the Levant Company. The trading Queen lent Osborne 10,000 lb. of Drake's silver. A profit of 300 per cent was made. In 1583 Newberry was sent from Aleppo down the Euphrates to establish an overland route to India; from 1583 to 1591 he, Ralph Fitch and their companions travelled overland, down the Persian Gulf to India, Burma, Malacca — an even more astounding feat, considering the difficulties of land travel, than any but the most spectacular sea voyages. This attempt came just after the failure of Fenton's voyage, which was intended to follow up the trading contacts established by Drake in the Far East on his way home round the world. But the real fulfilment of that was to come, after all, by sea and was not far ahead.

Defeated by Harborne at the Porte, the Venetians tried reprisals by forbidding the entry of English merchants into the Adriatic. The Queen waited for ten years while the Venetians took no notice, then in 1592 she cracked down on them by prohibiting all import of currants by Venetians. The Levant Company thus gained a highly lucrative monopoly — which the

[1] A. C. Wood, *A History of the Levant Company*, p. 7.
[2] *Ibid.* p. 14.

Crown ultimately shared — to offset losses by the war. By 1592 the Company had a membership of 53 merchants, with an option for 20 more; by 1599 it had 87 members and 189 servants, and 20 vessels operating in Italian waters alone. In Egypt the struggle was lost to the French: we had no Harborne there. The interest in Turkey and the Levant made its impression not only on the purses of Elizabethan merchants but in the minds of their dramatists. There is Marlowe's most popular play, that long held the stage, *Tamburlaine the Great*; Kyd presented the story of Suleiman and the fall of Rhodes; Shakespeare, less well educated than they, writes easily

> Not Amurath to Amurath succeeds,

and assumes his audience's response.

Meanwhile the Dutch were advancing their direct contacts by sea with India. The Dutch East India Company was formed and was very successful from the first. They took their opportunity to raise the price of pepper enormously.[1] The prospects of the Levant Company were depressed by the war in the Mediterranean, the uncertainties in the Levant most of all by the returns on the direct route to India. The Levant merchants got together with others to form the East India Company, which was given its charter in 1600: 218 members with the monopoly of all trade from the Cape to Magellan. It was difficult to collect instalments on the shares, and the English Company, unlike the Dutch — which continued to be disgracefully profitable — had bad luck with its first voyages. Ships were lost; there was a failure to float stock for the second voyage till the result of the first was known; when the ships of the second returned the country was in the grip of the plague of 1603. But when the accounts of both voyages were made up there was a dividend of 195 per cent while those who had paid up on both shares received a substantial bonus. The third voyage, the proceeds of which were distributed along with the first two, made a total distribution of 334 per cent, of which the profit was 224 per cent. The most profitable distribution of all was that in 1612 — some 320 per cent. That must have cured the sceptics and encouraged the adventurous. It is recorded that it put new life into the trade. No wonder! When the Company was attacked Dudley Digges was able to show that £200,000 worth of pepper had been re-exported, while the reduction of prices in England had saved the country £70,000 a year. Everyone then appreciated the bearing of such an argument;

[1] Scott, *op. cit.* II. 90 foll.

the Company enjoyed a period of undisturbed prosperity till towards the end of James's reign.

There is a clear distinction between voyages for opening up foreign trade and voyages for colonisation.[1] The former normally made money, the latter invariably lost it. Gilbert and Ralegh spent fortunes upon their dream of colonising North America with English folk. At last it was Joint-Stock that achieved it, but not until £36,000 had been spent in establishing the Virginia Colony. But it did not become successful or secure until the tobacco crop — unexpectedly, almost by accident — rendered a profit and trade became considerable. In Bermuda — the discovery of which suggested *The Tempest* — a rich find of ambergris worth £10,000 tided over the investors; but it was the profit on tobacco that saw the infant colony through. The old-fashioned and ineffectual hidalgo, Mendoza, said of the English: "Profit to them was like nutriment to savage beasts". Ralegh thought 100 per cent on a voyage a small return, and said in his proud way that he "might have gotten more to have sent his ships fishing".[2] But what was wrong with profit? The motive of profit has been responsible for far greater achievements in history than ever the absence of it has been.

We are in a better position now to estimate Burghley's policy in relation to the circumstances of the time. It had the great advantage of a mind of singular intellectual consistency directing the affairs of the country for forty years — an important element in its success. For we must admit that it had the justification of success, the most powerful justification known to history. Burghley was no doctrinaire: never was statesman more responsive to legitimate expressions of opinion, more aware of the changing pressure of circumstance. He was very English in the patient way he tried to seek always the public interest and welfare, to keep the balance of the whole, listening courteously to representations, trying to remedy grievances, bearing no malice when he failed to get his way, sometimes grieved and emitting a groan, but for ever trying to do his best. Hence the immense confidence everyone reposed in him, from the Queen downwards. His conception of the economic well-being of the country comes triumphantly through the test of a long reign, a long and exhausting war, and is an indispensable element in the success of the age. He attached importance to fundamentals: work and enterprise, the

[1] *Ibid.* p. 241 foll.

[2] q. *ibid.* I. 87.

returns from the soil, the opening up of its mineral resources, the acquisition of new skills and inventions, the harvest of the seas, the maintenance of the Navy, the sources of naval and military power, the discouragement of non-productive consumption, the achievement of a favourable balance of trade. " It is manifest ", he wrote, " that nothing robbeth the realm of England but when more merchandise is brought into the realm than is carried forth ", because the balance must be paid in currency. " The remedy hereof is by all policies to abridge the use of such foreign commodities as be not necessary for us." [1] Living at a time when the extent of the adverse balance undermines our whole economy and prejudices the safety of the nation, who can say that he was wrong? The Victorians could afford to ignore his point of view as that of a disproved and erroneous mercantilism. But it was his careful, sparing, capital-building policy that reared the foundations of their prosperity.

Nor, even as a very old man, was Burghley incapable of moving with the needs of the time. He was very much more aware of the mood of lassitude and strain, the actual burdens of the war as it dragged on, than ever the young men at Court were, the men of action who wanted it to go on for ever. In his earlier years he had used the methods of patents of monopoly to plant and encourage new inventions. There could be no objection to this: " Unlike the Continental system, the Elizabethan monopolies are broadly based upon considerations of the value of the industry to the realm ".[2] But he became more and more opposed to the monopolies which trenched upon the liberties or the necessities of the subject: those patents so hungrily competed for by the courtiers, those activities so bitterly described by Spenser in *Mother Hubberd's Tale*. If Burghley had lived in the reign of Charles I he would have been a Parliamentarian — as his descendants were. He refused to give his consent to a patent for making vinegar and aqua vitae to Richard Drake, " unless every poor subject might have liberty to make it in his own house and for their own use of what stuff best liked them ".[3] He was opposed to the Newcastle monopoly of the Tyne coal trade: Robert Cecil was informed of " the dislike my lord your father hath of it, holding the same to be an absolute monopoly; and in spite of much speech and writing I am void of hope to win him to anything of the same ". Robert Cecil continued his father's attitude: " And for monopolies . . . I hold them for the most part con-

[1] q. Cunningham, *Growth of English Industry and Commerce*, II. 71.

[2] q. Hughes, *Studies in Administration and Finance*, p.31. [3] *Ibid.* p. 59.

tentious and grievous to the subject, chiefly such as touch the poorer sort ".[1] The giving way of the government to the Commons in regard to monopolies, the conversion later of Ralegh to the idea of freedom of trade,[2] would not have been uncongenial to Burghley. He was a man who moved with the times in such things. A new age had other needs and circumstances, demanded a different outlook.

If we want to know what were the foundations of the prosperity that carried the Elizabethan Age upwards, here they are. If we want to know the secret of its miraculous achievement — as far as it can be explained — here is a part of it.

[1] *Ibid.* p. 62.

[2] Cf. Ralegh, " Observations touching Trade and Commerce ", *Works* (ed. Oldys and Birch), VIII, 351 foll.

CHAPTER V

LONDON AND THE TOWNS

IT is difficult to render the sense of movement in what is essentially a portrait. But in the case of the towns, especially of London, it is easier to grasp with the eye of imagination the pulsating rhythms of the life that passed in and out of them, the ups of some places, the downs of others, the emptying by plague and epidemics and the rapid filling up from the countryside, the movements like cloud or sun passing over the landscape which bring some areas into light where others are left in shadow. We can thus visualise pictorially something of the effect of the radiation of a money economy more widely over the country. Like water finding its own level, the balance of wealth becomes a little more equalised over the regions. In medieval England some regions were rich and others were poor: we have ocular demonstration of this in the splendid churches and finer domestic architecture of the eastern counties and the clothing district of the West, compared with the remoter West, Wales and the North. Now with the extension of a money economy and greatly increasing wealth, things were beginning to even out a little: one has the clear impression that the West is coming up, towns in the North are beginning to go ahead. The landscape is changing under our eyes.

For example, the smaller towns of Devonshire are going ahead. Exeter is bursting with activity, with trade and consequence and a crowded civic life. The clothing towns, Tiverton, Crediton, South Molton are thriving; Totnes, Dartmouth, Barnstaple are prosperous. The foundations of Plymouth's fortune were laid in Henry VIII's reign, but as a town it is an Elizabethan creation: it was then that it was fortified and grew strong — the maritime base at the Channel entrance, the starting-point for all those fleets and voyages. Poole was recovering from its decayed state with the growth of the Newfoundland fishery.[1] In the North, Newcastle with its coal trade

[1] J. Hutchins, *History of Dorset* (ed. Shipp and Hodson), I. 7. In 1574 it had 1373 inhabitants, of whom 165 were householders.

grew even faster than Plymouth: another characteristically Elizabethan town, at least in its growth. Berwick may be regarded as almost a creation of the time: it was then that it was surrounded by a second set of walls, which still remain, and that it enjoyed its heyday as a frontier town. Halifax, Leeds and Wakefield were just getting going; Manchester blossomed — if that is the word — rather suddenly into " the fairest, best builded, quickest and most populous town of all Lancashire ".[1] That was not saying much: Cheshire was still a more populous county than Lancashire. Birmingham, like Manchester, was just rising from very small manorial beginnings: it was still only one-sixth the size of Coventry.[2] These smaller Midland towns were starting their fabulous rise with Midland industry.

But we must not press too fast or too far. We must remember that we are in a country in which Totnes is more important than Liverpool, Maidstone twice the size of Manchester; in which Stratford-on-Avon is a borough with its corporation and its gilds while Birmingham is a manorial village governed by a court-leet and a couple of bailiffs. The small town of Sheffield is a manor of the Earl of Shrewsbury and governed as such, completely dominated by the castle within and the manor-house on its hill without. We have to keep in our mind's eye a map of England in which the East still is more important than the West, and the West than the North; in which the leading manufacturing town in the kingdom and the most populous — after London — is Norwich. Governmentally, the second town in the country, and one of the largest, is York: the administrative capital of the North, seat of the Council of the North, as Ludlow and Shrewsbury are of the Marches of Wales. Bristol is the third or fourth town in the country: active and very prosperous, but less populous than Norwich.[3]

Then, too, we must visualise an England in which London — though then recognisably a town, or rather two, instead of an octopoid sprawl — had a far greater ascendancy than today. No other town came anywhere near it in size or importance; it was of a different order of magnitude. Where Norwich had a population of perhaps 17,000, London's was nearing 300,000 and increasing rapidly.[4] The annual value of its customs was

[1] Leland q. in A. Redford, *Hist. of Local Government in Manchester*, I. 25.

[2] C. Gill, *Studies in Midland History*, p. 89.

[3] The Chantry Commissioners estimated the population of Bristol at not much over 6000. This was *c.* 1546–7 (J. Latimer, *Bristol in the Sixteenth Century*, p. 24).

[4] W. Hudson and J. C. Tingey, *Records of the City of Norwich*, II. cxxvi-cxxvii, estimate the plague mortality, 1579–80, at 5000, and the survivors at 12,000 to 13,000.

over twenty times that of Bristol, which came next.[1] Indeed its importance surpassed that of all the rest of the leading towns together. It was already the largest town in Europe, and one of the most beautiful. It may seem paradoxical that this was the case at a time when conditions were evening out a bit over the rest of the country. But it is not contradictory; it is part of the same movement: the commercial and financial effects of the metropolis are felt to the furthest extremities of the national economy. Everywhere there are complaints that London is absorbing the trade of the whole nation, and with some truth, even when we allow for the sixteenth-century habit of thought that if someone got the trade, someone else went without. (Little conception of reciprocal services, or recognition that they got anything in return. But there, too, the sixteenth century was at least as right as the nineteenth, with its opposite inflection.) Bristol complained; Norwich and Newcastle stood on their rights; Southampton moaned, very understandably, for London had taken away all its trade: the town was in visible decay. The whole country felt increasingly the economic pull of London; it may be seen in the individual careers of successful young men from the provinces, like Peter Blundell of Tiverton, Nicholas Mosley from Manchester, William Lambarde's father from Ledbury. The old medieval families of London, the Cornhills, the Faringdons, the Buckerels and Basings, had long ago died out, so long ago that their dust was no longer remembered in the churches. The city was more of a metropolis, to which people came from all over the country to make their fortune.

In the towns we can distinguish, even more clearly, what we observed in the country at large, the contrast between depression and decline in the earlier part of the century and the recovery and increasing wealth of Elizabeth's reign. We can observe even more vividly in them — in the wrecked and roofless churches, the cloisters turned into storehouses, the brasses ripped from their matrices — the grim time the country had been through with the Reformation. It was not without its effect upon the mind of one sensitive observer from the provinces:

> When I have seen by time's fell hand defaced
> The rich proud cost of outworn buried age;
> When sometime-lofty towers I see down razed,
> And brass-eternal slave to mortal rage. . . .

In general, the same thing happened here as happened with the country at large. After the upset, the dislocation and readjust-

[1] W. Barrett, *Hist. and Antiquities of the City of Bristol*, p. 186.

ments of the Reformation, the conversion of Church properties to more productive uses, the extinction of a good deal of non-productive expenditure on processions and wakes and ridings and what not, the towns for the most part absorbed experience with the property, profited by it and went ahead. There were, of course, towns that were losers by it, those towns whose prosperity stood by some great foundation: Bury St. Edmunds or Glastonbury, Malmesbury — though Stumpe's factory in the abbey tided it over for a time; ecclesiastical centres like Canterbury and York must have been losers by the downfall of their rich foundations — though that consideration did not prevent the townsmen welcoming the destruction of their ancient enemies under whose ascendancy they had long groaned. Smaller places went downwards with their smaller foundations: a crabbed little Cornish town like Bodmin was never much afterwards; a village like St. Germans ceased to be anything. But in general, like the country as a whole, the towns profited greatly: so many active animals, very much alive and kicking some little time after they had gorged themselves on a good meal.

Earlier in the century they were nothing like so prosperous; indeed there is a great deal of evidence of decline and decay. Here too we must distinguish. London was always an exception: and later on when the towns in general were prospering, some were languishing for special causes, some were going downhill as others came up. The Statute Book of Henry VIII is full of attempts to arrest the decay, both of particular towns and of towns in general. Numerous Acts were passed, though if this is evidence of distress it is also evidence of the will to repair and improve. The government was anxious to do its best for the towns, which gave it in turn such unquestioning, such unwavering support. Southampton, owing to the withdrawal of the Italians, the carracks coming there no more, the decay of trade and customs, is excused a former increase on the fee-farm it paid to the Crown.[1] Plymouth is burdened with a large annuity to Plympton priory, and the town is depressed by reason of the intolerable charges it has been at by adventure of sea and otherwise. So the priory is allowed to appropriate two advowsons in lieu of the annuity from Plymouth.[2] The government was inclined in favour of the towns against the Church; nor can we repine, though it means that there is nothing to see now in those nondescript meadows at Plympton.[3] This was in 1534, only a few years before the priory

[1] *Statutes of the Realm*, III. 351.
[2] *Ibid.* p. 475.
[3] Risdon laments its decay (*Survey of Devon* (ed. 1811), p. 196).

itself was extinguished. When we reflect that "the adventures by sea and otherwise" included William Hawkins's promising voyages to Guinea and Brazil, we take " the great ruin and decay " with a pinch of salt. But the upshot was an undoubted benefit to Plymouth, which from this time went forward.

York, by far the largest town of the North in the Middle Ages, was declining and the decay was not arrested. The Earl of Rutland consented to forgo more than half his annual rent on the city, and it was excused part of its remaining annuities to the Crown.[1] To offset the decline in clothing it was given a monopoly in making coverlets. So many benefices in that many-churched city could not be supported owing to the loss of tithes, so the Mayor and Corporation were permitted to pull down a number of superfluous churches and unite the livings.[2] Of forty parish churches, fifteen were destroyed. York lost its medieval supremacy, but not its population; the actual built-up area grew in extent in Elizabeth's reign, with the covering of monastic sites and gardens. In spite of the growth of Hull, of which York was very jealous, its trade was still three times that of Hull and its population much larger.[3] Canterbury was also in some trouble about its charters, " whereof not only the good civil policy of the said city is much decayed but also the wealthy occupying, the populous inhabiting and the beautiful building thereof be like to come in great ruin, depopulation and decay, not a little to the extenuation of that part of this Realm as well in the eyes of all strangers as in the eyes of such great personages as shall happen to have repair to the King's Majesty or otherwise ".[4] A characteristic Tudor motive for action! In these years there was a great drive to encourage and compel the rebuilding of decayed houses in nearly all the leading towns of the country: scores of them are named in four general Statutes of 1536–42.[5] Norwich, which still had many void spaces of ground after a fire years before, is told to get cracking: if owners do not rebuild within two years the corporation shall do so.[6] Lynn likewise.[7] One sees how much nearer the bone they were in medieval circumstances: the destruction of a quay — it is a frequent motif[8] — and a town may be ruined. Houses down, a town is grievously impoverished. Under a money economy the loss is spread over the country: in the sixteenth century there was nothing to disguise the raw facts of

[1] *Stats. of the Realm*, III. 582, 908.
[2] *Ibid.* IV. 14.
[3] C. B. Knight, *Hist. of the City of York*, p. 407.
[4] *Stats. of the Realm*, III. 917.
[5] *Ibid.* pp. 531, 768–9, 875.
[6] *Ibid.* p. 504.
[7] *Ibid.* p. 505.
[8] Cf. Scarborough, *ibid.* p. 1001.

economic life: people entertained the less illusions — at least in that sphere.

The author of the *Discourse of the Commonweal* gave what he thought to be the reasons for the decay of the towns: the fact that London had captured so many local markets and people bought their goods from thence, many of them imported from overseas when they might be made here.[1] The import of luxuries and trifles should be cut down, and " as for silks, wines and spices, if there came less over, it made no matter ". He was above all anxious that we should work up our own raw materials and export them in the form of finished manufactures, thereby creating the more employment within the country. This, which is sometimes called Mercantilism, might also be called common sense. He favoured those trades that brought most work to a town, as " making of glasses, making of swords, daggers, knives, and all tools of iron and steel; also making of pins, points, laces, thread and all manner of paper and parchments. I have heard say that the chiefest trade of Coventry was heretofore in making blue thread, and then the town was rich, even upon that trade only; and now our thread comes all from beyond the seas; wherefore that trade of Coventry is decayed, and thereby the town likewise. So Bristol had a trade by making points, and was the chiefest mystery that was exercised in the town." He was all in favour of the open door to foreign workers bringing new trades and crafts into the country, and showed progressive good sense against the obscurantism that would keep them out. It is noticeable how much these ideas from the reign of Edward VI are in keeping with Cecil's, who was in a position to act on them in the fifteen-sixties. The absence of further Acts for the repair of towns showed that the situation had improved. The boot was on the other foot now: the growth of London was beyond all bounds; neither proclamations nor statutes could stop it, though the government tried both.[2] Elizabeth was fortunate in that her accession coincided with a time of recovery; her government did everything possible to advance it.

What was happening may be seen from an unspectacular and all the more typical Midland county like Leicestershire.[3] It had only one town of any note, Leicester itself, with a population of 600 families — possibly three or four thousand people. The

[1] E. Lamond (ed.), *A Discourse of the Common Weal*, pp. 125-31.

[2] *Stats. of the Realm*, III. 852.

[3] For the information in this paragraph I am much indebted to the kindness of Dr. W. G. Hoskins.

population was rising steadily, especially in the last quarter of the century. A wealthy class of tanners, butchers and drapers was emerging, as in other Midland towns, like Rugby and Birmingham. There was prosperity at the top, and perhaps a larger number of poor at the bottom: a finer class-differentiation in consequence of increasing wealth. The prosperity of the town was based on the extensive cattle pastures round it. One or two of the smaller towns, Melton Mowbray and Loughborough, were growing also; each contained a few wealthy merchants and traders. Such lesser market towns in each county were important economic centres in their own countryside and add up to a considerable total of people and wealth, though each is negligible in itself. In Devon, for instance, such market towns were Torrington — the best market in Devon by the fifteen-eighties — Honiton, Ashburton, Tavistock, Modbury.[1] The clothing towns, Tiverton, South Molton and Totnes, owed something of their prosperity to their being food markets; and this was still more true of larger commercial towns, like Exeter and Plymouth.

We can now turn to the developments characteristic of the towns and showing their place in the country as a whole.

They are becoming stronger in themselves with growing prosperity and maturing experience, and this shows itself in the general movement to free themselves from the vestiges of their earlier dependence upon Crown, feudal lords or Church in matters of their internal government.[2] 'Independence' is too strong a word; for English towns — again with the exception of London — had never been strong enough to behave as independent potentates like many continental towns, as indeed Huguenot towns were behaving in France at this moment. In England the State was too strong and too well integrated. The development may be described better as a growth of administrative self-sufficiency. It meant not less, but more integration into the framework of the State. The towns ran themselves, but they did not run the country. The country was governed by the gentry, with the aid of the new nobility recruited largely from the gentry. The towns gave Tudor government consistent and loyal support, and no wonder after their experience of the brawls of fifteenth-century nobles, the faction fights between Courtenays and Bonvilles at Exeter, between Molyneux and Stanleys at Liverpool. Not a town cat mewed when a Tudor lopped off a noble (opposition)

[1] Risdon tell us that Modbury was noted for its happy ale (*op. cit.* p. 187).

[2] Cf. M. Bateson, *Records of the Borough of Leicester*, III. ix.

head — too many of them had been noble nuisances, from a good bourgeois point of view.

Again we must not go too far, if we are to hold fast to truth. The consolidation of internal self-sufficiency in the towns was by no means complete; and though the old nobles had lost their feudal lordship over them — where they had had it — the new magnates had much influence and even power with them. As usual, the English social order had conserved a good deal of what was useful beneath the changes of the time: English conservatism is always utilitarian rather than doctrinaire. In this matter, as in so many others, Elizabeth's reign was a transition — the word is hardly avoidable — between what is medieval and what is specifically modern. In the Elizabethan equilibrium there is invariable deference on the part of the town to the neighbouring magnate: sack and sugar whenever he passes through or pays it an official visit to view the musters or settle a dispute, hippocras and biscuits for my lady, payments to my lord's players, constant presents to keep his favour. On the lord's part he is apt to intervene a good deal in town affairs, sometimes at their request, sometimes not; in some instances he still wields power — though as with all Elizabethan government (and this is its secret) it was the power of prestige not of feudal rights. It was quite frequent for the lord to nominate one of the town's members of Parliament, the town the other. The pattern is subtle, various and shifting. The relation depended very much on circumstances. A large and powerful town like Bristol enjoyed the favour of the Earl of Leicester — which meant that he looked after its interests at the centre; he did not enjoy any power within it.[1] But then the neighbouring Berkeleys, who might have exerted it, were Catholics and under a shadow. The Duke of Norfolk had a good deal of influence in Norwich; but he resided there in his large, never finished and now vanished Palace by the Maddermarket with its gardens sloping down to the river. When his head fell, the town — by exception — regretted it, for he had made himself useful to it and kept great hospitality there, relieving many poor folk.[2] We must in short distinguish between the influence exerted by some leading figure at Court, whom the town had made its steward or such in return for his patronage and favour, and the real power exerted by a great magnate residing nearby.

An interesting example of the latter is the relation of the Earl

[1] He was High Steward of the city and was succeeded as such by Burghley, who was succeeded by Robert Cecil. The annual pension of the office was £10.

[2] F. Blomefield, *Hist. of Norfolk* (ed. 1806), III. 294, 296.

of Huntingdon to the town of Leicester.[1] One of the older nobility with royal blood in his veins, and in the line of possible succession to the throne, the Earl was yet of Puritan leanings — which are traceable in the family since. As Lord President of the North he was one of the inner governing circle. He was hereditarily Steward of the honour of Leicester, and from his great house at Ashby-de-la-Zouch evidently looked upon Leicester as his town. He built a house out of the materials of the abbey — fragments of it remain still on the site — and had a town house in the High Street. His relations with the town were amicable, eleemosynary and authoritative. As Lord-Lieutenant of the county he could determine the military levy on the borough, its contribution to poor relief, assess points in dispute with other towns. He interfered in small appointments, recommended (prematurely) a successor to the Recorder, made his wishes known in elections of M.P.s, along with the Chancellor of the Duchy of Lancaster and the Privy Council, while the town, whose chief motive was the avoidance of expense, modestly confined itself to wishing that the member might be one of the burgesses if possible. He defended the interests of the poor against the burgesses and gave money and coals for poor relief, aided the setting up of a workhouse, supported a preacher and controlled the appointment.[2] His players and his bearward, his jester and musicians often visited the town and received rewards from the burgesses for their entertainment. Now he lies in effigy on his mouldering tomb at Ashby, in the crumbling panoply of his greatness with all his titles and honours set out, in the church next the ruined and slighted great house — monument in its way to the social struggle of the Civil War.

There was a universal tendency on the part of the towns towards legal incorporation by obtaining a charter from the Crown.[3] In consequence, scores of charters were granted, many of them confirmations and re-grants of former charters with extended privileges. The avidity of the towns for them testified how important it was to them to have a charter. It was the hallmark of their self-government; the instrument defined their precise rights and privileges and made them secure. Those who had not a charter hastened to obtain one; those who had were willing to spend a good deal of money for a re-grant with extended privileges. Newcastle spent the very large sum of £635 : 10s. to obtain the

[1] Cf. Bateson, *op. cit.* pp. xxii-xxiv. [2] *Ibid.* pp. xxxiii, xlvii.
[3] M. Weinbaum, *British Borough Charters, 1307–1660*, p. xii.

Great Charter of 1600, though this was exceptional.[1] There were recognised ways of raising the money. At Shrewsbury twenty burgesses were taken in and made free of the town at £5 each, to meet the expenses of the suit for an extended charter.[2] The charter was worth money to the town in the privileges and rights it conferred or confirmed, to levy tolls and taxes, to regulate markets and fairs and take their profits, to receive rents and rates and so on. Regarded as a general development, incorporation was the objective of the towns. The perpetuity of status assured them permanent enjoyment of all their previous privileges; the power of suing and being sued protected the town officials and made possible the growth of a competent class of administrators. The Reformation gave the added motive of the desire to take over and use Church properties, often for schools or guildhalls or workhouses; the great impetus given to education was another motive, for many towns wished to make provision for a grammar school. The Crown was willing enough to leave local matters to them and used them as its agents in administering the local end of the country's affairs. "This elaborate piece of statecraft, the charter of incorporation, was the nucleus of British self-government." [3]

From the side of the government a charter was the sanction of a town's good behaviour. Maidstone, which was incorporated by Edward VI, forfeited its privileges for Wyatt's Rebellion under Mary. Elizabeth immediately restored them, adding further privileges, along with that of sending two burgesses to Parliament.[4] The town occasionally returned one official member and one local man.[5] For the manner of drawing up a charter we have a pleasant light from Shrewsbury.[6] Two of its agents, probably burgesses who had been sent up to London for the purpose, write to the bailiffs that they have been through the old charters and "taken a consideration of further things we want and do desire, and for help herein a search hath been made through all the best and latest renewed charters we could meet with, as well in the Rolls as by other help privately, that out of these posies (as it were) we might pick such flowers as might best serve our turns. These are now set forwards to be drawn together in good form." They report that they had been with the Lord Chancellor to favour the suit. The expenses were £94 : 9 : 8; we remember how the Corporation proposed to cover them.

From the point of view of the towns, the right to return

[1] R. Welford, *Hist. of Newcastle and Gateshead*, III. 132.
[2] H. Owen and J. B. Blakeway, *Hist. of Shrewsbury*, I. 378.
[3] Weinbaum, *op. cit.* p. xxvi.
[4] Hasted, *Hist. of Kent* (ed. 1798), IV. 272.
[5] *Ibid.* p. 281 foll.
[6] Owen and Blakeway, *op. cit.* p. 378.

burgesses to Parliament was a subordinate consideration compared with incorporation. Many of them, even considerable towns like Leicester, regarded it in the light of an expense to be avoided. Only the larger towns, that had interests of their own to safeguard or to push, were willing to go to the expense of maintaining two of their own burgesses — in the strict sense — as their members. The largest class were the middle rank of towns which divided their representation, with one member a resident, the other an outsider — more usually a local gentleman, less often a 'carpet-bagger' (to use the modern term for an ancient phenomenon), less frequently again an official member, a member or a nominee of the government. The small boroughs were glad to be represented by anyone who would save them the expense; that was apt to mean the local gentry or those from outside the county, lawyers of the Inns of Court with their way to make, or even townsmen from neighbouring larger towns.

From the country's point of view the increased representation of the towns was a chief and a remarkable phenomenon of Parliament.[1] Elizabeth added 32 boroughs, 64 members to Parliament. This was in response to varying impulses and requests: there is certainly no line of policy to be detected. The impulse came mainly from the localities, from the gentry and local people to whom it was convenient. Some boroughs that got the right to return M.P.s were obviously suitable: Beverley and Richmond in Yorkshire, for example, Maidstone, Andover, Cirencester, Sudbury. Even Fowey had something to be said for it. A number of other boroughs to be enfranchised were on or in the neighbourhood of Crown estates, the duchies of Cornwall or Lancaster.[2] But they did not return official members: for example, Eye in Suffolk was represented regularly by local people, Bacons, Grimstones, Gawdys — and even by a Bedingfield in 1586. There does not seem to be any particular rhyme or reason followed in it.

We have numerous examples of missives to the towns from magnates — courtiers and councillors, peers and gentlemen — requesting or desiring the nomination of a member to Parliament. It is much rarer to find the point of view of the town expressed in the matter. But this we do in the case of Liverpool in 1562.[3] The town was in the habit of reserving one nomination for their

[1] J. E. Neale, *The Elizabethan House of Commons*, chap. vii.

[2] These sentences are based on an examination of the returns in the Parliamentary paper, *Members of Parliament*, Part I, 1213–1702.

[3] J. A. Picton, *Memorials of Liverpool*, I. 53-4.

friendly patron, the Earl of Derby. On this occasion they had, exceptionally, nominated a Molyneux for one seat in return for a favour to the town. Now the Chancellor of the Duchy of Lancaster stepped in with a request for the nomination of a burgess. What were they to do? The Recorder records that the election of Mr. Molyneux had taken place before the Chancellor had communicated his wishes, and that they had " reserved the other for my lord the Earl of Derby, marvelling much that he sent not to the town as he was wont to do requiring the nomination of one burgess, which was a great stay and caused the town to meet in the hall divers times about the same ". Meanwhile the messenger bearing the Chancellor's letters was " willed to go to his dinner, and after that he should be answered ". After deliberation the mayor and his brethren promised that they would send the Chancellor an answer " after my lord the Earl of Derby's pleasure were known to us, whom always we were naturally beholden and bounden to ". So Ralph Seckerston, the leading townsman, rode post to London to see the old Earl. " My lord was well pleased with the town, giving us thanks, and gave his election to Mr. Seckerston. And he showed himself and kept time and hour, but was put back by the means of Mr. Chancellor. Yet he stuck to the matter still and obtained his room and served there. And when other town burgesses had and did retain speakers for them in the Parliament house, he retained none, but stood up after the manner there, and was speaker himself, to the great grief of Mr. Chancellor. So that in his fumes he caused privy seal made and was ready directed to fetch Mr. Mayor up to appear in the Duchy Chamber — but as God would — by means of the Earl of Derby, the privy seal was called in again, which, if it had not, the town would have been put to a great charge. In the meantime a cess was laid for Mr. Seckerston giving his attendance in the Parliament house, for the charges of him, after 2s. a day."

What a vivid revelation this episode is to us: the town's estimate of its representation in Parliament, the official pressure from the Chancellor though this was exceptional and, as we see, defeated, the Earl appearing as their *deus ex machina*. The towns — with one exception always — were as yet nothing like so important as the nobles or the gentry or even the Church.

The thing that strikes one most in getting to know Elizabethan towns is the frequency and tenacity of the disputes, disputes of every kind both within and without, with other towns but especially with other powers, rival jurisdictions. This last, mediēval feature is so ubiquitous as to suggest a general reflection. A large town like Bristol has all the more opportunity — or perhaps we should say in fairness occasion — to indulge the propensity. Of course, like all human bodies it was defending itself. It was engaged on many fronts: disputes with the Lord President of the Marches, with Gloucester, with the Lord-Lieutenant of Gloucestershire, with Lord Pembroke as Lord-Lieutenant of Bristol and Somerset, with the constable and keeper of its own castle. It may be readily seen that all of these disputes were over rival jurisdictions and conducted by the town in the interests of its own independence. There was a prolonged dispute with the Lord President over his claim for contributions to the expenditure of the Council of the Marches, dating from 1542.[1] In 1562 the claim was again raised and the Lord President succeeded in extorting 30s. for harness, pikes, etc. The Mayor and a deputation went to London and secured exemption for ever — at considerable expense. But everybody thought in that age that it was worth while to pursue such a dispute, however little was at stake: such trifles mounted up; money was scarce and worth a great deal; moreover dignity, right was at stake.

The conflict with the Lord-Lieutenant of Gloucestershire was over the town's claim to muster its own troops.[2] This was a frequent source of trouble: all the larger towns claimed the right to muster themselves. With London it was unquestioned. Exeter had sharp disputes with the Earl of Bath as Lord-Lieutenant of Devon over it, before it got its way. Bristol got its independence at once and the town mustered before the Mayor and his brethren. Not only civic pride was involved, but substantial burdens and charges. That it was militarily unsatisfactory went to the hearts of the Lord-Lieutenants, but did not greatly disturb the city fathers: they were not military men, but full of sturdy civilian spirit. (When the Civil War came, did they not defeat the professionals?) When the town's own Lord-Lieutenant, the Earl of Pembroke, came to view the musters along with Mr. Mayor, his reception cost £100.[3] But still piqued at not having been made High Steward — the town thought Leicester a better investment — he ignored the Mayor's right to precedence in his own city and took his upper hand: which gave great offence.

Newcastle spent such time as it could spare from its own internal factiousness, its disputes with the Lord Admiral over

[1] J. Latimer, *Bristol in the Sixteenth Century*, p. 33.
[2] *Ibid.* p. 38. [3] *Ibid.* p. 80.

admiralty jurisdiction in the Tyne and making money fast by the coal trade, in trying to extinguish the liberties of Gateshead which belonged to the Bishop of Durham and was a borough of its own. Whenever nobody was looking Newcastle tried to annex it. Northumberland's plan of abolishing the palatine Bishopric with all its special jurisdiction, and erecting two ordinary sees at Durham and Newcastle with part of the proceeds, has usually been put down to his own covetousness and irreligion. But it is evident that the plan had the enthusiastic support of Newcastle,[1] in which the older and richer townsmen were Catholic by sympathy. The fact was that the plan was a sensible and progressive step, a piece of rationalisation in government. But Northumberland was walking too far ahead of contemporary opinion, certainly in the North. And it is an interesting indication of Elizabeth's government being more conservative than Edward's that she did not go back on Mary's restoration of the Bishopric, though Newcastle would have welcomed its dissolution.

Edward's Act annexing Gateshead to Newcastle, and dissolving the palatinate of Durham, was passed in his last Parliament, and there was considerable opposition on Mary's accession to its restoration. To appease Newcastle Bishop Tunstall made the corporation a beneficial long lease of the Salt Meadows. Even so the repeal only passed in the Commons by 201 votes to 120. Twenty-three years later, in 1576, while the see was vacant, Newcastle made another attempt to annex Gateshead.[2] A bill was read in the Commons. Gateshead was thoroughly aroused and protested to Burghley that it was a borough of its own with 400 householders, holding of the Bishop. It also petitioned the Speaker and found a friend in Fleetwood, Recorder of London, the racy correspondent of Burghley: "I have always found your lordship the patron of that country". The bill was stayed. Burghley had learnt from his experience in the reign of Edward VI that it does not do to walk too far ahead of public opinion even in the best causes. Newcastle was again propitiated by a considerable sop. The Grand Lease of the rich coal-bearing manors of Gateshead and Whickham — of which the new Bishop Barnes had granted the Queen a long lease, a *quid pro quo* for his Bishopric — was granted to Leicester, who assigned it to Thomas Sutton, who conveyed it to Newcastle for £12,000 at the marvellously low rent of £90 per annum.[3] The Grand Lease became a wonderful source of disputes — and of profits — for Newcastle for a long time to come. But the town was not entirely

[1] Welford, *op. cit.* II. 293-306. [2] *Ibid.* p. 476. [3] *Ibid.* p. 501.

propitiated. Honour was involved, as well as profit: what more potent stimulants? Defeated in its second attempt to annex Gateshead, Newcastle tried two years later to prevent a market there.[1] It petitioned the Queen that Newcastle had a market every day of the week and that no other market was kept in any place adjoining the Tyne until this two years past, when Richard Nattras of Gateshead set up a market there, by which Newcastle would not be able to answer its fee-farm to the Queen. This — the usual threat — at a time of roaring profits from the coal trade! The case was heard at York, where the evidence was so conflicting that the poor battered Council could come to no decision.

York had its disputes with Hull and with the Council within its walls;[2] Liverpool with Chester — the younger town resented its subordinate position and receiving its orders from the older in regard to shipping troops to Ireland.[3] Yarmouth had a long and elaborate dispute with Gorleston across the water over the ferry rights there and other matters, a sharp contest with Lowestoft over the herring fishery, and a lingering quarrel with the Cinque Ports over the Yarmouth Herring Fair which was jointly regulated by them.[4] "Although we have lately tolerated your bailiffs to have prenomination to our discredit, whereby you seek advantage against us, we mean not to continue such injury against ourselves; but if you shall be contented with the use of such privileges here as your predecessors of old time", etc.: one sees the importance of legal precedent, of custom in all this. Nashe called Sestos and Abydos "towns that like Yarmouth and Lowestoft were still at wrig wrag and sucked serpentine hatred one against each other".[5] Dunwich struggled with Southwold over the cutting of a channel, but nothing could arrest its sea-fate.[6] Cardiff had a vexatious and intricate dispute with the earls of Pembroke as to their rights of lordship in the town — too complicated to go into here.[7] It was always cropping up and provided good business for the lawyers; after much consultation and disputation it remained much where it was. At Oxford and at Cambridge the town strove with the university authorities.[8]

1 Welford, *op. cit.* II. 504.

2 Knight, *op. cit.* pp. 406-7. In 1578 the city passed an ordinance forbidding citizens to bring actions within the city except before the city courts.

3 Picton, *op. cit.* pp. 70, 81.

4 F. Blomefield, *Norfolk*, XI. 287, 293, 350; *A.P.C. 1596–7*, pp. 66-7, 98-9.

5 *Works* (ed. R. B. McKerrow), III. 195.

6 *A.P.C. 1589–90*, pp. 340-41.

7 J. H. Mathews (ed.), *Records of the County Borough of Cardiff*, I. 390; III. 268.

8 Cf. *A.P.C. 1558–70*, *passim*, and subsequent vols.; and A. Gray, *The Town of Cambridge*, p. 102 foll.

Garrison towns invariably quarrelled with the captains of their forts. Those spiritual garrison towns, the cathedral cities, sometimes squabbled with their bishops; though much less often than in the Middle Ages, for now their forts were much reduced. When Bishop Alley thought to take his seat as a J.P. within the city of Exeter — how reduced a status compared with those great lords, his predecessors! — he found himself rebuffed by the bench.[1] Salisbury and Lincoln enjoyed tiffs with their bishops.[2] Quarrels with commanders of earthly troops were more serious. The Mayor of Portsmouth was locked in combat with the captain of the castle;[3] the disputes between Plymouth and the captains of its port and of St. Nicholas's Island were so embittered and distracting as to threaten good order. As for the eternal disputes between Weymouth and Melcombe Regis, one finds them as endlessly boring and tedious as the Council must have found them in its day.[4] One watches with sympathy the weary Council calling for order in the nursery. Again and again they are reduced to reminding such towns, as in the case of Burghley's own Stamford, that " these uncivil and unneighbourly divisions . . . have been the overthrow and decay of sundry good towns and corporations ".[5]

There is clearly some more specific explanation of such disputatiousness than the usual childishness of men, for that we have always with us. It is that jurisdictions and claims were still very inadequately defined: the Elizabethan world was in that respect still medieval: constitutional development was as yet primitive. Yet there was something primitive too about the people who fought so fiercely: they *were* children, for all their gifts and all their ability. For the wise and adult do not quarrel.

Within the towns the main line of division was one of class; in the larger towns between the moneyed merchant traders and the artificers and small retailers.[6] The lesser crafts spoke for the poor commons against the well-to-do. The larger towns had been full of these class-struggles in the previous century; in the sixteenth century they were much less fierce, partly owing to the fact that the well-to-do were so much more numerous and wealthy that they had won the game. Everywhere the tendency

[1] H.M.C. *Records of the City of Exeter*, p. 46.

[2] H.M.C. *Reports Various*, IV. 225, 230; *A.P.C. 1586–7*, pp. 220-21.

[3] *A.P.C. 1558–70*, *passim*; references to the Plymouth disputes are too numerous to cite, cf. many vols. *A.P.C.*; R. N. Worth, *Cal. of Plymouth Municipal Records*, *passim*.

[4] *A.P.C. 1571–5*, p. 355, and following vols. *passim*.

[5] *A.P.C. 1588–9*, pp. 91-3.

[6] A. S. Green, *Town Life in the Fifteenth Century*, II. 191.

was towards oligarchic government and the closed corporation; where there was any popular election it was hedged round with safeguards and usually indirect. There was much discussion in the nineteenth century about the early democracy of the towns, fostered by the liberalism of that age: theories that have subsequently lost their weight. We understand better now the natural oligarchic conditions of all government, the ordinary common sense that only a few in any community have the ability or the wherewithal to govern others. A grasp of the elementary facts of human nature obviates the necessity for much discussion. The men of standing in any given community will run it. The secret of the success of Tudor government was not that the few ruled, but that they managed to keep the good-will of the many.

The growth of wealth in the towns brought a large accession of support to the governing class: "In a thousand points their interests now coincided with the officials and the gentry in the counties; and their conservative instincts had won the confidence and sympathy of the Court".[1] (When the Civil War came, it came as the result of a split within the ranks of the governing class.) At the same time the growth of the artisans and of the mob increased the sense of danger and the emphasis on authority in every organ of sixteenth-century opinion. Rulers, to be successful, had to be *très sensible*. They were. Nevertheless plenty of jostling and faction and conflict remained. In Nottingham the struggle between the oligarchic Common Council and the burgesses in general had been going on for a century; in 1577 the latter seemed to score a victory, when the number of councillors was raised from 6 to 12 by order of the 45 burgesses of the Clothing.[2] But this increase only added strength to the well-to-do element and the Clothing became still more in effect mere nominees of the Council. In 1580 the Mickletorn Jury therefore asked for the abolition of all councillors except two coroners. The leader of the popular cause was a Millington, uncle of the regicide: one sees how our story hangs together, for the petite-bourgeoisie were a strong element in Cromwell's support. Throughout the years 1600–1604 there were different propositions to extend the Council, some accepted and then overturned, until the burgesses appealed to the Privy Council, who referred the matter to the Judges of Assize. In consequence an order was made establishing a Council of 24, 18 of the Clothing and 6

[1] A. S. Green, *Town Life in the Fifteenth Century*, II. 441.

[2] W. H. Stevenson and J. Raine (ed.), *Records of the Borough of Nottingham*, IV. ix-xviii.

Commoners. By 1606, with all its officers, the Council consisted of 55 members. But still the Mickletorn Jury complained that they were allotting the best of the town lands to themselves. (Why else be a town councillor?)

Nottingham was more democratic in constitution than most towns, and wealth more widely spread;[1] at least there was no one family that was dominant, like the Andersons and their relations at Newcastle. But the town that had the most democratic constitution of all was Norwich. The radical Mrs. Green pays a tribute to the intense vitality and popular vigour of the eastern towns and contrasts them with the apathy of the South, with a town like Southampton where the Mayor had singular pre-eminence and power and the people were completely subject to his authority.[2] At Norwich the hot conflicts of the fifteenth century produced a compromise, as in the government of the kingdom: the Mayor with his perpetual Council of 24, and the Common Council of 60; the ordinances of the upper Council had to be laid before the lower. The compromise worked well in the city, as it did in the kingdom.

In smaller towns the Privy Council was frequently called upon to intervene. At Carlisle, for example, in 1567 where an unsuitable mayor called Dalton had been elected, whose relations with the treasury were unsatisfactory.[3] In 1577 rival mayors were elected at Dover, one of them in opposition to the Privy Council's recommendation; both were called up before it.[4] At Doncaster there was a double election of mayor in 1590: the Common Council chose the old Mayor, Thomas Harrison, whereupon the commonalty elected another.[5] A petition went up to the Privy Council complaining of their "very outrageous and disorderly manner of proceeding". The Council referred the matter to a Judge, instructing him to enjoin them "to leave all factions, partialities and divisions, being a most uncivil and unchristian thing, and that will in the end be the overthrow of the town". The upshot was a compromise. The corporation was vindicated; the number was limited to 24, but on vacancies these were to be filled by election by the aldermen, common council and resident freemen. There was provision for participation by the people, but power was limited to few. At Sandwich

[1] Green, *op. cit.* p. 251.

[2] Green, *op. cit.* pp. 361, 319. But contrast Lynn, which had always been ruled by a small body of wealthy merchants (*ibid.* p. 403).

[3] *A.P.C. 1558–70*, pp. 323, 344, 347, 349-50.

[4] *A.P.C. 1575–7*, pp. 27-8, 39, 41.

[5] *A.P.C. 1590–9*, pp. 128-9, 258, 261-4.

there were such disorderly proceedings by the commonalty that the Lord Warden and the Privy Council deprived them of their votes in 1595.[1] Restored in 1599, they were taken away again in 1603 on account of "the insolence and disorder" of the commons. The common council was to be reduced to 24, and the jurats hereafter were to succeed to the office of mayor by seniority. The government had a horror of popular disorder and this provided a motive for extinguishing a democratic franchise in one of the Cinque Ports. But the movement was almost everywhere towards the closed corporation. In the numerous charters of the time where modes of election are laid down, they are almost always elaborate and indirect — the principle of election is not necessarily a simple thing and the Elizabethans used it with safeguards. Often the charters provided for simple co-option. The government felt that it could trust the upper class in the towns; its confidence was not misplaced.

The scars of the Reformation were still visible upon the face of the towns — at their worst in a famous ecclesiastical centre like York or Glastonbury or Bury St. Edmunds where Camden quotes Leland's shining description and says the abbey ruins still made a goodly show.[2] But the towns turned the losses of the Church into acquisitions for themselves and made some use of them, if only as quarries; often to some better purpose. York's loss of fifteen churches was, however, irreparable: it must have been a wonderful medieval city — it still has the grand air of a capital about it. On the Dissolution of the Chantries the hospitals, as usual, were saved: St. Thomas's was placed in charge of the corporation, St. Katherine's, the Merchant Taylors' Maison Dieu and the Cordwainers' continued.[3] The church of Our Lady in the Horsefair became the newly refounded St. Peter's School. Archbishop Holgate's regrettable lapse into matrimony did not prevent him from being the founder of a grammar school. While St. Mary's abbey became a quarry, the comfortable house of the abbot was adapted for the headquarters of the Council of the North. During Huntingdon's long rule as Lord President a new wing was added; and there it is today a composite monument to the Renaissance taste of the time. The first Elizabethan Archbishop, Thomas Young, signalised his activity in other directions. The family may be said to have been his foible, if not his vice.

[1] W. Boys, *Collections for a History of Sandwich* . . . (1792), pp. 700-702.
[2] W. Camden, *Britannia*, ed. cit. p. 460. [3] C. B. Knight, *op. cit.* pp. 388-9.

He enriched his offspring out of the prebendal estates — no doubt that was a gain to the country.[1] The splendid Treasurer's house descended to his son Sir George Young, who commanded a ship against the Armada. It can hardly be denied that it was a good thing that Archbishops nowadays had recognised (and recognisable) sons: Sir George was a better specimen than a previous Archbishop's son, Wolsey's " poor provost of Beverley ". Archbishop Young pulled down the hall of the Archbishop's Palace; no doubt it had ceased to be useful in changed circumstances, the cosier domesticity of episcopal arrangements — the long line of evolution that was to lead, in the fulness of time, to Mrs. Proudie. The gap there remains to this day at the north-west corner of the Minster: one misses it.

In the bigger towns the monastic establishments had meant that large areas were in the hands of independent corporate jurisdictions. In no case was this more notable — or more important in its consequences — than that of London. The extinction of these meant for the towns in general their integration into the town on a more efficient plane. Here again London was an exception, for these independent franchises fell to the Crown and not to the City, and this had unexpected consequences — one of them the development of the Elizabethan theatre. Bristol, like some other towns, was surrounded by monastic properties, which had cramped space for the development of suburbs. Besides the Castle, which belonged to the Crown, there were various monasteries, the priory of St. James which covered a large area, St. Augustine's abbey, Blackfriars, Greyfriars, the Carmelites, the nunnery of St. Mary Magdalen, and a couple of hospitals.[2] At the Dissolution the town brought off an interesting and far-sighted deal with the government. The Corporation obtained the grant of a large number of monastic properties; they had to raise the purchase money, £1790.[3] They proposed to the parishes to devote a quantity of superfluous plate to help pay off their liabilities, in return for their surrender of the right to levy tolls. (All corporate towns levied tolls at the town gates on incoming produce: it was a leading source of the town's revenue.) As compensation for the abolition of tolls and dues on victuals, a figure of £44 per annum was settled. The proposal was approved by fourteen parishes out of seventeen and these produced plate to the value of £523 : 10 : 8. (It is a popular delusion that much plate at the Reformation got into private hands; the government was too wide-awake and English adminis-

[1] *Ibid.* p. 399. [2] J. Latimer, *op. cit.* p. 2. [3] *Ibid.* p. 14 foll.

tration too efficient. The first great experiment in nationalisation was carried through in a business-like way and was much more of an incentive to production than any subsequent ones.) At twelve years' purchase this was a very good bargain for the parishes, especially since it was only at the cost of so much superfluous Church plate. For the town the purchase was an enormous benefit: it entered into full possession of considerable monastic properties and this enabled it to abolish tolls: a relief to the poor and an encouragement to trade. In Edward VI's reign the Corporation rebuilt the Tolzey (*i.e.* the toll-house) as a Council house, erected a block of warehouses in the old Jewry and built another block of houses on Bristol bridge. This was the way to Elizabethan prosperity. All which did not prevent the Corporation from being very mean, if not positively fraudulent, in withholding the property which Robert Thorne intended for the grammar school, for which purpose he had purchased St. Bartholomew's hospital.[1]

At Dover, where the haven gave infinite trouble and was a great expense over many years, the ruined church of St. Peter's was devoted, more usefully, to its repair.[2] At Yarmouth the changing channels of the river gave even greater difficulty. Seven attempts were made in the middle decades of the century to cut a satisfactory channel.[3] For the sixth attempt, in 1548, the money, plate and vestments of St. Nicholas' chapel, with the bells in the steeple and the rents of houses belonging to it, were sold to raise money; with the weekly contributions of the 24 aldermen and 48 common council men over £1800 was raised. The town worked at the site for eight successive years, until in 1555 they gave up in despair. In 1559 they began to make the harbour in the place where it had been in 1529. A thousand people were set to work to dig and it was completed in the following March. The stones of Our Lady's church were used to make a barrier at the mouth. By 1567, after £2600 had been sunk, the water broke through all the old works and made for the old channel. An experienced Dutch engineer was brought over, who drove in piles and forced the current in a north-east direction. But the Corporation could not bear the expense. It placed its hopes in a lottery:

> Yarmouth haven, God send thee speed,
> The Lord he knoweth thy great need.

The Queen granted them from time to time licences to export

[1] J. Latimer, *op. cit.* p. 40.
[2] *A.P.C. 1578–80*, p. 268.
[3] F. Blomefield, *op. cit.* XI. 266 foll.

corn on a large scale, which raised big sums. She lent them £1000 without interest, out of the customs, and remitted arrears of tenths and fifteenths. London lent them another £1000 without interest. This enabled the works to go forward. The result was the later prosperity that roused Manship's pride and Nashe's enthusiasm.[1] £5000 worth of nets might be seen drying at one time upon the Green. The town was able to contribute £800 to the State's charges in 1588, £1000 in 1589, and another £1000 in 1596. " Their whole harvest is by the sea." If other coasters were as industrious, we should have 20 eggs a 1d. and " it would be as plentiful a world as when abbeys stood ".

At Newcastle the Austin Friars — it had a fair church and cloisters — became the Queen's manor. In 1560 Cecil was lodged there during the negotiations that led to the Treaty of Leith.[2] By day he had consultations with the French commissioners, while slipping off at night to Alnwick to concert measures with Norfolk from Berwick against the enemy, and back in the early morning to Newcastle to meet the commissioners again. So like him — spry, inexhaustible, secret! Next year King Eric of Sweden stayed here, the great hall hung with tapestry from houses in the town and — what was apparently more appreciated — provided with a tun of beer.[3] Later, it fell from its high estate and became the Queen's storehouse; the incoming James gave it to a Scot. At Lynn — which was Bishop's, now King's — the four priories were sold, two of them bought by the Corporation, though this did not save their buildings.[4] A number of small chapels were defaced, though the most interesting of them, the remarkable octagon of Our Lady of the Mount, remains in a fair state of preservation on its bastion looking out over the green spaces of park and water-meadows. The nave and steeple of the large parish church of St. James were destroyed; but later the transepts were repaired by the town and fitted up as a workhouse for the poor to dress hemp and manufacture bags.[5] This venture in public works was, as elsewhere — and as might be expected — expensive and not much of a success. The little charnel chapel at St. Margaret's, in that spacious leafy churchyard, became a free school. All over the country these small chapels in towns were becoming grammar schools or town halls:

[1] Cf. H. Manship, *Hist. of Great Yarmouth* (ed. C. J. Palmer); Nashe's *Works* (ed. R. B. McKerrow), III. 169 foll.

[2] R. Welford, *op. cit.* II. 361. [3] *Ibid.* p. 370.

[4] C. Parkin, *Essay towards a Topog. Hist. of the County of Norfolk*, IV. 602.

[5] One can see what a tall upstanding building it was from seventeenth-century prints of Lynn.

inexpensive monuments to two characteristic developments of the age, the extension of education and of town self-government.

As time goes on we notice the upper class in the towns becoming more stiff-necked and Puritan. Where previously they had taken part in the jollity of May games and the customary performance of the town plays, a strong section now tries to suppress them; where they had been willing to welcome players coming to the town and pay them for their performance, they now pay them to go away; they support preachers instead and are ready to insist on the people's attendance at their sermons not only on Sundays — when everybody had by law to go to church — but even on appointed weekdays. Merry England was getting less merry in the towns. Was it all loss? Unattractive as we find it, and intolerable as some gay lads — congenial spirits — found it in their day, it was not all loss. The intolerably tedious sermons — though some must have been exciting, with their promise of hell-fire — were a form, if a rudimentary form, of education; and though their appeal was mainly to the emotions, they also stirred up the reason in the only form in which many had any experience of ratiocination. There is, too, the formative influence of the discipline in building up the morale and character that led to the heroic achievements of the Puritan Revolution. The more one studies these people in their time, the more one is impressed by their unyielding spirit: they were irrepressible, they would not give in, they were absolutely determined to have their way in the end.

At York the customary pageants were falling into disuse. The York Riding met with the disfavour of the Puritan-minded Archbishop Grindal, who protested against Yule and Yule's wife riding through the city " very undecently and uncomely ", drawing great crowds, to the neglect of sermons.[1] Upon which the Corporation resolved there should be no more Yule Ridings. The Corpus Christi festival was not observed there for the first year of the Queen's reign: perhaps because the town authorities did not know where the wind lay. But the Queen was no Puritan, and the festival was revived with its traditional plays. It was only the veto of Grindal's successor, Sandys, that overrode the decision of the Corporation and ended them. In 1575 the men of Coventry, famous for its cycle of plays, petitioned that when the Queen came to Kenilworth they might renew their old storial show, played yearly till of late it was put down by preachers " too sour in preaching away their pastime ".[2] So they came and

[1] C. B. Knight, *op. cit.* pp. 402-3.
q. in Owen and Blakeway, *op. cit.* I. 391.

performed before the Queen and her brilliant Court — almost the whole Court was there that summer. Of such were the

> Hard-handed men, that work in Athens here,
> Which never laboured in their minds till now:

Bottom the weaver, Peter Quince, Flute the bellows-mender, Snug the joiner, Snout the tinker. Shrewsbury enjoyed an annual fuss about the May games and the setting up of a green tree before the Shearmen's hall: preached against by the preacher in 1589. In 1591 there was again a disturbance, and the young men who had set up the tree were put on trial. Serjeant Owen decided that the usual tree might be set up as heretofore. But the fuss continued: there were two factions in the Council, the indulgent and the precisians. "Dost thou think, because thou art virtuous, there shall be no more cakes and ale?" was the attitude of the young men and the old Sir Tobys. Three years later the Council ordered that there should be no plays on any Sunday or at night; and that there should be no football, bear-baiting or bull-baiting within the walls.[1] The Quarry, looking down on the Severn, became the recognised place for these — and other — sports. No order was made against "the wonderful white horse of Mr. Banks of Staffordshire that could count".

Certain lusty young fellows of Lynn in 1582 began to set up bell-ringing again, which for some time had been disused.[2] Divers aldermen meaning to silence them, it turned to the Mayor's disadvantage and was the cause of much money spent. In 1603 the Merchant Adventurers of Newcastle made a new decree for the government of apprentices: young men learning to become merchants within sound of St. Nicholas' bells were forbidden to dance, dice or mum in the streets.[3] At the turn of the century Leicester had a series of disturbances about maypoles and morris dances.[4] For a number of years they had been forbidden by the town council, though apparently not everybody shared the views of the dominant faction, and the young men continued their games. The Mayor had to report that timber had been cut from the Earl of Huntingdon's woods, "and the stewards notwithstanding, there was the same night many maypoles by an unruly band and a confused multitude of base people set up in the street, and the stewards' watch too weak to suppress the outrage". A

[1] *Ibid.* p. 396. [2] B. Mackerell, *Hist. of King's Lynn*, p. 229.
[3] R. Welford, *op. cit.* III. 159.
[4] W. Kelly, *Notices of . . . Leicester*, pp. 98-106.

riot was the result of attempting to stop the fun. A shoemaker enjoying a holiday was heard to say that "if we do live we shall see other gates dancing and maying than is now"; and one of the Council said that "when he came to be Mayor of Leicester, he would allow a morris, being out of service time". And this was the view of the Privy Council, expressed apropos of maypole disturbances at Banbury: "We see no cause that these pastimes of recreation, being not used at unlawful times as on the sabbath day in time of divine service and in disordered and riotous sort, shall be forbidden the people".[1] That was not the point of view of the new bourgeoisie, who were determined to keep the people and popular manifestations down. And though the government might threaten to call up those who misliked its attitude before it "to show their reasons that doth lead them to be of that opinion", that did not frighten a class that was learning to stand up to the government. The Queen, who went a-maying to Highgate when an old lady in 1601, had much more popular sympathies than the Puritan middle class. But they were to win.

All these things are evidences of what has not been sufficiently observed or diagnosed: the sharpening class-differentiation in the towns, the drawing away of the middle class from the life of the people which they had so largely shared. Society was progressing.

We must postpone our depiction of the routine of administration in the towns, for it is properly part of that of the country in general, to which it had now closely approximated in character. We find the town authorities used in precisely the same way as in the country to carry out the purposes of government: to regulate employment, alleviate distress and provide poor relief; to control the prices and sale of food, and as far as possible safeguard its quality; to maintain public order and morals; to achieve a minimum standard of sanitation, water supply, street-lighting and paving; to muster the townsmen and train them for defence; to assess rates and aid in the collection of taxes. Even such an inadequate catalogue gives some idea of how busy the officials of a town of any size were kept. Civic life, like the life of the society in general, was controlled to a high degree: one is oppressed, one is almost stifled, by the completeness and the intimacy of the controls. Society, in every town, in every parish, was like one crowded, jostling family governed by paternal authority. There was no escaping it, except into vagrancy, the life of the road (with its whippings when caught), soldiering or sailoring (into which,

[1] *A.P.C. 1588–9*, p. 202.

as like as not, one was impressed), or flight abroad (which was regarded as treason, with its liability to extreme penalties). The society of the sixteenth century was in a good many ways more like that of the twentieth than that of the intervening period of civilisation.

The town authorities, like the J.P.s all over the country, were very convenient maids-of-all-work for the government and the pressure placed upon them enhanced the importance of their officials. With so much business of every kind on their hands, so many statutes, instructions, orders and regulations both from the central government and the town to administer, that legal official, the Recorder, comes into his own in the big towns. The most famous specimen of the genus was London's Recorder, Serjeant Fleetwood. One notes with pleasure Exeter's estimate of the value of theirs: " That Mr. Serjeant Hill, our Recorder, shall have given unto him yearly every year during his life eight salmons of the river of Exe, which is the like number that is allowed to the Mayor of the city for the time being ".[1] The Town Clerk was becoming a still more indispensable and highly estimated officer. It was not until the reign of Henry VIII that Nottingham had a clerk whose Latin went so far as to quote a line of Virgil: by 1587 it possessed a clerk who had Greek.[2] The archives and records of Leicester were kept in admirable order by William Dethick, town clerk for nearly half a century.[3] John Willis, Bristol's Chamberlain from 1566 to 1582, was said to be the best the town had ever known, a rich man whose administration of the city revenue was impeccable and who impaired his own fortune by his charities; he spent much on building causeways round the city.[4] Henry Manship, though not altogether satisfactory as town clerk of Yarmouth, was imbued with a proper spirit of pride in his native town, which inspired him to write one of the few contemporary town histories. But the best-known town clerk of the age, in whom the character of the office found complete expression, was John Hooker, Chamberlain of Exeter, scholarly, indefatigable, methodical, who had the affairs of Exeter under his thumb for most of Elizabeth's reign.

The growing organisation of the town councils may be seen reflected in their increased self-consciousness, the emphasis on their dignity. None can vie with the historic state and pageantry of London; but — perhaps by way of emulation — all over the country they are clothing themselves with scarlet or purple.

[1] H.M.C. *Records of the City of Exeter*, p. 322. [2] Green, *op. cit.* II. 20.
[3] Bateson, *op. cit.* III. lxiii. [4] Barrett, *op. cit.* p. 117.

Plymouth tells us that it is for the "better decency and reputation of the town", and follows with a detailed order as to the wearing of scarlet and how the council were to comport themselves.[1] In many places regulations are laid down for the conduct and due order of discussion; certain standards of courtesy, or at least forbearance, are insisted on; a tradition in carrying on public business is being formed. The council demands some measure of decorum in its members; Yarmouth expels a councillor for whoring.[2] Humbler officials attend upon their dignity and enliven the life of the town. Important towns have their band of waits, usually three or four minstrels, who play morning and evening. The town is very jealous of these delights and refuses to allow them to perform out of bounds without permission. As a special favour to Sir Francis Drake, the town waits of Norwich were sent to accompany him on the Portugal expedition of 1589.[3] It must have been regarded as a compliment, for the city was generous in providing them with new cloaks of stammel,[4] three new hautboys and a new treble recorder, money and a wagon to transport their instruments. At Leicester the waits broke into two factions and quarrelled long and bitterly.[5] Newcastle maintained a fool; there are many payments for his clothes in the town accounts, such as "shirts, ruffs and shoes for the fool against Christmas".[6] That nostalgic figure, the Town Crier, was becoming familiar: Shrewsbury instituted one in 1600 "to cry and call through the town in the night, giving all people the knowledge of the clock, to take heed of doors and locks, of fire and candlelight, and so bidding them all good night".[7]

London was then, and was to remain for some centuries, recognisably a town, with a town's proper articulation, anatomy and look; not a formless growth consuming whole countrysides, a great wen, a wilderness of bricks and ruins, a graveyard. It was beautiful, Gothic and irregular: not so beautiful as it was to become by the end of the aristocratic age, the Regency, nor even as it had been at the end of the Middle Ages before the Reformation destroyed so many churches and monuments and left so

[1] Worth, *op. cit.* p. 59.

[2] Blomefield, *op. cit.* XI. 396: "for that he is a whoremaster and liveth ungodly with sundry women, as he hath openly confessed and sworn to the same".

[3] Hudson and Tingey, *op. cit.* II. 195.

[4] Coarse red woollen cloth.

[5] Kelly, *op. cit.* pp. 137-9.

[6] Welford, *op. cit.* II. 382.

[7] Owen and Blakeway, *op. cit.* I. 401.

many gashes. Medieval London was particularly distinguished by its splendid monastic foundations and parish churches — over a hundred and twenty of the latter. When Dunbar wrote they were still in all their glory, and many of the parish churches were just being rebuilt in the greater magnificence of Perpendicular; so that his famous poem

London, thou art the floure of cities all

was no mere compliment but — so far as Northern Europe went — the truth. There was the situation of the city by its noble river brimming with craft and commerce; no other great city had such a river frontage, and the visiting foreigner was already impressed by the fact that nowhere else in the world was such an assembly of shipping to be seen.[1] There was London Bridge — none such so spectacular elsewhere — crowded with expensive shops and well-to-do houses; there was the fortress of the Tower, gloomy, forbidding, impregnable, which dominated the entry and impressed everybody, foreigner and native alike — Shakespeare has more references to it than to any other building in London. The great body of St. Paul's, a church much longer than the present building, with a spire one hundred and fifty feet higher than the existing dome, presided over it all.[2] Elizabethan London was the medieval city with some losses and many changes — changes brought about principally by two factors, the Dissolution and the immense building expansion now gathering force and that could not be checked.

The best way to visualise it is to look at contemporary bird's-eye views and maps, of which there are several. The first of them is Wyngaerde, less exact and finished than the later ones, Agas and Visscher, but more atmospheric and suggestive: if you step back from it you might be looking at the London the Elizabethans saw.[3] It is a free perspective view; let us begin from the east coming up the river as a foreign visitor might do — such as Wyngaerde himself was, probably in the entourage of Philip II. There are the gathered turrets of Greenwich, favourite residence of Henry and Elizabeth, where both were born and Edward died — shipping lying immediately before the Palace. We remember all kinds of episodes that crowd in upon the mind: Henry being rowed down the river to pay a visit to a lady-love housed in a lodge in the park and being shocked by some *propos*

[1] *Thomas Platter's Travels in England, 1599* (trans. C. Williams), p. 154.

[2] Until 1561 when the spire was destroyed by lightning.

[3] The original is among the Sutherland MSS. in the Bodleian. It has been reproduced by the London Topographical Society.

of Sir Andrew Flamock;[1] the children of Paul's acting comedies of Lyly's before the Queen there; Elizabeth in her barge rowing round young Richard Hawkins's ship, the *Repentance* (so called by his Puritan stepmother), and renaming her the *Dainty*;[2] Drake's ship the *Golden Hind* laid up by the Palace, one of the popular sights of London, until it began to rot with age and people carried off the timbers; Frobisher on his first voyage shooting off ordnance as a salute to the Queen, "Her Majesty beholding the same, commended it and bade us farewell with shaking her hand at us out of the window".[3]

Coming up the river we come to London proper with the church of St. Katherine's hospital, now under the water of St. Katherine's Dock; then the Tower, a province to itself, very much a stronghold with its cannon and the cranes on its wharf. There it is, not so much changed from what we know it, with pepper-pot turrets and grouped towers and so much of Tudor history going on under our eyes, where now all is but memories thronging. On Tower Hill the scaffold stands out very plain with the steps up which so many figures faltered or, more strangely, marched firm. Behind and beyond are the towers of various churches, St. Botolph's, the Minories and so on. Between here and London Bridge all is crowded with gables and churches, and along the river with quays and wharves and buildings; there are the inlets of Billingsgate and Queenhithe with small boats unlading at the wharves and warehouses. Here and there the artist has marked *grote scepe* — big ships lying alongside. The commerce of the river was the life of London and its highway. Then we come to the Bridge, which is depicted in detail. There are the numerous arches (there were twenty in all) and the packed gables of the houses on it with the narrow way occasionally clear in a breach between. There were only three such gaps from which you saw the river. There is the tall chapel of St. Thomas the Apostle on the bridge — formerly of the blissful Martyr, for this is the way leading to Southwark and the road to Canterbury along which the host of the Tabard and his jolly company went. On the south bank is St. Mary Overy's fine tower and the Bishop of Winchester's great house west of it.

Another stretch of crowded city brings us to St. Paul's, which dominates the scene magnificently with its tower, another and

[1] The naughty story is told in Puttenham's *Art of English Poesy*, Arber's Reprints, p. 275.

[2] *The Observations of Sir Richard Hawkins* (ed. J. A. Williamson), p. 9.

[3] q. in R. P. Cruden, *History of Gravesend*, p. 216.

more splendid St. Mary Overy, and with the spire and cross still intact. Beyond St. Paul's the open space of Smithfield is visible with a good deal of activity suggested, and with St. Bartholomew's nearby. Higher up the Bishop of Ely's palace stands out with great hall and chapel, around it the open courtyards and the acres of gardens which yielded so many roses that the reluctant Bishop, from whom the Queen wrung the lease for Sir Christopher Hatton, was able to reserve a rent of twenty bushels of them.[1] There is an empty space where Bridewell Palace should be: a narrow front to the river, and its main courts running along the Fleet river, which was at this time becoming a ditch, the noisomeness of which drove Henry to evacuate the palace he built, while Edward handed it over for the employment and correction of the poor. Now the houses are thinning out westward to the great houses along the river that join London to Westminster and have left their memorials in the street names of the Strand, Essex house, Arundel house, Somerset house, the Savoy hospital, Cecil house: mostly the former town houses of the bishops now taken over for the secular personages ruling the realm. Here Durham house stands out, an old-fashioned tall mass where Ralegh had his study and which his poor lady found so uncomfortable a home. The highway runs down to Westminster, the houses on the river each with its private stairs marked. Then the great hulk of Westminster Abbey stands out with transepts and apse; no towers of course. There is the long roof of Westminster Hall, and the tall chapel of Whitehall, unfamiliar to us, long since vanished. Whitehall stairs are marked, a very grand landing-place, with the gateway to the Court — St. James's on the outer edge — the jumble of courts and gardens making Whitehall and denominated 'the King's palace', the whole nerve-centre of the realm.

We can add further descriptive features from the pictorial map that used to be attributed to Ralph Agas.[2] We notice the bleaching grounds beyond the Tower with women tending the stretched cloths, the large fields that gave recreation to the citizens before you get into open country: Finsbury Field and Spital Field which used to be thronged at Easter-time for the open-air sermons at the Cross, here depicted with men shooting their arrows. In Bishopsgate and Lothbury are the big gardens of the houses of the rich merchants who live here. Up beyond St. Paul's

[1] E. St. J. Brooks, *Sir Christopher Hatton*, p. 149.

[2] Facsimile from the original in the City Archives, notes by W. H. Overall. But for the attribution to Agas, cf. H. B. Wheatley, *London Topog. Record*, II. 42.

are the splendid buildings of Greyfriars with the cloister still there. St. Paul's has lost its spire now. The chapter-house and St. Gregory's on the south side appear. One notes Cheapside as the broadest street, the chief east–west artery of the city: the Oxford Street of the Elizabethans, their chief shopping centre. Chancery Lane runs between open spaces with trees; the Inns of Court have their gardens. In mid-stream off Baynard's Castle is depicted the Royal barge, with Elizabeth's arms, being towed up to Westminster. On the Surrey side of the river Bankside, with its stews, runs along from Southwark to Paris Garden, opposite Bridewell and Fleet ditch. Half-way between are two large round houses: the Bear Baiting nearest Southwark, the Bull Baiting nearer Paris Garden. Those shapes perhaps determined that of the Globe Theatre, not yet built: all that triumph as yet unguessed at, undiscernible.

Norden's pretty pictorial maps of 1593 add further strokes to our picture. The first shows the walls of the city complete with the gates in good order:[1] Ludgate, which had been splendidly rebuilt in 1586 with statues and a picture of the Queen on the western face, Newgate, Aldersgate along the west; along the north, Cripplegate, Moorgate, Bishopsgate, Aldgate and so down to the Tower postern. Moorfields had been lately drained and laid out in walks. Bankside was handsomely embanked, with landing-stairs and a row of small houses. All beyond was country. The Bear house and the Playhouse are marked. Here Philip Henslowe lived, part proprietor of Paris Garden and manager of the Rose Theatre; Malone had evidence that Shakespeare lived here for a time: nothing improbable in that.[2] At Blackfriars Burbage's theatre was opened three years later. In Carter Lane was the Bell inn, whence Richard Quyny wrote to his " loving friend and good countryman Mr. William Shakespeare " in 1598, five years from now. Nearby was the great house of Coldharbour, which Edward VI had granted the Earl of Shrewsbury. We find among the accounts of Bess of Hardwick's favourite son, William Cavendish, frequent payments for boathire to visit his relations there when in town, and no less frequently to visit the Globe Theatre in Southwark.[3] The great house was pulled down in 1600 and the site given up to small tenements at large rents.[4] This was happening all over the city: index to

[1] Norden, *Speculum Britanniae: Description of Middlesex and Hertfordshire* (ed. 1723), p. 27.

[2] H. B. Wheatley, " Notes upon Norden and his Map of London, 1593 ", *London Top. Record*, II. 51.

[3] Hardwick MSS. [4] Stow's *Survey of London* (ed. C. L. Kingsford), I. 237.

prosperity and a thronging population. At Swan stairs next the Bridge most people alighted to walk to the east side and take boat again rather than shoot the Bridge. Norden's map of Westminster shows up the seat of government in admirably clear detail: the great houses of the nobility, including Burghley house on the other side of the Strand from the Savoy, Russell house, then Durham house, York house and Whitehall.[1] The Royal Mews occupy the site of Trafalgar Square. The banks of the river opposite Whitehall and the present Embankment are planted with trees. In St. James's park the deer are leaping.

When we come to Visscher's perspective view of 1616 we have something altogether more detailed and accurate than Wyngaerde half a century before. St. Paul's rises superbly over the whole. On the south bank the Bear Garden and the Globe are now depicted, octagonal open houses with flags at mast; further west nearer Bankside is the Swan. Above the gate-house on the Bridge entering London from the south is the ghastly decorative array of heads, like pins stuck in a pin-cushion, that arrested the attention of the traveller. It was all part of a London where public executions were frequent — as elsewhere in Europe. Stow had a man hanged on the pavement of his own door; but that was sufficiently rare for him to have noted it.[2] Fetter Lane had a gallows at either end of it.[3] Machyn mentions a gibbet being erected at the west door of St. Paul's for some offenders.[4] Every law day, Platter remarked — evidently rather impressed — twenty or thirty offenders were hanged.[5] Condemned felons on their way west to Tyburn were given a drink at the hospital of St. Giles', Cripplegate on their way: a touch of humanity that somehow makes the barbarity the more gruesome. The cheerfulness and nonchalance with which some went off, the cheap rate at which the people held their lives, were noted by more civilised foreigners. The rate at which life is estimated is an important, though not the sole, index to the degree of a people's civilisation.

The casual passer-by of today will observe little enough of the London of Elizabeth under the monumental bulk of Victoria's — only perhaps the most obvious things like the houses in

[1] *Loc. cit.* p. 46. This is conveniently reproduced in *Shakespeare's England*, II. 162.

[2] *Op. cit.* I. 144.

[3] H. B. Wheatley, *loc. cit.* p. 63.

[4] "The 10 day of January in the morning [1560] was a new pair of gallows set up without the west door of Paul's, and between nine and ten of the clock afore noon were William North and his man brought thither by the two sheriffs, and there hanged both till four at afternoon; and so the hangman cut them down and carried them into St. Gregory's churchyard, and there was a grave made and so they were stripped of all, and tumbled naked into the grave, in the east side of the churchyard" (*Diary o Henry Machyn* (Camden Society), pp. 222-3).

[5] *Op. cit.* p. 174.

Holborn that have survived so much. For the city is essentially the city of Wren and Dickens. Only nine pre-Fire churches survived to 1941: of these five remain intact.[1] But the more discerning will notice much more. The very names will excite the past for him: the streets that recall the localisation of medieval trades: "If we look up amidst the roar and bustle of our own Cheapside, the signs of Wood Street, Bread Street, Friday Street, Milk Street and Ironmonger Lane carry our minds back to the stalls and booths of a medieval market".[2] There are the names of wards, Bassishaw and Faringdon that recall medieval families; Candlewick and Vintry. So many streets enable one to follow ancient boundaries in the mind as one walks along London Wall or Moorgate or Houndsditch; one looks up in the Underground and the station is Aldersgate or Aldgate. The discerning traveller will see as he goes along Holborn the houses tapering out into the fields — Gray's Inn was the most favoured of the Inns of Court then, for it lay among fields and was the healthiest. He will see Moorgate opening on to low-lying marshes, and underneath Liverpool Street Station the hospital of St. Mary of Bethlehem, the original Bedlam. Everything will speak to him of the storied past, for everywhere there are memories to bring it back to him. Blackfriars will remember the crowded tenements and the liberty that permitted the development of the theatre; Lamb's Conduit Street speaks of the beneficent citizen who collected the waters into a conduit here in the year 1577;[3] Essex Street will recall the great house and its fatal owner, the tumult and the fiasco of that day in 1600, and before that it was Leicester house of which Spenser wrote,

> Next whereunto there stands a stately place
> Where oft I gained gifts and goodly grace
> Of that great Lord, which therein wont to dwell . . .[4]

and before that it was Paget house, where Mary's minister lived, and before that the town house of the Bishop of Exeter. He will see not the St. Paul's of Wren — that is the most difficult to exclude, Wren has so imposed it on our vision — but the three-portalled west front of the medieval cathedral, looking like Lincoln or York, with a congeries of buildings around it:[5] the Bishop's Palace at the north-west corner of the churchyard, the dean's house, the lodgings of the prebendaries, their brew-house and

[1] *Trans. London and Middlesex Archaeological Soc.* (1944), p. 69.
[2] G. Unwin, *The Gilds and Companies of London*, p. 35.
[3] Stow's *Survey*, II. 34.
[4] *Prothalamion.*
[5] Stow, *op. cit.* I. 326 foll.; II. 18-20.

bake-house on the other side; Peter's College now converted into Stationers' Hall — for this is the centre of the publishing trade. Only shortly before had the great cloisters with their frescoes of the Dance of Death been pulled down by Somerset to build his palace in the Strand, the Jesus bell-tower with its gilded spire and great bells by his follower, Sir Miles Partridge. It pleased Stow to think that these progressive and liberal-minded persons came to the end they did.

Penetrate the halls of the City Companies and there are still the treasures that go back to those days and before, the plate that garnished the cupboards at their feasts, the standing cups and salts that stood on the tables then as today, the funeral palls they used, like those possessed by the Merchant Taylors or the superb one of crimson and cloth of gold, with St. Peter crowned with tiara still giving his blessing, that belongs to the Fishmongers. The crystal mace that goes back to the Middle Ages is still borne before the Lord Mayor at his election. More intangibly, and surprisingly, the whole formal structure of the government of the city remains unchanged. The mode of election of the Lord Mayor — from two aldermen selected by the Livery Companies — goes back to the reign of Edward IV. The sheriffs of London held jurisdiction in Middlesex, by grant of Henry I, as late as 1888. There are still twenty-six wards, twenty-five of them each with its alderman and one, Bridge Ward Without, a sinecure since Southwark's existence as an independent ward lapsed in 1557 and still remains lapsed.[1] The powers of Common Council remain practically in abeyance — as they seem to have done since the Middle Ages. Southwark, in the reign of Edward VI, was the last extension of the city boundaries; the reason why the city's boundaries remained where they still are goes back to the Middle Ages and the City Corporation persistently refused any proposal to extend them.

We are exceedingly fortunate to have a description of Elizabethan London that is worthy of it: a classic. Stow's *Survey* is one of those rare books the author was born to write: a most happy conjunction of the man, the subject and the time. For eighty years he lived in the city — his father and grandfather were both buried in St. Michael's, Cornhill — loving every stone and monument in it, carefully, minutely observant, scholarly, noting down everything to his purpose. The result is a book

[1] W. J. Loftie, *London* (Historic Towns Series), pp. 107 foll., 145-7.

not only accurate and factual, but full of vivacity, sharp and personal, that conveys the author's temperament in the way only books that live do. The idea of making a survey of London, " my native soil and country ", was suggested by Lambarde's *Perambulation of Kent.*[1] Stow was a working tailor by trade and therefore was an amateur: but his work is a part of the antiquarian scholarship of the time. He was early troubled for his sympathies with the old departed order of things, but was protected by Archbishop Parker, good man, and afterwards enjoyed the friendship of scholars. Of his chief work, his *Summary* of the Chronicles, he wrote: " It hath cost me many a weary mile's travel, many a hard earned penny and pound, and many a cold winter night's study ".[2] The *Survey* was in a sense a parergon, which only appeared after his major works were finished; but it is all the more a labour of love, and, like such books, has a life denied to the others.

We see him as a boy fetching home from the nunnery farm in Goodman's Fields " many a half-penny worth of milk, and never had less than three ale pints for a half-penny in the summer, nor less than one ale quart for a half-penny in the winter, always hot from the kine, as the same was milked and strained ".[3] Or again, watching the disputations of the grammar-school boys in St. Bartholomew's churchyard under a tree, or the pitched battles of the Pigeons of Paul's against Anthony Pigs " with their satchels full of books, many times in great heaps that they troubled the streets and passengers ".[4] Or we see him as a sedate man dining with a friend at Westminster and walking back on the ice of the Thames to Baynard's Castle.[5] Winters were harder then. There is always this nostalgic note at the back of old Stow's mind: the sign of the true artist. " On May day in the morning, every man, except impediment, would walk into the sweet meadows and green woods, there to rejoice their spirits with the beauty and savour of sweet flowers and with the harmony of birds ", and he goes on to describe the May games of London when he was a boy and the maypole, taller than the steeple, that used to be set up before the south door of St. Andrew Undershaft — hence the name — where Stow himself has come to rest in effigy.[6] Earliest of all he can just remember the feast of St. Paul with " the buck being brought up to the steps of the high altar in Paul's church, at the hour of procession, the Dean and Chapter being apparelled in copes and vestments with garlands of roses

[1] Stow, ed. cit. I. xxxvi.
[2] *Ibid.* I. xxiv.
[3] *Ibid.* I. 126.
[4] *Ibid.* I. 74.
[5] *Ibid.* I. xxxvi.
[6] *Ibid.* I. 98, 143-4.

on their heads ", the vestments embroidered one set with bucks, the other with does.[1] The Reformation altered all that; Stow was no Catholic but he loved the old departed ways. The new age he thought " the most scoffing, respectless and unthankful age that ever was ".[2]

The recurrent themes of the book give us a good indication of what was characteristic of the London of the time. Most noticeable is the emphasis on the building going on: the precincts of the monasteries are becoming crowded with tenements, many of the great houses in the city are being divided up for them or pulled down to make way for them; there is constant encroachment upon open spaces, upon Smithfield or Tower Hill for example, upon the churchyards — Stow several times mentions buildings where he remembered a green churchyard, there is no room for willows to grow now at St. Anne in the Willows[3] — upon the very streets. Outside the gates there were rapidly growing suburbs, especially along Bishopsgate to Shoreditch, where the two early playhouses, the Theatre and the Curtain, were being built; outside Cripplegate, which had the effect of increasing the population of St. Giles' parish to some 4000 communicants;[4] eastwards from the Tower was one continual street to Radcliffe — where the mariners and their dependants dwelt — and from Radcliffe eastward "in place where I have known a large highway, with fair elm trees on both sides that the same hath now taken hold of Lime Hurst . . . corruptly called Limehouse ".[5]

A theme that touched Stow's heart is the destruction of monuments in the churches. This brings home to us the upset society had been through, and the hideous strain of Protestant iconoclasm continued for all that the government tried to hold it in check. This spirit got its head again with the Civil War and the Puritan ascendancy. The great time of spoil in this way was Edward's reign when government was not only weak but was led by the rapacious, and a good time was had by all the uncivilised. Again and again Stow has to record the destruction or the defacing of monuments in the churches: it would seem that the major portion of them had gone: he notices it as exceptional when a church has them still intact. From this point of view London must have looked almost a Protestant town: no incoming Huguenot from Antwerp or Orleans need have felt not at home. (They did, however, notice the ceremonies in the cathedrals as approximating more to Catholic rites:[6] reason for

[1] *Ibid.* I. 334-5.
[2] *Ibid.* I. xli.
[3] *Ibid.* I. 307.
[4] *Ibid.* II. 79-80.
[5] *Ibid.* II. 71.
[6] Platter, *op. cit.* p. 176.

the special Puritan animus against cathedrals.) With the large churches of the Friars hundreds of the finest medieval monuments went down — Stow lists them all — for those churches had been the favourite burying-places of the great. At Austin Friars the Marquis of Winchester, the Lord Treasurer, " sold the monuments of noble men there buried in great number, the paving above and whatsoever (which cost many thousands) for one hundred pound, and in place thereof made fair stabling for horses".[1] The house, cloisters and gardens of the Friars had been made into a great house by the Marquis's father, where Stow remembered him keeping great state with a retinue of two hundred gentlemen and yeomen in liveries of Reading tawny and giving great relief to the poor at his gate.[2] The church had not been pulled down: the choir and transepts were used for household purposes as a store for corn and coal; the nave was partitioned off and granted to the Dutch congregation for their church. It remained for the Germans to complete the destruction in 1941.

Stow frequently inveighs against the " bad and greedy men of spoil " who had done these things; it must have been a grief to him to have witnessed them. He took his own small revenge: in recording the remaining monuments he omitted many new ones, " because those men have been the defacers of the monuments of others, and so worthy to be deprived of that memory whereof they have injuriously robbed others ".[3] Sometimes the trouble was due to sheer pressure upon space, of the living upon the dead, of the newly dead upon those buried before them. At St. Botolph's without Aldgate the parishioners " being of late years mightily increased the church is pestered with lofts and seats for them ".[4] Aldermary Church in Cordwainer Street was much frequented by the Grocers and had been largely rebuilt earlier in the century by Henry Keble, Grocer and Mayor: now his fine monument had gone, " he gave by his testament £1000 towards the building up of that church, and yet not permitted a resting place for his bones there ".[5] His successors as Grocers and Mayors, Sir William Laxton and Sir Thomas Lodge, father of the novelist and poet, were ensconced in his vault, the one in Mary's reign, the other in Elizabeth's; their monuments took the place of his. It is curious: one gets the impression of people being shovelled in upon one another — the grave-digging scene in *Hamlet* must have been very true to life, probably a transcript from some actual experience. No doubt these churches needed

[1] Stow, *op. cit.* I. 176-7.
[2] *Ibid.* I. 88.
[3] *Ibid.* I. xxxi.
[4] *Ibid.* I 127.
[5] *Ibid.* I. 253.

a clearance by Elizabeth's reign; the grand clearance was to come in the Great Fire.

Stow's curious story of the renewed defacings of the great gilt cross that was the principal feature of Cheapside shows the unquenchable pertinacity of these nasty people [1] — so far from the people liking things of beauty, they hate them. On midsummer's night, 1581, the lowest range of images round the cross were broken and defaced. Proclamation was made offering a reward for the discovery of the offenders, but nothing came to light. In 1595 the figure of the Virgin was fastened and repaired, and next year a new figure of the Son laid in her arms. In place of the defaced image of Christ's Resurrection, a marble tabernacle was set up with an image of Diana "and water conveyed from the Thames prilling at her naked breast". In 1599 the cross at the top becoming decayed, it was taken down to make place for an obelisk. The Council sent letters by the Queen's express command to Sir Nicholas Mosley, then Mayor, to have the cross repaired and set up as it formerly stood. Nothing was done for more than a year, when the Council ordered the Mayor to carry out the Queen's wishes, "respecting especially the antiquity and continuance of that monument, an ancient ensign of Christianity" etc. After this a gilt cross was restored. "About twelve nights following, the image of our Lady was again defaced, by plucking off her crown and almost her head, taking from her her naked child and stabbing her in the breast etc. Thus much for the cross in West Cheap." It was impossible to defeat these people, as Charles I and Laud found.

Such efforts as were made at repairing and rebuilding churches were small and feeble enough: Elizabethans had other things to do. When the great spire of St. Paul's was struck by lightning in 1561, the roofs set on fire and a great deal of damage done, a special effort was made and the essential repairs quickly finished. But the steeple was never rebuilt: "Divers models were devised and made, but little else was done; through whose default God knoweth".[2] So Elizabethan London went without the crowning glory it had inherited from the Middle Ages — appropriately enough, in a way. The chancel of the little church of All Hallows the Less standing above the arched entry to Coldharbour, which had fallen, was rebuilt in 1594.[3] At Blackfriars where the parish church of St. Anne was pulled down along with the great Friars' church by Sir Thomas Carwarden, he had to provide a chamber over a stair for the worship of the inhabitants;

[1] *Ibid.* I. 266-7. [2] *Ibid.* I. 331-2. [3] *Ibid.* I. 235-7.

this fell and was rebuilt and enlarged for the increased number of parishioners in 1597.[1] St. Augustine's, Watling Street, was "lately well repaired".[2] It does not amount to much all told.

The building the Elizabethans did was secular, utilitarian, charitable. There was an immense amount of adaptation of monastic buildings for secular purposes, some turned into houses, others into hospitals or into government storehouses, a few into factories. A large number of great houses were turned into tenements, like Suffolk house in Southwark, the splendid house with its turrets that appears in the foreground of Wyngaerde, Worcester house, Ormonde house, Coldharbour, Berkeley Inn, the Bishop of Hereford's Inn which became a sugar factory, while other episcopal residences became, not less appropriately, glass-houses. The hall of the nuns at St. Helen's, Bishopsgate was purchased by the Leathersellers for their hall, and was panelled and given a rich plaster ceiling.[3] The nuns' aisle had its screen pulled down and was thrown into the church. The hospital of St. Thomas of Acre was bought by the Mercers for their chapel and free school, while their old chapel under the hall was let out for shops.[4] The Drapers bought for their hall the large house Cromwell had built in Throgmorton Street: everyone knows how he expropriated the small men, including Stow's father, from their gardens to make a large one for himself.[5] Yet Stow remembered the two hundred poor people that were fed every day at the great man's gate, the immense retinue of attendants in their master's livery of grey marble. It was a time of building of halls and warehouses. Blackwell Hall, the cloth-market to which clothiers sent their cloth from all over the country, was rebuilt in 1588:[6] you see its site on the right hand as you approach the Guildhall. All the Inns of Court were expanding rapidly: in their case the method was to allow their members to build on their own lodgings, staircase by staircase, and to occupy them for specified terms. The Inner Temple rebuilt its hall 1562–72; the splendid affair of the Middle Temple, in which *Twelfth Night* was performed in 1602, had been but lately finished.[7] Everywhere water is being piped and brought into the city; wells are being made into pumps, conduits enlarged, like the celebrated conduit at Fleet bridge with its chime of sweet-sounding bells. (The bridge had "certain lanterns of stone for lights to be placed in

[1] Stow, I. 341. [2] *Ibid.* I. 323.
[3] J. E. Cox, *Annals of St. Helen's, Bishopsgate*, p. 34.
[4] Stow, *op. cit.* I. 269-70. [5] *Ibid.* I. 179, 88. [6] *Ibid.* I. 288-9.
[7] F. A. Inderwick, *Cal. of Inner Temple Records*, pp. lxxi-lxxv.

the winter evenings, for commodity of travellers ".[1]) One sees London as a town of swift waters, running down its gravelly hills.

Somewhat surprising is the large number of almshouses built in the city, both by private persons, rich merchants living up to their responsibilities, and by the Livery Companies. The immense charitableness of the age may come as a new idea to those who have a preconceived opinion of it and think of the Elizabethans as only harsh, ambitious and grasping: they were that, but they were humane and charitable too: the interest is in the complexity of life and that they should have combined both, often in the same person. Sir Andrew Judde, Skinner, in addition to founding Tonbridge School, built almshouses in Bishopsgate; so did Sir Thomas Gresham.[2] By Grocers' Hall in Cheap Ward there were almshouses founded by various members of the Company; the Drapers built almshouses for widows of their Company in Cripplegate.[3] Indeed numerous citizens founded almshouses all over the city — ironmongers, salters, painter-stainers; there can hardly have been a ward without its complement of almshouses: they must have been a familiar feature of the city streets. The wards themselves give an impression of being proper organs of civic life, each with its alderman, its complement of companies' halls, its parish churches and its parishes. Everywhere the building of houses and shops was the order of the day: nothing could be more eloquent of the prosperity of the city, or of its character, secular, commercial, industrious. Every visiting foreigner was impressed by the busy traffic, the difficulty of getting along the streets.[4] The thronging citizens were more impressed by the difficulty of getting houses. It had been easy enough at the beginning of Elizabeth's reign, with all the Church property thrown on the market, and rents were low. By the end of the reign rents were high and, in spite of all the building, accommodation difficult. Thousands of foreigners had poured in and settled particularly in the eastern wards, along the Thames, and in Southwark. This was what impressed the natives, mostly unfavourably; many more thousands from the country had crowded into the metropolis — including the greatest Englishmen of the day, Shakespeare, Marlowe, Drayton, Drake, Byrd, William Gilbert, Hilliard. Spenser was an exception:

> At length they all to merry London came,
> To merry London, my most kindly nurse,
> That to me gave this life's first native source. . . .[5]

[1] Stow, II. 41; I. 26. [2] *Ibid.* I. 113-14. [3] *Ibid.* I. 263-4, 302.
[4] Cf. Platter, *op. cit.* p. 174. [5] *Prothalamion*, line 127 foll.

and it was right that he should celebrate the beauty of the city in an immortal poem, written within the gates of Essex house:

> Yet therein now doth lodge a noble peer,
> Great England's glory, and the world's wide wonder,
> Whose dreadful name late through all Spain did thunder,
> And Hercules' two pillars standing near
> Did make to quake and fear. . . .
>
> Sweet Thames! run softly till I end my song.

Let us peer a little more closely into the actual changes that were going on in a few chosen areas. The status and foundation of the hospitals of the city that were to become so famous had been already settled. In the changes brought about by the Dissolution the city authorities had been as public-spirited as could be expected — vastly more so than the government. Their chief concern was to provide for the poor and impotent on their hands. As early as 1538 the city had asked for three hospitals to be spared and for a grant of the abbey on Tower Hill (St. Mary Graces) as a poorhouse.[1] Nothing came of this; Henry was waiting for a better offer from the rich city; meanwhile he refounded only St. Bartholomew's hospital. On his deathbed he came to a grand agreement on the large scale, by which he became founder of the 'Royal Hospitals'; Edward VI on his deathbed added the fifth, St. Thomas's. By this agreement the city came into possession of a considerable amount of Church property which could now be devoted to social purposes. It provided endowment for five firm foundations: St. Bartholomew's for the sick, St. Thomas's for the permanently infirm, Christ's Hospital for the maintenance and education of children, Bridewell for the vagabonds and unemployed, Bedlam for the mad. At last the government had been shamed into generosity; the city had taken the lead all along, and pledged itself to raise an annual sum equal to the endowment. And this in addition to the £18,000 it provided to redeem the charitable trusts on dissolved chantries within the city.[2] It is true that the city was more affluent than the government. All this meant that Elizabethan London started out with a well-considered equipment for dealing with sick and poor, though its immense and rapid growth soon rendered this inadequate. One must remember, however, that the ground was covered by the parish organisations of over a hundred parishes.

[1] E. Jeffries-Davis, "The Transformation of London" in *Tudor Studies*, presented to A. F. Pollard, pp. 300-303; R. R. Sharp, *London and the Kingdom*, I. 449-52.

[2] R. R. Sharp, *op. cit.* I. 425.

Of the great complement of monastic churches which had been the pride of medieval London, ten were saved wholly or in part for parochial uses: like Grey Friars, of which the church became the parish church of Christ Church, the conventual buildings Christ's Hospital.[1] Five of the religious houses became great mansions, like Charterhouse, home of the Duke of Norfolk.[2] The convent buildings of St. Mary Overy were the house of the Catholic Lord Montague, and became a nest of adherents of the old Faith. St. John's, Clerkenwell was used as the headquarters and storehouse of the Master of the Revels; the Minories became an armoury, supplementing the Tower, St. Mary Graces a naval depôt with great ovens for baking ships' biscuit; glasshouses were established in the Black, White and Crutched Friars. The Bishop of Salisbury's inn went to the Sackvilles, the Bishop of Ely's to Hatton, Durham's to Ralegh, York House to the Lord Keeper; the prior of Tortington's to the Earl of Oxford, the abbot of Bury's to Sir Thomas Heneage, while Thomas Randolph, Sir Drew Drury and a couple of aldermen were seated in other abbots' town houses. Such is the picture. The storm had brought in a wholly secular crew stuck to the rafts.

Charterhouse had been granted to the Norths, who began the alterations turning it into a mansion.[3] They sold it to Norfolk, much of whose work remained up to the *blitz* of 1941: the fine screen in the great hall with the initials 'T.N. 1571', the brick cloisters leading to the tennis court, the Renaissance staircase with figured finials looking like so many that still remain in English houses, the Great Chamber to which Norfolk added the ceiling and the noble fireplace. The south wing of the Master's house was the long gallery in which Norfolk had his interviews with Ridolfi; the privy chamber — in which that ineffectual conspirator left a most incriminating letter under a mat and forgot it, having "given orders that it should be burned"[4] — overlooked the Master's Court. It was from here that the Duke was taken to the Tower, a "number of idle rascal people . . . running about him, as the manner is, gazing at him".[5] He was succeeded by his son Philip, Earl of Arundel, who was no more sensible than his father and added to it the impropriety of being under his wife's influence: he too found himself in the Tower, where he distinguished himself by hearing a Mass followed by a twenty-four hours' intercession for the success of the Armada. A precious lot

[1] E. Jeffries-Davis, *loc. cit.* pp. 305-6.
[2] *Ibid.* p. 310.
[3] G. S. Davies, *Charterhouse in London*, p. 114 foll.
[4] *Ibid.* p. 132.
[5] *Ibid.* p. 141.

of good it did! After these follies the house was occupied for a time by the gay, privateering Earl of Cumberland, then by Lord Thomas Howard, with whom the Howards resumed possession 1601–11; he sold it to Thomas Sutton for £13,000, who dedicated it to better purposes.

The site of St. Bartholomew's priory, Smithfield, provides an interesting example of how a monastic precinct was built up.[1] Sir Robert Rich, first Chancellor of the Court of Augmentations, bought the priory buildings and — what was most valuable — the profits of the annual fair: in consideration of his service to the King he got it for only nine years' purchase, £1064 : 11 : 3. Rich was an able, sycophantic lawyer, a nasty piece of work, whose service to the King was considerable. Sir Thomas More early had an ill opinion of him, which Rich requited by violating his promise in obtaining More and Fisher's views on the Royal Supremacy and then laying them in evidence against them. He was the chief witness against his friend Cromwell. It seems that Rich was a Catholic at heart, who conformed under Edward, then took an active part in the burnings under Mary, and voted against Elizabeth's Act of Uniformity. Before he died, Rich put himself right with his conscience by founding Felsted School — which became a favourite receptacle for the sons of Puritan families in the next century, including four sons of Oliver Cromwell. Rich died in 1567 and lies buried under his Renaissance monument at Felsted; his will provided for his illegitimate son. The family became a leading Puritan one. They must have made a pile of money from the building up of St. Bartholomew's, which the third Lord Rich began in earnest in 1583.[2]

The first Lord, our agreeable lawyer, had pulled down the splendid nave of the church to increase the accommodation for the more profitable fair in the churchyard. This was held 23–25 August and was principally a cloth fair, in which the Drapers and Merchant Taylors regulated the measurements — the latter still possess the silver yard used. The fair has its place in literature through Jonson's comedy, with his appropriate portrait of the Puritan hypocrite, Zeal-of-the-Land Busy. Rich, as Chancellor of the Court of Augmentations, collected a number of his officials conveniently around him in the close, and so Sir Walter Mildmay's father, auditor of the Court, came there to live. The son, Chancellor of the Exchequer and founder of Emmanuel College, lived in the frater with the cloister adjoining; he is buried in the

[1] E. A. Webb, *Records of St. Bartholomew's, Smithfield*, I. 263.
[2] *Ibid.* II. 232 foll.

church under a rich monument with obelisks, bosses and coats of arms. When St. Paul's was struck by lightning, Grindal tried to get the lead roof of St. Bartholomew's to repair St. Paul's, arguing — no doubt rightly — that the frater would make a sufficient parish church. Cecil was against it. Besides Mildmay was a friend and colleague. The Bishop scoffed to think "prayers more acceptable under lead than under slate".

Other distinguished persons came to live in the Close: Sir Roger Manwood, founder of the grammar school at Sandwich and chief Baron of the Exchequer 1578–92, when he was rebuked by the Queen for the sale of offices and, attempting to justify his action, shortly after died. Sir Philip Scudamore and the interesting young bachelor Sir Robert Chamberlain, lord of the delightful lordship of Sherborne in Oxfordshire, who perished on a journey to the Holy Land between Tripoli and Cyprus, to whom his friend put up a monument of him kneeling in effigy with a touching inscription. By the end of the Elizabethan Age there was a close connection of distinguished Puritan families living there, all stemming from Walsingham's grandfather: Mildmays, Carys and Fanes; Walsinghams, Manwoods and Cranfields; these were brought together by Lionel Cranfield marrying a Fane. The monks would hardly have recognised their (new) aristocratic successors. And all round, the green and leafy spaces were filling up with Rich's profitable tenements. In 1590 Lord Rich asked Burghley to persuade the Mayor not to stop his building operations; by 1595 the Court of Aldermen were protesting against his encroachments. By 1616 there were forty-six houses in Long Lane on the site of the monastic garner, eleven houses on the laundry green, three on the site of the north transept; in Cloth Fair, which was the churchyard, Longtiled House Row of sixteen houses, thirty houses on the north side; Kinghorn street, Middle street, Newbury street were built up on both sides, and from Sun Court to New Court. And so the precincts of that noble fragment of a church came to have the shut-in, enclosed appearance it has had ever since, where for most of the reign all was still open, spacious and green.

The Minories near the Tower, which had been a convent of Minoresses of St. Clare, Henry had granted the Bishop of Bath in exchange for his house near Temple Bar which he wanted for the Earl of Southampton; since, as the King agreeably explained, he was 'minded to have' his nobles and councillors near him, not the bishops.[1] Bishop Barlow, who had stripped the lead from

[1] E. M. Tomlinson, *History of the Minories*, p. 80.

the palace halls successively at St. David's and at Wells, sold the Minories to Somerset for ready cash.[1] After all, the poor man had a family of daughters — all of whom in Elizabeth's reign married bishops. (The Bench must have been quite a family party.) In 1563 the Lord Treasurer bought the property for the Queen's use, to house ordnance and stores for which there was no room in the Tower; the floors were breaking under their weight. He had great difficulty in persuading the Queen that it was necessary and had to call in Cecil's aid, " praying you to read her Grace the letter and show her that I am as loth to spend her Majesty's money otherwise than for the discharge of her debt and for her ordinary charges as herself is ".[2] That was the spirit. However, the Queen was persuaded, and the buildings were converted into storehouses and workshops for the Ordnance, and Sir William Pelham was installed in residence as Lieutenant-General. He was a soldier of vigour and experience, ancestor of the family at Brocklesby where is his portrait, an elderly bald man in black-and-gold armour with a large baton. When he came to accompany Leicester to the Netherlands in 1585 his official balance-sheet showed a deficit of £8000, while his personal debts were £5000.[3] The Queen would not hear of remitting them, but made him mortgage his own property as security before he went to the Netherlands. He was succeeded by Sir Robert Constable, 1587–91, and he by Sir George Carew who made a large fortune by peculation, became an earl and is buried beneath a sumptuous monument at Stratford-on-Avon. But that was in the palmy days of James I, after Elizabeth's careful vigilance had gone from the State.

A small community grew up within these precincts too: a number of good families, several of the Queen's musicians, a number of doctors, surgeons, silk-weavers, and a considerable foreign element, mostly Dutch.[4] There were Pelhams: Sir John Pelham was buried by torchlight 13 October 1580, Sir Robert Oughtred of Kixley in Yorkshire on 24 November 1590, " being on a Tuesday at even tide by torch light "; the Lucys of Charlecote and the Astons of Tixall lived here. So did Mark Antony Galliardello, who had been a Court musician to Henry, Edward, Mary and Elizabeth; his son Caesar was to James I; his daughter Frances married John Lanier, and Lucretia married Henry Truches, both musicians to the Queen. At St. Helen's, Bishopsgate, St. Katherine's hospital, Blackfriars and elsewhere the pattern was similar: a few grandees and their attendants, some pro-

[1] E. M. Tomlinson, *History of the Minories*, p. 107.
[2] *Ibid.* pp. 118-20.
[3] *Ibid.* p. 128.
[4] *Ibid.* p. 391 foll.

fessional people, a variegated crowd of hangers-on, craftsmen and a considerable foreign contingent. This was at its largest at St. Katherine's by the Tower: by 1567 there were within the liberty 425 foreigners, of whom 328 were Dutch and 69 French, mostly hatmakers.[1] Blackfriars had been granted to Sir Thomas Carwarden, Master of the Revels, who used the church of St. Anne to store his equipment. The theatrical associations persisted: Burbage opened his theatre there in 1596. Lord Cobham was its leading resident; for the rest, a crowded motley crew, players, recusant Catholics, conspirators — the usual Elizabethan *tohu-bohu*. Within St. Helen's, Bishopsgate resided Stanhopes, Delavals, and nearby Greshams and Reades; the foreign element was represented by Albericus Gentile, the eminent civilian and a secretary to the French ambassador. Sir Julius Caesar, Master of the Rolls, was a leading parishioner, and his fantastic monument remains to testify it.

The hospital of St. Katherine's provides a pretty story which shows up everybody in a characteristic light.[2] The liberty and franchises were parcel of the dowry of the Queens of England. When the English were driven out of Calais in 1558, many of the inhabitants settled here: by the eighteenth century Hammes and Guisnes Lanes had become Hangman's Gains, a more familiar idea. Elizabeth appointed her Secretary, Dr. Thomas Wilson, to the Mastership. Finding his patent void because he was not a priest according to Queen Philippa's charter, he surrendered it and took out a new one with a *non obstante* clause. Finding this a good precedent, he next surrendered the great charter of the hospital and obtained a new one, omitting the profitable liberty of the fair. He then sold the rights of the fair to the Mayor and commonalty for 700 marks (£466 : 13 : 4) which he appropriated to himself. (He was not a distinguished casuist for nothing.) This suited everybody — except the inhabitants. It suited the Queen — it was very much her way of rewarding her servants; it certainly suited Dr. Wilson; and it worked in well with the city's constant desire to extend its control and end the liberties, which were a nuisance from its point of view. The Doctor intended next to secure to himself all the properties of the hospital within the precincts. At this the inhabitants repugned. They presented a petition to Cecil complaining that it was the business of the Master to uphold the rights and privileges of the hospital, that the present inhabitants were a great commodity to it; where formerly the Master was charged with repairs they now bore the cost as tenants and the Master received the rents free. They had

[1] J. Nichols, *Bibliotheca Topographica Britannica*, II. 22 foll. [2] *Ibid.*

made whole lanes and streets where had been " dunghills, laystoffs and void grounds ". They paid all their parish charges, four offering days and clerk's wages; they shared the burden of the watch as a Tower hamlet — 28s. a month; they paid at least 5s. a week in poor relief. Many of their inhabitants were seafaring men serving at sea, as well as paying their charge to the Tower — *i.e.* for defence. Others were the Queen's servants, paying according to their fee and giving daily attendance on their Prince. This stopped Dr. Wilson's plans and the revenues of the hospital were preserved.

What a picture it affords: the legalism, the mixture of adherence to custom and charter, the connivance of Queen, Secretary and city authorities in getting round it, the readiness to halt when they found they had gone too far.

Conflicts of jurisdiction in London were relatively less frequent because of the immense authority of the Mayor, aldermen and Council. The Privy Council down at Westminster treated the city authorities with great circumspection and respect, they were liable to have so much need of them, especially financially, and in other ways. The respect was mutual; after all they were both involved in the common conspiracy, and the burden, of government. The way in which both co-operated was an admirable example of the relative maturity of English government compared with the Continent. In the end the authority of the Privy Council was overriding, but it was so well understood that it did not often have to be exerted. Where there was conflict it was usually over some question of jurisdiction, often in connection with the liberties that were left over from before the Reformation — small areas independent of the city authorities and more numerous in London than elsewhere. It is so like the conservatism of the English in the midst of revolutionary changes that these should have been preserved at all. Stow notices with some surprise that the privileges which had attached to the former College of St. Martin-le-Grand should now be claimed by the secular population that had poured into the precinct: " privileges granted to the canons serving God day and night (for so be the words in the charter of William the Conqueror) which may hardly be wrested to artificers, buyers and sellers, otherwise than is mentioned in the 21 of St. Matthew's Gospel ".[1] Into this liberty had crowded a large number of foreigners; the church

[1] Stow, *op. cit.* I. 309.

had been pulled down to build houses for them; the place was a hive of the luxury industries they had brought with them: they were mostly Dutch and French, leather-sellers, goldsmiths, tailors, button-makers, silk-weavers, bookbinders, virginal-makers and makers of printers' moulds.[1] Burghley himself was steward of the liberty, and when the aldermen of Aldersgate ward sent his deputy into it to impress men to serve along with others of the city he found himself admonished and told to take steps to prevent the molestation of anyone dwelling within that privileged place.[2] Respect for immunities and privileges was itself a stage in the development of responsible government.

Conflict between the authorities of the city and those of the Tower as to the bounds of the liberty went back to the fifteenth century. It was renewed when in 1582 one Hemming, servant to Sir William George, the Gentleman Porter, began to build tenements outside the Postern Gate, evidently with his master's encouragement.[3] Complaints flew between the Mayor and the Gentleman Porter, the Mayor and the Lord Treasurer; then the Privy Council and the Lieutenant of the Tower were drawn in. The Mayor complained that debtors sought refuge in the liberty of the Tower and that when the Sheriffs' officers pursued them "good citizens were taken prisoners into the Tower and there violently detained against all colour of law". The Privy Council did their best to meet the city authorities; they submitted the dispute to Queen's learned counsel, meanwhile ordering Hemming to stop building, and expressed their astonishment to the Gentleman Porter that "he or any under him should make any innovation or intermeddle in a matter not yet resolved but standing in question and doubt of law". The Lieutenant of the Tower also received an admonishment and was told to allow the Sheriffs to execute their office and to set the citizens at liberty. To all this was added a rumpus because the Mayor had had his sword carried before him when he went to take his oath outside Tower Gate, and two of the warders had tried to make him lower it. Recorder Fleetwood, however, had been equal to that. But the ancient boundary stone marking the Sheriffs' jurisdiction had been removed. The Mayor wrote to Walsingham asking for the redress of these injuries and that the stone might be replaced. And so it went on. The Council made an order for settling these controversies, but the question of the boundaries remained over for fools to fight about.

[1] R. E. T. and E. F. Kirk, "Returns of Aliens in London", *Proceedings of the Huguenot Society*, X. Part III. 434-9.

[2] *Remembrancia, City of London, 1579–1664*, p. 458.

[3] *Ibid.* p. 426 foll.

Where the Council was not willing to meet the wishes of the city authorities — or only temporarily in times of plague or other infection — was in regard to the theatres, for here was a plain conflict of interest between the tastes of the Court and the increasingly Puritan prejudices of the bourgeois. In 1580 the Mayor took the opportunity of some disturbance at the Theatre to inform the Lord Chancellor that " the players of plays . . . and tumblers and such like were a very superfluous sort of men and of such faculty as the laws had disallowed; that the exercise of the plays was not only a great hindrance to the service of God but also a great corruption of youth with unchaste and wicked matters, the occasion of much incontinence, practices of many frays, quarrels and other disorders within the city ".[1] He asked, therefore, that plays might be prevented not only within the city — where theatres were not allowed — but also in the liberties. This was asking for a lot. The sympathies of the Court and the nobility were, as often, more popular than those of the middle class. The Council responded only so far as to prohibit plays on account of the infection during the summer months, and now " as the sickness had almost ceased . . . in order to relieve the poor players and to encourage their being in readiness with convenient matters for her Highness's solace this next Christmas, they required them forthwith to suffer the players to practice such plays in such sort and in the usual places as they had been accustomed ". Next year the Mayor came back with a prohibition of plays on the sabbath and holidays. The Council replied with wary circumspection, invoking the sacred name: " Nevertheless of late, for honest recreation sake, in respect that her Majesty sometimes took delight in those pastimes, it had been thought not unfit, having regard to the season of the year and the clearance of the city from infection, to allow of certain companies of players in London, partly that they might thereby attain more dexterity and perfection in that profession, the better to content her Majesty, the said players being restrained from playing on the sabbath and only permitted on the ordinary holidays after evening prayer. . . ." They asked the Mayor to withdraw his prohibition. The Mayor replied " that although the players began not their plays till after evening service, yet all the afternoon they took in hearers and filled the place with such as were thereby absent from Church and attended to serve God's enemies in an inn. If they were restrained from letting in the people till after service it would delay the action of their plays to a very

[1] *Remembrancia, City of London, 1579–1664*, p. 350 foll.

inconvenient time of night, specially for servants and children." Moreover, the plague was increasing again and the meeting of Parliament near; these exercises would be dangerous, etc. In the summer months the plays were once more suspended. Then, in time for Christmas, the Council requested that "the players might be suffered to play as heretofore, more especially as they were shortly to present some of their doings before Her".

Ten years later the Court of Aldermen were still at it and calling in the aid of the Archbishop of Canterbury: the youths of the city were greatly corrupted, their manners infected with many evils and ungodly qualities by the wanton things they saw on the stage, apprentices and servants were withdrawn from their work, to the great hindrance of trade and religion (they went together); besides, harlots, cutpurses, cozeners, pilferers, etc., did their bad deeds under colour of hearing plays. The Archbishop did what he could; but by this time the theatres were established on a sure foundation and some of the theatre people on their way to achieve bourgeois respectability, to found a school or take out a coat of arms — both badges of having arrived. There were no doubt honest citizens like the couple in *The Knight of the Burning Pestle* who dearly loved a play and were proud of Ralph their apprentice, who "will act you sometimes at our house that all the neighbours cry out on him; he will fetch you up a couraging part so in the garret that we are all as feared, I warrant you, that we quake again: we'll fear our children with him; if they be never so unruly, do but cry 'Ralph comes, Ralph comes!' to them and they'll be as quiet as lambs".[1] But the conflict of the Puritan bourgeoisie with the Court on this point continued until the Civil War and the horrid Prynne had his way.

The corporate life of industrial and trading London was organised in the City Companies. These, too, were essentially medieval in character — they had developed out of the gilds and fraternities with which medieval life was honeycombed — and they had come through the Reformation virtually unchanged. The contribution of the sixteenth century to their development was to strengthen their organisation; various trades came together to form stronger associations; new companies came into being, like the Stationers — since the Reformation brought about a great increase in printing and the number of printers. About the middle of the century the number of the great Livery Com-

[1] Beaumont and Fletcher, *The Knight of the Burning Pestle*, Induction.

panies, which dominated all this side of London's life and from which it was customary to select the Mayor, was finally fixed, like the Apostles, at twelve.[1] These great Companies — Mercers, Grocers, Drapers, and so on in order of precedence — had a very strong and privileged position: they had had their own Royal charters and so had a good deal of independence. They were treated by the Mayor and aldermen, who were bone of their bone, as powers on their own, not subordinate branches of civic administration as the lesser crafts were apt to be. They were used as regular channels of administration and government, but on a voluntary basis. The relation of the civic authorities to them was rather like that of the Privy Council to the civic authorities. Mutual respect and understanding — but the authority of the Mayor was overriding and indeed becoming stronger in the later sixteenth century. It was used to support the Companies, which had only become subjected to the city's authority after a long struggle in the Middle Ages.

Everybody was supposed to be in his own organised craft, and there were very strong inducements to be so. The privileges of a freeman of London were jealously protected and they could not be attained except through membership of a gild. London would not suffer strangers to buy and sell there. And there were all the advantages attaching to membership once you were inside. In Elizabeth's reign, with the immense growth of industry and trade, the London population and the incoming of aliens, the bonds were much loosened and there was much shifting of boundaries among Companies. In some cases exactness of definition was difficult and crafts were shifting over to occupations allied to, but not always the same as, their primary ones. This was a fruitful source of dispute; the Clothworkers, for example, fought the incoming Merchant Taylors from their preserves long and furiously, but not in the end successfully; they had to allow the Merchant Taylors to finish cloth free from their right of search.[2] The Drapers were now almost wholly engaged in selling cloth, and in making hose — properly the work of the haberdasher. As the market extended there was more room: the Drapers were ready to compromise and allowed their apprentices to serve with members of the Merchant Taylors. Among the Drapers were a number of printers — some Companies wanted their own printers; in the end the Drapers were willing that they should join the Stationers.

[1] G. Unwin, *The Gilds and Companies of London*, p. 76.

[2] A. H. Johnson, *Hist. of the Worshipful Company of the Drapers of London*, II. 172.

The Companies continued to fulfil a number of most important functions. The primary purpose of gilds throughout Western Europe had been the control of industry and trade and the corporate protection of the individual — since the whole of medieval life was corporately organised. The Companies continued to regulate the conditions of industry and trade, standards of workmanship, recruitment — the admission of apprentices and the making of freemen, though naturally with less completeness and effectiveness as time went on and industry expanded. And this varied from Company to Company: the Goldsmiths and Pewterers, for example, had the right of search and thereby set the standards throughout the country, while the latter through their monopoly exercised a controlling influence on the tin industry. The Companies performed all the functions of benefit societies for their members: helping to set up their young men in trade, from the numerous benefactions they received for the purpose, providing almshouses and charities for their sick and infirm, founding schools for their children. They continued to give the corporate protection that was essential in the harsh circumstances of medieval life: everybody needed protection — even the players were organised into Companies under the protection of the Lord Chamberlain or the Lord Admiral, Leicester or the Queen. Writers had to have patrons; if these failed them they went under — like Greene or Nashe, or into the Church — like Marston or Donne. (Perhaps that might be regarded as the greatest of all Livery Companies.) They have been regarded as 'organisations for the accumulation of social prestige' — the more primitive the society the more important that commodity. In some respects their regulations — and their restrictive practices — were like those of a modern Trade Union, and they had some of its uses for their members. One aspect that can be dispensed with in modern society continued to be important: the religious. The Company still marched to its traditional, neighbouring church on the election day of its Wardens; only instead of hearing a Mass, it heard, more usefully, a sermon. The Grocers went further and kept the next day also as solemn, taking the sacrament together at St. Stephen's, Coleman Street.

It is remarkable how little the Companies were affected by the Reformation, once the disturbed period was over. They shook themselves, and found the confiscation of the Chantries Act quite tolerable after all. The government had only annexed that portion of their charitable trusts that was devoted to superstitious uses — *i.e.* Masses for the dead. It did not amount to more than £1000 a year in all.[1] There was only one hard case, the confiscation of the property of the Parish Clerks; and by the end of Elizabeth's reign they had set themselves up again in a new hall. But there was a good deal of saving of time and wasteful expenditure on non-productive objects. By the eve of the Reformation the Goldsmiths found themselves obliged to attend twenty-five anniversary services in different churches in the course of the year, to their great hindrance and trouble; while it was no unusual thing for thirty Masses or three trentals to be said for a deceased member.[2] It is necessary for all societies from time to time to cut out a certain amount of dead wood, and this the Reformation did. There was no break in their character or even in their records at the Reformation: once more, conservatism in the midst of change. They went to church as before; they had their funeral dinners to more point than their Masses.

Within the Companies, as within the industries they represented, there was a constant conflict of interests: between the ruling class of big merchants and middlemen and the dependent class of small master craftsmen. The distinctive feature of the fully developed Livery Company was a court, which came to be known in our period as the Court of Assistants. This body exercised jurisdiction over the members, regulated the number of apprentices, punished their offences or the offences of their masters against them, fined masters offending against trade regulations — above all, settled disputes among members. Control had passed into the hands of the Court; quite naturally: only a few fortunate members could afford the time to attend to so much business. The fully fledged members of the Company were known as the Livery; they were the well-to-do element from whom the officers were elected and who managed the Company's affairs. Beneath these were the yeomanry. They had formerly been the small master craftsmen. Here the immense economic and social development of the time was reflecting itself. Many of the yeomanry were no longer journeymen, but the younger sons of well-off members on their way up to the Livery, and to all the place and consideration in the city that entailed. The yeomanry now consisted of two different elements and had disputes enough within its own ranks. It usually had its own officers to settle them. It was all the more a triumph that the organisation maintained itself. But it had the authority of government behind it, both central and of the city. The government used the organisa-

[1] G. Unwin, *op. cit.* p. 209.

[2] *Ibid.* pp. 207, 118.

tion of the Companies greatly for administrative purposes — chiefly financial and for defence. It issued its orders to them through the Mayor, whose authority was thereby reinforced. It was such that the method of electing the officers in the lesser Companies was frequently prescribed by the Mayor and aldermen.[1] Government was inevitably, and quite naturally, oligarchical all through.

It is not surprising therefore that the Companies survived into a new world; in fact they flourished, added new lustre to themselves by taking in eminent persons as honorary members — Drake became a Draper; they feasted more largely than ever. When they were unwilling to contribute more to the costs of the war, in 1596, the Queen suggested that they might well suspend their sumptuous feasts and give half the money to the poor.[2] The august advice was heeded — at any rate there was no election dinner that year. They took to themselves new halls, or panelled and carpeted the old ones and laid out gardens; they did a great deal of undoubted good. Take the Drapers, for example, whom I cite out of piety. In Elizabeth's first year the number of the Livery had declined to only 43; by the end of the century they had increased beyond what they were before the Reformation — and those were only the well-to-do.[3] The yeomanry had quadrupled since the beginning of the century; they were 487 in 1574 — testimony to the prosperity of London. Though the question of the concealed lands was a troublesome one for all the Companies, they could well afford to pay the extra sums the government wanted to raise for them, since the annual rental of their lands had increased so much: in the case of the Drapers, by 50 per cent since Edward VI.[4] The Companies displayed great public spirit, both within and without. They founded schools; they maintained scholars at the universities; their members left numerous benefactions to help young men starting in life or those members in distress: "the gifts of such good men that be alive and they that be passed out of this world".[5]

The Drapers, in addition to maintaining almshouses, interested

[1] *Ibid.* p. 236. [2] R. R. Sharp, *London and the Kingdom*, I. 559.

[3] A. H. Johnson, *op. cit.* p. 191.

[4] *Ibid.* p. 234. 'Concealed lands' referred to a proportion of chantry revenues that had not been surrendered under the Chantries Act, owing to some difference of opinion as to what was liable to be surrendered. What made the question troublesome for the Companies was that the value of the lands had increased so much since 1547. The Drapers, for example, now paid the Crown an additional £584, more than half that originally demanded for their chantry properties (cf. Johnson, p. 207). [5] q. Unwin, p. 186.

themselves in poor relief. When the Mercers had purchased their hall they agreed with Henry VIII to found a school. The Skinners helped to found Tonbridge. The Merchant Taylors established their school in London by the munificence of a Master, Richard Hilles, who — a Protestant in his sympathies — was in the end charitable beyond his means.[1] Sir Thomas White, whose sympathies were Catholic, was no less charitable. He was the founder of St. John's College, Oxford, which he connected with his own Company, the Merchant Taylors, and he left a very large trust for the benefit of twenty-five towns by rota for the purpose of starting young tradesmen in life.[2]

To illustrate the business going forward within a Company let us look into the arcana of the Goldsmiths.[3] St. Dunstan's is their great day. They decide that their Wardens are to wear garlands on their feast day like other Companies. The Clerk loses his office for revealing the names of the Wardens-elect. The Wardens with the Clerk and their Beadle, Erasmus Clinkerdagger, set out on their periodic search journey — in 1571 through the western towns. A silver cross made for Sir Thomas Pope was done unskilfully: the price is reduced. A nest of gilt bells for the Earl of Worcester, badly done, are to be amended. A servant is beaten for taking his master by the beard; on the other hand, a servant complains to the Company against his master for breaking a pair of tongs on him and another leaves his master because he is not allowed a feather bed. Three masters are fined for allowing their apprentices to wear ruffs. One member has taught certain gentlemen of the Court the art of assay-making. The Wardens object that it is "contrary to his oath to open that or any other secret of his mystery to any man that is not free thereof".[4] The goldsmith stood stoutly to his defence and said that he would do it again for money. The Queen has had some of her plate stolen and it cannot be recovered; only two 'carcases of cruets' come back. A Cirencester man is apprehended for trying to sell plate with the arms cut away. When a Goldsmith is elected Mayor, he is granted £100 for his expenses. The Company raises a loan of £100 for arms, but keeps it secret lest greater taxation be imposed on them. A present of £100 in angels is given to Leicester for his favour. The Master of the Queen's barge furnishes them with a barge yearly for the Mayor's procession. A present of

[1] C. M. Clode, *Early History of the Merchant Taylors' Company*, II. 58 foll., 227.
[2] *Ibid.* II. 98 foll., 177 foll.
[3] W. S. Prideaux, *Memorials of the Goldsmiths' Company*, pp. 56-99.
[4] *Ibid.* p. 62.

29 nobles is given to their scholar at Cambridge on his proceeding M.A. Their Oxford scholar James Mabbe dedicates his book *The Diet of Health* to the Company and £10 is given him. (He was the grandson of a Goldsmith who was Chamberlain of London; he became a Fellow of Magdalen and famous for his translations from the Spanish.)

In 1570 there is mention of a book of portraitures Agnes Ruthgen has lent Nicholas Hilliard — apparently he is working at it. In 1599 he offers a fine of £20 and a picture worth 20 nobles for the renewal of the lease of his house in Gutter Lane. It seems that the Queen has to intervene through the lords of the Council on behalf of her jeweller and miniaturist: the house is leased to him for thirty years at a rent of £30 per annum, Hilliard to " bestow on the Company a fair picture of her Majesty to remain in the house for an ornament, and a remembrance as well of their humble duties and her princely favour towards him, as of his gratitude to the Company ".[1] We learn next that Hilliard wants the lease at once, promising to bring the money; but the winter is an unseasonable time to make a picture, he will make it in the summer and give security for it. We see that he had the artist's temperament as well as his genius. Here is some indication that Hilliard painted pictures as well as miniatures.

Such was the scene upon which there took place so many famous events that have left a living memory in the mind of the English people. There was the outburst of joy that welcomed Elizabeth's accession, that she made the most of and held on to all her life: the changed atmosphere, the sense of youth and gaiety and spring in the air, the melancholy winter with its burnings over. One cannot sense it better than in the pages of the diary kept by Henry Machyn, citizen and Merchant Taylor of London — actually he was a sort of undertaker, furnisher of the elaborate trappings that were proper to respectable funerals in those days. One sees Elizabeth going out on the Thames, across the water to the bull-baiting or down the river to watch the tilt at Greenwich, carefully cultivating the people and her popularity, putting Mary — whom they had rarely seen — out of mind. The friars and monks are sent away; there is a new spirit of enjoyment of life abroad, that could not be more marked than in the pages of this undertaker. " The 25th day of April was St.

[1] *Ibid.* p. 98.

Mark's day, the Queen's grace supped at Baynard Castle at my lord of Pembroke's place, and after supper the Queen's grace rowed up and down Thames, and a hundred boats about her grace, with trumpets and drums and flutes and guns, and squibs hurling on high to and fro, till 10 at night ere her grace departed and all the water-side stood with a thousand people looking on her grace." [1]

> Elizabeth and Leicester
> Beating oars
> The stern was formed
> A gilded shell
> The brisk swell
> Rippled both shores
> Southwest wind
> Carried down stream
> The peal of bells
> White towers
>   Weialala leia
>   Wallala leialala [2]

Or there was the unforgettable funeral procession of Sir Philip Sidney through the streets of the city to St. Paul's the year before the Armada: impossible to find a parallel for him — he was a kind of Nelson cum Rupert Brooke to the Elizabethans, combining an undying fame with youth, high birth and poetry. Or it is the spring of 1588 and the Lord Mayor goes with his aldermen down to Whitehall to assure the Queen of the devotion of the city.[3] He must have been impressed with all those chambers and galleries, being shown into the Lord Chancellor's chamber, then the Lord Steward's, then into the Council chamber, before he came into the Presence chamber where the Queen came to thank him for the city's contribution and the Lord Mayor replied with his old-fashioned oratory about the hairs of the head — getting few enough now under the red wig. "'I pray you, my Lord Mayor,' said her Majesty, 'tell them I thank them all for it, and desire them to pray for me and I will pray for them, and that I would be sorry mine enemies should have the like subjects, for', said her Highness, 'I think no prince in Christendom hath the like or can have better' . . . in which words her Majesty displayed her hands often times, as though she would have embraced my Lord Mayor, and after he had kneeled very long and was stiff there-

[1] *Diary of Henry Machyn* (Camden Society), p. 196.
[2] T. S. Eliot, *The Waste Land*, III.
[3] A. H. Johnson, *op. cit.* pp. 148-50.

with, her Highness willed one of her lords to help him up and came towards him herself to have helped him. 'O most precious Prince and jewel inestimable, whose hairs of her head her subjects are, I heartily pray unto God', said he, 'that if she have any loose hairs that will not stick to her head she may cast them into the fire.'" And so on. When all was over, and the ships of Spain lay scattered round the coasts of Britain, there was the great Armada procession to St. Paul's. And so to those March days in 1603 when the news of the Queen's death held London in a kind of numbness, only broken when in her funeral procession they saw her effigy carried by, and the sight of that so familiar figure going by for the last time caused all the people to break out in a universal lamentation and weeping.

This was the city that was now being so celebrated in literature. It is the citizens of London, the carpenters and cobblers, that pour into the streets in the first scene of *Julius Caesar*; it is the London mob of whom such a truthful and unflattering portrait is drawn in play after play of Shakespeare's, in *Henry VI, Henry IV* and *V*, in *Coriolanus.* A kindlier portrait is drawn in such comedies as *The Knight of the Burning Pestle* and *The Shoemaker's Holiday*, with its rollicking character of Simon Eyre, the poor apprentice who made good and became Mayor (there was such an historic person; he built Leadenhall and was buried in St. Mary Woolnoth in 1459).[1] Ben Jonson's canvases — himself a Londoner born and bred — in such plays as *The Alchemist*, *Bartholomew Fair*, *Eastward Ho*, depict the life of the city with a wryer humour, with a satirical and critical intention. In Captain Bobadil in *Every Man in his Humour*, one of his greatest creations, he gives us a caricature of a type of the time, a swashbuckling soldier, a 'Paul's man', with his following of young braggarts. Donne, a Londoner on both sides — his father an Ironmonger, his mother a daughter of John Heywood, a writer of Court interludes — has a satirical inflection in his comment on the time. The city authorities were themselves calling in the poets to celebrate its feasts and triumphs. Peele composed the device for the Lord Mayor's Pageant in 1585 and again in 1591. Munday and Middleton, Dekker, Webster and Heywood all composed pageants for such occasions. When the Merchant Taylors gave a great feast in 1607, Ben Jonson wrote the verses and Dr. John Bull provided the music. What we think of in the end, when we remember the London of those days, is its intense and jostling vitality, its uninhibited and native gusto for life: the Boar's Head

[1] Cf. Stow, *op. cit.* I. 153-4.

in East Cheap frequented by Falstaff and his boys, the Mitre and the Mermaid as the poets knew them and handed them down to us:

What things have we seen
Done at the Mermaid! heard words that have been
So nimble and so full of subtle flame,
As if that every one from whence they came
Had meant to put his whole wit in a jest. . . .

CHAPTER VI

SOCIAL CLASSES

We are now in a position to portray the classes that made up Elizabethan society, or at least to sketch the structure of social life — if such an image may be pardoned where so much is growth and movement, up or down. But at the outset we are confronted with what is the least studied, the most uncertain and difficult subject in these researches — that of Elizabethan population.[1] It would take a whole body of scholars, possibly a Royal Commission of both historians and statisticians, to get to grips with it, so vast is the evidence and so insecure its interpretation: thousands of parish registers all over the country, many hundreds of subsidy and muster rolls, most of them incomplete and many unreliable. All that can be done here is to provide an outline of a framework for our picture: such detail as we can provide is to be regarded as merely illustrative or suggestive. Figures can at least serve as a check on other evidences, as occasional boundary stones in these wide wastes.

It was not till the sixteenth century that quantitative problems came to be considered from a modern point of view;[2] and this attitude with regard to population, like so many other things, was first clarified and formulated in Italy.[3] By 1600 England had not yet arrived at general principles, but as usual our practice was better than our theory. From the beginning of the century enlightened opinion had been in favour of the registration of baptisms; but it came up against the irrational, though understandable, opposition of an illiterate people who feared new fiscal burdens.[4] It was not until the defeat of the Pilgrimage of Grace that Thomas Cromwell ventured to order a register of baptisms and burials to be kept in every parish. This was in 1538: France

[1] I should like to suggest this subject to intending researchers — perhaps the most important remaining in this field.

[2] A. M. Carr-Saunders, *The Population Problem*, p. 20.

[3] J. Bonar, *Theories of Population from Raleigh to Arthur Young*, p. 16.

[4] Cf. W. E. Tate, *The Parish Chest*, pp. 43-5.

followed next year with a similar ordinance.[1] A constitution of the province of Canterbury, approved by the Queen in 1598, ordered that parchment registers should be purchased into which the older entries should be copied, " but especially since the first year of her Majesty's reign ". It is for this reason that so many parish registers begin with Elizabeth's reign, and to this we owe the calculations that have been made of the population at the time. A contemporary estimate of the population of France placed it at some 14 millions; but since this greatly exaggerated the number of French parishes, of which in fact there were some 40,000, we should probably be not far wrong if we reduced our estimate to some 10 to 12 millions.[2] In England and Wales there were some 9000 parishes, and Rickman estimated the population in 1600 at 4,811,718.[3] A more modern estimate gives us 5 millions in 1603.[4] A conflation of these two estimates — and it is probably impossible to arrive at anything much more exact — yields the following scheme:

1558	4½ millions
1603	5 ,,
1625	5½ ,,

The interest of this is that it shows a considerable increase of the population during Elizabeth's reign, some 11 per cent; and double that rate of increase during the reign of James I, some 20 per cent, which is what we should have expected: the early seventeenth century was the great period of the hiving off of Englishmen to found colonies overseas, which the effort and success of Elizabeth's reign made possible.

It is when we come to distribute this population, to compare different counties and areas, that we find our present state of information most tantalisingly inadequate. The most ready source of information, the muster returns,[5] is notoriously defective — though not so unreliable as the endearing caricature of Falstaff's mustering methods would give us to suppose. We can at least get some comparative idea of the man-power of different counties, particularly in the South where the administrative apparatus was more efficient and where it needed to be. Even so we cannot get absolute figures on this basis — there are so many exceptions and defective returns, while other figures are

[1] A. M. Carr-Saunders, *World Population*, p. 11.

[2] E. Levasseur, *La Population française*, I. 190-92.

[3] Cf. G. T. Griffith, *Population Problems of the Age of Malthus*, p. 12.

[4] Cf. A. M. Carr-Saunders, *Population*, p. 7.

[5] Here is another subject that greatly needs to be worked at as a whole.

obviously conventional ones. But we can observe the comparative populousness of different counties. In the Armada year, when returns might be expected to be at their highest efficiency, we find four southern counties estimated to provide over 10,000 able men between the ages of sixteen and sixty: Gloucester, Somerset, Kent, Devon, in that order.[1] The next most populous group are Surrey, Cornwall, Wilts, Sussex. This is for the southern counties alone; it says nothing as to the Midlands and the North. There is this further factor of uncertainty — one suspects that the totals differed considerably according to the efficiency of the mustering authorities in different counties and at different times. The burden of defence against Spain fell on the exposed maritime counties of the South. The Midlands and the North got off lightly. As to the last we only learn that Cheshire was more populous than Lancashire, which we knew before; as to the East, that Norfolk and Suffolk were both rated higher than Lincolnshire.

Within counties the different balance of population presented from that today could be in some parts worked out from parish registers; though the historical imagination checked by common sense should give one a sufficient picture. One must think away the industrial and urban agglomerations of today. In general, the North was sparsely inhabited. Population adhered to subsistence. Where the soil was good, there were most inhabitants. The Elizabethan Age was beginning to make considerable exceptions to this in favour of power and industry; even so, the population was spread rather than coagulated. The water-power that facilitated the clothing manufacture of the West Country and the West Riding, the cutlers of Hallamshire and the scythe, sickle and sword-makers of Worcestershire and Staffordshire, did not lump them together but kept them strung out along their streams. Even the coal pits did not coagulate people. But the exploitation of local sources of power naturally increased population in those areas. In other ways, too, subsistence dictated a different balance. All along the coast, fishing counted relatively for much more. A return of 1582 gives us the number of ships, mariners and fishermen for different counties.[2] What is noticeable is the number of small boats of under 80 tons. London has the great bulk of ships over that tonnage; of those under, Norfolk has 145, Essex 143, Devon 109, Cornwall 65, Suffolk 60. Of the seafaring population London has 143 masters, 991 mariners, 957 wherry-men, 195 fishermen; Norfolk has 232 masters, 1438 mariners and seamen;

[1] S.P. 12/210/42; and cf. Harleian MSS. vol. 286.

[2] S.P. 12/156/45.

Devon, 150 masters, 1914 mariners, 101 fishermen; Cornwall, 108 masters, 626 mariners, 1184 seamen — evidently including a large number of fishermen. Another return enables one to visualise the Cornish coast, particularly the bay at home at St. Austell, with many more small fishing communities along its creeks and coves; one sometimes comes across the rubble of vanished fishermen's cottages, as at Trenarren or Porthpean, or the deserted beach at Hallane.

> The places that are empty now
> Were once so full of vivid life. . . .

From a cursory analysis of even a few parish registers some interesting things and one very important point can be established.[1] Let us take the registers of one or two country parishes in the North. Halifax — like Bradford and Leeds — was a huge country parish covering many square miles of moorland.[2] Every year from 1558 to 1583 shows a surplus of births over deaths; during the first decade at an average rate of just 100 a year, during the second at just over, and during the last five years at nearly 200 a year. The population was increasing fast. Then came the plague and the two years 1586 and 1587 show 566 more deaths than births. This pulls the rate of increase of the population back sharply. All the same the total increase for thirty years during which the records are complete is 2489, an average yearly increase of 83 on a population which we estimate as round about 6000: some 13 per cent. The parish of Ormskirk in Lancashire — the burial-place of the Stanleys — was much more visited by epidemics during this period, in 1558, 1559, 1563 and 1565 and again in the decade 1588–97; this pulled down its normal rate of increase so that over the whole period of the reign there was an actual overplus of 49 deaths over births, on a population which we estimate at about 2250.[3] But this was exceptional, as we can see from looking at other country registers. Take the little parish of Askham in Westmorland: its church in a dell with silver birches on the slopes and winter sunshine on the gravestones, the sharp edge of the North to its sweetness; close by is the River Lowther singing in the woods. In this remote place the names remain much the same from Elizabeth's day to this.[4] The decade 1568–78 yields a surplus of 18 births over deaths on a population of perhaps 320. Shap, high up on the fells, gives us a marked

[1] I am very much indebted to Mr. W. J. Rowe for help in analysing these registers.
[2] *The Parish Registers of Halifax*, ed. E. W. Crossley.
[3] *Ormskirk Parish Register*, ed. J. Arrowsmith.
[4] Mary E. Noble, *Registers of the Parish of Askham, Westmorland*.

surplus of 58 births over deaths for the decade 1563–71, on a population of some 650.[1] This is pretty good going; where did they all go? Subsistence on those fells must have been limited. They were healthy and invigorating. Six out of the 30 children baptized in 1569 are noted as base-begotten, 3 of them at the end of January. There must have been high jinks at Shap the preceding April: did they celebrate St. George's day with unwonted vigour?

Let us look now at some town parishes: they reveal a marked contrast. St. Oswald's, Durham, for the first decade of the reign shows a surplus of 9 births over deaths; for the second, a surplus of 10 deaths; for the third, of 80 deaths — 1587 was a plague year; for the fourth, a surplus of 3 births.[2] During the whole period 1560 to 1606 there were 78 more deaths than births. Yet the population estimate remains the same for the end of the period as at the beginning: about 800. One would not expect the results for another parish in the same city to be much different; nor are they. In St. Mary-le-Bow from 1572 to 1603 there were 128 more deaths than births; 1587, 1596 and 1597 were plague years.[3] There is a gap in the St. Oswald's registers for 1596 and 1597 or the results would obviously have been worse: it would probably double the size of the deficit in human lives. St. Michael-at-Plea, Norwich, makes a better showing: in the half-century 1558 to 1607, 55 more births than deaths; there were plague years in 1579, 1603 and 1604.[4] But London parishes seem to tell the same story as Durham. In the forty years from 1564 to 1603 St. Olave, Hart Street, shows 468 more deaths than births; there were heavy losses in the plague years 1593 and 1604, besides minor epidemics.[5] The registers of St. Peter's, Cornhill, follow the same pattern and show 317 more deaths than births during the reign.[6] At Exeter an analysis of the registers of eleven city parishes shows for the decade 1570–80, a surplus of 223 births, for 1580–90, 242 more deaths than births; then from 1590 to 1600 there is a slow recovery, with a surplus of 196 births,

[1] Mary E. Noble, *Registers of the Parish of Shap*. At the other end of the country a moorland Cornish parish yields similar results, windy St. Breward high up on the shoulder of Bodmin moor (cf. *St. Breward Parish Register*, ed. T. Taylor). For the eight years 1568–75 a surplus of 25 births over deaths; then in the plague year 1576, 23 more deaths than births; in the five years 1578–83, a surplus of 21 births.

[2] *The Registers of St. Oswald's, Durham*, ed. A. W. Headlam.

[3] *The Registers of St. Mary-le-Bow, Durham*, ed. H. M. Wood.

[4] *The Register of St. Michael-at-Plea, Norwich*, trans. by J. R. Tallack.

[5] *The Registers of St. Olave, Hart Street, London*, ed. W. B. Bannerman, (Harleian Soc. Reg.)

[6] *The Registers of St. Peter's, Cornhill*, ed. G. W. G. Leveson-Gower (Harleian Soc. Reg.).

and from 1600 to 1610 a rapid increase with 544 more births than deaths.[1] The epidemic of 1590–91 was very severe and must have greatly reduced the population of Exeter for a time. Yet by 1600 this was 8900, which shows that there had been a large influx, as happened in London after the plague visitations.[2]

The conclusion from all this is inescapable and important: the towns helped to absorb the surpluses of people from the country and in them deaths were apt to outnumber births, at times of epidemics very heavily. In short, they killed off people and helped to keep the population under. Further, there were swift changes, ups and downs, ebbs and flows of population, and that made for much greater mobility than has been attributed to Tudor society.

The more one lives into the past and becomes acquainted with its life as if it were one's own, the less possible it becomes to generalise. Even more so than with the life one actually lives, for there are added factors of uncertainty, ignorance, darkness. It is not merely hazardous to generalise — generalisations are apt to commit one to untruths. To be aware of this at every turn does not make for interesting reading: it is those who are prepared to commit themselves to summary generalisations who are more amusing. But at the same time as they make a joke at the expense of a whole class, they may be letting themselves in for what is not true. What is one to do? The responsible historian must adhere always to what is true and forgo the pleasures of generalised reflection, still more the indulgence of contemporary political prejudice in the form of moral indignation. The truth is often neither exciting nor amusing, and to arrive at it one needs endless patience and, above all, an essential justice of mind.

With these warning reflections, perhaps we may say that Tudor society was more highly diversified, more flexible and *mouvementé* than is altogether realised. It is true that society attached immense importance to degree, priority, place, and that it was hierarchical; but there was a good deal of moving up and down in the hierarchy.

Take but degree away: untune that string . . .

and we know all the terrible consequences that will follow. Such was the official theory, very generally accepted, so far as we can

[1] R. Pickard, *The Population and Epidemics of Exeter*, pp. 14-15.

[2] *Ibid.* p. 33; cf. F. P. Wilson, *The Plague in Shakespeare's London*, p. 114, for London's rapid recovery after the plague of 1603 in which London lost one-sixth of its population. It made fine opportunities for those who were not carried off or who came in from the country.

tell, by the society of the time. But the very strength of the emphasis on order and degree may reflect how necessary it was because of the forces that were in motion. People are never wholly ruled by their theory anyway, and we are concerned here not with their theories but the facts. The facts reveal a society in which there is not only an increasing degree of mobility but in which social classes are changing their relations. In it the nobility are becoming less important than the gentry as a whole — even though the decline of the nobility has been exaggerated; the gentry are going from strength to strength, recruiting considerable elements from the yeomanry: they are the most dynamic class in Tudor society; they are extending their hold in almost every parish in the land. At the same time as the yeomen are going up and joining the ranks of the gentry, their own class is not exhausted by the process: it too is prospering and going ahead. So also are many freeholders and leasehold tenants. That was possible with expanding resources. But it was also to some extent at the expense of the smaller folk and the poor, who became poorer, while the rich became much richer. Vagrancy and vagabondage increased greatly; poor relief became a question of the first importance for government; the roads swarmed with uprooted folk on the march, in spite of all the whippings; fairs and country markets were the hunting ground of many an Autolycus; London teemed with cutpurses and cony-catchers, rogues and harlots, and in fact gave birth to a vivid literature devoted to their pretty ways. Here were to be found some of the people squeezed out by the pressure of economic forces which they could feel if not conceive; here were victims who paid some part of the price for economic advances made elsewhere by others. There was a change going on in the balance of social forces which underlay the outward structure of the Elizabethan polity.[1] It led to many tensions, which were just contained without bursting their integuments so long as the external danger of the war with Spain continued and the Queen reigned. With her death and the coming of peace, they were free to break out into the open in the form of constitutional conflict: they led ultimately to the Civil War.

The mobility of the population varied very much from place to place, from one area to another, from one section of society to another. Whatever may be said of the declining fortunes of the nobility, it was a more stable thing to belong to it than anywhere

[1] Cf. on this R. H. Tawney, "Harrington's Interpretation of his Age", *Proc. British Academy*, vol. XXVII.

else in the social scale: you were more likely to stick. Primogeniture — though it had the effect of throwing "all of the kittens but one into the water" — did help to keep properties together, and it is property that makes for stability. It is obviously absurd to talk as if the Elizabethan aristocracy were on its last legs; if that were so, how is it that Howards and Percys, Berkeleys and Courtenays, Cecils, Cavendishes, Russells, Pagets, Paulets and others who were important in those days continued to decorate the landscape right up to ours? The same was true of the larger gentry, as anyone who knows the continuing life of English counties through the centuries is well aware: those families provided a more stable and continuous element than the next stratum. And so on downwards. The towns were the most mobile of all; London as mobile as quicksilver. Great urban families have a very short run: if they continue at all it is because they transplant themselves into the country, sometimes back whence they came. We have seen that in the towns there was an incessant ebb and flow in and out.

In the country, mobility was naturally much greater in progressive and economically changing areas like the Midlands than in the remote North or West, and in these last near towns and seaports much more than in moorland parishes and remote upland places. In South Nottinghamshire the majority of freeholders held their land less than two generations.[1] Their names drop out of the subsidy rolls very rapidly. Some families whose names disappeared must have remained in the parish, but poorer, or possibly having shifted their holding. In many rural areas there was not much numerical change in a hundred years or — what is more remarkable — up to the nineteenth century. That is the less surprising when one reflects that it is the subsistence that matters, the number of people the land can support. The population of the parish remains fairly constant, though the families change. In Nottinghamshire over the century "it will be found that names continually disappear, while new names occur, themselves in turn vanishing, leaving finally perhaps one family running through the series for a parish, a family which is generally that of the lord of the manor, or of a wealthy freeholder". Everything points to the conclusion that "the population of the county of Notts between the years 1558 and 1641 was in a highly mobile condition".[2] The same is borne out for Northamptonshire and Huntingdonshire. So too for Bedfordshire: in seven-

[1] S. A. Peyton, "The Village Population in the Tudor Lay Subsidy Rolls", *E.H.R.* (1915), p. 245 foll.
[2] *Ibid.* pp. 248, 250.

eighths of the parishes the names of at least half the subsidymen of 1545–6 have dropped out of the return for 1580–81.[1] And similarly for subsequent years. So too for Leicestershire, that mobile county. In general, in the Leicestershire village of the Tudor age only two or three families had been there since the fourteenth century.[2] Even the gentry there were more volatile. Of forty-five enclosing landlords only eleven came from long-established families; of those entering upon their manors only seven had succeeded by inheritance or marriage: the remaining twenty-seven had purchased their manors, half of which had belonged to the Church.[3] Behold the consequences of the Dissolution at work building up the gentry, recruiting their numbers, adding to their estates. In Lincolnshire, too, there was "a startling number of changes in the personnel of the county families" between 1562 and 1634.[4] By the latter year there are 78 new armigerous families in that roomy county, twenty-four of them coming from outside and possibly a half of them having risen from yeomen stock. In Staffordshire that old Catholic snob, Sampson Erdeswicke, felt it a personal grievance that so many new men, merchants and lawyers, had come in to take the place of the old stock.

Lower down the social scale the process is more interesting for it has been only recently revealed to us. It turns out that there was already a good deal of economic inequality among the small farmers in their villages. Take Leicestershire: "Even if we omit the squirearchy (who were less wealthy than many a yeoman, in personal estate at least) we find that 4 per cent of the rural population owned a quarter of the personal estate and 15½ per cent owned half of it".[5] In the ownership of land there was even greater disparity. One-half the farms were below 60 acres: which would give an average area of 30-35 acres, with a sown area in any one year of 10 acres. A great many of these small farmers lived very near the poverty line, as one sees from the pathetic picture drawn for us by Tusser. Only 4 per cent had more land: those were the yeomen, with 100 acres and more. Below were the cottagers and labourers with 1 to 15 acres. One easily sees the connection between mobility of tenure and periods

[1] Lydia M. Marshall, "The Rural Population of Bedfordshire, 1671–1921", *Beds. Hist. Record Soc.*, 1934, p. 54 foll.

[2] W. G. Hoskins, "The Leicestershire Farmer in the Sixteenth Century", *Leics. Arch. Soc.*, 1941–2, p. 34 foll.

[3] L. A. Parker, "The Depopulation Returns for Leicestershire in 1607", *Leics. Arch. Soc.*, 1947, p. 10.

[4] Mildred Campbell, *The English Yeoman*, pp. 37-8.

[5] W. G. Hoskins, *loc. cit.* p. 39 foll.

of depression: in human terms, a failure of harvest threw the starving peasantry on the country. Hence the riots and pinchbeck risings; hence the commissions: the government did what it could. The weak went to the wall, where there was no stay for them as in church; their holdings were snapped up by others, stronger in the race, more thrifty or luckier. For competition for holdings was keen among the peasants themselves, apart from what richer and greedier 'cormorants' — to use a favourite term of the time — might bid for them. Vast traffic in land was carried on by all classes of society, but most effectively by the strongest competitors for survival, successful yeomen and the gentry lesser and greater. These conditions gave a grand opportunity for laying field to field and acre to acre and we can follow the process now at every level of society. In Leicestershire "between 1540 and 1600 tens of thousands of acres of land passed into the hands of yeoman families by purchase, at first in parcels of two or three farms and then, by the fifteen-sixties especially, in whole manors. By the end of the century the greater yeomen had risen to the rank of gentry, many to that of esquire, owning the manors on which their fathers and grandfathers had been tenants half a century earlier. . . . The movement became wider and more rapid after 1550 and continued unabated throughout the rest of the sixteenth century and into the early years of the seventeenth." Dr. Hoskins calls it "the largest transference of land ownership since Domesday". This was the under-swell that bore up so many gallant cargoes in that age.

Here are a few random examples to illustrate the process. Into the village of Carlton Curlieu the Bales were newcomers in the reign of Henry VIII: the head of the family was a yeoman in that generation, a gentleman in the next, knighted in the next with a baronetcy by 1643 — all achieved within a hundred years.[1] (Nor was the ascent of the Cecils much different, though more spectacular and reaching more exalted heights. A nondescript man-at-arms, follower of Henry VII in one generation — for all Burghley's genealogical researches he was never able to provide him with a convincing ancestry — a knighthood in the next generation, a peerage in the next, with two earldoms at the hand of James, who was more generous with such things than Elizabeth had been. Really the sixteenth century provides more striking cases of *la carrière ouverte aux talents* than ours. Can it be that talents are not so much in request with us as they were with them?) The two most prosperous yeomen of Peatling

[1] W. G. Hoskins, *loc. cit.* p. 38.

Magna and Peatling Parva were the squires of their respective villages by 1567, owning practically all the land, yet they continued to call themselves yeomen as they had done all their lives. At Cosby, Thomas Bent, yeoman, bought up his neighbours' messuages, cottages, orchards, crofts, acres until in the eight years 1543–51 he had got possession of the manor, the village and over a thousand acres and was able to style himself, Thomas Bent, gent. His son spent his money on building a 'mansion house', which still stands "in the main street of Littlethorpe, a typical specimen of the more elaborate style of timbered dwelling that began to appear in several villages in this and the following decade, the homes of the rich yeomen who were no longer content to live in the comfortless manner of their fathers before them".

As yet there remained a good deal more social equality than strictly economic: social differentiation followed upon economic inequality. The squire's son often attended the same village school as the children of yeomen and husbandmen. William Faunt, son of the squire of Foston, went to school in the neighbouring village of Wigston; the young George Villiers, who had such an astonishing career at the hands of James I and became Duke of Buckingham, went to the little village school of Billesdon, near his home at Brooksby, of which his father was the squire.[1] (One catches sight of the ironstone Elizabethan manor-house from the high road between Leicester and Melton Mowbray, looking out over the broad valley of the Wreak stretching away into blue distance. The promoted young Duke — the handsomest man of his age[2] — was an exceptional case of social mobility: recommended to the susceptible King's favours by a cabal headed by the Archbishop of Canterbury.) In the first half of the century economic differences were not yet reflected in standards of housing and domestic comfort. The rich yeoman's wealth lay in the fields, in his crops; the surplus he spent in adding to his holdings and buying more livestock. He lived like any husbandman in the same kind of small house in the village street with a singular absence of comfort: a few pots and pans, a trestle table, a few stools, no chairs, and boards to lie on. Beds were beginning to come in for better-off yeomen to lie in: it is nice to think that the successful yeoman of Peatling Parva, the richest in the county, who lived very simply, did have feather beds and hangings — which few possessed. Elizabeth's reign

[1] *Ibid.* p. 37.

[2] "He was one of the handsomest men in the whole world" (Sir John Oglander *The Oglander Memoirs*, p. 48).

showed a great difference. There was money now for a good many to improve their houses and the " great period of house-building begins and coincides with the years in which the same class was making its most extensive purchases of land ".[1] If one casts one's mind over the country one realises that this was fairly widely true. The inventories to their wills reveal the simple standard of life prevailing, down to endearing details such as " the names of the cows that grazed in the ancient fields — like Py and Swallow, Nut and Marigold who belonged to Robert Colles of South Kilworth in 1558. We read of the favourite hawk of Mr. Anthony Faunt, the squire of Foston: Ringbell soaring on a blue-and-white morning in May high over the green pastures of South Leicestershire, the year before the Armada."[2]

Readers of Hardy's novels will best appreciate the character and diversity of rural life and of its complement the country town, for in essence it remained unchanged from Elizabeth's days to Victoria's. An investigation of Gloucestershire shows that rural society was highly differentiated and occupations very diversified.[3] Agriculture was naturally the largest; it employed two-thirds of the men whose occupations are stated, yet even so only one-half of the adult male population. The proportion of men engaged in agriculture varied widely in different parts of the country, as in Yorkshire, the West Country, East Anglia or elsewhere. Gloucestershire showed local specialisation in metal trades — there were the smiths of the Forest of Dean, the concentration of the woollen industry along the Cotswold escarpment. There was as yet no sharp line between wage-earners and independent producers and the number of the latter was surprisingly large in proportion to employees; they outnumbered the wage labourers by two to one. This is a matter of fundamental importance if one is to understand that society, especially when one considers the smallness of the population and the abundance of land available. Hence in a society that was strictly hierarchical and paternally authoritarian, that independence of spirit which has nevertheless characterised Englishmen through their history. From these ranks came Cromwell's plain russet-coats who defeated the flower of the aristocracy when it came to the test.

Of employees, two-thirds were to be found in agriculture and in the service of the gentry. It is not surprising that the latter employed such large numbers: a quarter or a third of the adult

[1] Hoskins, p. 42.
[2] *Ibid.* p. 34.
[3] A. J. and R. H. Tawney, " An Occupational Census of the 17th Century ", *Econ. Hist. Rev.* (1934), p. 39 foll.

males in one manor, five-sixths in another, all the men in a third in the service of one individual, as the Tawneys put it. (Is there not a Radical inflection here? From another point of view they were given employment by the lord of the manor and were no doubt glad to be: the comforts of life in the manor-house were greater than on the land and the opportunities not less.) One has to think of the greater houses as equivalent to villages, housing not only the whole family with their relations and dependants, but a large household of servants male and female, indoor and outdoor. We shall come to some examples later. Of knights, esquires, gentlemen, there were some 430, greater and lesser, their servants 750: this shows a relatively large ruling class, I should have thought, for the sons and brothers belonged to it, at any rate in the first generation — even though they moved into trade or the professions, the Army or the Church: sometimes they made a fortune in one or other of those callings and returned with improved status to the bosom of their own class. The class was large and its tentacles well dispersed: hence its tremendous hold in English society, such that it could fight a Civil War within itself, undergo a Puritan Revolution — the temporary emergence of the petit-bourgeoisie — and yet come out on top with the Restoration and stay there until the nineteenth century and the twentieth.

The leading occupations numerically in Gloucestershire followed this order: agriculture, textiles, masons and stonelayers, millers, farmers, vintners and innkeepers, glovers, mercers, bakers, and so on down to tinkers and bellows-menders. The clothiers, as we might expect, differed little from manual workers. The towns had an economic character of their own, however small, differentiating them from large villages: they had few farmers or farm labourers, miners or fishermen, nor were they primarily manufacturing — that went on in the countryside. They were finishing and distributing centres, their inhabitants engaged in dealing and retail trade. Some of them enjoyed special occupations. Tewkesbury had its bargemen, Cirencester its weavers. And over the country in general there were notable exceptions: Norwich, Tiverton and such were manufacturing towns, Coventry had its cap-makers, Sheffield its cutlers. But in general the towns — of which Stratford may serve as absolutely typical — were what Hardy described Casterbridge, " the pole, focus or nerve-knot of the surrounding country life . . . Casterbridge was the complement of the rural life around; not its urban opposite. Bees and butterflies in the corn-fields at the top of the town, who desired to get to the meads at the bottom, took no circuitous course, but flew straight down High Street without any apparent consciousness that they were traversing strange latitudes. . . . Casterbridge lived by agriculture at one remove further from the fountain-head than the adjoining villages — no more."

The yeomanry constituted a class of rural society of which contemporaries were proud as something peculiarly English. "An estate of people almost peculiar to England", said Thomas Fuller, "living in the temperate zone betwixt greatness and want."[1] "These were they that in times past made all France afraid", said Harrison,[2] and Bacon elaborated the theme. "Let states that aim at greatness take heed how their nobility and gentlemen do multiply too fast. For that maketh the common subject grow to be a peasant and base swain, driven out of heart and in effect but the gentleman's labourer."[3] It was the rural middle class that had his — and everybody's — approbation. "This . . . hath been no better seen than by comparing of England and France, whereof England, though far less in territory and population, hath been nevertheless an overmatch: in regard the middle people of England make good soldiers, which the peasants of France do not." The yeomen of England were applauded, both by writers of books and popular acclaim, for their upstanding pride in themselves, their honesty — in the Elizabethan, *i.e.* the classical sense of the word — and for their good feeding. "A man may find sundry yeomen", Lambarde wrote, "although otherwise for wealth comparable with the gentle sort that will not yet for all that change their condition, nor desire to be apparelled with the titles of gentry."[4] "He makes a whole line in the subsidy book", said Fuller; "when hospitality died in England, she gave her last groan amongst the yeomen of Kent."

Of the smaller type of free landowner, a class celebrated in a character and a Canterbury tale of Chaucer's, we have an illustrious example in the name of Benjamin Franklin. He tells us in his *Autobiography* that his family had lived "in the same village, Ecton, in Northamptonshire, for three hundred years, and how much longer he [his uncle] knew not (perhaps from the time when the name of Franklin . . . was assumed by them as a surname when others took surnames all over the kingdom), on a freehold of about thirty acres, aided by the smith's business, which had continued

[1] q. Campbell, *op. cit.* p. 62.
[2] Harrison, *op. cit.* (ed. Furnivall), p. 13.
[3] Bacon's *Essays*, "Of the true Greatness of Kingdoms and Estates".
[4] W. Lambarde, *The Perambulation of Kent* (ed. 1596), p. 14.

in the family till his time, the eldest son being always bred to that business. . . . When I searched the registers at Ecton, I found an account of their births, marriages and burials from the year 1555. . . . By that register I perceived that I was the youngest son of the youngest son for five generations back. My grandfather Thomas, who was born in 1598, lived at Ecton till he grew too old to follow business longer, when he went to live with his son John, a dyer at Banbury, in Oxfordshire, with whom my father served an apprenticeship. There my grandfather died and lies buried. We saw his grave-stone in 1758."[1] So short a step is it from the Elizabethan Age to the American Revolution.

Coke and the lawyers continued to make the out-of-date criterion of the forty-shilling freeholder their definition of yeoman status. In fact the definition was an economic one — as usually becomes the case, if after an interval. The yeomanry were the more prosperous range of farmers who had not become gentry. Sometimes they were better off than the gentry, their neighbours. But in general we may accept 100 acres as the dividing line: farmers who farmed more may be regarded as yeomen. They lived better than the husbandman; they ate 'yeoman bread', largely made of wheat.[2] They pushed its cultivation, for they were agricultural improvers as much as the gentry; they got down to making profits, not just subsistence out of the land. Robert Loder, farmer of what is now the Prince's Manor Farm at Harwell on the north slope of the Berkshire downs looking out on the Vale of the White Horse, is the classic type of this class: celebrated for the accounts he kept, three hundred years after his last account was closed.[3] But it is only the accident of his account-book having survived that has made him remembered. For there must have been hundreds like him. "He wanted as large a financial return for his expenditure of capital, managerial work and manual work as he could get, and he did his utmost to maintain it."[4] He was no mere subsistence farmer, dull and boring as the oxen he ploughed with. For one thing, he ploughed with horses; for another, he was out for profit in one form or another, motive force of progress. He depended for his profit on his arable crop. Realising that wheat and malt offered the best market, he increased his wheat acreage every year until it approached that under barley. His malt went from Henley down the Thames to London; for his wheat there were markets at hand at Newbury,

[1] Benjamin Franklin, *Autobiography* (Everyman Edition), p. 7.
[2] Campbell, *loc. cit.* p. 245.
[3] *Robert Loder's Farm Accounts, 1610–1620*, ed. by G. E. Fussell (Camden Society).
[4] *Ibid.* pp. xxiii-xxvi.

Wantage, Abingdon, Oxford. His profits were very considerable, ranging between £200 and £300 a year, a large sum in those days. He founded a county family: hence the preservation of his account-book and his memory.

The process of the rise of a yeoman family to the ranks of the lesser gentry is described as nowhere else in the delightful book that Robert Furse of Morshead in the Devonshire parish of Dean Prior wrote in the year 1593.[1] It tells the story of his family, gives us charming portrait sketches of its members, describes their properties in detail and how they were brought together piece by piece; what is more, it takes us into his very mind. His intention in writing his book was to let his descendants know " what our progenitors have been of themselves and specially those that have been within these seven score years. . . . And I do know that this book will be necessary and profitable for you considering that our lands lieth in divers parishes and come to us from divers persons and by divers titles, for by making this book perfect and keeping of the same in good order you shall always be able to make a perfect pedigree and to understand the right name of your lands and your writings and what you ought to have and what you ought to do." The naïveté, shrewdness and poetry are very Elizabethan: " Even like as the bees diligently do labour and gather together substance of divers sweet flowers to make their honey " — one sees the heather-coloured summer moorland of Herrick's Dean Prior,

> I sing of brooks, of blossoms, birds and bowers:
> Of April, May, of June and July-flowers —

" even so have I gathered together this book or matter herein contained some of your evidences, some by report of old ancient men and some of my own knowledge and experience ".

In the reign of Henry VII the Furses were small farmers owning a tenement of some 50 acres in Cheriton Fitzpaine and another of 40 acres in Cruwys-Morchard. But their descendants were not to be ashamed of their ancestors, " although some of them were but simple and unlearned and men of small possessions . . . for I am sure that the greatest ox was first a little calf and the greatest oak a small branch or little twig and the great river at the head which I do account the beginning is but a little spring or water; but by keeping of his own course and within his own bounds it groweth by little and little so that at last it is become

[1] Cf. H. J. Carpenter, " Furse of Morshead ", *Trans. Devon. Assoc.*, 1894, p. 168 foll. It is unfortunate that the original seems to have disappeared since.

an exceeding great river ". So the Furses had " always kept themselves within their own bounds that by these means we are come to much more possessions credit and reputation than ever any of them had ". There follow the precepts that Robert Furse considered led to success : " Be merciful unto all men, give alms of thy goods to the poor and needy and let always thy hired servant have his penny for his pain ". They were to have a delight in good housekeeping, to beware of usurers and borrowing money upon interest and of what bonds they sealed. They were to be careful, yet not illiberal, fair-speeched with all men but in friendship only with certain. Pretend not to take on many things at a time, nor take on anything above your strength but only what you can bring to pass. What a contrast this is with the Elizabethan aristocrat, magnificent and temerarious, for ever attempting the impossible, with Ralegh or Sidney, Oxford, Southampton or Essex ! Here we see displayed the middle-class virtues which have had so much greater survival value.

Robert Furse's advice on taking a wife, though characteristic, is common form, and need not detain us. More interesting is his respect for learning, especially in the scriptures, the laws of the realm and in the old chronicles and ancient histories, for " it is a shame for a man to be ignorant of that which he ought to know ". This is not surprising, for the family owed its leg-up in the world to Robert's grandfather, who had been sent to the Inns of Court when young and sworn an attorney. He did not practise, but it enabled him to serve as a clerk to various gentlemen, ending up with Sir Thomas Denis, the leading knight in the county, and the Marquis of Exeter, the greatest nobleman in the West. " But after the execution of my Lord Marquis he was never jocund nor merry in heart." His training qualified him to procure several profitable offices ; he was twice under-sheriff of the county, for many years steward of the Stannary, of the Duchy of Lancaster lands, of the courts of Tavistock and Buckland abbeys and chief steward to divers others " by means whereof his fees were large and his gains great ". He married a small heiress, and though when first married " they had but little . . . before she died they had 400 bullocks and great store of money and other stuff and were as well furnished of all things in their house as any one man of their degree was in all their county ". John Furse was buried under a blue stone in the chancel of Great Torrington church.

His son and heir married the heiress of Morshead in Dean Prior. The Morsheads had originally been called le Bond, which shows that they had been serfs before they became yeomen and took the name of their holding. The Morsheads had followed much the same course as the Furses, making prudent marriages and gaining a little land with each. Robert Furse's father-in-law had been a good sportsman, addicted in his youth to hunting, dicing, cards and especially to shooting and tennis, but with years and discretion he became a good farmer and pillar of the parish: "He was twenty years constable of the hundred of Stanbury, he was returned in many juries, he always maintained a good house, a good plough, good geldings, good tillage, good rearing and he was a good husband; indeed he would never be without three couple of good hounds: he would surely keep company with the best sort". He was buried with a fair blue stone upon him. One observes that yeomen had stone slabs over their graves where the gentry raised marble tombs. Robert inherited Morshead and married a woman who brought further parcels of land with her. He added further properties by purchase, chief among them the manor of Skirridon he bought from Philip Basset, a hopeless, feckless member of an old family. Robert was proud of his buy and details the manor at great length, along with the various improvements he had made out of doors and at home: "He made the porch and entry and ceiled the hall and glazed all the windows". Glazing windows was now coming into the West Country; the porch he built so solidly of great moorland slabs that it remains when the rest of the house is now a ruin. He arranged a good marriage for his son while yet a boy, by which "no doubt John Furse shall greatly increase his lands", and he details the burgages, closes, meadows and tenements, the third part of the manor of Rowcombe, all the small properties the girl-bride would bring with her. The projected marriage did not come off, but a better proposition with broader acres took its place. So did those long-vanished Devonshire yeomen build up the foundations that have enabled the family to make a distinguished contribution to the life of our day.

In tackling the question of the rise of the gentry — which must be a central theme in this book and one that is illustrated in many different fields — it is important to keep a proper historical perspective: the process did not begin, or reach its culmination, in our period. The gentry had been coming up markedly all through the fifteenth century, to a lesser extent in the fourteenth, and the process may even be traced back in small to the thirteenth century.[1] There was a good deal of mobility in English medieval

[1] I owe this point to Mr. K. B. McFarlane.

society: the upper ranks of the merchant classes were recruited from land-owning families; successful merchants acquired the status of *miles* or *armiger*, and usually they returned to the country as gentry.[1] A profound transformation in society was going on in the fifteenth century, when the manorial system was breaking down with its fixed labour services, villeinage and cultivation by the landlords through estate bailiffs: all this was being replaced by copyholds, leaseholds and a rent-collecting landlordship. The humbler ranks of rural society benefited and were on the up grade: wages rose, land became cheaper, average holdings larger. This movement continued and received an immense impetus with the Dissolution of the monasteries, chantries and gilds.[2] At one stroke, or at least within two decades, something like one-fifth of all the available land in the country came into the market for investment and secular ownership, besides a vast field for investment in tithes. A certain number of people got the ownership of lands which they previously leased from, or managed for, the monasteries. All the same it offered wonderful opportunities for increasing wealth and social advancement, the rewards of enterprise, industry, shrewdness or mere luck, the ground-swell that bore up a whole class. It greatly accelerated the rate of expansion of the gentry: one can trace that in every county. One can define the later sixteenth century as the constructive period, in which they went on acquiring, exchanging and consolidating, building their houses, forming their estates, licking them into shape and developing their resources. The period of enjoyment came after with their successors, a more cultivated and appealing generation — as the way is — with some reflections on what had gone before and a few regrets:[3] the Caroline age.

The rise of the gentry was the dominant feature of Elizabethan society. It was they essentially who changed things, who launched out along new paths whether at home or overseas, who achieved what was achieved, who gave what all societies need — leadership. One may fairly say that most of the leading spirits of the age, those who gave it its character and did its work, were of this class. Many of them belonged to it, or were recruited from it; some of them passed on, like the Cecils and the Bacons, the

[1] Cf. M. M. Postan, " Some Social Consequences of the Hundred Years War ", *Econ. Hist. Rev.* (1942), pp. 6, 10.

[2] R. H. Tawney's analysis of Dissolution properties in Gloucester, Northants and Warwick shows that from one-half to two-thirds went to the local gentry and humbler connections (*loc. cit.* p. 27). This agrees with my own findings for Cornwall, cf. *Tudor Cornwall*, chaps. viii and ix.

[3] Cf. for the well-known case of the Scudamores, H. R. Trevor-Roper, *Archbishop Laud*, pp. 95-6.

Russells, Cavendishes and Sackvilles, into the new nobility; others — a more numerous regiment — were recruited into it from the ranks of merchants or yeomen, successful soldiers or sailors, or churchmen who had done well out of, perhaps even by, the Church. In every field one is struck by the rich and dynamic contribution they had to make, their pullulating activity, their insatiable enterprise — whether it is a Cecil, a Bacon or a Walsingham at the centre of affairs, a Throckmorton or a Killigrew in diplomacy, a Norris, a Mountjoy or a Roger Williams in the field, a Leveson or a Hawkins at sea, a Cavendish or a Drake (a new recruit this) voyaging round the globe, a Hakluyt or a Lambarde in the world of scholarship, a Gresham, Smythe or Offley in finance or commerce, Carews, Grenvilles, Raleghs everywhere. An economic historian has reflected that " the topics of economic history have been determined by the interest of its founders in social reform, with the result that more is now known about the Chartists and trade unions than about the capitalists and manufacturers, and much more about the medieval labourer than about the medieval landlord ".[1] One needs no apology therefore for devoting most attention to the most interesting, most significant and rewarding of social classes.

Let us look, by way of illustration, at the movement in process in one particular county, that of Devon, once again try to photograph change on the wing. We are looking through the eyes of Tristram Risdon of Winscott near Torrington, himself one of the smaller gentry. Born about 1580 and educated at Oxford, " he would not but look upon it as a great indecorum to be knowing and curious in the rarities which are found abroad and a mere stranger in the things at home ",[2] began his *Survey of Devon* in 1605 and continued at it until 1630: so we can draw a fairly full, and quite representative, picture of the changes taking place, illustrate our themes from it. In the first place there is that of the break-up of certain great noble houses and the consequent enrichment of the lesser families who succeeded or got the spoils. The leading medieval family in the West were the Courtenays, Earls of Devon, with their castles at Okehampton and Tiverton, their houses at Colcombe and Boconnoc and their numerous manors in Devon and Cornwall and elsewhere. The attainder of the Marquis of Exeter in 1538 and the death without issue of his son, whom Mary had restored to the earldom, in 1556 brought to an end the senior line of the Courtenays. Their large estates mainly

[1] M. M. Postan, *loc. cit.* p. 11.

[2] From Prince's *Worthies of Devon*, q. in Risdon's *Survey* (ed. 1811), p. xiv.

went to improve the fortunes of four families among the Cornish gentry who represented four co-heiresses: Arundells of Tolverne, Trelawnys, Mohuns, Vyvyans of Trelowarren. These had been quite small gentry; they now moved up considerably. The junior branch of the Courtenays inherited none of the estates; they continued at Powderham, of which they had married the heiress, on the same footing as the rest of the Devon gentry.

At Colcombe, in the rich shallow valley full of cider orchards going down to Seaton, the Courtenays began, but never finished a great house: here the Princess Katherine, Edward IV's daughter, passed her long widowhood. With the manors of Colyton and Whitford it was bought by local families, Petres, Poles, Drakes of Ashe.[1] Observe here a new theme: the dividing up of old manors often with lands lying in different places to form new and concentrated estates, far more satisfactory to run. The Poles and the Drakes were forming two such estates out of the old diversity and complex pattern of holdings at this very time. Sir William Pole, the antiquary whose collections Risdon used, was building up his estate around Shute: one sees the woods on the sky-line from Colcombe down in the valley. Shute had belonged to the Lords Bonville, the great antagonists of the Courtenays during the Wars of the Roses; in Mary's reign it was bought by Sir William Petre, from whom Sir William Pole got it.[2] In place of medieval Courtenays and Bonvilles, the lesser family of Poles reigned, right up to our time of deliquescence and destruction; only their monuments in those churches remain. Meanwhile, down in the valley, the Drakes — very distant relations, if at all, of the *parvenu* Sir Francis — were building up an estate around their fine house of Ashe, in the parish of Musbury. They bought the manor of Uplyme, which had belonged to Glastonbury.[3] Netherton, which was part of the spoil of Canonsleigh, they bought and sold to the Prideaux. The Drakes were a prolific and active stock, throwing out a number of offshoots. One of them, at Wiscombe, sent two gallant captains to the wars in the Low Countries: "The first . . . of great esteem with the Prince of Orange and the States, for his valour, who in all his actions was said to make use of the spur of courage and the reins of judgment; the other a captain, of much hope, both taken away in the flower of their age, in defence of Ostende, to the great grief of their friends and loss of their country".[4] Of the parent house at Ashe only one wing remains, looking out among its

[1] *Ibid.* p. 28.
[2] Lysons, *Magna Britannia: Devonshire*, II. 443.
[3] Risdon, *op. cit.* pp. 24-5, 35.
[4] *Ibid.* p. 33.

orchards over the water-meadows, and with a more insistent memory, for it was here that John Churchill, Duke of Marlborough, was born: he continued their blood.

We cannot continue to survey Devon on this scale: it would need a whole book. Let this serve for illustration and let us concentrate on the general themes that strike the attention. What strikes one most is the remarkable way in which successful lawyers are buying up land. In the country in general everything points to the astonishing prosperity and expansion of the legal profession: the growth of the Inns of Court, the numbers of students and benchers, the increase of law-books, the number of legal fortunes, the social and political importance of lawyers. This too reached its apogee in the next generation or so.[1] Naturally the vast traffic in land, and the increased rapidity of its turnover, brought lawyers a great deal of business; but they took an increasing hand in the business too and neglected no opportunities to invest their gains in land. The great but uncongenial Coke — uncongenial in spite of his handsome looks and his pre-eminent abilities — provides the most spectacular example of acquisitiveness: everything he touched he turned into land — marriage, the law, politics, influence: all added up to the fifty-eight manors of the inheritance he left. Devon bears out (and Erdeswicke confirms it for Staffordshire) the success of the lawyers in this age, and the considerable contingent they mustered among the leading gentry. In Devon one member or another of more than a dozen families bought their estates from the profits of the law: Prideaux, Pophams, Heles, Pollards, Periams, Rowes, Harrises, Glanvilles, Whiddons, Williamses. Broad Hembury, which had belonged to Dunkeswell abbey and was granted to the Earl of Southampton by Henry, was sold under Elizabeth to Edward Drew, serjeant-at-law, "whose son Sir Thomas hath there a fair dwelling house, which he maketh his mansion".[2] Edward Drew also bought Killerton; his son sold it to Sir Arthur Acland.[3] The neighbouring manor of Columb John (which the railway line now skirts along the water-meadows of the Culm before the wooded heights of Killerton, running into Exeter) had belonged to the Courtenays. Reverting to the Crown, it was given by Mary to her faithful James Basset: his foolish son sold it and it too came into the hands of the Aclands, who were building up their inheritance in these parts. Sir John Acland, who was a younger son, made this

[1] Cf. R. H. Tawney, "The Rise of the Gentry", *Econ. Hist. Rev.* (1941), p. 21 the numbers engaged in the profession rose by two-thirds between the decade 1591-1600 and 1631-40.

[2] Risdon, *op. cit.* pp. 43-4.

[3] *Ibid.* p. 59.

his mansion house; " he was a great benefactor to the poor and did many charitable deeds worthy memory, amongst which he built a fair hall in Exeter College, Oxford ". In the church of Broadclyst are the monuments of both Edward Drew and Sir John Acland. Stowford, on the edge of the moorlands above Ivybridge, acquired by our old acquaintance Speaker Williams, was another legal trophy, dropped by the way from the Suffolk inheritance.[1]

A certain number of manors were bought by officials, whose fortunes were made out of service to the Crown. The outstanding example of this type among Devonshiremen was Sir William Petre, the obliging Secretary of State to Henry VIII and Edward VI, who managed to retain his office under Mary — even Cecil did not achieve such a triumph of conformity. The founder of a strictly Catholic family, Petre built up his estates entirely out of Church property. A younger son of a yeoman family of Torbryan — that perfect church in remote country in a tangle of Devonshire lanes, candle-lit with medieval and Georgian pews, painted rood-screen and pulpit, Petre monuments — he was educated at Exeter College, became a Fellow of All Souls, and made his way through the law into diplomacy and high politics. In the neighbourhood of his old home he bought the manor of Kingsbridge from the wreck of the Courtenays, the manor of South Brent from the spoil of Buckfast abbey.[2] Becoming a high personage in the State, he left his native county for good and seated himself at Ingatestone in Essex, which he got from the abbey of St. Mary's, Barking. He was a humane man, with a sensible latitudinarianism of mind; a patron of learning and a benefactor to both his colleges at Oxford. Another person of the same official class was James Basset, the clever younger son of Lady Lisle, protégé and confidant of Gardiner, who became one of Mary's inner official circle. During his brief heyday — he died young, before the Queen — he bought up half a dozen goodly Devonshire manors and left an orphan son, Philip, the King's godson, who, fool that he was, let them all slip through his fingers.[3]

Other officials held on to theirs: Eveleigh, feodary of the county, bought Holcombe and founded a family there.[4] The fortunes of Richard Duke, a clerk of the Court of Augmentations, were the most spectacular among lesser officials'. He got Otterton on the dissolution of Syon abbey, " and built a fair house upon

[1] *Ibid.* pp. 179, 184.

[2] *Ibid.* pp. 175, 178. The *D.N.B.* article on Petre is plainly wrong with its wild estimate of 36,000 acres in Devon.

[3] Cf. Lansdowne MSS. vols. 72, 77, 78.

[4] Risdon, p. 46.

the rising over the river ".[1] The river drove his mills beneath the house, of which fragments still remain. He left great possessions to his daughter, whom he married to the son of Lord Cobham; but this manor he left to a nephew of his own name, who married Sir Arthur Basset's daughter. The Dukes owned Hayes Barton in the parish of East Budleigh, the house in which Ralegh was born. It is wholly characteristic of the time that the moment Ralegh was securely entrenched at Court in the Queen's favour, he tried to get Richard Duke to sell Hayes to him: " I am resolved, if I cannot entreat you, to build at Colaton. But for the natural disposition I have to that place [Hayes], being born in that house, I had rather seat myself there than anywhere else." [2] But Mr. Duke would not oblige, so pressure had to be applied to the Bishop of Salisbury to make him relax his hold on the pleasantest possession of his see — Sherborne in Dorset. (After all, what did an Elizabethan bishop want with a castle in the country? Times had changed since bishops were on a footing with great lords; they were now on a reduced, but still respectable, footing with the local gentry and lucky to be so.) As yet comparatively few merchants in Devon go in for buying estates on any scale. They seem to be content with merchant and town life in Exeter and the towns for the most part, and when they buy land to buy smaller properties outside their towns where they may enjoy country life conveniently near and take the air in time of epidemics. Risdon says in general terms that they employ their gains " in purchasing of lands and attain to great estates worthy their endeavours . . . climbing up daily to the degree of gentlemen and do bring up their children accordingly ".[3] But this was more marked a feature of the home counties in Elizabeth's reign, and spread more widely in remoter counties subsequently.

Let us look briefly at a quite different area — Staffordshire — to see these themes borne out, if with a different inflection. One gets the impression that there was more marked social change in Staffordshire than in Devonshire: more examples of new families that had sprung up from nothing — at any rate in the eyes of Sampson Erdeswicke. Broadwall was the seat of Ralph Sneyd, who was the fourth in line from a citizen of Chester, founder of that family's fortunes in trade.[4] Now Ralph had " built a very proper and fine house of stone " at Keele,[5] and by his virtue, affability and lenity was increasing his patrimony.

[1] Risdon, p. 53. [2] E. Edwards, *Life of Sir Walter Ralegh*, II. 26.
[3] Risdon, p. 10. [4] S. Erdeswicke, *A Survey of Staffordshire* (ed. 1717), p. 9.
[5] It is characteristic of our time that this place should become the seat of a new university.

Evidently they were qualifying, even in Erdeswicke's eyes, for their place among the gentry. Some of their tombs remain in the rebuilt churches of the Five Towns. The owner of Darlaston was James Collier, " whose grandfather was first a tailor, then a draper, then a wool-buyer (for some staplers grew to such wealth) that he purchased Darlaston, a pretty market town, and a goodly farm which was a grange of abbey Combermere ".[1] At Stone the priory and demesnes, as well as the deanery of Stafford, were in the possession of William Crompton, son of a merchant " ex humili loco natus ", who purchased it soon after the Dissolution.[2] One hears the old Catholic gentleman's sniff of disapproval; but the Cromptons held on, leaving a small Elizabethan brass in the church, and in course of time contributing something more to the world than ever the Erdeswickes did. The Bagenals provided an interesting case of an old family which had been " brought down, I know not how, unto the plebeian state, until this our present age ".[3] Now they had come up again through the profession of arms; three of them had been knighted and Sir Nicholas, a distinguished officer in Ireland, had Fairwell, formerly a nunnery, for his seat. At Herracles, " one John Wedgwood, who advanced himself from a freeholder's son to the estate of gentleman, hath now seated himself; but his son, seeking further to advance himself, enters into a course contentious and I doubt will prove nothing commendable (if it be true that I hear) ".[4] The Wedgwoods in course of time were to do better than Erdeswicke expected.

The lawyers were not quite so much to the fore in Staffordshire as in Devon, but they were coming along. The leading family were the Gerrards of Gerrards Bromley: Sir Gilbert Gerrard had been Attorney-General and Master of the Rolls, and " in his old age built a very fair new house of stone at Bromley and lies buried in Ashley churchyard — whereof Thomas his son hath built a chapel and bestowed great cost on a monument for him ".[5] An elaborate Renaissance monument reposes on the son, but he had been advanced by James to the peerage. Lapley priory passed into the hands of the Manners family and thence to a son of Sir Robert Brooke, Lord Chief Justice of Common Pleas.[6] Norbury, a fine manor with much other land, was purchased by Thomas Skrymsher, a protonotary of the Common Pleas; he was enabled to settle seven sons with estates in Staffordshire and the neighbouring counties.[7] A daughter brought Norbury to the Barnfields, and here the poet, Richard Barnfield, was

[1] *Ibid.* p. 11. [2] *Ibid.* p. 13. [3] *Ibid.* pp. 6, 81. [4] *Ibid.* p. 181. [5] *Ibid.* p. 27. [6] *Ibid.* p. 64. [7] *Ibid.* p. 65.

born in 1574. If the lawyers were less pushing here than in Devonshire, the merchants appear to be more so. Look at the remarkable record of the Offleys.[1] William Offley was a burgess of Stafford. He sent his eldest son Thomas to London to be educated at St. Paul's. In turn, all Offley's brothers and half-brothers came to London; five of them became Staplers, one of them sheriff of London, Sir Thomas himself Lord Mayor. Three Offleys held posts in connection with the Royal Hospitals. Sir Thomas bought the manors of Mucklestone and Madeley, the latter from Lord Wentworth, and here he retired and established his family.[2] He became the ancestor of the Earls of Crewe, as Sir Gilbert Gerrard was of the Earls of Macclesfield. Perton was bought by James Leveson, merchant, of London; in Erdeswicke's time it was the seat of his great-grandson, Sir Richard Leveson, the naval commander and Vice-Admiral.[3] The south transept of Wolverhampton church became the Levesons' family chapel: there John and Agnes Leveson are buried beneath their table-tomb, and there is the splendid bronze statue of the famous seaman sculpted by a no less famous sculptor, Le Sueur, with its resounding roll of naval actions inscribed upon it.

One sees the social picture: how for the most part it is the sons of Staffordshire men who go up to London to make their fortune and, having made it, come back to found county families in their native landscape.

Staffordshire provides a parallel to the Petres of Devonshire in the rise of the Pagets. William Paget sprang from even humbler origins than William Petre; it is said that his father was a mace-bearer in the city of London: certainly his origins were often thrown up at him by his enemies and those who were jealous of the rise to power and fortune that his abilities brought him. He was educated, like so many of the leading spirits of the earlier sixteenth century, at St. Paul's and became a protégé of Gardiner. In Henry's last years and through Edward and Mary's reigns he was one of the inner ring that governed the country, ending up as Lord Privy Seal and Mary's chief — certainly her most intelligent — adviser. A humane and tolerant man, sufficiently cool in matters of religion to be regarded by the fanatics on either side as an atheist, he was yet too closely associated with Mary's policies to be continued in office by Elizabeth. So the Pagets, *écartés* from power, moved more and more into opposition; some of them remained Catholic and even went into exile.

[1] I am indebted for information about the Offleys to Mr. F. E. Leese of the Bodleian.
[2] Erdeswicke, pp. 17, 28.
[3] *Ibid.* p. 129.

The insufferable Charles Paget, an *émigré* in Paris, was one of Mary Stuart's advisers — he was a very bad adviser to that sanguine woman — and an underground conspirator, a constant thorn in the side of Elizabeth's government, for all the information that he volunteered to Walsingham on the activities of his fellow Catholics. The fortunes of the Pagets, like those of the Petres, were well founded on the spoil of the Church: in this case the superfluous possessions of the Bishop of Coventry and Lichfield. There was, Erdeswicke tells us, " Shuttleborough, the ruins of a goodly house, sometime the Bishop's and since Lord Paget's, who had the same, Cannock town and forest, with Haywood, Longdon, Rugeley, Beaudesert — another house also sometime the Bishop's and of late enlarged and now re-edified by the late Lord Paget, together with the park of Haywood and Beaudesert and a great number of hamlets and villages — all which were the Bishop of Coventry and Lichfield's and by him given in exchange of certain parsonages impropriate which the said Lord Paget had obtained of Edward VI, whereby he procured himself to be created Lord Paget of Beaudesert ".[1] After this, it was only right that he should repose in state in the cathedral at Lichfield — until Cromwell's troopers destroyed his tomb. The Pagets have reigned in Cannock Chase ever since, achieved a marquisate with the famous soldier of the Napoleonic wars, and made a place for themselves in English history. It remained for our own time to pull down the great house.

So one could go through county after county, tracing the mobility of social classes, the rise of the gentry and the foundations of English society as it remained up to the social revolution of our day. Wherever one looks it is the same, nor are the consequences of this social mobility and expansiveness confined to this country; they have their importance for the new society across the Atlantic that grew out of the old one here. The grandfather of the great Governor Winthrop of Massachusetts, Adam Winthrop, was a Lavenham clothier who founded the fortune of his family and got the freedom of the city of London. Like most others he went into land and obtained a grant of the manor of Groton, which had belonged to the abbey of Bury St. Edmunds.[2] His son Adam was trained to the law and became auditor of St. John's and Trinity Colleges at Cambridge; he took for his second wife the daughter of a clothier, at whose home the future Governor was born in the year of the Armada. His son again, the future Governor of Connecticut, was born at Groton. They all go back

[1] *Ibid.* p. 73. [2] *v.* article in *D.N.B.*

to Groton and the little Suffolk church with its beautiful hammer-beam roof and the brass — which was once taken away to America but has now come back again: " Here lieth Mr. Adam Winthrop, lord and patron of Groton, which departed out of this world the 9th day of November in the year of our Lord God 1562 ".

The social mobility of the age was well understood at the time: no doubt approved by those who had their way to make and thought they could make it, disapproved by conservative-minded persons like the old Duke of Norfolk who held that 'England was never merry since the new learning came up' — and indeed disapproved by the Howards as a whole (they had made their way up only just before): it is a clue to much of their political line. Judicious persons like Sir Thomas Smith, describing the facts of English society, were content to accept them as they were: " As for gentlemen, they be made good cheap in England. For whosoever studieth the laws of the realm, who studieth in the universities, who professeth liberal sciences and, to be short, who can live idly and without manual labour and will bear the port, charge and countenance of a gentleman he . . . shall be taken for a gentleman." [1] True, Sir Thomas felt it necessary to put up a defence for our easy-going empiricism in such matters: he did not mind that the Heralds were prepared to make out a coat of arms for the new-found gentleman in return for his money. The prince lost nothing by it as he would in France: here the yeoman or husbandman was not taxed as such, the gentleman bore greater charges, which he accepted for the sake of honour and reputation. " As for their outward show, a gentleman (if he will be so accounted) must go like a gentleman, a yeoman like a yeoman, and a rascal like a rascal." It was the appearance and the fact that counted with the English, as in so many walks, and not a preconceived or rigid doctrine on the matter. It was summed up in the popular saying which Burghley used in the precepts he gave his son Robert: " Gentility is nothing else but ancient riches ".[2] No nonsense about blue blood, or the status of a caste: one admires the good common sense of it.

With this background of social elasticity, perhaps all the more because of it, it was important to assert one's place in society, as high a place as one could pretend to. It did not do to be disregarded: that would be disadvantageous in the struggle for

[1] Sir Thomas Smith, *De Republica Anglorum* (ed. L. Alston), pp. 39-41.
[2] F. Peck, *Desiderata Curiosa*, I. 48.

survival that offered such rewards to talent and enterprise. Hence the constant, and to us rather boring, insistence upon gentility in all their writings. Innumerable persons find it necessary to harp upon it in their dedications; many will quarrel or fight about it; almost everyone is ready to take offence for some fancied slight to their gentility. Never can there have been more class-consciousness, one feels, in any age. Even Robert Cecil thought it worth while asseverating his gentility at Essex's trial, if only to point an oratorical contrast: " For wit, I give you the pre-eminence: you have it abundantly. For birth also I give you place: I am not noble, yet a gentleman." [1] Richard Bertie, master of the horse to the widowed Duchess of Suffolk, and who married his somewhat corpulent mistress, found his gentility impugned by the Earl of Arundel. He gave vent to his indignation in a letter to Burghley, the patient receptacle of everybody's complaints. " My Lord of A. (as I am informed, more of his accustomed good nature than of my desert) told the Queen I was no gentleman, which perhaps being otherwise unwilling, somewhat stayeth, but if that respect had stayed her ancestors in the time of Fitzalan, bailiff of London, my Lord should have lacked his lordship now to embroil others. As I have no cause, so I am no whit ashamed of my parents, being free English, neither villeins nor traitors. And if I would after the manner of the world bring forth old abbey scrolls for matter of record " — then, his indignation making him repeat himself — " I am sure I can I can reach as far backward as Fitzalan." [2]

All this provided a good target for the satirists to shoot at and for the dramatists to comment on. There is Philip Stubbes with his " every man crying with open mouth I am a gentleman, I am worshipful, I am Honorable, I am noble, and I cannot tell what: my father was this, my father was that; I am come of this house, I am come of that ".[3] The irreverence, the independent-mindedness of the Puritan has its value: it is very effective. Robert Greene, the scapegrace who had nothing to lose, could afford to be crude: " What is gentry if wealth be wanting, but base servile beggary? " [4] — a sentiment which must often enough have an echo in our time. The dramatists found it a piquant topic, particularly those like Jonson with a vein of social criticism. *Every Man out of his Humour* portrays one who would be a gentleman: " Now look you, Carlo: this is my humour now! I have

[1] Camden, *Annals*, sub. 1601.
[2] H.M.C. *Salisbury MSS.* I. 482-3.
[3] P. Stubbes, *Anatomy of Abuses* (ed. Furnivall), p. 29.
[4] Robert Greene, *Groatsworth of Wit* (ed. G. B. Harrison), p. 9.

land and money, my friends left me well, and I will be a gentleman whatsoever it costs me."[1] And from there the fun proceeds. The theme of *Eastward Ho!* is that of the foolish young woman, daughter of a goldsmith, who wants to be a lady and is taken in by the bogus, bankrupt knight, Sir Petronel Flash; the moral:

> What ere some vainer youth may term disgrace,
> The gain of honest pains is never base;
> From trades, from arts, from valour, honour springs,
> These three are founts of gentry, yea of kings.[2]

Shakespeare, who was no mere social critic — and took an early opportunity of success in London to sue out a coat of arms for his father, impaling those of his mother's family, the Ardens — displays his usual wise acceptance of the arrangements of society. The real hero of *King John* is the honest gentleman, the bastard Faulconbridge: through him speaks the English soil. *As You Like It* begins similarly with a dispute between two brothers: the elder withholds his rights from the younger: "He lets me feed with his hinds, bars me the place of a brother, and, as much as in him lies, ruins my gentility with my education. . . . My father charged you in his will to give me good education: you have trained me like a peasant, obscuring and hiding from me all gentleman-like qualities. The spirit of my father grows strong in me, and I will no longer endure it: therefore allow me such exercises as may become a gentleman."[3]

What that education and those exercises were we shall see later: let it suffice here to refer to Peacham's *Complete Gentleman*, first published in 1622, which sums up the agreed teaching on the subject and portrays an ideal of a gentleman not the less English for being recognisably Renaissance. There is all the Platonic emphasis on a just balance between mind and body, an Aristotelian insistence on temperance and moderation with an English regard for reputation and carriage and the reminder that the gentleman must be an amateur, not a professional. As to what younger sons felt about the subjection of their interests to the eldest, Thomas Wilson, as one of them, writes from the heart: "My elder brother forsooth must be my master. He must have all, and all the rest that which the cat left on the malt heap, perhaps some small annuity during his life or what please our elder brother's worship to bestow upon us if we please him and my mistress his wife. This I must confess doth us good some ways,

[1] Act I, sc. i. [2] Actus Primus, Scena prima. [3] Act I, sc. i.

for it makes us industrious to apply ourselves to letters or to arms, whereby many times we become my master elder brother's masters, or at least their betters in honour and reputation, while he lives like a mome and knows the sound of no other bell but his own."[1] Not even this somewhat disgruntled younger son could find it in him to disapprove of the custom of primogeniture; its importance in conserving families along with their estates, in providing a framework for, and a tradition of, social stability where circumstances are naturally so mobile and shifting, is fundamental and incalculable.

The rise of the gentry is interestingly reflected in the growth of heraldry and the corresponding importance of the College of Arms.[2] Henry VIII was a great patron; he was prodigal of arms to his wives, though he deprived them of their heads. He loved a full shield — so like a Renaissance prince; before that time simplicity characterised the arms of the gentry. The Dissolution of the monasteries led to the idea of the heraldic visitations of the counties, verifying grants of arms and recording pedigrees; hitherto the monasteries had been the repositories of genealogical concerns. The fondness of nobility and gentry for everything relating to heraldry, the mob of people pressing in an advancing society for grants of arms, brought great prosperity to the College. An Act of 1566 confirmed it in its privileges and regulated its orders. Under Elizabeth one observes a conscious attempt, in keeping with the Queen's determination to maintain a conservative social order, to control the traffic and keep it within bounds. She wished the different orders of her subjects to be kept exactly distinct, and by proclamation forbade the inferior gentry to assume the title of esquire, while those who had no pretensions to arms by descent were commanded not to use them unless legally procured from the College.

The traffic went merrily forward. Cook, Clarenceux king, granted five hundred coats of arms to different persons who applied in his time; the two Dethicks, father and son, granted more than that in theirs; Brooke, York herald, granted a hundred and twenty in ten years: all so much evidence of the increasing wealth of people who could support the rank and live like gentlemen. Nor were there wanting people who lived by dealing illegally in arms and making pedigrees: one William Dawkins, who was imprisoned and lost an ear for his irrepressible activities, compiled pedigrees for a hundred families in the eastern

[1] T. Wilson, "The State of England, A.D. 1600" (ed. F. J. Fisher), *Camden Miscellany*, XVI. 24.

[2] Cf. Mark Noble, *A History of the College of Arms*.

counties. The great joke was that Sir Gilbert Dethick, Garter king of arms, had constructed a descent for himself. He claimed to be descended from the Dethicks of Dethick hall in Derbyshire; in fact he seems to have been of obscure Dutch origin. (But what was a herald for if he could not make a pedigree for himself?) And what a career Dethick made out of it: embassies, gold chains and cups, a mansion at Poplar; he regularly made a New Year gift of plate to the Queen, and when his son was christened at St. Giles', Cripplegate, the Queen, the Earl of Shrewsbury and Lord Hunsdon stood godparents by proxy. Afterwards there was hippocras and wafers and ' much peeping '. Dethick was a very handsome man, of some skill in antiquities: we forgive him a good deal: after his long ascendancy the heralds quarrelled like mad among themselves.

The heralds' visitations of the counties were a more serious matter than has been supposed: it was no pleasant thing, especially in a society that attached such importance to prestige, to have one's pretensions to gentility publicly exposed and disclaimed. Yet that was the regular procedure. It was a way of keeping the class distinctions of an hierarchical society in some sort of order amid so much economic flux, and — perhaps of most importance — of regulating, though not obstructing, entry to the governing class. We find claimants binding themselves to make proof of their armigerousness within the next year.[1] As time went on the numbers of disclaimed grew larger. In Cornwall on the visitation of 1620 fifty-six altogether were disclaimed and written down as *ignobilis*, as against some two hundred and fifty families whose arms were allowed.[2] Practically all the disclaimed were of yeomen stock, not townsmen — of the latter the Robertses of Truro, Porters of Saltash, Marks of Liskeard are allowed. Among those disclaimed was John Tregagle of St. Allen, the unjust steward of Lord Robartes at Lanhydrock, whose name has such a sinister place in Cornish folk-lore. It is evident that the ranks of the gentry have not been rigorously or too exclusively drawn; on the other hand, hardly a single name among the disclaimed subsequently appears among the county families. On the other hand, we must remember that many disclaimed arms of their own will to avoid expense.

The original returns give us some idea of the occupations of the younger sons of the gentry.[3] Nicholas Roscarrock was an

[1] Cf. *The Visitation of Worcestershire*, 1569 (ed. W. P. W. Phillimore), Harleian Society, vol. VI.

[2] *The Visitation of Cornwall*, 1620 (ed. J. L. Vivian and H. H. Drake), Harleian Society, pp. 294-5.

[3] Harleian MSS. 1079.

antiquarian scholar, a lifelong Catholic recusant whom Lord William Howard ultimately took into his household at Naworth Castle.[1] The eldest son of Michael Vyvyan of Trelowarren served in the household of Charles, Earl of Derby, and was drowned on Passion Sunday 1520. In 1611 Peter Mundy travelled to Constantinople with two younger sons of that house who were apprenticed as Turkey merchants, members of the Levant Company.[2] John Mundy was a younger son of the Derbyshire Mundys and was settled in Cornwall by the kind offices of his uncle, the last prior of Bodmin, who gave him a long lease of the priory's fattest barton and married him to the well-dowered niece of the priory's steward. Peter, sixth son of John Michell of Truro, "did accompany Sir Francis Drake in his Voyage about the World and after returning died a captain at sea". Hugh, sixth son of Edward Herle of Prideaux, was an apprentice in London. John Trefusis' second son, Gavrigan, "died, being an ancient [ensign] in the Netherlands without issue". A younger son of the Bonythons was "Thomas Bonython of London, goldsmith in Cheapside". And others there be that have no name.

Gervase Holles, who was proud of his own descent from a merchant, pays a tribute to the calling and inveighs against those gentry "who, in the sickness of their understanding, apprehend this worthy calling of a merchant to be but ignoble and derogatory to the honour of a gentleman. All, especially the wiser sort, are not of this opinion, but the generality are." [3] He thought that the English had taken this infection from the French, and perhaps the seventeenth century grew more snobbish. "This value, in all ages, had the wisest and best sort of men for this worthy calling, and with reason enough. For no man conveys more advantages to the commonwealth than the merchant . . . transmitting both necessaries, wealth, intercourse and friendship to their own country from the places where they traffic." We have seen that the merchant families of the towns were on the whole content with the life of the towns where they ruled. It was the exceptional ones that bought land and migrated to the country. There was a social reason for that: in this age they were still very much the inferiors of the gentry. That was to change; but not yet. The characteristic townsman of the small class that ran the towns was a John Hooker, chamberlain of Exeter, a William Hawkins, Mayor of Plymouth in Armada year — neither of them

[1] Cf. my *Tudor Cornwall*, pp. 368-9.

[2] *The Travels of Peter Mundy* (ed. Sir R. C. Temple), Hakluyt Society, I. 15.

[3] G. Holles, *Memorials of the Holles Family, 1493–1656*, Camden Society, p. 18.

with a footing in the countryside. And we hear of Newcastle: "The names of the Newcastle merchants, Liddells and Riddells, Vanes and Tempests, Jenisons and Selbies were not very significant names in the reign of Queen Elizabeth; they could not even get a private act through her parliament. But when the evolution of the liberal aristocracy was complete, those names would be found to dominate the north, sometimes half concealed under earldoms and marquisates, and no longer buried in bourgeois comfort in the now unfashionable Fleshmarket or Sandhill of Newcastle, but glittering in the aristocratic splendour of castellated country mansions." [1]

The great exception was, as it always had been, London. The fortunes that could be made there were capable of rivalling the peerage and of promoting the next generation, though not the makers of them, into it. Customer Smythe, the yeoman's son of Corsham in Wiltshire, who went up to London, married the daughter and heiress of Sir Andrew Judde and made a large fortune out of his farm of the Customs, died possessed of a dozen manors in Kent, besides his smaller properties in Wiltshire and the mansion he built at Corsham.[2] The south transept of Ashford church became the mortuary chapel of the Smythes. There in a regular Janssen-style Renaissance monument the Customer lies, in long gown, skull-cap and ruff holding up a little book — presumably his eternal rather than his fiscal account. In the next tomb lies his son, Sir Richard of Leeds Castle; across the way lies Sir John, the eldest son, who succeeded his father at Ostenhanger. Though he was not knighted himself, three of his sons were; his grandson took the family into the peerage as Viscount Strangford. An even more celebrated London fortune was that of Sir John Spencer, 'Rich Spencer'. He came of small Suffolk origins, was engaged in Mediterranean and Levant trade, became Lord Mayor in 1594–5, made a vast fortune and had an only daughter. Greatly against her father's will, but it seems very much with her own, Lord Compton carried her off and married her without a dowry. But on the father's death the immensity of the fortune left him is said to have quite turned the head of the son-in-law for a bit. This match between landed nobility and City money, rare enough so far, is a pointer to what was to come. The union completed the foundations of the great wealth of the Northampton peerage. It forms a fitting pendant to the story that as I write

[1] H. R. Trevor-Roper, "The Bishopric of Durham and the Capitalist Reformation", *Durham Univ. Journal* (March 1946), p. 57.

[2] I am indebted for these particulars to the researches of Mr. L. L. S. Lowe.

these words the ancient manor of Finsbury, which was bought by the family in 1594 and has continued in it ever since, through all the changes of our history, is just being sold, the link at last broken.[1]

When we come to the nobility and knighthood we observe that it was no more a caste than the gentry. But the Queen was determined to keep it select and privileged — far more so than her father and brother had done. Their reigns were the heyday of new creations, apogee of the *parvenu*. Elizabeth was more conservative; she added very few to the peerage, none out of sheer favour, except the Dudleys and Hunsdon, her cousin, but for notable public service. The rest had to be content with knighthoods. For many years Burghley was the only person to be promoted to the peerage for political services, and, transcendent as those were, he never got beyond the lowest rank. She was chary too of creating knights: nothing annoyed her more in Essex's conduct than his cheapening the order of knighthood by taking advantage of his commands abroad, in Normandy, at Cadiz, in Ireland, to create a large number of new knights. In short, the Queen was careful of the social order, especially of the upper ranges that came within her immediate purview.

Again there is no rigidity even here: there was a complex gradation from the one solitary Duke left — and he disappeared in 1572 — down to the smallest knight, and many variations within the grades. To take perhaps the most obvious distinction that stands out: among the knights there was a section at the top, who by reason of birth or wealth, service or standing, were more nearly allied to the peerage. Such persons were those who belonged to the inner official ring and were eligible for the highest offices: these really belonged to the nobility, they lived on a footing with them and intermarried with them; James's generous creations of peerages merely recognised the position. Such were the Sidneys, for example, a high official family — all of them proud of their Dudley blood [2] — the equals of most peers and superior to some. Such were Sir John Perrot or Sir William Fitzwilliam, Lords Deputy in Ireland; Sir Francis Walsingham or Sir Francis Knollys, a distant cousin of the Queen and Comptroller of her household; Sir Walter Ralegh, Sir Christopher Hatton or Sir Edward Dyer among her courtiers; the Bacons,

[1] Cf. *The Times*, 7 December 1948.

[2] Cf. Sir Henry Sidney to his son Philip in E. Arber, *An English Garner*, I. 42.

Sackvilles, Egertons, Cokes, among the newly risen, chiefly lawyers; or such families as Arundells or Grevilles, Willoughbys or Fairfaxes not yet promoted to the peerage.

Within the nobility there is the obvious distinction — of which too much has been made — between the old families and the new. After all, they lived in the same way, they intermarried, they came very shortly to share the same social outlook: they both belonged to the nobility, which was one, not two. What distinctions there were worked in both directions. By no means all the old families were Catholic, or the new, Protestant. We have seen that two of the newest, and from the lowest origins, the Pagets and Petres, were Catholic. Conversely the Earl of Huntingdon, who had Yorkist royal blood and was of an old medieval house, was a very urgent Protestant. The Duke of Norfolk, head of the Howards — a comparatively recent medieval family — was no Catholic; his sons were divided in their religious sympathies. Still, on balance, it is fair to say that the Catholic were apt to be the old families, perhaps because they were the more conservative. A more effective division was that between big and small: between such potentates as the Earls of Derby or Shrewsbury, Northumberland, Arundel, Bedford or Southampton, whether new or old, and such comparatively landless or even indigent peers, the Earl of Bath, Lord Morley, Lord Vaux, to be joined by the thriftless Earl of Oxford. In addition, running through the nobility and knighthood alike was the rift of religion. But here we are only concerned with the phenomena of social class.

How to define the nobility? What are its distinguishing characteristics? What its function?

Gervase Holles, that good middle-class antiquary, tells us that "race and lineage are the matter of nobility, though the form (which gives life and perfect being) is virtue and qualities profitable to the commonwealth".[1] Peacham, like the schoolmaster he was, undertakes to define nobility for us: "Taken in the general sense [it] is nothing else than a certain eminency, or notice taken of someone above the rest, for some notable act performed".[2] In the Aristotelian tradition that has been so powerful in forming the mind of the English governing class, he asserts the superiority of the life of action to that of contemplation: "For since all virtue consisteth in action and no man is born for himself, we add — beneficial to his country; for hardly they are to be admitted to be noble who (though of never so excellent

[1] G. Holles, *op. cit.* p. 4.

[2] Peacham, *op. cit.* pp. 2, 14.

parts) consume their light, as in a dark lantern, in contemplation and a stoical retiredness". So, following out this superiority, Peacham specifies the pre-eminence and privileges that should be accorded the nobility and gentry: they should be preferred in honours, offices and other dignities of command and government before the common people; we ought to "give credit to a noble or gentleman before any of the inferior sort"; "he ought in all sittings, meetings and salutations to have the upper hand and greatest respect"; they may wear rich apparel and of what fashion they please, where sumptuary laws controlled what others wore, no less effectively than the rationing of today.

Bacon clinches the matter in a famous passage in the *Essays*: "A monarchy where there is no nobility at all is ever a pure and absolute tyranny: as that of the Turks. For nobility attempers sovereignty and draws the eyes of the people somewhat aside from the line royal."[1] But he is against a too numerous nobility on the ground that it "causeth poverty and inconvenience in a state; for it is a surcharge of expense". Then — "it is a reverend thing to see an ancient castle or building not in decay, or to see a fair timber tree sound and perfect. How much more to behold an ancient noble family, which hath stood against the waves and weathers of time. For new nobility is but the act of power; but ancient nobility is the act of time."

This pre-eminence involved the nobility in immense burdens and charges. In addition to the state they were expected to keep up, there were all sorts of social duties attaching to their position, honorific offices to fill — often all honour and no profit; the fearful expense of a foreign embassy on some special occasion with a retinue of a hundred gentlemen to maintain was apt to fall upon them; visiting grandees were put upon them to entertain, or there was the still more expensive honour — which some gentlemen begged off in a panic — of entertaining their Queen; the greatest offices of government, Lord Deputy of Ireland, Lord President of the North or of Wales, the charge of the Queen of Scots, Leicester's command in the Netherlands, all brought the occupants debts, not profits. Each time the Queen paid Burghley a state visit it cost him some £2000-£3000; he had that honour twelve times.[2] Multiply that by thirty. The Court's famous entertainment at Kenilworth in the summer of 1575 cost Leicester over £6000. When the Earl of Derby went on embassy to France in 1584 he had a train of 130 gentlemen in two liveries, one of purple and gold lace, one of black satin and taffeta, all with their

[1] "Of Nobility", *Essays*.

[2] F. Peck, *Desiderata Curiosa*, I. 25.

gold chains: 70 of these gentlemen were of his own retinue, even so he had none of his own council or country men with him.[1] It cost him a pretty penny: a year or two later we find him asking Burghley to put in a good word for him with Alderman Spencer to lend him £1000 for a twelvemonth.[2] The Earl of Northumberland begged off such an embassy on the score of deafness in a letter which comically betrays equal embarrassment and apprehension.[3] The Earl of Huntingdon, after twenty years of service as President of the North, died some £20,000 in debt to the Crown — which Elizabeth was not going to let his heirs off.[4] The magnificent Leicester — an interesting combination of magnificence and meanness, though the latter he could hardly help if he were to survive — is said to have died £70,000 in debt to the Crown; though the precise extent of Leicester's indebtedness is not clear, the Queen exacted the surrender of the great lordship of Denbigh to offset some of it.

Then there was the immensely increased luxury of society at the top, of which the Court set the example and the pace in that glittering dance: again the Renaissance impulse, a germ which was carried above all by Courts and to which courtiers were most sensitive. Richly elaborate and ostentatious as contemporary Courts were in Italy, France, Northern Europe, such a Court as that of Catherine de Médicis or Christian IV, it was observed that the English nobility stood out for the size of their households, the expense of their retinues. (Their servants made fortunes at their expense: a tribute to the more popular, if not democratic, nature of English society.) This same Earl of Derby, when residing quietly in the country at Lathom in 1587, had a household of 118 servants.[5] The simplification attendant upon the Reformation excused him from the necessity of more than 1 chaplain, where the pre-Reformation Earls of Northumberland had 11 priests. The Derby household was presided over by 3 officers, steward, comptroller and receiver general, each with 3 servants, while my lord had 7 gentlemen-in-waiting and a page. In 1590 the household had increased to 140 servants for a family of five. Nor was this very exceptional. Ostentation was the order of the day, in every respect: buildings, clothes, entertainments, hospitality, funerals, furnishing, travel, shows. When the Duke of Norfolk rode through the City in 1562 to take up his residence

[1] *The Derby Household Books* (ed. F. R. Raines, Chetham Society), p. li.

[2] T. Wright, *Queen Elizabeth and her Times*, II. 356.

[3] H. Percy, *Advice to his Son* (ed. G. B. Harrison), p. 14.

[4] Cf. L. Stone, "Anatomy of the Elizabethan Aristocracy", *Econ. Hist. Rev.* (1948), pp. 15, 18.

[5] *Derby Household Books*, pp. 23-7, 88.

he was attended by 100 horsemen in his livery with his gentlemen in velvet preceding him.[1] In the same year the young Earl of Oxford, returning from his father's funeral, rode through the City with 140 horse all in black. Funerals themselves were such an expensive affair that the indigent Marquis of Northampton lay unburied for many weeks since a person of such honour could not but have an honourable funeral and nobody could be found to support the expense of it.[2] In the end the Queen paid up, and the poor man was buried. The expense, and the extravagance, of clothes were frightful: seven doublets and two cloaks for Leicester were valued at £543.[3] When a lord's doublet, as well as a lady's stomacher, was sewn with pearls there were men who wore " whole estates on their backs ". " O, many have broke their backs with laying houses on 'em." [4] In such a scene, old Burghley in sober grey or black must have made a somewhat bourgeois figure.

Even he could not escape the touch of the time: he had his extravagance — building. There is the palace he built at Burghley to show that he was not untouched by the Renaissance spirit. He built other houses too, at Theobalds and Waltham. Other courtiers built on a splendid scale: Hatton built a palace fit for a king at Holdenby — where indeed Charles I enjoyed his only comfort during the last year of his life. Audley End, large as it is, is only a fragment of the immense house built by Norfolk's son, James's Lord Treasurer, Suffolk. Even the Countess of Shrewsbury, careful financier that she was, could not stop building. Sir Francis Willoughby well-nigh ruined himself over Wollaton. The entertainments that took place in these vast halls were according. Whole flocks and herds were slaughtered to feed such households and such retinues of guests. In the year 1561 the Derby household consumed 56 oxen and 535 sheep; the household expenses for the year were £2895 : 0 : 6.[5] Multiply by thirty! The household books of Sir William Fairfax of Gilling Castle in Yorkshire, whose family had swallowed the possessions in York of St. Mary's abbey, show just what such a household ate: for the year 1579, 49 oxen, 150 sheep, for food, £338 : 3 : 9½, and for the next year, £440 : 0 : 2½.[6] It is a lordly income spent on food alone. Hospitality was very lavish: dinners and suppers for the Archbishop of York, or the Earl of Rutland, with a host of guests: a first course of sixteen dishes, a

[1] *The Diary of Henry Machyn* (ed. J. G. Nichols, Camden Society), pp. 294, 291.
[2] *The Black Book of Warwick*, ed. T. Kemp, pp. 51-5.
[3] L. Stone, *loc. cit.* p. 5.
[4] Shakespeare, *Henry VIII*, I. i.
[5] *Derby Household Books*, pp. 1-5.
[6] H.M.C. *Various Coll.* II. 76, 78, 85.

second of fourteen. It was not unusual, as at Wollaton, for 40 strangers to come and dine along with the household; on a November Saturday in Lenton Fair time the Earl and Countess of Rutland with other gentry and their retinues to the number of 120 dined at the new house: that high confined hall must have been well filled.[1] Gervase Holles tells us that Sir William Holles "began his Christmas at All-Hallow tide and continued it till Candlemas; during which time any man was permitted freely to stay three days without being asked from whence he came or what he was. . . . And I have heard that his proportion which he allowed during the twelve days of Christmas was a fat ox every day with sheep and other provision answerable. . . . This liberal hospitality of his caused the first Earl of Clare to let fall once an unbecoming word, that his grandfather sent all his revenues down the privy house." [2]

There were many other modes of conspicuous consumption: costly furnishings, the velvets and silks coming in from Italy, jewels, lawsuits — to which a regular if varying proportion of income had to be devoted in the legal and economic complexities of such a society — dowers and jointures, expensive provision for children and their establishments, enterprises like the sea-voyages which cost the Earl of Cumberland a fortune or the colonising efforts which cost Ralegh £40,000. All these were obvious and striking enough. What is more complex is the economic position of the class as such.

It is important to keep a judicious balance in the discussion recently opened.[3] It is true enough that the wealth of the great nobles was impressive rather than immediate; often enough they found themselves without cash in hand. On his father's death, the ninth Earl of Northumberland found himself "so well left for movables as I was not worth a fire-shovel or a pair of tongs; what was left me was wainscots, or things riveted with nails; for wives commonly are great scratchers after their husbands' deaths, if things be loose".[4] But, as we see, this was a special case. What was true enough of great old-fashioned inheritances was that a certain amount of their wealth was locked up in unremunerative franchises, profits of hundreds, boroughs, fairs, markets. But these made a small item. Far more important were the overhead charges of administration of large scattered estates, the opportunities given to stewards and bailiffs to make

[1] H.M.C. *Middleton MSS.* pp. 418, 456. [2] G. Holles, *op. cit.* pp. 41-2.

[3] Cf. R. H. Tawney, "The Rise of the Gentry, 1559–1640", *Econ. Hist. Rev.* (1941); L. Stone, *loc. cit.* [4] *Op. cit.* p. 79.

money at every point at the lords' expense, the inefficiency of their estate management, their neglect of their own business affairs. All the evidence goes to show this, and to show something else — that, properly attended to, these things could be remedied. This is the simple answer to those people who talk of the Elizabethan aristocracy as a declining class on its way downhill.

There are indeed some striking examples in the Elizabethan Age of some great people losing a lot of money, and their fortunes tumbling downwards. But this has happened in all ages. In the Elizabethan cases there was nothing automatic in the process: in every case it can be traced to the foolery or the irresponsibility of the individual. And there is only one case that I can call to mind of a leading family that was permanently brought low by it — the de Veres, Earls of Oxford. Edward de Vere, seventeenth earl, was a very special case: light-headed, a fop — in spite of the advantage of having been brought up as Burghley's ward and married to his daughter — talented, with a taste for literature and the society of players, dissolute and with no head for money whatever: he was always ready to sell a manor at less than its value for ready cash; at the end, he had the mentality of a failed gambler. While still under age his clothing bills for four years came to £600; at twenty, returning from the North, he rode into London with 80 gentlemen in his livery of Reading tawny with chains of gold, and 100 tall yeomen also in livery; at twenty-four he was already £6000 in debt.[1] The truth about the de Veres is that they never were a very rich family; their lands were not extensive. It is not surprising that this young fool — whom his father-in-law described more kindly, but ruefully, as "in matters of thrift inconsiderate"[2] — ran through them all and ended up a pensioner, living on the Queen's bounty. What is more surprising is the long-suffering patience, the humility with which Burghley took this young man's intolerable treatment of his daughter.[3] (There is her pathetic monument on the wall at Stamford not far from her father.) Indeed Burghley's obsequiousness towards the nobility, and his paternal care of their interests, are indications of the change in the position of the class from the fifteenth century. The power was his: he could afford to be polite; but he always was polite.

The case of the Berkeleys has been a good deal canvassed; but the troubles of Lord Henry the Harmless are simple enough to explain: in large part the explanation lies in his name. It is

[1] B. M. Ward, *The Seventeenth Earl of Oxford*, pp. 1 31, 92.
[2] *Ibid.* p. 94.
[3] Cf. *ibid.* pp. 62, 119.

the usual story of a foolish young aristocrat, with no head for business and a head only for sport, overspending himself. He married the sister of the Duke of Norfolk; and John Smyth of Nibley draws a picture of this easy-going, extravagant young couple going about the country spending £1500 a year or so more than their income.[1] They had a household of 150 up to 1572, when it had to be reduced by 40, and again in 1580 — a great deprivation — to 70. Lord Henry had two large jointures to keep up, for his mother and grandmother, amounting to one-third of his income; in his younger years he had given improvidently generous leases to his officers — or they had helped themselves to them; he was dogged all his days by lawsuits, in particular by the great dispute which went on for over a century as the result of the Marquis Berkeley's will; his snobbish wife turned down overtures from Leicester to marry her daughters to his nephews and heirs, the Sidneys, with the consequence that Berkeley lost his suits with the Dudleys; in addition to his own troubles, his son turned out to be as extravagant as he had been himself in youth. The result of this was that Lord Henry had to sell a great many of his manors: in sixty years he sold lands worth £41,400. And yet in spite of this disastrous record John Smyth managed not only to see his master successfully through but to make a small fortune for himself out of Lord Henry in the process.[2]

The answer to it all was good estate-management: it could be done: the great estates of the nobles could be as successfully run as those of the gentry, if only they would learn to manage their own affairs or had someone whom they could trust to do it for them. It is the constant burden of the Earl of Northumberland's "Advice to his Son". He had learnt from bitter experience: his apprenticeship lasted a good many years. His father left him in ignorance of his estates, and much of his losses he put down to "not being taught the secrets of my estate before I had use thereof".[3] His officers and servants helped themselves to fat and favourable leases; his mother's officers had their rewards out of the western lands granted her in jointure in leases of three lives in reversion — which robbed him of subsequent fines. "Then were my felicities (because I knew not better) hawks, hounds, horses, dice, cards, apparel, mistresses; all other riot of expense that follow them were so far afoot and in excess as I knew not

[1] J. Smyth, *Lives of the Berkeleys*, II. 265 foll.
[2] I am indebted here to an unpublished essay on John Smyth by Mr. J. R. Cooper.
[3] *Op. cit.* pp. 80-84.

where I was, or what I did, till out of my means of £3000 yearly I had made shift in one year and a half to be £17,000 in debt." In a few years his losses in one way or another, by sale of woods, unfavourable leases and so on, amounted to some £60,000 or £70,000. Reduced to this pass he took his own affairs in hand and redeemed them: "I must confess I was forced to discard to the very kitchen boys before things could be settled as I wished; for you shall ever find it that servants will strive what they can to uphold any liberty winked at before if any of a former corrupt family be left". Having done this, Northumberland brought his estates round and left the inheritance unimpaired to his son.

There was no downward trend for the aristocracy, even if the gentry were coming up. In fact, conditions became increasingly favourable for the whole of the landed class with the growing returns from the land towards the turn of the century; and if the larger owners were capable of taking their opportunities, they profited more largely. We have been told that "the correspondence of Burghley, in the last decade of Elizabeth, reads like the report of a receiver in bankruptcy to the nobility and gentry".[1] This inference is not correct; they were not in liquidation. The point is indeed an elementary one: as long as they held on to their lands they could afford a great deal of indebtedness; indeed, in a society where cash was scarce, indebtedness was often a sign of considerable resources: if you had not the resources you would not have been given the advances. The actual burden of debts, which might be quite large, might mean little enough in relation to a large income from land: good management could pay them off in a few years. Burghley's real function in this regard was very far from a receiver in bankruptcy: it was to oil the wheels, "by occasion of his office he hath preserved many great houses from overthrow by relieving sundry extremities".[2] He could always be relied on to do his duty, and he conceived it his duty to do his best to maintain the great houses in the service of the State.[3] At Elizabeth's accession, we find among memoranda for the Parliament of 1559: "That an ordinance be made to bind the nobility to bring up their children in learning at some university in England or beyond the sea from the age of 12 to 18 at least. . . . The wanton bringing up and ignorance of the nobility

[1] R. H. Tawney, *loc. cit.* p. 12. [2] Cf. L. Stone, *loc. cit.* p. 26.

[3] There are many instances; cf. the Countess of Southampton, whose son was Burghley's ward, to Burghley (S.P. 12/233/96). Norfolk committed the oversight of his son's trustees to Burghley (H.M.C. *Various Coll.* II. 235); but the young Earl of Arundel set out on extravagant courses and came to no good. The Earls of Oxford, Essex and Southampton were all Crown wards committed to Burghley's charge.

forces the Prince to advance new men that can serve, which for the most part neither affecting true honour, because the glory thereof descended not to them, nor yet the commonwealth (through coveting to be hastily in wealth and honour) forget their duty and old estate and subvert the noble houses to have their rooms themselves." [1]

This is a very different inflection from the first half of the century, an important contrast. Henry VII and Henry VIII devoted themselves to subjugating the class which, possessing power, had made such a nuisance of itself in the fifteenth century. Now that it was reduced to submission, and was no longer a danger, the Crown could afford to conserve and protect its interests, make common cause with it against other challenging forces and use it with effect in the service of the State.

[1] H.M.C. *Salisbury MSS.* I. 163.

CHAPTER VII

THE GOVERNMENT OF THE REALM

ENGLISH government in the sixteenth century was authoritarian, but popular. It rested on the good-will of the people, and even — in a certain sense — on the will of the people. The Crown, the person of the monarch, was something they could all understand, especially with such an obvious personality as Henry VIII or one so recognisably his daughter as Elizabeth. A popular indication of that may be seen in the lasting impression their personalities made on the mind of the nation. For a people there was — and is — this great advantage in kingship.

In Europe the characteristic political development of the time was that of the strong State with an absolute monarch. Why did this not come about in England? The answer lies in the nature of English society: popular liberties were too much entrenched, the strength of the commons — gentry and people — too widely dispersed, a balance of power already achieved and subtly held, instinctively and tenaciously adhered to. On the Continent the doctrines of absolutism were in full flower; the classical principle *Quod principi placuit vigorem legis habet* expressed what was becoming the fact. The English sense of political restraint, the preference for stopping short of absoluteness even at some expense of clarity, stood the nation in good stead. For ultimately the simplicity of absolutism or totalitarianism of any kind is a less civilised thing than a balance of powers within a community (and perhaps without it as well); it means the mitigation and moderation of the whole force of society's impact upon the individual, so that he may get on with what is his proper business — to live life as fully as possible, to develop his potentialities voluntarily and co-operatively along with others: the proper end of society.

It was not until the powers of the monarchy were challenged and were on the down grade that the theory of the Divine Right of Kings began to bloom in all its finery. Elizabeth had been content to exercise them. But James, in touch with up-to-date continental thought, was out of touch with the common sense of ordinary people. Like the Franco-Scottish intellectual he was, he insisted with complete lack of tact in opening up awkward questions of principle which all good politicians know should rarely if ever be mentioned; and — what every Englishman's instinct is against — he persisted in pursuing these questions to their logical conclusions. He even wrote books of political theory about them: no wonder there was trouble. Not so Elizabeth: she had less learning and more sense.

That said, we must enquire more precisely what was happening in regard to government in our period. There is first the fundamental factor of continuity with the Middle Ages: no break, except for the revolutionary changes in the Church. Continuity indeed "has been the dominant characteristic in the development of English government. . . . Crown and Parliament, Council and great offices of state, courts with their judges and magistrates, have all retained, amid varying environments, many of the inherent attributes as well as much of the outward circumstance and dignity which were theirs in the medieval world of their origin."[1] The powers of the Crown were what they had been under Henry IV and Henry V; lapsed into the hands of the Council by the imbecility of Henry VI, they had been recovered and vigorously executed by Edward IV and Henry VII. Can we discern any new elements that characterise our period?

There is the obvious difference made by the Reformation, which meant an immediate extension of royal power and the concentration of executive authority in both Church and State in the hands of the ruler. But the effect of this concentration is liable to be over-emphasised: the Church even under Royal Supremacy retained an inner spiritual authority of its own, undefined — which Englishmen were too wise to try to define. Those who tried were apt to end up in the absolutism of Rome or Geneva. The greater concentration of power meant then a stronger emphasis on political sovereignty, as against some loss of feudal powers. Concentration of power, a simple and defined authority, efficiency of government: these were the keynotes of Tudor rule, and about all that the 'New Monarchy' of the Renaissance came to in England. For law and custom required royal authority to be carried on in conformity with rules which the personal act of the king was supposed not to transcend. Thus law, not the personal will of any ruler, ultimately formed the true basis of the State: a more mature and adult conception of political society. And the supremacy of law was coming to

[1] D. L. Keir, *The Constitutional History of Modern Britain, 1485–1937*, p. 1.

mean the supremacy of statute law, with its infinite flexibility for change in time to come. Already there were writers in Henry's reign who, during the swift and crowded experience of the Reformation Parliament, thought in terms of Parliamentary infallibility;[1] and Sir Thomas Smith, whose book enshrined the constitutional commonplaces of the time, wrote: "The most high and absolute power of the realm of England consisteth in the Parliament".[2] We remember that Parliament meant the King-in-Parliament. But the association of the two Houses with the Crown in responsibility for matters of high national policy was unparalleled elsewhere and surely made the English State already unique in Europe.

This was in part a consequence of the Reformation. It is somewhat paradoxical that the Reformation, which initially added so much to the power of the Crown, led in the unfolding of events to its decline. Abroad, in Catholic countries the Church remained normally a support of monarchy; in Lutheran countries it was an annexe of it. In England the gradual dispersal of the Church lands enormously strengthened the gentry and even some of the people. The Reformation Parliament, which was kept so long in session by Henry to share responsibility for his reduction of the Church, developed a sense of continuity and a claim in legislation and to have a voice in national policy that Parliament never forgot. The effect of the Reformation, which in the short run strengthened the monarchy and in the long run weakened it, was to weight the balance of the constitution further towards the property, rights and liberties of the people. And not in the very long run either: in the course of Elizabeth's reign the effect on the Crown's position was already turning from advantage to disadvantage. In its operation it was reinforcing the tendencies already inherent in the nature of English society.

With this background in mind, and always remembering the balance of social forces beneath the face of politics, we turn to the function of kingship. It has two aspects, social and political: impossible here fully to do the former justice. It was, however, the normal mode, along with religion, of holding society together in the sixteenth century as in the Middle Ages: it provided that sacrosanct centre which it seems a society must somewhere have — if not a king, then a sacred Book or written Constitution. There is indeed such a divinity that doth hedge a king: the

[1] Cf. F. Le V. Baumer, *The Early Tudor Theory of Kingship*, pp. 59-77.
[2] Sir T. Smith, *De Republica Anglorum* (ed. L. Alston), p. 48.

person of the monarch had an *aura*, a quasi-sacramental character confirmed by the anointing at his coronation. Touch not the Lord's anointed: the effect may be seen among primitive tribes or in the fact that in 1649 one or two persons are said to have died on hearing that the King's head had been cut off. The utility of the idea for government, in holding society together, in canalising its latent or overt violence into order, was immeasurable. No rebellions throughout the century dared challenge the name of the king: they all had to claim to be delivering the monarch from bad counsel: they were therefore hamstrung from the beginning and shattered in their inmost confidence when the king turned the light of his countenance upon them. "I am your anointed Queen", Elizabeth reminded Parliament, admonishing them for opposing her wishes. There is no doubt that she regarded herself as appointed by God to rule over her subjects, though the rational woman at the ceremony said of the oil that it stank. And yet —

> Not all the water in the rough rude sea
> Can wash the balm from an anointed king.

In truth, Elizabeth's own mind was not given to sacramentalism of any kind: hers was a mind positive, rational, political. But she understood all the more the political use of these things, and her reign saw a marked revival in the popularity of that sure sign of the sacramental function in the monarch — touching for the King's Evil.[1] For a period she discontinued the practice. The Papal Bull of excommunication was enough to determine her to call her powers into play again, and papal thunder does not seem to have affected them adversely. Catholics, of course, scoffed; not that they did not believe in such nonsense but that the Queen was excommunicate — for what that was worth. The Puritans were hostile — which was a step towards rationalism. But the people did not fail to be healed of their scrofulous complaints. The Queen kept up the traditional rite, only transposing it into English and omitting the invocation to the Virgin — doubtless she was virgin enough in herself. Amid the jollifications with Leicester at Kenilworth in 1575 she found time to touch nine persons for the Evil. She did not shrink from the duty of placing her hands upon the sore places of the sufferers. This horrified James when he came to it, and he had a scruple due to his Calvinist upbringing. Also, as a don, he was apt to take seriously what he thought he believed. But he soon suc-

[1] R. Crawfurd, *The King's Evil*, p. 64 foll.

cumbed and gave the idiot people what they wanted. Shakespeare, who had a way of putting into words what ordinary people thought, describes it:

> A most miraculous work in this good king:
> Which often since my here-remain in England
> I have seen him do.[1]

The mass of people did not think a king truly a king unless he healed. And Henri IV in France, like James in England, after his reception touched to great effect.[2] The sins of neither of these hoary old sinners — if in different directions — had any ill effect, for it is well known that the validity of a sacrament does not depend upon the grace of the performer.

"In pompous ceremonies a secret of government doth much consist."[3] The ceremony that surrounded the English monarchy was greater than that of any Court in Europe: all foreign observers commented on it. A Venetian ambassador was astonished to see the Princess Elizabeth kneeling before her father three times in the course of one interview. Anyone who came into the sovereign's presence knelt. Hentzner describes the Queen towards the end of her life passing on her way to chapel at Greenwich on a Sunday in 1598: "As she went along in all this state and magnificence she spoke very graciously to foreign ministers, in English, French and Italian. Whosoever speaks to her kneels; now and then she raises someone with her hand. Wherever she turned her face, as she was going along, every one fell on their knees."[4] All this had its use: it kept order in the nursery. For want of it the French monarchy lost in dignity and control. It too was popular in character, but there was a large element of familiarity in it, strange to English notions. The disadvantage of this may be seen in such an episode as Henri III and his young friends riding masked through the streets of Paris jostling and pushing the *bons bourgeois* about, insulting them and throwing their hats into the mud.[5] Such proceedings are unthinkable in a Tudor at the English Court in its sedate and rather solemn

[1] *Macbeth*, IV. iii. [2] Marc Bloch, *Les Rois thaumaturges*, p. 339.

[3] q. J. E. Neale, *Queen Elizabeth*, p. 67.

[4] q. M. Creighton, *Queen Elizabeth*, p. 282.

[5] *Journal de L'Estoile* (ed. A. Brette), p. 61: "Le cinquième jour de Carême-prenant, le Roi alla par la ville, accompagné d'environ cent chevaux et d'autant d'hommes, vêtus comme lui en pantalons de diverses couleurs, tous bien montés à l'avantage, et au surplus fort mal en ordre . . . lesquels, courant par les rues à toute bride, arrachèrent les chapeaux aux hommes, les chaperons aux femmes, et les jetèrent dans les boues; offensèrent chacun, ne donnèrent plaisir à personne; battirent et outragèrent tous ceux qu'ils trouvèrent en leur chemin. . . ."

splendour, its ordered ceremony and preoccupation with government.

All historians know now that it was Elizabeth who ruled in England; but no historian has had such a subtle understanding of her personality as Creighton: something in the sceptical nature of the prelate responded to the nature of the *politique* in her, a woman who was born, as Napoleon said of himself, *un être politique*. A woman of remarkable political understanding and force of will, endowed with great gifts, an actress to her finger-tips (which were much in play), a great exhibitionist, a woman at heart cold intellectually and emotionally and therefore always ultimately in control of herself and, as Queen, of others, she was more fitted for her position and time than any other monarch in our history. Hence her historic importance: " She represented England as no other ruler ever did ": [1] like Shakespeare, she too became identified for ever with that moment of awakening in the life of her people. But all this was the work of a lifetime and was only complete and made evident with its close. We must avoid thinking of Elizabeth as always the successful and famous old woman she became after 1588. For long it was not obvious that she would be successful; there were times earlier in her reign, and again towards the end, when she was not so popular. But when she was gone, her work stood clear and unmistakable. There is a most revealing sentence in a speech to her very first Parliament, when she was young, untried, still unknown: " What credit my assurance may have with you I cannot tell, but what credit it shall deserve to have the sequel shall declare ".[2] The sequel did declare it indeed! It was not possible for Elizabeth to make plain what she meant: her people must take her on trust as she, at the greatest crises and on the highest issues, trusted them. " When it came to decisive action she fell back upon her instinctive perception of what England wanted. As she could not explain this, she was driven to all sorts of devices to gain time. She could not, on the other hand, fully take her people into her confidence." [3] That was in the nature of her position, of ultimate responsibility, her own and alone, throughout forty-five years. That, and the character of her intimate personal life, have caused her to be thought of as enigmatic; in truth she has left us in her letters and speeches many evidences as to what she was and what she thought, particularly her conception of her role and rule. Let her speak for herself.

[1] Creighton, *op. cit.* p. 304.

[2] Sir Simonds D'Ewes, *Journal* (ed. 1693), p. 46.

[3] Creighton, p. 306.

At the beginning of the long war with Spain, the turning-point in her country's history, she made a speech to Parliament which is full of autobiographical interest and reflects back to what she felt on assuming the crown. With the constant plots against her life in mind, she said: "I know no creature that breatheth whose life standeth hourly in more peril for it [*i.e.* the Protestant religion] than mine own, who entered not into my state without sight of manifold dangers of life and crown, as one that had the mightiest and greatest to wrestle with. Then it followeth that I regarded it so much *as I left my life behind my care*. And so you see that you wrong me too much (if any such there be) as doubt my coldness in that behalf; for if I were not persuaded that mine were the true way of God's will, God forbid that I should live to prescribe it to you. Take you heed lest *Ecclesiastes* say not too true, 'They that fear the hoary frost, the snow shall fall upon them'. . . ."[1] She denounced both Romanists and Puritans: "I mean to guide them both by God's holy true rule. In both parts be perils, and of the latter I must pronounce them dangerous to a kingly rule, to have every man according to his own censure to make a doom of the validity and privity of his prince's government with a common veil and cover of God's word, whose followers must not be judged but by private men's exposition." That was intolerable: "God defend you from such a ruler that so evil will guide you".

As at the beginning, so at the end; never did her conception of kingship shine forth more nobly than in taking leave of the Commons for what she must have thought would be the last time: "I have ever used to set the Last Judgment Day before mine eyes, and so to rule as I shall be judged to answer before a Higher Judge. To whose judgment seat I do appeal that never thought was cherished in my heart that tended not to my people's good. . . . I know the title of a king is a glorious title; but assure yourself that the shining glory of princely authority hath not so dazzled the eyes of our understanding, but that we well know and remember that we also are to yield an account of our actions before the great Judge."[2] And then — weary of the long years' burden of responsibility and robbed of all pleasure in it by Essex's miserable end: "To be a king and wear a crown is more glorious to them that see it, than it is pleasure to them that bear it". She ended, speaking with great fervour and reiteration: "For I, O Lord, what am I, whom practises and perils past should not fear! O what can I do" — the report says that

[1] D'Ewes, *op. cit.* pp. 328-9.
[2] *Ibid.* p. 659 foll.

these words ' she spake with a great emphasis ' — " that I should speak for any glory ! " Thus she took leave of them, graciously inviting them all to kiss her hand before they departed into their countries.

Her inmost mind on government and kingship may be read in her private correspondence with the young James of Scotland. It does not leave a favourable taste, but it shows up an extraordinary character that compels admiration if only for its incessant energy of mind. Though intellectually subtle, her personality was coarse in texture and fibre — and that too was an asset; everything she had was turned to advantage; it was no use being refined or delicate in her position. The constant pose of the candid friend, the assumption of invariable rectitude, sometimes of outraged virtue, the condescending patronage, the chivvying, the advice, the censoriousness, the harping on her experience and success in the world — it all adds up to the portrait of an intolerable aunt. But it certainly offered an education in kingship, beginning with how to put up with things; and James took it in good part. After all she was a famous ruler and had the right to advise; moreover she had all the trumps, and was not the ultimate inheritance worth putting up with a great deal for? Perhaps we may make an exception for her who was herself exceptional and reproduce for once her own spelling: it is so full of character. Early on she warns him against any underhand dealings against her: " I have seen suche evident shewes of your contrarious dealings . . . and if you suppose that princes causes be vailed so covertly that no intelligence may bewraye them, deceave not yourselfe: we old foxes can find shiftes to save ourselves by others malice, and come by knowledge of greattest secreat, spetiallye if it touche our freholde ".[1] Elizabeth was constantly shocked by the evidences of indiscipline in Scotland — and no wonder when the irrepressible Scottish nobles were for ever running off with James: life was a difficult struggle for survival for a Scottish king: no small tribute to James that he did survive.

Elizabeth encouraged him to stand up for himself and enforce the authority of the crown. But sometimes " it is dangerous for a prince to irritast to muche, through evil advise, the generalitie of great subiectz ".[2] (This was disingenuous, for in fact she had been aiding some of them underhand.) She loathed Presbyterianism so much that her dislike went to her spelling: " A

[1] *Letters of Queen Elizabeth and King James VI of Scotland* (ed. J. Bruce, Camden Society), p. 17. [2] *Ibid.* p. 23.

secte of perilous consequence, such as wold have no kings but a presbitrye, and take our place while the enioy our privilege, with a shade of Godes word, wiche none is juged to folow right without by ther censure the be so demed. Yea, looke we wel unto them . . . *sapienti pauca.* I pray you stap the mouthes, or make shortar the toungz, of such ministars as dare presume to make oraison in ther pulpitz for the persecuted in Ingland for the gospel. Suppose you, my deare brother, that I can tollerat suche scandalz of my sincere govvernement? No." [1] As for the insolent Scottish aristocracy: " For all whoso you knowe the assaylers of your courts, the shamefull attempters of your sacred decree, if ever you pardon, I will never be the suter. Who to peril a king were inventores or actors, they should crake a halter if I were king. Such is my charitie. Who under pretence of bettering your estate, endangers the king, or needs wil be his schoole-masters, if I might appoint their universitie they should be assigned to learne first to obay; so should they better teach you next. I am not so unskylfull of a kinglye rule that I would winke at noe faulte, yet would be open-eyed at publyke indignitie. Nether should all have the whippe though some were scourged." [2] There speaks the daughter of Henry VIII; before she came to the throne, in Mary's reign, it was observed that she held her father in great admiration and was more like him than Mary was.

Elizabeth never ceased to be astonished at the mishaps that befell James; she felt that her good advice was all to no good; she was Cassandra, " but Cassandra was never credited till the mishap had rather chanched than was prevented ".[3] She knew not what to write, so little did she like to lose labour in vain; but she would pray for him that God would unseal his eyes that had too long been shut. She of course was always right; she had known what would happen, but if no-one would listen to her what could one expect? James knew a thing to that one: he asked for money: " If you thinke my frendshipe worthie that annuitie, remember, qui cito dat bis dat ".[4] The Queen sighed: " I had thoght that this wreached faitheles time, in wiche the subiects have license to deprive bothe life and land from princes rule, had yelded no cornar for my delyght. . . ." [5] But she did not mention the annuity; she spoke of the latter days of the world: " These lattar days of the world are to weke to retaine so sound bodies as may cary good minds, but rather al inclined to what may be worst thoght and wickedlest done ". James made love

[1] *Ibid.* p. 63. [2] *Ibid.* pp. 76-7. [3] *Ibid.* p. 70. [4] *Ibid.* p. 69. [5] *Ibid.* p. 174.

to the old lady with a sonnet, *incerto authore.*[1] She did not reply. She was not to be trifled with.

In the end, as her time draws near, they draw together and a genuinely friendly note steals into their correspondence. Her very last words to him were kind: " I hope yow will beare with my molestyng you to long with my skratching hand, as proceding from a hart that shall be ever filled with the sure affection of Your loving and frendly sistar, Elizabeth R." [2] And then one realises that though she had uttered no word with regard to the succession to her throne — and indeed doubt has often been expressed as to her intentions — all the while she had been schooling James in kingship and she meant him to succeed her. A tell-tale phrase, written when the Armada was off the coast of Scotland and James was giving her loyal support, offers a pointer — as was her way — to what was in her mind though she was too cautious to express it: " Yet if, by leaving them unhelped, you may increase the Englisch hartz unto you, you shal not do the worst dede for your behalfe ".[3] It was characteristic that the hint was equivalent to a bribe; she expected nothing for nothing, nothing from fortune, nothing from the world outside; for everything in this world one had to pay a price; whatever one achieved was won by effort and will: she had lived her life in a hard school.

For Elizabeth's part in government there is no shadow of doubt, in spite of what some writers have written to the contrary. Contemporaries had no doubt in the matter; they knew who ruled in England, and her greatest enemies often paid tribute to her sagacious, prudent government. She chose her own ministers and in the end stood by them, though they were often enough inconsiderately treated — a feature hardly avoidable in the possession of ultimate power and certainly not confined to royalty. Her judgment of men was almost infallible — an essential quality in a ruler — though she sometimes took risks for personal reasons understandable enough in any human being, particularly in one so susceptible to good looks in men. The new deal in Church and State, which she represented in her own person, undoubtedly had her backing and belief. She was neither a crypto-Catholic nor an atheist. Her concern was with authority, obedience, the unity and well-being of the country. The tendencies of her mind were humanist and sceptical: she would never trouble people for what they believed, provided that they had the sense to keep it to themselves and conformed outwardly. She was in funda-

[1] *Letters of Queen Elizabeth and King James VI of Scotland*, p. 171.
[2] *Ibid.* p. 156. [3] *Ibid.* p. 53.

mental agreement with William Cecil, not run by him; and though he was the only person who had any influence with her in the last resort over ultimate decisions, where they diverged he was ready to submit and obey. One can watch the growth of her self-confidence and command with experience and the exercise of her will. Cecil's influence was more active and forward-moving in the first decade or so; after 1572 he and the Queen grew more conservative together, though they did not fear to face the conflict with Spain when it came. Towards the end of their partnership Burghley advised his son Robert always to give the Queen his best counsel, as was his duty, but never to try and prevail over her own better judgment, so great were her knowledge of men and experience of affairs.

The actual work of government rested with the Council and the great officers of State. But all decisions of policy rested with her; the Queen's will was the prime motor of government. This meant that she had to be consulted about everything of importance, and she saw to it that she was. The mixture of short-temper and testiness, outbursts of royal wrath, with encouragement and praise, with kind words and words of majestic consolation — this was what was needed to keep people on their toes. As a ruler she could not afford to be sweet, people being what they are. The issues of peace and war rested with her; so did the choice of ministers, of all important appointments, civil, military, religious; the Church lay in the sphere of her prerogative and protection; she concerned herself especially with foreign policy, relations with foreign powers, contacts and discussions through envoys and ambassadors. The constitutional writers tot up the powers of the Crown in these matters, civil, martial, in affairs of administration, finance, the currency and in the realm of commerce. It is impossible to enumerate them; sufficient to conclude with Sir Thomas Smith's summary: "To be short the prince is the life, the head and the authority of all things that be done in the realm of England".[1] All these powers were hers and she continued to exert them until in the end she found herself — in Ralegh's touching phrase — a lady whom Time had surprised.

As to how she exerted these powers we have ample evidence. But it is precisely here that she has been most misinterpreted, least understood. Froude's *History of England*, a work touched by genius, yet does her a monstrous injustice: it is as great a misfortune as Macaulay's travesty of Marlborough. It is true that she was often dilatory, uncandid, obstinate, hesitant, sometimes

[1] *Op. cit.* pp. 58-62.

impossible. Frequently she would not make up her mind. There were other times when her mind was made up firmly and sharply enough. But sometimes it would have been fatal to precipitate a decision, and it became a habit to postpone difficult decisions. Undoubtedly she had luck, but I cannot but think that failure to appreciate her position is due to a want of political understanding. It might have occurred to her impatient modern critics that her long run of success could not be all luck. There is a profounder reason why her habit of mind in sixteenth-century circumstances turned to success. In those days, with far less control over the external world — the forces of nature, wind and weather — those who took the chances of aggressive action exposed themselves to defeat. Chances were strongly against them; they were all in favour of the defensive. As a woman she was naturally attuned to passive, defensive, insinuating action, underhand rather than overt. A man would have exposed himself more, probably to defeat. She exposed nothing, except a fine façade and a dangerous barrage of disingenuousness for the benefit of any fools who liked to be taken in by it. She would play the game on her own terms; like a woman, she was content with small gains, out of which she built up a position that, too late, was found to be inexpugnable. In fact she had displayed extraordinary courage and a cool nerve all along. "What credit my assurance shall deserve to have, the sequel shall declare."

It is indeed a piece of historical jejuneness to judge these things after they are all over and done with, and not to place oneself imaginatively before the events. One could not then know how they would turn out. It was a great decision to take the step of open intervention in the Netherlands that must mean war with the greatest power in the world, and perhaps alone. No wonder she hesitated long and always kept one ear open for possible peace negotiations. One would not dare to condemn her on our *ex post facto* knowledge, even if the events of history had not proved her right. Of course the way she behaved in detail was sometimes intolerable to her servants, though Burghley felt that there was intuition in her hesitations, that she had better have her own way, that things would work out all right — they almost always did. Even he was driven to complain to Walsingham, not long after the defeat of the Armada: "All irresolution and lucks [*i.e.* accidents] are thrown upon us two in all her speeches to everybody. The wrong is intolerable."[1] All the successes were hers,

[1] q. E. R. Cheyney, *A History of England from the Defeat of the Armada to the Death of Elizabeth*, I. 12.

all the mishaps were her ministers': that was what ministers were for. "Her wisest men and best councillors were oft sore troubled to know her will in matters of state. So covertly did she pass her judgment as seemed to leave all to their discreet management, and when the business did turn to better advantage she did most cunningly commit the good issue to her own honour and understanding. But when aught fell out contrary to her own will and intent, the Council were in great strait to defend their own acting and not blemish the Queen's good judgment." [1] Allowing for time and place, it might be Roosevelt that is being written about. She was a great *prima donna* in the realm of politics.

Again and again one can observe her in action; but never more characteristically or over a more crucial issue than the open intervention in the Netherlands that precipitated the war. She had hesitated long to make the decision; but it was inevitable, or the resistance of the Netherlands would be finally ended and Spain free for the invasion of England. She had shown great self-control in refusing, what no king would have done, the sovereignty of the Netherlands. Having made the decision to intervene, she issued a manifesto to Europe that her motive was not aggrandisement, but the preservation of the Netherlands in their ancient liberties. It is the first announcement of what became the secular objective of English policy and the secret of its success — limitation of objectives. Leicester was sent as the lieutenant-general of her forces with an express prohibition from taking on the supreme governorship offered by the States. He had not been there long before he accepted it. The Queen was furious; the more she considered its implications the more enraged she was. Anything that touched her personal authority was anathema, anything that looked like a slight unforgivable. But over and above this she saw something that her ministers' anxiety for the Protestant cause made them overlook: she had given her word of honour to Europe. As a Queen, she was more sensitive to European opinion; she realised the moral issue that was involved and that Leicester's acceptance made nonsense of her protestations.[2]

Every one of her ministers was opposed to her on this crucial issue. This was the beginning of war; they were terrified of discouraging the Netherlands and starting off on a wrong footing. The Queen was alone and isolated, against them all; she may even have been wrong, but she would not give way. Leicester

[1] *Ibid.* [2] *Leicester Correspondence* (ed. J. Bruce, Camden Society), p. xx.

should renounce the authority he had accepted or she would recall him. " We could never have imagined, had we not seen it fall out in experience, that a man raised up by ourself, and extraordinarily favoured by us above any other subject in this land, would have in so contemptible a sort broken our commandment, in a cause that so greatly toucheth us in honour . . . and therefore our express pleasure and commandment is that, all delays and excuses laid apart, you do presently upon the duty of your allegiance, obey and fulfil whatsoever the bearer hereof shall direct you to do in our name: whereof fail you not, as you will answer the contrary at your uttermost peril." [1] This, to Leicester, after all that had passed between them! All her ministers expostulated with her: to withdraw his authority now would be to destroy Leicester's credit with the Netherlanders and ruin the action. She stuck to her arguments: Leicester's acceptance of rule " was sufficient to make her infamous to all princes, having protested the contrary in a book which is translated into divers and sundry languages " and " I may not endure that any man should alter my commission and the authority that I gave him, upon his own fancies and without me ". [2] Messengers went to and from the Netherlands; government was held up; nothing could be decided. Burghley tried to bring pressure upon her and solemnly offered his resignation if she would not change her course. Amazed at such presumptuous " round speech " from him, she temporised; but she did not yield.

Having gained time she sent Heneage, her Vice-Chamberlain, reiterating her orders to Leicester. Arrived in the Netherlands, Heneage realised how fatal a public disavowal would be to Leicester's prestige and wrote back begging for delay. The Queen returned: " Jesus, what availeth wit when it fails the owner at greatest need? Do that you are bidden, and leave your considerations for your own affairs. . . . We princes be wary enough of our bargains: think you I will be bound by your speech to make no peace for mine own matters without their consent? It is enough that I injure not their country, nor themselves, in making peace for them without their consent. . . . I am utterly at squares with this childish dealing." [3] We see now that she was not only morally, but tactically, right: she was not giving the Netherlands a veto on her freedom of action with regard to English issues with Spain. She was safeguarding English rights as well as her own: the Crown was identified with the country, the defender of its interests, not the Protestant cause in Europe.

[1] *Leicester Correspondence*, p. 110. [2] *Ibid.* p. xx. [3] *Ibid.* p. 243.

Though a compromise in form was arranged and Leicester not publicly disgraced, the damage was done. He submitted completely and was forgiven; he returned to England, his credit broken.

Hardly less important in Elizabethan government than the Queen herself was Burghley. The long and complete partnership between them that endured for forty years is the most remarkable in English history, and, considering their joint effort in affairs affecting the formation of the modern English State, the most fruitful in effect. Actually the influence of the Cecils was prolonged in the person of Robert, the younger son, until 1612, by which date the union of the kingdoms was safely established — the secular objective of English policy brought about by that fortunate family. No political family can compare therefore with its influence on the English State. The Queen knew Burghley's worth: she said that "no prince in Europe had such a counsellor as she had of him".[1] It does not detract from the tribute that it was meant to reach his ears; moreover, it was the truth. On her accession the Queen made him her Secretary — another sign of continuity with Edward's government, in which he held the same office. When he took the oath, she said: "This judgment I have of you, that you will not be corrupted with any manner of gifts, and that you will be faithful to the State; and that without respect to any private will, you will give me that counsel that you think best; and if you shall know anything necessary to be declared unto me of secrecy, you shall show it to myself only, and assure yourself I will not fail to keep taciturnity therein".[2] How faithfully they kept that understanding the sequel did declare, though not what secrets they shared, that died with them!

In such a long association there were naturally divergences and jars. What is more remarkable is the extent of their agreement: where they did not agree they were complementary rather than opposed. At the very outset Cecil was set upon a forward policy in Scotland, taking the opportunity of the resistance of the Lords of the Congregation to clear the French out of Scotland, if necessary at the risk of open war. The Queen would not take the risk; she would give underhand aid, but that was not sufficient. Time passed; the opportunity seemed to be passing. Cecil's inner mind may be read in a petition of which the draft

[1] H.M.C. *Salisbury MSS.* II. 145. [2] q. Creighton, p. 46.

remains: "With a sorrowful heart and watery eyes, I your poor servant and most lowly subject, an unworthy Secretary, beseech your Majesty to pardon this my lowly suit, that considering the proceeding in this matter for removing of the French out of Scotland doth not content your Majesty, and that I cannot with my conscience give any contrary advice, I may, with your Majesty's favour and clemency, be spared to intermeddle therein. And this I am forced to do of necessity, for I will never be a minister in any your Majesty's service, whereunto your own mind shall not be agreeable, for thereunto I am sworn, to be a minister of your Majesty's determinations and not of my own, or of others, though they be never so many. And on the other part to serve your Majesty in anything that myself cannot allow, must needs be an unprofitable service, and so untoward as therein I would be loth your Majesty should be deceived. And as for any other service, though it were in your Majesty's kitchen or garden, from the bottom of my heart I am ready without respect of estimation, wealth or ease, to do your Majesty's commandment to my life's end." [1]

That describes the situation between them: complete respect and submission on one side with an equal self-respect on the other; an utter fidelity and no thought for anything other than her own and the country's best interests. It was that that gave him his hold on the Queen's mind; she knew that she could trust him absolutely, so she gave him her confidence as she did to no-one else. In Scotland, in France, in Europe in general, circumstances became more propitious; the French were otherwise engaged; the coast was clear. The Queen was now more ardently in favour of taking open risks than Cecil. Troops were sent over the Border; the Forth was blockaded; Leith reduced. Cecil went North to negotiate the Treaty of Edinburgh by which the French were cleared out of Scotland for good. It was a tremendous reversal of history and a resounding triumph for his policy. His journey and stay in the North had been very expensive. The Queen left him to pay the cost of it.

His reward was her confidence and support. The crisis of Cecil's career came with the duel between his policy and that of the old nobles pushing a marriage between the Duke of Norfolk and Mary Stuart, backed by Philip. It was the conflict between the new deal and the old order coming to a head, after a decade of success for the former. It is an intricate and labyrinthine plot, impossible to unravel here, but through which Cecil threaded

[1] T. Wright, *Queen Elizabeth and her Times*, I. 24-5.

his way without making a mistake or giving a point away to his opponents. They made a formidable combination: the great nobles, Norfolk and Arundel, joined by Leicester; the Catholic Earls of the North; Mary, and behind her, her European backers. The crisis passed through several phases from 1568 to 1569; it was not ultimately resolved till 1572. Here too Cecil took the offensive, though he proceeded with great dexterity. What is noticeable is the steady support he was given throughout by the Queen, against her own relations the Howards and her favourite, Leicester: a remarkable disjunction between the intellect and the emotions — not that there were not emotions also that Cecil could call into play, her jealousy and dislike of her rival, her fear of a marriage that would challenge her throne. One day at Greenwich when matters were under discussion the Queen was supporting Cecil's opinion against Leicester, who retorted that her throne would never be safe till Cecil's head was off his shoulders. The Queen in a passion threatened to send Leicester to the Tower. Norfolk remarked that Leicester was in favour so long as he echoed Cecil, but was in danger if he had an opinion of his own. There was the interesting situation. Then Norfolk threatened. He had the support of some of the greatest nobles; he was the candidate of the old nobility.

Cecil saw that he must bend temporarily. He neatly inserted a wedge between his opponents: he won over Norfolk by supporting his claims to the Dacre inheritance for his sons, whom he had married to the co-heiresses. The Catholic wing of the party, the Northern Earls, broke into open rebellion, were isolated and crushed. Norfolk could now be dealt with. He was dealt with moderately and with friendly consideration: he pledged himself never to marry Mary. Later he broke his word and entered into negotiations with her and foreign powers to intervene. Cecil unravelled the plots woven by the Papal agent, the banker Ridolfi; in this he was aided by Walsingham: it was the latter's introduction to the inner governing circle.[1] The Duke was brought to trial and his treason exposed; he was condemned to death by his peers, sentence being given by the Earl of Shrewsbury, the tears streaming down his face. The Queen long delayed the execution. Cecil behaved towards Norfolk with great consideration. The Duke regarded him as his friend — and indeed Cecil bore him no unfriendly feelings: that was his strength: he did not act from personal motives. The Duke thought he would be reprieved. But Cecil was in favour of the sentence

[1] Conyers Read, *Mr. Secretary Walsingham*, I. 56.

being carried out.[1] The Queen gave her warrant at last and Norfolk was executed. He was her cousin, through her mother, Anne Boleyn.

Cecil had won completely and henceforth was secure. He became a sated power, and, like all sated powers, increasingly conservative: less willing to run risks even than the Queen, in some respects. For example, he was opposed to Drake's voyage into the Spanish sphere of the Pacific; the Queen had her money invested in it. She was less respectable than he. The story of the great crisis of 1569–72, and Cecil's handling of it, is well known on the personal side. What has been less noticed are the class implications of the struggle. Throughout it the Queen and Cecil, who were faced with a break-away of the old aristocracy, or a section of it, with the North and Catholic backing abroad, were steadily supported by the body of the country, the gentry and the middle class, represented by the Commons. When Parliament was summoned in 1572 to give the government support — a move in Cecil's strategy — they demanded the execution of both Mary and Norfolk. The Queen was determined not to assent to Mary's death; her consent to Norfolk's was a sop to the Commons. These critical events were the last fling of the old order. In reality the combinations of the conservative aristocracy — apart even from the weakness of Norfolk, whose measure Cecil had taken exactly — had nothing like the force that they looked like having, dangerous though they might have been. The danger came from their being so highly placed in society, around the person of the Queen, her relations and associates. But her government was supported by, and was largely the expression of, those forces in society that were already much stronger and ever gathering greater strength.

The Queen, who had names for everybody, called Burghley her 'Spirit'; and indeed he was the spirit of her administration. We can read his character very clearly from his actions and the abundant evidences he has left us: a penetrating intelligence, a shrewd tactical eye, cool nerve, audacity combined with prudence and unsleeping watchfulness, he exposed the least possible target to his enemies. There was much more to him: an incessant industry, from those early days when he had paid the bell-ringer at St. John's college to wake him at four in the mornings. Only one indiscretion is known of him: his early and improvident marriage while still at Cambridge. (Even so, he could afford to marry, and the wife died young.) Temperance, self-control,

[1] *Salisbury MSS.* II. 11, 13, 15.

probity, a fantastic capacity for work, these were the clues to his success. He was a most secret man, no-one being admitted to his inner confidence — not his greatest friend; but, we remember, though he was affable and cheerful, he had no greatest friend. His household chaplain writes of him: "He was delighted to talk and be merry with his friends, only at meals; for he had no more leisure. He never had any favourite (as they are termed) nor any inward companion, as great men commonly have. Neither made any man of his counsel, nor did ever any know his secrets: some noting it for a fault, but most thinking it a praise and an instance of his wisdom. For by trusting none with his secrets, none could reveal them."[1] We recall his precept to his son Robert: "Trust not any man with thy life, credit or estate. For it is mere folly for a man to enthral himself to his friend, as though, occasion being offered, he should not dare to become the enemy."[2] There is something sad about this: he too, like his mistress, had been brought up in the dangerous school of the Courts of Henry VIII, Edward VI and Mary.

In the end we come down to his inner and outer integrity, his uprightness, the moral strength he got from religion. Unlike the Queen — and like Mr. Gladstone — he was a religious man. It all adds up to rather a Victorian character in that glittering Renaissance Court. He protested that he was no courtier, and he made a sober figure against that dazzling and jewelled background. All the same, he knew the ways of Courts through and through; we are apt to forget, in contemplating his sobriety, that he was the third generation of his family at Court since his grandfather came out of South Wales in the following of Henry VII to become yeoman of the guard. He much preferred to keep his own house or official lodgings, rather than endure the chatter and amusements, the intrigue and all the back-biting everyone in that environment enjoyed. A letter from Court in 1573 reports: "My Lord Treasurer, even after the old manner dealeth with matters of state only, and beareth himself very uprightly".[3] Lady Burghley had unwisely become jealous of the fancy the Queen had taken to the young Earl of Oxford — brought up in Burghley's household. "At all their love matters my Lord Treasurer winketh, and will not meddle anyway." Sometimes, as he grew older, he was got down by the back-biting he had to put up with: "Finding myself thus maliciously bitten with the tongues and pens of courtiers here, if God did not comfort me, I had cause to fear murdering hands or poisoning

[1] F. Peck, *Desiderata Curiosa*, I. 38. [2] *Ibid.* p. 49. [3] q. Creighton, p. 153.

pricks. But God is my keeper." [1] When he became too much discouraged the Queen would comfort him in her own way as no-one else could: "Sir Spirit, I doubt I do nickname you, for those of your kind (they say) have no sense; but I have of late seen an *ecce signum*, that if an ass kick you, you feel it too soon. I will recant you from being my spirit, if ever I perceive that you disdain not such a feeling. Serve God, fear the King, and be a good fellow to the rest. . . . And pass of no man as not to regard her trust, who puts it in you. God bless you, and long may you last, *Omnino*, E. R." [2]

But nothing could relieve him from the burden of his work and the ceaseless press of suitors. Sometimes he went into the country to avoid them, but there they were also. "Now that you and your wife are at the Court, and my youngest children at Theobalds, I am here as an owl, though companied with excess of suitors." [3] Again, "If I may not have some leisure to cure my head, I shall shortly ease it in my grave, and yet, if her Majesty mislike of my absence, I will about Tuesday or Wednesday venture to come thither".[4] We have a touching little picture of him in 1594, from his faithful secretary, Michael Hicks: "And truly, methinks, he is nothing sprighted, but lying upon his couch he museth or slumbereth. And being a little before supper at the fire, I offered him some letters and other papers, but he was soon weary of them and told me he was unfit to hear suits. But I hope a good night's rest will make him better tomorrow." [5] Later on, he could not read them: "I am become but as a monoculus, because of a flux in mine eye". In his last illness the Queen came and fed him with her own hand; the old man was deeply touched: he thought of his mother whom he had always revered. When he had gone, it was long before she could hear his name without weeping: she wept for the years that were over, for herself in the few years that remained, without him: the years that brought her greatest grief in the death of Essex,

[1] *Salisbury MSS.* III. 104.

[2] T. Wright, *Queen Elizabeth and her Times*, II. 201.

[3] *Salisbury MSS.* IV. 319.

[4] *Ibid.* p. 322. Cf. *Cal. S.P. Dom. 1595–7*, p. 71, for the Queen's inconsiderateness: Burghley to Robert Cecil, 14 July 1595: "I hear from the Lord Keeper that upon my departure yesterday night Her Majesty said that I wanted to go to Theobalds; I am well weaned from thence and without desire to see it for any contentment but only to be free from suitors. I have been fully occupied with Mr. Chancellor, the Barons of the Exchequer and all the officers that have charge to call for the Queen's debts, and have treated with the customers, receivers, surveyors, collectors of subsidies, tenths, fifteenths, bishops' first fruits", etc. etc. — and then the poor old man is not allowed a day or two at his own house in the country!

[5] *Salisbury MSS.* IV. 623.

who should have been her son: whose stepfather was Leicester.

All recognised the superiority of Burghley's intellect — 'wit' as they termed it then: "a person of the most exquisite abilities".[1] The foundation of his system was his intelligence service — the most efficient in Europe. Indeed he had the don's or the true civil servant's instinct (he was a mixture of the two) for acquiring information: some hundreds of volumes and thousands of memoranda remain to testify to his thirst for information. He knew the resources of the country as no-one else did, of every nook and cranny in it, of every creek along the coast; who were the families that mattered in every county, what their relations were with each other, their private affairs and quarrels: who could be relied on and how used; often he jotted down the genealogical trees of the greater families — important to keep their connections and ramifications in mind. All was grist that came to his mill. Of public money he was as careful as the Queen: another bond between them. They had learnt their principles of careful finance from the great reforming Lord Treasurer Winchester. These principles ran through the administration so long as they were alive to see that they were adhered to. Even so, it was a life-long struggle and the Queen and Burghley's eyes could not be everywhere. With regard to foreign affairs the same system obtained: Burghley's information service was unrivalled in Europe. But the increasing tempo of events abroad, their complexity and danger, made the burden too much for one man alone. Burghley brought Walsingham into affairs: in time he found, as others before and since, that he had provided himself with a rival.

The Spanish ambassador, Mendoza, observed rightly that though there were some seventeen or eighteen councillors the bulk of the business depended on the Queen, Burghley, Leicester and Walsingham.[2] A later observer wrote: "The principal note of her reign will be that she ruled much by faction and parties, which herself both made, upheld and weakened, as her own great judgment advised".[3] It was only natural that the Queen should seek to achieve a balance among her advisers or she would have been at the mercy of only one section — 'grouped', to use Castlereagh's word to Metternich as to Alexander I. And there were other advantages: each faction could keep in tow its own supporters, Burghley the moderates, the Anglicans, the com-

[1] Sir Robert Naunton, *Fragmenta Regalia* (ed. E. Arber, English Reprints), p. 31.

[2] Conyers Read, "Walsingham and Burghley at the Privy Council of Elizabeth", *E.H.R.* XXVIII. 38.

[3] Naunton, *op. cit.* p. 16.

mercial class, the peace party; Leicester the Puritans, the fighting men, the militants. These factions served the purpose of rudimentary parties: they canalised the conflicts of different interests and opinions; they represented them in the Council where their conflicts were fought out, in argument and intrigue, at the centre of power. Apprehensiveness, suspicion, a prevailing sense of insecurity were characteristics of so personal a government: no-one felt safe — it was desirable that no-one should feel too safe: everyone kept his eyes about him: at the centre of the web the Queen was watching. Distrust expresses itself in every accent of these men's words. Everybody leaving the centre of government was afraid of the enemies behind his back: correspondence is filled with their squeals, lamentations, protestations, assurances by which no-one was assured. The only thing was never to be away from the centre of power and favour. And that the Cecils contrived: one or other of them was always there.

Within the inner circle Leicester was Burghley's antagonist. To get Cecil out of power we have seen him join even with Norfolk and Mary in 1569. He was a dangerous *faux bonhomme*; he cultivated the religious — he of all people! "To take him in the observations of his letters and writings . . . I never yet saw a style or phrase more seeming religious, and fuller of the streams of devotion. And were they not sincere, I doubt much of his well being; and I may fear he was too well seen in the aphorisms and principles of Nicholas the Florentine, and in the reaches of Caesar Borgia."[1] It is possible that he may even have been partly sincere: it comes to the same thing. He spoke and read Italian; he was both splendid and mean; he carried himself like a Renaissance prince. Though he was no rival to Burghley in ability, he was also no fool; indeed intelligent and able up to a point, he was in many respects a useful member of the government.

It was Walsingham's accession to his side that gave Leicester's party the intellectual cohesion and leadership to withstand Burghley and oppose his policy. Though Walsingham had been Burghley's protégé, there was nothing underhand or mean about this: it was a matter of conviction. Walsingham was an ardent Protestant; an exile in Mary's reign, he knew the Europe of the Counter-Reformation; he knew the sufferings of the godly; he had been in Paris as ambassador during the dreadful days of the Massacre of St. Bartholomew, as such he had been able to save

[1] Naunton, *op. cit.* p. 29.

the lives of those who took refuge in his house. Such was his background: after that there was no compromise with him. Gradually he and Leicester built up a majority in the Council against Burghley and the Queen and their temporising policy hoping to keep out of war. To a large extent the situation in the Council reflected that in the country; as the danger grew, Protestant feeling strengthened and coalesced with that of national security. There were now in the Council the Earls of Leicester, Warwick and Bedford, Walsingham, Knollys and Mildmay against Burghley, the Earl of Sussex and Sir James Crofts, with the Queen in the background giving Burghley steady, though not unvarying, support. Sussex was entirely Burghley's, promising him " to stick as near to you as your shirt is to your back ".[1] He loathed Leicester; but " far the honester man, and far the better soldier ", he was no politician: " he lay too open on his guard ". In his last illness he warned his friends: " Beware of the Gypsy: for he will be too hard for you all: you know not the beast so well as I do ".[2]

Events came to the support of the majority in the Council — or the majority reflected them, in the manner of good politicians. We had to intervene in the Netherlands, or they would have been finished and our turn would have come next. Leicester and Walsingham had prevailed. With the outbreak of war the Council drew together. We have seen that Burghley gave Leicester in the Netherlands his support against the Queen. But also he did not fail to take the opportunity of his absence to bring in three new councillors who were supporters of his own: Whitgift, Archbishop of Canterbury, Lord Cobham to whose daughter Robert Cecil was married, Lord Buckhurst, a cousin of the Queen.[3] Age had not staled Burghley's infinite dexterity: the Queen's ' Spirit ' was called by less polite persons the ' old Fox '. Leicester protested; but from a distance could do nothing about it. We find him on his return, now altogether reduced, saying: " There hath been many that have sought to do evil offices between my Lord Treasurer and me, and my Lord Chancellor and me, but for my own part I will esteem of them as they are, for they are bad people, for I know they be my good friends ".[4] Between Walsingham and Burghley, too, there was a *rapprochement*, Walsingham presenting him with a springy coach for his gouty old bones to rumble over the London stones in.[5] Within a year both Leicester and Walsingham were dead. Burghley

[1] Conyers Read, *loc. cit.* p. 39.
[2] Naunton, pp. 29-30.
[3] *Salisbury MSS.* III. 137.
[4] *Ibid.* p. 251.
[5] Conyers Read, *loc. cit.* p. 58.

had provided for the continuance of his political system in the person of young Robert: it was astutely done, but it was also right and in the public interest.

The struggle between the moderates and the militants, between the men of peace and the men of war, was carried on in the next generation between Burghley's son and Leicester's stepson, Robert Cecil and Essex. The struggle between the factions, which the Queen's personal ascendancy had kept in control almost all her days, broke into the open towards the end of her life. This was due to Essex, whom she had spoiled. He would not accept the subordinate position to which Leicester was accustomed, and which the Queen wished to continue: Essex as her prime favourite, government dominated by her and the Cecils. He wished to be absolute in both spheres and he had a formidable party behind him. In close touch with the foremost young peers, Southampton, Rutland, Bedford, with a following of his own among the gentry, young captains on land and at sea, in the City; the candidate of both Catholics and Puritans, and all the irresponsibles, the darling of the mob — what made him dangerous was that he was in league with James and was his candidate for power. As the Queen grew old it became urgent to control the situation and effect a quiet transition. Cecil had a majority with him in Council and, in alliance with Nottingham (a Howard, Norfolk's son) and Buckhurst, was in control at the centre. But Essex's man, Archbishop Hutton, was on guard in the North as Lord President.[1] Cecil took the opportunity of Essex's absence in Ireland to have Hutton dismissed — he stood for toleration and incompetence — and replaced by his brother the second Lord Burghley with a policy of rigorous execution of the laws against Recusancy. Essex rushed back from Ireland, having accomplished nothing, and planned a *coup d'état* while James's envoys were moving south to back his demands on the Queen.

He allowed himself to be provoked into rebellion prematurely. Before the envoys reached London his head was off. Cecil stepped into his place, took the opportunity to reach an understanding with James's representatives and established a correspondence by which the ground was prepared for the great transition, with himself as the stage-manager and presiding genius. It was as neat an operation as ever the father had performed: the son was worthy of his place. The brother had to be sacrificed: he had the mortification of being dismissed in the

[1] R. R. Reid, *The King's Council in the North*, p. 230 foll.

hour of the younger brother's triumph. Burghley grieved that God had bestowed rarer gifts of mind on his brother than on him. But God — or his brother — also bestowed on him £100 a year out of his successor's salary. The dangerous politics of those days could hardly afford to be too kind to the second-rate.

The Council — it was becoming usual to refer to the inner body now as the Privy Council — was the focus of government and of the struggle for power at the top. Like its successor, the modern Cabinet, it was the permanent executive body dealing with government affairs. But it was unlike the Cabinet in several fundamental respects. It did not rest on a Parliamentary or popular basis, but on the will of the Queen. Of course it was responsive to political tendencies in the country, as we have seen, and even expressed them. Like any government it could not afford to walk too far ahead, or lag too far behind, its support and opinion in the country. To a considerable extent it had to proceed along a course determined for it by the character and relations of the social and political forces of the time. That reflection, if thought out, disposes of a great deal of the criticism and discussion of the Elizabethan government's proceedings in terms of sectarian or party prejudice of one kind or another: whole libraries of superfluous books which merely reiterate the *parti pris* of their authors, religious or political: too childish a proceeding to be regarded as history. A great deal of what Elizabeth's government did had to be done and could not be helped: if not inevitable it was, like so much in government, unavoidable. It follows from the Council's dependence on the Queen that many of the highest decisions on policy were not made within it; they might be made by her alone, or with the advice of one or other of her ministers, away from the Council board. Another respect in which it was fundamentally unlike our Cabinet was that it did not represent one party view, as we have seen: it had no necessary uniformity of outlook; they were all the Queen's servants, and that was the only thing that held them together and enabled them to function at all. Then, too, the Council had a most important summary jurisdiction, calling offenders of various sorts, usually important ones not otherwise provided for, from all over the country to attend upon it: this, in addition to its regular judicial proceedings as a court in Star Chamber. Beneath those simpler forms we can see in embryo many of the features and forms of government today; in the English constitution of today there are still interesting relics of those earlier forms; sometimes transmuted, sometimes atrophied.

An enormous increase in business before the Council is characteristic of the period: it must testify not only to the efficiency of what was the most efficient government in Europe, but to a healthy, regular and more active functioning of the society itself. In this country private wrongs did not go so often unrighted. Flexibility, immediacy, directness of action are what one notices about the English government, compared with the interminable delays in Madrid imposed by Philip's habit of having everything referred to him, or the confusion affairs fell into in France with the Wars of Religion. The Council complained of the press of business upon them. At the beginning of the reign they met on three days a week; later the Council met nearly every day including Sundays, and often both mornings and afternoons.[1] Those magnificent persons, Leicester and Warwick, Heneage and Hatton, were hard-working men. The press of suitors and cases continually increased: they were "so troubled and pestered . . . as at the times of their assembling for her Majesty's special services they can hardly be suffered (by the importunity of the said suitors) to attend and proceed in such causes as do concern her Majesty and the state of the Realm".[2] They ordered all such cases as were determinable by other courts to be taken there; they would only hear those which had been denied justice elsewhere, and those affecting the State.

The great part of the Council's work was executive or administrative. Impossible to describe it here in detail: it ranged from the highest issues of national policy to the minute concerns of private individuals — there is always this personal touch. We find, for example, that at the moment of repelling the Armada, amid all the press of work, sending instructions to the Council of the North to provide munitions for the Fleet pursuing the Armada, letters to the Dutch States warning them that the Armada might make for their coasts, to Hamburg and Denmark urging that no relief be given the Spaniards, orders for the squadron lying in the Narrow seas to prevent Parma from invading, the Council can pause to commit one Gill of Brighthempson [Brighton] for slanderous words against the Lord Admiral, or to deal with a *cache* of Popish vestments discovered near Reading.[3] This gives us a little idea of the variety of the Council's work: overlooking the conduct of the war, supplementing the administrative work of the offices conducting it. The normal administrative business

[1] Cheyney, *op. cit.* I. 67. [2] *Ibid.* p. 73. [3] *A.P.C. 1588*, pp. 218-29.

of the English counties proceeded through the regular channels of lord-lieutenants, sheriffs, justices of the peace; the Council supervised all this and weighed in where necessary. It was especially concerned with the outlying parts where government was less normal and regular, and in the nature of things had to be rather summary. This meant the northern counties and the Welsh Marches, the Scottish Borders and Ireland. In all these, except Ireland, we can watch government moving over to regular channels and normal courses. A still larger part of the Council's time was taken up with maintaining order and seeing that the laws were executed. This involved all kinds of activities: a constant watch for subversive and seditious movements, enforcing the laws against Recusancy, controlling the press, dealing with unemployment and repressing vagabonds, taking measures to relieve famine, with regard to public health, the theatres, the Church. The Council had also a certain legislative power by means of proclamations.[1] The Council's work was not only summary and controlling, but supplementary: its very flexibility made it an ideal instrument: wherever action was needed, no matter how small the affair, it stepped in. No wonder the Venetian ambassador considered that the lords of the Council behaved like so many kings.[2]

In the immense expansion of business the office of Secretary had the pivotal role. He had not the precedence and standing of the old great officers, the Lord Chancellor, Lord Treasurer, Lord Steward, Lord Chamberlain. But like these offices his grew out of the king's household and was to have an expansion in the fulness of time second to none in the modern departments of State.[3] In the reign of Elizabeth we can watch the evolution of constitutional organs at a very interesting stage, half medieval, half modern; wholly personal, yet in process of developing the regular forms and procedures of departments; an efficient secretariat, yet with all the flexibility, freshness and exposure to accidents of youth. This flexibility gave it great importance: with the long tenure of the two Cecils and Walsingham it became the key office in the State. With the vast increase of business that came to the Crown and the Council, the Secretary was the natural channel for the exercise of the prerogative; he was also the indispensable intermediary between Crown and Council. The growth of foreign business meant that the Secretary or Secretaries — some-

[1] Cf. R. Steele and the Earl of Crawford, *Tudor and Stuart Proclamations*.
[2] Cf. Cheyney, *op. cit.* p. 80.
[3] F. M. G. Evans, *The Principal Secretary of State*, pp. 2-9.

times there were two — had all the threads of foreign affairs in their hands, received and directed the intelligence, conducted the diplomatic service. Hence the Queen's nickname for Walsingham: he was her ' Moon ' — a respectful, if somewhat frigid sobriquet. The Secretary could take on anything — at a time when everything was coming along.

Robert Cecil himself describes the exceptional character of the office: " All officers and councillors of State have a prescribed authority by patent, by custom, or by oath, the Secretary only excepted ".[1] He has " a liberty to negotiate at discretion at home and abroad, with friends and enemies, in all matters of speech and intelligence. . . . As long as any matter of what weight so ever is handled only between the Prince and the Secretary, those counsels are compared to the mutual affections of two lovers, undiscovered to their friends." Always this language, or pretence, of love around the person of the Queen: an idiom, a mode, which as Bacon said (though not in her lifetime) she kept up far too long and late. Robert Cecil, hump-backed and undersized, knew and accepted the fact that he was not the kind of man she wanted, but very much the kind of councillor and Secretary: " for, excepting some of her kindred and some few that had handsome wits in crooked bodies, she always took personage in the way of her election ".[2] But so careful was she of the disposal of power that after Walsingham's death in 1589, Robert Cecil, aided at first by his father, did the work of the office for six years before he was awarded it and all that time they " touched not one penny of the emoluments ".[3] That was an irresistible recommendation to the Queen.

Separate Councils, off-shoots from the centre, governed Wales and the North, those exceptional backward areas, now catching up. In Elizabeth's reign the Councils of the North and of the Marches reached the apogee of their power and usefulness — and passed it. Their jurisdictions greatly expanded, their administration was successful in bringing those unruly areas into some order; their work having been done, its very success diminished their importance and opened the way for normal methods of administration. The gentry in those parts came to want to run

[1] Sir Robert Cecil, " The State and Dignity of a Secretary of State's Place ", *Somers' Tracts*, 4th Collection, I. 259. [2] Naunton, *op. cit.* p. 28.

[3] R. B. Wernham, " The Disgrace of William Davison ", *E.H.R.* (1931), p. 635. But this is not to say that the office was without profit. The official salary of £100 per annum would be worth much less than the fees and rewards. The office of master of the Court of Wards was a much larger source of profit to both Cecils. Cf. " Queen Elizabeth's Annual Expense ", *A Collection of Ordinances*, pp. 249-50.

things themselves instead of by leading-strings from Whitehall. In the heyday of the Councils Burghley's correspondence shows the minute care with which he supervised their work. The Elizabethans were proud of the Council's work in Wales, which had been " brought from their disobedient, barbarous and (as may be termed) lawless incivility, to the civil and obedient estate they now remain ".[1] This had been the work of the tough Bishop Rowland Lee, under Henry VIII, paving the way for the gentler, just administration of Sir Henry Sidney. Lee had hanged thieves in hundreds, right and left: yet " Thieves I found them and thieves I shall leave them ", he wrote.[2] We see how far the old folk-rhyme goes back:

> Taffy was a Welshman,
> Taffy was a thief;
> Taffy came to my house,
> Stole a leg of beef.

Cattle-thieving was endemic in these mountainous, pastoral areas, as on the Borders. To this the Welsh added another vice: the forcible carrying off of widows. Extreme poverty was at the root of it all, that and their unsettled, pastoral life with little arable — as again on the Borders.

Mary's leading minister, the Catholic Lord Paget — somewhat discredited by the events of her reign — had not thought it beneath him to ask Cecil, on Elizabeth's accession, for the office of Lord President of Wales.[3] But Sir Henry Sidney was appointed and ruled there in great state and with the good-will of the people till 1586. He was a gentle, courteous, just man, with an instinctive feeling — rare in Elizabethans — for the Celtic peoples over whom he ruled here and in Ireland. Celts themselves were apt to think that something tougher was needed. David Lewis, a Fellow of All Souls and civil lawyer, wrote: " In every commonwealth severity used with indifferency of justice to all men is more commended than lenity ".[4] Whitgift, when Bishop of Worcester and Vice-President of the Council, quarrelled with Sidney for his lenity: he would follow rather " justice and conscience, for sure he was that they would bring a man peace at the last and never be confounded. Whereas friendship often times failed and was very mutable." [5] The Queen's eyes were on Sidney, Walsingham warned him: " Your lordship had need to walk warily, for your doings are narrowly observed and her Majesty is apt to give ear

[1] C. A. J. Skeel, *The Council in the Marches of Wales*, p. 19. [2] *Ibid.* p. 63.
[3] *Cal. S.P. Dom. 1547–80*, p. 126. [4] Skeel, *op. cit.* p. 106. [5] *Ibid.* p. 111.

to any that shall ill you ".[1] Sidney loved his charge and the great position it gave him: " Great it is that in some sort I govern the third part of this realm under her most excellent Majesty; high it is for by that I have precedence of great personages and by far my betters; happy it is for the goodness of the people I govern; and most happy it is for the commodity I have, by the authority of that place, to do good every day ".[2]

High office was its own reward — such was the Queen's point of view: the honour of it and the privilege of serving her. And she was right in a way: " No prince's revenues be so great that they are able to satisfy the insatiable cupidity of men ".[3] Sir Henry Sidney complained that he had had from her " not so much ground as I can cover with my foot " [4] — but his family had been amply rewarded by her father and her brother.[5] He himself had spent his own money and sold lands to pay for his administration. He loved those coloured western counties where he ruled from the splendid castle towering above the Teme at Ludlow. His arms still remain upon the buildings he built there, amid those ruins where Milton's *Comus* was first performed, where Butler wrote *Hudibras*, in that town once busy with the comings and goings of attorneys that Baxter describes in his *Autobiography*. Sidney's little daughter Ambrosia died there and is buried in the church; he sent his son Philip to school at Shrewsbury. When he died, his heart was buried at Ludlow, " for the entire love he bare that place ".[6]

Between the trees in flower
 New friends at fairtime tread
The way where Ludlow tower
 Stands planted on the dead.

The North gave far more difficulty and was intrinsically more important: there was the frontier with Scotland, the Borders remained lawless till much later, the Marches there had the only standing troops always in arms.[7] But the Tudors pushed on the work of modernising the State: Henry VIII brought a large number of ecclesiastical franchises and liberties under the control of the Crown; Elizabeth took Norham, Crayke and Allertonshire that lay towards the Border away from the Bishopric of Durham:

[1] Skeel, *op. cit.* p. 102. [2] *Ibid.* p. 85.
[3] q. Neale, *Queen Elizabeth*, p. 114. [4] Skeel, p. 87.
[5] Sidney's father had been given large acres in Kent and Sussex for good service by Henry VIII, and Penshurst by Edward VI whose tutor and steward of the household he had been. [6] Skeel, p. 113.
[7] R. R. Reid, " The Political Influence of the North Parts under the Later Tudors ", *Tudor Studies Presented to A. F. Pollard*, p. 208.

these were steps towards more efficient government. At the beginning of the reign not ten gentlemen favoured the Queen's proceedings in religion: the North was very backward. Soon Archbishop Young reported that though the nobility there remained in their wonted blindness, the gentry were beginning to reform themselves: it seemed that, not wanting to ask for trouble, he was too sanguine.[1] Not until the Rebellion of 1569 had been suppressed could the execution of the religious laws be seriously taken in hand and the North brought into line with the rest of the country. In 1572 the Protestant Earl of Huntingdon went North as Lord President, an office which he held until 1595: another of those long administrations that mark the reign and were a considerable factor in the success of its government. After the Rising had been broken, the North conformed and gave little trouble over religion: there were no executions of seminarists until the Jesuit campaign began on the threshold of the war. Huntingdon was firm but moderate; he was anxious "lest too much rigourness harden the hearts of some that by fair means might be mollified".[2] Like Sidney in Wales he left behind him a tradition of even-handed justice to rich and poor. A more rigid and less congenial person than Sidney, he was a very faithful servant of the Crown and died many thousands in debt for his service. He had the capacity of attaching loyalty to himself: his own servants watched over his dead body for four months while his sovereign and his heir squabbled over the expenses of the funeral. In the end the Queen paid.

The execution of the government's social and economic policy gave much greater trouble: the North was set on its own way and indeed its economic conditions were different. The Statute of Labourers hampered cloth-weaving in country districts and held up countrymen from working in towns. Towards the end of the reign the J.P.s of the West Riding openly refused to execute the statute against the stretching of Yorkshire cloths: the industry was going ahead by hook or by crook.[3] The towns resisted the payment of Ship Money. Next, the West Riding gentry attacked the Council's authority to execute penal statutes except by Common Law. Its governmental powers were already shorn of authority: this was to attack its jurisdiction as a court. As the power of government at the centre increased, the Council became almost exclusively a court of justice: administration passed to the J.P.s. Now York refused to allow its citizens to

[1] R. R. Reid, *The King's Council in the North*, p. 195. [2] *Ibid.* p. 213.
[3] *Ibid.* p. 220 foll.

plead before the Council; Berwick won immunity as being under the jurisdiction of the Lord Warden of the Marches; now the local gentry were bent on restricting the Council's fiat to twelve miles from York.[1] Under James, Coke attacked the Council's jurisdiction successfully along with other prerogative courts;[2] by the end of the reign the gentry of the whole of Yorkshire, not only of the clothing districts, would gladly have seen this court dissolved.[3] It had fulfilled its function and outlived its usefulness.

The place of Parliament in all this was occasional, discontinuous and yet of the highest importance. The part it played already distinguished the English State from all other European States and its development in course of time was to constitute the main channel of the English contribution in the realm of politics. In this it reflected something profound in the nature of English society: a generalised instinct for freedom, the habit of self-government. Even the simplest people — *proletarii* as Sir Thomas Smith calls them — were not excluded: "These have no voice nor authority in our commonwealth . . . and yet they be not altogether neglected. For in cities and corporate towns for default of yeomen, inquests and juries are impanelled of such manner of people. And in villages they be commonly made church-wardens, ale-conners and many times constables, which office toucheth more the commonwealth." [4] The representative conception of Parliament was perfectly clear: it "representeth and hath the power of the whole realm both the head and body. For every Englishman is intended to be there present, either in person or by procuration and attorneys, of what pre-eminence, state, dignity or quality soever he be, from the prince (be he King or Queen) to the lowest person of England. And the consent of the Parliament is taken to be every man's consent." [5] Hence the authority of statute law: "That is the prince's and whole realm's deed: whereupon justly no man can complain, but must accommodate himself to find it good and obey it".[6]

Parliaments were called for only the greatest occasions and purposes: at the accession of a sovereign, to give warrant for some great change in national policy — as, for example, in religion — or to give support in waging war, and always for the purpose of voting supplies. Here was its great lever upon government, of which it made the maximum use in the next century. The Tudors'

[1] R. R. Reid, *The King's Council in the North*, p. 338. [2] *Ibid.* p. 354.
[3] *Ibid.* p. 372. [4] Smith, *op. cit.* p. 46. [5] *Ibid.* p. 49. [6] *Ibid.* p. 48.

use of Parliament gave it exercise, increasing experience and in the end confidence. At the beginning of Elizabeth's reign the Commons were still in a subordinate position: the Parliament chamber meant the chamber in which the Lords met; the essence of Parliament's meeting was still the medieval core of the sovereign in council with the peers of the realm, and at the opening of the proceedings as many of the Commons crowded in beyond the bar as could get in. Once there was a protest at most of them having been shut out and unable to hear the Queen's speech. But as the years pass one can watch, in the pages of D'Ewes' *Journal*, the proceedings of the Commons become ever more important, until by the end of the reign they are undoubtedly more decisive than those of the Lords. Many factors joined in making this so: perhaps, above all, the long continuance of the war, which necessitated the raising of large sums by taxation. In this very process the Commons, both in committee and in discussions of the whole House, were brought so intimately into the details of financial expenditure and ways and means of meeting it, that the House became a part of the machine of government.

The Queen was aware of this and reluctant enough; but so far as financing the war went, she could not help herself. Early in her reign she made a virtue of necessity — in her usual way — and took credit to herself for her unwillingness to summon a Parliament, burdening everybody with the expense of it and the country with the subsidies issuing from it; the Lord Keeper was put up to say with what difficulty the Queen had been persuaded — the assumption being that the country would not want it and only necessity forced her to call upon her good subjects.[1] For Parliaments raised awkward difficulties for her in the process: the Queen was in conflict with almost every one of her Parliaments over one issue or another — over her marriage and the succession, reform of the Church, Parliamentary privilege, especially that of free speech, Mary Queen of Scots, monopolies. In these circumstances her management of Parliament — or rather her conduct of the struggle — is not the least remarkable of her achievements.

It is amusing to watch the shocked attitude of the Spanish grandee who was Philip's ambassador at these proceedings. Of the Parliament of 1566, which was particularly intractable on

[1] Cf. the Parliament of 1562–3, D'Ewes' *Journal*, p. 61: "And notwithstanding all the disbursements of these her great charges, yet she was (as I right well know) very hardly brought to and persuaded to call this Parliament, in which she should be driven to require any aid, or by any means to charge her subjects, if by any other means it might have been holpen: and so her Majesty herself commanded to be declared".

the subject of her marriage, Don Guzman de Silva writes: "These heretics neither fear God nor obey their betters".[1] No conception that English liberties would produce in the long run greater results than those of Spanish orthodoxy. He took the opportunity of the Queen's anger with the Commons to underline the obedience and quietude of the Catholics compared with the turbulence of the Protestants.[2] Exactly. The Queen said that she did not know what these devils wanted; her words are not to be taken precisely *au pied de la lettre*: Elizabeth's circle, to the piety and simplicity of mind of the Spaniards at her Court, had nothing to learn from the Italians in Machiavellianism. "I said what they wanted was simple liberty, and if kings did not look out for themselves and combine together to check them, it was easy to see how the license that these people had taken, would end." Perhaps it would surprise Don Guzman, if he could revisit this world by the light of the moon, to see how things have turned out: the English monarchy and Parliament still with us — and Spain?

The relations between Crown and Parliament were more like those between President and Congress than those that subsist in England today. The Queen's ministers — like the President's Cabinet — were responsible to her and not to Parliament; and it followed from that that government had to keep in touch by various means, direct and indirect, with the two Houses. The Lords offered no difficulty once the Acts of Supremacy and Uniformity were through, restoring the Edwardian settlement, and Mary's bishops were out. It was the Commons that mattered and that were difficult. The group of Privy Councillors in the Commons — the Cecils, Hatton, Knollys, Mildmay, Crofts and others — acted together somewhat like a government: a closer link than that between President and Congress, in which the President's Cabinet has no footing. The distance between Whitehall and Westminster was not so great as that between the White House and the Capitol. The general management of Parliamentary business as a whole, even after he had moved to the Lords, was in the hands of Burghley acting as a kind of Prime Minister. But the Queen herself constantly exerted her personal influence: through messages prohibiting this discussion or graciously allowing that; through 'rumours' to which a House containing a large number of lawyers dependent upon her for promotion was noticeably sensitive (the analogy with Congress here leaps to mind); through sending for the Speaker — who was the government's choice rather than that of the House, and in

[1] *Cal. S.P. Span. 1558–67*, p. 589. [2] *Ibid.* p. 590.

three cases the Queen's Solicitor [1] — and giving him a wigging when necessary; receiving or summoning deputations from the Houses to Whitehall and there rating them in person; or descending magnificently upon Parliament in her coach or open chariot and addressing them through the Lord Keeper or in that clear, dry, authoritative voice we know so well, for all that it has so long been extinguished.[2]

Let us observe her for a little in action. Tact, tactical shrewdness, courtesy, consideration were keynotes of the government's behaviour in relation to Parliament: one notices it in the Queen herself, in Lord Keeper Bacon, who was a most politic speaker and much favoured by the Queen for his fun and facetious wit, in Burghley and again in his son. They deserved to succeed; they took such trouble to. Always they prepared the ground; when possible they took Parliament into their confidence, when not possible they pretended to, or — better — did as far as they could. They always put their case well and lost no argument that told. They took every opportunity of reminding Parliament of the state of affairs to which they had succeeded: the defeat into which Mary had run the country, an exhausted Treasury, a commonwealth sick and divided.[3] They praised the lenity of their own government; they knew better than to suppose that people would realise if not told. Bacon, in artful speeches, took credit to Elizabeth's government for permitting open discussion of the religious changes in Parliament: so much for foreign opinion abroad.[4] What made it all the cleverer was that it was true and nobody could deny it. And now: what was done publicly in Parliament could not be infringed publicly by any private man. Such was the ground of authority, the duty of obedience. The Crown's authority, the sovereign's part to rule, the subject's to obey — such were the insistent themes of the Queen, inculcated on her instructions by the Lord Keeper in his avuncular tones, wise and grave, full of sensible advice, treating the Commons like the new boys they were. They were " to fly from all manner of contentions, reasonings and disputations, and all sophistical, captious and frivolous arguments and quiddities meeter for ostentation of wit than consultation of weighty matters, comelier for scholars than councillors, more beseeming for schools than for

[1] Onslow, Popham, Coke. Three more Speakers, Wray, Puckering and Yelverton, became Judges.

[2] Cf. L. Antheunis, " La Maladie et la mort de la reine Élisabeth ", *Rev. d'Histoire ecclésiastique*, 1948, p. 162.

[3] Cf. D'Ewes, *op. cit.* p. 12.

[4] It is interesting to see Mary's bishops continuing to take part in the committee work of the Lords in the first weeks of Parliament (D'Ewes, pp. 1-36).

Parliament houses ".[1] But all that changed: by the end of the reign the school had grown up. If they had allowed themselves to be talked to like that by a great Queen it was another thing to put up with it from a Scots dominie.

To these notes of her government the Queen added other things: the advantage of being a lady, so that there were many things they could not say to her (though there was nothing she could not say to them); a gracious condescension, a royal wrath which could be applied in turn as the case demanded; the secrets of an enigmatic personality she was too wise to discover to any. But from the very first she had difficulties with the Commons: they were naturally worried about the succession: only one young woman's life stood now between the country and chaos: they pressed her to marry, and as soon as might be. She replied with a shrewd thrust: Mary had wanted to marry her off so as to be rid of her, out of the country. " From my years of understanding, sith I first had consideration of myself to be born a servant of Almighty God [her own way of reminding them of her divine right to rule] I happily chose this kind of life in the which I yet live . . . with which trade of life I am so thoroughly acquainted that I trust God, who hath hitherto therein preserved and led me by the hand, will not of his goodness suffer me to go alone."[2] What did she mean? That she would, or that she would not, marry? Perhaps not: " For though I be never so careful of your well-doing and mind ever so to be, yet may my issue grow out of kind and become perhaps ungracious. And in the end this shall be for me sufficient that a marble stone shall declare that a Queen having reigned such a time lived and died a virgin."

Before the meeting of her second Parliament she had had an attack of smallpox and for a few days her life was despaired of. Parliament redoubled its efforts to make her marry or declare her successor. Either course was dangerous. Whom to marry? To marry would be to throw away her best weapon in high policy and, perhaps, to give herself a master; it might be unfruitful, a failure and a tragedy like her sister's. (Besides, it was impossible for her to marry the man she loved: she accepted that, after a bitter struggle with herself.) To declare a successor would have been fatal; she had seen how it endangered her sister's position in herself. And so, to the Speaker presenting Parliament's petition: " For the first, if I had let slip too much time, or if my strength had been decayed, you might the better have spoke

[1] D'Ewes, p. 12. [2] *Ibid.* p. 46.

therein; or if any think I never meant to try that life, they be deceived. . . . For the second, the greatness thereof maketh me to say and pray that I may linger here in this vale of misery here for your comfort, wherein I have witness of my study and travail for your surety. And I cannot with *Nunc Dimittis* end my life without I see some foundation of your surety after my grave stone."[1] Parliament was prorogued.

It turned out to have been a mistake not to dissolve it; for when it was summoned again, the Commons, having learned from their previous experience, held up supplies until they got an assurance from the Queen that she would marry. She sent down her express prohibition from discussing the subject. They nevertheless persisted; the temper of the House was such that the Privy Councillors advised her to yield, if she were to obtain supplies. She gave them her assurance that she would marry. The Commons prayed that God would hasten its fulfilment. The struggle was at its height when the Queen addressed a deputation of Lords and Commons on — ironical date — November 5.[2] She strove to drive a wedge between them: "But therein Sir Domine Doctors with their long orations sought to persuade you . . . as though you, my lords, had not known that when my breath did fail me I had been dead unto you and then dying without issue what a danger were that to the whole state, which you had not known before they told you. So that it was easy to be seen *quo oratio tendit*. . . . Was I not born in this country? Were my parents born in any foreign country? Is there any cause that should alienate myself from being careful over this country? Is not my kingdom here? Whom have I oppressed? Whom have I enriched to others' harms? What tormoy have I made to this commonwealth that I should be suspected to have no regard of the same? How have I governed since my reign? I will be tried by envy itself."

As to declaring a successor, "I am sure there was none of them that was ever a second person as I have been and have tasted of the practises against my sister, who I would to God were alive again". She did not hesitate to bring home that there were some among the Commons who had made great motions to her during her sister's lifetime, "and were it not for mine honour their knavery should be known". "They would have thirteen or fourteen limited in succession and the more the better,

[1] *Ibid.* pp. 75-6.

[2] The cause of the struggle between Queen and Commons in this Parliament has been cleared up, and a fuller text of her speech given, by J. E. Neale, "Parliament and the Succession Question in 1562-3 and 1566", *E.H.R.* (1921), pp. 497-520.

and those shall be of such uprightness and so divine as they shall be divinity itself. Kings were wont to honour philosophers, but if I had such I would honour them as angels that should have such purity in them that they would not seek when they are the second to be the first and when they are third to be the second etc. . . . Truly, if reason did not subdue will in me I would cause you to deal in it, so pleasant a thing it should be unto me. But I stay it for your benefit, for if you should have liberty to treat of it there be so many competitors, some kinsfolk, some servants, some tenants; some would speak for their master, some for their mistress, and every man for his friend, that it would be an occasion of a greater charge than a subsidy." She meant that it would provoke bloodshed, perhaps civil war. "As for mine own part I care not for death, for all men are mortal, and though I be a woman I have as good a courage answerable to my place as ever my father had. I am your anointed Queen. I will never be by violence constrained to do anything. I thank God I am endowed with such qualities that if I were turned out of the realm in my petticoat I were able to live in any place in Christendom." She had called them to her presence without their Speaker, so that the Commons without him were unable, they complained, to speak. As to that, "She said she was a speaker indeed, and there ended".

After this, a compromise was arrived at, in the English manner: the discussion having been brought to this point she raised her veto on it; the Commons granted her supplies, though she sacrificed some for the sake of agreement. But she did not fail to dissolve Parliament this time. The victory remained with her. But the Commons had shown what they were capable of and how much they were gaining in experience and confidence. In fact the Queen was pursuing a course of policy abroad and at home which they were in agreement with, which became in time even more theirs than hers; she had made no mistakes, so wary had been her course. But what would happen with a king who made every mistake? The critics, the militants, the forward party in Parliament, would be proved right.

What all this portended may be seen from the career of Peter Wentworth, the leading protagonist of Parliamentary liberties, who foreshadows in voice and unyielding temper Sir John Eliot and Pym.[1] Like Eliot, he ended his days in the Tower — and this in the days of Elizabeth. It is strange that

[1] His Parliamentary career has been laid bare for us by J. E. Neale, "Peter Wentworth", *E.H.R.* (1924), pp. 36 foll., 175 foll.

not until our own day have people begun to appreciate the significance of the Parliamentary struggle under Elizabeth. It was already on: only the unfolding success of her policy and the increasing evidence that it was in line with the will of her people, the national unity imposed by the war and, it must be added, her incomparable skill in handling Parliaments, where opposition was often stifled by the terms of love in which their relations with her were supposed to subsist — language which no-one could challenge — only this prevented conflict reaching deadlock and postponed it until she was under her marble stone. In her day one or the other side gave way, usually the other. But the long war which came to her aid in increasing national unity made the fortune of the Commons in the longer run, by necessitating immense grants of money; the Queen was forced to sell a large proportion of Crown lands, not only those her father had taken over from the Church; the independent revenues of the Crown were rendered inadequate for government: the future was with Parliament, which represented property and the country and could raise money from it.

Peter Wentworth was descended from a junior branch of the tough Yorkshire stock occupying the pleasant fruitful lands around the snuff-brown stone churches of Woolley and Wentworth Woodhouse.[1] His father had been chief Porter of Calais under Henry VIII and acquired large estates, when the going was good, in Oxfordshire, Northamptonshire and elsewhere. A man of property, he was well placed at his manor of Lillingstone Lovell near Banbury in relation to that Puritan countryside, with his friend and associate Anthony Cope nearby at Hanwell, the Say and Seles at Broughton, the venue of the Parliamentarian consultations before the Civil War. Wentworth married Walsingham's sister; another sister married Mildmay; Wentworth's daughter married the son of Strickland. Walter Strickland, of another Yorkshire family, was another uncompromising spirit, a leading member of the Puritan group pushing Church reform and Parliamentary liberty against the régime. The prudent Burghley, whose personal relations with the Puritans were more friendly than his political position indicated, had married a daughter of his to Lord Wentworth, head of the clan. One sees Wentworth's standing and how representative his position was; his character made him exceptional: like Eliot later, he was irrepressible, fearless, self-opinionated. The Queen said that he

[1] I am indebted to Mr. Douglas Mackridge of Wombwell for taking me to see these delightful places.

had an opinion of his own wit. All the Puritans had: it was, so to say, their claim: no submission to anybody else's authority, priests' or kings'. It may well be — though there is an argument against the point [1] — that the liberties of Englishmen depended on their cheek.

Wentworth, in his Yorkshire way, never minced words: no South-country adulation or flattery of the Queen for him. In the Parliament of 1571, the first he sat in, Strickland and Norton brought forward motions for Puritan reforms in the Church. This, the Queen held, was to trench upon her prerogative. She had laid down in her opening speech that they were to meddle with no matters of State but such as were propounded to them. Later she sent them a command through the Speaker to spend little time in motions and to avoid long speeches. Though there were those who questioned her authority in religion as Supreme Governor, she certainly behaved in general as Supreme Governess. Sir Humphrey Gilbert, who was a courtier, made a speech making high claims for the prerogative.[2] This was disliked by the House and we do not find him speaking again. Several days later Wentworth attacked the speech and the disposition to flatter and fawn on the prince.[3] We notice that prerogative men are not popular; indeed no-one dares defend it in Gilbert's vehement style; the attitude of government supporters is defensive. It is the attackers who are popular: Wentworth, Strickland and Norton are very much to the fore and constantly speaking. Debate is noticeably on a high level.

To the Parliament of 1572 the Lord Keeper recommended that things there propounded might be " orderly and diligently debated, deeply considered and thereupon wisely concluded ".[4] Again, he emphasised that the Queen " doth employ her own treasure, yea and her own lands and credit, not in any glorious triumphs, superfluous and sumptuous buildings of delight, vain and chargeable embassages, neither in any other matters of will and pleasure: I mean no expense noted in a prince of thirteen years' reign, but as far as man can judge in the service of her realm and necessary defence for her people ". He recommended that " by the rules of good government, all officers both spiritual and temporal that have governance, during the time of their offices, ought to be preserved in credit and estimation ". He came to the defence of the bishops, whom the discipline and doctrine of the Church chiefly concerned. But bishops have never been popular with the Commons. The Queen commanded

[1] *v.* below, p. 302. [2] D'Ewes, p. 168. [3] *Ibid.* p. 175. [4] *Ibid.* pp. 192-5.

that no bills concerning religion were to be preferred in the House, unless first considered by the clergy. The Protestant temper of the Commons was sharply increasing with the exacerbation of the struggle abroad and the crisis of 1569–72 at home; they not only gave Cecil support but urged the government forward. The Queen imposed a halt when it came to the rights of another Queen or the Church. After a sharp tussle Elizabeth sent the Commons a gracious message, which pleased them much. Not so Wentworth: he did not think her Majesty deserved their thanks, so he spoke against any such motion.[1] This was a new note — if recognisably Yorkshire — in regard to the Queen.

But it is refreshing to hear in this age with its eternal insistence on authority and obedience: it is like a fresh moorland breeze blowing through those stuffy chambers tapestried and cobwebbed with adulation and flattery. Wentworth was a real believer in liberty — at any rate for himself, as was the way with Puritans. And that, though not a satisfactory halting place — as it proved — was the beginning of liberty for others. Here is something new, at any rate in high places, welling up from below in the spirit of the people; no doubt it too has its continuity, from the fractious independent-mindedness of the Lollards forward to the Independents of the seventeenth century and the Radicals of the nineteenth, of whom Wentworth was a precursor. One's heart almost rejoices, for once, to hear a Puritan speak. "Sweet is the name of liberty, but the thing itself [has] a value beyond all inestimable treasure. So much the more it behoveth us to take care lest we contenting ourselves with the sweetness of the name, lose and forego the thing. . . . The inestimable treasure is the use of it in this House." [2] So Wentworth begins the great speech which he delivered in the Parliament of 1575, stating the claim for freedom of speech in the House and no suppression of its right to discuss matters of State by the Queen. "Liberty of free speech", he claimed, as men of one idea are apt to, "is the only salve to heal all the sores of this commonwealth . . . and without it is a scorn and mockery to call it a Parliament house, for in truth it is none, but a very school of flattery and dissimulation."

He was conscious, as such fanatics are, of being a new and chosen vessel; he quoted Elihu: "Behold, I am as the new wine which hath no vent and bursteth the new vessels in sunder; therefore I will speak that I may have a vent . . . I will regard no manner of person", etc. Nor did he: especially bishops. He recounted how in the last Parliament he had been one of the

[1] Neale, *loc. cit.* p. 42.

[2] D'Ewes, p. 236 foll.

deputation sent to the Archbishop of Canterbury with the Puritan articles that had been passed. The Archbishop asked why they had omitted the articles for the homilies, the consecrating of bishops and so on. "Surely, sir," said Wentworth, "because we were so occupied in other matters that we had no time to examine them how they agreed with the word of God." "What?" said the Archbishop, "surely you mistook the matter: you will refer yourselves wholly to us therein?" "No, by the faith I bear to God," said Wentworth, "we will pass nothing before we understand what it is. For that were but to make you Popes. Make you Popes who list, for we will make you none." There speaks the Puritan spirit: intransigent, self-opinionated, fearless. It is possible that, human beings being what they are — or at least what they have been — such spirits are necessary to achieve such results. But it is also arguable that results might have been obtained, with far less loss, bloodshed and suffering, by the way of Laodiceanism, scepticism, indifference. Wentworth's speech, with its claims for the Commons against the Crown and the Church, foreshadowed the great conflict of the seventeenth century: King and Church against Parliament and People.

Wentworth was stopped by the House before finishing his speech, committed to ward and examined by a committee of its members.[1] He fully realised the gravity of the stand he was making: he had walked his grounds twenty times and more revolving and preparing his speech. Thomas Seckford, who, a master of the Court of Requests, was an official member, commented that Wentworth would never admit that he was wrong nor say that he was sorry for anything he said. In fact he was popular with the House and treated with lenity by the Queen, who soon restored him to his place: in time to take part in the Commons' assertion of their rights against the Lords.

The Parliament of 1580 began with a motion from Peter Wentworth's brother Paul for a public fast and daily preaching — one cannot discern for what misdemeanours in the eyes of the Lord: but how it looks forward to those horrible orgies of the Long Parliament during the Civil War! The idea horrified the Queen, who was, after all, a cultivated person. The House persisted and voted for it by a majority of 115 to 110: the orgy was to take place in the Temple Church. The Queen had other ideas, and before they could give themselves up to this enjoyment the Speaker was summoned to her presence and soundly rated. He came back and expressed his sorrow for the "error that had

[1] D'Ewes, pp. 241-4

happened in the House ", while the Vice-Chamberlain brought a message expressing her Majesty's own sentiments: " Her great admiration of the rashness of this House in committing such an apparent contempt against her Majesty's express commandment . . . as to attempt to put in execution such an innovation as the same fast without her Majesty's privity and pleasure first known ".[1] Not that she was against prayer and fasting, indeed she was accustomed " to the use and exercise thereof in her own person ". But she knew her Puritans, and she also knew how to deal with them. The House submitted completely and was received back into grace and love all round.

Mildmay, whose sympathies were Puritan, was put up to improve the occasion. " England was the only settled monarchy that most doth contain and countenance Religion."[2] He made an interesting survey of the reign, dwelling upon the " lenity of the time and the mildness of the laws heretofore made " and that this itself gave an opportunity for opponents to undermine them. Unhappily this was true: this was 1580: not only the seminaries but the Jesuits were seeping in, to sap and undermine. The only thing to do with fanatics on both sides, if one wanted any peace, was to shut them up; with subversives in a time of danger, if one wanted any security, to lay them by the heels. Mildmay concluded by pointing the contrast between what obtained in England and the state of affairs abroad: " Depopulations and devastations of whole provinces and countries, overthrowing, spoiling and sacking of cities and towns, imprisoning, ransoming and murdering of all kind of people ". Such was the Europe of the wars of religion, what was going on among our nearest neighbours; whereas in England " the peaceable government of her Majesty doth make us to enjoy all that is ours in more freedom than any nation under the sun at this day ". It was no more than the truth. When it came to the point they were aware of their good luck. Such were the rewards of government that kept fanatics in their places.

In the next few years we were drawn into the odious maelstrom: there was no avoiding it, for all that Elizabeth had wriggled and stalled and lied: the forces of human foolery were too strong for her sensible moderation. In 1584 William the Silent had been struck down by the assassin, as Coligny and the Regent Moray before him: the Protestant leaders in the Netherlands, France and Scotland respectively. Only Elizabeth remained, conspicuous and accessible. There was great fear for

[1] *Ibid.* p. 284. [2] *Ibid.* pp. 285-8.

her safety throughout the country, and associations were formed for her defence: unadventurous as she was politically, uncandid diplomatically, she was never afraid for herself and took no precautions. Parliament — much more aggressive than she — would have brought in a measure bringing to book one on whose behalf the Queen should be assassinated — a clear departure from justice, which she would not countenance: she would have no-one punished for another's fault. The bill to provide for government in case of the Queen's assassination proposed a Grand Council, and Parliament for a time would have been virtually sovereign.[1] The Queen would tolerate no such derogation from monarchy: she would trust to luck rather than that.

Her luck held good. The Babington plot implicated Mary Stuart fatally and Parliament was summoned to deal with her at last. With her out of the way the succession question was robbed of its urgency. At once, with the Puritan fever at its height, their leaders in the Commons renewed their campaign against the Church. When the Queen refused to allow these matters to be dealt with, Wentworth went to the root of the issue with a series of ten propositions on which he sought the ruling of the House as to their right of free speech and their place in the constitution: "Whether the Prince and State can be maintained without this court of Parliament? Whether there be any council that can make or abrogate laws, but only this court of Parliament? Whether free speech and free doings . . . be not granted to every one of the Parliament house by law?"[2] Further articles were directed against taking or receiving messages to or from the Queen against the orders and liberties of the House and against the Queen's punishing any member for any speech used in the House. It was a fundamental challenge: Wentworth would make the Commons their own arbiter as to their liberties. He pretty clearly regarded Parliament — in effect, the Commons — as the repository of the national will. There was little difference between his position and Pym's: it was time and circumstance that made the difference. The small group of irreconcilables around Wentworth swelled in the next half-century, with the growth of their class and the mismanagement of the Stuarts, into the overwhelming majority of 1640. Wentworth ended in the Tower, Pym with a State funeral in Westminster Abbey: the gentlemen of England had triumphed over the Crown.

The truth is that the House of Commons was the political instrument — indeed largely the expression — of the gentry and

[1] Neale, *loc. cit.* p. 181. [2] *Ibid.* p. 48.

was bound to become more important with the growth in power of that class. Already beneath the magnificent face Elizabeth put on affairs the balance of social forces was altering. The increased representation in the Commons in the course of the century was a leading feature of Parliament: 296 members at the beginning, 462 at the end.[1] Elizabeth herself added 32 boroughs, 64 members. In so doing she was granting favours to local persons, for the impulse came from them. The idea of the Crown packing Parliament at this time is an anachronism; the Queen held aloof from electioneering; and actually it was she who was responsible for the cessation in creating boroughs during her last four Parliaments: there were "overmany boroughs already", said her Secretary. The gentry were now in occupation of almost the whole representation in the Commons. By law there were 90 knights of the shire and 372 burgesses. But only 60 of the latter were *bons bourgeois*: only one-eighth were middle-class townsmen and some of those were connected with the families in the country at their gates. All the rest were country gentlemen. By custom and precedence, by right of their power in the country and the natural fitness of things, the heads of the leading county families represented the shire; junior members of the family, of cadet branches and lesser families sat for convenient boroughs. It was all very local and *familial*: all the more representative for that: the very stuff and texture of social life woven into the structure of politics. Often an important father and son sat in the same Parliament, the father for the county, the son for a borough. There were family groups of Cecils and Knollys, Grenvilles and Gilberts, Wentworths and St. Johns; and, as we have seen, by marriage and inter-relationship whole groups, like the West Country group of Grenvilles, Carews, Gilberts and Raleghs, or again the Puritan leaders.

It was these social ties, bonds of kinship or marriage, with the alliances they formed, that counted. That being so, bribery had no place. Representing the county bespoke the position and prestige of one's family in it, and that had to be maintained. "Play fair, play foul, in Montgomery a Herbert had to win."[2] As to that simple fool, the freeholder with his vote, it was very much as at Haverfordwest in 1571: "With whom wilt thou give thy voice?"[3] Answer: "Where my master, Thomas Tank,

[1] In these paragraphs I am much indebted to the Ford Lectures given at Oxford by Professor J. E. Neale in 1942, developed more fully since in *The Elizabethan House of Commons*.

[2] J. E. Neale, "Three Elizabethan Elections", *E.H.R.* (1931), p. 238.

[3] J. E. Neale, "More Elizabethan Elections", *E.H.R.* (1946), p. 25.

giveth his voice." Quite right, good fellow. With the growth of their power in the country, the gentry were becoming more desirous to sit in Parliament. With more money to spend they were willing to spend money on it. That suited the smaller boroughs, which did not want to be burdened with the expense of the wages of their members, a considerable item for places like Bossiney or West Looe, not much larger than crab-pots. Their chief concern was to find members who would serve for nothing and pay their own expenses. So we find them usually represented by their local gentry. Only the large and important towns could afford to return two of their own resident burgesses and pay them; and, if need be, refuse a neighbouring peer with a ready recommendation — as Cambridge and Gloucester did. Such towns had their own interests to look after and push — both Oxford and Cambridge, for example, against the universities within their gates — and it was worth their while to pay their own members. The largest class of boroughs were those that returned a resident as one member, while the second went to an outsider: a very nice example of English sense and compromise.

The overwhelming localism of representation in Parliament is its dominant feature and gives it vigour and reality. Everywhere the majority of members are local men, either gentry of the county or townsmen. The number of official members, privy councillors and such, is very small and even they have their roots. This is so even in Cornwall, to whose representation Elizabeth added six boroughs, with twelve members. An analysis of the representation shows a very small proportion of outsiders, and still smaller of officials.[1] Among these we find members like William and Henry Killigrew who, though officials, had roots in the county, or Ralegh who had connections there, or Sir Robert Carey who held property forfeited by a Cornish Recusant. Contested elections were very few and far between; in those jolly days room could be found for most of those who wanted to have a go in Parliament. When there was a fight, it arose out of some feud or ill-feeling in the county, more noticeable in Wales than elsewhere: for example, the endemic feud between Salusburys and Trevors in Denbigh, or between the Herberts and their opponents in Montgomery, the Perrot and anti-Perrot factions in Pembroke. It is these local factions that link up with the struggle for power at the centre and, of course, no question of principle: " I doubt whether political issues had any place in Elizabethan elections. What begat rivalry was the honour

[1] Cf. *Members of Parliament*, I. 400 foll.

associated with representing the county in Parliament."[1] In other words, prestige, the recognition of one's position and influence: an important factor in the struggle for power. Out of these elements, parties and their organisation came ultimately to be made: here they are in a very embryonic stage. 'Party' was a bad word to an Elizabethan, almost as bad as 'politician': "I have no affection to be of a party", wrote William Cecil, "but for the Queen's Majesty".[2] That was in 1565. By 1597 Essex was launching a campaign for Parliamentary seats, and Robert Cecil was countering him, taking a hand in Parliamentary jobbery in a way that would, perhaps, have shocked Burghley. Progress was being made, institutions growing and differentiating themselves.

This localism of representation and interest is naturally and sensibly reflected in the work of the House. The principle that obtains is that bills are committed to those most competent to deal with the subject. (One does not have to suppose that people centuries ago were any less naturally intelligent than ourselves: patronage of the past is a very naïf attitude, apt to go with too simple expectations of the future.) The bill for confirmation of Ralegh's letters patent for colonisation in America went to a committee heavily weighted with West Country members interested in voyages of discovery; Walsingham and Sir Philip Sidney were on it, so were Drake, Sir Richard Grenville, Sir William Mohun, Sir William Courtenay. What a committee![3] The whole age — or a great section of it — comes to life in it. It is something of a joke to us that a bill for restraint of excess in apparel is committed to Sir Walter Ralegh.[4] Bills concerning the law go to the lawyers — an increasing element in Elizabeth's reign: there are some forty to seventy practising lawyers in the Commons: the courts in Westminster are conveniently close by and the financial rewards of legal office are the highest in politics: there were great fortunes to be made and naturally much ability went into this channel. Francis Bacon is one of the leading Commons men at the end of the reign, on innumerable committees and a speaker always heard with attention. It is noticeable, too, what a prominent part the most famous figure among the new

[1] J. E. Neale, *E.H.R.* (1931), p. 211.

[2] q. J. E. Neale, "The Elizabethan Political Scene", *Proc. Brit. Academy* (1948), p. 12.

[3] D'Ewes, p. 339.

[4] *Ibid.* p. 581. Notice that in 1593 the Chancellor of the Exchequer takes it on him to defend the Queen's expenditure: "As for her own private expenses, they have been little in building; she hath consumed little or nothing in her pleasures. As for her apparel, it is royal and princely, beseeming her calling, but not sumptuous nor excessive" (*ibid.* p. 473).

gentry, Francis Drake — advanced by his own efforts — takes in the committee work of the House though, unlike Ralegh and Gilbert, he does not speak: evidently a good man of business.

The increasing importance of the House is marked by the greater definition and formalisation of procedure. There is no subject so boring — and yet to it we owe the order and regularity of proceedings which have made the English Parliament a more effective instrument of government than many more exciting assemblies. The regular procedure of three readings for a bill is established. There is far greater care in adhering to precedents as a means of advancing the position of the House in the conduct of business. From 1588 a standing committee for privileges and disputed elections exists as a regular feature.[1] The Commons' Journal itself takes form with the beginning of the reign; James's first Parliament completes the process by asserting direct control over it. The House is feeling its strength: several of the earlier Speakers are the Queen's Solicitors; the last two are not. But it was the growth of the committee system that was the most important development of the reign. "Between the days of Edward VI and Mary, when — a sure sign of immaturity — most bills were not committed, and the Parliament of 1597, when practically every bill was committed, what a transformation!"[2] The purpose of committees was to transfer discussion from the floor of the House to a place where it could be altogether more free and effective. In 1597 the bills for Poor Relief were "committed to all Readers at the Inns of Court, all serjeants-at-law, all knights of the shire, all citizens of cities, the burgesses for Hull, and forty-five other members by name". It became customary to hold some of these large committee meetings in the House itself; "in this unpremeditated way the Commons stumbled upon the substance of a new procedural device, the committee of the whole House, though realisation of its possibilities and formulation of the procedure did not follow until the next reign". To what a future that already pointed!

Parliament displays the personal touch, the familiarity, gross, naïf, endearing, of all Tudor government. When Sir William Knollys made his speech nominating Yelverton as Speaker in 1597, he spoke of his good abilities and made a little pause; "the House hawked and spat and after silence made he proceeded".[3] This was not by way of expressing disagreement: it was what we

[1] J. E. Neale, "The Commons' Journals of the Tudor Period", *Trans. R.H.S.* (1920), p. 166.

[2] J. E. Neale, *The Elizabethan House of Commons*, pp. 376-8.

[3] D'Ewes, p. 549.

should call a sympathetic murmur. When Yelverton was named, he blushed, and putting off his hat sat bare-headed; he then made a comic speech of self-deprecation. It was a tiresome piece of politeness always to depreciate your own performance: one longs for a bit of hubris. Even Ralegh, the most hubristic of persons — for he was a genius — when the monopoly of playing cards was mentioned, blushed.[1] One day the Speaker has wind in the stomach and looseness, so there can be no sitting — at least of the House — that day.[2] A lunatic is elected, very suitably, for a Cornish borough: Grampound, which so disagreeably distinguished itself in the later history of Parliamentary bribery and corruption.[3] A member, Sir William Bevil, is given licence to depart on account of his wife's extreme sickness.[4] Members are admonished that none is to come into the House wearing spurs.[5] At the end of the session the Speaker presents the subsidy book to the Queen in person, the gift of her faithful Commons. The Queen herself — playing to the gallery as usual — interrupts when the Speaker says that the realm has been defended "by the mighty arm of our dread and sacred Queen" and says "No, but by the mighty hand of God, Mr. Speaker".[6] And yet it was observed on her very last appearance in Parliament "as she went through the Commons very few said 'God save your Majesty' as they were wont in all great assemblies".[7] This — after all she had done for the country: an old woman and alone. They were on better ground, and speaking out of their better selves when the Speaker of 1592–3 — his name was Edward Coke — said, "We have cause daily to praise God that ever you were given us".[8]

If English-speaking people anywhere want to know the source of the self-government which is their peculiar contribution to the world in the sphere of politics, it is to be found as far back as the Tudor tradition — perhaps even earlier — of co-operation between government and subject: a co-operation to be found nowhere else in the Europe of that day. For the origin of English liberties we have to go back further to the fact — paradoxically enough — that the medieval English kings were more powerful than their continental counterparts, the country more integrated and more governable.[9] The reason is to be found deep in the

[1] *Ibid.* p. 644. [2] *Ibid.* p. 470. [3] *Ibid.* p. 126. [4] *Ibid.* p. 507.
[5] *Ibid.* p. 550. [6] *Ibid.* p. 600. [7] *Ibid.* p. 602. [8] *Ibid.* p. 459.

[9] In these paragraphs I am much indebted to a course of lectures, the most illuminating I have heard, given at Oxford in 1944 by Professor C. H. McIlwain; and to the suggestions of Miss Mary Coate.

character of English society: in factors as general, and all the more important, as the size of the country and the nature of the people — we should not exclude such considerations for not being exactly ponderable. England was small enough to be governable — there was no part which the King's writ could not usually reach — and therefore it came in time to be governable in a freer kind of way, that was not possible for continental countries. This slow working out of free institutions, of the negative constitutional safeguards of liberties, was the great inheritance the English people took to the New World, where their descendants have brought about what is the world's greatest experiment in the working of free institutions on a continental scale.

Here we are not concerned with origins nor their ultimate developments, but with that fascinating period when difference emerges and becomes clear: the difference between this country and the rest of Europe. In the sixteenth and early seventeenth centuries liberties are losing ground in Spain, France, Central Europe. England is the one country in which they remain: it is what makes our constitutional history unique. Aragon, Castile, France, Hungary, all possessed medieval representative assemblies that had the germ of future growth in them: why did they not develop? I cannot but think that the explanation lies at a deeper level than that of constitutional forms, though they have their part. Government was always easier in England than abroad, if only because of the smallness of the country. By the end of the Middle Ages there was nothing in England comparable to the great feudatories of France, or the deeply entrenched *fueros* [franchises] of Spain — while the experience of centuries had shown that Germany was ungovernable and Russia as yet exemplified the primitive barbarism that astonished Elizabethan travellers. To confine ourselves to civilised western countries that alone are comparable: under Philip II the Cortes of Castile had dropped in representation to only 18 towns with 2 proctors each: 36 in all: a number that could easily be bullied. There was no bullying 462 English M.P.s. In Aragon, representation was more broadly based; but any hope of independent corporate action was stultified by the rigid division into Houses according to class. In England we have seen how widely representative the Commons were and how tough a social texture it made: no division according to class: the sons of nobles, great gentlemen along with lesser, well-to-do townsmen along with a poor burgess who can only afford to contribute half a crown to the levy for wounded soldiers' relief: all sit in the House together and share in its corporate sense. It is unthinkable that this vigorous institution — so characteristic of English society — should not have a great future before it.

The sixteenth century brought about an emphasis on monarchy in Europe rare in European history, due largely to the conflicts of the fifteenth century, the anarchy, and the need for order. England was not unaffected by it: we see the influence at its height under Henry VII and Henry VIII. But in England the constitutional inheritance from the Middle Ages was larger than anywhere else. Parliament, in addition to representing estates, was the supreme court of jurisdiction. It comprised the body of all the realm. The king — by contrast with France — did not make Acts alone, but with the assent of Parliament. In course of time, with the change in the balance of social forces in the country, there came from that, Parliament's power to make Acts, with the assent of the king. Parliament came to make the law: a long course of evolution lies between that and the medieval conception of the king in Parliament merely declaring a law that exists. But to the medieval idea of an over-riding law we owe our liberties: they are very deeply rooted and they go back very far. No wonder "lesser breeds without the law" — we may disclaim any racial significance in the phrase — have no conception of what has been the heart of the English peoples' experience.

CHAPTER VIII

ADMINISTRATION: CENTRAL AND LOCAL

ENGLISH administration has been a no less remarkable achievement, though less visible and altogether less well known, than the development of our constitutional liberties. "The history of English political liberty has long since passed from the domain of special research into the political creed of the whole civilised world; it accomplished a great mission of liberation; it has surely not ceased to be a great political force. The history of English administration is much less known abroad, although it undoubtedly has a just claim to public attention. A powerful government, which attained great technical perfection, had been developed on the island at a very early date, and, according to the best authorities, was the unconscious nurse, if not the tender mother, of political liberty. . . . The success of the official surveys was also greatly dependent upon the habit of business routine which was so firmly rooted in the minds both of the central bureaucratic personnel and of the local agents of the state."[1]

This is an impressive tribute, coming as it did from a Russian scholar.

Yet Tudor administration, particularly at the centre, has been little studied compared with the work done on medieval administrative institutions. For a respectable reason: there is so much more material on more interesting subjects, in contrast with the frequent paucity of medieval records. In the field of Elizabethan administration the ground has not been cleared for us as elsewhere: we must pick our way carefully, hoping to let in a little light here and there, particularly in the thick forest of the Exchequer. If we keep to the facts of social life and regard administrative institutions as serving the needs of society, we shall not lose sight of our objective.

In default of such research, grave injustice has been done to

[1] A. Savine, *English Monasteries on the Eve of the Dissolution*, p. 17.

Elizabeth's government on the crucial issue of finance. Almost all historians have taken the side of those eloquent, expressive men, the soldiers and sailors, the men of action, against the hard-pressed, silent administration and the government always careful of the country's resources. The fighting men had no idea how easy it was to overstep the bounds of the latter and ruin all. Burghley's ear was constantly cocked to hear the cry of the merchants, of the ports and the seaboard counties burdened with the charges of the long war. The government did its best, the best possible in the circumstances — all that can be expected of government. The Queen's Navy was provided for in high efficiency. Her troops were paid — where others' went unpaid and mutinied. Vast sums were advanced to our allies — not all of which were ever repaid, as has happened since in our wars. Wounded soldiers were provided for, if scantily. The government always kept in mind the interests of the poor and did what it could to relieve them; though here they could not go further than the class-structure of their society permitted them; even so, there was a vast amount of private charity dispensed: it was a rule of the age, an accepted convention of a society more personally charitable than ours. So far from what Froude thought and many have repeated, the financial achievement of the government was among the greatest of the reign, for it was upon that that all the rest depended: not only the efficiency of government and what it could do, but the well-being of the country. It was only attained by incessant scrutiny at the top, by standards of conscientious administration being set by Burghley, who saw to it that they were adhered to throughout the radius of his influence. Where that was not felt, and when at last it was withdrawn, the difference was marked.

One sees the rhythm characteristic of the sixteenth century in administration no less than in government in general. There is first the adoption of more direct and summary methods by the Crown — by Henry VII — to recover from the damage of fifteenth-century disorders and restore the efficiency of the State. Then Henry VIII expands the operations of the Crown, lays hands on vast properties of the Church: it *looks* for a moment as if we are in for absolute monarchy of the continental kind. But in course of time the underlying habits of English society, administrative and governmental, come to assert their strength and, the advantages of the Crown's increased power having been absorbed, the older routine comes up again strengthened by the new methods. We have observed this in the case of Parliament; we shall now see it in the sphere of administration. It shows how deep those currents of habit and thought ran in English society to re-emerge after all.

The process may be observed precisely at the centre of administration in the Exchequer: we see how closely its development follows the constitutional movement of the time. To get quicker results Henry VII, who was his own Finance Minister, and brought to bear a notorious interest in the subject, by-passed the Exchequer with its ancient and cumbersome routine, its elaborate and conservative methods of accounting. In place of all that accounting by tallies, the detailed recording on the Pipe Roll, the checking by the Clerk of the Pells, the battledore and shuttlecock between the Exchequer of Account and Exchequer of Receipt (who can understand medieval methods of accounting in their beautiful and finished completeness?), Henry turned to the direct word-of-mouth methods, the simple issue and receipt of the King's Chamber, and used that.[1] He left the Exchequer to its old sheriffs and escheators' accounts from the counties and the collectors of Parliamentary subsidies. All the newer business went through the Chamber, the king's personal exchequer. This business grew greatly under Henry VIII until the enormous expansion of the Crown revenues, with the annexations of Church lands, necessitated a new department to deal with it. The Court of Augmentations was erected with a staff of officials in Westminster and receivers in the counties where the lands lay. Based on the speedy methods of the King's Chamber, the Court was a rival to the Exchequer, which now was reduced to little more than its ancient business. The Augmentations officials made hay while the sun shone. No doubt they conducted their business efficiently and summarily. But what a wonderful time they had of it! Great abbeys and their manors, fat priories and their pastures, desirable monastic buildings that could be made into comfortable country houses for up-thrusting families, pretty monastic granges for younger sons, hundreds of eligible properties and parcels of land in every county in England. They were, it is true, mostly paid for; all the same what grand opportunities the officials of the Court had of snooping the best: how many of them made their fortunes and set up country families out of the grants they mostly paid for.

In Mary's first year, under Lord Treasurer Winchester, the Court of Augmentations was abolished and its business annexed

[1] A. P. Newton, "The King's Chamber under the Early Tudors", *E.H.R.* (1917), p. 348 foll.

to the Exchequer. This was a measure of conservative reform, which restored its old ascendancy. The work of the ten auditors of the Augmentations was transferred to seven auditors of the Exchequer. But the new business continued to be done, not by the 'ancient course' of the Exchequer lumbering on its way, but in the simpler Augmentations manner. In Elizabeth's second year, still under the aegis of the remarkable octogenarian administrator, Winchester, two more Augmentations offices were revived in the Exchequer: the Auditors of Prests, whose duties were "to take the reckonings of the wars, buildings, ships, ordnance, and all other sums of money delivered in prest, and of the money and revenues of the hanaper, the butlerage and the Great Wardrobe".[1] Here also the newer methods of accounting were followed. So that within the Exchequer there were now two systems at work side by side, their conflict unresolved — as, one might almost say, in the constitution generally.

The Prests Accounts were gaining in importance with the expansion of their revenues and expenditure. But the entrenched Exchequer officials held, not without reason, by the greater security of the old methods. They were smug in their conservatism: "Behold then the quintessence of all invention in this Court . . . so perfect it is in all parts that the best wits cannot find what to add or take away in any particular without injury to the whole".[2] The Queen's Remembrancer, Fanshawe, and his colleagues were from the seventies urging that all accounts should be according to the ancient course of the Exchequer, through the offices of the two Remembrancers and ending with the final enrolment on the great roll of the Pipe. It did not detract from their conviction that fees were paid for each entry and enrolment, so that they had a pecuniary incentive for their campaign. But their case was also a strong one: they argued that these accounts should "have the ordinary controlment as others have, by remaining in the several custodies of others than those that made them, as the particulars in one office and the accounts in another, and by being briefly entered with both the Remembrancers of record, so as no alteration can be made; which sort of control seemeth by all precedents to have been used as necessary in the whole course of that service from the beginning".[3] Burghley was convinced by these representations, and in his last year as Lord Treasurer, in 1597, ordered that the accounts of the Auditors of the Prests were to be delivered into the Exchequer

[1] M. Dorothy George, "Notes on the Origin of the Declared Account", *E.H.R.* (1916), p. 41 foll. [2] q. *ibid.* p. 54. [3] q. *ibid.* p. 52.

and enrolled in the Pipe office. He restored the power of the Clerk of the Pells to control the receipts and payments of tellers: that official was authorised to compare every order with its respective authority under the great or privy seal and to mark it before money could be paid out by the tellers.[1] This signalled the end of Burghley's work for security and reliability in Exchequer administration: it was a victory for the old-established courses. Henry's erection of the Court of Augmentations had marked a new epoch in financial administration, consequent upon and necessitated by his revolutionary expansion of Crown revenues. Now all that experience had been absorbed and the ancient ways were re-establishing themselves. The rhythms within the Exchequer answered to the pulse of the country.

In its origin the Exchequer was primarily a place where the king's debtors were called to account, and, secondly, a court of law where cases touching the revenues of the Crown were heard.[2] Its name came from the chequered cloth covering the table upon which the final reckonings were made — so homely and simple these things were in their early days. Before that even it had been called the Tallies, from the notched sticks by which reckonings continued to be made right up to 1826, when a fine bonfire of these ancient accumulations was made. There were two departments: the Upper Exchequer, or Exchequer of Account, and the Lower, or Exchequer of Receipt. The latter was in intimate connection with the Treasury — one finds the Queen's treasure kept both at the Tower and at Westminster and consignments of it being made from time to time to the palace at Whitehall; the Treasury was continuous from Anglo-Saxon times and had the vitality to outlive the Exchequer, to become the dominant, the too active, department in government today. The Exchequer was the first department of State to acquire a separate organisation; when the King's *curia* began to develop different organs and to split up, and the Chancellor ceased to attend Exchequer sittings, in the reign of Henry III, his clerk became the Chancellor of the Exchequer. The only function that the modern Chancellor of the Exchequer performs by virtue of his ancient office — a solitary relic — is to preside at the annual nomination of sheriffs.

We are fortunate in possessing an Elizabethan account of the Exchequer, its organisation and procedure, written at the end of the reign by Thomas Fanshawe who was Queen's Remembrancer

[1] M. S. Guiseppi, *Guide to the Public Records*, I. 180.
[2] In this paragraph I follow Guiseppi, *op. cit.* p. 71 foll.

from 1568 to 1601.[1] He wrote it at the request of Lord Buckhurst, who succeeded Burghley as Lord Treasurer. Buckhurst, better known to us as Thomas Sackville, the magnificent rebuilder of Knole, was, as an extravagant young man, the finest poet of his generation: author of the famous " Induction " to the *Mirror for Magistrates* and of the last acts of *Gorboduc*, first of English blank-verse tragedies. We are more interested here in his fortune, for he succeeded to a vast patrimony in Kent, Sussex and Surrey made for him by his father Sir Richard Sackville, under-Treasurer of the Exchequer and Chancellor of the Court of Augmentations under Henry VIII and his children, from 1538 to 1566. 'Fill-sack' the people called him, and he could have filled many with what he (legitimately) made out of his office. He was a capable official and — what was rarer — a pleasant and agreeable one; agreeableness ran in the Sackville family until it went to seed in the third generation, the wildly extravagant second earl of Dorset, who almost ran the family on the rocks. But the family fortune was too solidly anchored in Church land for that; how appropriate that Sir Richard should be a first cousin to Anne Boleyn: that was no disadvantage to the Sackvilles with Elizabeth, who liked their cultivated society and affluent good humour.

The Fanshawes were even more strictly an Exchequer family than the Sackvilles. It is said that five generations of them were Exchequer officials. They sprang from old Derbyshire stock, of small gentry, with a John Fanshawe who was King's Remembrancer under Henry VIII; he, having only two daughters and not content with founding a free school in his native town, procured for his nephew the reversion to his office.[2] This was Thomas who succeeded to it in 1568, and from that the Fanshawes never looked back until they arrived at a peerage with the Restoration. Slow going, perhaps, but the foundation was as firm as the Exchequer. It was not the salary that made the money, which in this case was a mere £60 per annum, nor would any improper advantages be taken by so dependable an official; but there were the fees to be paid him on every enrolment and entry in his office, and there were still blissful opportunities for sagacious investment, though not what they had been under Henry and Edward. Besides his house in Warwick Lane and the old family property in Derbyshire, Fanshawe purchased two fine estates near London: Ware Park, famous for its garden, " none excelling it in flowers, physic herbs

[1] Sir T. Fanshawe, *The Practice of the Exchequer Court*, 1658.
[2] *v. D.N.B. sub* Thomas Fanshawe.

and fruit ", and the manor of Jenkins in Essex.[1] His second wife was a daughter of Customer Smythe, while his eldest son by his first wife married another daughter: one sees the tie-up of these Elizabethan official and financial families. His eldest son, Sir Henry, succeeded him as Remembrancer; his eldest by the Smythe marriage, another Thomas, became surveyor-general of Crown lands; the second, William, became auditor of the Duchy: all made independent careers and substantial fortunes. Both Sir Henry and his father were " happy in the favour of the princes of that time, for Queen Elizabeth said your grandfather was the best officer of accounts she had, and a person of great integrity ".

From a letter of his to Burghley, when both old servants of the State were nearing their end, one sees something of the standards of work and devotion these key-men at the centre exacted from themselves: " By my continually attending the business of my office all the term, I have too much neglected my health and business in the country and as my presence is urgently required there I have left all things in such a state that the duties may be as well performed without me. I hope I may repair thither and stay until the term. . . . If there shall be any occasion for my attendance, I will speedily return though to my hindrance both in health and profit."[2] We may hope that the Lord Treasurer was complaisant, since Fanshawe was always at his beck and call. One good turn deserves another: " If Burghley's coal-merchant is arrested for debt in the act of delivering his lordship's winter supply of fuel, Mr. Fanshawe is requested to settle the matter by an official stroke of the pen. If another honest tradesman has been informed against for breaking the statute by wearing a silk nightcap, he is sent, cap and all, to the obliging Remembrancer, with his lordship's private request that he ' will end the matter with the Customers and let him go '."[3]

From Fanshawe's book one derives an impression of a long-established and effective routine, of sufficient checks at every stage to ensure reliability and that the Crown was not defrauded. It is clear that the amalgamation of the Court of Augmentations with the Exchequer marked a new epoch: several new developments date from their uniting. Before that the Lord Treasurer sat very little in the Court: he left affairs to the Chancellor and Barons of the Exchequer, but since then he has to sit with them to consider all extraneous matters that have been brought in by

[1] *Memoirs of Lady Fanshawe* (ed. 1830), pp. 41-2.
[2] *Cal. S.P. Dom. 1595-7*, p. 413.
[3] H. Hall, *The Antiquities and Curiosities of the Exchequer*, p. 92.

the union. We must keep in mind the distinction between the financial and the judicial functions of the Exchequer. The Lord Chief Baron and the three puisne Barons are the legal officers, the judges of the Court; then there are the Queen's Attorney-General and his deputy the Queen's Solicitor, who consider all the hard cases and argue all demurrers for the Crown. Elizabeth's reign saw the equity jurisdiction of the Court established, when the Queen's Remembrancer became its registrar. Such was the legal side, with its minor officers; but the Lord Treasurer, the Chancellor and the under-Treasurer took part in the legal work too, sitting in court along with the Barons and joining in the decisions.

The powers of the Lord Treasurer were very great. He nominated all the escheators and all the customs officers, controllers and searchers, throughout England. He alone directed, reformed, punished all officers; directed all warrants for Exchequer commissions; granted warrants to revenue officers, receivers, surveyors of lands, etc. Burghley developed the habit of sending his serjeant-at-arms into the country to bring up defaulting or backward sheriffs and collectors. He alone gave warrants to individuals to have their (French) wines free of impost: a useful if somewhat invidious prerogative; we may be sure that with Burghley it was conducted with an eye to the public, or at least the Queen's, interest. His fee was a large one, £368 per annum, with robes out of the Wardrobe: what its indirect rewards and fees were it is impossible to estimate [1] — probably nothing like so much as the Lord Chancellor made, or as Burghley himself made, and Robert Cecil after him, as Master of the Court of Wards. This was a most lucrative source of income; we know that Burghley was moderate in the conduct of it.[2]

The Chancellor of the Exchequer was the next officer; a less important figure in the official hierarchy then than today —

[1] For Burghley's own opinion cf. his letter 14 August 1585: " In my whole time I have not for these twenty six years been benefited from her Majesty so much as I was within four years of King Edward. I have sold as much land of value as ever I had of gifts from her Majesty. . . . My fee for the Treasurership is more than hath been for these three hundred years. It doth not answer to my charge of my stall, I mean not my table " (q. in Froude, *History of England* (Everyman Library), *The Reign of Elizabeth*, IV. 64).

[2] Burghley made over £3000 in the last three years of his office from private suitors for wardships. But Mr. Hurstfield, who has studied the subject, concludes that Burghley's use of his opportunities was, as we should expect, temperate and his general policy in the matter " moderate and conservative ". Not so Robert Cecil; but then he had his way to make and Hatfield to build (J. Hurstfield, " Burghley and the Court of Wards ", *Trans. R.H.S.* (1949), p. 95 foll.).

secondary figures like Mildmay or Fortescue held the office — he was a kind of deputy for the Lord Treasurer. In Burghley's time the Chancellor was more active, since Burghley, having so much else on his hands, could not devote the whole of his time to this office as Winchester had done. Burghley made an order giving the Chancellor the rule of the Court of First Fruits and Tenths: all this business, the return of the first year's value of all ecclesiastical benefices with one-tenth of their revenues to the Crown, came into the Exchequer along with the other Church revenues of the Court of Augmentations. First Fruits had gone to the Pope before the Reformation: it was a great gain to the national revenue to retain them within the country. The under-Treasurer had the responsibility of the actual treasure remaining in the Exchequer, and of its accounting chest by chest. Then came the Barons of the Exchequer in order; they were judges of the Court, but other duties had been added. The two Chamberlains were responsible for the issue of money out of the Receipt, none could be paid out without their privity; with the Lord Treasurer they had charge of the treasury and kept the keys: all treaties of leagues with foreign powers and ancient records, among them Domesday Book, were kept there.

The two Remembrancers, the Queen's and the Lord Treasurer's, were the two chief accounting officers; they were the heads of their respective divisions. We may say, roughly, that the Queen's Remembrancer was responsible for the casual revenues of the Crown, which were much the larger, and the Lord Treasurer's for the fixed revenues, *i.e.* from the counties through sheriffs, escheators and bailiffs. Again roughly, the former's business dealt largely with the chief spending departments, the Cofferer of the Household, the Master of the Wardrobe, the Master of the Horse, the Master of the Revels, the Treasurer of the Mint, the Lieutenant of the Ordnance, the Receiver of the Ships, and so on. The sedate Lord Treasurer's Remembrancer took the proffers every Michaelmas and Lady day of all sheriffs, escheators, etc., and called them to account. (There were exceptions to this division of labour and further subtleties which we must ignore or perish.) These accounts were reckoned by tally — but only an accountant could understand the process, or perhaps explain: it is beyond my powers.

The Auditors of the Prests and the Auditors of the Exchequer were important active officials. As we have seen, Elizabeth revived the former from the Court of Augmentations to take the old great accounts, of Ireland, Berwick, the Mint, Ordnance, etc., which were never entered in the Exchequer nor went through its 'ancient course'. The Auditors of the Exchequer took and made all accounts of the revenue, riding every Michaelmas term to keep their audit at the Queen's court in every shire. Then there were the receivers and surveyors of Augmentations revenues, attorneys and clerks of the Remembrancer's office, of the Pipe and of the Pleas. There was that recherché officer, the Clerk of the Nichills, who made a separate roll of those sums upon which the sheriff returned 'Nichil'; and the Foreign Apposer who apposed his seal in green wax upon the sheriffs' accounts and received his fee for the same. And so the sheriff was discharged of his account, with *Quietus est* written upon it. (The rapacious mind of the poet seizes upon the word and turns it to another account, the last, and makes Hamlet muse

> When he himself might his quietus make
> With a bare bodkin . . .)

There were the Joiners of Tallies who were sworn to keep their tallies filed upon a string and kept under both their keys in their chests; they were to check their stock and file to see if they agreed and to prick them with a marking-iron. There were the Seal of the Court, the chief usher, the marshal, and the four ordinary ushers with their stick-in-waiting to attend on the great officers going to and from Westminster: an Alice in Wonderland world. There were the cutter of the tallies and the Clerk of the Pells. Burghley received a pathetic protest from the writer of the tallies against the revival of the Clerk of the Pells, so characteristic of this small place-world: "If this Pell should be revived in my time, that so long hath discontinued, I must think myself an unhappy man, having served for this twenty years past and more painfully and as uprightly as any that hath preceded me in that place: the world will judge and say that the same could not take effect without some great fault committed by me, the which would shorten the few days I have to live".[1] And so on down to the two parcel makers, the two under-chamberlains and the four ordinary messengers of Receipt to carry the Lord Treasurer's precepts to all customers, etc., in the country.

Such was the composition of the Exchequer staff and such it remained unchanged for the next century.[2]

Outside, in London and the country, the Exchequer had a more numerous body of officials subject to it than all the other

[1] H.M.C. *Salisbury MSS.* IV. 455.

[2] H. Hall, *The Antiquities and Curiosities of the Exchequer*, p. 88.

courts put together.[1] This was only natural, considering the nature of its business; even so they were only to be reckoned in tens, perhaps a couple of hundred who did the work over an area of England the same as it is today. Of the customs organisation London had a staff as large as all the rest together: two customers, of the small customs inwards and outwards, three collectors, all of these a clerk each, one searcher, fourteen surveyors and receivers, eighteen waiters. The ports around the coasts were grouped into some fourteen head-ports, each with a customer and a controller, sometimes a clerk or four waiters. Then there were the receivers of the Crown revenues in the counties: in all thirty receivers, each with a fee of £100 per annum. This is an indication that the office was an important one; it provided many opportunities for the advancement of local families, some of whose fortunes were based upon it. There were some forty-one surveyors of Crown lands, one for each county, two for Wales, North and South: the average fee £13 : 6 : 8. Along with the Crown lands, under the surveyance of the Exchequer, there went the duchies of Cornwall and Lancaster: each had a number of officials, the latter a considerable number of receivers, for it possessed lands in many counties. The Duchy of Cornwall was more concentrated, its lands lying chiefly in Devon and Cornwall; but it retained an attorney in the Exchequer and another in the Chancery, and paid fees to four counsel whom it retained and to the usher of Receipts in the Exchequer. The Duchy of Lancaster formed a small department on its own with its headquarters in the Savoy. There were, besides, two subordinate courts within the Exchequer: the Court of First Fruits and Tenths, with its chancellor, treasurer, auditor, clerks and messengers, and the Court of Wards and Liveries, with its small staff at Westminster and its feodary in every shire.

Such was the organisation of the Exchequer; it is not my purpose to describe the departments of State in detail, merely to take this central institution, upon which all the rest pivoted, as an illustration.

Of the troubles that could befall humbler officials of the Exchequer at Westminster we have a homely example in a document described as unique.[2] It is a letter written, 29 March 1573, to Sir Walter Mildmay, then chancellor, by W. Stanton, from the Marshalsea where he was in prison: "My humble duty with weeping tears remembered. It may please your honour to under-

[1] Cf. *A Collection of Ordinances* (ed. 1790), pp. 243-9.

[2] H. Hall, *op. cit.* p. 96 foll.

stand that on Friday being the 20th of this present March, all the tellers and other officers of the Receipt were in their several offices, where they continued till eleven of the clock . . . at which time they brake up, leaving their offices in safety . . . to my custody and charge. . . . After whose departure I shut the doors, barring and locking the same and brought the keys thereof into my kitchen, where I hanged the same upon an iron hook appointed and driven into one end of the mantel-tree of the same kitchen chimney." This kitchen was the living-room of the keeper, his family and servants; every night before going to bed he took the keys off the hook, unlocked the doors of the Receipt, made the round of it, looking under the boards and into all the corners, and then took the keys to bed with him. "This notwithstanding, my right honourable and singular good master, I considering this mishap and most unfortunate chance to come only through mine own fault and more than beastly negligence in so lewdly abusing myself . . . and further weighing the heinous offence by me committed against my very good lord, my lord Treasurer, whose great goodness both I and mine have often felt to our great comfort. . . . And lastly when I consider that I stand bound unto Sir Percival Hart, knight, gentleman usher of the Receipt and Star Chamber in the sum of £500 to save him harmless against the Queen's Highness for his said offices (unless I may taste the compassion of my said good lord Treasurer's help and your honour's) I certainly know and shall assuredly feel the utter destruction of me and mine in this world for ever. . . ."

The copiousness of the poor keeper's tears communicates itself to his pages; or, we begin to suspect, can it be something else? He gives us an account day by day of his doings over the Easter holiday, from Good Friday afternoon when "I with other the head-boroughs of Westminster did attend on Mr. Hodgson for the survey of the common sewer of Westminster by commandment of my said good Lord Treasurer". Next day his two servants being appointed to receive holy communion were given the day off "to prepare themselves, their clothes and necessaries for the worthy and decent receiving of the same". After dinner they walked abroad till evening prayer at church, "which finished they went into Westminster Hall and there played secretly by the space of one hour or thereabout, I and my wife standing by and beholding the same". On Easter even and Easter day the doors of the Receipt were locked as usual. On the latter afternoon the keeper took his family to St. George's Fields "by the boat of one Roger of Westminster, waterman", and so back to church to evening prayer and vestry with other head-boroughs afterwards. One begins to wonder whether the keeper was abusing himself with too much church-going. On Tuesday the keeper lay away from home with his servant, William Marshall. On Wednesday, when he was at church again, since it was Lady day, Mr. Hodgson "came and requested the opening of the Receipt doors, saying to William 'Have you not a bolt to this door?', who answered 'No'. 'Give me then the keys and I and my man Piers will be occupied here this hour.' But as soon as he came near the top of the Telling loft he spied dust in Mr. Freake's office; and going a little further towards his own office, spied his own chest to be spoiled and broken and a great hole over Mr. Freake's office: which so amazed him that he came running down the Telling loft stairs and sent his man to the church for me in all haste; and sent also for Mr. Petre, until whose coming he would not approach near his said chest." That was all the poor keeper knew about the matter, so he said. It is certainly all that we know about it; but it gives us a glimpse into the homely arcana of our forefathers: the Telling loft, the little offices one each to a teller, the chests, the keys on the hook by the chimney.

The originative figure in the financial administration of the country — the greatest of the century — was the Marquis of Winchester. The head of the younger branch of the Somersetshire Paulets, the family to which Mary Stuart's keeper Sir Amyas Paulet belonged, William Paulet was a favourite and dependable servant of Henry VIII, who made his fortune for him. A pliable, sensible man, who saw no point in making difficulties and treated everyone as well as he could, Paulet made his way forward through all the storms of four reigns and held the white staff under Edward, Mary and Elizabeth for twenty-two years, from 1550 to 1572. The truth is that there was a great deal more continuity in Tudor administration than is appreciated by those who look only at the surface excitements, the chops and changes of politics. Someone once asked the extraordinary old man — he retained his office and faculties until close on ninety — how he had stood up to so many storms: "'Why,' quoth the Marquis, '*Ortus sum ex salice, non ex quercu*, I was made of the pliable willow, not of the stubborn oak'".[1] It is possible that such men are all the more useful in such times: they keep their heads. His usefulness and his sense were well rewarded: Henry heaped offices and estates upon him — the mastership of the new court of Wards and Liveries; the control of the royal Household; the possessions of

[1] Naunton, *op. cit.* (ed. Arber, *English Reprints*), p. 25.

Netley abbey near Southampton. Under Edward VI, when the new nobility around the young king helped themselves to a vast share-out of Crown and Church lands, Paulet came in for a large grant in Wiltshire and Hampshire, the manors of Edington (with that splendid early Perpendicular church under the rise of the Wiltshire Downs), Steeple Ashton, the grange of Barton, etc.[1] The seat of this branch of the Paulets was at Basing in Hampshire, where the new Marquis proceeded to build the enormous house which was totally destroyed after the long siege in the Civil War.

All this did not mean that the Marquis was not an admirable public servant: he was a full-time professional administrator; he set new standards of exactness and method in financial administration and initiated all the reforms that bore fruit in Elizabeth's reign. In a sense Burghley and the Queen were his pupils: they did their best to walk by his precepts. A great financial reformer, his sympathies were conservative. But like a sensible man, he accommodated himself to the fact: his sense of things may be gathered from his comment to Cecil on a reverse, that "worldly things would sometimes fall out contrary, but if quietly taken could be quietly amended". He had taken a good deal very quietly. But he had possessed Mary's confidence and in her reign set about his work of economic reform. The uniting of the Courts of Augmentations and First Fruits to the Exchequer was his work. Having got them under his control, he proceeded to group the administration of the Crown lands by counties: a policy of centralisation and nationalisation which led to great improvement in the revenues.[2] In the Customs he introduced a new Book of Rates — many new commodities had not been rated at all: whence increased revenue.

The full deployment oı Winchester's programme came with Elizabeth's accession: Mary had been sentimental about the Church, to the detriment of the revenue and the strength of the State. In the financial crisis, the threatened bankruptcy, in which Philip's war had involved the country, and to which Elizabeth succeeded, the resumption of Mary's absurd Church grants brought back £25,000 per annum into the Exchequer. The Government pressed on with squeezing the bishops out of their temporal lands into spiritualties, *i.e.* making them exchange fat manors for tithes. Quite rightly: the bishops and deans and chapters were still fairly warm and squeezable; they had more

[1] *Cal. S.P. Dom. Add. 1580–1625*, p. 123.

[2] F. C. Dietz, *English Public Finance, 1558–1641*, p. 20.

than enough. The process was advantageous to the State — it is delightful to the student to hear the squeals emitted by the bishops — the Crown got rid of bothersome small parcels of tithes for lands which were increasing in value and yield. No-one could object save the bishops, and only then if they were not public-spirited. In his eighties the indefatigable Lord Treasurer concentrated his attention more on the Customs administration. He well knew, no-one better, how much the State was defrauded, how Customs revenue leaked at every seam, the ships that went in and out the creeks without making any entry. He appointed deputies in the ports, to check the collectors: to be paid by fees collected from the merchants making entries.[1] He introduced a general surveyor to inspect the Customs. In 1565 a new Book of Orders and Instructions was issued to catch up with new developments.[2] Commerce was steadily expanding, Customs revenue going up. The appetite of the Treasurer for administrative efficiency was still unassuaged: at the age of eighty-five he figured out the terms of Customer Smythe's first great farm of the Customs on imports at London and its subsidiary ports. It worked well and Burghley continued the plan when he succeeded Winchester. When near ninety he yielded up his white staff, but only with his last breath. Burghley as Lord Treasurer merely continued in the course set by his remarkable predecessor.

In Cecil and the Queen the old man had apt, if at first somewhat reluctant, pupils: Cecil had ambitious objectives in foreign policy, the Queen her favourites to reward and relations to provide for. Cecil had a war left him on his hands and opportunities to get the French out of Scotland which he could not but seize. The campaigns in Scotland and France were costly, the country ill-equipped. Gresham spent £139,000 for munitions in Flanders from 1559 to 1562.[3] The Franco-Scottish war cost £750,000. Gresham raised £300,000 loans in Flanders. Parliament voted a grant. But as early as 1560 the Crown had sold £90,000 worth of lands. The French, however, were out of Scotland. Winchester and Cecil worked well together: their friendly correspondence went back to Edward's government, like so much in Elizabeth's régime — interrupted by the parenthesis of Mary's. Now Winchester writes recommending that the obsequies of the late Emperor should be held at Westminster instead of St. Paul's: it

[1] The Venetian ambassador in 1557 commented on the inefficiency and waste of the Customs administration, to the great loss of the revenue (S. Dowell, *History of Taxation and Taxes in England*, I. 180).

[2] A. P. Newton, "The Establishment of the Great Farm of the English Customs", *Trans. R.H.S.* (1918), p. 134.

[3] Dietz, *op. cit.* p. 16 foll.

would be a great saving.[1] He makes out a wardship for Cecil and promises that his chimney at Court shall be amended. As soon as possible he recommends the discharge of 1000 men at Berwick and Portsmouth.[2]

Elizabeth was by no means ungenerous with her friends, particularly at the beginning, before she had learned her lesson. She treated Leicester like a prince — like the prince she would have liked to make him. In 1559 she gave him a couple of monasteries in Yorkshire and a house at Kew, following it up with four or five profitable licences to export cloth free of duty; this in addition to his offices, as Master of the Horse, Lieutenant of Windsor and so on. In 1563 she gave him the lordship and castle of Kenilworth, the vast lordship of Denbigh and lands in many counties; in 1564 manors in Bedfordshire; in 1566 sixteen estates in various counties.[3] She restored the Marquis of Northampton, brother of Katherine Parr who had been a kind stepmother to her, and commanded Winchester to prepare him a grant of lands worth £500 per annum.[4] Sir Francis Knollys, who married a cousin of the Queen, was provided for out of the Bishopric of Winchester: a grant of the great manor of Taunton, the jewel of the see, for three lives.[5] Warrants were always coming in from the Queen to reward this or that service with some little titbit: she was well within her rights: government was hers to make or mar. Winchester was driven to complain: Her Majesty was "too liberal in gifts before her Majesty knoweth what it is she giveth. And likewise in exchanges and licences."[6] That was one for Leicester. She rewarded her Exchequer officials with suspicion of their dealings: at the time of the recoinage Winchester and Sackville had to thank Cecil and Parry for removing from the Queen's mind the suspicion she had conceived of them.[7] At last the Queen and Cecil were convinced, and became converts to Winchester's policy. After his death they carried it on until the war with Spain forced their hands. By then Burghley had built up a war-chest of nearly £300,000. When at the end of his life he came to meditate on the success of the Queen's actions, he pointed proudly to "the parsimony of her Majesty" — with him the word was, as it should be, a compliment — which, with certain exceptions where she had spent wisely, "hath been a great cause of her

[1] *Cal. S.P. Dom. 1547–80*, p. 117. His plea was not heard: the magnificent memorial service for the Emperor Ferdinand took place at St. Paul's, 3 October 1564.

[2] H.M.C. *Salisbury MSS.* I. 251.

[3] *D.N.B. sub* Robert Dudley.

[4] *Cal. S.P. Dom. 1547–80*, p. 141.

[5] *Ibid.* p. 159.

[6] Dietz, *op. cit.* p. 32.

[7] *Cal. S.P. Dom. 1547–80*, p. 161.

Majesty's riches, able to perform these actions whereof heads are inquisitive ".[1]

During the frugal period, 1572–85, Burghley made a sharp cut in the budget for the repair of the royal palaces.[2] He scrutinised every detail of expense in the Winchester manner: it must have given him, who had no ear for music, pleasure but to sack the sackbut players of the Queen when the instrument declined in favour. Interlude players were axed — administratively. Later still, when financial pressure became acute again with the needs of the war, we can catch the Queen in a characteristic mood. Always under pressure day after day, year after year, from people wanting to get something out of her, she must have felt very much as Roosevelt described his attitude towards Harry Hopkins — grateful to one who wanted nothing for himself. Here Windebank, clerk of the signet, with her at Windsor, is describing to Burghley her reception of his memorial.[3] After learning the state of her treasure, she forthwith answered that there must be a loan, to which she had agreed. Windebank produced the warrants for privy seals, which would impose loans of certain sums upon those persons named. It was a regular enough procedure in an emergency, but it needed the Queen's own endorsement. She then hesitated, reflecting that she was loth to burden her subjects with a fresh charge. Perhaps the money could be otherwise provided. Anyway it was her opinion that the King of Spain would or could not attempt anything this year, 1590. On the other hand, if she were provided with a good sum by her subjects it might remain untouched until cause might happen to use it. Or she could repay it. Many unlooked-for occasions happen. She would speak to the Chancellor of the Exchequer in the afternoon. Windebank knew no further resolution: "Howbeit, I do mean to engross the warrant this day to be ready at any sudden calling for it, for I think her Majesty will sign it at length ". On another occasion the Queen took the dockets as read: she said " it was no matter, for she knew them already and so signed the bills, which I keep ". It was just as well, for a few hours later " her Majesty in the midst of the sermon sent a message unto me by Mr. Conway, the gentleman usher, that I should stay those things which her Majesty had signed ". One sees her, using the interval of the sermon, more profitably, to think things over.

The financial administration of the reign falls into three periods. There is, first, that from 1558 to 1572 while Winchester

[1] S.P. 12/255/84. [2] Dietz, *op. cit.* pp. 34-6.
[3] E. Hughes, *Studies in Administration and Finance*, p. 80.

was still Treasurer; second, from 1572 to 1585, the frugal period during which debts were paid off and a reserve laid up for contingencies; third, from 1585 to 1604, the war years during which an increasing strain was placed upon government finance. And yet, in spite of the burden, the English government — almost sole in Europe — did not go bankrupt: a remarkable tribute to the soundness of the administration. It was not only the wealth of her country but the excellence of her administration that made the Queen of England the most desirable *parti* in Europe. Neither she nor Burghley nor anybody else that was sensible liked the idea of heavy taxation. And in fact — in spite of the considerable expense of the Franco-Scottish war, of forces on the Border and in Ireland, of the Northern Rising and the tension with Spain, 1569–72 — taxation was held low and Parliament was not much called on to aid the Crown. Parliamentary grants were conceived as exceptional measures to meet emergencies; normally the Crown was expected to subsist and provide for government out of its own revenues. For the special purpose of the Franco-Scottish war the Parliaments of 1559 and 1563 voted a subsidy and two tenths and fifteenths, some £250,000 in all.[1] When these grants came to an end, in 1566, Cecil tried a third appeal for supplies and perhaps hoped to make Parliamentary grants a regular measure. The thought opens an extraordinary vista of what might have happened had it been successful: would it have ensured the Crown's independence? would the constitutional conflict of the seventeenth century have been avoided? But it was just this that was not permitted. Parliament was restive under any attempt to depart from the custom that subsidies were war measures and to make Parliamentary taxation a regular routine. Cecil yielded and the government made concessions: it accepted one subsidy and one tenth and fifteenth at a reduced rate of one-third; *i.e.* a rate of 2s. 8d. instead of 4s. in the £ on land, 1s. 10d. instead of 2s. 8d. in the £ on goods. When this ran out, there was no further grant of tax for several years, until the Parliament of 1571. This meant that the government was hard put to it to meet the crisis with Spain; it marked the withdrawal of England from the Netherlands money-market and her reliance on her own resources: that was a gain to the merchants of the City. And the government had the sense always to remember that what it forewent was a positive gain to the Queen's subjects. It also meant that the Crown had to sell more land: another gain to private persons. The country at large benefited all round.

[1] Dietz, *op. cit.* p. 22 foll.

This was still more true of the frugal period from 1572 to 1585, when the government set itself the desirable objective of leaving as much money as possible in Englishmen's purses. (Adventurous individuals at sea set themselves the objective of raiding the pockets of foreigners. The respectable Burghley strongly disapproved. The Queen thought it a *quid pro quo* for the conspiracies against her. The war reserve in the Exchequer told its own tale: £263,790 in ready money, gold bullion, pistolets at 6s. apiece, double milreis and double ducats each at 13s. 5d. apiece.[1])

The main interest of these years was in Customs administration. Impossible to go into its complexities here: it suffices to show that it reflects precisely the same rhythms as we have observed elsewhere, running through administrative as in constitutional channels, in political as in economic life. There is first the increasing unification and co-ordination under the early Tudors: the country emerging out of the medieval town economy. The greater efficiency of government made the new duties that were imposed more enforceable. But, from the moral elevation of the throttling efficiency of our own time we must not entertain an exaggerated idea of sixteenth-century administration, least of all in the Customs: scores of little ships moved in and out the creeks every year without paying dues; a little of everything they brought in stuck to the mariners' fingers; everybody along the coasts got whatever they could, hand in glove with the collectors their friends and cronies, for as little as they could conveniently pay. Can one blame them? Certainly no West Country descendant of theirs can. London was rather exceptional here, and since it dealt with half the country's trade we can take comfort in the thought that the government was not equally fleeced all round.

In the nature of things there was less administrative uniformity and regularity than in the land revenues.[2] Then, too, if the collection of duties was to be rendered speedier it was necessary to remove their accounting from the lumbering system of the Exchequer. This pointed to farming out the Customs: more efficient collection, the incentive of private gain, no roundabout Exchequer delays. Winchester was opposed to farming the Customs to the municipalities, as a backward step away from national control and uniformity. He tried out the idea of general

[1] H.M.C. *Salisbury MSS.* II. 384.

[2] F. C. Dietz, "Elizabethan Customs Administration", *E.H.R.* (1930), p. 35.

surveyors as with the land revenue. Great was the outcry, not only from the localities but from the Exchequer, which, as we have seen even if we did not know, could be very obstinate. But constant private offers to increase the revenue for a share in the profits from persons who knew, as everybody did, how the government was defrauded encouraged it to try the experiment. There were one or two experiments before the government found its man: this man was Customer Smythe. Burghley well understood the risks involved: the government was bound to be cheated, but perhaps less this way, and what he wanted was certainty of revenue. The experiment was a great success and marks an epoch in Customs administration.

What was necessary was a man of immense proficiency, with experience in this line, and sufficient financial strength to back his rent to the government. These conditions were fulfilled in Thomas Smythe.[1] The husband of Alice Judde, heiress of Sir Andrew Judde, and the successor to many of his business interests, Smythe had been collector of tonnage and poundage in the port of London since 1557. Leicester made over his farm of the impositions on sweet wines, at an increased rent, to Smythe: it answered well at £3500 per annum. Burghley added the French wines to the farm. In 1570 a great bargain was struck: Smythe was to farm the import duties at London and its subsidiary ports for six years for roughly £17,500 per annum and a fine of £5000. Smythe was immensely professional at his job and he raised the efficiency of Customs collection at once. He put in his own officers and more of them, and began by raising their wages. His efforts, and the risk he took, were well rewarded. Customs revenue went up every year with the expansion of trade: he got the increment in his sphere, but the government got its rent punctually and in full. There were constant allegations against the Customer's honesty, and there were certainly no flies on Smythe. But the government would have been defrauded anyway: this was the most profitable way of being defrauded. The government did its best to catch as much of the (earned) increment as it could, by negotiating ever larger rents out of Smythe with each renewal of the farm. His last farm, from 1584 to 1588, cost him the enormous sum of £30,000 a year. But he could meet it, and in spite of it cleared a profit of £16,000. Altogether from his four farms he made a net gain of £50,000: hence all the manors in Kent, the setting up of his sons' families.

[1] I am indebted here to a thesis by my research student Mr. L. L. S. Lowe on "Mr. Customer Smythe".

But it is noticeable that for all his wealth, and his piety, the Queen never made him a knight.

At the end, Burghley tried to extract a figure that even Smythe would not agree: an old man now, perhaps he had had, and made, enough. But this experiment in Customs administration had great importance; it paved the way for government, it increased Customs efficiency. No-one else was successful like Smythe. Walsingham headed a syndicate for leasing the Customs in the outports: he had not Smythe's professional experience and he lost money over it heavily: he died in debt to the Crown and the rent had to be remitted. Notice that the Customs on exports from the port of London had never been farmed. The conjunction of these events, the uncertainty of the time — for it was 1588 — and the urgent need of the government for more revenue induced it to undertake the direct management of the Customs under a system of general surveyors, which prevailed for the next ten years. Where the Customs were farmed there was no accounting to the Exchequer, merely the rent was returned. Fanshawe, like the good watch-dog he was, was opposed to this, and Exchequer officials fought it all along. Now they won, and Customs officers accounted again at the Exchequer. On Burghley's death in 1598, there was a return to farming; Robert Cecil headed one such syndicate. All this culminated in the Great Farm of 1605 which brought about a higher degree of centralisation and unification than had ever before been attained. The fruit of the experiments and experience of Elizabeth's reign, the Great Farm marked the end of the medieval system and inaugurated that which lasted right up to the end of the eighteenth century.[1]

During Burghley's long administration it is said that he was successful in creating a sense of public spirit among Customs officials and in improving standards of honesty. The Queen too took a hand. According to Naunton's story, Richard Carmarden when an under-officer in the Customs presented her with a paper showing that they were under-rented by Smythe and that two or three of her councillors had been bribed. We do not know if this was true, though Naunton's conclusion may have been: "that there were of the Queen's Council that were not in the Catalogue of Saints".[2] Certainly Carmarden was a trusted officer; he became surveyor of Tonnage and Poundage dues. Of the diffi-

[1] A. P. Newton, *loc. cit.* p. 155.

[2] For the details of this well-known story *v.* Naunton, *op. cit.* pp. 22-3. Ralegh wrote later (*Works*, ed. Oldys and Birch, VIII. 195) that Burghley, Leicester and Walsingham were pensioners of Smythe. This may be malice on Ralegh's part; but the acceptance of a fee would not have been against the usage or morality of the time.

culties and worries that Burghley had we have evidence in the case of Thomas Phillips, collector of petty customs on exports at London. In 1594 Carmarden wrote to Robert Cecil: "As her Majesty hath a hard account of Young's customership, so we find little better of Phillips. But my lord your father hath taken order, in the presence of Mr. Chancellor, Mr. Fanshawe and myself, that no more money shall come to his hands; and I have dealt with him to offer satisfaction in payment to her Majesty for this debt, which is £10,000. . . . Your father is much disquieted therewith, which doth not a little hinder his health; yet he placed none of them."[1] When Phillips was retired in 1597 he was owing the Crown nearly £12,000; in 1600 it was found that he could not pay. In the outports defrauding the Customs must have been constant and regular. In 1598 the searcher of Ipswich reports that he had seized the goods of certain rich merchants, laden at London for Hamburg, on which no custom had been paid, and that they were threatening to sue him in the Exchequer Court: he desired protection.[2] Of the scale of fraud in the Customs at Exeter we have pretty evidence for 1575–6. A commission granted to Sir Gawen Carew to search into the import of wines during that year, found that there were "in all landed 275 tons, whereof entered as by note appeareth 77 tons; and so remaineth unentered 200, save two".[3] Looking through the faded difficult parchments one comes constantly, familiarly, affectionately, across the names of the Topsham barks, the *Trinity*, the *Falcon*, the *Greyhound*, the *Dragon*, the *Saviour* of Northam, the *Gift of God* of Fowey, the *Katherine* of Looe: one sees the tiny craft bobbing up and down on the seas between the western coasts and Bordeaux or La Rochelle: in those dry entries what courage and endurance, what gallantry in those vanished lives. And no less frequent are the names of the merchants one knows from their sedate memorials in the churches: Blackallers, Midwinters, Peryams of Exeter, Hawkins and Peperells of Plymouth, Rashleighs of Fowey.

The aim of Elizabethan taxation was to take only as much from the subject as was absolutely necessary for the extraordinary expenses of government. All the highest authorities were agreed in desiring to keep taxation low and were proud of their success in doing so. The Englishman then could take pride in being the lowest taxed subject in Europe. Bacon wrote: "He that shall

[1] H.M.C. *Salisbury MSS.* V. 40. [2] *Ibid.* p. 49. [3] E122/46/21.

look into other countries and consider the taxes, and tallages, and impositions, and assizes and the like that are everywhere in use, will find that the Englishman is most master of his own valuation and the least bitten in purse of any nation in Europe ".[1] Burghley was strongly opposed to heavy taxation and held that the country ought not to be impoverished by taxes and imposts after the manner of France.[2] The Queen who, unlike James, had a proper valuation of money, was always loth to burden her subjects unnecessarily — indeed her standards of government in general were such as to make it difficult for her successors anyway. The Venetian ambassador noted with surprise that the sums levied by subsidies on individuals were paid within two months without any complaint or tumult. The English have long been notably docile in this respect, at any rate since the end of the fifteenth century: a factor in the strength of the State.

Parliamentary grants took two main forms, fifteenths and tenths, and subsidies. The produce of a fifteenth and a tenth had become fixed at about £30,000, of a subsidy at £100,000. But the tendency of both was to yield less, not more. This may be surprising to a modern ear; it is in its way, as all taxation is, very revealing of the essence of the society. It was here that Elizabethan government felt most the want of a trained and professional bureaucracy. The leading classes assessed themselves, and the government was really in their hands: it could not make them pay more than they were willing to pay. Hence Elizabethan government was ultimately government by persuasion. Then, too, there was the inert force of custom: the grant became a fixed sum apportioned out by the commissioners in every county, who were the local gentry, so that every hundred and ward, every parish and township raised its usual sum from the same lands. If one looks into any subsidy books or rolls in detail one sees the same names, or the same houses or farms, answering the same amounts, with small variations, over years.[3] There was this social advantage, that though the yield to the government declined, it allowed expanding income to accrue to the individual who made it. Many rising individuals escaped notice and were not brought within tax. Those who were, the subsidymen, enjoyed the doubtful honour of the income-tax payer today and were the subjects of rueful jokes by the dramatists: " He that hath a cup of red wine to his oysters was hoisted

[1] q. Dowell, *op. cit.* p. 158. [2] Dietz, *op. cit.* p. 380.

[3] Cf. *e.g. Constantine Subsidy Rolls* (Devon and Cornwall Record Society); or Henry Best's *Farming Book* (Surtees Society).

in the Queen's subsidy book".[1] The subsidymen were the substantial householders in a parish.[2]

Since assessment was in the hands of the gentry, poorer people paid to the uttermost value relatively to their income. The richer paid proportionately less. Again and again we find the government doing its best to redress the balance and protect the poor: it is no recent phenomenon. The Queen herself, and those who took their tone from her, constantly urged the interests of the poor. Ralegh tells us that she had always much desired to spare the common people.[3] In the levy on the counties for arms and armour in 1592 the Queen desired the meaner sort to be spared and the burden laid on those best able to bear it, rich farmers, landed men and the wealthy by trade.[4] Burghley wrote on the eve of the Armada: "If these demands for musters and powder and new weapons were not demanded of the poor in towns, the matter were of less moment for the rich may well bear greater. I see a general murmur of the people."[5] Ralegh always spoke up for poor people in the Commons — though precious little reward he got from them: he remained unpopular; as a genius they hated him; they adored the hopeless, the irresponsible Essex, who had the advantage of being an earl. In the Parliament of 1592–3 when a new survey of all men's goods was proposed and an annual proportion levied for the war, Ralegh urged that the £3 men be spared and Parliament itself make a general grant of three subsidies.[6] Again in 1601 we find him saying: "Call you this *par jugum*, when a poor man pays as much as a rich, and peradventure his estate is no better than he is set at, or but little better; when our estates that be thirty pound or forty pound in the Queen's books are not the hundredth part of our wealth?"[7]

But there was no arguing with these hard-faced men. Not that they were any more hard-faced than usual (they were dominantly Puritan); they were merely following their own class-interest: it happened that that worked out best for the country. In 1576 the commissioners of subsidy complained at being asked to set a good example in rating themselves.[8] The commissioners of 1594 were taken to task by the Council for undervaluing themselves, in spite of the direction given them. How it worked may

[1] John Lyly, *Mother Bombie*, Act II, sc. v.

[2] For methods of imposing and collecting the subsidy cf. Dowell, *op. cit.* I. 151 foll.

[3] *Works*, VIII. 187.

[4] Dietz, *op. cit.* p. 66.

[5] *Ibid.* p. 59.

[6] D'Ewes, *Journal*, p. 491.

[7] *Ibid.* p. 633. The phrase *par jugum* may be translated by the phrase 'equality of sacrifice'.

[8] Dietz, *op. cit.* p. 386 foll.

be seen from Lord North's report from Cambridgeshire in 1589: "I have made an end of the assessment for the half-shire where I dwell, and have well advanced the subsidy, with reasonable contentment of all men. I fear you will adjudge me over-liberal to the subject, seeing the law is the best and most value of lands and goods. There is no man assessed before me but is known to be worth at the least in goods ten times as much as he is set at and six times more in lands than his assessment; and many be twenty times, some thirty, and some much more worth than they be set at, which the commission cannot without oath help. If your lordship [Burghley] blame me not for the Queen, the country will bear this well."[1] In his Meditation, Burghley regarded the relaxation of the oath as a feather in his cap: "Yet her Majesty in her time remitted the usual manner of assessment by oaths of the assessors, so as the taxation of men's values was voluntary without any inquisition by oath or other coercion".[2] In these circumstances, was it any wonder what happened? The county of Buckingham was rated at £4000: by 1623 it could bear an increase to £15,000.[3] Gloucester, "though rich in landowners by recent purchase, derived from the ranks of the prosperous merchants of Bristol, shows a subsidy roll with only 79 names of persons charged £10 or more".[4] It was impossible if you were a commissioner to raise the assessment of one of your own class; it was as much as your life was worth: it led to 'challenge of words', an affray, a county feud; besides, you reflected, your turn might come next when your enemy became commissioner for the next subsidy.

In such circumstances, with no professional administrative staff to deal with taxation, it is a great tribute to the government that it got in as much as it did. Every kind of excuse was offered, especially from the remotest areas. In 1587 the receiver of Northumberland has to report that divers collectors near the Border have never appeared to account or pay.[5] He has had a commission from Mr. Fanshawe's office for enquiring into old debts, but there was no appearance for a jury nor of the gentry warned to be there. In 1596 Francis Courtenay writes from Cornwall that he has only been able to gather £16 this term, as against £54 last term, "as that part of the country which is in my collection is so poor, and so much burnt by the Spaniards,

[1] H.M.C. *Salisbury MSS.* III. 429.
[2] S.P. 12/255/84.
[3] Dietz, *op. cit.* p. 388.
[4] Dowell, *op. cit.* p. 156.
[5] *Cal. S.P. Dom. 1580–1625*, p. 218. It would seem that this refers to land revenue.

that at least £40 of the £200 will be wanting ".[1] Now we happen to know that the Spaniards only burnt some houses at Penzance, Paul and Mousehole. Courtenay prays for his discharge, that no process be issued against him, and adds disarmingly, " I will send some fresh fish for your master, my very good friend ". That meant the indispensable Mr. Fanshawe.

In view of all this, the old line of attack, and the popular misconceptions that still continue, on the Queen's financial administration are seen to be wholly unjust, or just not to understand her problem. The men of action never understood — and their historians still do not understand — Burghley's anxiety and his and the Queen's desire for peace. " I pray God we have not cause to remember one thing," wrote Howard of Effingham, " that we do not curse for this a long grey beard with a white head witless, that will make all the world think us heartless — you know whom I mean." [2] How unjust men are to those in positions of ultimate responsibility! — this, after all Burghley's services to the State, the constant struggle he had with the Queen to spend anything on action. Still he went on making preparations for the country's defence, finding the money to aid allies — one and the other of them, the Dutch, Alençon, Henry of Navarre — with subsidies. The old man was not afraid to face the challenge when it came, though he constantly found the Queen making " means at small holes to stop her own light and so I must tell her today with what danger she seeketh to spare ".[3]

But the Queen too had her own justification. Incessant war ruined the finances of the State. To pay for it she had to sell £876,332 of Crown lands in the course of her reign.[4] Any action whatsoever in Tudor circumstances left money sticking to the fingers of all the intermediaries between the Queen and the common soldier: these two were the victims in the end. The experience of the war in the Netherlands showed that she could trust no-one there to watch over her finances.[5] Without proper accounting there was no check whatsoever, and she could not get accounts rendered. " You know my old wont, that love not to discharge from office without desert: God forbid." She found it impossible to get accounts out of the men on the spot — " God knows by whose default. . . . It is a sieve that spends as it receives, to little purpose." She did her best for the common soldier as she did for

[1] *Cal. S.P. Dom. 1595–7*, p. 246.
[2] q. Dietz, *op. cit.* p. 55.
[3] *Ibid.* p. 57.
[4] *Ibid.* p. 298.
[5] J. E. Neale, " Elizabeth and the Netherlands, 1586–7 ", *E.H.R.* (1930), p. 382 foll.

herself, but without accounts she was helpless: money simply disappeared in thousands. At last she went on strike and said she would send no more treasure until she saw the check-books of the muster masters. Discovering the frauds on dead-pays and a dozen different ways the officers had of cheating the Queen of her money and the men of their pay, she sent out circular letters from local committees to protect the common soldier. No wonder the solvency of her government has been held 'the miracle of the age'.

She was as careful of her own personal expenditure as any queen could be expected to be: after all, the state kept up about the person of the sovereign was an instrument of government. No-one could complain that from the point of view of show they did not get value for money where she was concerned; but in fact she kept her Household expenses within bounds. Every decade or so Burghley or she undertook a campaign, and then back came the swarm of unauthorised attendants, serving-men whom no-one could account for, pilferers from kitchen and spicery and cellars which stood open to all comers, the extravagant suppers sent up to lords and ladies in their rooms, the embezzling of her supplies. She could not look into it all herself; her officers were not very helpful; but she did manage to live within the annual budget of £40,000 allocated to the Household, without recourse to Parliament, which she always wished to avoid, and in spite of the rise in prices. We see her at work in the last year of her life, in a most vivid interview with the clerk comptroller.[1] She asked him to explain why £40,000 was not enough to pay for the Household. He reminded her of the rise in prices. She asked him "to examine the difference of some year at the beginning of my reign and one year's expenses now". He found that the charges for bread, beer, wood, coal and wax had grown by £12,000. At this the Queen, "greatly moved", said: "And shall I suffer this? Did I not tell you, Brown, what you would find? I was never in all my government so royally with numbers of noblemen and ladies attended upon as in the beginning of my reign, all offices in my court being supplied which now are not, and all those then satisfied with my allowances agreed upon by my council, and signed by me, by that care as by all former princes hath been used. I will not suffer this dishonourable spoil and increase that no prince ever before me did to the offence of

[1] Miss Allegra Woodworth first brought this interview to light in her "Purveyance for the Royal Household in the Reign of Queen Elizabeth", *Trans. of the American Philosophical Society*, pp. 16-17.

God and the great grievance of my loving subjects, who I understand daily complain and not without cause, that there is increase daily of carriage and provisions taken from them at low prices and wastefully spent within my court.[1] And now, myself understanding of it, they may justly accuse me to suffer it. But my speedy order for reformation shall satisfy my loving subjects grieved; for I will end as I began with my subjects' love. It is no marvel though these grievances were complained of in Parliament. . . ." She characteristically laid the responsibility home to the whitestaves and officers of the Green Cloth: "I myself will speak unto them and give them charge, and then let me see or learn what he is in my house that dareth break and disobey my orders and commandments!" Whereupon her Majesty sent certain notes in writing to the whitestaves to be put into execution. In the meantime, "before the perfecting whereof it pleased God to take her Majesty to His Mercy".

Many and various were the links that bound administration at the centre to that in the localities. At one end was the Privy Council, with the Queen occasionally taking a hand and putting more than a word in; nothing was too small for these great persons to take notice of—we shall have an amusing example presently from Burghley himself. At the other end were the counties. The English counties had, as they have always had, an existence as true social groupings, with their own character and inflections, all expressing itself in social life and culture, in politics and administration. They were of the greatest importance as units of administration in almost every respect: in taxation and defence, the organisation of the country's man-power, the regulation of wages and food supplies, provision for the poor and unemployed, the administration of justice. In all these matters the period saw a great extension in administrative activities and powers; at the same time, since the country was very far from being over-administered, one may take it as a sign of the efficiency and soundness, the robust vigour, of the society. The links and lines holding it together had the effectiveness of a system without its rigidity; there were always residual powers that could be exercised to fill a gap, and leading persons did not

[1] This refers to the royal right of purveyance, by which the counties had to provide their portion of cattle, corn, etc., at fixed prices to the officers of the Household. One sees what opportunities of cheating both Queen and subject were there. By compounding with counties over this, Burghley in 1597 managed to effect a saving of £19,000 per annum (Woodworth, *op. cit.* p. 15).

hesitate to intervene at any point where action was necessary. There were many delays, much slacking and malingering, many injustices and inefficiencies in particular, in so raw and crude a society; but there was no red tape. Life was not stifled; it was indeed too effervescent, violent and tumultuous.

Of these links the most glittering was the Lord-Lieutenant. He stood at the apex of the system of local administration, himself usually a peer and often a privy councillor, one of the governing circle, held responsible for a county or a group of counties under his supervision — almost always where he had interests and estates. For example, in the Armada years Burghley was Lord-Lieutenant of Lincoln, Essex and Hertford, Hatton of his own county of Northampton, Ralegh of Cornwall, Hunsdon of Norfolk and Suffolk, the Earl of Derby of Lancashire and Cheshire, the Earl of Pembroke not only of Somerset and Wiltshire where he lived but of all the Welsh counties and the Welsh Marches, where the Herberts had estates.[1] This exalted office was a characteristic Tudor creation: it combined great *panache* with utility and responsibility. It arose out of the local emergencies and dangers of the Reformation years, the rebellions of 1549; it was found useful, since it provided direct contact between the government and the provinces, a means of exerting direct authority on the spot, and so the office was extended and perpetuated. It was particularly valuable in times of emergency, and so with the outbreak of the war with Spain the system reached its full extension: by 1595 there were twenty-nine English counties under some seventeen Lords-Lieutenant.[2] What more effective than that the councillors themselves and the inner governing circle should take under their wing their own areas where they were looked up to as the powers they were? The supervision of the whole administration of these localities was in their hands; theirs was the responsibility and the residual authority.

Naturally the most important of them, like Burghley himself, or Huntingdon or Hunsdon, could not be much on the spot, and so deputies came to be appointed for them by direct commission from the Queen. They were chosen from the foremost and most active gentry in each county, the cream of the Justices of the Peace. They were found so useful during war-time that they too became regularised: a judicial decision stipulated that each county should have two; in fact the exposed coastal counties had many more, a busy area like Middlesex had the two sheriffs of London and ten

[1] Cf. G. Scott Thomson, *Lords Lieutenants in the Sixteenth Century*, pp. 49-50.

[2] E. P. Cheyney, *op. cit.* II. 362.

other deputy lieutenants.[1] By 1595 there were some 200 appointed in England and Wales and they bore the burden of the work; their job was to carry out the instructions they received from the Lords-Lieutenant and often directly from the Council. The bulk of their work was military: they had to muster the men of the shire, select the trained bands, provide them with armour and weapons, see that the gentry provided their quota of light horsemen, attend to the beacons. All this was laborious enough, but it was complicated by the endemic conflict of jurisdictions, claims to privilege and exemption and so forth. It took great persons to reconcile these quarrels; and then they too sometimes joined in them and a fine *fracas* there was. The financial duties of the Lieutenants and deputies came next in importance, especially with regard to emergency measures such as collecting loans imposed by government: the Lord-Lieutenant received the privy seals for stated sums, which the deputies and J.P.s distributed — invidious duty — among their neighbours. Here was further opportunity for dispute: one could work off old grudges against opponents by selecting appropriate recipients for these demands. One's activities might be sobered by the thought that on the next round, with a reversal of office, one would be exposed to similar tactics. Hence, in part, the competition for office, onerous and disagreeable as it was apt to be; still more was it a question of local prestige and social esteem. (Asses like carrots. Still, the world must go round.) Other duties were more unpleasant — like routing out Recusants or sitting on religious fanatics; or more boring — like seeing to the corn supplies of the districts, regulating the markets, preventing export from the area in time of dearth. All these and other activities, in addition to their ordinary work as J.P.s, kept the deputy lieutenants busy. To it we owe the fact that such a busy one as Richard Carew, just outside of Plymouth, never got round to the promised second edition of his *Survey of Cornwall*, or wrote — and such a delightful writer — any more books.

Beneath and around these grandees were the ordinary J.P.s, the characteristic figures in local administration from then right up to our own time. It was in this age that they flowered in all the powers conferred by "so many, not loads, but stacks of statutes that have . . . been laid upon them".[2] The J.P. is such a familiar figure in the English scene, and yet so unique outside it, as an unpaid local magistrate, that it is difficult to

[1] *Cal. S.P. Dom. 1595–7*, p. 124. Berks. had four, Oxon. five.

[2] W. Lambarde, *Eirenarcha, or of the Office of the Justices of Peace* (ed. 1602), p. 33.

know where to begin to describe him; and again, in the English way, this centuries-old figure continues to fulfil some of his purposes in hardly recognisable social surroundings. In the sixteenth century he was the *clou* of the whole local administration; the great increase in the numbers and powers of the J.P.s reflected, in part, the rise of the gentry to a dominant position in the landscape, along with the increased efficiency in administration. Throughout the country the J.P.s were the leading local gentry, those who accepted the régime or at least did not actively oppose it. This meant that notoriously Catholic families were apt to be excluded, since J.P.s were supposed to swear to the oath of the Queen's supremacy. But the government wisely forbore to scrutinise too closely and many slipped into the Commission of the Peace.[1] It was an indignity, an affront to your family, to be left out; and in a highly competitive society, where prestige mattered so much, people were very touchy about such things.

By the end of the reign the number of Justices in the Commission of the Peace had, according to Lambarde, increased to "the overflowing of each shire at this day".[2] Numbers varied with the size and importance of the county: large counties like Norfolk and Devon had between fifty and sixty, Staffordshire under twenty. In 1595 the Queen herself took a hand and, according to the Lord Keeper, since there were "many insufficient, unlearned, negligent and undiscreet, her Majesty therefore, like a good housewife looking unto all her household stuff, took the book in her own hands and in the sight of us the Lord Keeper and Treasurer went through and noted those Justices she would have continue in commission and whom she thought not meet and willed us to consider of the rest".[3] A typical reaction may be observed at the other end in a letter from Sir Henry Killigrew to Robert Cecil: "It pleased your Honour to favour my cousin, this bearer's brother, William Treffry, as to procure him to be a Commissioner of Peace in Cornwall. Since, as I understand from these assizes, he is left out of the Commission by direction of the Lord Keeper, to his no small disgrace and our discredits. I know the gentleman to be of very sufficient living, of sound religion, and learning and judgment to execute such authority, and no Justice to the west of his house within thirty miles, nor to the north within twelve, nor to the east within six; the town where he dwelleth [Fowey] being a place subject to many disorders through the common recourse of men of war to that harbour, I am bold to desire your honour to be a means to the Lord Keeper for his

[1] Cf. Lambarde, p. 53. [2] *Ibid.* p. 32. [3] Cf. Cheyney, II. 318.

re-establishment, as well in regard to her Majesty's better service in that shire, as to salve the credit of the gentleman." [1]

From that, and from the immortal caricature of those Gloucestershire J.P.s, Shallow and Silence — Shakespeare was careful not to make them Warwickshire Justices, since that might have invited a rejoinder upon a local resident — we may read much as to their social position. Shallow, we remember, was "Robert Shallow, esquire. In the county of Gloucester, justice of peace and 'Coram'."

SHALLOW: Ay, cousin Slender, and 'Custalorum'.
SLENDER: Ay, and 'Rato-lorum' too; and a gentleman born, master parson.

A small select number of J.P.s in each county were of the 'Quorum': one of whom was indispensable for certain actions to be taken or powers exercised. The qualification here was supposed to be some skill or learning in the law; and we know that Justice Shallow had been at Clement's Inn, where he often heard the chimes at midnight, and knew Jane Nightwork and other bona-robas, and lay all night in the windmill in St. George's field. All that was fifty-five years ago, when he was as lean as a forked radish and you might have thrust him and all his apparel into an eel-skin; and now he is become a squire and has land and beefs — to the envy of Sir John. The Lord-Lieutenant was usually Custos Rotulorum, but the records were in fact kept for him by the Clerk of the Peace. We have seen something of the qualifications for office from Killigrew's letter: the essential thing was that the J.P. should have sufficient living and countenance and not be utterly discreditable even if a fool. It was desirable that he should not be a retainer of someone else and that he should live in the county. The Queen sometimes complained of the incompetence and negligence of J.P.s; she took the opportunity of a session of Parliament to remind them that the proper execution of her laws was more important than making new ones; and the moment the session was over she ordered them off to their counties to be about their business instead of hanging about London three-quarters of the year.[2] She would not have approved of Justice Shallow.

A string of text-books attests the desire of the country gentry to be informed as to their duties and powers — very necessary since one was liable to be sued for overstepping the limits: it was a frequent thing for someone to run off to Westminster to sue

[1] *Salisbury MSS.* VI. 335.
[2] Cf. D'Ewes, *Journal*, p. 619.

out a writ of *supersedeas* to stop proceedings. The country gentleman needed to be something of a lawyer to protect his own interests: hence the flocking to the Inns of Court for education. Of these books we fortunately have a classic from the age in Lambarde's *Eirenarcha, or of the Office of the Justices of Peace.* One sees in the book the logical mind and method of the trained lawyer, and also the amount of learning at the back of it all, in the Latin moralists, Cicero, the medieval English legal writers, in the statutes and the Bible. What gives the book convincing reality and a certain country charm is that the precepts and commissions it cites are directed one by one to the J.P.s in the commission for the county of Kent. There they all are, friends and neighbours as they were in life, meeting in the dry pages of this black-letter book as they did at quarter-sessions and musters and assizes when they were alive: George Multon of Ightham, whose daughter Lambarde married; George Byng of Wrotham; William Sedley of Aylsford; Sir Edward Wotton, half-brother of the famous Sir Henry; Roger Twysden; Sir John Scott of Scottshall, now vanished in the fields below the church at Brabourne; Sampson Leonard, Sir Edward Hoby, Lord Cobham, whose family was to have such a tragic end, and that splendid house to know them no more.

The whole clue to the J.P.'s function is given at the outset: it is not to reduce people to a universal unanimity, it is the negative one of repressing force and violence, taking measures to see that they are not given their head.[1] That means that there is a large positive sphere for the exercise of the moral influence of the J.P.s in pacifying controversies between neighbours. One cannot over-estimate the violence latent in society; and in the palpitating, ragged, vigorous life of the Elizabethan Age, just emerging from the insecurity and endemic strife of medieval society, the violence of men's impulses was as often as not uninhibited and released. Only the law and the Church restrained them; with the bulk of people, even the great and the good — one can see it in a Ralegh or a Philip Sidney — the idea of self-restraint was little enough realised. Stealing and robbery were endemic; they constituted the bulk of the offences for which men were hanged in numbers at assizes. Murder and manslaughter were frequent, there were constant fights and affrays ending in wounding or death; the bastardy rate was high; rape does not make much of an appearance in the records — no doubt because sex-life was much more free and easy in the blissful medieval ways

[1] Lambarde, pp. 7-10.

before Puritanism had won its battle and the ravages of syphilis brought home its warnings. Life, in a world where pestilence and famine were regular, was indeed very cheap. Those who know the Middle East today know what the Middle Ages were like in these respects with us.

The powers and duties of the J.P. were multiplied by Elizabethan legislation: he was the instrument ready to hand to operate the new laws regulating labour and apprentices, seeing that people attended church and punishing those who did not, and dealing with the poor, the idle and unemployed. But always his fundamental concern was to maintain and provide for the Queen's peace. He was sworn to do equal right to the poor as well as the rich, not to be of counsel in any quarrels brought before him, not to conceal fines or forfeitures or let people off for any gift.[1] He was to support the established order and swear to the Royal Supremacy. Any one J.P. could call upon a rout to disperse; he could decide disputes between masters and servants as to terms of work; in harvest-time he could call upon labourers and artificers to help; he was to suppress unlawful hunting and games, such as football and casting the stone;[2] to seek out seminary priests and Jesuits, to certify absentees from church, to have beggars and vagabonds whipped, to apprehend spreaders of rumours and slanderous news. Two or three J.P.s together had further enlarged powers to punish riots and unlawful assemblies, to punish masters and servants for giving and taking higher wages than those allowed by statute.[3] Servants might be punished for departing from work contrary to their engagement, but employers might also be admonished for not adhering to the terms and their servants allowed to depart from them: there was a rough fair-play in the matter and work-people were certainly not treated as chattels; they had their rights and their due independence of spirit. There were many offences for which J.P.s could convict and commit to prison without bail: offences against the statute of liveries, against the statute of musters, for abusing licences to export, for refusing to work for wages appointed by order or to perform a bastardy order, or for practising witchcraft or conjury or uttering foul prophecies. J.P.s might try misdemeanours with regard to tithes, assess the parish for contributions to the relief of persons robbed in it, hear causes against rogues and vagrants. There were very few corners in local life into which J.P.s might not pry;

[1] *Ibid.* pp. 50 foll., 170 foll.

[2] At Devizes trolemadame and rifling were condemned as unlawful games (H.M.C. *Various Coll.* I. 68).

[3] Cf. Lambarde, *op. cit.* Book 3.

it was some consolation that they were human and liable to err themselves. In addition to these corrective powers there was the field of positive social influence and administrative responsibility that fell upon those who were the natural leaders in their localities.

The focus of these activities was at quarter-sessions when the J.P.s of the county met and could give directives to the individual J.P.: not that there was any disjunction between his private and their collective capacities: the latter merely filled out and reinforced the former.[1] Easter sessions were most important, for then the J.P.s, of whom one was to be of the quorum, nominated 4, 3 or 2 substantial householders to be overseers of the poor in every parish; and rates of wages were fixed for the ensuing year. The specific point of sessions was that causes were there heard and determined, not merely enquired into. The sheriff, clerk of the peace, bailiffs and constables of the peace ought to attend, and especially the jurors who were summoned; for the jurisdiction was very wide and practically every offence against the criminal law was only punishable on indictment and before a jury. There lie the roots of the safeguards the liberties of the individual have in English life: they are very deep. The number of sessions varied from county to county: four times a year may be regarded as normal, but six, eight or more than a dozen times a year occur.[2] In the West Riding it was usually six or eight times a year; in smaller counties like Stafford or Cornwall usually four times. The burden of the work was carried, as usual, by the few, the really active J.P.s, from half a dozen to a dozen, who ran most counties. Serving on juries was no sinecure either, a duty that fell regularly and frequently on the substantial yeomen: fortunately it was taken as an honour as well as a duty, a tribute to social status. How long-continuing these themes and habits are in the life of our country: from Butterton in North Staffordshire a Sampson Stubbs frequently made the journey to quarter-sessions at Stafford in the years after the Armada; from the same farm a Sampson Stubbs was making the same journey in the years before the Battle of Britain.[3] Tuesday was sessions day in Stafford in Elizabeth's day; Tuesday it still is. Though the old right of traverse was abolished a century ago, the jury is still the 'traverse jury' at Stafford.

Let us look at quarter-sessions there in the last years of Elizabeth. The number of J.P.s who could be relied on to attend

[1] Lambarde, *op. cit.* Book 4. [2] Cheyney, II. 324.

[3] *Staffordshire Quarter Sessions Rolls*, ed. S. A. H. Burne (William Salt Archaeological Society), II. xxxii; I. xxv; II. xxix.

was small, about seventeen; that is partly due to a considerable number of leading families remaining Catholic — Fitzherberts, Wolseleys, Erdeswickes, Giffards, Maxfields, Draycotts, Wrottesleys, many of whom would have been in the Commission of the Peace. J.P.s received 4s. a day for their attendance. With regard to the cases that came before them we must remember that, underneath, the old immemorial routine of manorial courts still continued and was not yet superseded: innumerable petty cases still came before them, a layer of communal life not yet submerged. One of the most important tasks at quarter-sessions was the licensing and regulating of ale-houses. The number of inns, taverns and tippling-houses varies a good deal from place to place. Stone seems to have been a thirsty neighbourhood.[1] When a victualler is prohibited from keeping a tavern without a licence, the constable gives notice in church, the effective meeting-place of the whole parish. Catholic Recusants are indicted in scores, but the majority seem to have got off fairly lightly. Only the rich could pay the increasingly exorbitant fines; some of them, like the Fitzherberts, were gradually squeezed out of existence; many among the smaller people conformed in course of time. The Earl of Stafford, inhabiting his castle hard by, took no part in these proceedings and made no appearance: he was a Catholic sympathiser himself: we remember his disdainful, if inaccurate, reproof to the busy Mr. Bagot, Essex's agent and the most active J.P. the government could rely on: "We have been nine descents Barons and Earls of Stafford before any Bagot was known in this shire".[2] Family pride was a melancholy consolation persons in his position resorted to; his lordship's history was wrong. Later, the Recusants' jurisdiction was taken away from quarter-sessions; it became so burdensome, and raised such difficulties, that special commissions were appointed to deal with it. And indeed special commissions became a favourite administrative device as more and more tasks devolved upon the J.P.s.

A lot of people slipped through the rough meshes of justice and, though cited, do not appear and cannot be found: some compensation for the severity of the law and the brutality of its punishments when caught. The truth is that there was no *finesse* about administering justice then: you were liable to be hanged or else get off scot-free. One must not under-estimate the dangers, particularly to health, of imprisonment; but there was little sense of the remedial in justice: plain objective punishment was the purpose of the law. Naturally, when such very heavy

[1] *Ibid.* I. 283. [2] *Ibid.* II. xxxvi.

punishments were inflicted for felonies, large numbers of offenders got off by one means or another. It was observed that simple country people would not procure any man's death for all the goods in the world.[1] The hand of the law was very heavy upon life. Take the figures for one county alone, Devon in the year 1598:

Epiphany Sessions:	prisoners	65,	hanged	18
Lent Assizes:	„	134,	„	17
20 were flogged, 11 claimed benefit of clergy, were branded and set free, 16 pardoned.				
Easter Sessions:	prisoners	41,	hanged	12
Midsummer Sessions:	„	35,	„	8
Autumn Assizes:	„	87,	„	18
October Sessions:	„	25,	„	1

That is to say, altogether there were seventy-four persons hanged in one county in a single year, of whom one-half were condemned at quarter-sessions.[2] Historians are less surprised at the brutality of the world, outside the happier West: it is the human condition; it was once our own. Indeed foreigners commented on the cheapness with which life was held in Elizabethan England.

It was necessary, in such conditions, to support the lower officers in the execution of their duty and to keep them up to it. At Stafford Sessions the constables of Wolverhampton are presented for not punishing rogues.[3] An obstreperous person of West Bromwich, a disorderly type, is indicted for beating a bailiff: he sent for the bailiff to his house and there beat him to his knees with a truncheon and said " he would teach him to proclaim him outlawed being a gent, etc." Strumpets are dealt with, on the complaint of the parish: one Ellen Smith of Norton by Cannock, wife of an ale-house keeper, seems to have converted the house into a stews. " And the silly man her husband being spoken unto to reform the said abuses is ready with this answer, ' God's blessing on his heart which taketh pains for me in that I cannot perform myself '. And for the rest he either cannot reform or will not." No doubt her easy ways brought the house custom. She was in the habit of making " a solemn night's dancing to recreate her customers withal ", and so " hath five or six of her servant women and others that have accustomly used the night's dance in her

[1] Edward Hext, a Somerset J.P., writing in 1596. He was of the opinion that only a fifth part of felonies were brought home to book (E. M. Leonard, *The Early History of English Poor Relief*, p. 126).

[2] A. H. A. Hamilton, *Quarter Sessions from Queen Elizabeth to Queen Anne*, pp. 30-32.

[3] *Staffordshire Quarter Sessions Rolls*, II. 255, xxviii, 51 foll.

house within these three years been gotten with child". And "finally her great shows of overmuch familiarity towards many men within the parish hath bred such disquietness between them and their wives that they hath been ready to part company, whereupon she hath greatly rejoiced". There were evidently some spoil-sports about; but the parish could not put up with that sort of thing. Bastardy cases are, not unnaturally, frequent. But an amusing slant is given to the insistent problem of poor relief when three of the four overseers at West Bromwich complain that their colleague has aggravated the situation by begetting and then refusing to support two illegitimate children.[1] At Eccleshall one Jackson was in the habit of hiding "himself from all musters and very lately hid himself three days on a rye mow of William Rodon's and was victualled by Rodon's wife". A local character at Wolverhampton, given to drink and brawling, was committed to prison by a J.P., but procured his release by some means or other, in time to return to town and mock the J.P. who committed him, wearing a feather in his hat on one side and the J.P.'s *mittimus* on the other; and on Easter day in church mocking the constable who had arrested him, "and to the great astonishment of all the assembly made very low obeisance to the said constable . . . in derision of the said constable and his office". How odd it is to think of such goings-on in St. Peter's church there, now empty and silent enough, with the bronze statue of the Elizabethan Vice-Admiral, Richard Leveson, looking serenely upon the scene.

In Devon, quarter-sessions appoint and dismiss the constables of the hundreds. We find Ralegh complaining of "slanderous and scoffing speeches touching his late occasion at sea".[2] He gets a cool reply from the Justices: there was not much love lost between him and them; there were frequent disputes between them over his claim as Lord Warden of the Stannaries to muster Devon tinners.[3] But we know that Ralegh was a very touchy person, quick to resent any fancied slights: due to something in his make-up and background, the restricted circumstances of his early years, the passionate ambition, the long-enforced wait for an opportunity for his superb gifts, his resentment at the refusal of others to recognise what they had not got, and then his taking it out of them when he got the chance. Not wise, but so very understandable in him. We find certificates for maimed soldiers

[1] *Ibid.* IV. xviii, xix; II. 112 foll. [2] Hamilton, *op. cit.* pp. 4-5.

[3] Cf. A. H. A. Hamilton, "The Jurisdiction of the Lord Warden of the Stannaries in the Time of Sir Walter Raleigh", *Trans. Devon. Assoc.* (1876), p. 380 foll.

and sailors signed by the single-minded and more successful Drake: the county had fifty-two such pensioners in 1602.[1] A separate rate was levied for them, and two J.P.s were appointed treasurers annually for the purpose. The county was much troubled by fires at this time: the clothing towns of Tiverton and Cullompton were practically destroyed, one in 1596, the other in 1602. It fell to the J.P.s at sessions to levy a benevolence throughout the county and supervise its collection, and to quarter the homeless poor on other parishes. Similar collections were made in other counties for the relief of these towns. The Queen's loan of 1597, to tide the government over until the subsidy began to come in, was apportioned and collected through the usual channels, Lord-Lieutenant, deputy lieutenants and J.P.s. Licences to buy and sell small quantities of grain, butter and cheese, and to exercise all kinds of trades, fell within the purview of sessions. So also did church ales and May games, which were regarded with increasing disfavour by the gentry and the Puritan bourgeois: one can observe the growth of the disfavour in the documents of towns like Plymouth, Ipswich, Leicester, but it was general to the ruling interests in all towns. The Devon Justices took the step of abolishing church ales and revels on the Sabbath in 1595; four years later they utterly suppressed them.[2] To decree such measures was one thing; to carry them out was another, we are happy to say. The church ales went, but nothing could subdue the spirits of the people.

Innumerable papers, public and private, remain to attest the activities of the J.P.s: we may pry for detail into the work of such a one as Nathaniel Bacon.[3] While their clever half-brothers, Anthony and Francis, sons of a clever mother, had their way to make in London, the elder brothers confined themselves to county affairs: Nicholas to Suffolk, where he succeeded to his father's estate at Redgrave and now sleeps under the large effigy in the barn-like church looking across the fields to the site of the Lord Keeper's vanished house; Nathaniel to Norfolk, where he got his father's estate at Stiffkey on the coast, and where the tumbled fragments of his house remain. Nathaniel Bacon became the leading Justice in Norfolk towards the end of the reign. We find him taking on the usual jobs, going through the usual routine of offices: commissioner for restraint of the export of grain, then of wood and leather, sheriff of the county, as collector of the loan on

[1] Hamilton, *Quarter Sessions*, p. 18 foll.
[2] *Ibid.* p. 28.
[3] Cf. *The Official Papers of Sir Nathaniel Bacon*, ed. H. W. Saunders (Camden Society).

several occasions distributing the privy seals among his neighbours. A Puritan in his sympathies, he was a commissioner for searching out Recusants and made suggestions for tightening up the machinery against them: there were ways and means by which they sometimes managed to soften the impact of their fines. But he was also called upon to discourage the Puritan 'prophesyings' in church; this must have gone against the grain, since he was regarded as a "zealous favourer of the preachers of the word".[1] Here he was no doubt less active, since the prophesyings continued, with the usual Puritan rudeness about the poor Bishop who was doing his best to execute orders from above.

As commissioner of sewers Bacon had a great deal to do to keep up the sea-banks and waterways in this area. When it came to raising money for these purposes the regular thing was for the inland hundreds to throw the onus on the coast. The Privy Council was entirely defeated in its attempts to finance Terrington sea-bank: the episode shows how dependent it was upon the local gentry and towns, and how, if they were refractory, they could obstruct the government's endeavours in the public interest. When hogsheads of wine were cast up on the coast they lost no time in claiming them as their own: it is pleasant to think that a score of them found their way to the Hall in time for Christmas 1592: one hopes that the celebrations were of not too Puritan a character. It is rather surprising to learn that the slackest side of administration was in regard to musters at this time: that may have been special to Norfolk, which was less exposed than the southern coast counties, or it may reflect a relaxation after the Armada years. Poor relief was probably the greatest single problem of internal administration: we have some evidence of its size when we learn that in the small town of Aylsham "there be of poor people that have need of the charity of others to the number of 300 persons".[2]

Attempts to found a system of Poor Relief were common to most countries of Western Europe in the sixteenth century.[3] It is the continuous existence of the system worked out in England at that time that distinguishes this country: tribute to, and evidence of, efficiency of administration, for it certainly was a most intractable and difficult problem. It engaged the combined efforts of government, Privy Council, the towns and the J.P.s all through

[1] *Ibid.* p. xl. [2] *Ibid.* p. 60. [3] Cf. E. M. Leonard, *op. cit.* p. vii.

the second half of the century until at the end a satisfactory code was worked out, which remained the basis of our Poor Law right up to modern times and unabrogated until its break-up in our own day. In the medieval world begging was endemic, and in the early sixteenth century government interfered very little with the matter. But the profound disturbances that overtook society, economic even more than religious, immensely aggravated the problem. It was a complex one: there were the aged and impotent poor incapable of fending for themselves; there were the children; there were the able-bodied who, people thought, should provide for themselves; there were vagrants, gypsies, rogues, the incorrigibly wandering and idle. What people think of under the simple heading of Poor Relief in fact involved not only the poor, but the unemployed and rudimentary health and social services. It was a triple question, and no wonder it taxed the administrative resources of the time, was a constant headache to the authorities and took the best brains and the wisest experience to solve it. It really is very interesting to watch how it was done — not the least achievement of the age to have accomplished it; there is no room for more than a brief summary of a vast national undertaking here. What is so characteristic is that the famous legislation of the age on the subject followed the experiments that were made and did not initiate them. That is very English — and a good recipe for success.

There are three elements in the gradual evolution of the Poor Law system: first, the regulations that the towns were forced to make to deal with the problem; then the Parliamentary statutes which took the experience accumulated by the towns as their basis to extend over the whole country; thirdly, the incessant activity of the Privy Council in encouraging and supervising national administration.[1] It was in the towns that the problem first became acute and intolerable; thither that the countrymen pushed off the land took refuge, along with the flotsam and jetsam of soldiers returned from the wars, beggars, the thieves and rogues who battened on Tudor society, and increasingly — towards the end of the century — the Irish. We have seen that London evolved something of a system as early as Edward's reign: St. Bartholomew's hospital for the sick and bedridden, St. Thomas's for the aged, sick and infirm and with some 500 out-pensioners dependent on it, Christ's hospital for the children, Bedlam for the insane, Bridewell — Henry's fine Fleetside palace — as a house of correction, training and setting on work. As such, Bridewell

[1] Leonard, p. 23 foll.

became the model for scores of houses of correction and workhouses all over the country in course of time. But a municipal system was not enough: it meant that vagrants and poor flocked to London for what was going, from the places that should properly have supported their own. Other towns followed London's lead, among the earliest the progressive and forward-looking towns of Ipswich and Norwich.

Both these towns developed very successful methods of coping with the problem. The clue to success was a compulsory rate: it was nothing like enough to trust to charity or even to church collections accompanied by hortatory sermons. There were far too many of the poor, infirm and unemployed. By 1569 Ipswich had established a combined hospital and house of correction on the site of Black Friars: an asylum for the old, a training school for the young.[1] Beggars were surveyed and badged, the poor organised, compulsory payments for their relief established. The achievement of Norwich was remarkable.[2] In 1570 there were more than 2000 beggars in the city. Drastic measures were necessary. The citizens took them, but they were constructive ones. An elaborate census of all the poor in the city was taken: those who could were to be set on work, those who could not were to be supported. This the authorities achieved by imposing a compulsory rate, ordering away all the beggars they found did not belong to the city and setting the employable to work, the women to spin, the men to weave, carpenter, etc. It is worth noticing how many of the children were sent to school: popular education is no recent innovation. Ipswich sent two of their citizens to study the working of the Dutch settlement there. The result was that a stock of money was granted to a Dutch weaver to set forty people on work making bays and says in the great hall of the hospital. The good townsmen of Ipswich were not limited in their ambitions; they made efforts to establish a new mart whereby "Ipswich should become Antwerp".[3] The citizens of Norwich were proud of the model they had set, and rightly; though one may opine that the degree of its success owed much to the expansion of the cloth industry in the city at the time. One may still see there a complete, and beautiful, example of a Tudor hospital for the infirm: the great nave and aisles of St. Helen's church converted into little almshouses, the chancel into a women's ward, the transept into the chapel, and all round the

[1] *Ibid.* pp. 42-3. [2] *Ibid.* p. 101 foll.

[3] From Vincent B. Redstone's Transcripts from the Headborough Books of the town at the Borough Library, Ipswich.

gardens filled with flowers and fruit-blossom in spring.

It was only gradually that the law groped towards compulsory payments for the poor as the solution — naturally since they were to come out of the tax-paying classes. In the end their public spirit forced them to recognise its necessity, and perhaps their sense of efficiency in government. Compulsory rates then accompany increased relief. One observes a clear transition from the hard and bitter Reformation years in the middle of the century to a milder and more civilised atmosphere as time goes on. In those middle years the possessing classes were appalled and frightened by the growth of the problem; the Peasants' Revolt in Germany was their spectre of a Soviet Revolution. They reacted brutally: persistent vagrants might be taken as slaves, and, though that was inoperative, they might be and were in numbers burned through the ear;[1] but the regular punishment was whipping until 'their backs be bloody', and all over the country they continued to be whipped out of the parish back to where they came from. Lambarde gives us a specimen of such a certificate: "John at Stile, a sturdy vagrant beggar, of low personage, red-haired and having the nail of his right thumb cloven, was the sixth day of April in the forty and one year of the reign of our sovereign lady Queen Elizabeth openly whipped at Dale in the said county [Kent] for a wandering rogue according to the law, and is assigned to pass forthwith from parish to parish by the officers thereof the next straight way to Sale in the county of Middlesex, where (as he confesseth) he was born . . . and he is limited to be at Sale aforesaid within ten days now next ensuing at his peril".[2] The country was crawling with such characters: repression had little effect on them: the more the question was studied the more it was realised that remedial measures and effective administration of them were the answer.

The question reached a culminating crisis in the years 1594–1597: all years of bad harvests, great scarcity and distress. From all over the country the cry goes up. The deputy lieutenants of Hertfordshire write: "It is pitiful to consider the great multitude of poor in most of the towns in the shire, who having the last year spent the greatest part of their substance are now driven to live upon relief; the wealthier sort are thereby so overburdened that many protest they shall not be able to continue it long".[3] At

[1] In two months of 1591, seventy-one vagrants were whipped and burned through the ear in Middlesex alone (Cheyney, II. 333). But this duty became distasteful to the authorities and it was dropped in favour of whipping.

[2] Lambarde, p. 190.

[3] *Cal. S.P. Dom. 1595–7*, pp. 10, 62.

Newcastle the town buried nine "poor folks who died for want in the streets" in September, and sixteen in October 1597.[1] The Parliament of that year, which devoted much of its time to social legislation — the increase of tillage, providing for maimed and wandering soldiers, restraining luxury in apparel — thrashed out the whole question of Poor Relief. A great committee containing a large proportion of the House met in Middle Temple Hall and hammered out the necessary legislation, throwing over the dozen or so draft bills they had before them in favour of a new bill, simple and bold.[2] The essence of it was the national enactment of a compulsory poor rate; the J.P.s were to appoint from two to four overseers of the poor in every parish, to levy the poor rate by distress, to assent to the binding of poor children as apprentices. Quarter-sessions were empowered to take order for the erection of workhouses, to set the able-bodied on work and provide for the infirm. The solution now was to put this system into effect all over the country; the Privy Council saw that it was, and exercised a constant pressure and supervision. In every county and town one can observe the efforts made: the workhouses set up, the widespread development of the practice of setting the poor on work; pressure was applied on employers to keep their folk at work in times of depression. Almshouses were founded by private charity in many places. Hundreds of wills, and inscriptions in churches, thousands of documents, remain to attest the benefactions of people to town or parish, to lend out money to deserving apprentices, to set up a stock to employ people in work. Altogether the spirit in which this tremendous problem for a small society with limited resources was tackled, and a solution worked out that endured through centuries, provides us with a remarkable achievement in the realm of administration.

The main responsibility fell on the J.P.s, quite properly, since they were the ruling element in local life. They were supported in all their works by a small and homely hierarchy of lesser officials: overseers, with the aid of the churchwardens of the parish, for the poor; constables, headboroughs or tithingmen, in towns beadles and the watch, for maintaining the peace and other duties.[3] With the loosening of manorial ties, the decline and gradual increasing disuse of the manor courts, the parish becomes

[1] Leonard, *op. cit.* p. 125.

[2] D'Ewes, *Journal*, p. 561. Nicholas, Nathaniel and Francis Bacon were among the members.

[3] Cf. Lambarde, *The Duties of Constables, Borsholders, Tithingmen, etc.* (ed. 1602).

the essential unit or cell in local administration. A proclamation of the Queen revived and encouraged one useful sort of pre-Reformation procession: beating the bounds of the parish. (To this day, on Ascension day, the choir-men and choir-boys of St. Mary's, with the vicar and wardens, beat the bounds of the parish through the quadrangles of All Souls.) Churchwardens were becoming more important: though we have not yet moved into the Churchwarden Age, they were truly representative of the parish. Chosen by the parishioners in Easter week, they were the substantial farmers, the leading yeomen, some of them moving upwards into the gentry. They were legal corporations for holding the Church goods; in addition they held the parish stock, were responsible, along with the overseers, for the poor and the bastards of the parish, for the destruction of vermin under the Act, and for keeping up the highways.

The constables were declining in importance; they had been appointed by the court leet but were now increasingly by the J.P.s, the residuaries of all government in their localities. The job of the constables and headboroughs was to aid the J.P.s in keeping the peace: raising the hue and cry after a robbery or an assault, any breach of the peace, or after a suspect. They had some other small responsibilities: a labourer or artificer wishing to work in another parish was supposed to get a testimonial from the constable and two honest householders; at harvest-time the constable could call upon work-people to help; he collected the assessments made on the parish to recoup a person robbed; he was to see whether the malt put on sale was good or no. It was all small beer, very neighbourly and amateurish, and varied with country humours. What it was like we can see nowhere better than in Shakespeare's portrait of Dogberry and Verges: we gather from Aubrey that it was taken from the constable at Grendon Underwood in Buckinghamshire. Dogberry knew that it was the business of the watch "to comprehend all vagrom men; you are to bid any man stand in the prince's name". And though he did not know much else, he knew a rascal when he saw one. "Stand thee close, then, under this pent-house, for it drizzles rain," said Borachio; "and I will, like a true drunkard, utter all to thee." [1]

How true this picture is to the facts may be seen from a letter of Burghley, almost Shakespearean in its vivid portrayal of the scene, written in August 1586 at the height of the Babington conspiracy, while the conspirators were still at large in the neighbour-

[1] *Much Ado About Nothing*, III. iii.

hood and the hue and cry was up. "Sir, As I came from London homeward in my coach, I saw at every town's end the number of ten or twelve standing with long staves, and until I came to Enfield I thought no other of them but that they had stayed for avoiding of the rain, or to drink at some alehouse, for so they did stand under pentices at alehouses. But at Enfield finding a dozen in a plump, when there was no rain, I bethought myself that they were appointed as watchmen, for the apprehending of such as are missing. And thereupon I called some of them to me apart and asked them wherefore they stood there. And one of them answered, 'To take three young men.' And demanding how they should know the persons, one answered with these words, 'Marry, my lord, by intelligence of their favour.' 'What mean you by that?' quoth I. 'Marry,' said they, 'one of the parties hath a hooked nose.' 'And have you,' quoth I, 'no other mark?' 'No,' saith they. And then I asked who appointed them. And they answered one Banks, a head constable, whom I willed to be sent to me. Surely, sir, whosoever had the charge from you hath used the matter negligently. For these watchmen stand so openly in plumps as no suspected person will come near them; and if they be no better instructed but to find three persons by one of them having a hooked nose, they may miss thereof. And thus I thought good to advertise you, that the Justices that had the charge, as I think, may use the matter more circumspectly." This letter is endorsed "To the right honourable my very loving friend Sir Francis Walsingham Knight, her Majesty's principal Secretary. At London. W. Burghley. Haste, haste, haste, haste: Post." [1]

Nevertheless, it is satisfactory to relate, the Babington conspirators were apprehended — not far away, in Harrow parish.

Other local officers had their importance as links in the administrative chain that connected the counties with the centre, though their functions were more specialised. The sheriff still was important and he took precedence at the head of the county immediately below the Lord-Lieutenant. His name was pricked annually by the sovereign — as it still is — from a small select list of three suitable personages: the office was very honourable, unavoidable and a great *corvée*. It involved its holder in a good deal of expense, and sometimes considerable financial risk; for it was the sheriff's business to collect the old fee-farms and payments due to the Crown, and also Crown debts; all this was heavily increased by the business of Recusancy fines, the extending of

[1] S.P. 12/192/22.

their lands and distraint upon their goods for default.[1] On the legal and financial side the bulk of the work fell on the under-sheriff. At a Parliamentary election the sheriff's office was important: he might turn the scale in the election of the knights of the shire; it was then very much worth having and a competitive point of honour amid the factions of county society to secure it. The coroners also were important: normally there were two in each county. Their chief functions were investigating cases of sudden death, impanelling juries to take evidence and bringing to trial suspect persons: in a society where murders and manslaughters, fatal affrays and deaths by misadventure were frequent, it was a whole-time and responsible job. Vice-Admirals of the coastal counties — usually again there were two — formed another link with the centre: in this case with the Lord Admiral who appointed them and with the Court of Admiralty to which there was an appeal from their own local courts that dealt with wreck, salvage and marine causes. The high constables of hundreds, now on their way out, had become tax-collectors. All these offices were, of course, the perquisites of the local gentry.

But the government kept its eye on them. Administration was still interwoven with justice, out of which it originally came. The circuits of the Judges of Assize through the country were used, not only for gaol-delivery and the execution of justice, but to keep the J.P.s up to the mark. The Queen herself sometimes took a hand in their choice and gave instructions as to the directions she wished them to give to the J.P.s in their counties: her constant theme was the execution of the laws, the repression of rogues and vagabonds. Burghley took credit to the Queen for increasing the allowances to the judges " for their riding charges and diets besides their former fees " and for allowing two judges for the Welsh shires instead of one.[2] The judges, indeed, were representatives of the Crown on circuit, and, in addition to their prerogative of pardon, they exercised disciplinary powers over the J.P.s and reported as to their qualifications and conduct to the Lord Chancellor. We have an interesting survival of the kind of private report they made in a " Certificate touching J.P.s in Devon and Cornwall, which displaced and which not: October

[1] There are many evidences of the financial risk attaching to these offices. Richard Carew was liable for £100 by statute as collector for a subsidy when a deputy collector nominated by him failed to pay in his amount (E 134, 2 James I, Mich. 20). When Henry Lyte was under-sheriff of Somerset in 1559, the principal clerk of the officer of first fruits to whom Lyte had paid £95 : 16 : 8 fled into Ireland with it, and Lyte was forced to pay the sum in again (*Som. Arch. and Nat. Hist. Soc.* (1892), p. 54).

[2] S.P. 12/255/84.

1587.[1] Gentlemen removed out of the Peace:—Mr. Coswarth: of a good disposition but hath a weak brain not able to bear drink. Peter Courtenay: proud, undiscreet, self-loved, malicious, covetous, ignorant. Mr. Coryton: a man ridiculous to all men for his folly. Gentlemen yet in the Commission and to be considered of:—Mr. Carmynow: an old fornicator, a common drunkard, corrupt and ignorant. Mr. Chyverton: of no ability but by that office. Francis Courtenay: very infamous, corrupt, fraudulent and accounted a Papist. Mr. Moyle: envious, proud, corrupt, inconsiderate and the furious maintainer of factions in that country. Mr. Kempthorne: of no living, shifted into the Commission for his vehement disposition to all innovations. . . . Hugh Acland: a poller and piller of the people. Humphry Specott: in times past a great Papist, now in the other extreme, a server of the time, extreme, covetous, corrupt, and a great maintainer of stentons and factions."

It brings home to one how difficult a path in life it was for even an Elizabethan J.P. to live up to public expectations.

[1] Lansdowne MSS. 53/83.

CHAPTER IX

LAW IN THE SOCIETY

It would not be possible here to describe the whole complex legal system of the day and its working, even if I were capable of it; nor do I propose to traverse the field of the law, a science to itself, proper only to lawyers. My aim is rather to estimate, and to illustrate, the place of the law, its organs and members, in that society, to extract the juices of its social significance. Again, following my usual method, I ask what characterises the period; and I would point out the advantage of reading the contemporary law-books, for there was a whole school of literate lawyers, and their works enable us to breathe their climate of opinion, even when they are inaccurate and out of balance in the picture they draw.

What most obviously strikes the attention is the great expansion of legal business and of the legal profession. Everything witnesses to it: the enormous increase in the business of the courts; the growth of the Inns of Court, the amount of building they were obliged to undertake; the numbers at the bar and the fortunes made there — of which we have already given some indication in one or two counties. Other evidences are the growing number of books this expansion called forth, the remarkable legal literature of the age, and the ever greater prominence of lawyers in public affairs. All this was continuous with the fifteenth century — the age of Fortescue and Littleton — but the fuller development of these things reflected on one side the prosperity and expansion of the society, after the revolutionary changes of the Reformation, and on the other the increasing order, since many matters were now taken to law which would have been fought out in factions and private warfare earlier.

Holdsworth tells us that " the policy of the Tudor sovereigns accentuated the causes which, in the preceding period, were making for a purely native development, and gave to English law and institutions a form which differed fundamentally from the law and institutions of continental states ".[1] There is no

[1] Sir W. S. Holdsworth, *A History of English Law*, IV. vii.

doubt as to the upshot; but as to what brought it about, I should put the emphasis the other way round. Government policy as much arises from social circumstances as it imposes a course on them. And this development of the law expressed the character of English society and the forces at work in it. It is not possible to go into detail here — that is for lawyers themselves to do; but one recognises how the jury system responded to the facts of rural life, and how the instinct, deeply planted in the English, for a certain freedom and a regard for the individual brought it about in the later Middle Ages that the rights of tenants might be pursued against their landlords in the king's courts.[1] The more one reflects on the history of other peoples, the more remarkable that fact becomes. The great social fact of English medieval history is that the monarchy was strong enough to look after the interests of small men against the power of the great. Of course there were innumerable injustices and exceptions — that is to be expected; what was remarkable was the general assumption underlying English life and the force it had. It was what marked us off from abroad; and it was brought home to the two leading writers in describing the English polity — Fortescue in the fifteenth century, Sir Thomas Smith in the sixteenth — by the accident of their writing their books in France.

The influence of the society in moulding all its institutions is clear from Holdsworth himself in relation to the local administration we have been describing: "The manner in which it was organised in the sixteenth century has affected the whole of the public law of the state from that day to this. . . . The continental organisation was fundamentally different from the English."[2] But, of course, it expressed the difference in the societies: one has only to think of the French State with its military forces and bureaucracy against the English State with no standing army and the voluntary service of its subjects, not only of the gentry. "Thus on the continent the medieval system of local government gave place to a highly centralised bureaucratic régime. With the disappearance of the medieval system there disappeared also those ideas of the supremacy of the law and of local self-government which were inherent in it. The people at large had nothing to do with the government except to obey its orders. Criticism was not tolerated; and they gradually ceased to take an intelligent interest in its conduct. When the burden came to be too heavy the only resource was revolution."[3] The English develop-

[1] Cf. F. W. Maitland, *The Constitutional History of England*, p. 204.
[2] Holdsworth, IV. 108. [3] *Ibid.* p. 111.

ment was in contrast to this: continuity, a regard for the rights of small as well as great, the grafting of new institutions upon old, were characteristic of it. The result was the successful, eclectic blend of our institutions as in our language and in our art, absorbing what was wanted from wherever it came. No instance is more remarkable than trial by jury itself: an institution characteristically Frankish that became in time peculiarly English and had already by the end of the Middle Ages become a theme of national pride. "Fortescue contrasts it favourably with the procedure of the French courts, where there was no jury and where torture was freely employed."[1] One sees in our law, as in so much else, the enormous English capacity for adapting to itself and absorbing what it needs, with no repinings or regurgitations.

The class that was behind the movement of the time, and was now emerging as having the formative influence upon society, shows itself in the most significant field affecting its interests — that of the land law. It was not the nobility but the gentry. We may watch them at work, like so many moles in a field, over a fascinating tract — their operations with regard to Henry VIII's legislation as to uses, *i.e.* trusts tying up property and devising it for purposes willed by the owner. The enormous development of uses in the past century led not only to a great expansion in the business of Chancery — which had an altogether more flexible procedure than the somewhat ossified and cumbrous ways of the Common Law courts — but also to a marked depletion in the feudal revenues of the Crown. Henry VIII at the beginning of the Reformation Parliament proposed to deal with this by allying himself with the nobility to carry through a measure which would have simplified and revolutionised the law at the expense of the gentry. All entails were to be abolished, except for the lands of the nobility; "so that all manner of possessions be in state of fee simple from this day forward for ever".[2] If this position could have been held it would have altered the whole balance and structure of English society: it would have made transactions in land freer for the lower ranks of society, yeomen and such, but it would have reinforced and riveted the hold of the nobility from the top downwards; the middle elements would not have had that freedom of action to make our society what it was already on the way to become. But the balance was already in their favour, and not even the most autocratic and powerful of our kings could get his way in the matter. The proposed measure would have deprived the gentry of their freedom to make family settlements

[1] Maitland, p. 213. [2] q. Holdsworth, IV. 450.

and secret conveyances of their property, and the lawyers of a great deal of profitable business. The lawyers were allied to the gentry: they came from them and went back to them with their gains. Together, in the Reformation Parliament, they defeated Henry's plans. A great opportunity for reform of the land law, and for the registration of all such uses in the king's courts, was lost. As for making up the Crown revenues, everyone preferred to look to the Church.

Henry, as a good politician, knew what he could and could not do, and he slipped over into alliance with the gentry and the lawyers. The Statute of Uses gave him some of the benefits of a compromise: he got back some revenue; even so the statute was a factor in bringing the Northern gentry into the Pilgrimage of Grace — so far are the motives of the more intelligent from being pure and holy. (Reginald Pole, like the backward-looking aristocrat he was, favoured keeping entails as a privilege of the nobility;[1] but he was out of touch with his own country.) After this dangerous corner had been turned, Henry took note of the discontent, and the Wills Act of 1540 allowed free liberty to all whose lands were held in socage to dispose of their lands as they pleased. He reserved his own feudal dues, but "the landowner retained a large part of the power to devise which he had enjoyed for upwards of a century".[2] Indeed, the upshot of it all was "a large addition to the powers of the landowner, and an improvement in the means by which these powers were exercised. Since the Statute was not accompanied by any large reforms of the land law, landowners retained all their existing powers of dealing with their property, and, in addition, gained the new powers and the improved modes of exercising them which were rendered possible by the machinery of the use. The skill with which the conveyancers took advantage of the position which the Statute had thus created enabled landowners to make full use of their opportunities and with very little interference on the part of the legislature. The chief limitation on their freedom of action came not from the legislature, but from the courts."[3] Naturally, for the legislature was theirs; the courts were the king's. It is a most significant episode: henceforth the future was theirs — right up to the social revolution of our time.

In legal development we observe the same contrast, as in other respects, between the early sixteenth century and the later: no

[1] Thomas Starkey's *Dialogue*, (ed. S. J. Herrtage), II. 112.
[2] W. S. Holdsworth, *op. cit.* IV. 466.
[3] *Ibid.* p. 473. For subsequent effects on the landowners as a class, *v.* pp. 475-6.

doubt reflecting the same movement in society. Up to the middle of the century the Common Law seems at a standstill, and relatively to the Civil Law is losing ground. The prime necessity for orderly government, which reinforced the power of the monarch with the early Tudors, brought out the powers of the prerogative courts and the supplementary jurisdiction of Council and Chancellor. The Council exercised a most effective summary jurisdiction, all the more so for being direct and informal. " The same body which issues ordinances, which controls the execution of the law and the administration of the state, acts also as a court of justice with a comprehensive penal jurisdiction — one day it can make an ordinance, and the next day punish men for not obeying it. Its jurisdiction it exercises without any lengthy formalities — there is no trial by jury before it — the accused person is examined on his oath, a procedure quite strange to the courts of common law, in which (as the phrase goes) no-one can be compelled to accuse himself. And it uses torture."[1] The Council exercised its jurisdiction both informally at the council table, and more formally in the Star Chamber. We must not be guilty of remembering anachronistically the Stuart unpopularity of the court: all the evidence shows that under the Tudors it was highly popular. The essential thing was that it brought to book great offenders who might not be dealt with otherwise; Sir Thomas Smith called it the poor man's court, in which he might have right without paying any money, and he added, with pride, " of the which that I can understand there is not the like in any other country ".[2]

Just as the Council, with its outliers in the North and the Welsh Marches, made up for the deficiencies of the criminal law, so the inadequacies and delays in the old private law administered by the Common Law courts were filled in and shortened by Chancery. A great increase in Chancery business of all kinds, not only in regard to uses and trusts, was a feature of the century, and the rules that prevailed in the court — rules of common sense and conscience, enriched by resort to the treasury of Roman law, and in course of time systematised by formulation of its own precedents and procedure — developed and built up a system of Equity complementary to the Common Law. The Court of Requests dealt with poor men's causes, mainly debts, and was a kind of dependency of Chancery: its procedure was that of the Civil Law. So was that of the Court of Admiralty, which dealt

[1] Maitland, *op. cit.* p. 221.

[2] Smith, *De Republica Anglorum* (ed. Alston), p. 115; cf. the whole chapter, Book III, chap. 4, and Hawarde's *Les Reportes des Cases in Camera Stellata*, p. lxi.

with maritime cases, and experienced a notable expansion with the growth of commerce and enterprise of all kinds at sea. The Church courts administered canon law: after the Reformation, as much of it as was allowed by the laws of England. But the Reformation had the somewhat unexpected result of increasing the powers of the Archbishop; and the Court of High Commission, when founded, exercised a summary jurisdiction with a procedure most uncongenial to common lawyers. All these courts were largely under the influence of Roman law, and the business of most of them was greatly expanding. Contemporaneously in most countries of Western Europe there was a significant Reception of Roman Law, at the expense of their older customary law, strengthening the hand of monarchy and pointing towards absolutism.

By the middle of the century the Common Law was marking time, the Civil Law pushing forward. Henry VIII encouraged its study by founding professorships at the universities. "Tunstall, Gardiner, Bonner, Sampson and Clerk, to say nothing of the Leghs and Laytons, were doctors of law and took their fees in bishoprics and deaneries. Certainly they were more conspicuous and probably they were much abler men than those who were sitting in the courts of the common law."[1] In 1535, the year of More's execution, the splendid series of medieval Year Books, which had reported the cases of the Common Law courts, came to an end. Reginald Pole favoured a reception of Roman law, not only to end the infinite delays, remove the uncertainties, and flex the rigidities, of the Common Law but because the Civil Law had now become the "common law almost of all Christian nations".[2]

Why did it not come about here, alone of the countries of Western Europe?

It has long been regarded as a problem of the first importance. We now see more clearly that the answer lies in the nature of English society. Maitland suggested that it was due to the corporate strength of the Inns of Court and their system of legal training. And that was an important factor. But there were deeper reasons. The instinct of the English for fact led them to prefer case-law and to resort to general principles only when driven to them. This ultimately — when the formalities of procedure were somewhat abated — made for greater adaptability, allowed flexibility and scope for common sense. (Coke's defence

[1] F. W. Maitland, *English Law and the Renaissance*, p. 15.
[2] q. *ibid.* p. 43.

of the Common against the Civil Law reads like an exact rebutment of the charges made by Pole: they must have been those usually made.) The gentry increasingly objected to the interference of the prerogative courts because they restricted their economic freedom; they resented the efforts to regulate prices and control enclosure. Their indignation was more than shared by the common lawyers, who to their common class-interest added the piquancy of professional jealousy. From 1547 we have a petition of Common Law students particularly directed against Chancery for taking away business from their courts and staying their processes "insomuch as very few matters be now depending at the common laws".[1] They complained that this was "such a discourage" to them that numbers were falling off and within a few years there would not be sufficient learned men to serve the king in that faculty.

Within a few years the trend was reversed; the numbers at the Inns of Court bounded up: the Elizabethan era was the golden age in their history; the Common Law resumed its forward movement to a complete ascendancy. What happened was very much parallel to what happened in the constitutional and political sphere: the deeper, stronger forces in our society, temporarily halted, asserted themselves; they came up again, having absorbed a good deal in the interval, to re-establish themselves, stronger than ever. We now realise that the Common Law was not in danger in the sixteenth century, though its supremacy was temporarily in doubt. At the end of the century there was an unstable equilibrium in law, which was like — and reflected — that in society and the Constitution, between the Crown and the dominant class of the gentry. It could not last, and, the facts being what they were, it could only be resolved in one direction: idiotic of the Stuarts to oppose it. The fact that the Common Law suited the economic and social interests of the middle elements of society did not mean any the less that the future of English liberties was bound up with them: such is the way of things. In fact, the Common Law itself was liberalised by a kind of Reception — it learned so much and absorbed so much from the new modes and procedures; but what emerged was as national in character as the English Reformation. The result was that our law emerged as the fusion of diverse systems, like the fusion of stocks at the base of the English people. "The political ideas in the Common Law became the constitutional law of the English state and formed the political theory of English-

[1] F. W. Maitland, *English Law and the Renaissance*, pp. 79-80.

men "[1] — and not only of Englishmen either: it formed the common core at the heart of the political experience of the English-speaking peoples overseas. In our period all that lay in the undiscoverable future: no-one guessed what an achievement it was to be — " big in the history of some undiscovered continents ".[2]

There was no absolute disjunction between the spheres of Civil and Common Law, between prerogative and people's rights; it was all a question of emphasis and balance. It made a great difference that almost all lawyers, including those practising in the new Civil Law courts, had been trained in the Common Law at the Inns of Court and they helped to give technical shape and detailed application to the new principles coming in. " Thus it happened that the principles of the Common Law had as great an influence upon the new law of the Chancery as the new law of the Chancery had upon the development of the Common Law."[3] Neither Council nor Chancery administered purely Civil or purely Common Law, but a kind of equity peculiar to themselves. A Common Law judge often sat to assist the Lord Chancellor or his deputies.[4] The influence of the Common Law, expressing English instincts and prejudices, may be seen in the publicity given to the proceedings before Council and Star Chamber, so exceptional for such courts abroad. Conversely, there was the considerable influence of Star Chamber proceedings upon the growth of criminal law. The truth would appear to be that there was a modified Reception in England, only the English took just as much of the Civil Law as they needed and worked it into what was already going.

One can see the process very well with regard to the Law Merchant and the Court of Admiralty. The growth of trade and enterprise at sea made the reception of civil law doctrines — since they were the common law of Europe — necessary in England. The Council delegated to the Court matters concerning salvage, spoil, wreck, piracy and privateering, prize and mercantile cases generally. The Court prospered; its judges made fortunes. It exercised a great influence on the development of our commercial and maritime law. The Common Law courts contested its jurisdiction, and there were frequent conflicts, but it served far too useful a purpose for the Council to allow it to be scuppered. The result was a concurrent jurisdiction that was not finally resolved in favour of the Common Law till after the Civil War. In the Tudor

[1] Holdsworth, IV. 288. [2] Maitland, *op. cit.* p. 27. [3] Holdsworth, IV. 277.
[4] J. Ritchie, *Reports of Cases decided by Francis Bacon*, p. viii.

period the boundaries of the various courts and their respective jurisdictions were never settled: the equilibrium continued. Separate Merchant courts were never developed in England as abroad, for here the towns, even London itself, were less independent and there was a far greater number of royal courts with general jurisdiction throughout the country. In short, the explanation is again a social one: the greater integration of the country. So it was that " in England alone among the nations of Europe commercial and maritime law became simply a branch of the ordinary law " of the land.[1]

The Court was located at Southwark, conveniently near the waterside. Thither were rowed the bustling, complaining merchants with their outlandish names — Spaniards, Italians, Flemings — the sea captains, the West Country sparks out for a quick profit from a prize, the mariners still clutching their doubloons or pieces of eight, the mere pirates condemned to be hanged at the water's edge. What a hullabaloo there must have been within the Court — so many different lingos, so much life and vivacity. It is not surprising that the Welsh civil lawyers, Dr. William Aubrey and Dr. David Lewis — both University lawyers and civilians, both Fellows of All Souls — should have been to the fore in it, while a third was the Italian, Sir Julius Caesar. Upon the front of his tomb at Abergavenny, Dr. David Lewis bears the curious nautical emblems and decorations of his office, with the sculptor's name across the stem of an anchor.[2] Sir Julius Caesar has his appropriately classical tomb in St. Helen's, Bishopsgate, with the curious fantasy of the inscription in the form of an enrolled deed, in proper diplomatic style and with seal affixed: " by this my act and deed I confirm with my full consent that by the Divine aid I will willingly pay the debt of Nature as soon as it may please God ". At the bottom, one notes, the deed is enrolled in Heaven: *Irrotulatur Caelo*.[3]

The assumption among the writers of the time is that the Common Law is the norm, the Civil Law exceptional and supplementary, to be resorted to only when the Common Law does not provide a remedy. This is true of Sir Thomas Smith, though he was a civilian: he says of the Chancery procedure — which was by bill and rejoinder in writing, and where the trial was not by jury — that " in this court the usual and proper form of pleading

[1] Holdsworth, V. 151-3.

[2] Cf. *Trans. Bristol and Glos. Arch. Soc.*, 1934, p. 36.

[3] Cf. J. E. Cox, *The Annals of St. Helen's, Bishopsgate*, p. 69; *Roy. Com. on Hist. Monuments: London*, vol. IV. plate 127.

of England is not used ".[1] Lambarde regarded it as a good dispensation that " men no less learned in the Common Laws of this Realm " should be placed in Chancery.[2] He was a Master in Chancery himself, but he thought that Equity should be subordinate and infrequent: " the most part of causes in complaint are and ought to be referred to the ordinary process ". The Common Law course was that commonly held; men were called before the Council in exceptional circumstances; Star Chamber was ordained because Common Law proceedings were held up by the greatness of offenders; even so, Council did not determine finally concerning freehold and inheritance.[3] That is to say, the Common Law was the great protection of property rights, and not only of property in kind but of man's property in his own life. The assumption common to the writers was that acted upon by the government: they used the prerogative of the Crown and the new courts to supplement, and not to override, the Common Law. We find the Queen herself intervening to stop certain suits undertaken in Chancery to overthrow a settlement: she writes to the Lord Chancellor that " her pleasure is the validity of the same assurance be tried only by the courts of Common Law and that the suits be dismissed out of the Court of Chancery ".[4]

Sir Thomas Smith had spoken of the future of the conquering Civil Law. What the situation looked like in the year of the Armada to an intelligent young lawyer, who was a friend of Spenser and the poets, may be seen from the curious book, *The Lawyer's Logic*, which Abraham France published in that year.[5] After eight years at Cambridge, bred up at St. John's College — that fruitful seminary of eminent Elizabethans — France entered Gray's Inn. The Herberts took him under their wing and he found a haven in the Court of the Marches of Wales. While at Gray's Inn he rewrote his book on the new logic, of which most of the quotations and examples had been taken from his friend's *Shepherd's Calendar*; to these he now added legal examples from Plowden's *Commentaries* and Stanford's *Pleas of the Crown*. " If the Civil Law be elegant and delectable," he writes, " the Common Law is neither barbarous nor unsavoury. . . . Our Common Law is as easy, as short, as elegant and as delightsome as is the Civil, which every man extolleth. . . . But the Civil Law, will

[1] Smith, *op. cit.* p. 71.

[2] W. Lambarde, *Archion, or a Commentary upon the High Courts of Justice in England* (ed. 1635), p. 83 foll.

[3] *Ibid.* pp. 155, 205.

[4] H.M.C. *Salisbury MSS.* XIII. 264.

[5] Abraham France, *The Lawyer's Logic, exemplifying the Precepts of Logic by the Practice of the Common Laws* (ed. 1588).

some man say, is both in itself more constant and philosophical, and also by Justinian more methodically and by later writers more eloquently put down." Such objections were made " by them that heard somewhat at the University of the Civil Law but never read anything of our Common Law ". The Common Law has a procedure answerable to the Civil Law; one must remember with Aristotle the imperfection of all laws and not impute as a special blemish to our law what is incident to every law. Justinian was not so perfect but that the civilians " daily contend with new innovations and continual printing of new methods to bring it unto better order ". This was an opening of which the great Coke took full advantage: he said roundly that the law decided in court by the judges had greater authority and certainty than that argued by the doctors from their texts.[1] France urged them then not to discourage those " which hope to see the Common Law of England brought to as good and easy a method as ever was any ". This was to be the life-work of Sir Edward Coke, greatest of English lawyers.

From the middle of the century there came about a striking revival of strength in the Common Law. The vitality of the Common Law reflected the vitality of the English people. Its renewal was not so much due to a new formulation — that came rather as a consequence; it was rather an upsurge from the sea of social life: this was the law of the people administered in hundreds of courts all over the land. It was the Common Law that ruled in local life, its rules and processes that were decisive in local administration. All the same it needed bringing up to date, it needed expansion and refinement. This process called forth the energies of a remarkable series of great lawyers, who distinguished Elizabeth's reign by contrast with Henry VIII's. The new use of the Civil Law was gradually absorbed, a fertilising influence from which the Common Law emerged capable of meeting the needs of the most efficient State and the most active people in Europe.

The law dispensed at court leet and court baron, at sessions and assizes throughout the land, concentrated upon the High Courts of Justice at Westminster. There they had their place in Westminster Hall, as they had right up into the reign of Queen Victoria. At the entry on the right-hand side was the Common Pleas, " where civil matters are to be pleaded, specially such as touch lands or contracts. At the upper end of the hall, on the

[1] His point was that the Civil Law doctors were advocates and their interpretations in a manner private ones. But his expositions were based on resolutions of judges reported and were therefore *Regula*: Proeme to Second Part of the *Institutes* (ed. 1670).

right hand, the King's Bench, where pleas of the Crown have their place" — both civil and, still more, criminal actions.[1] In previous centuries Common Pleas was much the busier of the two courts; in our period King's Bench was attracting more business to itself, until in the seventeenth century it got the major portion of civil business.[2] On the left hand at the upper end was Chancery, where the Lord Chancellor sat, accompanied by the Master of the Rolls. No place to go into the organisation of the courts here: of the three Common Law courts, King's Bench and Common Pleas had each a Lord Chief Justice and three ordinary judges, the Exchequer a Lord Chief Baron and three ordinary barons.[3] Under the Lord Chancellor there were twelve Masters in Chancery, of whom the Master of the Rolls was the head; dear William Lambarde, we remember, was one. To the Masters were referred questions of fact and precedents. There were six Clerks of Chancery, who filed pleadings and acted as solicitors for litigants. Among the Registrars in our time was one Lawrence Washington, Registrar of the court from 1593 to 1619, whose cousin was that other Lawrence Washington of Sulgrave, ancestor of the First President.[4] The Registrar had a house in Knightrider Street in Maidstone, played his part as burgess both on the corporation and in Parliament, and now lies under a stone slab in the church of All Saints there.[5]

Law-terms were four in the year: for centuries they had been fixed so as to avoid seed-time and harvest, and the major festivals of the Church. The vacations amounted to more than half the year. In addition, the judges went on circuit, in general visiting each shire in the South twice a year, to hear and determine cases pending at the Common Law, and for the purpose of gaol delivery. A characteristic development of our period was the rise of the barons of the Exchequer to an equality with the judges of the other two courts: the increase in litigation necessitated their services being used for general judicial purposes. To resolve knotty and disputable points the judges met in Exchequer Chamber, as a kind of court of appeal. This arrangement was given statutory organisation by Acts of 1585 and 1589. We have already seen that the Queen increased the salaries of the judges and improved their treatment. The oath they took was to do justice and not to

[1] Smith, *op. cit.* p. 68.

[2] M. Hastings, *The Court of Common Pleas in 15th-century England*, p. 16.

[3] For salaries, allowances and expenses of the courts *v.* Peck, *Desiderata Curiosa*, I. 51-3.

[4] J. Ritchie, *Reports of Cases decided by Francis Bacon, 1617–1621*, p. vii foll.

[5] *Records of Maidstone* (1926), pp. 34, 35, 38, 56, 67, 133.

delay to do so even though the monarch should command by letters or word of mouth to the contrary. A remarkable degree of independence of the judiciary was built up. Much care was taken over appointing judges — competition for office became acute and standards higher; but after appointment they had practical security of tenure. *Esprit de corps*, competitiveness, the strenuous training they had been through at the Inns of Court, the watchful Argus-eyed atmosphere of the legal community kept them pretty virtuous, if not wholly pure according to our more enlightened ideas. Even in the confusion and uncertainty of the fifteenth century there was only one clear case of a royal dismissal of a judge from office.[1] Not even Henry VIII dismissed a judge; nor did Elizabeth: she kept on Mary's judges, Rastell and Saunders, though they were Catholics. Even with regard to subordinate appointments in the courts, the Crown was very tender of the judges' rights: in the end Elizabeth gave way completely to the judges over Cavendish, a servant of Leicester's whom he wished to foist into the Common Pleas.[2] The judges had refused, and on being summoned before her law officers to hear her case had pleaded their oath to obey the law and reminded her that she was sworn to keep the laws as well as they. Nor were the judges afraid a few years later to make a joint protest against subjects being committed to prison, against the law, at the command of any councillor or nobleman.[3] In these circumstances it made all the more a sensation when James dismissed Coke from the bench: it had a deplorable effect.

Coke began his classic *Institutes* with a tribute to the eminent judges who adorned the bench in his young days and to the Queen who had appointed them: such as Sir Nicholas Bacon and Sir Thomas Bromley in the Chancery, Burghley and Mildmay in Exchequer Chamber, Sir Christopher Wray and Sir John Popham in King's Bench, Sir James Dyer and Sir Edmund Anderson in the Common Pleas, Sir Edward Saunders and Sir Roger Manwood in the Court of the Exchequer. The rugged Coke becomes eloquent when he thinks of the dead Queen, " who now by remembrance thereof since Almighty God gathered her to himself is of greater honour and renown than when she was living in this world ".[4] The unspoken thought was no compliment to James:

[1] Hastings, *op. cit.* p. 94.

[2] *v.* Anderson's *Reports*, p. 154. It is regrettable that there is no reference to this significant case in either Prothero or Tanner's *Documents*; all the more so since Hallam had expounded its significance, *Constitutional History* (Everyman ed.), I. 160-61.

[3] Cf. Hallam, *ibid.* I. 220-21.

[4] Sir Edward Coke, *Institutes of the Laws of England* (ed. 1670), Preface to Part I.

what a world of contrast there was between her and her rival's son!

Let us bring back for a moment some of these vanished figures.[1] Dyer, C.J., belonged to Middle Temple. When called serjeant he gave a ring, the first with a recorded inscription — *Plebs sine lege ruit*: true enough, after the Elizabethan fashion. On the Midland circuit his impartial administration of justice, even though somewhat heavy-handed, was unpopular with the gentry: the J.P.s of Warwickshire complained against him. His *Reports* were lucid and concise, and helped to bridge the gap between the Year Books and the modern reports. But a greater lawyer was Edmund Plowden, whose *Commentaries* was the most important law book, a standard authority, before Coke. Since he was a Catholic, he could hardly be made a judge; he seems to have conformed, like almost all Catholics, until the Papal Bull of 1570 forced too clear a break. After that, Plowden heard Mass privately, often in Lord Browne's house, and his family at Plowden in Shropshire have been Catholics ever since. He remained the leading figure in Middle Temple, and was treasurer when the magnificent hall was begun. Plowden's eminence in Middle Temple enabled him to protect Catholics there and we hear of it as "pestered with Papists". Nor did the fact interfere with his successful career as an advocate: he triumphantly defended the egregious Bonner against Bishop Horne; he was successful as counsel for the Dean of Westminster in retaining Westminster as a sanctuary for debt. He married the daughter of William Sheldon of Beoley, another Catholic, and he made a fortune, buying estates at Burghfield, Shiplake and elsewhere in Berks and Oxon. He was buried in the Temple church under a Renaissance tomb — himself upon it in lawyer's robes under a coffered alcove, flowers and obelisks and coat of arms — which remained in beautiful preservation until the late barbarism fell on London.[2] In the preface to his *Reports*, dedicated to students of the Common Law especially his companions of Middle Temple, he tells us that he had collected them for his own instruction, but that all the Common Law judges had asked him to print them.[3] The book contained only cases involving points of law which had been tried and decided, and he had shown his reports to the judges and serjeants who were concerned in them. So these *Reports* "excel

[1] In the following paragraphs I follow the accounts in the *Dict. Nat. Biog.* except where otherwise stated.

[2] *Roy. Com. on Hist. Monuments: London,* vol. IV. plate 188.

[3] Plowden's *Reports* (ed. 1761), pp. iv-v.

any former book of Reports in point of credit and authority ". No Elizabethan thought it worth while to write himself down. Plowden's *Reports* were the most elaborate and the most methodical yet reproduced; they became an indispensable text-book. One can see the importance they would have at this moment of expansion, of growing opportunity and confidence, of need for definition, of the Common Law.

Anderson, C.J., who was of Scots descent, was a quick worker, but harsh and brutal in manner. At the trial of the Essex conspirators he bullied both Cuffe, Essex's secretary, who was being prosecuted, and Coke, the Attorney-General, who was prosecuting. He was especially severe on religious sectaries, who, it must be admitted, deserved it more than most. Yet he had certain qualities of the great judge: he was even more independent than Coke; it was he who stood up to Leicester over the Cavendish case and drew up the protest of the judges against arbitrary imprisonment. He came down strongly against a Puritan mayor of Leicester for imprisoning a man for setting up maypoles: the Puritans considered this a pagan survival. One finds the judge's action congenial. At the age of seventy-two, while on circuit in Somerset, confronted with a disturbance, he snatched a sword from a man-at-arms, laid about him and quelled it. A man of spirit, he gave judgment according to reason; if he considered there were no reason in the old books, he threw them over. He made a large fortune, multiplying many times the thousand pounds inherited from his father. He lived in some state at Harefield Place in Middlesex and Eyworth in Bedfordshire, where he founded a family whose monuments are in the church, where he lies in effigy in his judge's robes beneath an elaborate tomb.

Sir Roger Manwood rivalled Anderson in severity. He was rigorous against Puritans and was in favour of punishing those who spoke against the Queen " with all extremity of irons and other strait feeding and keeping ", or by burning in the face or tongue, or by public exposure " with jaws gagged in painful manner " or rooting out the tongue.[1] One must, of course, judge that in the environment of the time: breaking on the wheel was a common punishment abroad. As a young man at the Inner Temple he played the part of the Lord Chief Baron in the masque " Palaphilos " at the Revels of 1561. In 1578 he became Lord Chief Baron, by the influence of Walsingham. On Dyer's death Manwood offered Burghley a large sum for the office. (One must remember that right up to the Victorian Age, and the reign

[1] For his conduct of Cuthbert Mayne's trial *v.* my *Tudor Cornwall*, pp. 348, 352.

of the middle class, office was regarded as a form of property: the offer to buy, or sell, must be seen in that context.) But Burghley was too virtuous: it was given to Anderson. In 1591 Manwood was censured by the Queen for selling an office in his gift. She had regarded him with favour and given him the manor of St. Stephen's, Canterbury, where he built a magnificent house. Several charges were made against him: they were not necessarily true; but like everybody, in that age, he was acquisitive. He was unrepentant, and was impertinent to the Council in defending himself; after all, there were many perquisites and rights attaching to office: no-one could be too sure of the rights and wrongs. The Council confined him to his house. This did not deter him from offering Burghley 500 marks to be made Chief Justice of King's Bench. Burghley took no notice. Shortly after, Manwood died and was buried under a splendid monument at St. Stephen's. As a man, he had not only face but facetiousness: a good many quips are attributed to him — such as, " In the Common Pleas there is all law and no conscience; in the Queen's Bench both law and conscience; and in the Exchequer neither law nor conscience ". He was a judge in the Exchequer: he would know. Now the interesting thing about this grasping, avaricious judge is that he was a most generous benefactor. Besides the house of correction he built at Canterbury, he gave a peal of bells to St. Stephen's and built the transept chapel in which he was buried. He gave money to augment the living, he built and endowed seven almshouses in the parish and left money to set the poor on work. Above all, he was the chief founder and benefactor of the grammar school at Sandwich; himself the son of a draper, he had a lifelong interest in education and took part in the foundation of the grammar school at Lewisham. Such is the duplicity of life.

A more congenial character was the Queen's last Lord Keeper, Sir Thomas Egerton, Lord Ellesmere. He early won the Queen's favour: it is said that she heard him plead against the Crown. " In my troth he shall never plead against me again ": he was made Solicitor-General and conducted a number of famous prosecutions. Next, Master of the Rolls, he was promoted Lord Keeper in 1596, " The Queen's own choice without any competitor or mediator ". Burghley was not pleased, for Egerton was a friend of Essex. A kindly man, he helped Francis Bacon all he could along the uphill discouraging path of preferment; he worked hard to have him made Attorney-General in 1606. The Queen had absolute confidence in him, and he entertained her sumptuously in the last year of her life at Harefield, which he bought from Anderson. James made him Lord Chancellor and supported him and Chancery against the onslaught of Coke and the Common Lawyers in 1616. As Manwood had been a friend of Archbishop Parker, so Egerton was a friend of Whitgift, a lover of learning and the clergy. A cultivated man, he enjoyed the society of literary men: John Donne was a member of his household and might have gone far if it had not been for the *contre-temps* of his marriage; Ben Jonson and Samuel Daniel, to whom he had been good, praised him. His widow survived him at Harefield, where Milton's *Arcades* was presented before her. Ellesmere and she began the great Bridgewater Library. He left behind him a great mass of papers — now in the Huntington Library — and the nucleus of the enormous Ellesmere fortune.

Even these careers are put in the shade by the fantastically long and important, the epoch-making, career of Sir Edward Coke: the central figure in the history of English law. Most of it falls, in any detail, beyond our scope; but its general import has to be estimated. Born in 1552, he was entirely an Elizabethan; yet he lived to take a leading part in Parliament against Charles I. The alliance of the Common Law with Parliament, both expressing the interests and outlook of the gentry and yet vehicles of the liberties of the people, was incarnate in him. Nor was that all: in his immense literary work, single-handed he surveyed the whole field of our medieval law, public and private, criminal and constitutional, brought it up to date and adapted it to modern conditions. He is the great figure of the transition: he harmonised the medieval doctrines that formed the basis of the Common Law so that they were fit to go forward into the uncharted future and take the strain of the unborn societies across the seas. His great rival, Francis Bacon, was haunted by the idea of a new re-statement of English law, a kind of codification on general principles. But it was Coke who achieved it on the opposite lines of adhering to custom and case-made law, following the facts and their implications instead of imposing a theory on them and making them fit. Though a far less subtle mind, it was a subtler way. He was very English and essentially historical, not philosophical, in outlook. "But the historical lawyer preserves the ideas of past ages; and these ideas often come into their own again in a future age. Coke's writings preserved for England the medieval idea of the supremacy of the law." [1] It was he who was in keeping with the forces and characteristics innate in

[1] Holdsworth, *op. cit.* V. 480.

English society and therefore exerted a prodigious influence on it; the mere ideas of the man of genius that Bacon was were without effect.

Over most of their careers they were in curious and pleasing antithesis. Both were East Anglians, those tough litigious countrymen who were said to carry Littleton's *Tenures* at the plough-tail. (Soon it was to be Coke upon Littleton, several volumes of it.) Bacon was born in the purple of the law, son of the Lord Keeper, the favoured child of Gray's Inn; Coke was the great man at the Inner Temple. Bacon was nine years younger; but he got less than no help towards his advancement from his uncle Burghley, who was jealous for his son Robert and probably disapproved of the young man's ways. The old man took Coke under his wing and pushed him for all he was worth. It was Coke, and not Bacon, who got the Attorney-generalship in 1594; Bacon could not even get the second place as Solicitor-General. Coke had married a Paston heiress with £30,000; she further enriched him with ten children. Bacon, though willing to marry an heiress, preferred the company of stable-boys and, not unnaturally, had no children. On the death of Coke's wife, there was great rivalry between them for the hand, or rather the fortune, of Burghley's granddaughter, Lady Hatton, who had the attraction of being exceedingly rich. Coke, who was very handsome, won the prize, though the marriage ceremony of the great lawyer was clandestine and doubtfully legal. Bacon was well out of it, for she turned out a tartar and gave Coke nothing but trouble. When, years later, he wanted to marry his daughter he had to carry her off by force from her mother; Bacon supported the Lady Hatton in the matter — but it was he who got ticked off by the king. On the other hand, James was much more sympathetic to Bacon, and gave him the high office his abilities merited. It was by Bacon's advice that Coke was kicked upstairs from being Chief Justice of the Common Pleas, where he was too popular and opposed the king's interests, to the King's Bench where he might be expected to defend them. "My Lord Coke", Bacon advised, "will think himself near a Privy Councillor's place, and thereupon turn obsequious."[1] Never was subtle calculation more misplaced, and Coke guessed to whose advice he owed his remove. His place was taken by another East Anglian, Hobart, the builder of Blickling, whose melancholy Puritan visage looks down still upon the splendours of that palace.

In his new place Coke proved himself more intractable than

[1] *The Life and Letters of Francis Bacon* (ed. J. Spedding), IV. 381.

ever, and his arrogant self-confidence brought about his downfall, for he had no friends outside the Common Lawyers. All his professional life he had pushed the claims of the Common Law to be supreme and restrict the activities of other courts, and he was an arrant bully. He surpassed even the standards of the time in his monstrous conduct towards the prisoners in the trials of Essex and Ralegh. Bacon was above this crudity of behaviour; he behaved with courtesy, even when he was being false; he was an intriguer — but then so was everybody else; his transcendent powers of mind had gone long unrewarded and he was desperate for preferment. Coke's arrogance played into Bacon's hands: from the King's Bench he proceeded to attack the Court of Chancery and challenge its jurisdiction: the Common Law should be supreme: he was its prophet. The king upheld the Lord Chancellor, Ellesmere. On his death the lawyers would have liked Coke to succeed. Bacon, in a letter to the king, stated all the objections to the appointment of Coke, erasing the words that spoke his inner mind: "who I think in my mouth the best choice". Instead, upon further evidence of intractability and opposition to the king's wishes, Coke was dismissed from office. Coke's fall coincided with Bacon's triumph: in quick succession he became all that he had so long desired, Privy Councillor, Lord Keeper, Lord Chancellor, a peer. He had come into port. But not for long. After only four years of highest office charges of bribery were made against him and sustained. It does not seem that he was fully aware of their extent: he was generous to his favourites and they took advantage of it to make hay while the sun shone on him. And no-one doubts that the bribes had not affected his judgments: he had given sentence against the givers. But the full extent of the charges was brought home by the committee of investigation, of which Coke was a member. Bacon had no other course but to plead guilty: he was ruined. His enemies did not need to press him any further; "even Sir Edward Coke", says Macaulay, "for the first time in his life behaved like a gentleman".

They make an interesting foil for each other, these two: the one such a great philosophical mind, taking all knowledge for his province, and so missing somewhat of his effect; the other no genius, yet inspired with a devouring passion for the Common Law, sticking to his last and never dispersing his energies, and so achieving the reward of being the greatest single influence there has ever been in the history of our law. Bacon was a man who could be generous, was extravagant, of large ideas, something of a visionary, ambitious, corruptible; Coke was mean, ungenerous, of narrow though long ideas, avaricious, incorruptible. It was the man of genius who was fallible. One of Coke's fellow Templars told him when Attorney that " he was the best cook and licked his fingers best of any cook the Queen had ".[1] He had indeed beautiful hands and they were exceedingly acquisitive: there was the great house at Stoke Poges, all the fifty-eight manors, the vast inheritance of Holkham. " Five sorts of people he used to foredesign to misery and poverty: chemists, monopolisers, concealers, promoters and rhyming poets ", says Fuller.[2] " For three things he would give God solemn thanks: that he never gave his body to physic, nor his heart to cruelty, nor his hand to corruption." As to the last he did not need to: he had well provided against the temptation. " In three things he did much applaud his own success: in his fair fortune with his wife, in his happy study of the laws and in his free coming by all his offices, *nec prece, nec pretio*, neither begging nor bribing for preferment." It may be seen that he had more than his share of Elizabethan smugness; but no Elizabethan objected to that.

Coke's chief works are his *Reports* and his *Institutes.* The former, of which there are thirteen books, were in course of publication from 1600 onwards; they represent a lifetime of practice and observation in the courts. They contain innumerable cases, now famous, in which he had been concerned. The Preface to Book VII gives us some idea of his method: no sooner had he ended Book VI than " the greatest case that ever was argued in Westminster hall [that of the Post-Nati] began to come in question . . . while the matter was recent and fresh in mind and almost yet sounding in the ear, I set down in writing, out of my short observations which I had taken of the effect of every argument (as my manner is and ever hath been) a summary memorial of the principal authorities and reasons of the resolutions of that case ".[3] Book VIII enforces the point that " the grounds of our Common Laws at this day were beyond the memory or register of any beginning " and that the laws William the Conqueror found within this realm were good and ancient laws he swore to observe. One sees the *tendenz* of this. It is followed by a long historical interpretation, Coke's view of the Middle Ages, which is continued in Book IX. Coke's view was extremely tendencious, but the *tendenz* was good: it was all in

[1] *Journal of Sir Roger Wilbraham* (ed. H. S. Scott), *Camden Misc.* X. 13.
[2] T. Fuller, *Worthies of England* (ed. 1811), II. 129.
[3] Coke's *Reports* (ed. 1738), Preface to Book VII.

favour of the supremacy of law in the State and of the liberty of the subject. The Common Law was held up as the safeguard. One cannot doubt that his instinct was right though his history was faulty, inaccurate, one-sided. But there was no-one who could follow him in his vast readings of medieval law. The result was that he was taken for an oracle, both by the lawyers and Parliament, and his reading of the past, of Magna Carta and the rest of it, became of cardinal importance for the future. Bacon, as usual, put his finger on the weakness of the *Reports*, even though he praised them: " those of my Lord Coke's hold too much *de proprio* ". This did not prevent them, in addition to being an indispensable study for generations of students, from having over the ensuing centuries " an intrinsic authority in the courts of justice ".[1]

The *Institutes* are even more important: they provide a complete survey of the whole Common Law. One sees something of Coke's spirit of exclusive personal loyalty in his tributes to the communities with which he had been associated and which continued to honour him: the Inner Temple, Clifford's Inn, Lyon's Inn; the University of Cambridge and especially Trinity College, which he loved; " and to my much honoured and beloved allies and friends of the counties of Norfolk, my dear and native country; and to Suffolk where I passed my middle age; and of Buckinghamshire where in my old age I live. In which counties we out of former collections compiled these Institutes." [2] It too was the work of a lifetime: Coke in the course of his span got through the work of three full lives. The first Book contained his translation and exposition of Littleton, and covered the land law. This was the volume that became famous as Coke upon Littleton and the law student's first text-book. The second Book dealt with Magna Carta and other ancient statutes, citing medieval authors and records never before printed — Bracton, Britton, the *Mirror*, Fleta — no wonder Coke was an oracle, nobody else had been here or could check him. He depended on Lambarde for his Anglo-Saxon laws. The third Book covered treason, pleas of the Crown and criminal cases. Here too the patriotic note is struck: the English language is " as copious and significant and as able to express anything in as few and apt words as any other language that is spoken at this day. And (to speak what we think) we would derive from the Conqueror as little as we could." This theme was to have an extraordinary future, right up to Cobbett

[1] Blackstone, q. *D.N.B. sub* Coke.
[2] Coke's *Institutes* (ed. 1670), Preface to Part I.

and beyond to Robert Blatchford. And in Coke's eloquent praise of the Navy "that doth excel the shipping of all other foreign kings and princes . . . so many large and spacious kingly and princely palaces . . . so many moving and impregnable castles and barbicans termed of old the walls of the Realm" one sees the continuity of the Elizabethan spirit through him with Parliament and the Commonwealth.[1] And indeed he has a chapter "Of the Power and Authority of the Protector and Defender of the Realm . . ." Among the law students in London at this time, reading Coke like everyone else, was the young Oliver Cromwell.

The fourth Book was posthumous. It contained gunpowder and could not be brought out till long after his death. It dealt with the jurisdiction of the courts and made no bones about the supremacy of the Common Law courts: "If one court should usurp or encroach upon another it would introduce incertainty, subvert justice and bring all things in the end to confusion". The assumption was that which he had tried to enforce in practice — and been defeated by Bacon and the king: the Common Law as the arbiter between courts. He declared roundly that the jurisdiction of the Church courts was bounded by the king's laws — he meant the Common Law; and of the Court of Admiralty that its jurisdiction was confined to only things done upon the sea. In the epilogue to the great work the old man at last strikes a note that is congenial: "Whilst we were in hand with these four Parts of the *Institutes*, we often having occasion to go into the city, and from thence into the country, did in some sort envy the state of the honest ploughman and other mechanics; for the one when he was at his work would merrily sing, and the ploughman whistle some self-pleasing tune, and yet their work both proceeded and succeeded. But he that takes upon him to write doth captivate all the faculties and powers both of his mind and body, and must be only intentive to that which he collecteth, without any expression of joy and cheerfulness while he is in his work." At last the old man wins our sympathies — at least those of us who know the labour of writing books as against those who do not.

It was through this unpleasant man, selfish and opinionated, greedy of power and money, rasping and grasping, pedantic and shrewish, for all his good looks crabbed and inaesthetic (he loathed poets), that English liberties were upheld and defended. A less combative, more attractive type would not have stood up so

[1] *Ibid.* Part IV, p. 147.

effectively — as one frequently sees in history. In spite of everything he deserves our admiration. He was always an advocate and had little real justice of mind, far less than Bacon, who had a certain nobility of mind in addition to his genius. But Coke was in tune with the innate sense of his people — what genius was apt to overlook — that the liberty of the subject was something precious, an inalienable possession of the Englishman. Here he was simple and sincere. He alone of them all had the humanity to lament the innumerable hangings: "What a lamentable case it is to see so many Christian men and women strangled on that cursed tree of the gallows; in so much as if in a *large field* a man might see together all the Christians that, but in one year throughout England, came to that untimely and ignominious death, if there were any spark of grace or charity in him, it would make his heart bleed for pity and compassion".[1] Again, when as late as 1611 Archbishop Abbot was set on burning a couple of unfortunate heretics, it was to Coke's credit that he was much averse to it.[2] No doubt it added a spice to Coke's opposition that he was obstructing an Archbishop: he had the ordinary English layman's dislike of bishops and their pretensions. He was, like most of his class, out to get the Church under.

Coke's later career under James and Charles saw the conflict fully extended. While Elizabeth lived the equilibrium was held. Dismissed from office, the great Chief Justice — he had been obsequious enough in Elizabeth's day as her Attorney-General — came out as a political leader in open opposition to James and Charles. His last important work was in drafting the Petition of Right. But it was the campaign in and through Parliament that gave the Common Law its position in the English State: they were the two wings in the battlefront of gentry and middle class and they won at the centre. There is no doubt that the English monarchy was not an arbitrary one; the phrase 'Tudor Despotism' is quite contrary to the truth: it was a monarchy subject to the law and operated through law. The Tudors never justified their prerogative by a theory of absolutism — not even Henry VIII;[3] only James and Charles were fools enough, or un-English enough, to do that. It was fashionable abroad; but it did not go down here. The Tudors, with their infallible political sense, never put forward the prerogative as above or outside the law; it was always there, held in reserve for exceptional cases, in time

[1] q. in *Shakespeare's England*, I. 398.
[2] *Egerton Papers* (ed. J. P. Collier), pp. 447-8.
[3] F. le V. Baumer, *Early Tudor Theory of Kingship*, pp. 178-9.

of danger and emergency — and as such was sanctioned by the Common Law.

The position is implicit in the facts and the actual record of Elizabeth's reign. It is stated perfectly clearly in an interesting book that came out in the first year of it: John Aylmer's *An Harbour for True Faithful Subjects*, which was a reply to Knox's unforgivable (and unforgiven) *First Blast of the Trumpet against the Monstrous Regiment of Women.*[1] Aylmer states: " The regiment of England is not a mere monarchy, as some for lack of consideration think, nor a mere oligarchy, nor democracy, but a rule mixed of all these, wherein each one of these have or should have like authority ". He uses this to defend the rule of the Queen: " for first it is not she that ruleth but the laws, the executors whereof be her judges, her Justices of the Peace and such other officers ". He rests the defence of the Common Law on the best possible ground: " our law must direct us because it best agreeth with our country ". He recognised fairly that it has some disadvantages compared with the Civil Law, is in some ways inferior. The latter condemned no man unless he confessed his guilt, and so was driven to use torture to extract it — often wrongly. Whereas English law relied on the sense of the country expressed in the verdict of a jury: " Twelve men being indwellers in the country and men of skill shall learn by the circumstances as by the life of the man, the common fame of the people or their own search in the matter, whether he be such a one or no, and so without racking, wresting and tormenting the deed may be found ".

It was this that made contemporary Englishmen proud of their law — especially when they were abroad and could compare it with other peoples'. It was answerable to the nature of our people and the character of our society. There was a rough common sense and a sort of popular fairness in the institution of the jury: they were selected from the local community in the best position to know the facts; as against its obvious dangers of bias and prejudice, it was an institution profoundly educative of the community. And Sir Thomas Smith makes it clear that putting pressure on a jury was " accounted very violent, tyrannical and contrary to the liberty and custom of the realm of England ".[2] He has an interesting passage that reveals the social background of the institution. Writs of attaint to question the verdict of a jury " be very seldom put in use, partly because the gentlemen will not meet to slander and deface the honest yeomen their

[1] Perhaps I should say that the word regiment = regimen, or rule.

[2] Smith, *op. cit.* pp. 110-11.

neighbours". They would rather pay the fine and not appear to put their lesser neighbours out of countenance. "And if the gentlemen do appear, gladlier they will confirm the first sentence, for the causes which I have said, than go against it." So English society held together, in a comfortable spirit of neighbourliness.

Smith noted, with contemporary France before his eyes, that there were fewer punishments in England — and we know how many there were! "Heading, tormenting, demembering, either arm or leg, breaking upon the wheel, impaling and such cruel torments as be used in other nations by the order of their law, we have not: and yet as few murders committed as any where."[1] In England, beheading, which has made such a disproportionate impression on the popular mind, was reserved for great personages guilty of treason: it was rather a privilege of their class. And, indeed, Harrison notices that there was a certain class rationale in trial and punishments.[2] Smith expounds and rationalises the English objection to torture: "For what can he serve the commonwealth after as a free man, who hath his body so haled and tormented, if he be not found guilty, and what amends can be made him? . . . The nature of Englishmen is to neglect death, to abide no torment. . . . In no place shall you see malefactors go more constantly, more assuredly and with less lamentation to their death than in England. . . . The nature of our nation is free, stout, haught, prodigal of life and blood: but contumely, beatings, servitude and servile torment and punishment it will not abide. So in this nature and fashion, our ancient princes and legislators have nourished them, as to make them stout-hearted, courageous and soldiers, not villeins and slaves; and that is the scope almost of all our policy."

The exacerbation of the conflict in Europe, the relentless forward drive of the Counter-Reformation, the resistance of the Protestants driven on the defensive but reacting militantly, aggressively — forced the government here in self-defence to resort to weapons in themselves unpopular and alien. The underground campaign of Jesuits and seminaries directed from Rome had to be met by underground, as well as overt, methods. It was extremely difficult to deal with: under the guise of religion, and quite genuinely, they were sapping allegiance. In the acute circumstances of a struggle for survival against Spain they formed, willingly or unwillingly, a Fifth Column. The government was forced, much against its will, to employ continental methods of torture against the most dangerous, the most unyielding and

[1] Smith, *op. cit.* pp. 104-6. [2] Cf. Harrison, *op. cit.* p. 239.

political of them. The anguished conflict of loyalties all this led to within individual hearts and consciences — too familiar in the similar circumstances of our own tragic epoch — will be dealt with in the following chapter. But that the resort to torture, the rackings in the Tower, were alien to the English tradition as they were foreign to the Common Law, is clear from the defence of the government's acts Burghley thought necessary to issue at the height of the conflict in 1583: three years after the first Jesuit mission, two years from open war with Spain.[1] It is an extremely effective, indeed unanswerable, statement. He cites the gentleness with which Elizabeth had dealt with her opponents by contrast with Mary's burnings, until with the Bull of 1570 her position as Queen was denied and her subjects absolved from allegiance. Burghley enumerates the opinions for which these men were tortured, and many died: that Elizabeth was not the lawful Queen of England; that all her subjects were discharged of their oaths and obedience; that all were warranted to disobey and conspire against her rule. There is no doubt that those who adhered to such a position were traitors; no government in Europe would have tolerated it; no government could tolerate it unless it were to abdicate. One can appreciate the tragedy of a riven and divided Europe: killing, murder, torture was no way to close it. It is impossible for the historian to sympathise with lunatic human conflicts for power in the guise of opinion. Elizabeth's government was forced to cruel measures in defending itself; but oh the human tragedy of the necessity for it!

[1] "The Execution of Justice in England", *Harleian Miscellany* (ed. 1808), I. 489 foll

CHAPTER X

THE CHURCH

HOW to do justice to the theme of the Church in the space of a chapter? For at that time the Church was almost one-half of society; or if not a half, it was society as a whole, regarded, at least in relation to end and intention, in one aspect — the non-temporal.[1] And yet it springs out of the temporal, is conditioned at every point by it, given its character by it — for the religious organisation of a people but expresses its social and economic character. We can recognise readily enough that the constitution of the Elizabethan Church represented that blessed balance between Crown and gentry that made for the success of the age. The natural expression of the interests of the gentry would probably, left to themselves, have been Presbyterian; certainly their tendencies were more Protestant than suited the monarchy, which had in episcopal organisation an indispensable support for its own position in society. " No bishop, no king ", said James. He knew: he had had it in Scotland at the hands of impertinent presbyters. Elizabeth did not say it; she was no don: she acted on it. The Church of England, then, reflected the Elizabethan equilibrium in society that was broken in the next age by the social shift going on underneath. Something of the conflicts that raged round and within it, something of the stresses and strains that bade fair at times to split its structure, was due to this.

It is not my purpose to write a narrative of these events. There are many such church-histories already — mostly written from some particular sectarian point of view. My own, like Maitland's, is that of a dissenter from all the sects:[2] I subscribe to none of their *partis pris*. Looking at them from the outside should at least give one the advantage of some objectivity. The high themes of their beliefs are not here my aim; I prefer the lower,

[1] Cf. R. Hooker, *Works* (ed. Keble, Church and Paget), I. 273: " The Church being a supernatural society doth differ from natural societies in this, that the persons unto whom we associate ourselves, in the one are men simply considered as men, but they to whom we be joined in the other are God, angels and holy men ".

[2] F. W. Maitland, *Roman Canon Law in the Church of England*, p. vi.

the more intimate, to ferret out the secret, to reveal the life beneath the documents, the passions behind the formularies, the human beings enclosed within the institutions. The thirst for life leads one into these dusty records, the more poignant and strangely satisfying because it is the lives of men dead these hundreds of years, whose eyes we yet look into — and find ourselves.

Then, too, this way we avoid much of the endless, the sterile and stultifying, conflicts of doctrine and theory, of what men think they think: one attaches less importance to their notions than to themselves. The men are more important than what they suppose.

The background, or rather the ground-swell, of our subject is the tragic human inability we know so well — and recognise so sickeningly in our own time — to bring about necessary and desirable reform without conflict, destruction and mutual killings on the grand scale. The record of man, as the historian knows, is not the record of man's sin (a concept which has no meaning apart from a superfluous hypothesis), but of man's, or rather of most men's, ineffable stupidity, irrationality and foolery — " the crimes, follies and absurdities of mankind ". The sixteenth century is full of the endless fooleries of disputes about doctrine, even more senseless — since they were largely over things by definition unknowable — than those of Marxism in our own time. Flesh and blood can hardly now stand the reading of them: no wonder the Scottish divines of the next century cost Buckle a paralysis of the brain. No-one who does not know the literature of the time would believe the whole libraries written for and against transubstantiation, for and against the presence of Christ in the sacrament of the eucharist, the precise nature of the presence, whether local or general, whether a sacrifice or merely commemorative or what not. There are similar libraries of controversy about other doctrines — and the amenities of these controversies, the rudeness, the grossness, the vulgarity, the obscenities! — when all this intellectual energy might have gone into channels that were remunerative: to understand and increase our control over Nature, to learn about human psychology and the problems of society, to alleviate human suffering instead of adding to it. It makes one sympathise all the more deeply with Elizabeth's Laodiceanism: like all the truly intelligent and humane in her time, she was a *politique*. Whether she wrote the well-known lines or not, they speak for her.

> Christ was the word that spake it,
> He took the bread and brake it;

And what his words did make it
That I believe and take it.

Creighton comments: "It was a saying the theological truth of which has become more apparent as controversy on the point has progressed".[1] He was a bishop: he should know.

The Church of England is so characteristically English that it has been little understood on the Continent. Naturally enough both Catholics and Puritans have been better appreciated, since they have their European affiliations. The Anglican case historically has been allowed to go rather by default. And yet it is the Church of England that carries the character of the English people and is more difficult — perhaps also more rewarding — to understand. It chose the middle of the road, it stood for comprehensiveness, within its external framework for greater tolerance and forbearance; it was far less persecuting than Rome was or the Puritans revealed themselves to be when they had the chance; it was gentler and kindlier, like the English people themselves. This essential character may be seen coming through the troubles, the disturbances, the *fracas* made by fanatics in the course of the Queen's reign.

But it is a mistake to think of the Church in too negative terms as merely concerned with avoiding either one extreme or the other: the disadvantage of too great a stress on the *via media*. There was a positive intention in the Tudor conception of an English national Church which may be seen developing from Cranmer through Jewel to Hooker intellectually, and administratively from Cranmer again through Parker to Whitgift: with Whitgift on one side and Hooker on the other its essential character and ethos become established.

It is curious to think that but for the dreadful accident of being burned by Mary, Cranmer would have lived on to be Elizabeth's Archbishop, a figure symbolising the continuity from Henry and Edward. Cranmer was Elizabeth's godfather, chaplain to her mother, like Matthew Parker after him. They all belonged to the Edwardian circle whose rule Elizabeth's accession perpetuated. Mary's was for them but a disagreeable and dangerous interlude. Cranmer was its martyr: the Elizabethans looked on him as such and as a saint of the Church. He was a very fallible and human saint — all the more congenial for that. A Cambridge scholar, he was not made for high politics: he was all gentleness and humility, with a certain temporising quality that

[1] M. Creighton, *Queen Elizabeth*, p. 37.

increases one's respect for him. He bequeathed something of this spirit to the Church for which he died; his inner soul may be read in the prayers he composed for it. His very weakness and shrinking from the fire increased people's feeling for him — it was all so human: the pathetic figure in Bocardo, the stripping off of his vestments and degradation at Christ Church, the last stand in St. Mary's, his coming to the fire and holding out his right hand that did offend, an ageing man white-bearded and " sore broken in studies ". That was the kind of thing that burnt itself upon the mind of the English people and reversed Mary's régime for ever. Like many moderate men caught in the course of a revolution, he found that he reaped the whirlwind — we can only sympathise the more. When young, men are too ignorant of life to know, but it is astonishing that they should not have the imagination, or the knowledge of history, to tell them what always happens.

Scant justice has been done the Elizabethan Church. Attacked from both sides, Catholic and Protestant, it has come in for more criticism, and that criticism has made more noise, than was ever warranted. As over enclosures in agrarian history, far too much attention has been paid to the critic. What was vastly more important, as with the land the slow working of innumerable processes of custom and habit, so with the Church: people hear the tiresome, unjust voices of the critics and forget the infinitely larger area of life that is covered, the complex organisation, the burden of work and toil, the patience and sense of duty, the piety and pastoral care of unnumbered officers — bishops, clergy, clerks, churchwardens — which gave the people a rule of life. So too, subsequently, the Elizabethan Church has come in for attacks from Left and Right, from Catholic and Socialist writers, from the clever who make fun of the Elizabethan bishops and their troubles. Few historians have even tried to be just, certainly not Macaulay or Froude, not to mention the lesser crowd of pseudo-historians. Even Frere speaks of " the corrupt character of the episcopate of the day ",[1] and Archbishop Lang had a low view of his Elizabethan predecessors at York. This is mistaken: I do not know a single Elizabethan bishop who was a bad man. Some were failures, some muddled; if several of them founded families on a modest scale, what was wrong in that? The great majority of them were conscientious hard-working men struggling in difficult circumstances with a heavy burden of administrative toil.

What emerges from a serious study of the Church in detail,

[1] W. H. Frere, *Visitation Articles and Injunctions*, I. 168.

the detail of life with its vexatious problems, its efforts and failures, is that the Elizabethan Church was, as human institutions go, a success; an unexpectedly great success in the end. Through the cautious humble spirit of Hooker there gleams for one single moment a careful qualified pride — as far as any such emotion was permitted to so delicate a conscience — in the achievement of the English Church by the end of the reign, especially as compared (he compares it) with the far less satisfactory state of affairs in France or Scotland — or for that matter in the Low Countries or Germany, Italy or Spain.

What, in the first place, did the Elizabethan settlement achieve? The maximum amount of unity for the English people that could be combined with probably the greatest amount of liberty of opinion that was possible in the circumstances. On both extremes there were fools (or knaves) arguing for their own idea of liberty, Catholic or Puritan — each wishing, of course, to impose it on the other. Nothing more boring in history than men's identification of universal good with their own interests. Elizabeth made it clear that she did not wish to interfere with men's inner convictions: it was her duty to maintain an external order, in the interests of society, if only to prevent men from persecuting each other. Naturally that meant a diminution of enjoyment for some, since some men like persecuting, others being persecuted. For one man who is prepared to die for his convictions — often enough when no-one has asked him to — there are a score who will kill for theirs. The two sides are interchangeable: one does not respect either; nor did Elizabeth: she liked those who knew how to live. There was, no doubt, greater unity achieved in Spain and Italy. But at what a cost! — no liberty of thought at all: the Inquisition burned out all dissent, with the consequences to be expected in intellectual stultification, in moral and political decline for those countries.

In England, Catholicism did at least survive, and not insignificantly. The same religion that burned Protestants in *autos-da-fé* in Spain and Italy, and killed thousands in Alva's persecution in the Netherlands, was allowed a certain quiet latitude in England, in characteristic English fashion, provided it was discreet and did not flaunt itself. Every county had its Recusants, numerous in Lancashire, Cheshire, Yorkshire. There were Catholics in position at Court: the organist of the chapel royal was one, William Byrd. It was a privilege of noblemen not to have to take the oaths and not to be interfered with in religion, and a number of the gentry maintained their private chaplains.

But the rule of *general* observance was strictly pressed and the national Church included the great bulk of the English people in its discipline and rule.

It is no less right that we should do justice to that discipline. A great deal of effort and hard work went into its administration. The working system of the medieval Church went on, in some respects tightened up and made stricter. Where a great deal of energy and wealth had been dissipated in unproductive ways — a vast number of people, far too many, in holy orders, innumerable rites and ceremonies, saints' days and ringing of bells, consecrations of holy oils, of every blessed thing — clerical energy was now employed more efficiently. The Reformation meant an immense simplification, a cutting out of dead wood such as all societies need periodically: all the more energy for the expansive energies. The bishops were no longer absentees as they had been — great officers of State kept away long years from their dioceses ruling the country. Here was a great difference. The Church no longer ran the country: the country ruled the Church. No longer — save for the two Archbishops and the bishops of Durham, London, Winchester — on a par with the greater nobles, reduced to the more modest level of the country gentry, the bishops were yet not without honour and position, and they were full-time at their job. The medieval bishops in their dioceses had been much employed by government: they were on all kinds of commissions. This continued, and as the work of secular administration increased with the war so did the burden upon the bishops: they became hard-worked civil servants. The penitential system was more effectively enforced right into the seventeenth century, as one can see from the extant proceedings of the Archdeacons' and other courts. Gradually the bishops got their dioceses into order and improved the condition of the parish clergy. The changes of the last two decades had to be made good and routine once more established on a basis that was largely the old one, as it affected the bulk of people, though with a new inflection. One can see something of this in the transition from the old Latin service books to the Prayer Book: from the idea of sacrifice for the quick and the dead and the life of the world to come to the needs of this world.[1] A more useful emphasis: after the jolts and changes of direction, the discomforts and ardours of a religious revolution, the English people were settling down to profit by a Reformation which — so like them! — kept more than with any other people to the old ways.

[1] Cf. J. Dowden, *Further Studies in the Prayer Book*, p. 300.

Underneath the chops and changes there was more continuity than might be supposed from reading history in terms of political narrative. A better guide is to go into the churches and observe how many clergy continued in their parishes. The major disturbance was Mary's reign, which temporarily arrested the momentum set towards reform; after that it resumed control again, but Elizabeth's government held it in bounds, tried to moderate it so that its impetus was driven underground — to emerge again stronger than ever with the Puritan Revolution. Mary's reign meant an immense upheaval for the clergy, the deprivation of many hundreds of them for marriage: so many, indeed, that they had to be used elsewhere and, on putting their wives away, were transferred to other livings. Under Elizabeth they came back to their old parishes, or stayed where they were; there was nothing like such a general post. The new disturbance was severe enough, but it was greatest at the centre and at the diocesan centres, the cathedral cities. Naturally the intelligent and the conscious, people forced to commit themselves, were more upset than the simple, ordinary creatures of habit. The leadership was what was changed. Mary's reign was a watershed, if the expression be not too inappropriate; her bishops could hardly deny the position for which they had burned — others. So there was a new episcopate. It looks as if Elizabeth's government was rather surprised by the virtual unanimity of the refusals at the top — they entertained hopes of Tunstall, for example: after all, he had conformed with the previous breach with Rome; most of them had. But it was an advantage in that it made way for a new alternative leadership. The country was thereby committed. The Queen, naturally rather conservative and wishing to stand above factions, was no doubt disappointed. She might have wished Archbishop Heath to continue — he was no burner; and she always treated him with respect and kindness in his retirement. Still, he could not have given, even if he could have followed, the desired lead. As for Bonner, Elizabeth's government could not have continued him in his see, even if he had gone over. It was noticed that, on her entry into London, Elizabeth withdrew her hand when he knelt to kiss it. His very name was loathed by the Londoners — though this, as we have seen, did not prevent him from getting justice in his dispute with Bishop Horne, the Catholic Plowden acting as his counsel.

We have to begin then with the overwhelming defeat, the collapse, of Mary's régime. It would simply not have been possible to go on with it: the country could not have been carried.

True enough that the bulk of the people could, and two-thirds of them may have been Catholic, as the Spanish ambassador estimated;[1] but they did not matter. It was the leadership that counted, and they could not have been carried, even if Elizabeth and Cecil had wished it so; in fact they belonged to it. The most active and energetic elements in the leading areas of East, Midlands and South — gentry, towns, but, above all, London — were pushing forward; they had always regarded Mary as a temporary aberration: the proper momentum of society, which had been held up for a bit — heroically perhaps, but in the end unavailingly — resumed its control. Back from exile flooded the religious refugees, the Edwardians, to give the movement intellectual direction, to preach and stir up the people — among them Foxe, whose *Book of Martyrs* was the great propaganda work of the time. Elizabeth's reception by London was such as to surprise even her friends and to force the pace of change. When Parliament met there was an undoubted Protestant majority in the Commons, pushing the government forward. Perhaps already there was a Puritan nucleus, and as the years went on the Commons became more and more Puritan. The whole development of the age bears the impress of an irresistible impetus. The problem of the government — of any government, since no government can cut itself off from its own basis of support — was to keep in with it and keep it within bounds. The latter of these two objectives was as much as Elizabeth could aim at, and even in that she was not wholly successful, as we shall see.

Nothing is more obvious than the weakness of the Marian remnants: the bishops and their sympathisers among the old nobility were isolated. Mary's circle had been prematurely old, sickly and failing: the Queen herself, her cousin the Cardinal, Bishop Gardiner, her friend and bed-mate the Marchioness of Exeter, even the young Earl of Devon and the promising James Basset — all were gone. This was the new deal, in the hands of the young and hopeful. The Spanish ambassador wrote to Philip: "What can be expected from a country governed by a Queen, and she a young lass who, although sharp, is without prudence? . . . The kingdom is entirely in the hands of young folks, heretics and traitors."[2] It is delicious to observe the incomprehension of this really stupid Spaniard, to watch his eyes growing rounder day by day. On Mary's death: "It is very early yet to talk about marriage; the confusion and ineptitude

[1] W. H. Frere, *History of the English Church in the Reigns of Elizabeth and James I*, p. 15.
[2] *Cal. S.P. Spanish, 1558–1567*, pp. 1-10, 22-6, 37, 62.

of these people in all their affairs make it necessary for us to be the more circumspect. . . . Your Majesty understands better than I how important it is that this affair should go through your hands. . . . Everything depends upon the husband this woman may take. . . . Really this country is more fit to be dealt with sword in hand than by cajolery; for there are neither funds nor soldiers, nor heads, nor forces, and yet it is overflowing with every other necessary of life." Of Elizabeth: " She is very much wedded to the people and thinks as they do. . . . The whole of London turned out and received her with great acclamations. They tell me her attitude was more gracious to the common people than to others." A week later: " She seems to me incomparably more feared than her sister and gives her orders and has her way as absolutely as her father did ". De Feria thought " the best thing will be to get my foot into the palace, so as to speak oftener to the Queen as she is a woman who is very fond of argument ".

The result of this was a discussion in which de Feria told her his Majesty had ordered him to beg her to be very careful of religious affairs, as they were what first and principally concerned him. " She answered that it would indeed be bad for her to forget God, who had been so good to her, which appeared to me rather an equivocal reply." It was indeed: she meant all the dangers she had escaped at Mary's hands. Philip decided that the only thing to do was " to place on one side all other considerations which might be urged against it and . . . to render this service to God, and offer to marry the Queen of England ". But she would have to become a Catholic and uphold and maintain Catholicism in England: " She will have to obtain secret absolution from the Pope and the necessary dispensation so that when I marry her she will become a Catholic, which she has not hitherto been. In this way it will be evident and manifest that I am serving the Lord in marrying her and that she has been converted by my act." Apparently God thought not; certainly the Queen of England didn't: she told de Feria that she could not marry the king as she was a heretic. De Feria had another little discussion with her about religion: she said there was very little difference between them, only three or four things in the Mass from which she dissented, and ended the colloquy by saying she hoped to be saved as well as the bishop of Rome. " In Scotland," wrote de Feria, " I believe they are ill-treating the English. I am sure they are not doing it so much as I could wish." Not long after he received his *congé*.

What was the situation as it presented itself to the government? As always, to take a course consistent with its own support, while not letting the forward elements carry it too far out of touch with the backward North and West. At the same time Elizabeth wanted to keep in with Philip abroad and keep his protection against France. With him, therefore, she puts on as Catholic a turn as possible; the candles on her altar are lighted or extinguished, the crucifix appears or disappears, as the political situation demands, in the delightful fashion described by Maitland.[1] Philip rewarded her with his protection; perhaps he was, as a man, relieved at not having to marry her, after his taste of one English queen. He held up the Papal excommunication for years and, when it was at length fulminated, long prevented it from being published in his dominions. As for the Pope, Cecil was of the opinion that they need fear only " evil will, cursing and practising ". Henry had survived all that very well. The way was clear for the government to restore the Edwardian Church system. This was done, when Parliament met early in 1559, by enacting the two fundamental statutes of Supremacy and Uniformity. The first occasioned no difficulty: Rome was more unpopular than ever; national spirit exacerbated by frustration and defeat. The oath of Supremacy, which was to be sworn by all officers in Church and State, had a significant difference: the Queen was not described as Supreme Head of the Church, as her father and brother, and even her sister had been (to her great disgust, for Mary was a simple, pious woman): Elizabeth was described as " Supreme Governor of this realm . . . as well in all spiritual and ecclesiastical things and causes as temporal . . ." It made little practical difference: it was a degree more swallowable by the reluctant, and Elizabeth got all the diplomatic use out of it she could in her representations to Catholic powers, probably with some conviction. Heresy was to be only what had been declared to be so by the authority of the canonical Scriptures, or by any of the first four Councils or any General Council, or such as hereafter shall be determined by Parliament with the assent of the clergy in Convocation. Such was English good sense that these powers did not need to be called on.

The Act of Uniformity, re-enacting the Second Prayer Book of Edward VI, gave much more trouble. It was ultimately passed by a majority of only three in the Lords; it would never have got through if, providentially, a number of sees had not been left vacant by Pole, at the end dispirited, defeated and ill. The

[1] F. W. Maitland, " The Anglican Settlement and the Scottish Reformation ", *Camb. Mod. History*, vol. II; *Cal. S.P. Spanish, 1558–1567*, p. 105.

Spanish ambassador had reason to curse the dead Cardinal. The explanation of the government's difficulties seems to be that the Protestant sentiment of the Commons was driving harder than the government wished; hence the vote of Winchester and six other of the lay Peers who were not Papists, among the large minority who voted against.[1] The government tried to broaden the acceptance of the Prayer Book as widely as possible in the crucial matter of the eucharist, by adding to the words of the Protestant commemorative formula, "Take and eat this in remembrance that Christ died for thee, and feed on Him in thy heart by faith with thanksgiving", the Catholic doctrine of the Real Presence, "The Body of our Lord Jesus Christ which was given for thee, preserve thy body and soul unto everlasting life". Surely no reasonable person could now complain? And, in fact, it reconciled the great body of reasonable persons to the established order; especially over the first decisive eleven years, when issues were left rather unclear, until the excessive clarity of the Papal Bull *Regnans in Excelsis* in 1570 ended Elizabeth's long honeymoon.

The Act further permitted greater latitude with regard to vestments and ornaments by going back to the more Catholic practice of the First Prayer Book of 1549. But this was unimportant compared with the national enactment of attendance at church on Sundays and Holy days on pain of a fine of 12d. for every abstention. This was the beginning of a new policy which became more rigorous as religious conflict grew fiercer later on; the effect of compulsory attendance at church over many generations upon the morale of the nation must have been incalculable. In his speech on the dissolution of Parliament, Lord Keeper Bacon was able to point artfully to "what freedom of speech hath been used and permitted, for the plain declaration of every man's knowledge and conscience . . . and with what nigh and universal consent they [the statutes] have been by you enacted and established".[2] That was a bull's eye for public opinion abroad. The fat Lord Keeper executed a quick turn to public opinion at home: "For now her Majesty verily trusteth that like as no manner of determination in Parliament neither can nor ought by any private man to be infringed or undone . . . so the laws being made and passed her Majesty doubteth nothing but that they will, like good, humble and obedient subjects, willingly and humbly submit themselves to the law as to life". Such were the twin struts of the Elizabethan church-system; nothing much new in essence: a slightly conservative return to

[1] Cf. D'Ewes, *Journal*, p. 30. [2] *Ibid.* pp. 32-4.

what had been interrupted by Edward's premature death. It remained to put the laws in force, to clear up the débris of the old and discarded, to get things into working order on the new revived basis. Now it had come to stay, for, as the Duke of Norfolk reminded the Queen — no doubt unnecessarily: "Let your Highness assure yourself that England can bear no more changes in religion, it hath been bowed so oft that if it should be bent again it would break".[1]

The way of instituting the new order was that of royal visitation and injunction, followed up by diocesan visitations and the establishment of a permanent court of High Commission. Henry's Royal Visitation of 1535 had been a new departure of prime national importance — prelude to the greatest measure of nationalisation ever undertaken in this country, that of the monasteries. Characteristically it had had some precedent in the right of royal visitation of royal peculiars; with the Reformation it was given national extension.[2] (There is an interesting contemporary parallel in France with the Parlement de Paris visiting religious houses.) Immediately following the passing of the Act of Uniformity the Royal Injunctions were issued, dealing with Church order: clerical marriage, though permitted, was discouraged (old prejudices in the country were against it); the clergy were to obtain licence from their bishop and two J.P.s of the shire.[3] (Herein spoke the voice of the Queen, who never reconciled herself to the idea that they should marry at all.) Other articles dealt with the dress of the clergy, conduct of services in church, the removal of altars and the substitution of Communion tables. (Here the Queen gave way: she preferred stone altars.) There followed the appointment of commissioners to visit the dioceses and put the Injunctions into practice. It showed a politic wisdom and a genuine desire for conciliation on the part of the government not to administer the oath of Supremacy pure and simple but a form of general subscription to the religious settlement.[4] The commissioners appointed were almost wholly laymen; it is fairly certain that clerics would not have achieved such moderation.

The government reaped its reward in the overwhelming acceptance of the settlement by the clergy. No doubt it represents in part that exceptional degree of conformity with the require-

[1] H.M.C. *MSS. of the Marquis of Bath*, II. 17.

[2] Frere, *Visitation Articles and Injunctions*, I. 119.

[3] For these in full *v.* H. Gee, *The Elizabethan Clergy, 1558–1564*, p. 46 foll.

[4] *Ibid.* p. 45.

ments of the State that led a French observer to say once that if Henry were to declare Mahomet God the English would accept it. No doubt, too, there was a shift of opinion going on in these years; the world was becoming more modern: as against Mary, Elizabeth had luck — or, as some people would say, Providence — with her. The crisis of 1559, during which the royal visitors went through the country from diocese to diocese, passed without any disturbance: a great contrast with Edward and Mary's changes: the black years were at last over: conciliation and hope were the prevailing mood and actually lasted for a blissful decade. In the event only some 200 clergy were deprived: Camden's figure of 194 is confirmed by modern research. The great upheaval of Mary's reign had affected 1 in 6 of all the benefices of the kingdom.[1] In London 120 beneficed clergy had been deprived in one year only, mostly for marriage; from 1561 to 1564 there were only half the number of deprivations, mostly to make way for Mary's ejected. In the diocese of Gloucester 54 incumbents had been deprived for the offence of matrimony in one year: a greater number than for the whole of Elizabeth's reign for all causes together.[2] So far as the ranks of the clergy were concerned the question of marriage was far more important than doctrine: it had occasioned the great upheaval. Now, though we need not go so far as to say that it "wrecked all chances of success for the Marian reaction", it certainly was a great consideration with the clergy to accept Elizabeth's.

Most of the deprivations for reasons of religion were of dignitaries — bishops, their chancellors and important officials. Even so, there were cathedral chapters where there was hardly any change. At Norwich, for example, only the dean, who made way for the Edwardian dean, John Salisbury, now restored; the four archdeacons and six prebendaries all took the oath.[3] Several of the pre-Reformation monks were still going happily on as minor clergy of the cathedral establishment. At Gloucester there was only one certain deprivation, or at most two, for recusancy. Naturally the greatest changes were at the centre of things, in London, where the chapter of St. Paul's was almost completely reconstituted.[4] "It seems to have been the policy of the government, while taking care to eject very stiff and perverse opponents

[1] Frere, *The Marian Reaction*, pp. 77, 86; and cf. G. Baskerville, "The Married Clergy and Pensioned Religious in Norwich Diocese, 1555", *E.H.R.*, 1933.

[2] G. Baskerville, "Elections to Convocation in the Diocese of Gloucester", *E.H.R.*, 1929, p. 11.

[3] Baskerville, *loc. cit. E.H.R.*, 1933.

[4] Cf. Gee, *op. cit.* pp. 279-80.

of its policy from posts in the universities and cathedrals, to let them go on in subordinate positions."[1] In the country even known opponents were given the benefit of the doubt: Maurice Clennock, though living at the English College at Rome, retained the rectory of Orpington in Kent till 1566; James Hargreaves, rector of Blackburn, though a 'noted Papist', was not deprived till 1562.[2] It was all very wise and well-considered: one sees the cautious, unfaltering hand of Cecil.

Meanwhile the government had taken steps to provide the Church with its new leadership. The exiles came flocking back from abroad. It is notable that those who were made bishops were drawn from the more conservative congregations: Jewel, Parkhurst, Pilkington from Zürich, Sandys and Grindal from Strasburg, Cox, Horne, Berkeley from Frankfort.[3] Of the Genevan group, who underwent the magic influence of Calvin and agreed with John Knox, Whittingham got only a deanery, Goodman and the too celebrated preacher, Lever, nothing at all. Still more notable, the two chosen for the sees of Canterbury and York had never left England, but had remained quietly at home through Mary's persecution. These were Matthew Parker and William May; the latter died on the day of his election to York: too much for him. Parker was exceedingly reluctant to become archbishop or indeed to take on any high office. A shy, retiring Cambridge scholar, bashful of speech and of public appearances, he was no courtier. An accident that had happened by a fall from his horse one night in Mary's reign when escaping from his pursuers brought on a malady — it seems a rupture — that gave him frequent pain. What he liked was the life of the University of Cambridge and scholarship (Wolsey had wanted him, as he had wanted Cranmer, for Christ Church): "Of all places in England I would wish to bestow most my time in the University".[4] He was bidden up to London: he begged to be excused; he did not wish his friends to procure him anything above his ability. He was alarmed at the thought of the archbishopric — as well he might be, considering the times and the fates of Cranmer and Pole. "Put me where ye will else." A resolution was made in the Queen's presence that he was the man. He made a last appeal to the Queen herself, entreating her to discharge him. But Parker had owed his early fortunes to Elizabeth's mother: it

[1] Baskerville, *E.H.R.*, 1929.

[2] *V.C.H. Lancaster*, II. 50.

[3] G. Williams in *Journal of the Hist. Soc. of the Church in Wales* (1947), p. 90.

[4] *Correspondence of Matthew Parker* (ed. J. Bruce and T. G. Perowne, Parker Society), p. 51 foll.

seems that Anne in the last words she ever spoke to him had recommended her daughter to his care.[1] He could not now refuse the Queen. Years later, after varied experiences at her hand, sometimes unjust, often discouraging, he said, "Yea, if I had not been so much bound to the mother, I would not so soon have granted to serve the daughter in this place".[2] He found the archbishopric no bed of roses, but once having submitted, he served her and the Church faithfully to his life's end.

The Church of England owes Matthew Parker a great debt; Elizabeth's advisers, as usual, had made no mistake in fixing on him for the post of prime responsibility. Personally modest and in his views moderate, meticulous and methodical in his ways, he was a fair-minded man, of a simple piety and no dogmatist; an orderly, conscientious administrator by nature, he belonged to the central tradition of the English Church; a man of principle yet broad in his sympathies, firm yet sensitive to the ill-treatment he received — not only at the hands of opponents either — apt to be discouraged at times, but in spite of everything holding on to the end. What consoled his heart was scholarship: there was his inner sanctum; there fanatics ceased to rage, lunatic clergy to torment, the Queen to be unfair. Ensconced among his books, the scholars he kept in his house at Lambeth, writing his book *De Antiquitate Britannicae Ecclesiae* — which he would not publish in his lifetime for his enemies to tear to pieces — he could forget the enemies who had bored holes in his barge to sink him in the Thames. The Queen had placed him in position and then left him to face the wolves; she forced him privately to take measures for which she would give him no open backing if they were unpopular. The Queen's popularity must never be risked: quite right in a way; and yet how intolerable for him, year after year. "Her Majesty told me that I had supreme government ecclesiastical; but what is it to govern cumbered with such subtlety?"[3] He was a plain, blunt, honest, middle-class Englishman; his father a worsted weaver of Norwich, who had left his family comfortably off. A contrast with the frail, refined, princely figure, his predecessor at Lambeth: Reginald Pole, with the blood of Plantagenets in his veins, Cardinal of the Holy Roman Church, of the title of Santa Maria in Cosmedin. The Cardinal's hat and his arms still hung in the cathedral at Canterbury. In this contrast how much there was of the English Reformation.

In Parker's *Correspondence* we grow used to his phrases, almost

[1] Parker's *Correspondence*, p. 400.
[2] *Ibid.* p. 391.
[3] *Ibid.* p. 478.

overhear his voice. He does not " care three chips ", we hear him say, or another time " three points ".[1] He did not like 'Germanical natures' among the returned exiles — understandably enough. Of the Puritans at Norwich there is Johnson " cocking abroad " with his four prebends, as they say, both against statute and his oath.[2] " The world is much given to innovations; never content to stay to live well. In London our fonts must go down, and the brazen eagles, which were ornaments in the chancel and made for lecterns, must be molten to make pots and basins for new fonts. I do but marvel what some men mean, to gratify these puritans railing against themselves. . . ." As for himself, he would love to recover the " great notable written books of my predecessor Dr. Cranmer . . . I would as much rejoice while I am in the country to win them, as I would to restore an old chancel to reparation ".[3] Alas, " the world is full of offences and displeasure contained . . . I may not work against precisians and puritans, though the laws be against them. Know one and know all. . . . Though I have a dull head yet I see, partly by myself and partly by others, how the game goeth."[4] Then at the end, discouraged and ill: " I toy out my time, partly with copying of books, partly in devising ordinances for scholars to help the ministry, partly in genealogies and so forth; for I have little help (if ye knew all) where I thought to have had most ". The Queen had left him to bear the brunt of it all.

There was the work of his diocese, of the province, overseeing its affairs as well as administering those of vacant dioceses, of his position as Archbishop and Metropolitan. Then there were the awful tiffs with the Queen, from which he emerged flustered and bedraggled but not always worsted. There were the crucifix and the lighted tapers in the royal chapel: these things had been abolished by law out of the churches and there was the Queen herself setting the laws at defiance. Everyone pressed the Archbishop to intervene; Knollys, Vice-Chamberlain of the Household (there was still a Knollys in the Household of Edward VII), agitated Parker against " the enormities yet in the Queen's closet retained ".[5] The 'offendicle' was removed. Ten years later, when the Archbishop was not looking, back came the crucifix again — and the Puritans held him responsible for it.[6]

Suddenly, there descended in 1561 the royal order prohibiting women, whether wives or not, from residence in cathedral closes or colleges: a piece of the Queen's own mind.[7] She would have

[1] *Ibid.* p. 475. [2] *Ibid.* p. 450. [3] *Ibid.* p. 186. [4] *Ibid.* pp. 473-4. [5] *Ibid.* p. 97. [6] *Ibid.* p. 379. [7] *Ibid.* pp. 146-61.

gone further: "Her Majesty continueth very evil affected to the state of matrimony in the clergy. And if I were not therein very stiff, her Majesty would utterly and openly condemn and forbid it." Bishop Cox of Ely protested: he was a family man, too much so in the Queen's eye. He had refused to officiate at the Queen's altar, with crucifix and lights; he was rapidly exhausting his credit at that treasury of merit: she was to take it out of him by squeezing several manors out of his see. If their wives were driven out, Cox wrote, deans and prebendaries would cease to reside: "There is but one prebendary continually dwelling with his family in Ely church. Turn him out, doves and owls may dwell there for any continual house-keeping." The Archbishop was carpeted by the Queen, and was shocked by the Henrician language he heard: "I was in a horror to hear such words to come from her mild nature and Christianly learned conscience, as she spake concerning God's holy ordinance and institution of matrimony. I marvelled that our states in that behalf cannot please her Highness. . . . Insomuch that the Queen's Highness expressed to me a repentance that we were thus appointed in office, wishing it had been otherwise." She threatened to follow the matter up with further injunctions. The Archbishop for his part wished that he had never entered on his office and feared he would "rue the time to be the head" when such hourly complaints poured in upon him. He took refuge in writing Cecil all his troubles: "I have neither joy of house, land or name, so abased by my natural sovereign good lady". Cecil and he consoled each other: the Secretary wrote, if it were not for maintaining the Church "before God I this write, I would not contentedly abide in this service, to have a thousand pound a month". This storm blew over: the clergy kept their wives.

He was married himself, to the daughter of a Norfolk gentleman: Margaret Parker was a quiet woman, who kept properly behind the scenes at Lambeth. In the *Correspondence* there are only two references to her. In the account of the Archbishop's household she is referred to as her Grace: a title that failed to establish itself. It is likely that there is something in the celebrated story of Elizabeth's leave-taking from Lambeth once, "Madam I may not call you; mistress I am ashamed to call you, so I know not what to call you; but yet I thank you" — since it comes from Harington and he was likely to know.[1] Parker was deeply downcast by her death in 1570: he survived her five years. His tomb in Lambeth chapel was destroyed by the agreeable

[1] Sir John Harington, *Nugae Antiquae* (ed. 1779), I. 4.

Puritans in the Civil War, his poor old bones thrown out upon a dunghill.

More serious was the struggle to keep the Puritans within bounds, particularly in the diocese of London where Grindal's laxity encouraged them to grow apace. Here the Queen left Parker to his own authority. She upheld his position by visiting him, dined with him to honour him, listened to his representations, sometimes acted on them, often accepted his suggestions for appointments; but when it came to unpopular measures of repression, which she herself urged, she left him to it. "Must I do still all things alone?" he wrote. ". . . I trust her Highness hath devised how it may be performed. I utterly despair therein as of myself, and therefore must sit still . . . alway waiting either her toleration, or else further aid."[1] The result was that "I was well chidden at my prince's hand; but with one ear I heard her hard words, and with the other, and in my conscience and heart, I heard God. And yet her Highness being never so much incensed to be offended with me, the next day coming by Lambeth bridge into the fields, and I according to duty meeting her on the bridge, she gave me her very good looks, and spake secretly in mine ear, that she must needs countenance mine authority before the people, to the credit of my service. Whereat divers of my Arches then being with me marvelled", etc. That was just like Elizabeth: there was something irresistible about her, a touch that reconciled the victim just when he despaired. So she jollied along her bishops, and sometimes jockeyed them on: it was all part of her incomparable technique of getting the most out of everybody for the purposes of government.

Though a Reformer, Parker was always one to uphold authority: a right inflection for the Church of England, a continuing character in its unfolding history. "God keep us from such visitation as Knox have attempted in Scotland: the people to be orderers of things!" he wrote.[2] We know what Knox thought of things in England: "*Among many sins that moved God to plague England* I affirmed that slackness to reform religion, when time and place was granted was one. . . ."[3] (What Knox's phrase meant was *among the many things I did not approve of* . . .) It is amusing to recall the discomfort that even Northumberland complained of at the hand of this fanatic,[4] and not surprising that the Queen would not have him in England at

[1] Parker's *Correspondence*, pp. 279-80, 311. [2] *Ibid.* p. 105.
[3] q. in *Journal of the Hist. Soc. of the Church in Wales*, p. 85.
[4] *Cal. S.P. Dom. 1547–80*, p. 48.

any price.[1] Parker himself was no sycophant: when the Queen demanded the resignation of an unpopular official of his he refused outright.[2] He was not afraid to make representations to her out of his own conscience; he did not wholly follow her in her authoritarian ideas, her affection to govern 'princely'; and though he did not question her own dispensing power, he doubted whether she might pass it on to him: "whereas somebody may say that the bishop of Canterbury may dispense, I think for myself I take some heed not to extend my sleeve beyond mine arm".[3] He was a moderate man: his high position did not move him out of the way of moderation.

He lived at Lambeth in considerable state. The Cardinal had had a patent to retain 100 servants, an Italianate household presided over by Signor Priuli. Parker had a patent for 40 retainers, but he kept a great many more.[4] His household had a chancellor with 3 servants to wait on him, a steward with 2 men and 2 geldings, a treasurer with the same, a controller with one man and a gelding, a chief almoner, a doctor and other chaplains, a chief secretary, and Dr. Drewry, master of the court of Faculties, each with a man-servant. There were gentlemen of the horse, gentlemen ushers, yeomen and grooms of the hall and great chamber, of parlour and chapel, a clerk of the kitchen, a master cook and so on. In the private lodgings lived the Archbishop's family, with sixteen servants. The Archbishop dined publicly in hall thrice weekly, when he entertained persons of quality and called to his table some of the reluctant guests who had been placed on him by the government: Marian officials like Dr. Boxall, or Bishop Thirlby who was his guest for more than ten years, or others committed to him from time to time, like Lord Henry Howard. Parker chose for himself the company of students and antiquaries he delighted in and whom he had always living with him: notably John Joscelin, his Latin secretary and one of the earliest of Anglo-Saxon scholars, who was an invaluable assistant in all Parker's antiquarian enterprises, in collecting and editing manuscripts, publishing medieval chronicles and so on. There was a whole succession of scholars in the house at this work, a number of them afterwards being preferred to bishoprics

[1] Knox on Elizabeth: "And yet is she that now reigneth over them neither good Protestant nor yet resolute Papist". *John Knox's History of the Reformation in Scotland* (ed. W. C. Dickinson), I. 369.

[2] *Registrum Matthei Parker* (ed. W. H. Frere), I. xxii.

[3] Parker's *Correspondence*, p. 351.

[4] Ducarrel, "History and Antiquities of Lambeth" in J. Nichols, *Bibliotheca Topographica Britannica*, vol. II.

or deaneries. The tradition of good scholarship, which has always been so strong in the Anglican Church, was given a noble start by Parker; his munificent benefactions to his Cambridge college, Corpus Christi, are beyond praise: through them alone his fame would endure. The gentry of Kent and Sussex were glad to have their sons brought up in attendance in the Archbishop's household: one sees the function it performed: like Cecil's household, it was a school of virtue.

Parker's Register, the most instructive and complete of Elizabethan episcopal registers — much fuller than Pole's and more orderly than Cranmer's — gives us a window into the administration of the Church at the top. Our dominant impression is that whatever the changes brought about in doctrine and practice, life and habit continued in the old ways. What is remarkable is how much of the old order and routine remained. On Parker's accession Anthony Hussey was still registrar, as he had been for the past twenty years throughout all the changes and chances.[1] The machinery of the Archbishop's courts both as metropolitan and diocesan continued: the Arches dealt with business of the province, the Auditors with less technical, more personal affairs, the Prerogative court with wills from the whole province, the court of Faculties, which gave licences and dispensations, became more important than before since the Archbishop had succeeded to some of the Papal powers in these matters — though carefully hedged by Act of Parliament. In addition there was the consistory court at Canterbury, like any other diocese. It was the privilege of the archdeacon of Canterbury to enthrone bishops of the southern province, as it had been in the Middle Ages and as it still is today. In the vacancy of the see of Canterbury the Dean and Chapter acted; in the vacancy of a see of the southern Province the Archbishop acted. Similarly in the northern Province the Archbishop of York. After the jolts and interruptions of the past two decades the machinery, still intact, was creaking along. Elizabeth's refusal to be Supreme Head of the Church had a certain importance: it meant that the bishops did not look to the Crown as the source of their spiritual jurisdiction. They were not appointed by letters patent as under Edward VI; the old conservative routine of *congé d'élire* was restored: in practice no such matter. With the Reformation, as subsequently in our history, it seems as if the Channel imposed a time-barrier, enabling us to adopt as much as we wanted from abroad and no more.

The regularity of ordinations had gone to pieces in the

[1] *Registrum*, I. xxiv.

dioceses in the years immediately before the Reformation.[1] There were far too many people in orders of one sort or another anyway, as Sir Thomas More thought. The supply, what with the ex-religious and the chantry priests who had settled more usefully into parish life, lasted through the disturbed mid-century. Ordinations had not yet become a regular routine again in the dioceses and Parker provided for a large number to be ordained in London, taking advantage of any of his suffragans who happened to be there to hold them and relieve him.[2] All the formal documents relating to his own appointment and election are there in elaborate detail, the first and second citations of opposers and the replies thereto — purely formal, and yet they gave an opportunity to object, in the English way. There is a careful, circumstantial account of his consecration at Lambeth on the third Sunday in Advent 1559, followed by his enthronement at Canterbury. The Church of England had its active head: the machine could go forward. The administrative record follows the old ruts, like any medieval bishop's register. A good many documents relate to the appointment of other bishops of the Province, with their confirmations at St. Mary-le-Bow, the head church of the Archbishop's peculiar in the City, where they still take place. The bulk consists of institutions to benefices in the diocese, and in others of the Province in the vacancy of the sees. There are the usual licences for schoolmasters to teach, doctors and midwives to practise; dispensations for scholars under age to hold a benefice while at the university — for example in 1570 Scipio Stucley, aged nineteen, was allowed to hold the rectory of Westworlington, provided the cure was served meanwhile.[3] The lad had a certificate from the Queen: he had been presented by Lewis Stucley — that family has always had a good time in presenting its sons to the family livings. The keys of the Church, the power to excommunicate, are still in evidence: there are letters to the Crown requesting the arrest of various persons who have been excommunicated, usually for contumacy. There is one such, of 25 August 1560, to take Thomas Washington, clerk, of Peterborough diocese, for not appearing before the Archbishop's vicar-general when cited and who, though excommunicated publicly in his parish church of Benefield, took no notice for forty days: *claves sancti matris ecclesie* descended upon him according to the old form.[4]

Other entries testify to the changes of the time: a licence is

[1] W. H. Frere, *The Marian Reaction*, p. 102. [2] *Registrum*, p. xxvi.
[3] *Ibid.* I. 318. [4] *Ibid.* p. 352.

granted to pull down the remains of the priory church at Stone to build another aisle on to the chapel there and make it a parish church.[1] The decayed church of Holy Trinity adjoining the north side of Ely cathedral is demolished and the Lady Chapel made into the parish church: a sensible measure which preserved a masterpiece of the early fourteenth century. Licence is given for a disused chapel in the church at Wingham in Kent to be made into a pew and place of burial for the Oxindens, that family which wrote such charming letters in the next century: one notes the continuity of it all, the descendants of William Oxinden sitting there Sunday by Sunday above the coffins of their ancestors, until the family came to an end and the place knew them no more. Many documents relate to Merton and All Souls, of which colleges the Archbishop was Visitor. All Souls was reluctant to hand over its Mass-gear, its vestments, ornaments and Latin service books: Parker had to jog the college twice before it consented to drag them out of their hiding-places. We can trace the career of Robert Hovenden from the day, 10 June 1571, when he was made deacon in Lambeth chapel, by Bishop Jewel of Salisbury; on 28 November he was made priest by Bishop Cooper of Lincoln.[2] In that same month Hovenden was presented to the Archbishop, and admitted, as Warden. Next year Parker considerately collated him to the country rectory of Newington with Britwell at the foot of the Chilterns. There are the tables of fees received by the Archbishop's officials, for absolution, for examination of tithe defaults, decrees, licences, all the things that had made the Church unpopular before the Reformation and were to make it not much less so after. The Church itself has to bear some of the burdens of the State: there are regular returns made to the Exchequer of all preferments in the diocese during the year for payment of First Fruits, and returns of levies upon the clergy for light horse when the war with Spain grew hot. These were made by the bishops in all dioceses: it was part of the regular grind of administration they had to accept, along with so much else.

It is possible to make too much of a contrast between the social origins of the pre-Reformation and post-Reformation episcopate. If the former included Arundels, Courtenays, Bourchiers, it also raised up those eminent founders, William of Wykeham and Richard Foxe, from obscure origins; while Wolsey, who thought himself the equal of kings, popes, emperors, was the

[1] *Ibid.* pp. 456, 431, 1036. [2] *Ibid.* pp. 611, 617, 884-90, 1102.

son of an unsavoury butcher and tavern-keeper of Ipswich. Conversely, a number of Elizabethan ecclesiastics were of gentle birth: Archbishop Sandys, Bishop Pilkington and Nowell, Dean of St. Paul's, all came from the small gentry of Lancashire. Aylmer, Bishop of London, belonged to a family long established at Aylmer hall in Norfolk;[1] Archbishop Bancroft was the son of a Lancashire gentleman and the fortunate great-nephew of a bishop who, being a bachelor, could take an interest in his nephew. The most gentlemanly of them all was dear Bishop Cooper, the Oxford tailor's son, born in Catte Street, upon which I look out as I write: the little houses were demolished to make way for the great quadrangle of All Souls. The bulk of the Elizabethan bishops came from the middle range of society: such people as Whitgift, whose father was a well-to-do merchant of Grimsby; Grindal — his was a good yeoman of St. Bees; Parker's a prosperous worsted weaver, Jewel's a respectable North Devon yeoman. What we can perhaps conclude is that there was less variety in the Elizabethan episcopate: none of the nobility or greater gentry, fewer from the humblest origins: the middle ranks of society were running it.

On the whole, the bishops were a respectable lot, for all that they were traduced by their enemies at the time — the Puritans had a pretty line in personal abuse — and for all that some of the mud has stuck. Let us look at a clutch of them. The bishops of Exeter, my own diocese — which I know best — were good men enough.[2] William Alley, the first of them, was a learned man and an admired preacher: his lectures on the First Epistle of St. Peter, published as the *Poor Men's Library*, was a popular work.[3] Like other officers of the Church he was strong against the occult arts: let there be "some penal, sharp, yea, capital pains for witches, charmers, sorcerers, enchanters and such like".[4] It must not be supposed that his diocese was any more addicted to these arts than any other at that time; the clerical attitude, for all the nonsense that they themselves believed, represented some

[1] It is interesting to observe Aylmer establishing his own family. In 1584–8, a very difficult time for Catholics, he and his son Samuel acquired the manor of Claydon in Suffolk from Sir Robert Southwell of Woodrising, a leading Recusant. They also acquired the manor of Akenham, where Samuel lived — to become high sheriff in 1626. In 1594 he bought the manor of Knight-thorpe, Leics., from the Earl of Huntingdon (*Proc. Suffolk Inst. Arch.* XXIII. 9).

[2] Cf. G. Oliver, *Lives of the Bishops of Exeter*, pp. 138-44.

[3] Alley was a protégé of the Puritan second Earl of Bedford, to whom he dedicated the book. To us it is a nightmare of theological reading and citations on all kinds of themes, *e.g. Bonum mulierem non tangere*: a precept to which he did not adhere. He was married.

[4] q. F. O. White, *Lives of the Elizabethan Bishops*, p. 143.

advance in rationality. The Bishop was merry and accessible, much addicted to bowls and did not lose his temper over the game, as Bishop Aylmer did: one sees him playing in that green and shadowed garden between the cathedral and the city wall. If he made his son archdeacon of Cornwall, what of that? — he may have been as good at the job as anyone else.

His successor, Bradbridge, was not a bad man, though a feeble bishop. He had conformed under Mary; at Exeter, bothered and badgered by Puritans and Papists alike, he gave up the unequal struggle, retired to his living of Newton Ferrers and betook himself to agricultural operations, which prospered no better: he became bankrupt and died £1400 in debt to the Queen. This was quite easy: if a bishop did not hold on to his see long enough, especially if it was a poor one, he could not raise the money to pay back the Queen's First Fruits.[1] Bishop Woolton, of good Lancashire stock, nephew of Dean Nowell, was a tougher type. As prebendary at Exeter, he was the only one to stick at his post during the terrible plague of 1570. He wrote a remarkable anticipation of Bunyan's *Holy War*, with his *Castle of Christians and Fortress of the Faithful*. The candidate of the Earl of Bedford, he had in fact earned his bishopric. It fell to him to deal with a number of the Family of Love, who had spread from the Netherlands and East Anglia into these parts: this sect held the abominable doctrine that the people of God — which they, like all sects, peculiarly were — were exempt from the law of sin, which, it is well known, governs human nature but for divine grace. One of their clerical sympathisers even thought the first chapters of Genesis an allegory and the Church of England as imperfect as the Church of Rome. Bishop Woolton dealt with him.[2] The Puritans were more pestiferous and tenacious: they stuck to him: they laid all sorts of charges against him, of having an illegitimate child born in his own household — as if the Bishop himself were responsible. His own son, whom he had presented to a living, lapsed under Jesuit influence; the Bishop sent him to gaol and put him in irons: he soon saw the light. A man of action, he got the Crown to restore the lands which had been

[1] The revenues of the see of Exeter had been reduced by the activities of the State from some £1560 to £500 per annum. Elizabeth therefore usually allowed the bishop to hold one or two livings *in commendam* to add to his income.

[2] Woolton wrote Burghley, 6 June 1581, asking that his sentence might stand for the quietness of the Church, " and for that Randall hath many complices and that hurtful sect, the Family of Love, beginneth to creep in this country, of the which company I have brought twenty to open recantation in this cathedral church " — his proceedings against the rest would be much weakened if his sentence against Randall were not allowed to stand (Lansdowne MSS. 38/15).

given to the Chapter for obits and most of the lands which had belonged to the College of vicars choral (alas, today a heap of rubble). A good manager, he was able to purchase the pleasing little estate of Pilland to establish his family. Babington was at Exeter for two years only: time enough to make a grant of Crediton, the see's best manor — which Mary had restored — to the Crown on behalf of William Killigrew, groom of the Chamber. William Cotton came of an old Staffordshire family: he was shocked by the " wildness and wickedness of the country in some parts ", his rule being " in the midst of so tough and stubborn a people ". He set to work with a will to reduce them: with success as regards recusant Catholics, with no success at all in the case of the sectaries who " spawned fast " in that diocese, as they always have done.

Of the bishops who have left in some part a bad name, in other cases merely a bad smell, this was usually due to hard luck rather than wicked deeds. Kitchin, Marian bishop of Llandaff, has been thought ill of for conforming under Elizabeth; we think worse of him for burning under Mary. Bishop Scory, who had had a variegated past in conformity, was not a pretty piece of work though he had a pretty financial sense; he presented three sinecure prebends to his wife, and his son to a prebend in his cathedral: a convenient arrangement for the family. The son disgraced himself by becoming a Catholic; the father redeemed himself by making large charitable bequests out of his episcopal fortune. Bishop Cox of Ely, of the celebrated squabbles between Knox and Cox at Frankfort, was of a type that has become more frequent since: the headmaster-bishop. And, indeed, he was a censorious person, who dared to be so with the Queen. She awaited her opportunity, which did not fail to come, for the Bishop, like others, had a weakness for matrimony. At the time of her order against resident women in cathedral closes, Bishop Cox had dared to address a general expostulation to the Queen: the institution of marriage, he said, had been " blessed by Christ himself ". This did not impress the Queen of England. In his seventieth year the Bishop fell into the error of a union with a too marriageable widow, years younger than himself. He was disgraced; the royal indignation was worse to him than death, he wrote to Cecil. He confided to him, in the decent obscurity of Latin, his reasons for marriage: [1] he would have incurred the anger of God, he said, without it — really, at his age!

Some years later these backslidings were brought home to him.

[1] *Cal. S.P. Dom. 1547–80*, p. 324.

Sir Christopher Hatton was in want of a town house, if he were to fulfil his functions — whatever they were — at Court: what more eligible than Ely Place in Holborn with its acres of gardens that produced bushels of roses and immortal strawberries? It was far too splendid a place for a bishop under the new dispensation: more important that a high official, or an intimate servant of the Queen, should occupy it. The Bishop resisted and appealed to the Queen: he thought it sacrilege to grant away Church property; he had not thought so years earlier when he took a profitable part in Henry's Reformation. Nor did the Queen think so now: she forced him to lease the manor, if not to Hatton, to the Crown and herself made the lease over to her useful favourite. The Bishop had better luck with the campaign waged by Lord North to get possession of one of the Cambridgeshire manors of the see. To aid himself Lord North raked up a large budget of diocesan scandal of the usual sort — easy enough, for Cox was unpopular: he was both rich and mean. But the Council found there was no substance in the charges: the tough old man held on and was given a sumptuous funeral in his cathedral. Twenty years later his monument was defaced: he was not loved in Ely. But he had done well: he had established a family: his son was a knight, his daughter the wife of Archbishop Parker's son, another knight.

Clerical dynasticism was well on the way: an institution that has much to recommend it. But that the Queen's dislike of episcopal, if not of clerical marriage in general, was not without reason may be seen from the horrid experiences of bishops Cooper and Freake. Mrs. Cooper was no better than she should be — in fact a great deal worse. Like the patient scholar he was, her husband put up with a great deal — or perhaps, engrossed as he was in his great Dictionary, which gained him his preferment, he did not notice. Harington pays him this tribute: " His life in Oxford was very commendable and in some sort saint-like; for, if it be saint-like to live unreprovable, to bear a cross patiently, to forgive great injuries freely: this man's example is sample-less in this age ".[1] It seems that it was his brother who took his place by his wife's side, while he slept with his Dictionary. " In the end taking him both in place and fashion (not fit to be named) that would have angered a saint, he drave him thence (not much unlike) as Tobias drove away the spirit Asmodeus, for that was done with a roast, and this with a spit." The university was so sympathetic as to offer the aggrieved husband a divorce. But Cooper admitted, like Cox, that he could not live thus without sin

[1] Sir John Harington, *Nugae Antiquae* (ed. 1779), I. 71-3.

— so far had the breach with celibacy slackened clerical standards. " He would by no means agree thereto, alledging he knew his own infirmity, that he might not live unmarried ; and to divorce and marry again, he would not charge his conscience with so great a scandal." So he went on carrying his cross into the episcopate.

Mrs. Freake was more of a public nuisance at Norwich : an early example of the species Proudie.[1] She ruled the diocese ; her servants called her Mrs. Bishop and if she wanted anything done the poor Freake had to do it, 'will he, nil he'. The Bishop complained with tears that if he did not do as his wife wanted "she would make him weary of his life ". One recognises the kind. Palace life gave great opportunities to such : all who came were first interviewed by Mrs. Bishop, but if any came without a present she would " look on him as the devil looks over Lincoln ", and woe betide the Bishop if he looked with favour on any of whom Mrs. Freake disapproved. The Bishop had a favourite steward " who loved and favoured the gospel and frequented sermons " ; Mrs. Freake, who had the merit of disliking those who pretended to be better than she was — herself was not religious — gave her husband no rest until the offending steward was thrust out of doors. All this made a fuss in Norfolk ; one sees that there was a certain Puritan animus at work against the palace. The fact that the Bishop had his own trials did not prevent him from trying a crazy Arian for heresy and condemning him to be burned.

Archbishop Sandys when at York had a narrower escape from a frame-up against him. It should be said to his credit that he had not wished for episcopal preferment ; but when he got it, his appetite grew on it. At Worcester he made a very good thing for his family out of the possessions of the see, leasing lands on very long leases for inadequate rents to members of his family, putting pressure on the dean and chapter to make over valuable leases of their lands to himself and his wife. When he left Worcester for London he stripped the episcopal residences of everything he could carry away : his successor died deeply in debt to the Queen owing to Sandys' activities. He was not a North-countryman for nothing. He managed to settle his family on the great manor of Ombersley, where his descendants still live ; at the end of the next century the family moved up into the peerage. Wherever he went squabbles and quarrels followed him : in London with Aylmer over dilapidations, a fertile source of clerical rows ; at York and Durham over his rights of visitation as metropolitan. A cataclysm may have taken place in the Church, but still the

[1] *Cal. S.P. Dom. Eliz. Add. 1566–79*, pp. 548, 551-2.

Archbishop pressed his claim to visit Durham and still Durham resisted — as in the Middle Ages. On his arrival at York an attempt was made to wrest Bishopthorpe from him, as a residence for the President of the Council of the North.

A more dangerous enemy was Sir Robert Stapleton, who was after a lease of the best manors of the see, Southwell and Scrowby.[1] Thwarted in this, he laid a plot. When sleeping in an inn at Doncaster, the Archbishop was conveniently discovered one night by the innkeeper in bed with the innkeeper's wife. What made things more difficult was that she had been a favoured maidservant of Mrs. Sandys. (Father Parsons, of course, made the most of this — he would — and supposed that the Archbishop had been too familiar with her in earlier days.[2]) Sir Robert Stapleton was waiting conveniently near, and the Archbishop was fool enough to hand over a large sum of money to the innkeeper and a lease to Stapleton. But when the latter continued to press for Southwell, Sandys was driven to inform the Council of the whole story. Stapleton spent a year or two in the Tower and the Fleet; the Archbishop turned to works of piety. At Hawkshead, at the head of Esthwaite Water, he had a tomb erected for his parents: his father had been receiver-general of the liberty of Furness and he himself had received his schooling at Furness abbey. By the roadside under the hill he built the little grammar school so celebrated in the history of our literature and lovingly described in *The Prelude*. He died in the year of the Armada and sleeps — oddly enough, considering his fierce Protestantism — under his effigy in full vestments, mitre and chasuble, in Southwell Minster, unique for Elizabethan England: a curious piece of conservatism, or did they economise to the last by using a vacant tomb?

With such difficulties about from women, it is not surprising that the Queen was anxious to spare her favourite ecclesiastics from danger. Such a one was Richard Fletcher, who was a very handsome man; the Queen was pleased to take an interest in the trimming of his beard. She made him her Almoner; she promoted him from Bristol to Worcester and thence to London in rapid succession.[3] He had been already married once, and the

[1] For the whole story *v.* Strype, *Annals*, III. i. 142-58.

[2] Harington, *op. cit.* I. 211.

[3] These rapid promotions were advantageous to the Crown, which got the First Fruits of the sees. Bishop Fletcher died in debt to the Queen as the result of these preferments which kept him in continual payment of First Fruits — £3000 in three years; besides, it was said, £2000 in gratifications at Court, to Lady Stafford, Sir Edward Denny, etc. Financially, if not spiritually, speaking he should have resisted temptation and stayed where he was (cf. *Cal. S.P. Dom. 1595–7*, p. 247).

Queen exacted some sort of promise that he would not do it again. But he would not be warned: he had no sooner got the see of London than he married a taking young widow, of dubious character, whose husband was but recently dead. This was the end for the bright and promising Bishop: he was banished from Court and suspended from his (spiritual) functions.[1] Worst blow of all, the Queen gave his Almonership to someone else: he could console himself with his widow. This was what he was doing when death came upon him but a year after — he was only fifty-one: "The Queen being pacified and he in great jollity, with his fair lady and her carpets and cushions in his bed-chamber, he died suddenly, taking tobacco in his chair, saying to his man that stood by him, whom he loved very well, 'Oh boy, I die'".[2]

We must not allow that the Queen was wholly right: whatever the disadvantages of women in the Church they had their uses. Clerical celibacy, though no such loss to the Church, would have been a great loss to the State. Bishop Fletcher died leaving eight orphans; but one of them, to whom he left half his books, was the dramatist, the inseparable companion of Beaumont — with whom there was such a "wonderful consimility of phancy", according to Aubrey, that they shared everything in common. The State would have been much the poorer without the sons of Archbishop Sandys, and not this country only but America; for of the seven of them, three of whom became knights, Sir Edwin Sandys became the leading figure in the Virginia Company and the most effective planner and promoter of its colonisation. He had other interests in the East India and Somers Islands Companies. From the dissolution of Furness abbey to India and America in two generations: there lies the story of the age, the kernel of this book, in a phrase. The seventh son of the Archbishop was the admired poet, George Sandys, friend of Falkland and his circle. He was treasurer of the Virginia Company and a planter there; it was in America that he completed his translation of Ovid's *Metamorphoses*, two books of it "amongst the roaring of the seas".

What is more difficult to overlook than marriage in these persons is their iconoclasm, their indifference to things of beauty, their theological contentiousness: these went together, different

[1] For the Bishop's pathetic *cri de cœur* to Robert Cecil *v.* H.M.C. *Salisbury MSS.* V. 106-7: "If it [his sequestration] be for marriage, it must be the cause of many, and then I trust my case will not prove singular. . . . And surely I must needs confess that her Majesty's motive and prudent advice to me in that behalf should have been to me as an oracle from Heaven, if that other oracle, *Omnes non capiunt verbum hoc*, had not enforced me to another resolution," etc.

[2] Harington, *op. cit.* I. 31.

aspects of the same attitude. When one looks at their portraits, high-shouldered with their furred tippets, their puffy, lined faces with their atrabilious, constipated expressions, always grave, often sour, one cannot find them congenial. Only one of Elizabeth's bishops seems to have been a merry old soul, who wrote comic letters, Bishop Cheyney of Gloucester; and he was much disapproved of as a Lutheran, the only one on the bench, who held a high Anglican view of the eucharist: all the rest were Calvinists in doctrine. Nor did he hold Calvin's ugly doctrine of Predestination: he was a believer in free-will. As a sensible moderate he came in for a double dose of abuse on both sides, the Puritans attacking him as a 'papist' and the Blessed Edmund Campion, to whom he had been kind when young, describing him as an "object of loathing to the heretics, and of shame to the Catholics".[1] Of course. The poor Bishop, attacked by forty *bons bourgeois* of Bristol, who insisted on their diocesan swallowing Calvin whole — good bourgeois are apt to think alike — devoted such time as he could spare from being abused by everybody to the neglect of his duties. He left them to be performed by his chancellor, who also abused him by taking money right and left for the commutation of penances.[2] Hardly anybody was punished in the Gloucester diocese: a pleasant contrast with the severities of the nasty martyr, Bishop Hooper: a jolly, lax spirit prevailed under good Bishop Cheyney.

He had never wanted a bishopric, or any high preferment;[3] he was without ambition and had no love of money; a generous hospitable bachelor, he died poor, in debt to the Queen. He had never liked the Calvinistic Thirty-nine Articles, and protested in the Lords against the twenty-eighth on the doctrine of the sacrament. He quoted Bishop Guest as agreeing with him. Bishop Guest wrote to Cecil to make clear the difference between them. "I suppose you have heard how the bishop of Gloucester found himself grieved with the placing of this adverb 'only' in this article: 'The body of Christ is given, taken and eaten in the supper after an heavenly and spiritual manner only', because it did take away the presence of Christ's body in the sacrament. . . .

[1] Cf. F. O. White, *op. cit.* pp. 172-7.

[2] For his agreeable career cf. F. D. Price, "An Elizabethan Church Official — Thomas Powell, Chancellor of Gloucester Diocese", *Church Quarterly Rev.* (1939), p. 94 foll.

[3] As early as 1563 Cheyney was willing to resign: "I had much rather live a private life, like a poor man, as I did before I was drawn to office. . . . I have already enough of lording wherein I find nothing but *splendidum miserium*" (Cooper, *Athenae Cantabrigienses*, I. 401).

As between him and me I told him plainly that this word ' only ' . . . did not exclude the presence of Christ's body from the sacrament, but only the grossness and sensibleness in the receiving thereof. For I said unto him though he took Christ's body in his hand, received it with his mouth and that corporally, naturally, really, substantially and carnally, as the doctors do write, yet he did not for all that see it, feel it, smell it, nor taste it." And so on: we see that this provides ground for infinite dispute. And so it has done: whole libraries of it. This will have to do for a sample; we cannot give any more space to it here.

The more tangible subject of iconoclasm is more distressing. This, like the other, has a long history behind it. The saddest thing about the Reformation, sadder perhaps than the loss of lives, was the enormous loss in things of beauty, for they were in no way responsible for the fate that befell them. In the later Middle Ages there had been growing a spirit of hatred for images, in stone and wood and glass, ostensibly because of the veneration paid to them; but also no doubt because among many human idiots there is a loathing for things of beauty they cannot comprehend. We may take as the most celebrated European expression of it the hateful spirit of a Savonarola. The destruction of the monasteries and chantries, the carrying overseas of shiploads of precious manuscripts, vestments, books, carvings, must have been heart-breaking to those who loved objects of beauty and antiquity: no wonder Leland went off his head. Mary did what she could to repair the damage: we find foreign workmen brought in to help repair the screens and the images. Elizabeth's accession was the signal for a renewed outburst of this disgusting spirit of the Protestant mob. Within the first weeks Bow Church was gutted. Iconoclasm was, of course, a natural expression of the Protestant spirit: it hated these things, not only in themselves, but for what they stood for. Pulling them down was the strongest possible argument, for the people, against the doctrines they signified. In the celebrated words of Bishop Latimer: " As the founding of monasteries argueth purgatory to be, so the putting down of them argueth it not to be " : a revealing, if somewhat crude, statement of the relative importance of deed and thought in human affairs.

Elizabeth's government could not but go some way to meet the Protestantism which was its support. It held to a middle way: monuments of superstition should go: that is, those to which discarded beliefs were attached: chalices, images, the roods in their lofts, stone altars; paintings were to be whitewashed; the old service books and most of the vestments were no longer wanted.[1] On the other hand, the screens without the roods were to remain, so with the painted glass, tombs, fonts, lecterns and some vestments. There is no doubt that if the Queen could have had her way there would have been no destruction at all — cultivated, sensible woman that she was. But she was young when the worst of it happened and had not the control and authority that came with years: the forces of human foolery, as often in politics, were too much for her. She did, however, stop the horrid Puritans from carrying it a great deal further: they would have had the churches in the deplorable barn-like state of Scottish churches today. As early as 1561 a Proclamation was sent out against " defacing monuments of antiquity set up in the churches for memory, not for superstition"; ordinaries were to enquire into losses since the first year of the reign and to cause the offenders to set up again what they had broken, and restore the bells and lead they had made away with.[2] One cannot think the order was very effective. Sometimes the Queen herself put in a word, as on her visit to Worcester, where a defaced panel with the crucifixion in the choir was tidied up and plastered over.

But what losses of medieval art the country suffered — paintings, frescoes, manuscripts, alabasters, statues, chalices, jewels, needlework. Alas that people should take their absurd beliefs so seriously! It is a pity that the Elizabethans were not archaeologically, or even historically, minded. They took these things too seriously in one sense, in another not seriously enough. A modern preference would regard their aesthetic value as more important than their religious, or irreligious, use. Some of Elizabeth's bishops, in their gayer days, had taken part in the enjoyable work: the egregious Horne, when Dean of Durham, had destroyed the windows in the cloisters depicting the life of St. Cuthbert; the unattractive Bishop Pilkington defaced many monuments in the cathedral and pulled down chapels and bells

[1] For an insight into the division of opinion within a parish cf. Throwley in East Kent in 1561: " Richard Goteley was warned by name, by Mr. Sonds and the most part of the ancients of the parish, to be at the pulling down of the rood-loft, as well as others, for that he was an accuser in Queen Mary's time. Then Goteley, thus admonished, did not only stubbornly absent himself, but spake these words of Robert Upton, being churchwarden, because he said that the rood-loft must come down: 'Let him take heed that his authority be good before it be pulled down, for we know what we have had, but we know not what we shall have'. . . . Richard Goteley said unto George Overy, 'I will see the Queen's broad seal or I have it down'" (*Home Counties Mag*. X. 181). It is evident that in this progressive area the majority of the ancients of the parish were for pulling down. In less progressive areas there would be a different sentiment. For a contemporary description of the change in the internal appearance of the churches *v.* Harrison, *Elizabethan England*, ed. cit. pp. 77-8.

[2] S.P. 12/13/32.

at his palace of Auckland. He did not fail to leave a fortune to his daughters. The most splendid of all English cathedrals suffered the greatest losses: Durham is a magnificent architectural shell of what it once was. No wonder the anonymous author of the *Rites of Durham*, writing in 1593 and remembering the old days, wrote a book filled with such nostalgia: the innumerable roods and altars, the Black Rood of Scotland brought from Holyrood by King David Bruce, the Jesus altar where Jesus Mass was sung every Friday throughout the year, the great silver basins that hung before the high altar, the frontals of gold and silver thread, the "candles which did burn continually both day and night, in token that the house was always watching to God", the crucifixes and all the rites of creeping to the cross on Good Fridays, the images with their inscriptions *Virgo mater dei miserere mei*, the bells that ceased not day nor night.[1] No wonder Nicholas Roscarrock wore out his last years with Lord William Howard at Naworth, in that tower looking to the Scottish border, in remembering and piecing together all the saints' days and their feasts, the holy wells and their rites and customs, of his youth in Cornwall, growing more remote in the distance and yet ever present in his mind.[2] There must have been many left all over the country, but especially in the North, who regretted the bells of the monasteries ringing out from the dales across the fells to reach people's hearts in the far uplands and tell them that the monks — their sons and brothers — were praying for them, in Lanercost or Rievaulx, Bridlington or Fountains or Cartmel. A passing phrase in a document brings it home to one: some witness or other remembering a date by when the bells still hung in the steeple of Roche abbey.[3]

Parker's example was admired, if not always followed by some of his colleagues. Bishop Cox advised Mary Stuart's agent, the Bishop of Ross, "at my returning into Scotland to recover all the ancient books that was in the abbeys and cathedral churches, as the Archbishop of Canterbury has done in England".[4] But too much was being lost almost adventitiously. The canons of Chester were said to have carried off glass from the cathedral to their private benefices, and prebendaries to have set their houses to rent.[5] At Coventry Harington notes that the whole floor of the

[1] Cf. *Rites of Durham*, Surtees Society.

[2] Cf. *Household Books of Lord William Howard*, Surtees Society.

[3] A. G. Dickens, "An Elizabethan Defender of the Monasteries", *Church Quarterly Rev.*, 1940, p. 237.

[4] q. C. H. and T. Cooper, *Athenae Cantabrigienses*, I. 441.

[5] H.M.C. *Marquis of Bath MSS.* II. 20.

cathedral had been paved with fine brasses, now stripped off.[1] We come across individual instances like that of the vicar of Islington, Meredith Hanmer, who converted several brasses into coin for his own use; he then went into Ireland and had a successful career as treasurer of Christ Church, Dublin: he died of the plague in 1604.[2] Habington's survey of Worcestershire is full of a Catholic antiquary's nostalgic regret for such depredations and losses. Pre-Reformation inventories show Essex churches as particularly rich in alabasters, those specialities of English medieval art that went all over Europe.[3] Few are left in England now.

We can watch the ordered policy of Church administration through the regular machinery of visitations and Church courts, in this respect as in others covering the whole field of Church policy. The effect of the change at the centre may be read in affecting detail in hundreds of parish accounts; one must serve for them all, Barnstaple in North Devon.[4] John Peard and Nicholas Wichalse, churchwardens, received from the church-ale in the year 1559, £12 : 10 : 8; of which they "paid William Gyble for dressing of the places where the images were [it is the term one applies to wounds] 16d.; item for defacing of images and whiting where the altars were; item for 2 English psalter books 3/-; item for the communion-table and ceiling for the same 13/-; item for pulling down of altars and carriage away the rubble thereof 3/4; item for a book of the English service 5/4; item for a skin of parchment to make the inventory of the church goods 6d.; item for making of a carpet for the communion table with buckram to line the same 6/4; item to David Bedman for making of communion bread, cleansing the churchyard and attendance upon the Queen's Visitors [the famous Jewel was one of them] 2/2; item for wine for the Communion 5/1; item for wood to burn the images 11d.; item for setting up a desk in the church for the Bible 4d." There in those speaking entries one sees the picture of the change-over, pretty complete in one sweep in a town church.

In remote country areas it took some years. In Yorkshire, for example, at Ross in 1567 "the holy water stock, pictures, paintings in the rood loft is reserved"; at Burton Pidsey, "a holy water stock, a cope with images upon it, 6 banner staffs, 11 banner cloths, an amice, the sepulchre and paschal is reserved".[5] The gloomy note follows: to be defaced, the churchwardens to appear

[1] Harington, *op. cit.* I. 99.
[2] J. Nichols, *Bibl. Top. Brit.* vol. II.
[3] *V.C.H. Essex*, II. 20.
[4] H.M.C. *IX Report*, p. 205.
[5] J. S. Purvis, *Tudor Parish Documents of the Diocese of York*, pp. 31, 63, 150.

before the commissioners. At Kirkby, near Richmond, in 1570, "all the monuments of idolatry be undefaced and the cross standing in the rood-loft and no Bible neither other books that are appointed to be in the church". At Wilberfoss in 1571 Roger Wilberfoss and Edward Harlings were charged "that they keep undefaced the timber which was the rood-loft . . . and have felled and put into the ground the cross stones of the church of Wilberfoss being unwilling to have them broken and defaced, contrary to the laws". Old sympathies were rife in the North; but the reluctant churchwardens spent a few days in York Castle. There were Catholic Recusants among the Wilberforces at this time. The regret of the parishes may be seen in such actions as the burying of the figures on the beautiful pulpit of Trull in Somerset beneath the floor, to emerge into light again in better days. In still more remote areas the rood lofts went on: among the inaccessible hills of Wales, in Devon and Yorkshire, a few still remain, and very beautiful they are.

The old observances lingered on in country places, in some areas long and tenaciously. It was understandable enough in the early days of the transition that at Canterbury — where the visitation began with morning prayers for Whit Sunday, following in the old tracks of Mass of the Holy Ghost with which visitations had always begun — the bell-ringers had to confess that they had rung on Becket's even, while a canon admitted that an *anime omnium fidelium* sometimes slipped out by mistake.[1] The natural instinct to pray for the dead remained strong, and for a long time parishes continued to ring for the souls of the faithful departed on All Hallows even. At Weverham in Yorkshire as late as 1575 "the people will not be stayed from ringing the bells on All Saints' day".[2] At Ripon money and candles were collected for the ringers on All Hallows night; they drank ale in the church and had good cheer abroad in the town afterwards. In the diocese of Chester there was too much ringing for the dead at funerals still; at Tilston in 1567 "Ralph Leach useth prayer for the dead and willeth the people to pray for them and say a pater noster and de profundis for the dead when the people do rest with the dead corpse". All over the country rush-bearings and mummings and disguisings continued, Yule-ridings and pilgrimages to old shrines and wells, for all the efforts of the authorities; it is possible that in this sphere of folk-lore the propaganda of the Puritans was more effective: another small advance in a rational-

[1] W. H. Frere, *Visitation Articles and Injunctions*, I. 149, 153.
[2] J. S. Purvis, *op. cit.* pp. 65, 73, 174.

ist direction, for what that is worth with the people. The inhabitants of Aldborough in Yorkshire " having followed their vanity all the night in seeking their mommet [this proceeding presented its opportunities], commonly called the Flower of the Well, would needs bring the same on a barrow into the church in prayer time . . . with such a noise of piping, blowing of an horn, ringing or striking of basins and shouting of people . . .": one realises how near we are to Darkest Africa.[1] At Clynnogin in the diocese of Bangor bullocks were sacrificed at Whitsuntide to Beyno, the patron saint of the parish.[2] It was too much to expect that the comparatively superficial conscious changes of a Reformation should interfere with the deeper layers of the instinctive, subconscious behaviour of the people; the far longer perspectives of the secular paganism of the countryside held up to our own time.

For the pressure of the Church for order, discipline, education and improvement of standards among clergy and people, let us look at a diocese — the large diocese of Lincoln. It had had Northamptonshire cut out of it by Henry VIII to form the diocese of Peterborough: it now fell into a northern half, Lincoln, Leicester and Rutland, and a southern consisting of Bedford and Huntingdon. The bishop lived chiefly in the last county at Buckden, midway between Lincoln and London: in that fine moated palace of red brick with its great quadrangular tower now ruined, looking down upon the parish church beyond the wall. The bishop's itinerary shows him residing here most of his time, then at Lincoln, then at Lambeth, only once at Leicester, sometimes at his manor of Nettleham.[3] Here in his parlour or his great chamber, the bishop sat as judge in the cases that came before him, relating to misdeeds of the clergy, testaments, defamation — such a case as that against William Snasedale of Ramsey who had said " that he sent upon Monday was fortnight . . . his servant a maid to milk at his close, whereas his maid told him one John Hyde came behind her and took her by the hand requiring *corpus eius habere ut cum ea carnalem copulationem haberet*, and strove with her in such sort as he got her neck under his arm and with his leash would have bound her; wherewith she cried out and he let her go, saying he would teach her to come at due time and not to rob his traps; and saith there be two maids moe in the town that in like sort he hath attempted ".[4] The bishop enjoined Snasedale to make

[1] *Ibid.* p. 169.
[2] *Cal. S.P. Dom. 1581–90*, p. 603.
[3] *Lincoln Episcopal Records . . . 1571 to 1584* (ed. C. W. Foster), pp. 336-8.
[4] *Ibid.* pp. 123-4.

public confession of having overshot himself: insufficient evidence to bear him out. The rector of Cranoe had allowed puppets to play in his church: 3s. 4d. fine to the poor of his parish and "in no wise hereafter shall suffer any such order either by morris dance or otherwise to be in his church".[1] The vicar of Tilton had "committed adultery with Elizabeth Wilmot (as she saith) and she claimeth marriage of him"; whether he married her or not, he resigned his living.[2] There were no doubt plenty who got away with it. Licences for clergymen to marry were given up to the end of the reign; we find one for a parson to marry the daughter of an innkeeper. By 1576 two-thirds of the clergy were married.[3]

At the beginning of the reign the educational standard of the clergy was very low and a constant pressure was maintained, chiefly through triennial visitations, to improve it. Many of them knew very little Latin and little enough of the Scriptures; it was as much as most could do to read the services out of a book: for the rest farmers, like their neighbours. Very few could preach: in 1561–2, only 15 out of 129 in the archdeaconry of Leicester.[4] It was for this reason that Cooper, like other bishops, winked at or positively encouraged the exercises disapproved of by the Queen as Puritan in inspiration and leading to the spread of Puritanism. No doubt they had that effect, but they offered a means of mutual stimulus and edification for the clergy meeting in them. A number of bishops were prepared to risk the displeasure of the Queen for the spiritual improvement of their clergy. She would have preferred no sermons at all: she did not share the contemporary mania for sermons: perhaps because she had to listen to too many. She evidently regarded them as a great bore; she heard them from within her closet, often transacting business with the window closed; for on one occasion we catch her out: a bishop had taken a line she afterwards much disapproved: after the sermon she opened her window and to everyone's surprise thanked him: she had evidently not been listening.[5]

The Puritans, who were a small minority, were treated with a great deal more patience and toleration than might have been expected: infinitely more than they extended to others. Of the small number suspended in this diocese, not one was deprived of his living.[6] The Puritan survey of this diocese was moderate and fair: one knows how disgracefully abusive and defamatory those of Warwickshire, Norfolk and Cornwall were. Bancroft was quite

[1] *Lincoln Episcopal Records . . . 1571 to 1584*, p. 138. [2] *Ibid.* pp. 137, 139.
[3] *Ibid.* p. xii. [4] *Ibid.* p. xiii. [5] Harington, *op. cit.* pp. 217-20.
[6] *The State of the Church*, I. (ed. C. W. Foster), Lincoln Record Soc. vol. 23. xxv.

right to regard them in general as mere libels. By one means or another the bishops improved the educational standards of the clergy out of all recognition by the end of the reign; by instituting a number of readers, giving licences to preach, suspending an ordinand's cure for a year or two until he could satisfy the bishop after examination. As things settled down under the new deal, the country became more prosperous and the Church more efficiently run, the ministry became recruited more and more from the universities: men with degrees, hitherto a small minority of the clergy, came to fill the livings. By 1600 there was a striking decrease of curates: less pluralism, the livings filled by functioning pastors. In the visitations and injunctions great emphasis was placed upon the clergy instructing in catechism.

All this is borne out by the diocese of Norwich.[1] In 1561 there was a royal order to set up the Ten Commandments in the churches for the people to read: one notes the government's economical idea of improving instruction and morale at one go. By 1597 the furniture and fittings of the churches were regarded as satisfactory. There were still eighty-eight parishes with no monthly sermons. On the other hand, only seven clergymen were presented for unseemly conduct: one of them a rector who was too much addicted to husbandry and spent his time, unsuitably clad for his profession, stamping apples for Lady Higham.[2] There were fourteen cases of suspected witchcraft brought up at this visitation. It had become quite common not to use the font, but to put a basin and baptise from that. A woman in Norwich cathedral refused to allow the sign of the cross at the baptism of her child. It was fairly usual for clergy not to wear the surplice. Norwich was a diocese where Puritan sympathies were strong. But it is evident that very decent order had been established in the Church by the end of the reign: the result of incessant toil and labour by the government, High Commission, diocesan authorities and courts. Those much-tried men, the bishops — for whom nobody had a good word — had done their duty and established the Church in a fair way.

The supervision of all classes of society was close, astonishing

[1] Cf. *Bishop Redman's Visitation 1597* (ed. J. F. Williams), Norfolk Record Soc. pp. 11, 17, 20, 26, 14, 144.

[2] The clergy were liable to be presented by their churchwardens at visitations for going about unsuitably clad. Cf. the vicar of Preston in Kent, 1572: "He is a common cow-keep and one that useth commonly to drive beasts through the town of Faversham, being a town of worship, and in other open places, in a jerkin with a bill on his neck, not like a prelate but rather like a common rogue, who hath oft-times been warned thereof, and he will not be reformed". He was charged also with other things (*Home Counties Mag.* IX. 205).

in its detail, the moral disciplining of the people so thorough it would be intolerable to us. It was only tolerable to them because there were large loopholes through which to escape — into life on the roads, the life of pedlars, tinkers, fairmen travelling from fair to fair, into serving in the forces abroad in Ireland or the Netherlands with its high mortality, or returning home to join the large ranks of thieves or vagabonds, scallywags and impostors who crowded into the towns, London above all, making a whole section of society on their own and contributing a whole thieves' language to the rich diversity of tongues; or going to sea with the Queen's ships, as often as not deserting and being pressed again, or crowding the ships adventuring to strange oceans, from which few enough returned. The stay-at-homes, the stable elements of society, were strictly supervised, watched by their neighbours in country parish or town alley, from the cradle to the grave. The Church courts provided the machinery through which this moral discipline was enforced; its punishments were bothersome, chiefly by way of open penance and fine, rather than strenuous. But as the people grew out of their medieval nonage so the Church's supervision came to be more and more resented; it was probably a greater cause of its unpopularity among people at large than any of the doctrinal issues, which are given so much place in the books and which they did not comprehend.

For the operation of the Church courts let us look at Oxford.[1] At Carfax, in St. Martin's church, the archdeacon held his court every week; coming down the High you came to All Saints where the bishop's court sat; a step or two further was St. Mary's, the university church, where the vice-chancellor held his court. In the long vacancy of the see of Oxford — the machinery continuing to run all the same — the most important figure was the archdeacon, John Kenall, an interesting character, a Cornishman.[2] The Puritans, those denigrators, tell us that " his con-

[1] We are indebted to Dr. E. R. Brinkworth for opening up the subject of the archdeacon's court with his admirably edited volumes, *The Archdeacon's Court: Liber Actorum 1584*, 2 vols.: Oxfordshire Record Society. It remains for someone to explore the interesting territory of the bishop's consistory court. The actual procedure has been well described in detail by F. S. Hockaday, " The Consistory Court of the Diocese of Gloucester ", in *Trans. Bristol and Glos. Arch. Soc.* (1924), p. 195 foll.

[2] Kenall took a sensible line about conformity. According to Fr. Parsons, Derbyshire, chancellor of London, " found a great conflict in himself " on the subject. On the day that appearance had to be made before the commissioners in St. Paul's, Derbyshire going in met Kenall coming out. Kenall asked Derbyshire what he meant to do. The chancellor replied that he intended to follow his conscience and refuse the oath. Kenall said, " What, surely you are not such a fool as to sacrifice all your fat livings ? " Derbyshire was. What good it did him history does not declare (C. G. Bayne, " The Visitation of the Province of Canterbury ", *E.H.R.*, 1913, p. 655).

versation was most in hounds"; Carew, more affectingly, that in him the principal love and knowledge of the Cornish language "lived and lieth buried". He was, it is true, a much beneficed man, a busy official, assiduous in his duties: alas, much too busy to put down all that he knew of Cornish. From his house within Christ Church, he supervised the moral life of his archdeaconry; but a few steps up St. Aldate's and he was in his court from which he meted out justice to the erring. Dr. Brinkworth assures us that in his court fair and considerate dealing prevailed.[1]

Many and various were the misdoings that came within the purview of the Church. Attendance at Church on Sundays and holy days was enforced on everyone; if you did not come, you had to have a good excuse, or be punished.[2] Thomas Harwell of Islip had sometimes been abroad hunting hares during service time; Joan Milman of Launton washed a few clothes on Sunday last "because she had no time to do it in the weekdays". Cuthbert Atkinson, of St. Peter's in the East — the next parish going down the High — sets his rack on Sunday mornings as do "most of the fullers in England . . . because otherwise they cannot keep promise with their customers, for that there is sometimes scarce one fair day in the whole week". The English climate is held responsible; but it seems that he was in the habit of carrying cloth on Sunday too.[3] In church the sexes were usually separated — the tradition still remains in some remote country places; and the seating held strict regard to social status. Hence there were many occasions for brawling in church over one's seat. After service people went forth to games, as they always had done. The churchyard itself provided occasion for cases, over dancing and bowling there, shooting at butts or playing football, allowing cattle to feed or pigs to rootle. At Duns Tew the churchwardens had allowed interludes and plays in the church. Everyone in the parish had to communicate at Easter; Richard Turland of Bloxham gave the unusual excuse for going to King's Sutton that his own vicar would not receive him because of his inability to say the catechism by heart.[4]

But the largest class of cases deal, naturally enough, with sex; they have the reality of a Hardy novel, of life itself.[5] John Gill of Adderbury gets Mary Spenser with child. Penance: "To come into the church on Sunday sennight next and there tarry the whole evening prayer and after evening prayer in some con-

[1] Brinkworth, *op. cit.* I. xv.
[2] *Ibid.* II. xvii.
[3] He made several appearances before the court (*ibid.* I. 167, 169, 192, 212, 219, 225).
[4] *Ibid.* II. xvii, xxi, xv.
[5] *Ibid.* I. 11, 16, 12.

venient place of the church before Mr. Rawlins the vicar, the two churchmen and four honest parishioners, confess his fault and there deliver 6/8 to Mr. Rawlins to the use of the poor and undertake 6/8 more to the same use at the feast of St. Michael next". Hundreds more, thousands all over the country, did like John Gill: the sole importance of such misdoing was the economic burden of the child upon the parish in simple communities living close to the soil with little enough to spare. Mary Marsh of Steeple Barton refused to lie with her husband "because he hath abused her divers times and did (about three years ago) send one John, then his man, to her bed for to have lain with her and doth continually ever since abuse her in words and calleth her whore and other railing words so that she cannot live in quiet by him". The joyous people sing rhymes about each other's naughtinesses, though they commit them themselves or would if they could. Anne Wrigglesworth of Islip — a good name — repeated a certain rhyme for good-will to goodwife Williams and her daughter, and to goodwife Cadman and her daughter because it was made to their discredit: she had heard it coming to Oxford last Christmas of Robert Nevill "who did sing it by the way, and the rhyme is this, viz. 'If I had as fair a face as John Williams his daughter has, then would I were a tawdry lace as goodman Bolt's daughter Mary does; And if I had as much money in my purse as Cadman's daughter Margaret has, then would I have a bastard less than Butler's maid Helen has'". Not very good poetry, but O *le bon temps*!

Not all the clergy were above reproach; but the licence to marry had relieved the strain and led to what district visitors would call an 'improvement' in morals.[1] Only five in the archdeaconry were actually up for incontinence. The curates of Bampton and Brize Norton were a bright pair: both mixed up in an unseemly row on the highway, then the first is involved with one Jane Pusey and has to pay for her child's maintenance, while the other is in trouble over a certain Dorothy May. Curates were counted quite low in the social scale: they were none the less human. These revelations of life have their humours and their country charm: the Shakespearean countryside looks out at us from the dusty records of an archdeacon's court: "Sir Hugh Evans was serving English cures, Dogberry and Verges were walking the streets . . . Peter Turf and Henry Pimpernel and old John Naps were in the congregation".[2] On a soberer level

[1] Brinkworth, *op. cit.* II. xi.

[2] A. Hamilton Thompson, *Visitations in the Diocese of Lincoln, 1517–31*, I. xxxvi.

we have to register that by this time, the fifteen-eighties, there had been a great improvement in the keeping of churches; the worst days of neglect and disrepair, of ruinous chancels and gaping roofs were over. The community was prospering; the gashes of the upheaval were in some way staunched; the demon- and angel-haunted world of the Middle Ages, figured on the walls of the churches, was receding under the sober whitewash and the scriptural texts.

What the upheaval had meant, when one comes down to the living detail of a parish, may be seen from the curious memoir of High Ham in Somerset, written by its rector in 1598.[1] This fine Perpendicular church had been built within the year 1476–1477 by the parishioners, local worthies like the Paulets and others; the chancel by the abbot of Glastonbury, its patron. The abbot was out to annex the rectory and for some years before the Dissolution the cure was served by the monks, who " transported from thence out of each parsonage barn by the space of 40 years . . . for the maintenance of the abbey all the corn to Glaston by boats and litters through a ditch made by hand for that purpose — which ditch at this day they commonly call Harding's ditch ". Defeated in their attempts to annex the rectory and turn it into a vicarage, the abbots managed to impose an annual pension of £2 on the living, which after the Dissolution went into the Exchequer. The parson appointed by the abbot was an absentee; the twelve men of the parishioners, when it came to rating the benefice, took their revenge by rating it far too high, " by reason of the hatred and ill will of the parishioners " for his absenteeism and his polling and pilling them of all he could. The next incumbent was an honest ex-monk of Glaston who was only there two years when he died of a surfeit of " fat sow's meat commonly called brawn being fried by an old woman, a meat very hard of digestion ". Queen Mary presented an absentee chaplain, whose revenues were collected for him by a London skinner or pelt-monger of his own kindred. There next succeeded for a short time — who but John Kenall? Next followed an absentee chaplain of the Grey family, who compounded the living for £35 per annum, who spent all his substance on a notorious harlot, then married a rude and ignorant Frenchwoman, and died miserably in the suburbs at St. Giles in the Fields.

To him succeeded the writer of the memoir: a German, Adrian Schaell, from Saxony, a protégé of Grindal. For the

[1] C. D. Crossman, " Adrian Schaell's Memoir of High Ham Church and Rectory, A.D. 1598 ", *Proc. Somerset Arch. and Natural Hist. Soc.* (1894), pp. 113-22.

first time for a century, this charming parish with its village on the high hill rising steeply from the marshes of Sedgemoor, had a resident pastor: the serious-minded German, come into port at last and determined to make the best of it, set to work to reclaim and repair. The parsonage houses, with their hedging and fencing, were utterly decayed: it cost him eight years' value of the living to set all in order. He had fenced and stopped his orchards and gardens, grafted trees and introduced new herbs and vegetables; he had himself cultivated the glebe, instead of letting it out negligently. "By this means I have sustained a greater family, I have entertained my richer neighbours more bountifully, and have not been unmindful to relieve the poor." The old church-house had been turned into a school. As he looked back over the years of his ministry, writing it up in the few spare leaves at the end of his register, the rector could contemplate it with the complacency of a Victorian: truly, his lot had fallen in a pleasant place, of which he was duly appreciative: "The church being placed on the top of an hill, the clear firmament (in chief time of the year) through the wholesomeness of pure air and pleasant prospect on every side, it doth marvellously delight the comers thereunto". Being a German, he was more expressive than most: one cannot think that his responsiveness to the beauty of nature, though hardly ever expressed outside poetry, was unique.

The fact is that for the Church, socially speaking, things were getting better; and this is not a matter of opinion: it can be shown in concrete detail. The incomes, and the social status, of the lower clergy were improving. The increase in the price of corn benefited holders of livings doubly: as farmers themselves, cultivating their own glebes along with their neighbours, and as recipients of tithes when the return from the land was going up. In Leicestershire the value of benefices multiplied by nearly four between 1534 and 1603.[1] Naturally the increase was not uniform: the value of rectories, since they gathered the greater tithes, on corn and such, increased generally more than that of vicarages, which usually had the lesser tithes, on stock, poultry and so on. Again we note greater differentiation with an advancing society: so much better than greater equality with lowering standards. Marriage was an advantage in a farming economy, even if the

[1] W. G. Hoskins, "The Leicestershire Country Parson in the Sixteenth Century" reprinted from *Trans. Leics. Arch. Soc.* (1939–40), p. 19.

wives of the clergy were a trifle too fruitful: more hands to help with house and farm. And now, in the generation after the Reformation, the parsonage house was recognisably superior to the neighbours: it possessed a study with books in it. Few enough of the clergy had any books before the Reformation: about one in seven.[1] Now, what with their education at the university, " by 1590 practically every parson had books and a study ". The simple furniture of the interior, so beautifully described by Traherne, was being added to:

> As in the house I sate
> Alone and desolate,
> No creature but the fire and I,
> The chimney and the stool, I lift mine eye
> Up to the wall,
> And in the silent hall
> Saw nothing mine
> But some few cups and dishes shine:
> The table and the wooden stools
> Where people used to dine:
> A painted cloth there was
> Wherein some ancient story wrought
> A little entertained my thought
> Which light discovered through the glass.

Framed tables were taking the place of trestle tables; joined stools in place of the rough things knocked together by the carpenter. Chairs and cushions make their appearance in vicarages; but the principal object was the vicarial bed, often an expensive affair with its hangings, valued at as much as the entire furniture of many a farmhouse. When one thinks of the contribution of the clerical bed to English life, the number of great men alone produced by it, one feels that perhaps it was worth all the turmoil of the Reformation to achieve. Many of the clergy now had their cupboards of plate, mainly pewter, but with some silver. They kept bees on a considerable scale — not only in their bonnets. Dr. Hoskins gives us a delightful picture of the domestic interior of the vicar of Barrow-on-Soar, who died in 1588; and then — " up in the orchard, where the vicar was wont to stroll, were his bee-hives. We may imagine him tending these on some summer morning, while the cuckoo's ancient plain-song echoed from a vanished spinney and the air was heavy with the scent of the hawthorn that hedged off the orchard and gardens from the

[1] F. W. Brooks, " The Social Position of the Parson in the Sixteenth Century ", *Journ. Brit. Arch. Assoc.* (1945–7), p. 32.

village fields. Beyond the orchard hedge, the vicar would see his barley, rye and wheat ripening in the Midland sun, and somewhere out of sight his tethered livestock grazed in the common pastures."[1]

Tithes were the foundation of the clergy's support all over the country; for their collection let us look at my native parish of St. Austell: it so happens that it possesses a rare tithe-book going back to the last years of the reign.[2] The living was a vicarage, since the rectory had long been appropriated to the priory of Tywardreath across the bay; so the rectorial tithes, on corn, came into possession of the Crown and ultimately that of the Tremaynes of Heligan. Impropriated tithes of this kind opened up an enormous new field of investment for the gentry, and the law courts of the time are filled with tithe-cases of all kinds, very revealing of social life. Not only the gentry, but still more cathedral chapters, colleges, bishops and (decreasingly) the Crown derived large revenues from impropriations. So that many interests and classes of society were intricately interwoven with the Church in the tithe system. In the parish of St. Austell, the rectorial tithes were less valuable than the vicarial: corn-growing less important than other agricultural operations; in other words, the vicar got more than the lay-impropriator. The balance would be the other way in corn-growing areas. Custom decided how the tithe was apportioned: room for great diversity in detail from parish to parish.

At St. Austell grass and hay fell among the small crops and tithe on it went to the vicar; so did tithes on cattle of all kinds, poultry (not on turkeys, since they were *ferae naturae*), private earnings such as servants' wages or from handicrafts or mills, fish. The last was an important item in this coastal parish: at Trenarren in 1603 the tithe of fish taken by the boat the *Trinity* (the dedication of the parish church) was compounded for 12s., the *Pearl* for 6s. at Michaelmas and another 6s. at Easter next; and so on all round the bay. In 1600 the vicar compounded with John Rowse and John Young for their boat the *John* for 20s. "Rowse and Pendrea owners" paid 15s.; "for Rowse's seine and Young's that day shared and the women 15s. 3d.": there must have been a very good catch that day: the vicar got his share. Servants paid on their wages: the highest being £6 per annum, the same amount as Sir Martin, the curate at St. Blazey, received. They were hired annually at Easter from year to year. Often they did not stop so long: of one the vicar records *dudum venit et*

[1] Hoskins, *loc. cit.* pp. 17-18.

[2] Cf. J. H. Hammond, *A Cornish Parish*, chap. xiii.

non stetit mensem. Tinners paid on their earnings; husbandmen on their agistments, the profits made by feeding their cattle on the common pastures. Mortuaries were paid on the death of every householder, and an Easter offering of 2d. was payable by every adult parishioner. The vicar or his deputy sat in church all Easter week receiving offerings. Honey and wax were brought to the church porch or deposited at the altar. In those days it was as busy as a market-place, where all is silent enough now.

If we are to look into the very hearts of the clergy, let us take, not some celebrated divine, the saint-like Jewel or Hooker, or the famous Bernard Gilpin, rector of Houghton-le-Spring, who refused a bishopric in order to become the 'Apostle of the North', but a more ordinary figure whose name is known to few today: Dr. John Favour, vicar of Halifax.[1] He was a Fellow of New College, who took over the charge of this immense, this rude and — it is not too much to say — barbarous North Country parish in 1593. It was not forty years since a predecessor, vicar Holdsworth, had been murdered there. His successor, Christopher Ashburn, cheated Holdsworth's representatives of their dues, sold off a good deal of the vicarage buildings, then resigned to get his son appointed in his stead. There followed Dr. Ledsam who resigned and went to London to get murdered. After these northerners there followed a southerner and a don, who worked manfully all the rest of his life for the benefit of his rough parishioners, though his heart was still in the South; he gave a Bible "out of the love he beareth unto his dear country . . . that it may be chained to a desk in the council chamber of the Audit House [at Southampton] for the edification of those that shall read therein". Favour had a tough struggle to get his huge parish into order, as we can see from the vivid entries with which he characterised those whom he buried. A man is killed by his kinsman in drink; an infant is found dead on Halifax moor; William King is buried, "a swearer, drinker, a most filthy adulterer, among others he kept long one Dorothy Brigg, a widow, in whose house and hand he was stricken with sudden death, his last words were oaths and curses, he lived after about forty hours but never spake word". Richard Commons was an Irish goldsmith, "a common drunkard, a blasphemer of God's holy name. When he spent all he could make he set fire to straw in four corners of his house and hanged himself in the midst . . . but by God's merciful providence the straw took not fire and so

[1] Cf. *Memorials of Ripon II* (Surtees Society), p. 277 foll.; W. J. Walker, *Chapters on the Early Registers of Halifax Parish Church, passim.*

both house and the town were preserved which he purposed to burn." David Dison was killed by a sword suddenly in drink while he was following a prostitute. Of the marriage of Elizabeth Grave — "this quean had five bastards before she wed". It may be seen that life in Halifax was not without incident.

Nor was it all of this kind. Parishioners are written up as well as down: some are noted as kind neighbours, or pious and religious, doing good works for the poor or for education; the vicar's niece dies, *quae ut pie vixit, ita sanctissime dormivit in Domino,* leaving £20 to pious uses and other bequests to Favour's family. The vicar married in the North and gathered round him a circle, Favours, Foxcrofts and Powers, to help him in good works. He worked strenuously to get Heath grammar school going; there were no less than twenty bequests to it during his vicariate. He took great interest in the extension of industry in his parish and encouraged his flock in their cloth-making, turning himself into both their lawyer and their doctor. The inscription on his monument bears witness to his work:

> Corpora et aegrotant animae; fremit undique rixa
> Scilicet orba suo turba Favore jacet.
> En Pastor Medicusque; obiit Jurisque peritus . . .

Only a long sickness gave the vicar the opportunity to write his book: he had had so many impediments, "preaching every Sabbath day, lecturing every day in the week, exercising justice in the commonwealth, practising of physic and chirurgery in the great penury and necessity thereof in the country where I live, and that not only for God's sake, which will easily multiply both clients and patients . . ." It is evident how dearly this southerner won the confidence of his flock by the many bequests they left in his oversight and care in their wills, often leaving them entirely to his discretion to apply. The Doctor's sympathies were Puritan: he held an exercise every month in Halifax church at which neighbouring ministers and strangers preached; he sheltered two lecturers, one of whom had had to leave Kent on account of his nonconformity. He looked after the material wants of his parishioners as well as their spiritual; we find his memoranda of shirts and sheets distributed to the poor: he kept strict watch over the measurements of his drapers as over the morals of his people. He writes to Mr. Baron Savile to let a man have money for work well done, for he has left himself none to spare.

There in that sombre great Yorkshire church, after thirty years of toil and moil, *pastor vigilantissimus . . . placide in Domino obdormivit.* On the south wall of his chancel one sees his bust, in ochre-red and black: there is the Doctor in gown and hood with black skull-cap and ruff, one hand on his breast, the other on a skull before him. One goes down to the vestry below; there is the library of theological books brought together by him and his successors. Outside is the grey smoke-laden atmosphere of that hiving industry of which he saw but the beginnings. The church and the great hillsides remain the same, up which the clothiers climbed pack on back in his time. As one looks out on the scene, changed yet familiar, one does not forget him. He was a good man.

Among the mingled mass of humanity serving the Church and commonwealth all over the country, there were, as always, many such doing their duty humbly and obscurely. It is impossible to over-estimate the influence of the Church's routine of prayer and good works upon that society: the effect upon imagination and conduct of the liturgy with its piercing and affecting phrases, repeated Sunday by Sunday.[1]

> We have left undone those things which we ought to have done, and we have done those things which we ought not to have done, and there is no health in us.
>
> O Lord our heavenly Father, almighty and everlasting God, which hast safely brought us to the beginning of this day: defend us in the same with thy mighty power, and grant that this day we fall into no sin, neither run into any kind of danger.
>
> Wherewithal shall a young man cleanse his way: even by ruling himself after thy word.
>
> Wash me throughly from my wickedness: and cleanse me from my sin.

And then the consolation and comfort of the last collect before the closing of Evening Prayer:

> Lighten our darkness we beseech thee, O Lord, and by thy great mercy defend us from all perils and dangers of this night, for the love of thy only son our Saviour Jesus Christ.

These things have for us today the pathos not only of the unbelieved but of the almost forgotten. For our forefathers in their day they provided a system of belief, making a whole world of experience within which to live, giving satisfaction to the inmost

[1] Cf. *The Prayer Book of Queen Elizabeth* (1559), ed. E. Benham.

impulses of the heart while not disturbing the critical standards of the mind, setting a guide to conduct in all the concerns of life, instructing in duty to God, one's neighbour and oneself, offering such consolation as nothing else in grief, in sickness and in the hour of death.

Simpler societies cannot live without a myth to support them; more sophisticated societies are the poorer without one.

The change-over from a religion of which the sacrifice of the Mass was the heart and centre to that in which sermons held the first place meant — however less attractive outwardly — an increase of reflection and edification, a stimulus to education and the active virtues. One needs only common sense and a little imagination playing upon the facts to see the kind of effect it had on society, the nature of the change. The facts may be gathered in armfuls: the endowment of preachers, the push for lecturers and support of them, the insistence by corporations in busy towns upon attendance at a weekday sermon, the refusal of a congregation to allow a favourite preacher to stop after two hours and making him go on for a third, the voluminous publication of sermons which became the staple mental diet. However unappetising we should find it, it was greatly appreciated by the Elizabethans. They crowded to sermons; they lapped them up; not content with that, they bought and read them too. In the course of it they produced classics, like the sermons of Donne or Andrewes or Hooker. But our point is the difference it made to society. It marked a mental advance; it gave the mind something to feed on, it stimulated thinking, it gave an impulse to action, it helped to educate the raw illiterate masses, many of whom cried out for such: it was a great force in the change from the sixteenth century to the more self-conscious, aware, awakened seventeenth century.

A classic defence of the Church of England in its new relation to Europe was made by Jewel in his *Apology* in the first years of the reign.[1] The task could not have fallen to a more suitable person: he was an excellent scholar, widely read in both the early Fathers and the schoolmen, with a touch of humanism to make it more agreeable; a trained logician, he was a good disputant; what was better, his well-known gentleness of disposition made him a less acrid and more convincing controversialist than most. And in fact his book set the tone — taken up and given deeper reverberations, more haunting echoes, by his pupil Hooker — of Anglican apologetics ever since. There is no doubt that Jewel's

[1] *Works of John Jewel*, ed. J. Ayre (Parker Society), vol. III.

mind was in a different class from his tenacious and opprobrious opponent, the Romanist Harding. Each of them bandies about the word ' truth '; each of them acknowledges, teaches and is reviled for the sake of ' truth '. ' Truth ' always means your own point of view: the assumption runs through the dead controversies of these people on both sides, on all sides. With them all, it is easy to observe, ' God's will ' = one's own will, ' God's truth ' = what one thinks oneself. One may omit the superfluous concept and devote one's attention to concrete considerations.

Jewel begins characteristically with two common-sense points, rebutting the charges that the change in England was disorderly and increased dissension among Englishmen, and that the intention was to overthrow the existing order in Europe for the rule of the people. So far from that, he was able to argue, all had been done orderly and soberly: " The matter hath been treated in open parliament, with long consultation, and before a notable synod and convocation ".[1] The Pope should have listened to their reasons instead of condemning them outright. There was a good case for reform: a reformed England meant stricter living than before; Protestant marriage was better than previous concubinage — a point that made a great impression with Protestants. He is strongly against the country maintaining droves of monks, who " for all they do nothing " yet live well on other folk's labour: a sound Protestant emphasis. Elizabeth's government was conducted by laymen, not by ecclesiastics neglecting their proper duties for it. It was the duty of churchmen to preach the gospel; as to the rites abolished, " they have not that antiquity, they have not that universality, they have not that consent of all places nor of all times ".[2] As for the relation of the Church to the State, it was in essence a continuation of the medieval position in regard to the two spheres, spiritual and temporal, with the Papal ascendancy omitted. Nor was this so very strange and new, " for we have had ere now in England provincial synods and governed our church by home-made laws ".[3] And this was not the only country to opt to rule its own branch of the Church. It was in truth part of the secular movement of the Northern peoples away from the tutelage of Rome.

The aim of the English Church was to get back to something nearer the simplicity of primitive Christianity, behind the subsequent accretions of time. Their appeal, therefore, was to the Scriptures, and they asked to be tried by them. All this part of Jewel's argument is tactically very skilful: he suggests first what

[1] *Ibid.* p. 93. [2] *Ibid.* p. 89. [3] *Ibid.* p. 102.

he is going to argue: there are centuries of scholastic disputation behind him. One notices, too, how much the argument is within one tradition and training, citing the same authorities and going round and round, like any Marxist, over the same ground. He tactfully elides the central difficulties of doctrine over the Mass. His appeal is to the success of the English Church. There could not be a more important historical argument; it says nothing to the truth or not of the theological propositions at issue, since these belong to the realm of the unprovable. So much the better. The success or not of the Church of England was to be the practical test: all the labour and devotion, the administrative good sense and piety that went into it. It must be pronounced to have had the better of the argument historically: it suited the English people, and neither of the two alternatives would have done better — or anything like so well. At the same time Jewel's hopes were not wholly fulfilled: Protestantism generated a number of sects. He concludes with an eloquent appeal to the mind of Europe for a fair judgment of the English Church.

In sixteenth-century circumstances, and certainly on the assumptions they accepted — the identification of civilisation with Christianity, of Europe with the Christian Church, of its unique revelation in that chosen environment — it was not nonsense to think that the Church of England had a stronger intellectual case than Rome. It was Christianity reformed. The conversion of a number of distinguished intellects bore witness to that. (In the collapse of the whole world of such assumptions in our time the case is altered.) It is interesting that with Jewel the position is argued on intellectual grounds, on Church considerations: natural enough in a cleric, who had come out of the same tradition as his antagonists. It was also the mode in which people *thought*. But there were plenty of more mundane considerations to account for, and justify, the breach with Rome. There was the geological shift of Northern Europe away from dependence on its ancient primacy: something impersonal, a movement so immense — like the social revolution of our time — as to dwarf, if not remove, personal responsibilities. There was the determination of a country reaching maturity to have all its affairs under its own control. (One may compare the revolt of the American colonies from the mother country.) There was the economic benefit of stopping payments overseas; the enormous increase of wealth consequent upon the secularisation of Church lands, the productive emphasis as against the non-productive and the wasteful. There was the simplification of a top-heavy, too elaborate ecclesiastical structure, both of government and institutions, of beliefs, rites and observances, cutting out the dead wood and the waste: an economy of mental energy as well as of material resources. Hence the greater efficiency and achievement of Protestant English society, as well as its moral toning up for action and the part it was thereby to play in the world. The losses were chiefly aesthetic, not merely in architecture — of churches, of music and works of art, but in certain charming mystical types such as the defeated cause generated, like Campion and Southwell. But such is the inextinguishable creativeness of human impulse that the English Church was itself to produce them shortly in a Nicholas Ferrar or a George Herbert.

The Christian myth has been a wonderfully creative one, the most creative that Europe has ever known, or is ever likely to know. The change in England, though it was disturbing to aesthetic creativeness for a time, soon proved itself sufficiently propitious to the arts. Catholicism is, of course, by far the most propitious of all forms of Christianity, for it is a religion of acceptance of man's experience, of all that wells up in his nature from the earth. The English Church showed that it too provided an atmosphere gracious to the arts, though naturally not on such an oecumenical scale. It did not have the repressive inhibitions, the positive hostility to the arts, of Calvinism: it was too humane, too Catholic for that. In truth it was a representative expression of the English people, the moderation of its nature its characteristic note, not the ecstasies of a St. Teresa or an El Greco, the moral extremism of a Pascal, the sublime *innerlichkeit* of a Bach, but the rich and kindly humanity of Hooker, Herbert and Vaughan, of Orlando Gibbons and Purcell, of Wren, Newman and Thomas Hardy. These things show that for the English it provided a sufficient habitation for the spirit.

CHAPTER XI

CATHOLICS AND PURITANS

I

THE chief difficulty in treating the question of Catholicism and of Catholic Recusancy is that of seeing it in proper proportion. It has usually been treated on sectarian lines, either on one side or the other: not so here. Then the intrinsic interest of the subject means that there is a vast literature on it. In fact the great bulk of the population was not touched; it only concerned a small percentage of the people. But real importance does not go by percentages, and this minority consisted of people who mattered — peers, landed gentry, university men, priests, scholars, poets. The awkwardness, the exacerbation of the conflict, in the end its significance, are due to the fact that it was a cleavage within the governing class. Hence too its interest: for these were men who could not only think and argue for themselves, had an intellectual position to hold, but the estates and place in society to maintain it. What made it more acute and tragic was that it was part and parcel of the international dispute raging between the Counter-Reformation and Protestantism, of the Roman Church and the Spanish Empire with the Northern heresy.

In this conflict for power, which grew desperate and flamed into open war in the last half of the reign, here within the country was a Fifth Column, part of it actual, conscious and determined, part potential, part passive victims, caught irremediably and tortured by the ineluctable — often unendurable — conflict of allegiances. It is a situation that we can all too readily understand, far better than the innocent, civilised Victorians; it is all so familiar in our own deplorable time: we know those refinements of torture, the prison life, the spies and counter-spies, the seminaries of mutually exclusive faiths, the cult of martyrdom; invasion and resistance movements, the planned projects for exterminating the liberties of peoples, sometimes carried out, sometimes successful; the implacable hates, the use of assassination, the division of families, the riving asunder of friends and — what is at root most reminiscent of today — the conflict within the individual conscience itself, which tore men's hearts open and exposed the quivering, bleeding flesh for the historian to feed on for his daily fare.

For the great mass of people these things did not apply: fortunately, in England they would follow the government's ruling. The curious commonplace book kept by a North Country cleric of old-fashioned sympathies — a perhaps unique document — reveals the way in which the new orders from the government in London are obeyed at once in the country: no more candles, ashes and palms at Candlemas, on Ash Wednesday, Palm Sunday; no more creeping to the cross on Good Friday or lighting the Paschal candle on Easter even.[1] The English State was pretty efficient and did not like waste. It was a useful habit of mind politically. A few years after Elizabeth's religious changes we have some indication of the attitude of the gentry from the surveys of the dioceses which the government demanded of the bishops. The rough figures give us: J.P.s favourable 431, indifferent or neutral 264, hostile 157.[2] This was very early on, the year 1564; most of Mary's appointments were still going. It was a sufficient majority among those who mattered; for it may be taken that of the indifferent the great bulk would go with the government — especially after the oath of Supremacy was put to them from 1569, while of the hostile minority many would die off and not be replaced. Every county had some Papists, but in only one county, Lancashire, were they and their sympathisers a possible majority. It is noticeable that the areas where they were strongest were in the North and the West. At this early date there were still Papists among the leading figures of some towns: they are mentioned at Winchester, Hereford and Leicester, while the Bishop of Coventry and Lichfield found the greatest disorder to be in the 'towns corporate'. But this was rapidly to change, until no more solid support for the government was to be found than in the towns.

What is striking from any point of view is the extraordinary leniency of the first decade of Elizabeth's government. It was very politic and wise, but it could not have been maintained if the government's course had not been popular and, even so, aided

[1] Cf. A. G. Dickens, "Robert Parkyns' 'Narrative of the Reformation'", *E.H.R.* (1947), p. 58 foll.

[2] "Letters from the Bishops to the Privy Council, 1564" (ed. M. Bateson), *Camden Misc.* vol. IX.

strongly by the reaction from Mary's. At a time when mutual massacres for the sake of religion were taking place in the Netherlands, and wars of religion in France, not a life was lost in England for these causes. The Queen and her ministers were rightly proud of their record and, in the Elizabethan manner, were not ashamed to boast of it. There was no persecution of Catholics; the legislation of 1559 and even of 1563 did not amount to more than exclusion from office and, even so, we have seen how many remained J.P.s.[1] So long as there was no declaration against the Queen from Rome, Catholics seem mostly to have gone on going to church, as we have seen with the great lawyer Plowden. There were various practices: priests might say the Communion service in church and a private Mass for the old-fashioned faithful at home; or a household like Lady Monteagle's would have a Protestant chaplain and private Masses by a priest.[2] Boundaries had happily not yet become rigid and the government exerted itself to keep the ways open.

In the Northern Province, where Catholicism was strongest, the visitation of 1559 ended by depriving not more than a dozen beneficed clergymen of their livings.[3] In Lancashire, which was strongly conservative, only three were deprived.[4] Laurence Vaux, warden of Manchester College, went off to Ireland, taking the plate, vestments and muniments of the church with him for a better day, which never came; only one other Fellow of the college refused submission. It was not until three years later that James Hargreaves, vicar of the important parish of Blackburn and a 'noted papist', was deprived. One of the most important of the exiles at Louvain went on enjoying his living for several years undeprived. The government was anxious to hold its hand, to leave the door open for return and not to have to drive people out. For absence from church the fine imposed was 12d. for each offence, for the benefit of the poor: 52s. a year was no hardship to the landed gentry and it was reported from Lancashire, which was more recalcitrant than any other county, that the Recusants regarded not such light penalties.

In that county the authorities were far too lenient. There is no doubt that the survival of Catholicism on such a considerable scale in Lancashire — quite exceptional for any English county — was due to the slackness of the Earl of Derby and Bishop Down-

[1] Cf. A. O. Meyer, *England and the Catholic Church under Queen Elizabeth* (trans. J. R. McKee), p. 124.

[2] Nicholas Sander, *Rise and Growth of the Anglican Schism* (trans. D. Lewis), p. 267.

[3] J. S. Leatherbarrow, *The Lancashire Elizabethan Recusants* (Chetham Society), p. 19.

[4] *V.C.H. Lancs.* II. 50.

ham in that decade. " They that have the sword in their hands under her Majesty . . . suffer it to rust in the scabbard ", wrote a Protestant clergyman two decades later.[1] By then the situation was beyond repair: it should have been taken in hand in the fifteen-sixties. But the Earl, who was responsible for the area, was in rather an equivocal situation: his wife and his relations were largely Catholic; there were said to be priests in his household; as late as 1569 the Northern Earls looked to him to join them. After their failure he came out more actively in execution of the government's policy. The majority of the Lancashire gentry were Catholics, and as against the supineness of the authorities the leading priests were very active: above all, William Allen and Laurence Vaux. Allen was a Lancashire man: his grandfather had received from a benevolent abbot of Dieulacres, his kinsman, a convenient lease of the monastic grange at Rossall. The family — unlike so many others — were gratefully and undeviatingly Catholic. (The farm is now under the sea, what remains of the buildings a part of the school.) Allen gave up a promising career at Oxford to go abroad in 1561 to Louvain, where he became the leader of the exiles. Next year he returned to Lancashire, where he worked hard and successfully to resist the tendency to conform, to keep Catholics sternly to their separate path. Thence he moved to the vicinity of Oxford and later to the household of the Duke of Norfolk, himself a Protestant but with Catholic connections and dependants. In 1565 Allen went abroad and never returned. By this time, with the accession of Pius V, there was a change in Papal policy, which became definite and aggressive: it was declared mortal sin to frequent the Protestant service. Laurence Vaux crossed over to Lancashire to circulate the order. By 1567 it was reported to the Council that a number of gentlemen had taken an oath not to come to Communion; leading families like the Molyneux and Blundells were reconciled and absolved.[2] The tragedy had begun.

This was precisely what the government had wished to avoid. The withdrawal from the Roman obedience, after the Marian experience, was inevitable; even Mary had had to confess with humiliation to Pole that there was more difficulty over the authority of the Apostolic See than over the true religion, and that his legation was hateful to her subjects.[3] Elizabeth could not but break, but she was anxious to avoid open war and especially any condemnation by Rome. Long delayed and held up by

[1] Leatherbarrow, *op. cit.* p. 87.
[2] *V.C.H. Lancs.* II. 52-3.
[3] Pole, *Ep.* IV. 119; Foxe, *Acts and Monuments*, VI. 114.

the diplomacy of Philip and the Emperor, it came in the most brutal and offensive manner possible with the Bull *Regnans in Excelsis* in 1570. Elizabeth was declared excommunicate and deposed, a heretic and a bastard; her subjects were absolved from their allegiance and encouraged to resist and to rebel. St. Pius V was not the less a fool of a friar for being a saint. He should have thought first of means of executing his Bull before publishing it. As it was, both he and his successor, Gregory XIII, were reduced to approving of projects for the Queen's assassination.[1] Whatever else may be thought of her government it had no part nor lot in projects of assassination — such as the Catholic princes, Spanish, French and Roman, made such use of. It was not until the reign of Sixtus V — himself a man of great personality — that the merits of the Queen began to be appreciated at Rome; but by then there was a European war and the Armada for the forcible conversion of England was in preparation. It was observed that this Pope did not entertain great hopes of its success.

The Bull of 1570 was the last occasion on which a pope deposed a reigning prince. It was perhaps a mistake that it should have been tried against England. At the same time there is a perfection in its symbolism: it was the last, ineffective gesture of the medieval world against the scandalous and unprecedented young nation which more than any other symbolised the new. But at the moment the Pope scandalised his supporters rather than his opponents: Philip and the Emperor were taken completely by surprise; the politicians were horrified by the ineptitude of the move. In itself the Bull was irregular and indefensible from the point of view of canon law; it condemned Elizabeth for taking the title of Supreme Head, which she had expressly refused.[2] It certainly showed great ignorance of English affairs at Rome, complete failure to grasp the elements of the situation inside the country. Regarded as a political declaration, the Bull was a catastrophe. It is usual to defend it as having served a certain spiritual purpose: as preserving, at a terrible cost in human lives (those, of course, are less important), a Roman Catholic remnant in England. From a wider point of view of Christian unity, it made the breach between England and Europe irremediable.

Within the country it marked the turning-point for the Catholics. It made a fatal dilemma for them: either they were traitors to the State or they were disobedient to the Church; within this contradiction they had to live. Gripped in a vice, they twisted and turned, tried various attitudes for comfort or

[1] Cf. Meyer, *op. cit.* p. 90 foll. [2] *Ibid.* pp. 82-3.

compromise, broke into differing sections of opinion, in the end developing an open conflict between the secular priests, upon whom the worst sufferings fell, and the Jesuits under the control of the famous Father Parsons, who had the ear of Rome. The seculars came to hate him worse than the government: it was they who fixed on him the sobriquet of Machiavellian (he was a brilliant intriguer, his hands were calloused with wire-pulling). Europe was treated to the strange spectacle of the government and the appellant priests in collusion over an appeal to Rome against the Jesuits: of course in vain. But this was after twenty years of sublime struggle and suffering, until flesh and blood could endure it no longer and the government was sickened by the butchery it could not escape. The Queen was never in favour of the execution of priests; she preferred banishment. The circumstances attendant upon the execution of the Jesuit Campion, whom she had taken particular notice of as a young man of great promise at Oxford, seem to have shocked her as they shocked a great many people. A drop of blood from his mangled body as his members were being thrown into the cauldron fell upon the young Henry Walpole and sealed his vocation: it led him to a similar death fourteen years later, at York. This last outburst of executions about this time is said to have wrung from her the cry — was there to be no end of the shedding of blood?

But what else could the government have done? From the moment of the Bull there was open war between England and Rome. The crucial question was the issue of allegiance. The Queen had been excommunicated and deposed by the Pope, her subjects encouraged to rebel, invasion of the country promoted. What was the attitude of Catholics? The government was perfectly genuine — it was on strong ground — when it took the line that " the Queen would not have any of their consciences unnecessarily sifted, to know what affection they had to the old religion "; it was the acceptance of her sovereignty, the assurance of their allegiance, that it demanded.[1] It was for withholding that that the Catholic martyrs died. From the government's point of view they were traitors. And indeed it is noticeable in the numerous trials that make such sadly contemporary reading, that it is always when a priest falters over this question — ' the bloody question ' they called it — that his death is sealed.[2] Some priests spoke their treason openly, like Cuthbert Mayne, the first of

[1] *Ibid.* p. 128.

[2] Cf. the examinations in E. H. Burton and J. H. Pollen, *Lives of the English Martyrs*, vol. I. 1583–1588; *e.g.* that of Edward Shelley, p. 418.

the seminarists to be executed: he said that if the country were invaded by a Catholic prince to reclaim it to Rome, all Catholics should aid and assist the invader.[1] One need not doubt that the bulk of the Catholic laity was loyal enough to the Queen, nor that the main purpose and work of the mission in England was religious, not political. The conflict remained ineluctable and it had been made so by Rome: if the mission had succeeded in its purely religious objective, in reconciling England — *per impossibile* — to the Roman obedience, that would have been the end of Elizabeth's rule.

Penal legislation against the Catholics and the practice of their religion became sharper as the conflict grew more acute and tension mounted. No persecution at first, merely exclusion; but after the Bull of Excommunication it was made high treason to bring in any Bulls or to reconcile anyone to Rome. This did not deter people; the seventies saw a marked Catholic revival, the first onrush of the Counter-Reformation's offensive against England. Allen's foundation of an English College at Louvain in 1568, subsequently transferred to Douai, was a great and lasting success: for two centuries, until the French Revolution, Douai was the seed-bed and centre of English Catholicism.[2] Scores of students flocked thither from Oxford and Cambridge, and from Catholic families all over the country. In the fifteen-seventies they came seeping back as priests in scores, to reconcile, to persuade, to subvert. The English College at Rome was founded to take a hand in the promising work. In 1580 the accession of the Society of Jesus to the task was signalised by the scandalously successful mission of Campion and Parsons. For months these famous priests were at large, preaching and converting, writing their tracts, printing and circulating them; Convocation at Oxford assembled to find Campion's *Decem Rationes* awaiting it on the benches in St. Mary's. The government was greatly alarmed by the campaign, and the success, of the Jesuits. In 1581 a new Act of Parliament made it high treason to withdraw anyone from the Church of England to Rome; anyone saying or hearing Mass was liable to a large fine and a year's imprisonment; a fine of £20 a month was imposed for abstention from church. It was this last provision that gave the government an effective financial weapon to use against Catholic families, and from now on we find them liable to pay £260 a year or to have two-thirds of their lands extended.

[1] Cf. my *Tudor Cornwall*, p. 350.

[2] Cf. T. F. Knox, *The First and Second Diaries of the English College, Douay*, p. xxviii foll.

With the outbreak of war, all Jesuits and seminary priests were ordered to depart the realm; any priest coming in was guilty of high treason, anyone maintaining him, of felony. A last measure, when there was a threat of a new Armada in 1593, restricted all Recusants to within five miles of their dwelling: they were not to move beyond without special permission.

The tightening up of these repressive measures proceeded step by step with the mounting of the crisis. They were never so uniformly enforced as ordinary legislation; they were designed rather as weapons which the government could press or slacken as occasion demanded. As the struggle got fiercer, Parliament became more Puritan and was always prepared to go further: there was a proposal to take away the children of Recusants and have them brought up as Protestants. The converse would certainly have been done by the Inquisition in Spain or Italy. The Queen would not have it in England. There always remained a residual moderation in the government on the strictly religious issue, amid all the hangings and quarterings. No compromise on that of allegiance: no mercy for those acting with the enemy in time of war. One could draw a graph of the number of executions showing how they go up and down with the crises of the time, increasing from 2 in 1583 to 15 in 1584, the threshold of war, reaching their apogee in 1588 with a holocaust of 34 victims.[1] With the comparative security of 1589 the number falls to 9, increases next year to 11, next year to 15, for the remainder of the reign, with the slackening of danger, never to rise above 10; for the last years 8 were executed in 1601, 6 in 1602 and only 1 in 1603. There were altogether much the same number of executions, something under 300, for the last thirty years of Elizabeth's reign as there were burnings during the last three of Mary's.

The Elizabethan persecution was not much more successful than the Marian: neither of them prevented people from thinking what they wanted to think. Meyer concludes that the Elizabethan persecution did not in any way damage the country: it went from strength to strength, its energies increased and its achievements in every sphere. All the same, one cannot but regret the devotion, the spiritual energies, that went into sterile and futile conflict: if only, instead of obfuscating each other, they had gone positively and constructively into making the Church and society better! One must not read history backward from what happened subsequently. People took a line — easily enough in the early days — against the government; they could not know to what it would lead in

[1] *Catholic Record Society*, V. 8 foll.

the future — the miseries, the tortures, the divisions, the ending of families — or they would have drawn back. With families as with individuals, some particular loyalty or conservative attachment, or just a quirk of mind, or an accident like reading a book when a young man at Oxford — particularly in the case of young men, who are prone to take a leap in the dark — and the decision is made before they are aware of it, with all the hideous consequences they would have shrunk from if they could only have known; then pride and loyalty, fidelity to the group and its members, enter in to keep them to the course they chose, leading to a future of exclusion, insulation, conspiracy, martyrdom, all unforeseen when the line was taken in the usual human way, unthinking, not imagining what could happen in the future, or even reflecting on the knowable past, but merely reacting to the present condition like any creature without reason, animal or termite.

The government too had its difficulties, its disillusionments and failures — Catholic Recusancy became an intractable problem. Its worst failure was in Lancashire, the only English county where Catholicism survived continuously on any scale. This " so unbridled and bad an handful of England " — as Lord Strange, Derby's eldest son, called it — gave the government any amount of trouble, and is thereby, for our purposes, all the more interesting.[1] The explanation of Catholic survival there is a social one, and offers one more illustration of our leading theme as to the place of the gentry in Tudor society. Without the agreement of the local gentry the government in Westminster could not get its policy carried into effect or its orders effectively executed. Up to the failure of the Northern Rising, Derby's attitude was equivocal and the great majority of the Lancashire gentry were with him. If he had thrown in his lot with the Northern earls, as they hoped, Lancashire would have been reduced as the other Northern counties were. Thereby hangs, perhaps, a moral. The government, none too sure of the Earl, was content not to press matters too far early on — until it was too late. In sixteenth-century society everything shows that it is the successful exertion of force that counts. In Lancashire the fulcrum was wanting: social influence and power were all on the other side, at any rate in the country. The towns of East Lancashire were strongly Protestant, especially Manchester, to which the harassed Bishop Chadderton would gladly have removed his stool. West and North Lancashire were under the domination of their gentry, who

[1] J. Peck, *Desiderata Curiosa,* I. 141.

remained conservative and Catholic. Of the J.P.s in 1564, only six are returned as favourable to the government's proceedings; eighteen, and those all the really important ones, were against.[1] In the hundred of Blackburn not a single J.P. was in favour; all the leading gentry were against: Sir John Southworth of Samlesbury, John Towneley of Towneley, John Osbaldeston of Osbaldeston; and the fact that Richard Ashton and John Bradyll had done well out of the dissolution of Whalley abbey did not prevent them from being good Catholics. In the hundred of Amounderness, which was dominated by Sir Richard Shirburn of Stonyhurst, who was a conforming Papist, the Bishop could recommend no-one trustworthy to add to the bench.

Everywhere in Lancashire the old usages cropped up: the people of Farnworth were shriven and burnt candles on Candlemas day; at Preston they would not take the sacrament in their hands but, after the old fashion, in their mouths; they had their children christened in private by priests; at burials prayers were said for the dead; old women told their beads at the Communion.[2] As late as 1585 we have a pathetic picture of 'Uncle James', an old Henrician priest, travelling with his few trinkets about the countryside administering Catholic rites: his chalice and paten of tin, his girdle of thread, his two little boxes for singing bread and an old Mass-book. In 1568 the Council pressed Bishop Downham into a show of activity: he informed them that "from Warrington all along the sea-coast the gentlemen were of the faction and withdrew themselves from the religion".[3] Sir Richard Molyneux of Sefton, the leading figure in the hundred of Derby, and the Blundells of Ince had been reconciled. The Bishop reported that the people were tractable and obedient, but this was pure indolence on his part. The Earl and the Bishop were stimulated into having six gentlemen up before them: who promised conformity, were let off leniently and went off to do as they liked. Nowell, Dean of St. Paul's, a famous Lancashire man and brother-in-law of John Towneley, was sent on a preaching mission which did some good temporarily. Yet several of the clergy, disappeared, were reconciled, about this time.

The soil was ready for Allen's seminary priests, and indeed Lancashire contributed a greater number than any other county. When the Jesuit Campion came on his mission he spent some time in safety there, with the Southworths, Houghtons, Talbots and

[1] *Camden Misc.* IX. *loc. cit.* 77-8.
[2] Leatherbarrow, *op. cit.* pp. 12, 25, 45, 121-2, 138.
[3] *V.C.H. Lancs.* pp. 52-3.

Westbys; it was not until he came south to Berkshire that he was caught. In 1579 a new bishop was appointed: Chadderton, a Cambridge don with Puritan sympathies and a declared intention of doing well out of his see. From his correspondence with the Council we can follow the now insuperable difficulties with which he was faced.[1] Derby and he as the leading figures on their ecclesiastical Commission were urged to take action. The first thing that came to his notice was the dispute that raged in the parishes as to whether common bread or wafer bread was more proper for the sacrament: the bored Council ruled — each parish according to taste, until Parliamentary order. Burghley's sage advice was to feed children on milk. The Council understood well that it was " the obstinacy of the great that prevents the lower orders conforming ". Not one Recusant had been presented at quarter-sessions, save only at Manchester: naturally enough, since the J.P.s' sympathies were Catholic, they were not going to present each other, or themselves. The Commission was urged to act, and at last Sir John Southworth and John Towneley were laid by the heels.

But great interest was made on behalf of such persons. Lady Egerton was a Recusant, but hope was entertained of her conforming; a respite was begged to give her time. Some months later the Lord Chancellor himself was begging a further respite for preachers to confer with her and persuade her. It is to be feared that the obstinate old woman went on as before. Sir John Southworth was treated with much consideration: he was to be confined to his own house on bonds, if willing; he was permitted to take the air with his keeper in the grounds of Alport lodge, Derby's house in Manchester. All to no avail, he went to prison — the new Fleet at Salford. Here a great fuss was made about his treatment by Robert Worsley, the capable and reliable keeper — who had infinite trouble getting payment of the fines of the richer Recusants to support the poorer in prison. Strong suit was made for Sir John on account of his former good services; his eldest son asked that he might be removed to London for better treatment. All to no avail: Walsingham had to enquire whether it were true that Sir John intended to disinherit his eldest son for conforming. (This was precisely what Milton's grandfather, under-ranger of Shotover Forest, did to his son: a stiff-necked stock.) No doubt Sir John preferred his younger son, the priest whose putative bones now repose under the blood-red pall of a martyr in a chapel of Westminster cathedral. For the luxury

[1] Peck, *op. cit.* p. 81 foll.

of not attending church John Towneley paid some £5000 in Recusancy fines up to 1601: an enormous sum, but he was very rich and very pious.[1] Dean Nowell himself interceded for his brother-in-law and petitioned that he might have leave to come to London to consult physicians for his health.

The situation in Lancashire did not improve for all the government's efforts: in 1590 there were some 700 Recusants presented (in Cheshire 200): there was nothing like such a proportion anywhere else.[2] The Recusancy fines could not conceivably be collected with any fulness; large debts to the Crown accumulated on the part of the leading prisoners; the poorer Recusants had to be freed, since their retention was only an expense to the Crown. The Bishop got into trouble: some of his fellow Commissioners had the kindness to report that he was retaining £3000 of recognisances and bonds in his own hands. This, on account of his unfortunate announcement of his intention to make a fortune, was believed. Burghley sent him a sharp reprimand; he was to return all such moneys at once into the Exchequer: "My lord, to avoid doubtful reports made of you in this matter, you shall do well to make answer speedily".[3] The report was untrue. Walsingham somewhat wryly consoled his Puritan confrère: "I know men of your calling are most subject to ill reports than others. And so God, for the best, will have it. To the end you direct all your doings with greater circumspection."[4]

The Bishop had a supporter in the Earl's son and heir, Lord Strange, between whom and his father there was a certain tension: "To be constant is no common virtue," wrote the son, "although it be most commendable, most fit and least found in noblemen."[5] It seems that they both thought that the Earl's temporising policy was responsible for the ill-success of the campaign in Lancashire. He sat on the Commission, was the leading commissioner, took part in examinations of priests and Recusants, condemned them when he could not help it, hung back when he could. A Stanley, he continued his family tradition of being on both sides. But from the social point of view — and that was probably what weighed with the Earl — how could the campaign succeed against the embattled gentry of the shire? In Derby hundred as late as 1590, out of seventy-one names among the gentry, only ten were reliable supporters of the reformed religion.[6] The most slippery customer was the conforming Papist: Sir Thomas Gerard of

[1] Leatherbarrow, *op. cit.* p. 34.
[2] *V.C.H. Lancs.* p. 56.
[3] Peck, *op. cit.* p. 134.
[4] *Ibid.* p. 146.
[5] *Ibid.* p. 147.
[6] Leatherbarrow, p. 115.

Bryn was one such, father of the famous Jesuit, who in the course of his long mission in England had greater success as a proselytiser than probably any other priest. In the year 1585 twenty-one priests were returned as at work in the county: they had things their way: the Church itself had only ten preachers in all that county to confront them. The government came to the conclusion that more preachers were wanted to present the case. The trouble with them was that they were apt to be Puritans: only Puritans could get up the requisite enthusiasm. Bishop Chadderton encouraged them, and even the government allowed their exercises. But this had its dangers. Archbishop Sandys thought that Bishop Chadderton gave way to them too much: "The devil is crafty, and the young ministers of these our times grow mad".[1]

Away in Westminster, Burghley, with his professional thirst for information, had a detailed map of Lancashire which gave him a complete picture of the situation; but it gave him no prise on it. As the years pass we can watch the Catholics consolidating themselves into a conscious minority, cut off increasingly from the public life of the country, driven in upon their own defences and working out their own methods of survival. These must necessarily be economic. The economic weapon of fines for Recusancy — since extermination was not to be thought of — was the most powerful means of bringing pressure to bear. But there were ways and means of evading it. Often the head of the family went to church occasionally, while his wife and children abstained. Recusant women offered a peculiarly difficult problem. They were usually more obstinate than the men, and had no property to get hold of. It was one such *dévote* who persuaded the poor priest, James Bell, who had been an Anglican minister for twenty years, to revert and so led him on to his martyrdom at Lancaster, 20 April 1584.[2] It was quite common for Lancashire families to have a Recusant schoolmaster, who was sometimes a priest, in the house: Mrs. Houghton of the Lea kept one of the Blundells as such, who taught her children to sing and play upon the virginals.[3] When children of these good Catholic families grew up they were sent abroad to Allen's foundations at Douai or in Rome, to Brussels or St. Omer, Valladolid or Seville. One

[1] Peck, p. 102.

[2] Burton and Pollen, *op. cit.* p. 107 foll. His case provides another instance of the governing political distinction in condemning to death. When asked "Whose part wouldst thou take if the Pope or any other by his authority should make wars against the Queen?" he answered, "We ought to take part with the Church of God for the Catholic religion".

[3] Leatherbarrow, p. 104.

sees the formation of the English Catholic tradition, a self-contained minority with its affiliations abroad, with its own idiosyncrasy and peculiar place in the subsequent life of the country.

When Recusants failed to pay their fines and continued to be so openly recalcitrant that it was thought desirable to pursue them, two-thirds of their lands were liable by statute to be taken into temporary possession. It was here that all kinds of tricks were playable. Naturally members of the family got a lease where possible, to keep the lands in the same hands. Or Recusants made over their lands to other members of their family before they became liable to forfeiture. In Lancashire — and no doubt elsewhere — the practice grew up of J.P.s and even ecclesiastical commissioners themselves taking grants of Recusants' lands and goods in collusion, while the Recusants retained the use of them. All was fair in this kind of war; thus when John Bridgewater, the author of the *Concertatio Ecclesiae Anglicanae*, a well-beneficed man and a chaplain of Leicester, went abroad to become a Jesuit, he had the financial prescience to lease out his livings before going.[1] The operation of the Recusancy fines is one of the most complex and specialist subjects in the whole period; it has been very little studied.[2] The truth seems to be that the operation of the whole thing was very irregular and apt to be spasmodic, with occasional drives against the Recusants as the government or a local sheriff thought fit. But though the system was haphazard in operation, the financial penalties were in the long run such as to squeeze the lesser people out of existence. Only the greater Catholic landowners could survive, they and the tenants dependent upon them. They did what they could for their dependants: we find a large landowner like John Arundell making over property to co-religionists;[3] it was in the natural order of things that their tenants should be good Catholics like their lords. So we come back to the social bonds, the intricate threads of interest and affection, that kept the Catholic minority together through the heroic days of persecution to the hebetude of the eighteenth century.

It was thus that Catholicism survived on a geographical basis, where it survived at all: in Lancashire notably, in three areas — in Ribblesdale about Stonyhurst, in the Fylde country and along the fertile coastal area from Liverpool to Southport. In Cornwall,

[1] Sir C. Chadwyck-Healey, *History of Part of West Somerset*, p. 167.

[2] The source for such a study is the Recusants' Rolls in the Public Record Office (E 377/1 foll.). The first Roll, for 1592–3, has been published with a useful introduction in *Catholic Record Society*, vol. XVIII.

[3] Cf. E 377/15, *sub* Cornub.

for example, it survived among the tenantry of the Arundells of Lanherne, in the parishes of St. Columb and St. Mawgan, until the family was absorbed into the Wardour branch and the last embers flickered out among the farmers in the eighteenth century. So too in Yorkshire Catholicism was localised to a few areas where the leading gentry were of the old faith and formed a community with their servants and tenants. This great county was second in importance only to Lancashire in English Catholicism: the Diary of the English College at Rome from 1579 to 1673 shows 130 Yorkshire students to Lancashire's 200.[1] Yet the actual proportion of Recusants to the rest of the population was small, even in centres of Recusancy. There was a marked increase in the numbers presented through the seventies and eighties, with the seminary priests active in reconciling and the government getting sharper on their tracks. By the outbreak of war something near 600 were identified, though by no means all were routed out, or indicted.[2] The peak of Recusancy was reached in the year after Elizabeth's death. Hundreds who had not dared to show their hands came into the open: there was a general expectation of a change of policy and a measure of toleration with Mary Stuart's son on the throne — until all that was blown sky-high with the Gunpowder Plot. The Yorkshire Survey of 1604 may be taken therefore as the high-water mark reached by Recusancy.[3] It reveals altogether some 2500 Recusants and non-communicants, of which total the latter provided some 600. The Yorkshire population has been estimated at 300,000; and though that may be too high, the proportion of Recusants can hardly have been 2 per cent.[4]

These figures are very striking and enable us to get the question of Catholic Recusancy in a better perspective than any amount of sectarian dispute. It was none the less vexing to the government, since it concerned chiefly a section of the governing class, or dangerous, because of its peculiar relation to the international conflict raging. In Yorkshire, as elsewhere, the Catholic remnant was markedly localised. In the East Riding, open to the new influences blowing up the Humber, dominated by the towns Hull and York, there was hardly any: only in the south-western extremity around Hemingborough, where the leading families of Metham and Babthorpe held sway. Sir William Babthorpe's son,

[1] *Records of the Society of Jesus*, ed. H. Foley, VI. xxii.

[2] A. G. Dickens, "The First Stages in Romanist Recusancy in Yorkshire, 1560–1590", *Yorks. Arch. Journal* (1941), p. 170.

[3] *A List of the Roman Catholics in the County of York in 1604*, ed. E. Peacock.

[4] A. G. Dickens, "The Extent and Character of Recusancy in Yorkshire, 1604", *Yorks. Arch. Journal* (1948), p. 24 foll.

crippled by fines, had to sell the family estates and died overseas fighting for Spain; and that was that. Not far away in the country towards Leeds, in the West Riding, there was a group of half a dozen parishes where the gentry were Recusants, around Ledsham and Kippax: such families as Watertons and Barnebys. Thomas Barneby, head of the family, was conforming; but the women were Recusants and his son was a seminary priest about the place; so was the son of Margaret Champney, the other family in Caythorne parish. The Lilburnes were Recusants, the family that in the next generation produced the radical John and the regicide Robert Lilburne: anything to be out of step. Further north, the Ripon area contributed several knots of Recusants: attachment to the old faith here went back through the Rising of 1569 to the Pilgrimage of Grace. The Nortons, who had suffered so much for their part in the Rising and are commemorated in *The White Doe of Rylstone*, continued to be Catholic: with such families it was a point of honour to remain so.[1] The Inglebys of Ripley produced a martyr: Francis, fourth son of Sir William, who suffered at York, 3 June 1586: that kept them true, and a good many others in that parish too, servants and tenants of the big house, whither there continued great resort of Recusants and priests. In the south of Craven a few parishes were affected; the leading family were the Tempests of Broughton, who were allied to the Percys by marriage, so that that reactionary tradition accounted for them. But like the Throckmortons of Coughton in Warwickshire, and many others, the family was divided and had a Protestant branch: a measure of security and sense.

In the North Riding were two strips of disaffection. There was the Richmond district running from the high, remote north-western dales, where such people could not be much interfered with, to the vale of York. Here were Markenfields, also inculpated in 1569, and Gascoignes, who had married with the too devout Nortons. At Rokeby, by the sounding brown waters of the Tees, not far down the dale from the lonely ruins of Eggleston abbey above the turn of the river, Sir Thomas Rokeby and all his family were non-communicants. Though some of the younger branches were Protestants, Sir Thomas was imprisoned and ultimately sold that wood-hung, water-loud domain. Lastly, there were the high wolds of Cleveland, especially about Whitby where the influence of the Cholmleys was paramount. Sir Richard and his son after him were church-papists, sufficiently conforming; but their

[1] It is not generally realised that the sub-title of Wordsworth's poem is "The Fate of the Nortons".

women were active Recusants: the widow of the first a daughter of the Earl of Cumberland, obstinately pious, the wife of the second a Babthorpe. At Lythe the leading figure was another noblewoman, daughter of the exiled Earl of Westmorland. The women largely outnumbered the men; not only because of their greater natural piety, but because they survived them. Several of these women were responsible for the devotion — and the sufferings — of their families: the earls of Northumberland, Westmorland and Arundel all owed their troubles to being under the thumbs of their women: more fools they for listening to them. There was even a certain *cachet* attached to belonging to the old faith in the highest circles — at Court, for example, in the immediate vicinity of the Queen, whose presence gave a certain protection: the Howards, the earls of Arundel, Oxford and Southampton, the Berkeleys, Vauxes, Monteagles, Brownes, Pagets, Arundells were almost all Catholic or crypto-Catholic. Similarly in the country a number of the best, though not always the oldest, families adhered to the old faith; among the complex play of motive an element of snobbery is not to be excluded. In Yorkshire as in Lancashire there are hardly any Recusants from the towns or among the middle class.[1]

Similar conclusions emerge whatever area we study: they are beyond the bounds of sectarian prejudice. East Anglia — a forward Protestant region for the most part, with Puritanism strong in the towns — had its pockets of Catholic resistance: again, a localised gentry. The Queen's progress into these parts in 1578 had the secondary purpose of asserting the authority of government. Means had been taken to have the Queen lodged at Euston, the house of Edward Rookwood, a Catholic: which did not prevent him from being sued by the Council in attendance.[2] Hunsdon, the Lord Chamberlain — who had been granted the use of the forfeited estates of Francis Tregian, Cuthbert Mayne's patron — called Rookwood before him, commanded him to leave the Court and had him committed at Norwich. We have a vivid and characteristic account from the Catholic-baiter Topcliffe: " A piece of plate being missed from the Court and searched for in his hay-house, in the hayrick such an image of our Lady was there found, as for greatness, for gayness and workmanship, I did never see a match. And after a sort of country dances ended, in her Majesty's sight the idol was set behind the people, who avoided: she rather seemed a beast, raised upon a sudden from hell by

[1] A. G. Dickens, " First Stages ", *loc. cit.* p. 179.
[2] A. Jessopp, *One Generation of a Norfolk House*, p. 67 foll.

conjuring, than the picture for whom it had been so often and long abused. Her Majesty commanded it to the fire, which in her sight by the country folks was quickly done to her content, and unspeakable joy of everyone but some one or two who had sucked of the idol's poisoned milk." [1]

This little campaign had the effect of routing out a group of Recusant gentry: a Bedingfield, a de Grey, Lady Style, a Drury, Robert Downes. This last was the builder of a splendid house at Great Melton.[2] He spent the next twenty years in and out of gaol at Norwich castle, becoming year by year more heavily embarrassed; first his Suffolk property went, then his lands in Kent, at last his life interest in the Melton estate was surrendered to the Queen. In 1609 he was compelled to sell house and estate outright: it may be hoped that his religious convictions were a sufficient compensation for his losses. Norfolk sported a small Catholic area within a ten miles' radius of Grimston: Townshends of Rainham, Cobbs of Sandringham, Bastards of Dunham and lesser gentry were touched by Recusancy.[3] Into this neighbourhood descended the Jesuit, Father Gerard, who lived with Edward Yelverton at Grimston and made that the centre of his remarkably successful mission. Young men are notoriously susceptible to this kind of thing, and ten young men of the best East Anglian families left England for the Society of Jesus. Some twenty fathers and mothers of Norfolk families altogether were reconciled by this plausible Jesuit; and though he was imprisoned in the Tower and hung up by the wrists — he has left us a vivid account of what it felt like — he ultimately died safely in his bed. His greatest success was with the Walpole family. Three branches of this indigenous family, at Houghton, Anmer and Herpley, occupied a tract across fifty miles of Norfolk heath. Of the six sons of the family at Anmer three became Jesuits, one of them the martyr, Henry Walpole. Father Parsons wanted martyrs for his new seminary at Valladolid, so he sent Henry Walpole, who was apparently not much good for anything else, into England. Before leaving Spain he had an audience with the great king, who was now so low and weak that Walpole could hardly catch what he said, save the words "*Dios os encamina*": Philip must have become disillusioned with his efforts by this time.[4] Edward Walpole, the heir of Houghton, was reconciled by Father Gerard and gave up his fair prospects to become a priest abroad, so forfeiting his estates. Fortunately for the family his interest was a reversionary

[1] *Ibid.* pp. 79-80.
[2] *Ibid.* p. 197 foll.
[3] *Ibid.* p. 138 foll.
[4] *Ibid.* p. 187.

one, and his more sensible brother was able to buy them back for a large fine. Otherwise what an historic future around Houghton would have been sacrificed: the great Sir Robert, the filial Horace who has painted the picture of it all for us in his Letters.

Suffolk and Norfolk really make one unit, their families were so much allied; but there was this difference: the Suffolk Catholics were not concentrated in little areas of their own, but scattered over the western half of the county; there were, characteristically, none in Ipswich or to the east, open to the sea and trade.[1] The Rookwoods were Suffolk people; Ambrose Rookwood of the Stanningfield branch was educated abroad and was a leading Gunpowder Plot conspirator. Such people made their worst enemies right. The Bedingfields, though Catholic, were loyal: they survived. The Queen did not hold it against Sir Henry that he had been an irritating keeper when she was her sister's prisoner: she made his son a gentleman pensioner. Everards, Yaxleys, Jermyns, Hares, a branch of the Rouses at Dennington, which produced the priest Anthony Rouse, another convert of Father Gerard; [2] Martins of Long Melford, Mannocks of Stoke-by-Nayland: such were the Suffolk faithful.

Most interesting to us are the Timperleys of Hintlesham, for they have been studied. As a family they seem to have come down from the North in the wake of the Mowbrays and to have made their fortunes in the following of the Howards, who succeeded. What is interesting is to see that they followed their patrons into Recusancy, the original dependants of the great house following its fortunes: though free and substantial now, they were allied by marriage. Nicholas Timperley married a Rookwood: here again we notice the building up of the self-conscious minority allied by marriage. "Constant intermarriage with families of similar religious convictions cannot but have strengthened their persistence. . . . The influence exercised by Audrey Hare, Elizabeth Shelley, Frances Bedingfield and Audrey Mannock must all have been thrown into this same scale; and, indeed, the staunchness of women papists generally is a matter of certainty." [3] It may be added that they did not have to go to prison. Nicholas Timperley entertained the priests Ballard and Tyrrell, who were involved in the Babington conspiracy. The

[1] Sir Gerald H. Ryan and L. J. Redstone, *Timperley of Hintlesham*, p. 109.

[2] The secular priest, Watson, said that Father Gerard got £1000 from him (Jessopp, *op. cit.* p. 220).

[3] Ryan and Redstone, *op. cit.* p. 92. Notice the adherence to the old cult of St. Etheldreda in the Christian name Audrey — a characteristic fidelity.

renegade Tyrrell confessed that he had said Mass at Lady Waldegrave's and that several of these Suffolk gentry knew of his intended visit to Rome — upon which, he said, the Pope had approved the project of the Queen's assassination. "It is the more remarkable in a county of strong Puritan feeling, such as Suffolk, that the whole force of the law was not pressed more quickly and more forcibly against a Papist family. The Timperleys lived in a countryside which was even then breeding the unbending and intolerant Puritans who founded the states of Massachusetts and Connecticut, and governed New England as a strictly Puritan Commonwealth. Hintlesham lies but a few miles from Groton where, in Sir Thomas Timperley's time, the John Winthrops, father and son, gathered together their neighbours to venture to the New World; and the Timperleys lived almost within hearing of the persuasive doctrines of Timothy Dalton at Wolverstone, and the fulminations of Samuel Ward at Ipswich."[1] But it was difficult to get a jury and witnesses against their own lord of the manor: a reason, perhaps, for the direct action of the government on the royal progress here in 1578. It all points to the charmed privilege of the gentry in Elizabethan society. But they were not sacrosanct.

If we wish to peer into the heart of such a Catholic group there is plenty of material: none better than the correspondence of Sir Thomas Tresham, a leader of the loyal Catholics.[2] He was a Northamptonshire magnate, who built the fine quadrangular mansion in that county's rich limestone, cream shading into tawny, at Rushton. It seems that his correspondence was walled up in a passage off the great hall at the time of the Gunpowder Plot. Tresham came of notably loyal old stock, of which he was very proud, and all through his troubles was ready to assert his loyalty to the Queen, to fight in the van for her, etc. But all his protestations were nullified by his son, a violent fool, who first took part in Essex's conspiracy, and then became a ringleader in the Gunpowder Plot. Both father and son died in that same tragic year for English Catholics. Sir Thomas succeeded his grandfather, the last Prior of St. John of Jerusalem; the sympathies of the family were conservative, which did not prevent them from doing well out of Church lands. Sir Thomas was reconciled in the course of the Jesuit mission of 1580–81, probably by Campion himself, and with this his troubles began. He estimated in 1588 that he had

[1] *Ibid.* p. 94. [2] Cf. H.M.C. *Various Coll.* vol. III.

paid £2800 in fines over the last eight years, besides other contributions to the service and defence of the State; but all through this he went on with his remarkable, somewhat fantastic, building operations: he was very rich, but it pulled him down in the end.[1] His reconciliation made a breach between him and the other Northamptonshire gentry, like his cousins the Montagues of Boughton and the Comptons, not to mention the Spencers, whom Sir Thomas despised as *nouveaux*. (Again the element of snobbery in the old Catholic.) The Montagues had been much to the fore on the Edwardian side, supporters of Queen Jane; and Sir Thomas, in his quarrel with his cousin Sir Edward Montagu, remembered the help his grandfather had been to them at the beginning of Mary's reign.[2] He remembered too the old kind entertainment at Boughton. There was, perhaps, the most serious aspect of Recusancy: the breach it entailed in the social order. Again and again one comes across evidence of the resentment it entailed among the rest of the gentry locally — this withdrawal from their responsibilities in society, from their proper place in Church and State.

This did not mean that a Catholic could not get justice at the hands of the State he was in some sense deserting. Sir Thomas recovered a goodly estate which his ancestors had not enjoyed for nearly eighty years: "I recovered it by many years' suit albeit the then Marquis of Northampton (my near kinsman and one of my mightiest adversaries) and the judges of that circuit, also all the puritans and preachers, combined therein against me".[3] He seems to have been a good man of business, dealing in enclosures and Church advowsons like anyone else. On his sister's marriage to Lord Vaux, he became a trustee of the marriage settlements and that involved him more and more in that easy-going, impecunious nobleman's affairs. The eldest son, Henry Vaux, absolutely refused to marry — which was understandable enough; he preferred the religious life — which was less so. This enraged Henry's sisters, who accused Sir Thomas of encouraging these unnatural propensities in order that his own sister's son might succeed. Actually Sir Thomas succeeded to a hornets' nest with these religious women. Anne Vaux took advantage of his "last long close imprisonment; she joying, whereas true Catholics ought to have had Christian commiseration. . . . Rather than I would have seconded my suit by taking such an irreligious advantage against any Christian whosoever, I would have permitted it to have quailed, than thereby to have prospered;

[1] Cf. H.M.C. *Various Coll.* III. 46. [2] *Ibid.* p. 128. [3] *Ibid.* p. 98.

but if against one of my religion, a Catholic, I sooner would have begged my bread than in such sort have been my fellow's bane." [1] But they could not dispense with his help: "They term me a Machiavellian, but they seem to trust me as reformedest Christian, devoid of spleen and fraught with charity". Enough of these unedifying quarrels among the faithful.

Sir Thomas is indeed a delightful character: good-natured, whimsical, loyal, fantastic, cheerful in misfortune. He has a long-winded, euphuistic style all his own, which makes one delight in his gossip. To his wife, while sequestered at Hoxton: "Jesus. Maria.[2] This present weeping All Souls day (which exceedeth all the extreme wet days of this long matchless wettest season) here arrived (as my petty Hogsden common was coming for my dinner) my now kind, former unkind cousin, accompanied with old Brokesby and a pettifogging former solicitor of hers, with a retinue of many servants, I having then none here but Hilkton and my trusty cook." (How we can sympathise today.) He was fascinated by the Tre in his name and took it for a symbol of the Trinity; the triangle was therefore his favourite figure. The Triangular lodge which he built to punctuate the western sky-line from the great house at Rushton is a riot of such symbolism, verbal and numerical, of emblems and monograms, triangles and trefoils. He built another lodge in the Hawkfield, of which the ground plan was a duodecagon intersected by an equal-armed cross, the well-known Lyveden New Building and the charming little Renaissance market-hall, looking like a diminutive Italian palace with a Northamptonshire accent, in the square at Rothwell; all this in addition to his work on the great house, and gardens everywhere. His creative vein gave him occupation during imprisonment. The Catholic gentlemen confined in the Palace at Ely during the dangerous years amused themselves by decorating their chambers with painted work. Sir Thomas undertook the west window in the gallery and covered it with his favourite devices. St. Etheldreda was much invoked, the patron saint of Ely: *uxor et virgo, regina et sancta, beata Etheldreda, ora pro me miserrimo peccatori Thoma Tresame.* His devotion to the Trinity was corroborated one night in unusual but unmistakable manner: "Having my servants (here allowed me) to read nightly an hour to me after supper, it fortuned that Fulcis my then servant reading in the *Christian Resolution* in the treatise of proof that there is a

[1] *Ibid.* pp. 82, 86.

[2] *Ibid.* p. 84. It was common for Catholics to head their correspondence in this way.

God etc, there was upon a wainscot table at that instant three loud knocks (as if it had been with an iron hammer) given to the great amazing of me and my two servants ".[1] That must have fortified his faith, more than the learned preachers with whom he was all too ready to confer: it did them no harm, and him no good. But he was very polite; he was quite willing to be convinced, if possible, that it was not a damnable sin to frequent " others' services than our own ". Quartered upon the Bishop of Lincoln at Buckden, he made great friends with him: they professed the language of love to each other. What was perhaps more difficult, he had great respect for the Master of Balliol, to whom he was much beholden, " not only for your readiness to impart unto me some part of your much skill in divinity, but also was contented that I should rudely and preposterously with thwart and misshaped arguments offend your learned ears ".[2]

The loyal Catholics, of whom Sir Thomas was a leading spokesman — and they were the great majority — well understood the Queen's position. She could not possibly have allowed her claims to be pronounced upon by Rome. " The Papal declaration against the legality of her mother's marriage, the very doubtful force (as the Catholics believed) of the Acts of Parliament passed to legitimize her, and the almost certainty that if she had accepted the Catholic position and submitted her claim to the Pope, his Holiness would have given sentence against her and in favour of Mary Stuart " — such at least was Sir Thomas's opinion.[3] At the outbreak of war with Spain he and his friends petitioned the Queen, expressly denying the Papal claim to depose her: " We for our parts utterly deny that either Pope or Cardinal hath power or authority to command or licence any man to consent to mortal sin. . . . Much less can this disloyal, wicked and unnatural purpose by any means be made lawful, to wit, that a native-born subject may seek the effusion of the sacred blood of his anointed sovereign. . . . We do protest before the living God that all and every priest and priests who have at any time conversed with us have recognised your Majesty their undoubted and lawful Queen *tam de jure quam de facto*." [4] They asked for a toleration of their religious rites. But no toleration would have been granted by Rome: the very idea is always qualified by the Counter-Reformation as deplorable, detestable, damnable. As to the Queen and her sovereignty, Rome had already spoken. The tragic contradiction in which the English Catholics were

[1] Cf. H.M.C. *Various Coll.* III. 92.
[2] *Ibid.* p. 20.
[3] *Ibid.* p. xxiv.
[4] *Ibid.* p. 40.

caught was due to their leadership being outside the country: the conflict of loyalties in the individual heart rendered acute, the public issue of allegiance absolute.

So long as he lived William Allen was the leading English Catholic figure.[1] He was a mild, scholarly, rather dull man; more fit for the university than for international politics. And, indeed, the seminary side of his life, his college at Douai and the English College at Rome, were of the greatest importance in the continuity of English Catholicism and made him an historic figure; while his dabbling in high politics was a uniform failure. At least it was contrary to his nature, though owing to the high position he occupied he could hardly help himself. At first he had intended to devote his life to "scholastical attempts for the conversion of our country and reconcilement of our brethren to the Catholic Church". But he was drawn into correspondence with Guise and Mary Queen of Scots over the project to place Mary or James on the English throne; and after the collapse of those hopes he turned to Spain. On the outbreak of the war he was summoned to Rome, to take part in the preparations for the attack on England. In these high political matters he came under the influence of Father Parsons, essentially a political spirit; his elevation to the cardinalate in 1587 was acclaimed at Rome as a signal for the crusade against England — which it was. Allen said later, more modestly, "under Heaven Father Parsons made me Cardinal". He was cast for the part that Pole had played thirty years before — but those thirty years had made a world of difference in England and the posture of her affairs in the world. On the eve of the invasion the Cardinal issued his "Admonition to the Nobility and People of England", in which Elizabeth was declared "a most unjust usurper and injurer of all nations, an infamous, depraved, accursed, excommunicate heretic, the very shame of her sex and princely name, the chief spectacle of sin and abomination in this our age and the only poison, calamity and destruction of our noble church and country". It would be amusing if it were not so tragic, to observe what fools people's convictions make of them. There is no doubt the Cardinal was a traitor; and in a public letter in defence of Sir William Stanley, Allen defended his fellow Lancashireman's treason in surrendering Deventer to the Spaniards and called upon all Catholics to abjure the heretic Queen and her allegiance.

This marked the height of Parsons's influence with him. After the collapse of their cloud-castles in 1588, there was a coldness

[1] Cf. T. F. Knox, *Letters and Memorials of Cardinal Allen.*

between the Cardinal and the Jesuits: Parsons was of "too hard and violent a nature", Allen truly said.[1] The atmosphere in Rome changed with defeat, and Allen with it. Though he had been responsible for calling the Jesuits into the English mission, he did not wish them to control it. In his heart he had not ceased to be an Englishman; but he was old and tired and found the ways of God inscrutable. What he felt may be seen from the kindness with which he treated visiting Englishmen, Protestant as well as Catholic, in Rome in his last years. On his deathbed he felt remorse that he should not have died the martyr's death to which he had sent so many others.

We cannot be sure that no such regrets visited the undescried heart of Robert Parsons. The brilliant Balliol man stepped into the position of the quiet ex-Principal of St. Mary's Hall as the leading English Catholic at Rome. As Prefect of foreign missions he had the control of all Jesuit seminaries; even at Douai, Dr. Worthington was under a secret oath of obedience to him. He was a sort of cardinal *in petto*, with immense backstairs influence; but he was only the head of a party: in England he had far more enemies among his co-religionists than friends. From 1588 to 1597 he was in Spain, where he had great influence with Philip. In 1591 he published his book on the English Succession, in which he argued Philip's claims, as a descendant of the house of Lancaster, on behalf of his daughter the Infanta: any clever fool, it seems, can find arguments for anything that he wants. Like everything he said or did — for he had a fatal touch where his countrymen were concerned — the book created fury in England and did enormous harm to the Catholics. The sense of personal superiority, said a secular priest who hated him, was the root of his trouble. Laid on the shelf at last, his influence waning, his schemes disregarded, when he came to die he asked that he might be buried by the side of the Cardinal, whom he had pushed forward so remorselessly in the glad days of the crusade for the conversion of England.

He was indeed a fascinating character: we should say nowadays that he was a man with a complex.[2] A Westcountryman of low origins, it was said by his enemies that his father was a blacksmith, of Nether Stowey (that village of other, more endearing memories) — though why that should have been held against him passes comprehension: it is the way of enemies. At Balliol

[1] q. Meyer, *op. cit.* p. 388.

[2] For Parsons's career to 1588 *v. Letters and Memorials of Father Robert Parsons, S.J., 1578–1588* (ed. L. Hicks), Catholic Record Society.

he distinguished himself as a tutor, and was made dean and bursar of the college; as such he twice took the oath of Supremacy. Popular and successful with pupils, he quarrelled with the other Fellows — one sees the familiar psychological pattern; in the end he either resigned in a huff, or was dismissed. Accounts vary; the effect was the same. A sense of social inferiority, consciousness of great abilities, resentment at opposition, especially from people he must have considered his inferiors, frustration imposed upon a temperament naturally aggressive and designing, made for command though not naturally and easily like those, often far less able, who are born to it: all these must have stored up the desire to be revenged upon the country that had disconsidered him and upon which he had turned his back. In the circumstances of sixteenth-century belief, the desire for revenge transmuted itself easily into the idea of mission; it made it all right with God.

And an almighty revenge the blacksmith's son from Nether Stowey had upon his heretic country; scores of people went to their deaths — perhaps, indirectly, hundreds — because of him; rejected at Balliol, disregarded in England, he became one of the most famous figures in Europe. Since he was not much loved, he became one of the best hated men of his day. The man who was not good enough for Balliol became a marvellous insinuating courtier, the intimate of cardinals and popes, of the King of Spain. The bursar who bungled his relations with a lot of dons became the cleverest intriguer, the most finished diplomat in Europe. When irreconcilable disputes broke out in the English College, between the supporters of the Jesuits and those of the seculars, he had to be sent for from Spain to reconcile them; it was the leading spirit of the Jesuits who won over his opponents, the great majority: he must have had something irresistible about him. Like all such characters touched by a hidden flaw to genius, he was a man of contradictions: the most uncompromising of Jesuits, he had great flexibility and tact when he chose to exercise it; an ultramontane and leader of the extreme pro-Spanish faction, he was prepared to switch to James ("the forces of the Spaniards do not correspond to either their wishes or ours", he wrote in 1597 after the last failure);[1] a man with a great faculty for business and intrigue, he had no political judgment where it was warped by his complex, took the impress of his deep (and concealed) grievance; a personality that attracted public hostility and distrust, he had a singular capacity for winning men's private confidence; a writer of the best prose of his day (commended by

[1] q. Meyer, p. 372.

Swift, another conjured spirit), he lived his life in exile and spent his talent on the bitter Dead-sea fruit of political controversy (like Swift it was power that he wanted); a man whom all the world took to be a Machiavellian, he had an inner spiritual life, simple and secure, which made his book, the *Christian Directory*, a book of devotion even for Protestants.

II

The chief difficulty in writing about the Puritans — apart from the unattractiveness of the subject and the usual nimiety of material (for they have been too much written about, disproportionately to their place in society) — is one of definition. Who were the Puritans? Whom are we to regard as Puritans? The shadow of this question of delimitation hangs over most books on the subject; it accounts for the very varying estimates of the numbers and support for the Puritans in the country. Some writers give the impression that they had a large number of the laity with them, as they certainly had in the House of Commons; others that they were a small minority, an essentially clerical movement. It all depends on how one delimits them — exact definition, in history as in life, is perhaps impossible.

Puritan sympathies and sentiments were fairly widespread, though not popular in the exact sense, in certain districts and some strata of society: most widely, perhaps among the governing bourgeois of the towns, especially the more prosperous merchants and tradespeople in commercial centres like Norwich, Ipswich, Leicester, Bristol, Plymouth, Hull, Manchester, Newcastle. Then there were the Puritan-minded gentry, who formed a minority in a good many counties, very much stronger in some areas, like Northamptonshire, Oxfordshire, Bedfordshire, Essex and East Anglia, than in others like the North and West. In the highest circles a small but powerful group gave the Puritans consistent support and protection: the Bedfords and Huntingdons; Knollys, Walsingham, Mildmay; the formidable Lady Russell, the disapproving aunt of the Bacons (the expression of disapproval and moral censoriousness were her characteristic pleasures); Leicester was on their side and kept in with them, spoke their somewhat nauseating language (to them, not to the Queen), while Burghley, who was pledged to the execution of the laws and wished to follow a middle course, was privately sympathetic and did them many a good turn. Lower class elements — tailors, cap-makers, shipwrights, Dutch immigrants [1] — were liable in their clownish way to shade off into various sorts of separatist sects, Brownists, the Family of Love, Anabaptists; but they were very few. Cambridge was the intellectual centre of Puritanism and provided — though there were representatives of it in Oxford — its choicest spirits.

Again, with regard to its class affiliations, there are writers who speak of it as a middle-class manifestation; others, thinking of its aristocratic patrons, suppose the exact opposite. In fact, the centre of the thing is to be found in the middle class and its leading spirits were middle-class men. In so far as it gave birth to a way of life, that was capable of being shared in by people of all classes; in so far as it was a system of ideas and ideals, by people of all kinds who were capable of apprehending them. Dr. Knappen regards it as a form of idealism, that " powerful social force, comparable to race, nationalism and class, and as worthy of serious study ".[2] Idealism may be an important and even, in some circumstances, a valuable element in society. In our own time we have reason to be more aware of the wreckage due to it and can appreciate better the value to society of maintaining things, if not as they are, as well as may be. The onus of change rests on the prophets and preachers; and when they come into power we see that so far from their doing any better, they may do a great deal worse. It is Dr. Knappen's phrase that the culmination of all this activity, with the Commonwealth, was " the fatal parliamentary Erastianism of 1646–7 "; and we know how the rule of the Saints failed to hold, or to represent, the country.[3] When Robert Browne, the separatist leader, patron saint of Congregationalism, left England under episcopal tyranny for the freedom of Presbyterian Scotland, he found that " the preachers having no names of bishops did imprison me more wrongfully than any bishop would have done ".[4] Well, of course; no wonder he ended up, a sadder if not much wiser man, an Anglican parson for some forty years in the country.

These are generalities; it is no use defining Puritanism as an ' attitude of mind ' — anything may be that. We must delimit those whose sympathies were with the Puritans from the Puritans proper: those who subscribed to and took active part in the movement for change of order in the Church. That is something quite definite; for the movement in course of unfolding its objectives

[1] Cf. the interesting list of a Barrowist congregation in London in 1592 (C. Burrage, *The Early English Dissenters*, I. 145-8).
[2] M. M. Knappen, *Tudor Puritanism*, p. vi.
[3] *Ibid.* p. 223.
[4] Burrage, *op. cit.* I. iii.

made it clear what was the order it desired. When fully defined, it was the Presbyterianism of Geneva: Cartwright, the intellectual leader of Puritanism, went there to study it at the fountain source and came back with the idea of transplanting it to English soil. In a general sense the Reformed ideal was a nice combination of clerical leadership and lay responsibility designed to produce a people intelligent and disciplined, a community united in the service of a common principle.[1] (One thing — and not the only thing — wrong with it was that that was too much to hope for. On the other hand, such strenuous disciplines produce iron men, individuals unflinching and independent, whether facing authority at home or the enemy abroad. It is fairly indicative that the greatest seamen, Drake and Hawkins, were touched by the Puritan spirit; Monson, who was not, was made of altogether weaker stuff.) More particularly Puritanism came to object to the whole hierarchical order which the Church continued intact, minus the Pope, from the pre-Reformation Church. The Puritans felt that the Reformation had been stultified of its proper and full development; and there was a good deal in what they thought. The greatest stumbling-block — in the end it proved an insuperable one — was that the Queen thought that it had gone too far already and was determined to hold to the compromise of 1559 to her dying day. She was far more determined than the bishops, who had to bear all the unpopularity, growing to an intense hatred, for the execution of her policy: she herself would never come into the open in this region where the irrational element in human beings is capable of anything. Dr. Knappen says truly of her character, nothing ever changed her; what she had accepted as a young woman of twenty-five she was still holding to as a middle-aged woman when the Puritan campaign was at its height; she had not changed when she laid down her task, sick and weary of it, though by then the Puritans had been defeated and scattered, driven underground or out.

Puritanism started as a movement for reform and became, as such movements do, a campaign for power. The stages are easily marked. It is usual to go back for the origins of the movement to the famous troubles at Frankfort, where it was revealed that there were two parties among the English exiles. The left-wing, led by Knox, wished to identify itself with the pure Genevan principles, rites and organisation of Calvin. The right-wing, led by Cox, wished to adhere to the Edwardian Prayer Book of 1552: " They would do as they had done in England, and they would have the

[1] Cf. Knappen, *op. cit.* p. 92.

face of an English church ".[1] A revealing phrase: there was the conception of an English national Church, which was ultimately to prove more in keeping with the English people, a truer expression of the nation, than ever the Puritans were. The left-wing Reformers were more international in outlook: they attached more value to their kinship with Geneva and the Huguenots: they looked abroad to France and to Scotland. " Is a Reformation good for France and can it be evil for England? Is discipline meet for Scotland and is it unprofitable for this realm? "[2] It may fairly be said that, compared with England, the state of affairs in neither France nor Scotland was any recommendation for it: endemic religious wars in the one, assassination, privy conspiracy and rebellion in the other.

It is noticeable how comparatively reluctant the returned exiles were to take high office in the Church on Elizabeth's conditions. It makes one wonder the more what would have happened if Mary's hierarchy, or a substantial part of it, had continued under Elizabeth: it would certainly have strengthened her hand in making the Church settlement more conservative. But Protestant feeling was too strong, and already in the sixties many clergymen were ceasing, as a matter of conscience, to wear the vestments and perform some of the rites prescribed by the Prayer Book. It was the Queen who insisted on Parker issuing his " Advertisements ", and enforcing them on reluctant clergy. The task occupied him for the rest of his life. That was the first stage.

Something of the defiant spirit of the Puritans, and something of their reforming objectives, may be seen in a passage from a sermon preached before the Queen by a celebrated Puritan preacher, Edward Dering: of benefices, " Behold some are defiled with impropriations, some with sequestrations, some loaden with pensions, some robbed of their commodities " ; of patrons, " Some are selling their benefices, some farming them, some keep them for their children, some give them to boys, some to servingmen, a very few seek after pastors. . . . Look upon your ministry, and there are some of one occupation, some of another, some shakebucklers, some ruffians, some hawkers and hunters, some dicers and carders, some blind guides and can not see, some dumb dogs and will not bark." [3] There was indeed a good deal in Dering's criticism: the Puritans had a high, or at any rate an exacting ideal of the ministry: they wanted a preaching ministry of active

[1] *The Troubles at Frankfort* (ed. E. Arber), p. 62.
[2] q. Knappen, p. 235. [3] *Ibid.*

pastors who directed their sheep. (One sees how the famous lines of " Lycidas " give permanent form to decades of Puritan complaint.) There were many cases of pluralism; all too many of the higher clergy, like our friend Dr. Kenall, occupying half a dozen places when there were, according to Puritan figures, nearly 200 graduates at Oxford and 140 at Cambridge without livings: clerical unemployed.[1] And that provided a motive for some of the criticism, no doubt; there were Puritans who accumulated benefices when they had the chance. But that does not invalidate their charges. What stultified them was that, in spite of the efforts of the bishops to improve the standards of the clergy, the Queen did not want a preaching ministry: in her experience preachers only stirred up trouble for government. Dering was not afraid to point the conclusion — no Puritan was afraid: " And yet you, in the meanwhile that all these whoredoms are committed, you at whose hands God will require it, you sit still and are careless, let men do as they list. It toucheth not, belike, your commonwealth, and therefore you are so well contented to let all alone." So like the Puritans, so like their tact: that did them no good: they got nowhere that way.

With the seventies Puritanism entered a second, a fully developed, phase. Its leaders, notably John Field, who acted as organising secretary of the movement, made contact with the Commons to advance the cause. An effective propaganda was undertaken; two 'Admonitions' to the Parliament of 1572 were issued, stating the Puritan case. In the same year the first presbytery was established at Wandsworth. Later on, a whole 'classis' movement — organisations of a number of presbyteries — came into being, such as the Dedham classis, the minutes of which remain.[2] Exercises, fasts and prophesyings came into vogue in Puritan parishes, often with the connivance — and sometimes, as we have seen, with the encouragement — of the bishop. These meetings of clergy at which they edified each other with their sermons, their commentaries on passages of scripture, their criticisms of each other's comments, their ardent and extempore prayers — all these were helpful means to a better trained clergy. The Queen looked on them with disgust: to her they were trumpets of sedition. In this same decade the Puritans found intellectual leadership in the works of Cartwright and Travers.

It was Travers — at one time Burghley's chaplain and tutor to Robert Cecil — who produced the classic statement of Presby-

[1] *The Seconde Parte of a Register* (ed. A. Peel), II. 199.
[2] Ed. by R. G. Usher, *The Presbyterian Movement, 1582–9.*

terian discipline and organisation as applied to England.[1] But it was Cartwright who became the undoubted intellectual leader of the Puritans, partly through his position at Cambridge, seed-bed of the movement, but still more through his long controversies with Whitgift who took the lead on the other side. The duel bore at first the character of a domestic squabble between dons, but it came to involve the fate of the Church. Cartwright, Lady Margaret Professor of Divinity, had a large and enthusiastic following at Cambridge; not necessarily, or even probably, the majority, but the most devoted. He proclaimed that Presbyterianism was the constitution of the early Christian Church, and that it was the model for all time. No historic sense, no conception of historical development; but no Puritan ever had much historic sense. The conclusion was the abolition of episcopacy and the radical alteration of the Church. Cartwright's sermons and lectures produced a great sensation, as they would in such a place. The authorities were seriously alarmed, and Whitgift as Vice-Chancellor — besides replying to Cartwright's arguments — got him removed from his professorship: which was more effective. This was the beginning of a long literary duel that consumed many hundreds of pages in folio. Theologically, Whitgift was as much of an orthodox Calvinist as Cartwright: a firm believer in predestination, the salvation of God's elect, the damnation of those not chosen from all eternity. The intellectual position of the Church, as described by its more eloquent spirits, was more Calvinist than Lutheran; though not so the Thirty-nine Articles, which, based mainly on the Lutheran Confessions, were closest to that of Augsburg. A Church Catholic in structure, in most of its doctrine and many of its rites; Lutheran in the emphasis of its formularies; Calvinist in its theological flavouring — what more English a compromise for the Church of England?

What are more interesting are the differences between Cartwright and Whitgift. Cartwright held that the Old Testament death penalties for adultery, blasphemy and heresy still held good as for murder and should be put into force.[2] Whitgift believed that under the Gospel there should be less severity and that repentance and mercy had their place; Cartwright would have hounded Catholic priests to death: " He that killeth a man and taketh away his corporal life ought to die: it followeth much more that he which taketh away the life of the soul should die ". The usual argument: it is only fair to say that the Inquisition would

[1] A. F. Scott Pearson, *Thomas Cartwright and Elizabethan Puritanism*, p. 257.
[2] *Ibid.* p. 90 foll.

have done as much for him. " If this be bloody and extreme, I am content to be so counted with the Holy Ghost." (Of course: the Holy Ghost = Cartwright. It is the argument of the loathsome Luther against Erasmus: 'the Holy Ghost is not a sceptic'.) Cartwright held " that Princes should be excepted from ecclesiastical discipline, and namely from excommunication, I utterly dislike ". This was much more awkward for him, and Whitgift made the most of his advantage. He strove to show that Puritanism led to Anabaptism; but the Puritans abhorred the Anabaptists, said Cartwright. Of course. Everyone was shocked by Anabaptists; the fires of Smithfield were relit in these years for a couple of Dutch Anabaptists, who denied the truth of the Trinity and " died in great horror roaring and crying ".[1] The truths upon which society rests must be maintained. It is pleasanter to record that after many years of weary controversy, and some vicissitudes, Cartwright returned home to England to make a modified submission to his old enemy, now as Archbishop of Canterbury responsible for order in the Church; Whitgift treated him with kindness and courtesy, and Cartwright spent his last years prospering in a sphere of usefulness in the Church. After all, were they not both Englishmen, both Trinity men?

Before this agreeable conclusion was reached, a remarkable episode had taken place in the government of the Church — Grindal's archi-episcopate. The Puritan agitation went on growing, while the government's attention was occupied by the more serious danger of the Romanist campaign; and, indeed, that played into the hands of the Puritans, forced the Queen to let up on them. On Parker's death Grindal was appointed to succeed him. He was really Burghley's candidate; and this marked the apex of Burghley's influence: he was never to exert so much influence in Church affairs again. We find the two men consoling each other over their ailments: Cecil showing Grindal his doublets " cut and voided in the back " for fear of the stone; Grindal responding with advice and a glass of Thomas Gibson's balsam: " thus much of physic, whereof all sick men love to hear ".[2] Grindal was a suitable man: pious and eminently respectable, elderly and experienced, having held the sees of London and York: moreover, he was unmarried. He had expressed himself in favour of dealing with Puritans by authority, and " although Cartwright would revoke, he is never to be permitted to read again in the university; for he hath a busy head,

[1] A. F. Scott Pearson, *Thomas Cartwright and Elizabethan Puritanism*, p. 155.

[2] *The Remains of Edmund Grindal* (ed. W. Nicholson, Parker Society), p. 281.

stuffed full of singularities ".[1] At York he was not troubled by Puritans: " The uniform order allowed by the Book is universally observed . . . but the bishop of London is always to be pitied; for if burning were the penalty of these curiosities, yet should he never lack a number of that generation ".[2] Cartwright was at that moment being entertained by a Cheapside goldsmith. There was always support for Puritans among the aldermen and fathers of the City.

But Grindal had an English fairness of mind and gentleness of temperament;[3] he was personally charitable and gave the surplus of his income to the poor. There was much in the Puritan demand for reform with which he sympathised: " The bishops should be stirred up by letter to persuade and urge the Queen's majesty, by all convenient methods, to amend those things which breed offences and hinder the course of the gospel; and also, if they cannot obtain all they wish, that in inflicting penalties upon their brethren and fellow ministers . . . they would be somewhat more gentle and more disposed to toleration ".[4] This was the man who came to the chief executive position in the Church just as the Puritans were getting into stride and their 'prophesyings' grew hotter. No sooner was he in the saddle at Lambeth than the Queen sent him a series of orders to be executed: these exercises were to be brought under the rigid control of the bishops, none held except under their hand and seal and with their nominee to moderate them; no lay person to speak at them, and no-one to reflect on matters of State or Church government. One recognises the hand of the Queen: this was her settled opinion; she considered three or four licensed preachers enough for a county and for the rest the reading of homilies should suffice.[5]

The Archbishop considered, and then refused to execute the orders. He justified himself in a letter, the like of which the Queen can never have received.[6] " Alas! Madam, is the Scripture more plain in any one thing, than that the Gospel of Christ should be plentifully preached? . . . Public and continual preaching of God's word is the ordinary mean and instrument of the salvation of mankind." In that the Archbishop agreed with the Puritans; to the Catholics, the sacraments were the means of salvation; to the Queen, obedience. During his six years at York

[1] *Ibid.* p. 305. [2] *Ibid.* p. 347.

[3] We find him, for example, moving the lords of the Council in 1569 to spare Sir John Southworth his imprisonment for a time, " for the prison sicknesses reign usually at this time of the year " (*ibid.* p. 306). Everybody was considerate to Sir John Southworth. It did no good.

[4] *Ibid.* p. 342. [5] *Ibid.* pp. 372-5. [6] *Ibid.* pp. 381-90.

Grindal had himself placed forty preachers. " The reading of homilies hath his commodity, but is nothing comparable to the office of preaching." In short, " I am forced, with all humility, and yet plainly, to profess that I cannot with safe conscience and without offence to the majesty of God, give my assent to the suppressing of the said exercises: much less can I send out any injunction for the utter and universal subversion of the same ". He besought her that " when you deal in matters of faith and religion, or matters that touch the church of Christ, which is his spouse . . . you would not use to pronounce so resolutely and peremptorily, *quasi ex auctoritate*, as ye may do in civil and extern matters ". He reminded her that she was but a mortal creature. " God hath blessed you with great felicity in your reign, now many years; beware you do not impute the same to your own deserts and policy, but give God the glory." Elizabeth knew very well what she owed to her own ability.

What a letter for a mild man to write to the daughter of Henry VIII! She meant to depose him, and would have done if she could. But that would have been too open a scandal, for the supreme Governor to turn out an archbishop: it would have destroyed the moral authority of episcopacy, the view held by the English Church that the bishops did not hold their spiritual powers (whatever they were) from the Crown, but that they had a certain *jus divinum* attaching to their office and by virtue of it. It would have contradicted her own position. It was very awkward. The longer her settlement of the Church lasted, the more opportunity there was for these underlying implications of Catholic order to grow their crop in belief and doctrine. It was that that infuriated the Puritan laity and made them so urgent: they saw that time was against them. The Church *was* becoming more Catholic again. In society it is the nature of institutions that counts, far more than what people (temporarily, illusorily) think about them: give the institutions time and they will mould what people think. Sir Francis Knollys saw the point, and under Whitgift — who was winning the battle for the Church — kept agitating Walsingham and Burghley on the issue, who were largely with him already.[1] Knollys wished the bishops to be forced into admitting that their superiority over other clergy came direct from the Queen's grant, and was therefore not *jure divino*. In other words, his was the position of a complete Protestant Erastianism. If Elizabeth had deposed Grindal she would have proved him right. Like the clever and controlled woman

[1] Cf. his letters (S.P. 12/223/23 and S.P. 12/233/62).

she was — controlled where her passions were concerned, which was so singular, no passion touched her so nearly as a challenge to her power — she drew back. Grindal was not deposed; he was confined to his house for six months and sequestered from exercising his office. This deplorable situation lasted for five years; until, just when arrangements were being made for the old man (now blind) to retire, he died. Meanwhile, Puritanism went from strength to strength.

This episode, however, brought into the open who it was at the back of it all that held up the Puritans. It was not the bishops, it was the Queen who was the greatest anti-Puritan in the country. She never lost sight of their implied challenge to monarchy: had she not Scotland under her eyes, the harassed James under her pen? The Puritans were personally antipathetic to her, as well as politically: a civilised woman, she hated their cant; a tolerant one, she was disgusted by their hateful, Biblical intolerance; with her Renaissance view of life she could not bear their narrowness, their limitations on others' enjoyment of it, their denial of the pride and glory of life; a Queen, and a great one, she would have no challenge to her rule. She was sure that she knew better how to rule — and she did.

The next archbishop was her own personal choice: Whitgift, the antagonist of Cartwright: a man wholly devoted to the interests of the Church, to a degree that robs his private life of any interest (he had none, unlike Parker), rather inscrutable as a person, completely sure of himself, resolute and determined, as able a man of affairs as he was intellectually — above all, unmarried: her " little black husband ". A complete Churchman, he might have been a medieval archbishop. He needed all his strength of mind and character to deal with the Puritan campaign, now at its height in the eighties. An influential group of the most active and devoted clergy — such men as John Knewstub and Ezekiel Culverwell in Essex, Dudley Fenner, Richard Greenham, William Perkins at Cambridge, Edward Gellibrand at Oxford, with outlying representatives in the Midlands, East Anglia and the southern counties, all kept in touch by the indefatigable, elusive John Field, with Cartwright as their mentor — pushed forward the Puritan propaganda. Books were published; their *Book of Discipline* was set out and, even though they could never agree about it,[1] it provided an alternative form of organisation

[1] Cf. the *cri de cœur* of Cranmer years before: " If such men were to be heard, although the Book were made every year anew, yet should it not lack faults in their opinion " (q. Knappen, *op. cit.* p. 96).

for the Church. The Parliament of 1584–5 had a strong Puritan representation; for its benefit an alternative Prayer Book was produced, based on Geneva and omitting the rites and ceremonies to which Puritans objected. The organisation also produced a series of surveys of the state of the Church in various counties — Bancroft, Whitgift's right-hand man at Lambeth and ultimate successor there, called them 'libels' rather. Disobedience to the Prayer Book order was spreading; if the hiatus at Lambeth had lasted much longer it might have been impossible to recover the position.

Whitgift was sworn by the Queen to reduce the Puritans and restore order in the Church: "Her Majesty moveth and earnestly exhorteth me thereunto with straight charge as I will answer the contrary".[1] He went some way to meet the demands for reform, produced three articles to which all the clergy were to subscribe, as the basis of uniformity. These acknowledged the Royal Supremacy, accepted the Thirty-nine Articles and the Prayer Book as containing nothing "contrary to the Word of God". It was this last provision, the Puritans found, that "killed them in their souls". Recalcitrants were brought before the Court of High Commission — ecclesiastical commissions of various kinds had become the instruments for putting the Royal Supremacy into action.[2] Here the procedure was the Civil Law one of an *ex officio* oath, by which evidence was gathered from the mouth of the accused. Burghley made a celebrated protest to the Archbishop against his use of this method: it savoured of the Spanish Inquisition, he said. An exaggeration characteristic of the layman's reaction to clerical authority: old Burghley was typical of his countrymen: therein lay his strength. We must remember that hatred of clerical immunity, clerical privilege and, above all, clerical authority had been mounting up for two centuries before the Reformation and provided the strongest psychological force in carrying it through.[3]

All this latent feeling was being directed against the bishops again. Burghley wrote the Archbishop drily that "he saw much worldliness in many that were otherwise affected before they came to cathedral churches that he feared the places altered the men".[4] The Privy Council itself was opposed to Whitgift's course; they did what they could to obstruct and hold him up,

[1] H.M.C. *Marquis of Bath MSS.* II. 26.
[2] Cf. R. G. Usher, *The Rise and Fall of the High Commission.*
[3] Cf. *e.g.* the importance of Richard Hunne's case, A. F. Pollard, *Wolsey*, p. 31 foll.
[4] q. Knappen, p. 276.

encouraging prophesyings in Chester diocese, as we have seen. Robert Beale, the redoubtable Clerk of the Privy Council, engaged in a campaign against the Archbishop, circulating two whole volumes of objections to the legality of Whitgift's actions. (He told the Archbishop that he had found he was very popular with the Queen of Scots.) The Archbishop protested: "The laws are with me whatsoever Mr. Treasurer [*i.e.* Knollys] and some lawyers (whose skill is not great) sayeth to the contrary".[1] He was threatened from several quarters, but nothing would move him: "I am at a point and I say with David *in manibus tuis Domine sortes meae*".

Whitgift's motto was *Vincit qui patitur*. He needed it, and it was justified in him. He had to bear an intolerable campaign of abuse from the Puritans, a constant stream of insults from their underground press (the 'Protestant underworld'), refusals to recognise his position or authority or even, when a separatist like Barrow was brought before him, that he was a Christian;[2] then there were, more important, the backstairs intrigues of councillors and courtiers, the campaigns of Knollys, Walsingham, Beale, the disapproval of Burghley. Nothing could shake him. Only the Queen's unwavering, and unspoken, support enabled him to win through. How often she had given Parker the hint and expected him to understand the position and go forward on his own! Here was a man who understood perfectly and was not afraid. He had a first-class *aide* in Richard Bancroft, who did brilliant detective work in tracking down the surreptitious Puritan press, the authors and printers of scurrilous literature, the proceedings of the Classis movement. He surpassed himself in getting hold of the private papers, written in Scotland, of John Penry, upon which he was condemned for treason.[3] But not even Bancroft could ever discover who was the author of the famous Marprelate tracts, nor has it ever been discovered since. These made the greatest sensation of their day; they were works of literature, scandalous, amusing, bubbling with mirth and mischief. Bishop Cooper, unfortunately for himself, replied with a long-winded *Admonition*. The rejoinder *Hay any Worke for Cooper?* did not spare the bishop's leading liability, his lady. Sparkling pieces of Elizabethan prose, as naughty as Nashe, they are very secular productions and did the Puritans no good. They were not welcomed by the elect: too amusing; it was irreligious to be amusing:

[1] H.M.C. *Bath MSS. ibid.*
[2] Cf. Usher, *High Commission*, pp. 133-4.
[3] *The Notebook of John Penry, 1593*, ed. A. Peel.

Martin Marprelate made sin ridiculous when it should be made odious.[1]

By the end of the eighties Whitgift had won. He had made some slight concessions, but his undeviating course wore down the opposition. Cartwright himself made a modified subscription, was received well and made Master of Leicester's Hospital at Warwick. (Not much changed, there is the little chapel above the town-gate looking to Stratford, where the great Puritan preached and carried on his ministry: in harbour at last.) The death of Field, the collapse of the Classis movement, the silencing of Marprelate, the submission of so many recalcitrants marked the defeat of the party for Elizabeth's lifetime. The Hacket 'conspiracy' — the proclamation of this religious maniac as the Messiah in Cheapside — added a ridiculous comment and a salutary warning. (How it looks forward to the lunacies of the Commonwealth!) In fact, for all that sectarians have said subsequently, when one thinks of the circumstances of the time, what was happening abroad, what was happening to Catholics at home, the Puritans were treated with great forbearance and liberality. It is generally allowed that the Anglican control of the press was fairly widely tolerant and placed no shackles on the creative development of literature. It would have been otherwise had the Puritans won: they hated the stage, for example. In the fifteen-nineties the fact that the Church had won its battle is witnessed by the flood of apologetic literature on its side, culminating in a great work, Hooker's *Laws of Ecclesiastical Polity*.

What Puritans thought of their fellows in the ministry, and something of their own spirit, may be learned from their Surveys.[2] The most spicy and vindictive appears to be the Cornish one; perhaps it was written by that bitter spirit, Eusebius Paget. Let us take a more moderate and representative one: Warwickshire.[3] At Warwick the vicar of the Lower parish, Humphry Waring, "is thought to be unsound in some points of Christian religion, loveth the alehouse well, and very much subject to the vice of good

[1] This was Richard Greenham's opinion. Far too secular and amusing to have been written by the earnest Penrys of this world, were they, I wonder, written by such a person as Michael Hicks? They were clearly written by someone in a position to know everybody who was anybody, and the absolute certainty of Martin that he would never be brought to book points to someone safely ensconced high up at Court. Michael Hicks, Burghley's secretary, was a supporter of the Puritans, and he had a merry facetious pen. But who could Martin have been? The secret seems lost for ever.

[2] Cf. *The Seconde Parte of a Register* (ed. A. Peel), II. 89 foll.

[3] *Ibid.* pp. 165-74.

fellowship ". One hears the sniff of the self-righteous: that vice the Puritans were certainly not subject to. At Stratford was a preacher, " learned, zealous and godly . . . a happy age if our Church were fraught with many such ". (It would seem that Shakespeare escaped his ministrations.) At Snitterfield the minister was a hireling, dumb and unlearned, though honest; " he teacheth to play on instruments and draweth wrought works ". The vicar of Wootton, " negligent and slothful, a man defamed and of tainted life ", had two livings besides, " which he supplieth by his hirelings, whereof one upon rumour of a change in religion in Monsieur's days did shave his beard ". An interesting country reflection that, if true, of the expectations and rumours set going by the negotiations for the Anjou marriage. The parson of Oldberrow, dumb, idle and popish, had had a more varied experience: " He married first another man's wife, got a maid with child, married a third; a common alehouse haunter and useth to play after a sort the reconciler amongst the simple ". Poor man, the last at any rate was a useful function to perform. The vicar of Tachbrook " bendeth himself wholly to the plough and cart, whence he is many times called to burial and churching ". The vicar of Grafton was an old priest whose " chiefest trade is to cure hawks that are hurt or diseased, for which purpose many do usually repair to him ". A charming picture of an old parson turning his country lore to the good use of his parishioners. At Lapworth the minister " sometimes playeth the serving man in a livery coat, sometime the minister ". The vicar of Baddesley was " a secret persuader of the simple to popery, one that prayeth for the dead, a blasphemer of the name of God, vicious and licentious of life, a companion at all games ". The poor old minister at Honiley " can neither preach nor read well; he could not one day read the commandments for want of his spectacles. A wool-winder and girthmaker by his usual occupation. An old pardoner in Queen Mary's time and yet remaineth popish." The occupations of the vicar of Packwood were different, though he too was an old priest and a Mass-monger: he was, " as it is thought, a sorcerer ". Biased and spiteful as these Surveys are, so that we cannot be sure of their truth, they do give us a living picture of the variousness of the clergy, and they prove to us how much of a minority the active Puritans were.

Opposed as they were to the remnants of Catholic rites — the use of the cross, of the ring in marriage, processions, baptism in fonts — they made what havoc they could of the works of men's hands that expressed these things. In many places the stone fonts were broken or thrown out: the font in Stratford church (in which Shakespeare was baptised) is a case in point, whether damaged under the blessed Mr. Barton I do not know. At Ashford in Kent the minister thought good " to deface a monument of superstition, to put away a font-case, coloured, gilded and pictured story-like with the seven popish sacraments, the bishop giving holy orders and confirming children, the priest saying Mass and christening with exorcisms, marrying, shriving and annealing . . . these things being slubbered over with a whitewash that in an hour may be undone, standing like a Diana's shrine for a future hope and daily comfort of old popish beldames and young perking papists, and a great offence to all that are Christianly minded ".[1] It must have been a delightful object — and how few of them are left. In the cathedral at Chichester, the Puritans complained, " there standeth the passion of Christ . . . even whole, saving that about two or three years past, it was washed over with some white colours; but since that time some well-wishers of that way (as there are too many) have taken some pains that it is almost as bright as ever it was ".[2] This was the eighties: the Church was becoming more Catholic again. These are the frescoes that we take such trouble to uncover again in our own time. The Queen herself was admonished that the walls and windows of the royal chapels were filled with images and pictures which should be " cleansed and purged away ".

Nothing daunted their spirits. We have an amusing example from the little book that the Puritan Mr. Fuller left upon the Queen.[3] He had asked one of her ladies-in-waiting for leave to write to her and Elizabeth answered 'Yea, with all her heart'. This was what the tactful Puritan wrote: God's command against swearing was clear, " and yet notwithstanding your gracious Majesty in your anger hath used to swear sometime by that abominable idol the Mass, and often and grievously by God, and by Christ, and by many parts of his glorified body, and by saints, faith, troth and other forbidden things; and by your Majesty's evil example and sufferance, the most part of your subjects and people of every degree, do commonly swear and blaspheme, to God's unspeakable dishonour, without any punishment ". He was very strong on punishment — like most Puritans — for others. The Queen had been far too slack in executing murderers — this was aimed at that great rock of offence, Mary Stuart — and in punishing adultery and fornication. Elizabeth herself in Mary's

[1] Cf. *The Seconde Parte of a Register* (ed. A. Peel), I. 239.
[2] *Ibid.* II. 191.
[3] *Ibid.* II. 49 foll.

days went " to the anti-Christian abomination and travailed to bring all your family also thereunto " ; afterwards " your Majesty in process of time was so marvellously altered in mind, manners and many things, that there was no hope of any such reformation (when your Majesty should come to the Crown) as was before hoped for ". Therefore, seeing that in so many ways the Queen had put herself outside the right course of God, he was unable to approach her ! One sees — no sycophancy among the Puritans : in that the ancestors of the democratic spirit ; one catches too that smugness which is the characteristic smell of Nonconformity.

How much of the little book the Queen read we do not know. She told Burghley of it, " and it lying in a chair, as he went out he took it with him, and then her Majesty coming to the chair, asked the lady for the book ; and she answering that my lord took it, her Majesty willed her to call for the book and said ' I will have it again ', but the lady durst never ask it ". Tactful old Burghley to take it away and sit on it : it might otherwise have been the worse for Mr. Fuller.

To be fair, one must see Puritanism at its best, as well as on its average form. (I have not depicted it at its worst, for the good reason that I like it so little.) Puritanism has no more choice spirit to show than Richard Greenham, rector of Dry Drayton, a few miles out of Cambridge on the Huntingdon road.[1] A Puritan parallel to George Herbert, he made that little place a sort of Bemerton, or more, a place of pilgrimage for many afflicted souls. Like Herbert an ailing man, he had the intensified spiritual life that often goes with ill health. " His masterpiece was in comforting wounded consciences " — in Catholic parlance, he was at his best as a confessor. Dear Bishop Hall, no enemy to the Puritans, describes him as knowing well how to stay a weak conscience and how to raise a fallen. He was charitable to a fault, often leaving himself short of money for his own housekeeping. " If he saw a poor body at a distance from him as he rode abroad he would send his man with money to him, and when he rode by the castle at Cambridge the prisoners would never ask him for anything, for if he had any money in his purse they were sure to have part of it." He kept only two beasts that the poor might have his straw. He was a famed preacher, exhausting himself with the effort. And yet in his own parish it was of little effect : its ignorance and obstinacy were matters of general comment : " Greenham had pastures green but sheep full lean ". In a way it made the Puritans' opponents right : so little to be

[1] Cf. Knappen, p. 383 foll.

done with mankind in general. Yet such a man was the salt of the earth. Though a supporter of Cartwright, and standing firm with his brethren, telling Bishop Cox " I neither can nor will wear the apparel nor subscribe unto it or the communion book ", he would not quarrel: he had perceived " by experience that dissension of reasons doth cause alienation of affections ". His gospel was, as so rarely, that of love; his life the achieved life of the Christian saint.

Beyond his parish, he wielded a wide spiritual influence. When he died his sermons and commentaries were published and taken to heart by many faithful readers.[1] The preface of his editor makes interesting reading: " The devil in elder ages in blind Papacy fed blind souls with fables and idle friars' inventions: now men's wits be refined they can no more feed on such dry stubble. He feeds dainty ears with choice of words and unclean hearts with the unchaste and wanton love-songs of Italian poetry. Such food breeds many unclean beasts in city and country. Such men cannot love the truth and holiness; because they are replete with error and uncleanness." That is what the Puritans thought of Elizabethan poetry. Ascham is quoted: " These enchanters of Circe's brought out of Italy mar men's manners in England . . . more papists be made by your merry books of Italy than by your earnest books of Louvain ". There was the Puritan hatred of the arts. When Greenham's son-in-law was passing by Holdenby, he was invited to see the splendid great house built by Hatton; he desired to be excused, and to sit still looking on a flower he had in hand: " In this flower I can see more of God than in all of the beautiful buildings in the world ".[2] Richard Greenham was a kindred soul to Herbert's; and yet there is a contrast: he was no poet.

Contrary to what is widely supposed, the Puritans were not preoccupied with the next world (as mystics like Robert Southwell or John Cornelius were, their hearts desiring the crown of martyrdom: they got their desire). Their concern was with this world, with the interminable struggle to reach the standard of conduct they set themselves. Their interests were not metaphysical or even theological; only the brilliant young Dudley Fenner wrote a systematic treatise on divinity; their concern was unswervingly, excruciatingly ethical. Even intellectual curiosity was not to be approved: it was apt to encourage the sin of pride. Nothing but this appalling concentration on ideal conduct. We

[1] Cf. *The Works of Richard Greenham*, 3rd ed., 1601: the Bodleian copy was Robert Burton's, author of *The Anatomy of Melancholy*, with his beautiful signature, 1608.

[2] Knappen, p. 387.

can see what this ideal was, we can look into their very hearts, in the few diaries that have come down to us.[1] Richard Rogers was one of the knot of Puritan ministers in Essex, preacher or reader at Wethersfield; a close friend of Culverwell at Felsted, an admirer of the redoubtable John Knewstub at Cockfield. This last was his ideal, whose great strength lay in prayer: " in this he is unwearied if it were to pass the most part of days and nights in it ". Not unnaturally, such people had often to complain of spiritual dryness. Tears were regarded as a great sign of God's favour, almost indispensable to it; and their meetings together for spiritual exercises provided occasions for horrible emotional display, not unlike a modern Buchmanite house-party. All this combined, of course, with the usual smugness: in a neighbouring gentleman Rogers saw " such unsavouriness in him in godliness that, though I confess I might praise God highly for a better portion, yet I was very heavy and dull after, even in good company. I see good cause to be thankful for not being tied to attend or to have much to do with such." Rogers's father had been a joiner, his grandfather a carpenter; he was born at Chelmsford, " that dunghill of abomination " — poor place! All the same, one has to recognise the constant moral effort to live up to a standard, the devotion and self-sacrifice demanded by it: it engendered great strength. One sees the poor minister bracing himself to undergo imprisonment and separation from his family.[2] Thus were stoked up the energies to move mountains and make empires.

A more attractive picture of the disciplined Puritan life is that of the Lady Hoby, first of English women diarists — she wrote her diary evidently with the religious purpose of keeping herself up to the mark, though it is pleasant that secular concerns come breaking in.[3] An East Riding heiress, she was brought up in the household of the Puritan Countess of Huntingdon and married off to Sir Thomas Posthumus Hoby. A son of the formidable Lady Russell — one sees the enclosed Puritan circle — he was spindle-shanked and a hunchback, not able to get children, it was thought. One might have said that his lady consoled herself with spiritual exercises, but that the marriage turned out an affectionate one. Hoby as a Puritan was a useful government outpost at Hackness — where he and his wife now lie buried in the chancel of the church — near Scarborough, countryside where the Catholic Cholmleys and Eures were accustomed to

[1] Cf. *Two Elizabethan Puritan Diaries*, ed. Knappen.

[2] Actually he was treated leniently by Bishop Aylmer and restored to his ministry (*ibid.* p. 29).

[3] *Diary of Lady Margaret Hoby, 1599–1605*, ed. D. M. Meads.

hold sway. Regarded as an interloper by them, the little man had plenty of spirit and no fear in raking in Recusants. The strenuous Puritan ideal is announced on the first page of the diary: this "day was deadness in prayer, and my greatest offence was want of sorrow for the same: the Lord of his mercy increase true and fervent mourning unto God that he never take his spirit from me. Amen. Amen." Here is her Sunday routine: one sees how it was the Puritans who prevailed in the Victorian Age. "After I was ready, I went to private prayers, then to breakfast; then I walked till church-time with Mr. Hoby, and after to dinner. After which I walked and had speech of no serious matters till 2 o'clock. Then I writ notes into my bible till 3. And after 4 I came again from the church, walked and meditated a little and again writ some other notes in my Bible of that I had learned till 5, at which time I returned to examination and prayer. And after I had read some of Bond of the Sabbath, I walked abroad. And so to supper, after to prayers and lastly to bed." [1]

There was not much difference between the Sabbath and weekdays: the routine of prayer, self-examination and pious reading formed the framework of every day that passed, except that on weekdays the interstices were filled in with the occupations pertaining to a lady's housekeeping. We find her engaged in preserving quinces, setting aside tithe apples, seeing her honey ordered, making sweetmeats, winding yarn or working with her maids or busy in the kitchen. Sometimes she visits Mrs. Brudenell in her coach, or goes to York to the manor where Burghley's eldest son kept state as Lord President; now Sir Edward Hoby comes to visit them, bringing with him the Puritan divine, William Perkins of Christ's, who had such an influence on Cambridge men and their New England following. But wherever she was the real routine of her life was given by the stated times for prayer, self-examination and reading. Sometimes she has to accuse herself: when she neglected her custom of prayer, "it pleased the Lord to punish me with an inward assault. But I know the Lord hath pardoned it because he is true of his promise and if I had not taken this course of examination, I think I had forgotten it." [2] Or at night-time, poor lady: "Lord, for Christ's sake pardon my drowsiness which with a negligent mind caused me to omit that meditation of that I had heard, which I ought to have had". Mr. Rhodes, the Puritan preacher at Hackness, lived in the house as a chaplain and frequently read to her; Foxe's *Book of Martyrs*, Greenham's *Works*, sermons by Udall or

[1] *Diary of Lady Margaret Hoby, 1599–1605*, p. 62. [2] *Ibid.* pp. 69, 71.

Broughton or Perkins, the writings of the great Cartwright — such were the regular fare. Sometimes Mr. Rhodes was joined by another preacher, Mr. Ardington, who shared the pious duty of prayer and reading with him; or Mr. Fuller, my Lord's chaplain at York, would expound to them a sermon he had come from hearing, a morsel they had missed; or they would sing psalms together. One day she learned from Mr. Rhodes's reading that the title of Lord Archbishop was unlawful, and that no minister should be made without a ministry and cure of souls.[1] We hope that the former did not impede her religious converse with Mrs. Hutton, the Archbishop's wife; and shortly after, we find Mr. Rhodes enjoying the cure of souls at Hackness as its parish priest. So life passed for the Lady Hoby, one day like another in this (to us) intolerable routine, until one day she passes out of it for ever.

Before the century closed these controversies produced the first instalment of a great masterpiece, Hooker's *Laws of Ecclesiastical Polity*. This book rose far above the level of the controversy to which it was addressed: we are in a different world. With it, and with Bacon's *Essays*, by the turn of the century, Elizabethan England may be said to have achieved intellectual maturity. From the first words of the famous opening paragraph the work has all the air of being a classic: and in spite of its being unfinished at the author's death — he died on All Souls' day, 1600 — it is so. Hooker had at his command not only all the patristic scholarship of his time, his Oxford training in Aristotle and the schoolmen, in logic and divinity, but a wide reading in classical literature, especially in Plato, which gives his book its humane appeal. He seems to have read everything — Machiavelli, the *Vindiciae*, Bellarmine — except, perhaps, the contemporary poets who were doing even greater honour to the country (had he but known it) than he was himself. But Hooker did not think in such terms; for though he must have known he was writing a great work — as others knew it at the time and helped all they could (Whitgift, George Cranmer, Edwin Sandys) — he was a deeply humble man. He well understood, if not the duplicity of things, their uncertainty, human fallibility — what none of the controversialists of the age on any side would allow, the liability to error. He was ready to admit that he was liable to err himself: "wherein I may haply err as others before me have done".[2] He

[1] *Ibid.* p. 166.

[2] *The Works of Richard Hooker*, ed. by J. Keble, revised ed. by R. W. Church and F. Paget, I. iv.

was different: he had a truly philosophical mind, where the others were but dialecticians, logic-choppers for ever chopping the chaff of religious controversy. For himself he was weary of it and once and again expresses his heartache: "Shall these fruitless jars and janglings never cease? Shall we never see end of them?"[1] He regarded his great task as laid upon him by authority; his desire to find rather what was commonly agreed upon by the whole Christian world.

It is difficult to express the essence of Hooker's mind in brief; what is absolutely characteristic of him is his readiness to state, and say what is fairly to be said for, the position he is opposing before he pronounces. He goes further: he often sees into the position he is opposing more sympathetically than his opponent. He had more than fairness, he had imaginative sympathy and all that flows from it in psychological understanding, in tact and humanity. His was a very English — one might say a very Anglican — mind. Caution was characteristic of it: he was careful never to state the position exclusively, without taking all possible objections into account, providing for every contingency. But such was his transparent candour that people have never accused him of equivocation, or of giving with one hand and taking with the other: the usual objection that is made to, and sometimes lies against, the moderate middle view, the *via media*. He well understood the difficulties of the central position, under fire from both wings, misrepresented alike by left and right — of defending an established order against those who criticise it: so much easier than to make it work. "He that goeth about to persuade a multitude that they are not so well governed as they ought to be, shall never want attentive and favourable hearers; because they know the manifold defects whereunto every kind of regiment is subject, but the secret lets and difficulties, which in public proceedings are innumerable and inevitable, they have not ordinarily the judgment to consider. And because such as openly reprove supposed disorders of state are taken for principal friends to the common benefit of all and for men that carry singular freedom of mind; under this fair and plausible colour whatsoever they utter passeth for good and current. . . . Whereas on the other side, if we maintain things that are established, we have not only to strive with a number of heavy prejudices deeply rooted in the hearts of men, who think that herein we serve the time, and speak in favour of the present state, because thereby we either hold or seek preferment; but also to bear such exceptions as

[1] *The Works of Richard Hooker*, III. 235.

minds averted beforehand usually take against that which they are loth should be poured into them." [1]

From this point of view Hooker traverses the whole Puritan position, often with sympathy. Like Whitgift he was nearer the Puritan point of view doctrinally than he was to the Roman. He took a moderate view about episcopacy; there were exceptional circumstances that might justify ordination without a bishop — a point of view which could be taken to open the gate to Wesley. But his whole tone and temper were different from the Puritans': he had an historical sense and he had reason. The Puritans insisted on the literal interpretation of Scripture and the return to the practices of the Apostles. Hooker pointed out that the practice of the Apostles was frequently uncertain; that the commonly accepted traditions of the Church were something to go by; that reason was necessary to the study of the scriptures; that human authority, not only scriptural, must be received. He showed that the actions of the Separatists, who would break up the unity of the Church, flowed directly from the doctrines of the *Book of Discipline*. Harrison, Browne's follower — who afterwards quarrelled with him — had said it might be better were all dumb ministers hanged up in their churches. This was where Puritan propaganda against the Church led: to an episode like that of Hacket, of whose fate he spoke with pity and commiseration.

His defence of the ceremonies the Puritans so much disliked is marked by the same reasonableness. They were not so important as all that: "Ceremonies have more in weight than in sight, they work by commonness of use much, although in the several acts of their usage we scarcely discern any good they do. And because the use which they have for the most part is not perfectly understood, superstition is apt to impute unto them greater virtue than indeed they have." [2] For prevention of which we should always plainly express the end whereunto the ceremony serveth, as with the cross "for a sign of remembrance to put us in mind of our duty". Doctrines like those of the Trinity or of the Eucharist had much better not be disputed about. Articles about the Trinity were matters of mere faith; and as for the sacrament: "All things considered and compared with that success which truth hath hitherto had by so bitter conflicts with errors in this point, shall I wish that men would more give themselves to meditate with silence what we have by the sacrament, and less to dispute of the manner how". [3] He was very wise to remove these matters to a region where there is no testing or proving: "This heavenly

[1] *Ibid.* I. 198. [2] *Ibid.* II. 319. [3] *Ibid.* II. 350, 351, 354.

food is given for the satisfying of our empty souls, and not for the exercising of our curious and subtle wits ". His recommendation was rather: " Take therefore that wherein all agree, and then consider by itself what cause why the rest in question should not rather be left as superfluous than urged as necessary ". It was a truly English inflection and was in the long run to prove itself more so than Puritan dogmatism and conceit. He well understood how little real humility there was among the Puritans, any more than among their descendants in modern Nonconformity.

By the time he had finished with the Puritans he had left them — in the gentlest, most reasonable manner — with hardly a foot to stand on. But they went on standing, since few people are ever persuaded by rational argument. Power was — as usual — what they wanted; and therefore the issue of Church government was the important one. Hooker's book develops, then, from being a discussion of the points at issue with the Puritans into a positive statement of the Anglican, indeed the English, view of Church government, as between Rome and Geneva. This is indeed the main substance and purport of the book, as witnessed by its title: not to be gone into here since it develops beyond our bounds into the realm of political theory, where it occupies a central place in the English tradition, mediating between the Middle Ages and John Locke and modern England. No theory of royal absolutism with Hooker: the English monarchy is a limited monarchy, resting on consent of the governed and ruled by law. He gives us a precious hint that his conception of the Christian polity was similar and consistent. As a good Aristotelian he knew that different circumstances and peoples required difference of social institutions. He thought that different nations might have their appropriate ecclesiastical structures and organisations without the underlying unity of Christ's Church being broken. The place of Papal absolutism might be taken by an agreed common law within Christendom. (Perhaps it was too Anglican a conception, and rested too much on the good sense and co-operative capacity of peoples to be practicable.) At any rate, so far as we were concerned, the fact that we had found it necessary to reform a good many things in the pre-Reformation Church did not mean that we ceased to belong to " the church we were of before ". It took some courage to say that in the circumstances of dissension and war and mutual hate we have been illustrating. Hooker was ready to go further in detail and say that there were many respects in which it was better to follow the prescribed forms of prayer, the devotional rites of Rome (always shearing them of the elements of superstition with which they were corrupted) than those of Geneva. He saw that the issue with Rome was far more important than that with the Puritans, and as the book went on developing under his hand — until the pen dropped with his task still unfinished — his mind moved into the European region of the Roman argument. We find him taking up the pen against the great Bellarmine, an opponent more worthy of him than Cartwright, for all the latter's " sharpness of wit ".

In fine, Hooker's mind was exceedingly capacious and well-rounded, sensitive rather than subtle, deeply judicious, but not — except perhaps in the combination of his qualities — original. He never considers whether the Christian faith may be, after all, not true. Like Newman in his *Essay on the Development of Christian Doctrine*, his view is confined to Western Europe in the last two millennia, in which Christianity has occupied a central place. But that is not the same thing as being true. Hooker speaks again and again of the 'true' religion; but its truth is assumed, not discussed. He appreciates the social utility of religious beliefs and refers to Machiavelli, though not by name: " There are of these wise malignants some who have vouchsafed it their marvellous favourable countenance and speech, very gravely affirming that, religion honoured, addeth greatness, and contemned, bringeth ruin unto commonweals; that princes and states which will continue are above all things to uphold the reverend regard of religion, and to provide for the same by all means in the making of their laws ".[1] But this is not to answer such persons: he does not deal with the fundamental difficulties or answer the fundamental doubts. He deals only with religious believers accepting the same assumptions — far easier game; he remains within the safe world of Christian belief.

It is difficult for us today to explain in rational terms the crucial importance for all brands of Protestantism, earlier, of the twin doctrines of Justification by Faith and Predestination. In any case we do not have to limit ourselves to purely rational explanation. There is no nonsense that human beings have not been prepared to die for at all times, and the fact that a man is prepared to die for his creed is no evidence of its truth. But what *is* the explanation of the hold of these doctrines on their believers? The election of the individual is the kernel of Protestantism. It must be that without it, a proper emphasis on Works opens the door to the institution of the Church, its system of sacraments and a priesthood, and makes the individual dependent on it. Hence

[1] *The Works of Richard Hooker*, II. 22.

the insistence on Justification by Faith, the doctrine of the priesthood of all believers. Many have found it curious with regard to the Protestant attachment to Predestination, as they do today in the case of Marxist determinism, that it should be precisely these deterministic creeds which create the greatest energy of will in their adherents and drive them on to make the greatest efforts. It seems paradoxical in those who are at such pains to deny freedom of the will. The explanation can only be that to identify your desires and wishes with the march of events is the greatest assurance, comfort and reinforcement that human egoism can command. It stores up and releases untold energies; for, as we all know, human egoism is the greatest motive force in the world.

CHAPTER XII

EDUCATION AND THE SOCIAL ORDER

EDUCATION follows the same rhythms that we have observed at work in so many areas in Tudor society — in agriculture, industry and commerce, in politics and administration, in regard to religion. Nor should we expect it to be otherwise, for education is apt very intimately to reflect, or to betray, the characteristic movements, even the movement of mind, in a society. It was the Reformation, here as in so many other things, that made the great divide. Before that there had been a steady increase of educational facilities, new foundations of schools and of colleges at Oxford and Cambridge, on a medieval basis. The profound upset of the Reformation affected education as it did other sectors of the country's life: adversely in the first instance, advantageously in the long run. The Dissolution of the Monasteries was not so much of a loss educationally, since those schools attached to monasteries were small affairs. The new cathedral foundations — both those which from being monastic were made secular and those newly created by Henry VIII — were constituted on a basis that made much more of their schools, strengthened them and made them an integral part of their foundations: here was a great advance, though limited: it was not general.

On the other hand, the Dissolution of the Chantries and Gilds overthrew a large number of schools, even if they were small and amateurish in themselves, all over the country. This was a bad blow; it meant a great set-back. Neither Henry nor Edward's government intended it; indeed their intentions were the contrary. But they could hardly help themselves: they were caught by adverse economic circumstances which rendered their government virtually bankrupt. Henry's last French war forced him to go back on his intentions: he had to withdraw his over-generous endowment of divinity scholars from his new cathedral foundations to the universities. Edward VI's Commissioners for the continuance of schools provided for a certain number to be continued on a skimpier allowance and had to postpone the rest to " further order ", which was never taken. Scores of small schools, especially song-schools, must have come to an end during what I have called the " black years " of the century. And yet during these very years a certain number of important foundations, like Shrewsbury and Tonbridge, were set on foot and other schools were refounded. Elizabeth's government carried on this good work; the stability and prosperity of the reign gave it such an impetus that by the end there were as many grammar schools as ever there had been, and for the most part established on a surer and more effective foundation. Harrison was able to say that " there are not many corporate towns now under the Queen's dominion that have not one grammar school at the least, with a sufficient living for a master and usher appointed to the same ".[1]

The same rhythm is observable in the universities: a number of new foundations up to the Reformation; then the loss of the friaries, a hold-up and considerable uncertainty reflected in the diminution of numbers with each new accession and change of policy; with Elizabeth's long reign, the return of confidence, reform, expansion, prosperity. An even greater degree of expansion and prosperity, reflecting the circumstances of the profession and its place in the society, is to be seen in that legal university, the Inns of Court. It is not too much to say that the age had a genuine enthusiasm for education, from the Queen — herself one of the best educated persons in the country — downwards. The leaders of Elizabethan society — statesmen, churchmen, gentry, merchants, countrymen in their parishes — realised that it was necessary to be educated to cope with the modern world and the country's new situation, its opportunities opening out on every side. For the continental background and the atmosphere of the time must also be borne in mind: the later sixteenth century saw a tremendous impulse towards education, in which the Jesuits took the lead in Catholic Europe, while Protestants were equally ardent in their own dominions. We may say that the impulse of the Reformation was greatly to advance popular education, though on somewhat narrower and more dogmatic lines, where that of the Renaissance naturally appealed to choicer spirits; while — in the tedious way in which human societies move, by aggression and reaction — the Counter-Reformation went in for education only too effectively as a reply to the Protestants.

With this background in view let us observe in more detail the actual effect of the Reformation; it may turn out somewhat contrary to popular notions so long received. Those schools

[1] W. Harrison, *Elizabethan England*, ed. cit. p. 258.

which some monasteries maintained — most of them did little for education, it was not their function — were not all swept away by the Dissolution.[1] That at Evesham remained. At Bruton the convent had held lands in trust for the school; in 1549 the town got a grant of these lands; the school continued and flourished. At Sherborne and at Leominster the school was not maintained by the monastery; at the latter the townspeople paid £100 for some lands of the priory to endow the school. At Cirencester the school had been supported by a yearly pension of £10 from Winchcombe abbey, which was discontinued after the suppression and the school with it: a 'great discommodity' to the town. In general, the suppression of religious houses was intimately connected with the founding of educational institutions: in place of monks more scholars was one (good) intention. Alas for men's good intentions: the government was overtaken by war, economic depression, near-bankruptcy, political insecurity and constant crises. But Henry's refoundations of cathedral establishments and his erection of some monasteries into new cathedrals reveal his mind. At Westminster, where the abbey was transformed into a secular college, the school was made an integral part of it and became very much more important: in place of the abbot and 24 monks, a dean and 12 prebendaries, 2 masters and 40 scholars.[2] The school became, along with Shrewsbury, St. Paul's and Merchant Taylors', a leading Elizabethan school. The refoundation of Canterbury was on a very generous scale: provision was made for 50 scholars on the foundation — and so their chance came to Marlowe, Hovenden, Stephen Gosson, William Hervey.[3] The more usual number of scholars at these refoundations was 20 or 30; but these formed only the nucleus to be provided for: the majority of the pupils would not be scholars.

How things worked out — the difficulties and dangers of the transition period, the fulfilment of some hopes, the disappointment of others — may be traced from the case of Worcester.[4] There the cathedral monastery had maintained a small school for its boys, while the Trinity gild supported a school for the children of townsfolk. At the refoundation of the cathedral in 1541, for a Dean and Chapter in place of monks, provision was made for 2 schoolmasters, 10 scholars and (perhaps too generously)

[1] A. F. Leach, *English Schools at the Reformation*, I. 18.

[2] J. Sargeaunt, *Annals of Westminster School*, p. 4.

[3] C. E. Woodruff and H. J. Cape, *History of the King's School, Canterbury*, p. 48.

[4] A. F. Leach, *Documents Illustrating Early Education in Worcester* (Worcester Hist. Soc.), p. xxx foll.

12 divinity scholars to the university:[1] a total of 154 persons in place of 54. Instead of 18 persons engaged in education there were now 65: education was made a prominent part of the institution, as at Westminster, Canterbury, etc. The 40 scholars were only the nucleus: no limit was placed on the number of town boys. Scholars were to be between nine and fifteen years old, except in the case of choristers whose voices had broken, who might be older; the scholars were to be *mediocriter docti* — like the (early) Fellows of All Souls. Of the university students four became Fellows of this Oxford college; but in 1546 the King had to withdraw his too liberal provision for divinity students and the foundation had to surrender the manors that provided for them. The headmaster was assigned a good salary, £15: 2s. per annum, with liveries of cloth; but he was not made a member of the Chapter and that reacted unfavourably upon the school in later centuries, for in unreformed days he continued to receive the salary fixed by Henry VIII, the school's endowment remained static and did not increase with the value of land. The eighteenth-century Dean and Chapter bloomed upon the increment: it may be seen, happily, in visible form in the pleasant Georgian houses of the College.[2] For the sixteenth century all was well: among the scholars ("poor boys without friends") were to be found Lygons, Folliotts, Coningsbys along with the townspeople's children. Those young children who were yet ignorant of grammar were to form an extra class before admission to the first class. The monks' refectory at Worcester still serves its purpose as the school hall.

It is evidence of the success of these provisions that Edward's Commissioners for the continuance of schools took the view — strictly in accord with the Chantries Act — that the Trinity gild school was no longer necessary. Not so the townspeople: the city would not submit to their adverse ruling. The Trinity gild was a civic institution, practically coterminous with the corporation: its gildhall was their hall. The townsmen sent deputations to London and undertook legal proceedings; meanwhile having lost one headmaster through these discouragements, they paid for another out of the town's own funds. With Elizabeth's accession they got their charter refounding the school — "at the

[1] Perhaps one should in fairness say that such a provision, had it been maintained, would have promoted an educated clergy earlier and forestalled some of the criticisms of the Elizabethan Church — though nothing would have stopped Puritans from criticising. They would not have taken even Yes for an answer.

[2] At Worcester the close is called the College.

request of the inhabitants and of many subjects in the country": Cecil was careful to include the districts round about in the school charters he approved. The restored school was intended to be of a lower grade than the cathedral Grammar School and complementary to it—it was a 'Free School', not a 'Grammar School': it was to teach ABC and grammar, for small children preparatory to going on to the Grammar School and those going no further. Gifts were made by the citizens and the Queen for the endowment; the former gave their gildhall for the school-house, the Queen's annuity was prudently allotted out of former monastic income. By the fifteen-eighties the school was doing well: it could pay £18:13:4 a year in salaries; the masters were university men. It was in the unreformed eighteenth century that it declined to the status of a Ragged School, not until 1850 that it was revivified and has since enjoyed great growth and prosperity as the Royal Grammar School. In the story of these two schools, this and the cathedral monastery school which became the King's School from Henry's refoundation, may be read much of the history of English secondary education.

We can gather what was going on in obscurer places in those dark years of the mid-century from what happened at Abingdon.[1] The suppression of the abbey was a blow to the town and meant temporary impoverishment. Sketchy provisions had to be made for the town's government and its schooling. Until the incorporation of the borough in 1556 the town was governed by officials appointed by the Court of Augmentations. The abbey had maintained a school, and the last monk to be master carried on after the Dissolution, with the support of the townspeople. It was all very natural but had no permanency. Early in Elizabeth's reign John Royse, an Abingdon boy of the old school, who had prospered as a mercer in London, established the school on a permanent footing: gave the corporation money to buy a new school-house and an endowment for the master's salary. In 1563, in Royse's sixty-third year, the school was refounded for sixty-three boys with a schoolroom sixty-three feet long: the sort of conceit the Elizabethans loved. And there the building is to this day, crushed up against the gatehouse to the vanished abbey that nourished it for so many centuries. In the earlier years of Elizabeth's reign the master had only one chamber in the almshouses there for his lodging. In these infected premises four headmasters, Oxford men, died of plague in the years 1573–84: the other side to the

[1] A. E. Preston, *The Church and Parish of St. Nicholas, Abingdon* (Oxford Hist. Soc.), p. 290 foll.

age. At the end, in 1600, the premises were swept away and a proper house built. Royse did not ordain the teaching of Latin, but the teaching of nurture and good manners, of virtuous living and literature, especially Christian literature. In fact, practically all the headmasters had a degree. The school prospered and produced many good men.

The general picture to be drawn is this. The Dissolution of the Chantries contemplated a large transfer to education. The financial stress of the government made this impossible. The distinction was made — and too rigidly enforced — between that part of the chantry endowment which was intended for education and that for superstitious uses, *i.e.* Masses for the dead. The latter, not unreasonably, was annexed to the Crown: in a word, nationalised. But the enforcement of the policy was not left to the Chantry Commissioners for each county: they would have represented the interest of the county, local spirit would have made them far too liberal. The government appointed two central Commissioners to decide which schools and what endowments should be continued: Robert Kelwey and Sir Walter Mildmay, Augmentations officials. Observe the name of the latter: in Elizabeth's reign he became a great educational founder and benefactor in his own right. These two officials worked under the pressure of the government's financial stress: they had to interpret their instructions rigidly, ungenerously. Sometimes they made improvements, as when they moved a school from an inaccessible place like Week St. Mary to a populous town like Launceston, or moved a school to a better centre, from Bradford-on-Avon and Trowbridge to Salisbury. What they continued was settled on a surer foundation; but it meant the cutting down of educational facilities. In Herefordshire, for example, which had had some fifteen schools, they continued ten and refounded one.

The greatest loss during these dark years was of elementary and song schools: some forty-five elementary schools are mentioned, and their endowments suffered worst.[1] The gentry and the middle class believed in education for their children and they made strenuous efforts to rectify the position. They thought education less important for the people, and they were right. What is noticeable is that where ground had been lost it was only recovered by local pressure on the government.[2] Where there was no public spirit, as in Cornwall — where there never has

[1] A. F. Leach, *English Schools at the Reformation*, p. 92.

[2] A. F. Leach, *Educational Charters and Documents*, p. xliv.

been much — the ground was lost irretrievably: in time to come the six schools of the county sank only to one.[1] In three instances, — Berkhampstead, St. Albans, Stamford — local spirit expressing itself through Parliament got their schools re-established by statute. The sale of Sedbergh and the hanky-panky played with its endowments created a scandal: it was animadverted against in a sermon before Edward VI by Lever, the well-known Protestant Master of St. John's, Cambridge, and the school was restored with a new endowment. But already under Northumberland's administration the government was setting its hand to repairing the damage: some thirty schools were founded or, more usually, refounded — such schools as Grantham, Louth, Morpeth, Birmingham, Macclesfield, Sherborne and, most successful of all, Shrewsbury. It was indeed unthinkable that the government should not have intended and wished to provide for education. We are already on the highway to the recovery under Elizabeth.

How this worked out may be seen in innumerable instances. Take Faversham in Kent.[2] John Cole, Warden of All Souls, had founded a school there for the novices of the abbey. (One may say at once that the essential part of 'founding a school' was the provision of the money, either by a grant of land or by a rent-charge on land.) At the Dissolution the school revenue was annexed by the Crown along with the other revenues of the abbey. The Faversham people petitioned Henry to restore this small revenue — without success. When Elizabeth was stopping a couple of nights in the town in 1574 the townsfolk took their opportunity to renew their petition. The Queen was very willing to give them back their endowment. The school's charter was granted in 1576; the town rated itself to build a school-house, which was erected on the north side of the churchyard in 1582. The Warden and Fellows of All Souls were to nominate and remove the headmaster; Warden Hovenden made the orders by which the school was governed up to the nineteenth century. At Sandwich in 1563 the mayor, jurats and principal inhabitants agreed to raise a sum to erect a school-house, upon the promise of Roger Manwood to give the school a permanent endowment.[3] They raised the large sum of £286 : 7 : 2. (A contrast with the comparatively small sum raised by Plymouth for its school.[4])

[1] "God knows the people be very ignorant", wrote the Commissioners of Edward VI. They have not ceased to be.

[2] N. Carlisle, *Endowed Grammar Schools*, I. 573-5.

[3] *Ibid.* pp. 595-615.

[4] R. N. Worth, *Calendar of Plymouth Municipal Records*, pp. 50-51.

Archbishop Parker got the Dean and Chapter of Canterbury to grant land for the site at the low rent of 20d. per annum. In 1568 Mrs. Trappes, widow of a merchant, left four scholarships to Lincoln College, Oxford, of which two were to be from Sandwich. In 1570 Thomas Manwood left £10 per annum for the endowment of an usher, *i.e.* an under-master. In 1581 Roger Manwood arranged for four scholarships to Caius, to be nominated alternatively by the governors and the college. The mayor and council were made governors; in 1580 Manwood himself drew up the statutes. The master was to have £20 per annum, a good salary, and was not to board more than twelve pupils, nor the usher above six. (It was usual for most boarders in Elizabethan schools to board out in the town: a practice that continued in small country schools up to this century.[1]) Here was a good record of generosity and public spirit.

This was widespread all over the country. There was a general recognition on the part of the leading elements in society of the leeway there was to be made up and of the utility in going beyond that. The Speaker made a great point of this in his speech to the Parliament of 1563: "I dare say a hundred schools want in England, which before this time have been. And if in every school there had been but an hundred scholars, yet that had been ten thousand. . . . The universities are decayed, and great market towns, and others without either school or preacher."[2] He put it down rightly to the impropriation of Church revenues by the laity at the Dissolution. The Queen no doubt considered that they had done very well out of it all, and it was not the Crown's business to produce schools, but the country's. In fact, she could usually be prevailed on to restore an educational endowment that had been annexed by the Crown, when the case had been made out and the claimants had shown themselves willing and able to establish a school. The country in general rose remarkably to its duty; there was a great deal of enthusiasm among private persons for education. By 1600 the leeway had been more than made up: there were now some 360 grammar schools in the country, of which over 100 have ceased to exist since then.[3] That is to say, one such school for every 13,000 of the population. Not that there is much point in saying it, for provision varied from county to county: it merely establishes that there was twice as favourable a ratio in this matter as in Victorian England. It

[1] Cf. Anne Treneer, *Cornish Years*. [2] Sir S. D'Ewes, *Journal*, p. 65.

[3] Cf. A. M. Stowe, *English Grammar Schools in the Reign of Queen Elizabeth*, pp. 9-11; J. H. Brown, *Elizabethan Schooldays*, pp. 7-8.

is probably fair to say that there was a greater rate of school foundations in this than in any other period of our history.

All kinds of people took part in the movement: gentry and well-to-do yeomen; churchmen, lawyers, officials; most notably, prosperous merchants and local boys who had made good. Even one or two of the nobility took a hand. Lord Williams of Thame — who had had the disagreeable job of presiding at Cranmer's burning and now lies peacefully magnificent upon his alabaster tomb in Thame church — founded the free school outside the churchyard, the 1569 building of which still remains pretty and undisturbed. Frances Sidney, Countess of Sussex, left £5000 to found a college at Cambridge. Sir Walter Mildmay, one of Edward's school Commissioners, was a great benefactor; engaged in making up from his private pocket what he had not been able to perform as a public servant. Besides founding Emmanuel College single-handed, he gave scholarships to Christ's, an annuity to Christ's hospital, and helped in establishing the grammar schools at Chelmsford and at Middleton in Lancashire. The careful Burghley founded neither school nor college, but both he and his bluestocking wife founded scholarships. On the whole, the nobility did not take much of a hand; they left it to lesser, more prosperous folk — like Peter Blundell, the clothier, who founded the school at Tiverton, with scholarships at Oxford and Cambridge; John Royse or Laurence Sherriff of Rugby; Richard Platt, the brewer, of Aldenham; Sir Andrew Judde, skinner, founder of Tonbridge; Richard Hilles of Merchant Taylors'; Thomas Sutton of Charterhouse. John Lyon, of an old prosperous yeoman family of Harrow, for many years spent 20 marks a year on the education of poor children. Like Peter Blundell, having none of his own, he exemplified the saying of Bacon: "The perpetuity by generation is common to beasts, but memory, merit and noble works are proper to men; and surely a man shall see the noblest works and foundations have proceeded from childless men".[1] (Bacon was a childless man himself.) "So the care of posterity is most in them that have no posterity." In 1572 John Lyon obtained a charter to found a free grammar school at Harrow, which he endowed with lands. Among churchmen, in addition to Sandys' and Grindal's foundations, Bishop Pilkington of Durham founded Rivington; Robert Johnson, Archdeacon of Leicester, Uppingham; Archbishop Parker, Rochdale grammar school and scholarships at Cambridge besides his munificent benefactions to Corpus; Whitgift his school at

[1] Bacon, *Essays*, "Of Parents and Children".

Croydon along with the almshouses. The leading educational adviser of the age was Alexander Nowell: he had a hand in many foundations, drawing up their statutes, besides re-establishing Middleton school and greatly benefiting Brasenose College: the Dean of St. Paul's was certainly the dean of educationists.

Naturally the towns themselves were chiefly to the fore in providing for their children; and in many places in England one can detect the original buildings under the detritus of the present. At Leicester in High Cross Street, muffled up as a carpet store, is the building of 1573 which the town built out of the stones and timber of the superfluous church of St. Peter. At Ashbourne in Derbyshire there is the gabled school-house in the main street opposite Dr. Taylor's house where Dr. Johnson used to visit: founded in 1585. Or at Dorchester in St. Peter's church one notices still the tablet commemorating Thomas Hardy of Melcombe Regis who endowed the school in South Street in 1569 with the monastic rectory he purchased for the purpose.[1]

Let us look at the educational provision in a forward county like Essex [2] and a backward one like Lancashire. The medieval prosperity of Essex is reflected in the large number of schools: no less than nineteen presented by the Chantry Commissioners, besides other smaller affairs. In most cases, after the Chantries Act the endowment was insufficient to maintain a grammar school; perhaps it would have been any way. At Chelmsford, of two chantry endowments one had been continued for a school. In 1551 Mildmay's influence got the school refounded with other properties of greater value. His father had bought the refectory of Blackfriars and leased it for a school-house. His uncle left a generous endowment, a rent-charge of £25 a year out of tithe-corn — which later successors neglected to pay. The Elizabethans, however, were not at fault: they had done their duty. John Dee and Philemon Holland, "translator general of the age", were early scholars under the wing of the Mildmays. At Colchester Henry VIII granted the properties of two little chantries to the bailiffs of the town on condition that they erected a free school; Lord Audley, a Colchester man, to make the statutes. Between 1561 and 1583 eleven scholars from this school entered St. John's and Caius. At Saffron Walden the chantry foundation was continued and a new charter procured by the influence of Sir Thomas Smith, a local boy. His brother became treasurer of this school that had the three remarkable Harvey brothers, Gabriel, Thomas

[1] Cf. J. Hutchins, *History of Dorset* (ed. Shipp and Hodson), I. 370.
[2] *v.* C. Fell-Smith in *V.C.H. Essex*, II. 501 foll.

and Richard, as pupils. At Halstead, William Martyn, clothier, had left houses in reversion to found a school in 1573, but since this did not take effect they were given to the poor; Dame Ramsey established the school with a manor in 1594.

Brentwood grammar school was founded by Sir Anthony Browne in 1557; Walthamstow by Sir George Monoux, draper and Lord Mayor, in Henry's reign. At Felsted, in Mary's, Lord Rich founded a chantry which under Elizabeth he converted to a school for eighty boys, with preference to those born on his manors. The school-house was completed in a year on the edge of the churchyard: it still remains there. Rich died and, after his various changes, was buried beneath his motto *Garde ta foy*: whatever it meant, it is still the school motto. At Dedham, Dame Joan Clark gave a school-house and a house for the master in 1571; William Littlebury added an endowment and a scholarship to Cambridge. Further funds came in for exhibitions and a house in which elementary instruction in the three R.s could be given. Newport provides a story told by Nowell himself of how grief was turned into good works. The rich Mrs. Frankland of Rye House, twice widowed, had an only son who was thrown by an unbroken horse and killed. Dean Nowell hurried to comfort her but found her inconsolable. At last " God, I think, put me in mind to say ' Comfort yourself, good Mrs. Frankland, and I will tell you how you shall have twenty good sons to comfort you in these your sorrows . . . who would be in love towards you as dear children ' ".[1] She listened and left the bulk of her property to founding Newport grammar school and scholarships at Oxford and Cambridge. The school was placed under the government of Caius, with an inscription to say that it was founded by her and her son.

Lancashire, Nowell's native county, was a favourite field of action.[2] He and his brother Robert were brought up at Middleton school. Robert was the real re-founder of it: he left the whole of his fortune to charity and good works — he had done well as attorney of the Court of Wards. He left his educational charities to the execution of his brother. The Dean provided six scholarships from Middleton to Brasenose, his Oxford college. In 1572 Nowell petitioned the Queen that he might refound the school. She was prepared to reward generosity with generosity, and to his surprise granted a rent-charge of £20 a year out of the dissolved chantries of St. Paul's freely, " which I would have purchased of her Majesty ". Thus the Queen gave six scholarships

[1] Cf. J. Venn, *Caius College* (College Histories), pp. 90-91.

[2] A. F. Leach and others in *V.C.H. Lancs.* II. 561 foll.

and Nowell seven more. With £912 from his brother's estate he bought the manor of Upbury and the rectory of Gillingham to endow the school; in 1586 he bought a field and built a fine school-house. By 1600, with nearly 200 scholars, it was at the height of its prosperity.

A county late in developing, Lancashire had few schools in the Middle Ages, and those of the fifteenth century: Lancaster, Preston, Middleton, Manchester. The early sixteenth century added Liverpool, Blackburn, Leyland, Whalley. By the Reformation there were little schools at half a dozen other places, Bolton, Warrington, Winwick, Kirkham. In Edward's reign there was one new foundation: Penwortham, primarily an elementary school for ABC and catechism, only secondarily for grammar. Under Mary, Clitheroe started a school. With Elizabeth there were four schools founded by three archbishops and one bishop: Rochdale, Rivington, Hawkshead, Warton. Seven more schools were founded by laymen: Blackrod, Urswick, Halsall, Wigan, Heskin, Churchtown, Burnley. Under James ten more were founded, eight by joint parochial effort. Manchester had a well-known headmaster, Thomas Cogan, who wrote medical books and made a text-book Epitome of Cicero's Letters. At Blackburn a small chantry endowment had been continued; in Elizabeth's reign a school was built and £250 subscribed by the townspeople was invested in a rent-charge of £20. Small boys of five might be admitted, but these were to be taught by the grammarians — the older boys.

Liverpool exhibited no public spirit: the corporation could only collect a sum of £5 : 13 : 6 for the wages of a master, over and above the stipend continued by the Commissioners: the school was no doubt not free but fee-paying. It occupied the chapel on the town quay, which the eighteenth century allowed to fall down and in 1800 the school was discontinued. Hence there was no public provision for secondary education till the Act of 1902: it had to be supplied by semi-private institutions. That is not unrepresentative of the later history of secondary education in England: the eighteenth century was the classic period of decline, until things were at their worst in the first thirty years of the nineteenth century, just before Reform got going. St. Michael's-upon-Wyre reveals a curious story. Leach calls it "a school which was cut off in the flower of its youth". Why? The Schools Commissioners had ordered the continuance of the chantry endowment of the Butlers. In 1595 these lands were leased to Henry Butler of Rawcliffe, who bought them outright in

1606! There must have been something fixed there, for he was a Catholic: the school was extinguished, but a private Catholic schoolmaster maintained by the family. At Kirkham in the early seventeenth century long disputes raged on the governing body between Catholics and Protestants. The religious bugbear affected Lancashire schools thus early; but Lancashire people showed as much enthusiasm as elsewhere for founding schools.

Such was the movement in force over most of the country: no doubt there were backward, as there were poorer areas. It answered to the great expansion in the middle ranks of society and equipped them to play their part in it. The grammar schools were essentially schools for teaching Latin, for Latin was the key to all the professions. The need for it was not confined to the Church and the university. "The diplomatist, the lawyer, the civil servant, the physician, the naturalist, the philosopher, wrote, read and to a large extent spoke and perhaps thought in Latin. Nor was Latin the language only of the higher professions. A merchant, or the bailiff of a manor, wanted it for his accounts; every town clerk or gild clerk wanted it for his minute book. Columbus had to study for his voyages in Latin; the general had to study tactics in it. The architect, the musician, everyone who was neither a mere soldier nor a mere handicraftsman wanted, not a smattering of grammar, but a living acquaintance with the tongue as a spoken as well as a written language."[1] Nothing more useful, nor more up to date, than the Latin education then of the grammar school — though there were forward-looking minds, like the remarkable schoolmaster Mulcaster, who envisaged the time when there would be enough knowledge and books of every kind in English for education to be in and through our own tongue.

As to elementary education there is far less evidence, and what there is has not been collected. Leach tells us that a considerable number of elementary schools were founded in the latter part of the reign, like that at Henley-in-Arden by George Whately of Stratford in 1586, to teach the three R.s to thirty children, and that in James's reign the number of them greatly increased.[2] We have seen that at Worcester there was a grammar school and a free school to teach both those going on to grammar and those who were not. There was the same provision at Southwark: St. Saviour's had the grammar school, St. Olave's the elementary.[3]

[1] A. F. Leach, *English Schools at the Reformation*, I. 105.

[2] A. F. Leach, *Educational Charters*, p. xlvi.

[3] J. W. Adamson, "The Extent of Literacy in the 15th and 16th Centuries", *The Library*, X. 184.

In 1561 the churchwardens of St. Olave's were instructed to get a schoolmaster to teach reading, writing and counting. A parish minute of 1566 says that children should attend until they were able either to go to service or else to grammar " as their friends shall think for them most fittest at that time ". At Dedham we have seen a school that provided elementary instruction chiefly, though it was possible to go on to grammar: there must have been many such. At Wigston near Leicester, the chapel of St. Wistan's at the other end of the village from the parish church becoming disused, the little building was used for a free school.[1] There the son of the squire, Sir William Faunt, went to school with the village boys and girls; a husbandman leaves his son 20s. " and my will is that he be kept to school until he can write and read ". We learn only by chance that girls were taught as well as boys; for a drunk lurched in one day and broke the hour-glass that stood near the font: the schoolmaster gave one end to a boy, the other to a girl.

It is fairly clear that in these elementary schools in town or country, and perhaps in the preparatory forms of the grammar schools, girls were taught as well as boys. The best educational opinion was in favour of it. Mulcaster was strongly in favour of the education of women — " myself am for them tooth and nail ".[2] But custom was against their attending grammar school and university, otherwise Mulcaster might have been in favour, for he had a high opinion of feminine capacities — which was as well with such an example of a well-educated woman as the Queen at the apex of society. He did not fail to produce a panegyric of Elizabeth: she was such a credit to her schoolmasters. There were a number of other learned ladies of the time besides the Tudors and the Greys: there were the Russell, Sidney, Dudley, Knollys, Hoby, Cooke ladies. For these and others in high position other studies than those usual for women were appropriate. The point is that people should be educated according to their position and aptitude: sixteenth-century education did not leave the ground of common sense in these matters. And since for girls marriage and the home were the ends in view, reading, writing, music, needlework and housewifery were the essential subjects. Women have little aptitude for geometry or mathematics; they are not called upon to be lawyers, physicians, preachers; they have no leisure for philosophy. Who shall say, with our subse-

[1] Cf. Dr. W. G. Hoskins's *The Midland Peasant.*

[2] Cf. Dorothy Gardiner, *English Girlhood at School*, pp. 191-3.

quent experience, that Mulcaster was wrong? In fact it would seem that there was a higher level of literacy among women than at any other time until the later nineteenth century. It may be that the Civil War had an ill effect in this as in other respects.

It is Dr. Hoskins's opinion that "England had far more schools in Elizabethan times than we know of. Many Leicestershire villages had these village schools, like Wigston, which do not come into any official report. One finds them by accident. And if they existed in Leicestershire there is reason to suppose they were to be found all over England."[1] Educational provision was far more widespread and various than appears from the books. There were many private schools — like the extremely successful school kept in Goldsmith's Alley by Thomas Farnaby, the leading schoolmaster of the early seventeenth century. But this was a grammar school to which sons of the nobility and gentry were sent. In many country parishes the parson was very helpful, like Dr. Moreman, the well-known vicar of Menheniot.[2] The clergy was an important factor in education. At the simplest level there was in many towns somebody, sexton or bell-ringer, to teach poor men's children their ABC, like the old men paid 13s. 4d. a year by the mayor at Launceston for the purpose, or the bell-ringer at Penryn. Such is the picture that emerges out of the evidence and common sense.

Far more interesting than the education of the simple is that education which amounts to something in itself, which has an intrinsic interest: that conducted in such characteristic schools of the age as Westminster and Shrewsbury, St. Paul's and Merchant Taylors', by remarkable schoolmasters like Ashton and Camden, Udall and Mulcaster. Shrewsbury was the most successful, "the best filled school in England", according to Camden.[3] With its accidence and preparatory forms it must have had nearly 400 pupils. It owed much to its situation: as a residence of the Council of Wales a lot of people came there: it became the leading school for the gentry of North Wales and the north-west of England. This in addition to the children of the townspeople, as elsewhere. The table of fees reveals the interesting social mixture of the age: sons of the nobility and gentry, of the burgesses and other inhabitants of the town. This social mixture at school must have strengthened the fibre of the nation, as in the

[1] From a letter to me on the subject. [2] Cf. my *Tudor Cornwall*, p. 151.
[3] G. W. Fisher, *Annals of Shrewsbury School*, p. 12 foll.

theatre it gave force and variety to the drama. At Shrewsbury the oppidans were a minority; all the gentry in the counties round about sent their children there. The boys were lodged in the town. The Lord President, Sir Henry Sidney, sent his son: the young Philip, aged ten, entered on the same day as Fulke Greville and James Harrington, 17 October 1564. The great man sent his son a letter of advice, the whole theme of which was obedience: " Be humble and obedient to your master, for unless you frame yourself to obey others, yea, and feel in yourself what obedience is, you shall never be able to teach others how to obey you ".[1] What the Elizabethan ideal was we may read in Greville's tribute to his dead friend: " Though I lived with him and knew him from a child, yet I never knew him other than a man: with such staidness of mind, lovely and familiar gravity as carried grace and reverence above greater years. His talk ever of knowledge, and his very play tending to enrich his mind: so as even his teachers found something in him to observe and learn above that which they had usually read or taught."[2] It reminds one of the young Milton at St. Paul's.

The master to whom Shrewsbury owed its success was Thomas Ashton.[3] Edward's School Commissioners had not allotted a school to the town: the townspeople themselves obtained a charter and an endowment. Ashton was the first headmaster and virtually a founder. His success gave him such credit that the town left him to make the orders by which the school was governed: he was careful to bring the town into the government of the school without giving them absolute power: they shared it with the headmaster and St. John's, Cambridge. In quite a number of schools the appointment and dismissal of the master was given to an Oxford or Cambridge college: a useful provision. The masters at Shrewsbury, of whom there were four, were the best paid in England. School hours were, as usual, some eleven a day: in summer from 6 A.M. to 5.30 P.M., in winter from 7 A.M. to 4.30 P.M., with an interval for dinner. Elizabethans began, and ended, their day early. Ashton, like all the best schoolmasters of the time, had a passion for plays: he wrote plays himself and the performances in the Quarry were famous.

A leader in this was the celebrated Nicholas Udall, headmaster of Eton, 1534–42.[4] He was an early Lutheran, a friend of Leland

[1] G. W. Fisher, *Annals of Shrewsbury School*, p. 10.
[2] Sir Fulke Greville, *Life of Sir Philip Sidney* (ed. 1907), p. 6.
[3] Fisher, *op. cit.* p. 4 foll.
[4] Cf. H. C. Maxwell Lyte, *History of Eton College*, pp. 117-22.

with whom he wrote pageants for Anne Boleyn: a fierce beater, commemorated as such by Tusser. His great interests were in literature and theatricals. Perhaps his tastes savoured a little too much of the stage: his relations with his pupils were not what those of a schoolmaster, or at least a headmaster, should be. Cooling his heels for a time in the Marshalsea, he yet held on to his livings and his literary work. Favoured by Edward VI he was made tutor of Edward Courtenay: not that it seems to have done that young man any good. Bishop Gardiner was a patron and made Udall schoolmaster of his household; he received privileges from Mary, for whom he produced revels and interludes, and ended up by succeeding Nowell as headmaster at Westminster. As the author of *Ralph Roister Doister* he is a creator of English comedy; he wrote other plays that have not survived; he must have been rather hard to resist.

Plays, as we all know, have remained an essential part of the Westminster tradition; the statutory obligation to perform them saved them in later times.[1] Gager, the brilliant author of the Christ Church Latin plays, was a Westminster scholar, and Ben Jonson as a schoolboy may have played in them. Udall's *Flowers for Latin Speaking gathered out of Terence*, based on his school practice, was published there; and it is possible that he first introduced the teaching of Greek, which was given a much larger place in the curriculum than at Eton. Under Elizabeth the school greatly prospered: the clause in the statutes excluding sons of the wealthy was ignored and that restricting the numbers to 120 became obsolete.[2] The Queen provided three scholarships to Christ Church and three to Trinity, Cambridge. Burghley, as High Steward of Westminster, took some interest in the school and gave 20 marks a year to scholars at the universities, while Lady Burghley gave two scholarships to St. John's, Cambridge.[3] The Elizabethan Deans paid much attention to the school, Lancelot Andrewes taking a regular part in its work, teaching the elder boys Greek and Hebrew in the Deanery and giving lectures to classes every week. He had been himself well brought up at Merchant Taylors' by Mulcaster.

St. Paul's was the largest and most important school in the City in the early sixteenth century; Colet's refoundation and the high-mastership of William Lily — a distinguished figure among the Oxford humanists — gave it the lead in English education.[4] It produced a number of able and brilliant men: Paget and

[1] J. Sargeaunt, p. 48 foll. [2] *Ibid.* p. 11. [3] *Ibid.* p. 60.
[4] M. F. J. McDonnell, *A History of St. Paul's School*, p. 69 foll.

North, Lupset and Leland. It had a larger nucleus of scholars than any school and its standards were high: it was not for poor men's children, but the children of citizens: these must be able to read and write Latin and English before admission, and there was the sensible provision in the statutes that those who made no progress should go, to make room for those who could. In Elizabeth's reign Merchant Taylors', under the rule of Mulcaster, caught up with St. Paul's, though it was more mixed as to class.[1] A large school of 250 boys, in the Marquis of Exeter's old mansion in St. Laurence Pountney, it consisted of 100 children of well-to-do parents, 100 poor men's sons and 50 poor men's children — no doubt ' petties ' occupying a preparatory form. A hundred were free scholars, the rest paid fees. There were four masters. Mulcaster himself was in favour of the incentive derived from fees: " Sure experience hath taught me that when the Master is left to the uncertainty of his stipend to increase or decrease with his diligence that then he will do best and the children profit most " — provided that he did not take on too many.[2] Brought up at Eton under Udall, Mulcaster imbibed his love of literature and dramatics. There was not much scope for play in Tudor schools — not even football was allowed — hence perhaps the importance attached to plays. All good schools, and colleges at the university, performed plays in Latin and English, and Mulcaster's boys were specially famous. Every year they played either at Court or in Middle Temple hall. On Candlemas night 1574 they played " Timoclia at the siege of Thebes by Alexander " before the Queen at Hampton Court; on Shrove Tuesday next year " Perseus and Anthomiris ".[3] In 1583 Mulcaster's children from Merchant Taylors' were still playing before the Queen; but performances were given by St. Paul's and Westminster too. No wonder Ben Jonson chaffs: " They make all their scholars play-boys. Is't not a fine sight to see all our children made interluders? Do we pay our money for this? We send them to learn their grammar and their Terence and they learn their play books."

Mulcaster had the final justification, for a schoolmaster, of the pupils he produced and their opinion of him.[4] Five of them became bishops — one of whom was Lancelot Andrewes. There were Edwyn Sandys, Matthew Gwynne, professor of music at Oxford and of physic at Gresham's College, and Judge Whitelocke, who paid tribute to his training under Mulcaster " in the

[1] C. M. Clode, *Early History of the Merchant Taylors Company*, II. 161 foll.
[2] *Ibid.* p. 166. [3] *Ibid.* I. 234.
[4] T. Klahr, *Leben und Werke Richard Mulcaster's*, p. 23.

famous school of the Merchant Taylors' in London, where I continued until I was well instructed in the Hebrew, Greek and Latin tongues. His care was also to increase my skill in music, in which I was brought up by daily exercise in it, as in singing and playing upon instruments, and yearly he presented some plays to the court, in which his scholars were only actors and I one among them, and by that means taught them good behaviour and audacity."[1] Two boys who were to become stars in the heavens passed through his hands: Thomas Lodge who left in 1573, and Edmund Spenser who left in 1569. With the last we observe the good work done by Robert Nowell's benefactions to poor London scholars: they helped to educate the poet of the age both here and for seven years as a sizar of Pembroke at Cambridge.[2] Dean Nowell often took part in the examinations at the school and in the selection of scholars. After a quarter of a century Mulcaster retired at Christmas 1586. Ten years of retirement, of private teaching and struggle to make ends meet, and he emerged to become high-master of St. Paul's, 1596–1608. For St. Paul's he wrote his *Catechismus Paulinus*, dedicated to the Mercers' Company, with verses in praise of William Lily. His was indeed a remarkable career; he died a poor man in 1611 and is buried in a nameless grave.

His work lives after him: his ideas are enshrined in two books, *Positions*, dedicated to the Queen in 1581, and *The First Part of the Elementary*, dedicated to Leicester in 1592: neither of which seems to have had much influence in his own day. His great advantage as a writer on education — as against Ascham or Milton — lies in his immense practical experience.[3] Like the good Oxford Aristotelian he was, he had a clear insight into the realities of human nature and an enlightened perception of the conditions determining culture. What is characteristic of him is his combination of sound traditional sense with original modern ideas. He well understood that children should be well grounded when they were young and the memory empty. "Children know not what they do, much less why they do it, till reason grow into some ripeness in them; and therefore in their training they profit more by practice than by knowing why, till they feel the use of reason which teaches them to consider causes. . . . We must keep carefully that rule of Aristotle which teaches that the best way to learn anything well which has to be done after it is learned

[1] *Liber Famelicus of Sir James Whitelocke*, ed. J. Bruce (Camden Society), p. 12.
[2] Clode, *op. cit.* pp. 357-8.
[3] Cf. J. Oliphant, *The Educational Writings of Richard Mulcaster*, p. 210.

is always to be a-doing while we are a-learning."[1] But grammar "in itself is but the bare rule and a very naked thing. . . . In grammar which is the introduction to speech, there should be no such length as is customary, because its end is to write and to speak." A good linguist himself, he yet thought that "we attribute too much to tongues, in paying more heed to them than matter". He looked forward to the time when all teaching would be in English, "a tongue of itself both deep in conceit and frank in delivery. I do not think that any language . . . is better able to utter all arguments, either with more pith or greater plainness than our English tongue is."[2] *The First Part of the Elementary* is mainly an exposition of how to write and teach English: little enough use seems to have been made of it. As against the usual academic denigration of the age, Mulcaster took great pride in it and — very perceptively and unusually — compared it to that of Demosthenes or Cicero: "Such a period in the English tongue I take to be in our days for both the pen and the speech".[3] He spoke more truly than perhaps even he knew.

Among his practical ideas his interest in elementary education and sympathy with the schooling of girls stand out. He wished that wealthy men would erect elementary schools for the young: such should be in the centre of towns near their homes, grammar schools in the suburbs near fields and open country.[4] He criticised the imperfection of elementary teaching: it was left to the meanest and therefore worst, while the first grounding of children should be handled by the best.[5] For girls he thought that teachers of their own sex would be fittest, in some respects — an original idea for the time; "but ours frame them best" — nor was he perhaps wrong.[6] Mulcaster was a complete professional with a high sense of the importance of the teacher's task and he made the original suggestion of special training colleges at the universities for teachers, "inasmuch as they are the instruments to make or mar the growing generation of the country . . . and because the material of their studies is comparable to that of the greatest profession".[7] He wished colleges to specialise in particular studies and to plan definite and comprehensive curricula. He wanted the State to have a free hand in controlling the uses of private endowments according to the needs of each generation. We see how much he was a man of the time in his insistence on

[1] q. Oliphant, *op. cit.* pp. 239, 219.
[2] R. Mulcaster, *The First Part of the Elementary* (ed. 1582), p. 258.
[3] R. Mulcaster, *Positions* (ed. R. H. Quick), q. p. 306.
[4] *Ibid.* p. 222 foll. [5] *Ibid.* pp. 233-4. [6] *Ibid.* p. 182. [7] *Ibid.* p. 237 foll.

uniformity: as in the Church so in education: he praised Henry for bringing all grammars into one form, imposing Lily's Pauline Latin grammar as the King's grammar, and he wished the Queen to reduce school books and teaching to better choice.[1] No doubt it would be convenient and lead to greater efficiency.

Mulcaster was no totalitarian and did not favour much beating — any more than Ascham did. He was essentially a man of the Renaissance: like Montaigne he thought that education should be based not on what was to be learned but on the nature of the learner. A good elementary course should " follow nature in the multitude of its gifts . . . and should proceed in teaching as she does in developing. For as she is unfriendly wherever she is forced, so she is the best guide that anyone can have wherever she shows herself favourable." Many of the teachings of the sainted Comenius were anticipated by Mulcaster. Where Comenius laid stress on education as a preparation for eternity, we prefer the common sense of the Englishman, of the Oxford man grounded in Aristotle, who laid stress on fitting the individual for his place in society. " The end of education and training is to help nature to her perfection in the complete development of all the various powers . . . whereby each shall be best able to perform all those functions in life which his position shall require, whether public or private, in the interest of his country in which he was born and to which he owes his whole service." [2] It is a more useful emphasis and has a more lasting claim, at a time when preparation for eternity has faded from our eyes and even from our thoughts.

The same rhythms are observable in the universities as in the schools — only more closely, since those sensitive barometers went up and down with every change of régime and policy at the centre. Very naturally, since the clerkly leadership of the country was recruited from them and they did not cease to be intimately associated with the Church. They became, however, less exclusively clerical. The general change in society affected them in the same way: the secular element at the universities expanded greatly, their interests became richer and more diversified. Here again we notice the general rhythm of the century: hope and promise in the early decades, reform and the first wind of the Renaissance in the air, kindness and liberality, the foundations of the Lady Margaret at Cambridge, of Fox and Wolsey at

[1] *Ibid.* p. vii.

[2] . Oliphant, *op. cit.* p. 237.

Oxford; then the bitter years of theological contention, the raging of factions, mutual extrusions, loss and destruction, burnings of people and (what was more valuable) works of art; with Elizabeth's reign recovery, the damping down of factions though by no means with complete success, expansion of the colleges and a more efficient system of teaching, greater diversity of interests so that the universities make a remarkable contribution not only to the Church, to politics and the law, but to literature and — quite significantly — to the drama. The Elizabethan metaphor applied to the universities of the 'two eyes' of the State was well deserved.

These institutions so characteristic of medieval society — among the most agile and vital bequests of the Middle Ages to us — underwent some marked changes that better fitted them to fulfil the purposes of a more modern society and emerged essentially as they are today. The central change came about with the development of colleges. The medieval colleges at Oxford and Cambridge were small affairs, sometimes less than a dozen men, while even Merton — which set a new model for both — had only twenty-four.[1] It was the university with its 'schools' and lectures that mattered; the great bulk of the students lived in hostels or lodgings. The colleges were not for undergraduates, they were for graduates occupied with higher things: All Souls is the only example, and exemplar, that remains of a medieval college, complete and perfect.[2] The medieval university was much more democratic — it was actually governed by its Masters of Arts, most of them quite young — more turbulent and disorderly, full of fights and rows: a good indisciplined time was had by all. Organisation was elementary; there was much coming and going between universities, and much changing and chopping within them. In the sixteenth century students were organised more and more into colleges, until none was left outside: in Elizabeth's reign ordinances at both Oxford and Cambridge forbade any residents at the university who did not belong to a college. This was aimed at Catholics, who took themselves more and more abroad, to Louvain and such places. Undergraduates were young: the usual age of admission was from thirteen to sixteen and the normal length of their course was some seven years. A consequent change too was a great in-

[1] H. Rashdall, *The Universities of Europe in the Middle Ages* (ed. F. M. Powicke and A. B. Emden), Introduction, p. xxiii.

[2] With the exception of its four bible-clerks reformed away in 1921. It is interesting that this medieval institution should have provided the model for the twentieth-century foundation of Nuffield College.

crease in the authority of heads of houses. At Oxford they got more power over the business in Convocation; while Leicester as Chancellor restored the practice of nominating the Vice-Chancellor.[1] At Cambridge the new statutes of 1570 gave the heads the power of electing the Vice-Chancellor — after 1583 none but a head of a house was ever elected — and of virtually nominating the *Caput*, the body that conducted university business.[2] These measures at Cambridge were most unpopular, but they succeeded: order prevailed against medieval democracy and disorder.

The government kept closely in touch with what happened at the universities — as was fitting considering their importance to society, both as seminaries of opinion and recruiting grounds for the professions. But it did so in the English way, leaving it to people on the spot in whom it could have confidence, operating indirectly for the most part and intervening in important matters when its authority was needed. There were effective channels of communication: Leicester was Chancellor of Oxford — as usual less than justice has been done to him as such: he filled the office conscientiously, took time and trouble over it and was frequently called upon to intervene; no doubt he thought the occasional granting of a favourable lease no more than his due for his pains. The Queen intervened similarly.[3] No such recompense was solicited by Burghley: a devoted Cambridge man, he was familiar with all its affairs, and no service was too great or too small for him to perform for it as Chancellor throughout most of the reign. Then, too, there were the activities of successive archbishops, especially Parker and Whitgift, by virtue of their office and as Visitors of various colleges; and to a lesser extent of other bishops as Visitors, or of laymen and ecclesiastics alike — Cecils, Bacons, Dean Nowell — who kept contact with their old friends and foundations. One way or another, the government was in constant touch. At intervals a royal visit, when the whole Court came down, made history with its disputations and entertainments, the grand opportunities it afforded the royal scholar of performing upon the academic stage; but its purpose was well-conceived: to keep an eye on the well-being of the universities,

[1] C. E. Mallet, *A History of the University of Oxford*, II. 116.

[2] J. B. Mullinger, *The University of Cambridge from the Royal Injunctions of 1535 to the Accession of Charles I*, p. 222.

[3] For an instance cf. H.M.C. *Various Coll.* II. 98-100. The Queen ordered Trinity, Cambridge, to grant a lease of a parsonage to Sir William Fairfax. The Master, in complying, prayed Fairfax for a lease of certain lands for himself and a poor friend. Good: always take your opportunity.

to foster and promote young talent for future service in Church and commonwealth.

The immediate effects of the Reformation are obvious and indeed visible enough; the long-term effects pass beyond our ken. Henry's intention to use some of the proceeds for the benefit of education is evident: it was in part fulfilled. On the transference of First Fruits and Tenths upon all benefices from the Pope to the Crown, the universities were made exempt: in return they were required to contribute to the support of new public lectures.[1] Beneficed clergy there were either to study or to return to their cures; the wealthier to maintain scholars at the university — this remained a dead letter. Oxford was chosen for one of Henry's new sees. At the end of his reign he was hurrying to catch up with his intentions: five Regius Professorships were endowed, in Theology and Hebrew, Civil Law, Medicine and Greek — observe the accent of the New Learning. Christ Church was refounded on a scale hardly less magnificent than Wolsey had designed. At Cambridge, Henry founded a comparable institution in Trinity College, in time to become — with his daughter Mary's munificence — the noblest of all English academic bodies. In itself it furnished " a striking example . . . of the change from the medieval to the modern conception of education and learning ".[2] It was founded on the site of the Franciscan friary, " and even now the Franciscan water is still used for the College Fountain, whose splash at midnight has been grateful to the ears of so many generations of dwellers in the Great Court ".[3]

Relatively to Cambridge Oxford lost by the Reformation: it made the fortune of the younger university. In the Middle Ages there had been no comparison. Oxford was one of the great universities of Europe and from the middle of the thirteenth century to the mid-fourteenth its schools of philosophy enjoyed a European ascendancy, its thinkers the greatest of their time, from Roger Bacon to Duns Scotus and Occam. After Wycliffe the palm passed to Paris and to Padua, the Renaissance on the horizon. The fortunes of the Reformation were bound up with Cambridge, which lay open to the new winds blowing from Europe. Though Tyndale was an Oxford man — like his great antagonist, Sir Thomas More — he made his way to Cambridge. It was more affected by the second wave of the Renaissance impulse. Erasmus refers to the flourishing state of the three

[1] Cf. Mullinger, *op. cit.* p. 310. [2] *Ibid.* p. 81.
[3] G. M. Trevelyan, *Trinity College*, p. 14.

foundations of the New Learning, Queens', Christ's, St. John's; More himself comments invidiously on the greater enthusiasm for Greek there. It was from St. John's that the propaganda for Greek and the enthusiasm for the new pronunciation came. That college enjoyed a distinguished ascendancy in the second quarter of the century: the brilliant group of men within its walls included Sir John Cheke, the first Greek scholar of the day, Roger Ascham, William Grindal — both tutors to the Princess Elizabeth — William Cecil, whose first wife was Cheke's sister: Edwardians all, their impulse maintained itself long into the age of Elizabeth. By that time the ascendancy had passed on to Trinity, at its beginning a '*colonia deducta*' out of St. John's, which gave it its first and third Masters, and such Fellows as John Dee and Cartwright.[1]

Even physically Oxford suffered more, the splendid necklet of monasteries along the Thames on the western approach from charmingly placed Godstow down to Rewley and the towering mass of Osney unroofed and falling into ruin. Within the town, "Durham and St. Bernard's College laid void, and were kept for Dr. Wright's and Dr. Kenall's bachelors, called by the waggish scholars of these times 'the two kennels of hounds and gray-hounds'".[2] Mary's reign saw the restoration of these two as Trinity and St. John's respectively, by the Catholic Sir Thomas Pope, an Augmentations official who made a large fortune out of Church lands, and by Sir Thomas White, who made his out of trade. The Carmelites' refectory became a poor house for the parish. It was not until James's reign that the site of the Austin Friars was occupied by Wadham. Both universities had hoped that the religious houses within their walls, with their properties, would fall into their laps and Cambridge had petitioned several times in vain. If she could not get their properties she made much more use of monastic materials. The Great Court of Trinity was built of materials from the Grey Friars and from Barnwell priory. The chancel of St. Radegund's priory became the chapel of Jesus College. Mildmay's Puritan foundation of Emmanuel rose on the site of Blackfriars; the Dominican refectory became its hall. The Grey Friars' site was bought to build Sidney Sussex on: the chapel in which the young Oliver Cromwell worshipped stood where the friars had fed in their refectory. The Catholic-minded Dr. Caius bought stone to build his courts from Ramsey abbey: he bought it of Oliver's grandfather.

[1] J. B. Mullinger, *St. John's College* (College Histories, Cambridge), p. 43.
[2] q. Mallet, *op. cit.* p. 72.

More subtly Oxford must have suffered a certain spiritual and even intellectual loss — though we must not exaggerate it — from the exodus of so many Catholics, some of them men of distinction. Louvain earlier, Douai and the English College at Rome later, were staffed by them. Allen wrote to the Jesuit General in 1576 that Oxford was " more responsive to the ancient faith, and from thence we mostly recruit our seminary at Douai ".[1] In addition to the leading figures Allen and Parsons there were such noted men as the controversialist Harding — Jewel's voluminous antagonist — and Bridgewater; Gregory Martin of St. John's, the main translator of the Douai Bible; the scurrilous Nicholas Sanders of New College, author of *De Visibili Monarchia Ecclesiae* and Nuncio to Ireland where he found it was not so visible and died of exposure in the woods. Many Oxford men became Jesuits, many more became martyrs: some combined both activities like Edmund Campion — who might have had a useful career and done good service in the English Church — and young Briant, a youth of singular beauty, who died with him at Tyburn. Cambridge produced a number of Catholic exiles, particularly Caius under the rule of its founder whose sympathies were with the old ways; but it did not amount to an actual drain on the university. Oxford has reason to be remembered in the prayers of Catholics.

In spite of these disadvantages Oxford recovered and prospered. There was only one foundation of a college, that of Jesus in 1571, which had a struggle to begin with; its first four principals came from All Souls. The new colleges, Trinity and St. John's, consolidated themselves; other colleges, like Queen's, much increased their numbers. Oxford was still the larger university, with 216 admissions in 1558 to 175 at Cambridge.[2] The disparity was narrowing however: by 1570 Cambridge numbered 1630, Oxford not many more.[3] Harrison was about right in estimating the university population altogether at some 3000. The great hall of Duke Humphrey's Library stood empty and disconsolate for most of the reign, since the rifling and dispersal of the medieval manuscripts in the dark days of the Reformers. In 1598 Sir Thomas Bodley, a distinguished diplomat retired from service, began his work of restoration; by 1602 he had gathered a nucleus of 2000 manuscripts and books, a collection to which accrued such

[1] *Catholic Record Society* vol. VII.

[2] J. B. Mullinger, *The University of Cambridge*, vol. cit. p. 168.

[3] Ducarrel, " History and Antiquities of Lambeth ", p. 53, in J. Nichols, *Bibliotheca Topographica Britannica*, vol. II.

later glories. He made it fashionable to make gifts: in 1603 Ralegh gave £50; from Essex there came the library of the Bishop of Osorio, scuppered on the coast of Spain, on the Cadiz Voyage; then came such treasures as Bacon's *Essays* annotated by the Queen and her own manuscript translation of Cicero. In the same period the University Press became established; at Cambridge earlier.

To the leading spirits of the age Oxford made a fair contribution: among men of action, Sidney and Ralegh; among scholars, Camden; the great propagandist of overseas empire, Hakluyt; the chronicler of the Protestant martyrs, John Foxe, whose book had an influence on the mind of the people only less than that of Bible and Prayer Book — a very powerful, if astringent, ingredient in the formation of the specifically Elizabethan outlook; among mathematicians, the greatest, Harriot; of writers, poets and dramatists, Donne, Samuel Daniel, Florio and Sir John Davies, Peele, Lyly, Lodge, Beaumont and Marston. Oxford made nothing of medicine at this time, but, perhaps owing to the revised study of the Civil Law, she was already to the fore in the field of diplomacy, with such figures as Dudley Carleton and Sir Henry Wotton and that marvellous adventurer and *blagueur* Anthony Shirley of All Souls. Among schoolmasters Mulcaster was a Christ Church man; among musicians, John Bull, Morley, Weelkes, Dowland make an agreeable quartet. Most of the leading figures in the Elizabethan Church were Cambridge men; but it is interesting that its two great apologists were Oxford men, Jewel and Hooker. The Church's theology was dominantly Calvinist. But institutions have a way of growing their own ethos and their appropriate thought; the underlying implications of the structure in course of time push aside the top-dressing of doctrine they may have been given. The conservative Aristotelianism of Oxford formed the mind of Hooker, and it is fascinating to observe that it was his formulation, not the Cambridge Calvinists', that became the central tradition of the English Church.

Cambridge was, however, more to the fore in the age itself. The Queen might be regarded as a Cambridge figure: she was taught, like her brother and unlike Mary, by Cambridge men, William Grindal and Ascham. The first royal visit she paid to a university was to Cambridge in 1564; Oxford came two years later. Her inner circle of ministers were all Cambridge men: Burghley and his son Robert, Lord Keeper Bacon and all his family, Sir Thomas Smith and Walsingham. Burghley, who was a strong believer in university education, sent his wards to

Cambridge: the young earls, Oxford, Essex and Southampton, and Norfolk's younger sons. The great financier, Gresham, as became a sprig of Norfolk, was a Gonville man. As against Wolsey, More and Pole, the Church was governed by Cambridge men from Cranmer to Bancroft. Almost all the leading Puritans belonged to Cambridge and were true to the place in their outlook, anti-historical, inaesthetic, full of the easterly winds of moral rectitude and searching of conscience, uncompromising, doctrinaire, undeniably energetic, keen and biting: Cartwright, Travers, Dering, Fenner, Perkins, Greenham and a host of less agreeable saints. A far greater glory were the poets: Spenser and Marlowe, the unrespectable, the irresistible Nashe and Greene. Among navigators, one of the two Englishmen to circle the globe, Cavendish; among scientists, John Dee and William Gilbert; of lawyers, the greatest, Bacon and Coke. Such were the constellations of talents Cambridge contributed to the age: the firmament itself was of a Cambridge shade.

One gets the unmistakable impression that Cambridge was intellectually more active and vigorous: there the issues in controversy could be fought out and were. The main issue at Oxford could not be discussed openly by the Catholics and their sympathisers: they could only keep quiet or get out. The struggle with the advanced Protestants and Puritans, which was the main issue at Cambridge, was an open one. Quite early there was an outbreak of iconoclasm and resistance to Parker's Advertisements. The leading colleges, St. John's and Trinity, had advanced sympathies: windows and monuments were broken; the whole college in each case, fellows and undergraduates, refused to wear the surplice in chapel; the heads of houses would not use the Latin Prayer Book. Among those who signed the protest against Parker's Advertisements was Whitgift.[1] In 1567 he was appointed Master of Trinity. It now fell to him to administer the orders to which he was sworn. A man of his word, who came genuinely to see the point of view of government when called on to take responsibility, he took the lead in resisting Cartwright. The latter as Lady Margaret Professor of Divinity had a great following: all the young fools in the university were for an attack on an existing institution — a point Hooker put in his magnificent way. Whitgift took up what was a cudgel rather than a pen: writing did not come so easily to him as action. But he managed to push through his *Defence* of the Church against the Puritan *Admonition* and a long-winded controversy with Cartwright.

[1] Mullinger, *op. cit.* p. 198.

Better still, since Cartwright would not take orders, Whitgift got him out of his Fellowship and out of Cambridge. He was mainly instrumental in drafting the new statutes of 1570 that got power into the hands of the heads of houses. There was an uproar. Among those who protested was Richard Bancroft.[1] Not twenty years later he was Whitgift's right-hand man at Lambeth in tracking down the Puritans and ultimately succeeded him in his responsibilities. Such are the ironies of life: the gay partisanship of youth transformed by the gathering responsibilities of years.

Whitgift's ten years as Master of Trinity marked the transition to it from St. John's as the leading college. His success brought thither many students, sons of nobles as well as of the gentry; the young Essex was lodged with him and did not fail to remember Trinity. When the Master left Cambridge for Worcester (*en route* for Lambeth) he was given a notable send-off both by town and gown: a long cavalcade of horsemen accompanied him on the first stage of his journey. He had won his first great battle. Trevelyan says: "Thus the great struggle of Anglican and Puritan . . . may almost be said to have originated, certainly to have been rehearsed in the chambers and the chapel of Trinity".[2] It is a pardonable exaggeration, for, though there were Puritans at Oxford, Cambridge was their capital and their spiritual fortress. Nor was this the end of the theological contentions which the young Bacon described in his essay on "The Controversies of the Church" as "such as violate truth, sobriety or peace. . . . The universities are the seat and continent of this disease, whence it hath been and is derived into the rest of the realm."[3] Sensible old Parker summed up the lesser dons' rows within the colleges: "Scholars' controversies be now many and troublous; and their delight is to come before men of authority to show their wits etc."[4] He did not wish Cecil's time to be withdrawn from better doings by these internal squabbles.

An important subject of dispute that testifies to the intellectual vigour of Cambridge was that over the new logic of Ramus.[5] Ramus, an advanced Protestant who had been killed in the Massacre of St. Bartholomew, was an anti-Aristotelian. He regarded logic as dialectic, synonymous with reasoning; though somewhat formalistic, this had the advantage of ridding the subject of many preconceptions. The Socratic method was the

[1] *Ibid.* p. 236. [2] Trevelyan, *op. cit.* p. 18.
[3] Bacon's *Works*, ed. J. Spedding, VIII. 82.
[4] *Correspondence of Matthew Parker* (ed. J. Bruce and T. T. Perowne), p. 249.
[5] Mullinger, *op. cit.* pp. 404-13.

only model to follow: away with the rules and routines of Scholasticism! This, of course, was honey to Cambridge: the *jeunesse* was ravished by it: it was the logical positivism of the time. Gabriel Harvey, always anxious to be in the fashion, was entranced; Spenser was attracted by it; Abraham France applied its methods, somewhat fatuously, to the law. More serious dons took it more seriously and wrote books about it. The greater minds of the age were not convinced: Bacon disapproved, Scaliger and Casaubon were hostile. Hooker spoke of it with unwonted contempt; it was not received at Oxford.

Even literary controversies were brighter and more fruitful at Cambridge. There was the important discussion that went on in the circle of Gabriel Harvey and Spenser as to the applicability of classical measures to English verse; it led to developments in literary criticism, like Webbe's *Discourse of English Poetrie*, and cleared the way for Spenser's own practice. The literary fracas between Gabriel Harvey and Nashe — very much a Cambridge quarrel — was both bitter and joyous. Nashe could always be relied on to be scandalous and the much-tried Whitgift, now arrived at Lambeth, had to exert his control over the press to stop the contestants. In the end the most significant development was in the field of theology. Before the close of the century the authority of the almighty Calvin was called in question — at Cambridge of all places. (He had never been quite such a deity at Oxford.) Peter Baro, the new Lady Margaret Professor, was heterodox on the sacred doctrine of Predestination — a liberty Whitgift would not have dreamed of permitting himself.[1] Indeed he thought it necessary to reaffirm the full position in a set of Lambeth Articles, which remained a dead letter: though they may have represented the Reformation past, they did not the Anglican future. The institution of the Church was sprouting buds of Free-Will, after the invigorating winter of Reform. Whitgift's successor, if not positively rude to Calvin, dared to be less deferential to the monster.

The evidences of greater expansive activity remain strong at Cambridge: hence its Tudor look compared with the medieval appearance of Oxford. Neville, Master of Trinity, 1593–1615, carried through a vast work of reconstruction: he cleared away the medieval buildings on the site, moved back the Edward III gate-tower stone by stone, formed and completed the Great Court, built the cloisters at his own expense. " It needed a man of unusual imagination, authority and strength of will to form and

[1] Mullinger, *op. cit.* pp. 347-50.

carry through his conception."[1] Bishop Hacket wrote of him: "he never had his like for a splendid, courteous and bountiful gentleman". Over the wall from these operations St. John's was building its second court, for which Bess of Hardwick's daughter provided £3400. In addition two new colleges were building, Emmanuel and Sidney Sussex; Dr. Caius was erecting his courts with their Gates of Humility, Temperance and Honour. Cambridge must have rung not only with theological controversy but with the sound of hammer on stone and brick, the scene a forest of scaffolding reflected in those waters.

The foundation of Emmanuel and Sidney Sussex was intimately connected with the Puritan impulse. Sir Walter Mildmay had already shown his charitable inclinations — scholarships and a Greek lectureship for his own college of Christ's, stone for the completion of Great St. Mary's — when he resolved on the founding of Emmanuel.[2] It was expressly designed as a seed-plot for the supply of the Church, to bring up ministers and preachers of the Word. The Queen questioned whether he were not erecting a Puritan foundation. Mildmay equivocated, but in fact he was. The buildings were rushed up in a short space; the master and fellows recruited from Christ's — Chadderton the first master, brought up under Laurence Vaux, had been converted from Catholicism and cut off by his father. In some town-and-gown row Chadderton had saved Bancroft's life, and later the Puritan customs of Emmanuel — sitting at communion, an unconsecrated chapel, their own deviations from the Prayer Book — were never interfered with. Puritan families flocked there and the college was early a success. Sidney Sussex was founded in imitation of it, for the same purpose and following its statutes.[3]

What gives Emmanuel its place in history is its extraordinary part in the formation of the mind of New England. By far the largest contingent of any college, and the most influential, came from this to become pastors in the new England across the Atlantic. John Cotton became the leading divine of Massachusetts, its most admired preacher, a virtual Pope, of whom Roger Williams remarked wryly that many "could hardly believe that God would suffer Mr. Cotton to err".[4] A comet appearing in the skies foretold his death (retrospectively) to the faithful. But they had more sense than to follow his idiotic proposed

[1] Trevelyan, *op. cit.* p. 21.
[2] E. S. Shuckburgh, *Emmanuel College* (College Histories), chaps. i-iii.
[3] G. M. Edwards, *Sidney Sussex College* (College Histories), pp. 5, 24.
[4] Louis B. Wright, *The Atlantic Frontier: Colonial American Civilisation*, p. 119.

statutes for the colony based on the Ten Commandments: it was too much even for them. They turned to another Emmanuel man who gave them a nice blend of Magna Carta, the Old Testament and Coke's Reports: their *Body of Liberties*. Nor were these the full tale: Samuel Stone and Thomas Hooker went over with Cotton, Hooker to become the Luther to Cotton's Melanchthon, according to Mather. Over a score of these Emmanuel men went to become pastors in the bleak New England Church: Mildmay's 'seed-ground' has had an influence altogether beyond what he could ever have imagined. Nor was the influence of Cambridge confined to the Church. The Winthrop family was closely connected with Trinity, and the first Governor was an undergraduate there 1602–5. All his life he remained under the influence of the gloomy, self-accusing Puritanism of Culverwell, another Fellow of Emmanuel. But far the most influential spiritual leader was the converted sinner, the celebrated Perkins of Christ's: a great preacher, the author of some forty works — some of them important, like his *Exposition of the Apostles' Creed* and the *Reformed Catholic* — he fortunately died young.[1] Of a liberal tendency in some respects of doctrine — he was apparently not sound on the descent into Hell — he yet believed that atheists should be put to death. Of course, the horrid barbarian! The influence of his personal life was carried by his disciples and his teachings both by them and his books far beyond the bounds of Cambridge to New England where he was much read and admired.

To the influence in the realm of education of this wonderfully expansive period in Cambridge history — calling in the New World to redress the balance of the Middle Ages — there is no end. When Ireland at last got a university with the foundation of Trinity College, Dublin in 1591, it was, as Fuller says, "a *colonia deducta* from Cambridge and particularly from Trinity College therein . . . as may appear by the catalogue of the provosts thereof".[2] All the first five Provosts were Cambridge men. And as for America, was not John Harvard another Emmanuel man?

Commentators at the time observed that the social composition of the universities was changing; but one must not exaggerate this. It provides another example of how misguided it is to take literary opinion for fact. To listen to people like Harrison one would suppose that poor scholars had been driven out to make

[1] J. Peile, *Christ's College* (College Histories), pp. 99-101.

[2] q. Mullinger, *op. cit.* p. 353.

way for the sons of the gentry.[1] The truth is that the gentry were sending their children increasingly to the university, but they remained a minority; the interesting thing, as so often in English life, is the extent and intimacy of the social mixture. Caius has the completest record of its students: of the first hundred from 1564, there was one nobleman's and one knight's son, twelve sons of esquires, seventeen sons of gentlemen, fifty-nine of the middle class, the rest poor men's sons.[2] Sizars at Cambridge, servitors at Oxford enabled the sons of poor men to come to the university: they waited at table in return for tuition. Four out of eight masters after Dr. Caius began as sizars. It is true that distinctions of rank had increased, and there was a great growth in the number of commoners, *i.e.* fee-paying students. But it was precisely the varied social contacts of college life, and between seniors and juniors, that sharply differentiated the English universities from the Continent.[3] Sir Henry Wotton, who knew both, preferred residence in college and the tutorial system to the foreign method of the solemn exercise for a degree, as who would not? The gentry certainly saw the value of a university education to equip themselves for their place in society, and the middle class appreciated its aid in gaining them one. University men — unlike today — predominated in Elizabethan Parliaments: Cambridge in the earlier, Oxford in the later.[4] It is another indication of Oxford's recovery.

With the organisation into colleges and halls there went the development of the tutorial system. Every undergraduate was in the charge of some tutor who stood to him *in loco parentis*: all very necessary considering that they came up from thirteen onwards. The college was more like a school, with a rough, rumbustious discipline and much beating. Life was rude and hard, as it was at school: variegated by horseplay, country expeditions, music and play-acting.[5] Though the organisation had changed, the content of the education was still medieval. The method of disputation still prevailed and was the royal road to success — sometimes proved to be so in the presence of the Queen, who did not fail to attend the tedious disputations our predecessors found so exciting and to take note of promising performers. Logic was the staple of education at the university, as grammar at school: it was the central study for the undergraduate and the ground-

[1] Cf. the too much quoted passage in Harrison, ed. cit. pp. 252-3.
[2] J. Venn, *Early Collegiate Life*, pp. 129-30.
[3] R. H. Hodgkin, *Six Centuries of an Oxford College*, pp. 84-6.
[4] J. E. Neale, *The Elizabethan House of Commons*, p. 302.
[5] This will be discussed in Vol. III.

work of everything. Hence the interminable logic-chopping of theologians, moralists, everybody. Not that anybody ever proved anything or convinced anybody else by it. What convinced other people in Hooker was not his dialectics but his sweet reasonableness, that illative quality which has nothing to do with logic. In the Middle Ages there had been no theology for the mass of the clergy, indeed the great bulk of them did not come to the university; only a small proportion of the lesser clergy had a university degree, the higher took arts and the Canon Law and went on into administration and office. Here the Reformation made a great difference: there was more teaching of theology, of the Bible and Calvin, and the lower ranks of the clergy became more instructed as the result of a constant effort on the part of the bishops. By the end of the century the clergy consisted more largely of men who had been to the university, with or without degrees.

In London was the third university of the realm: the four Inns of Court, with the nine smaller Inns of Chancery, of which Staple Inn remains — and some of us remember, alas, Clifford's Inn with its melancholy, ruined charm. This was indeed the golden age of the Inns, when all was pulsating with vitality and *joie de vivre*. The gentry and prosperous middle class were sending their sons in ever greater numbers to acquire a legal education: so useful an equipment not only to look after their property and estates in so litigious a world, but to fill their place in society, as J.P.s and M.P.s, stewards, officials, what not. As the universities provided for the Civil and Canon Law, so the Inns had a monopoly of education in the Common Law — vastly more important.[1] Some parents sent their sons first to the university, then on to the Inns of Court: the young Walter Ralegh was sent first to Oriel, then to Lyons Inn, thence to Middle Temple, whence he betook himself to the wars. But the majority of the students received the whole of their education at their Inn: it was their college, and a very complete and efficient course they got if they attended to it.

Life in the Inn was very much like that at Oxford or Cambridge — with the educational advantage that they had the town to run loose in. The lads came up young and were placed under the wing of their seniors, often relations or neighbours. Local connection counted for a great deal: a John Treffry of Fowey

[1] W. S. Holdsworth, *History of English Law*, IV. 229.

would be bound with a Trevanion and a Glyn, a Kendall of Treworgy with Glyn and Moyle, an Edgcumbe with a Grenville. Sons followed their fathers; brothers went up together; there were whole dynasties of legal families: Beaumonts, Fortescues, Pophams, Cokes, Bacons. The young men who were going to be professional lawyers stayed from six to nine years as students, then became utter barristers; after five years more they began to practise in the courts at Westminster; ten years after their call to the bar they were admitted ancients of their society and had the agreeable privilege of choosing their bedfellow, for everywhere Elizabethans shared beds.[1] Their education was amply provided for by readings and exercises in the morning, moots and bolts in the evenings, while there is the suggestion of " some Elizabethan wit that the lawyers should be obliged to the players for giving them something to do of an afternoon ".[2] Above all there was the common life in hall and chapel and court, the friendships and factions, the revels, the feasts and junketings, the play-acting. It all added up to " the liveliest, the most intelligent, and certainly the most influential society England could furnish " [3] — save for the Court itself.

One has only to turn over the records of the Inns to realise what the swiftly developing literature and drama of the time owed to that mercurial, vivacious fraternity. " Walter Ralegh of the Middle Temple " writes his earliest verses in commendation of *The Steel Glass* of George Gascoigne of Gray's Inn — and with strange clarity, as sometimes happens, the young man saw what was to be his own fate:

> But envious brains do nought or light esteem
> Such stately steps as they cannot attain.
> For whoso reaps renown above the rest
> With heaps of hate shall surely be oppressed.

One notes in passing such names as Francis Beaumont of the Inner Temple — it was their family Inn — and Arthur Golding, who made the translation of Ovid so much adored by the poets. John Davies of the Middle Temple dedicated his beautiful poem *Orchestra* to his fellow Richard Martin; it was a literary quarrel that made Davies break a cudgel over his friend's head in the hall, after which he returned to Oxford to write his poem *Nosce Teipsum*, dedicated to the Queen. She so much appreciated its quality

[1] R. J. Fletcher, *Pension Book of Gray's Inn, 1569–1669*, p. xxxiii.
[2] G. M. Young, " Shakespeare and the Termers " (*Proc. Brit. Acad.*), p. 5.
[3] *Ibid.* p. 7.

that she had him reinstated and promised him preferment: the impulsive, sensitive poet was enabled to forsake the Muses for a lucrative legal career. Philip Sidney was a member of Gray's Inn; Francis Bacon spent many of his happiest years there. Richard Hooker was Master of the Temple, where he preached his sermons; preacher at Lincoln's Inn was John Donne.

The first of English blank-verse tragedies, *Gorboduc*, was produced in the Inner Temple on Twelfth Night 1561: it was by two members of the society, Thomas Norton and Thomas Sackville, later Lord Treasurer.[1] Next year it was performed by the same company before the Queen at Whitehall. In 1568 *Tancred and Gismunda* was produced: also written by members of the society and long remembered by William Webbe, who got it printed twenty-four years after. In 1594 ambassadors from Inner Temple went to Gray's Inn to see their *Comedy of Errors*, but they were shabbily treated and there was much bickering in consequence. Shakespeare's *Twelfth Night* was acted in the grand new hall of Middle Temple in 1602. The young Templar Manningham has a note of it in his Diary, along with the notes of sermons he heard and stories, like that of Burbage when playing Richard III so taking the fancy of a citizen's wife that she gave him an assignation: "Shakespeare overhearing their conclusion went before, was entertained and at his game ere Burbage came. Message being brought that Richard III was at the door, Shakespeare caused return to be made that William the Conqueror was before Richard III."[2] It is evident from the Plays how much Shakespeare was in touch with his lively public from across the water and how much he appealed to them. We remember Justice Shallow:[3]

And is Jane Nightwork alive?
FALSTAFF: She lives, Master Shallow . . .
SHALLOW: Doth she hold her own well?
FALSTAFF: Old, old, Master Shallow.
SHALLOW: Nay, she must be old; she cannot choose but be old; certain she's old; and had Robin Nightwork by old Nightwork before I came to Clement's Inn.
SILENCE: That's fifty five year ago.

Gray's Inn was the largest of the Inns: in 1574 it had 220 fellows of all kinds, Middle Temple 190, Inner Temple 189,

[1] F. A. Inderwick, *Calendar of Inner Temple Records*, p. lxx.
[2] *Diary of John Manningham* (ed. J. Bruce, Camden Society), p. 39.
[3] *2 Henry IV*, III. ii.

Lincoln's Inn 160: what with the Inns of Chancery, something under a thousand in residence in London's legal university, besides others unorganised outside.[1] But the numbers were constantly increasing: Hatton as Lord Chancellor said in 1588, " There are now more at the bar in one house than there were in all the Inns of Court when I was a young man ".[2] There was great building activity: the hall of the Inner Temple was building from 1562 to 1572, the grand screen finished in 1575; the magnificent hall of the Middle Temple with its forested roof was going up at the same time. Since the Inns had no revenues from lands, members ran up their own buildings with right of occupation for life and afterwards bequeathed them their names. Prosperity declared itself in greater comforts, though such was the crowding to the Inns that chambers had to be divided; ashen mugs were discarded for green pots made of white Farnham clay; pewter plates and dishes took the place of wooden platters. The legal education given was much improved and regularised under the aegis of Coke, the great man at the Inner Temple as Bacon was of Gray's Inn.[3]

Gray's Inn, on the edge of the country, was noted for the healthiness of its air. It was the family Inn of the Cecils and Bacons: Burghley wrote of it, " the place where myself came forth unto service ";[4] Nicholas Bacon was Treasurer when the hall was rebuilt in 1556. Francis Bacon was treated as a favoured child of the house for his father's sake: suffering from indigestion and late rising, he was given the privileges of an Ancient and allowed to choose his own diet. His Puritan mother wrote in 1594 to his brother Anthony, who lived with him there: " I trust that they will not mum, masque, nor sinfully revel at Gray's Inn ".[5] But they did. Francis took a foremost part in arranging the masques and revels; nor were these the only, or the least innocent, diversions the brothers enjoyed, in spite of all the old tartar's solicitude for their spiritual welfare. In return for the kindnesses he received Francis Bacon gave the Inn devoted service over years: he went through the routine of office, Dean of Chapel, Lent Reader, Treasurer for eight years and he only ceased to attend business pensions when he became Attorney-General. He laid out the walks and planted them with trees; as Treasurer he set up a mount, laid out with flowers: " I like also little heaps, in the nature of molehills (such as are in wild heaths), to be set, some with wild thyme, some with pinks, some

[1] Inderwick, *op. cit.* p. lxxviii. [2] q. *ibid.* p. lxxxiii.
[3] *Ibid.* p. xcvii. [4] Fletcher, *op. cit.* p. xxvii. [5] q. *ibid.* p. xxxix.

with germander that gives a good flower to the eye; some with periwinkle, some with violets, some with strawberries, some with cowslips, some with daisies, some with red roses, some with lilium convallium, some with sweet williams red, some with bearsfoot, and the like low flowers, being withal sweet and sightly ".[1]

There are other touches derived from his residence there that appear in the famous little book of *Essays*, dedicated to his brother Anthony " from my chamber at Gray's Inn this 30 of January 1597 ".[2] Many of his works were written in that congenial society; he dedicated his *Arguments of Law* appropriately to it: " Few men are so bound to their societies, by obligation both ancestral and personal, as I am to yours ". After his belated triumph in the world, his brilliant if somewhat insecure transit across the public scene, the Lord Chancellorship, Whitehall and York House, the peerage and the fall, he came back to his old familiar haunts: " Myself for quiet and the better to hold out am retired to Gray's Inn; for when my chief friends were gone so far off, it was time for me to go to a cell ".[3]

Among Bacon's contemporaries was our old friend Lawrence Washington:[4] they must have been well known to each other, for they were admitted utter barristers together on the same day, with Roger Wilbraham, 27 June 1583.[5] Four years before, Washington had been allowed to make a door for his chamber into the court " so that the same be not to the impair of the chapel wall ". On 7 February 1589 they were elected together into the great society as Ancients. Ten years later " Mr. Lawrence Washington, Esquire, Register of Her Majesty's High Court of Chancery, is admitted to the table and commons of the Readers of this Society ". In the slow progress towards office Washington had so far got home before his ambitious contemporary: he had got his niche: he did not get further.

We have an interesting insight into the education and career of a successful lawyer in the Autobiography of Sir John Savile, Baron of the Exchequer.[6] The eldest son of the house at Bradley near Eland in the parish of Halifax, he was born in 1546. In the time of Edward VI he learned his alphabet and catechism under the parish clerk and the curate of Eland, and at Huddersfield.

[1] Bacon's *Essays*, " Of Gardens ". [2] *I.e.* 1598. [3] q. Fletcher, *ibid.* p. 72.

[4] Washington, as a good Northamptonshire man, had come up from Oxford where he had been a demy at Magdalen, 1560–67 (J. Foster, *Alumni Oxon*).

[5] Fletcher, *op. cit.* pp. 55, 34, 83, 145.

[6] *Yorks. Arch. and Top. Journal*, XV, 420 foll.

At the end of Edward's reign he was learning his accidence under Robert Ramsden, a relation. In Mary's first year he read through *Aesop's Fables*; in her second, part of Castellion's *Dialogues* at Halifax; in her third, Cato's *Moralia* at Huddersfield and at Okes farm under Ramsden; in her fourth and fifth, he read through Vergil and the grammar rules at Newhall and at Eland. The first three years of Elizabeth's reign he spent at Halifax reading Ovid, Vergil, Horace, Cicero and the *History* of Eutropius. Then he entered Brasenose, leaving after two years because plague was imminent. He now began his legal education under his father, reading Littleton's *Tenures*, the *Natura Brevium*, John Parkin's book and the Statutes, Rastall's *Abridgements* and the Year Books of Richard III, Henry VII and Henry VIII. On All Souls' day 1561 he was entered at Clement's Inn — Shallow's old Inn; he remained there till 1566 when he was admitted to Middle Temple by Plowden, then treasurer. In 1573 he became an utter barrister and practised first on the Northern circuit. Settled in his career he married two years later: Dean Nowell preached on the text "Marriage is honourable amongst all, but whoremongers and adulterers God shall judge".

We do not need to follow the dreary succession of childbirths and wives' deaths — he ran through three. We notice his progress up in the world from the status of his infants' sponsors — wives of judges, the Master of the Rolls. By the fifteen-eighties he is himself a judge, on the commission of the peace for the West Riding and inhabiting the new house at Bradley. In 1598 he is appointed a Baron of the Exchequer by Sir Thomas Egerton during Burghley's last sickness; in the same year he buys Methley and rebuilds the house. At Bradley he built a chapel. He died in Serjeants' Inn in 1607 and was buried in St. Dunstan in the West, his heart at Methley in the fine Jacobean tomb: *cor vero hic inter antecessores.*

An Elizabethan foundation that had a distinguished history for more than a century and might have had an immense flowering — for from it might have sprung a university for London, had it not been wantonly destroyed by the City authorities in the eighteenth century — was Gresham College.[1] Sir Thomas Gresham had hesitated between founding a college at Cambridge and one in London; in the end he decided in favour of a foundation

[1] J. W. Burgon, *Life and Times of Sir Thomas Gresham*, II. 515 foll.; J. Ward, *Lives of the Professors of Gresham College.*

in the modern spirit, in the City, in touch with the currents of commercial life and to advance modern subjects. By his will he left, after his widow's death, his great quadrangular mansion in Bishopsgate to house, and the rents of the Royal Exchange to support, a college of seven professors in the up-to-date subjects of divinity, astronomy, geometry, music, law, physic, rhetoric. The professors were to be unmarried and to reside; they were to give regular weekly lectures in their subjects to their City audiences. In 1596 the will came into operation with the City corporation and the Mercers as trustees. They took their duty conscientiously and wrote to the universities for two nominations each to each chair: " we have thought good to derive our choice from the very fountain ". Oxford responded with alacrity; Cambridge was suspicious, " doubting that in time it may be greatly prejudicial to our university ".

All played their parts, however, and excellent appointments were made: three from Oxford, the professors of astronomy, physic and rhetoric; from Cambridge, divinity, geometry and law; the Queen recommended Dr. John Bull, organist of her chapel, as professor of music: since he could not speak Latin he was allowed to lecture in English. The Gresham professors were a distinguished body of men. Henry Briggs, first professor of geometry, was a remarkable mathematician who co-operated closely with Napier in working out the theory and method of logarithms. Matthew Gwynne, first professor of physic, was a very clever man, who wrote a Latin tragedy, *Nero*, among other things; Edward Brerewood, first professor of astronomy, a retiring researcher, wrote on meteors and on optics. In the mid-seventeenth century two men of genius were professors in the college: Robert Hooke and Christopher Wren. The whole bias of the institution was modern: the professor of divinity was to deal specially with the points in controversy between the Church of England and other churches and sects; the professor of law to handle the topics most useful to merchants and citizens; the physic lectures were to follow the modern methods of Fernel, physiology, next pathology, then therapeutics; the professor of astronomy to deal with instruments and subjects of interest to mariners, and to devote one term to geography and navigation. It is a thousand pities that in the unreformed age of George III Gresham College was virtually confiscated: its site was handed over by the City to the Crown for a rent of £500 a year. The ultimate value of its site and that of the Royal Exchange would have been enough in the next age to form a nucleus for a university in London. As things are, a few lectures are all that remain today from this noble foundation, so characteristic an expression of the desire of that age for knowledge.

The Court itself was a centre of education, in the arts of culture and manners, in worldliness and sophistication, intrigue and treachery. There were some who threaded their way through it unscathed, though with many a weary sigh, Burghley and Walsingham, Hatton, the Sidneys and the virtuous Knollys. They were the professionals, the politicians. With others, it went to their heads and they lost their balance. Sometimes they foundered completely, like Philip Earl of Arundel, who lost fortune following the Court and, finding no favour, took to the no less dangerous consolations of religion; or the Earl of Oxford who spent his entire patrimony and lived humiliatingly on a pension at the Queen's hand; or the glittering and tragic career of Essex. Others lost their footing temporarily, experienced greater or lesser set-backs, like Southampton or Bacon or Ralegh. We hear the laments they emitted in prose or verse, in genuine regret or hope of a come-back. There is Ralegh's " Farewell to the Court ":

> Like truthless dreams so are my joys expired
> And past return are all my dandled days:
> My love misled and fancy quite retired,
> Of all which past the sorrow only stays.

Or it is:

> Say to the Court it glows
> and shines like rotten wood . . .

Whatever the mood, it held their eyes, for to them the Court was the world, the power and the glory. It was literally so: the fountain of power and influence, the source of fortune, magnet of all eyes, the stage which concentrated all the elements in their society and held them lit up for the public gaze, at home and abroad.

Elizabeth herself set a high standard of education to her Court. In her brother's reign she was distinctly the learned Princess, the bluestocking, hope of the stern unbending Protestants. (They got rather a surprise.) In those retiring days Roger Ascham read the Greek Testament and Sophocles with her every morning, in two years got through all Cicero and most of Livy. Then he quarrelled with her steward and there was a coolness with the Princess. On her accession he was reinstated and continued to read Greek with her until his death.[1] Elizabeth was brought up on his method of double translation, from Latin into English, from English back into Latin. She was an apt pupil: she had natural duplicity of mind.

Ascham was a kindly, congenial man; the first among Grecians, he was no mere bookworm, but addicted to sports of every kind. Indeed, Camden said that it was his addiction to dicing and cock-fighting that kept him a poor man. He wrote a book, *Toxophilus*, on archery and intended to write one on cock-fighting. But it is by his *Schoolmaster* that he lives. The book arose from a discussion at Cecil's table at Windsor one day in December 1563. Ascham describes the scene: Mildmay and Sir Richard Sackville were there, Sir John Mason and Sir William Petre, both All Souls men (Mason was the son of a cowherd at Abingdon), Dr. Wotton and some others. That day several scholars had run away from Eton for fear of beating, and the conversation turned to the subject of beating in schools. Cecil, with his gentleness of nature, deplored it, so did Wotton and Sackville; Petre, "as one somewhat severe of nature", was in favour of the rod; Mason "after his manner, was very merry with both parties".[2] After dinner Sackville came up to the Queen's privy chamber, where Ascham was reading Demosthenes with her, and besought him to write his book.

The whole book is a plea for gentleness and against beating: Ascham's theme is always to observe nature and disposition. Even he thought that young gentlemen were allowed too much liberty in England: they were brought up well enough as boys from seven to seventeen; "but from seventeen to seven and twenty (the most dangerous time of all a man's life, and most slippery to stay well in) they have commonly the rein of all license in their own hand, and specially such as do live in the Court".[3] Ascham inveighs against Court life: sophistication leads to naughtiness: young men are made bold and brash. (They certainly learned to be insolent and quarrelsome — when one thinks of the quarrels of Philip Sidney and the Earl of Oxford, of Oxford and Ralegh.) The qualities to cultivate there were "where the swing goeth, there to follow, fawn, flatter, laugh and lie lustily at other men's liking. To face, stand foremost, shove back . . . to think well of himself, to be lusty in contemning of others, to have some trim grace in a privy mock."[4] Not unnaturally, too, Ascham did not like the literature in favour at

[1] R. Ascham, *English Works* (ed. W. A. Wright), p. 219.
[2] *Ibid.* p. 176. [3] *Ibid.* p. 203. [4] *Ibid.* p. 207.

Court: "More Papists be made by your merry books of Italy than by your earnest books of Louvain".[1] He follows it up with a famous attack on the literary influences coming from Italy: it was nothing to him that it was precisely these that matured and ripened the splendid harvest of our own Renaissance literature. Nothing of that was yet to be seen. He preferred the religiosity and *Ernstheit* of the Germans — a Protestant bias which has led Europe away from civilisation indeed.

On the other hand, Ascham's view of the ideal education for a gentleman was by no means one-sided: it was itself the product of the Renaissance grafted upon the English tradition and common sense. "To ride comely, to run fair at the tilt or ring, to play at all weapons, to shoot fair in bow, or surely in gun, to vault lustily; to run, to leap, to wrestle, to swim; to dance comely, to sing and play of instruments cunningly; to hawk, to hunt, to play at tennis and all pastimes generally, which be joined with labour, used in open place and in the daylight, containing either some fit exercise for war, or some pleasant pastime for peace, be not only comely and decent, but also very necessary for a courtly gentleman to use."[2]

The idealistic Humphrey Gilbert, reflecting on these matters, produced a scheme for an Academy in London for the education of the Queen's wards and sons of the nobility and gentry.[3] Nothing less than the proper instruction of the leadership of society was in view; one observes the twofold character of the instruction and the modern emphasis. Not only the ancient but modern languages were to be taught: French, Italian, Spanish, German. An eloquent speaker himself, half-brother of Ralegh, Gilbert attached special importance to the speaking and writing of English. The young men were to be practised in making English orations; they were to learn "the choice of words, the building of sentences, the garnishment of figures, and the other beauties of oratory". A philosopher was to give instruction in policy, in peace and wars and in the commonwealth; the reader in natural philosophy and the mathematicians were to instruct also in fortification, in cosmography and astronomy. There should be an engineer, and a doctor in physic who would also instruct in first aid and experiment in chemistry. To the library all printers should deliver one copy of every book printed. It is characteristic of Humphrey Gilbert's schemes — so soaring that they foundered in the event — that some suggestion should take seed and flower: here is one that did.

[1] *Ibid.* p. 230. [2] *Ibid.* p. 217.
[3] W. G. Gosling, *Life of Sir Humphrey Gilbert*, p. 115 foll.

In the end it was the society itself, as always, that was the chief school of education. As to this, Dr. Hotson says well: " The Elizabethan world was more spacious than ours; why? Because their morality had little room for hypocrisy; because their life embraced unafraid traffic with painful emotions, that is, with passions. Unable to reduce or control physical suffering, they had to face the worst. Consequently education of children was severe, and they were taught not to fear the hardships of life, and to tackle them young. Their way of meeting life sharpened their senses, quickened their wits, and gave them a grasp of human experience that we can only envy." [1]

The constant theme of Elizabethan thought and teaching on the subject of society is the necessity of order and degree, and the consequent insistence upon authority and obedience. The lesson was enforced through all the institutions of society, through a thousand channels: in Church and school, courts and musters, sermons from pulpits, speeches from the Queen and her ministers, in Parliament, and on the stage; from the pens of poets as well as by the writers of prose. It is the theme of one of the most splendid passages of Hooker,[2] which is paralleled by — indeed may be the source of — one of the most famous speeches in Shakespeare:

> The heavens themselves, the planets and this centre
> Observe degree, priority and place . . .[3]

Now the interesting thing is that this insistence had no inhibiting effect whatever on the creative energies of their society. It would seem that the very insistence, and the necessity of it, is so much evidence of the abounding energies contained within it. For a divine moment the tension was held: national unity imposed by the danger from abroad and the struggle; the personality of a celebrated Queen. Ascham himself gives us the word: " No perfection is durable. Increase hath a time, and decay likewise, but all perfect ripeness remaineth but a moment: as is plainly seen in fruits, plums and cherries; but more sensibly in flowers, as roses and such like, and yet as truly in all greater matters." [4] It is probable, indeed I think it certain, that the hierarchical nature of that society was no bar, but a stimulus, to creative achievement; authority, by setting bounds, gave form and channel to those energies, stimulated their action, increased their

[1] L. Hotson, *Shakespeare's Sonnets Dated*, p. 173.
[2] R. Hooker, *Works* (ed. Keble, Church and Paget), I. 207.
[3] *Troilus and Cressida*, I. iii.
[4] Ascham, *op. cit.* p. 286.

force; difference excited emulation, diversity gave colour and character, achievement received recognition, ambition was admired, genius and greatness of spirit adored.

We were, in the Elizabethan Age, a small people of only some five millions. But a society that had Elizabeth at its head, Burghley as its statesman, Philip Sidney as its pattern of chivalry, Drake for its sea captain; whose poet was Spenser, whose philosopher Bacon; that had Shakespeare for its dramatist, may well bear comparison, so far as civilisation is concerned, with any of the larger societies of our time. While for us it will always have the dew of morning upon it, for it was then that our people passed, in a decade, to maturity and awakening, awoke to self-consciousness and self-questioning. For

> What good is like to this
> To do worthy the writing, and to write
> Worthy the reading, and the world's delight?

INDEX

THE END